PATTERN AND PURPOSE IN INSULAR ART

*Proceedings of the Fourth International
Conference on Insular Art
held at the National Museum & Gallery,
Cardiff 3-6 September 1998*

Edited by
Mark Redknap, Nancy Edwards,
Susan Youngs, Alan Lane, Jeremy Knight

Oxbow Books

Published by
Oxbow Books, Park End Place, Oxford OX1 1HN

© Oxbow Books and the individual authors, 2001

ISBN 1 84217 058 9

A CIP record for this book is available from the British Library

This book is available direct from

Oxbow Books, Park End Place, Oxford OX1 1HN
(Phone: 01865-241249; Fax: 01865-794449)

and

The David Brown Book Company
PO Box 511, Oakville, CT 06779, USA
(Phone: 860-945-9329; Fax: 860-945-9468)

and

via our website
www.oxbowbooks.com

Cover: The Garryduff bird (Photograph: Cork Public Museum)
Background image is taken from the South Cross, Castledermot, Co. Kildare
(Photograph: Dúchas, The Heritage Service, Ireland)

Printed in Great Britain by
The Short Run Press
Exeter

Contents

Preface

This volume presents papers read at the *Fourth International Conference on Insular Art* which was held in Wales at the National Museum & Gallery, Cardiff, in September 1998. Over 100 people attended from many European countries, and North America.

The papers in this volume are concerned with Insular art in its broadest sense, encompassing studies of metalwork, manuscripts, sculpture and textiles, both recent discoveries and new investigations of well known objects. Geographically they include material associated with Anglo-Saxon England as well as Scotland, Wales and Ireland; discoveries of Insular metalwork in Scandinavia are also considered. Temporally they are concentrated within the early medieval period, though the later use of Insular motifs on Scottish metalwork is also included. The conference was divided into five themes which have been retained in the publication. These were intended to reflect the many recent advances in the study of Insular art as well as some new examples of more traditional art-historical methods. Using case studies, papers in the 'Politics & Patrons' section draw attention to the importance of considering the historical, cultural and political context of Insular art objects. The theme 'National & Regional Identities' considers to what extent it may be possible to identify patterns for the national and regional production of Insular art objects. The papers concerned with 'Art & Archaeology' emphasise the significance of archaeological excavations, which have not only brought much new material to light (from fragile textiles to decorated metalwork), but have also provided contexts for their production and use (themes which are also reflected in a number of other papers in this volume). 'The Implications of Scientific Analysis for Insular Art and its Production' demonstrates the growing importance of both scientific and microscopic investigations in Insular Art studies and indicates the potential for both metallur-

gical analysis and experiment in order to understand ancient technologies. The theme 'Style: Analysis, Methodology & Meaning' embraces a wide range of techniques which are currently being used to study Insular illuminated manuscripts, sculpture and metalwork. These include traditional methods of stylistic analysis. However, the increasing importance of an understanding of Biblical exegesis and other texts in the interpretation of Christian artistic symbolism is also recognised, as are new ways of analysing ornament and understanding its visual impact. The importance of studying the political and social context in which earlier scholars were writing and the influence which this may have had on their interests and interpretations of Insular art is also recognised.

It is a pleasure to record our thanks to colleagues and friends who have helped to make both the Conference and these proceedings a reality. We would like to thank all those who gave papers at the Conference and who have submitted their papers for publication. As editors we have attempted to standardise spellings and references wherever possible, but we have not tried to reconcile differing views or opinions, which remain those of the individual authors. We are also grateful to the following for papers delivered at the Conference, which for various reasons are not included in these proceedings: Martin Carver on 'Art and archaeology in partnership: interpreting Sutton Hoo and Tarbat'; Ian Fisher on ' Local styles and international motifs in the sculpture of western Scotland'; Perette Michelli on 'The Crozier of St Patrick – guardian of Ireland?' and Charles Thomas on 'The Llanlleonfel (Brecs.) slab – a unique Insular monument?' Some of these have recently been published elsewhere. We would also like to thank the staff of Oxbow Books who agreed at an early stage to publish the volume and have waited patiently during the long editing process.

We are particularly grateful for the support and assistance of the Department of Archaeology & Numismatics, National Museums & Galleries of Wales, who hosted the Conference, and Cardiff University, who hosted the inaugural lecture by George Henderson and helped with the bookings. Tony Daly of the Department of Archaeology & Numismatics designed the conference icon and the cover of this volume, and provided advice on the illustrations. Administrative support was provided by Morag Redman of the National Museum & Gallery, Cardiff, Kathleen Rees of the School of History and Welsh History, University of Wales Bangor and the staff and students of the School of History and Archaeology, Cardiff University. We would like to acknowledge the generosity of individual scholars who, on the initiative of Professor Charles Thomas, provided a number of student bursaries. We would also like to thank the University of Wales Board of Celtic Studies for a generous grant, without which the conference and publication would not have been possible.

Mark Redknap & Nancy Edwards (for the editors)

List of Contributors

Dr Edel Bhreathnach
Scoil na Gaeilge
National University of Ireland
Galway
Ireland

Dr Shirley Ann Brown
Department of Fine Arts
Atkinson College
York University
Toronto M3J 1P3
Canada

Victoria Anne Bruno
History of Art Department
35 Goldwin Smith Hall
Cornell University
Ithaca NY 14853
USA

Judith Carroll
Judith Carroll Archaeological Consultancy
Pine Forest Art Centre
Pine Forest Road
Glencullen
Co. Dublin
Ireland

Dr Paul Craddock
Department of Scientific Research
The British Museum
London WC1B 3DG
England

Dr Penny Dransart
Department of Archaeology
University of Wales Lampeter
Lampeter
Ceredigion SA48 7ED
Wales

Dr Virginia Glenn
National Museums of Scotland
Chambers Street
Edinburgh EH1 1JF
Scotland

Professor James Graham-Campbell
Institute of Archaeology
University College London
31–34 Gordon Square
London WC1H OPY
England

Hero Granger-Taylor
22 Park Village East
London NW1 7PZ
England

George Henderson
Emeritus Professor of Medieval Art
University of Cambridge
Cambridge
England

Michael W. Herren
Distinguished Research Professor
Classics & Humanities
York University, Toronto M3J 1P3
and Centre for Medieval Studies
University of Toronto M5S 2C3
Canada

Eamonn P. Kelly
Keeper of Irish Antiquities
National Museum of Ireland
Kildare Street
Dublin 2
Ireland

Dr Lloyd Laing
Department of Archaeology
The University of Nottingham
University Park
Nottingham NG7 2RD
England

David Longley
Gwynedd Archaeological Trust
Craig Beuno
Ffordd y Garth
Bangor
Gwynedd LL57 2RT
Wales

Martin McNamara
Woodview
34 Mt Merrion Avenue
Blackrock
Co. Dublin
Ireland

Dr John F. Merkel
Institute of Archaeology
University College
31–34 Gordon Square
London WC1H OPY
England

Professor Nancy D. Netzer
Department of Fine Arts
Boston College
Chestnut Hill
Massachusetts 02167
USA

Raghnall Ó Floinn
National Museum of Ireland
Kildare Street
Dublin 2
Ireland

Caroline Paterson
Powbank House
Powis Loan
Stirling FK9 5PS
Scotland

Michael Pinder
Manchester Metropolitan University
Faculty of Art & Design
Department of Three Dimensional Design
Chatham Building
Cavendish Street
Manchester M15 6BR
England

Emmanuelle Pirotte
Chargée de Recherches F.N.R.S.-U.L.B.
68 rue A. Danse
1180 Bruxelles
Belgium

Frances A. Pritchard
The Whitworth Art Gallery
University of Manchester
Oxford Road
Manchester M15 6ER
England

Dr Robert D. Stevick
Department of English
University of Washington
Box 354330
Seattle
Washington 98195–4330
USA

Dr Catherine Swift
Department of History
National University of Ireland
Co. Kildare
Ireland

Dr Gabor Thomas
Research Officer
Sussex Archaeological Society
Barbican House Museum
169 High Street
Lewes BN7 1YE
England

Dr Kees Veelenturf
Katholieke Universiteit Nijmegen
Opleiding Kunstgeschiedenis & Archeologie
Afdeling Kunstgeschiedenis van de Middeleeuwen
Erasmusplein 1
NL – 6525 HT Nijmegen
The Netherlands

Jonathan M. Wallis
Derby City Museums and Art Gallery
The Strand
Derby DE1 1BS
England

Dr Niamh Whitfield
47 Faroe Road
London W14 0EL
England

Dr Jonathan M. Wooding
Theology and Religious Studies
University of Wales Lampeter
Lampeter
Ceredigion SA48 7ED
Wales

The Editors:

Dr Nancy Edwards
Department of History and Welsh History
University of Wales, Bangor
Bangor
Gwynedd LL57 2DG
Wales

Jeremy Knight
21 Warren Drive
Caerphilly
Wales

Dr Alan Lane
School of History & Archaeology
Cardiff University
PO Box 909
Cathays Park
Cardiff CF1 3XU
Wales

Dr Mark Redknap
Department of Archaeology & Numismatics
National Museum & Gallery
Cathays Park
Cardiff CF10 3NP
Wales

Susan Youngs
Department of Medieval & Modern Europe
British Museum
Great Russell Street
London WC1B 3DG
England

Part I

Politics and Patrons

1 Patrons and Politics: Art, Artefact and Methodology

Raghnall Ó Floinn

Introduction

The brief given to me by the organisers of this conference under the title 'Patrons and Politics' was to emphasise the importance of looking at the political and social background to material culture and the creation of important works of art in the Insular area using a wide range of sources. It was surprising to learn that, while there was great interest in the other themes to be explored, very few papers had been offered for this section. I confess to being puzzled as to the reasons for this as, over the years, one can detect an increasing interest in the question of context in the study of Insular Art – a welcome move away from the well-trodden paths of stylistic analysis and motif comparison.

What I will attempt to do here is to take two examples of well-known artefact types in different media and from different periods – Insular dress fasteners of the fourth to sixth centuries and Irish high crosses of the eighth to ninth centuries – and look at them from a different perspective. Central to my argument is the need to look in detail at the context of each artefact as an archaeological object whether it be a simple brooch, a piece of sculpture or a piece of fine metalwork and to examine critically the first-hand accounts of its discovery or its location. As will become evident below, the provenance and distribution of artefacts of early medieval date have never been accorded their due importance. For the early medieval period, especially in Ireland, there is a rich variety of written sources which extends well beyond the main series of annals. Genealogies, origin legends, hagiography and, in particular, place-name studies can be combined to create a political and geographical landscape against which the archaeological artefact can be placed.

Penannular brooches

My first example consists of a group of artefacts which carries the first expression of an early medieval Insular art style – the earliest of the Insular penannular brooches and some related stick pins. Studied first in detail by Howard Kilbride-Jones (1937) over 60 years ago, he returned to the subject in his 1980 monograph *Zoomorphic Penannular Brooches*. The latter work appeared on the surface to be comprehensive but scant attention was given to object history, find location and context, the author being more concerned with questions of typology and chronology. An early series of brooches, first identified by Kilbride-Jones, has been refined and added to in recent papers by Knight (1984), Graham-Campbell (1991) and Youngs (1995). These so-called Class 1 brooches (to use Graham-Campbell's term, combining Kilbride-Jones' 'Initial Form' and some of his 'Group B1' brooches) were developed in Britain and are derived from smaller penannular brooches of Roman type.

Youngs (1995, 128) has noted how the pins of these early brooches lie parallel to their terminals, thus indicating how they were worn, though not the orientation of the whole brooch on the garment. The significance of this observation is that these brooches were most likely worn singly on the breast. In the seventh- or eighth-century Irish law tract known as *Bretha Étgid* ('Judgements of Inadvertence') there is a section dealing with injury caused by the pin of a brooch (Kelly 1988, 150; translated in *AL*, III, 291). It is stated that men are exempt from liability if they wear their brooch on the shoulder and women if they wear their brooch on the breast. Thus, in the written sources a distinction is made between male and female dress – women wear brooches on the breast and men at the shoulder. This is also evident on contemporary sculpture – the female rider on the

Pictish slab from Hilton of Cadboll, Easter Ross, wears her brooch horizontally on the breast (Stevenson 1959, pl. VI.1), while the male figure on the monument from White Island, Co. Fermanagh wears his on the shoulder (Ó Floinn 1989, fig. 2). Therefore, although there is no burial evidence from British or Irish contexts to substantiate the point, it is likely that these early brooches were primarily items of female dress and that they were worn singly. Where they occur in Anglo-Saxon burials, British penannular brooches appear to have been worn in pairs although a substantial number of single brooches are also known (White 1988, 24–5). The only burial of the period from Ireland with pen-annular brooches is from Betaghstown, Co. Meath and is dated by radiocarbon to between the fourth and seventh centuries. This female was accompanied by a number of grave goods, which included a pair of iron brooches of Fowler's Type B1 worn on either shoulder in the Anglo-Saxon manner, and is in-terpreted as a rare intrusive Anglo-Saxon burial (O'Brien 1993, 96–7, fig. 3a, b; O'Brien 1999, 179, fig. 29A).

Of the 50 or so Class 1 penannular brooches, 30 are from Britain, the remainder from Ireland. Their distribution is of some interest (Fig. 1.1). In Britain, two concentrations are evident, the first around the hillfort of Traprain Law (which produced no less than three examples) in the territory of the British Votadini. The second is in the lower Severn Valley area in the lands of the Dobunni (see maps in Davies 1995, fig. 35; Dark 1994, fig. 25). The distribution in Ireland is more diffuse, but it is worth noting a cluster in the east midlands.

For a number of reasons, it is clear that these brooches originate in Britain and that the Irish series represents an introduction from there. In Britain, their find contexts vary: the East Lothian finds come from hillforts at Traprain and North Berwick, while others in Scotland come from brochs. In the south, a number come from Anglo-Saxon graves (White 1988, 18–9). In some instances only the pins were de-posited in the grave and in one case the hoop was reused as a bracelet (*ibid.*, 25). Published work has tended to concentrate on these grave finds. This has obscured the fact that a greater number have, in fact, been found on Roman settlement sites. These include the fort of *Segontium*, Caernarfon, Gwynedd and *Bravoniacum*, Kirkby Thore, Westmorland (Kilbride-Jones 1980, nos 8, 24); villas such as Witcombe (*ibid.*, no. 10) and Frocester Court, Gloucestershire (Gracie 1970, fig. 13, 39) and Feltwell, Norfolk (Gurney 1986, fig. 22, 2); and towns, as in the cases of the brooches from *Venta Silurum*, Caerwent, Monmouthshire (Kilbride-Jones 1980, no. 11) and *Aquae Sulis*, Bath (Cunliffe 1988, 23 and pl. XVIII). One was found in a hillfort at Oldbury, Wiltshire (Kilbride-Jones 1980,

no. 21). The southern British finds and their contexts suggest that these brooches were used by the native Romano-British population.

A similar pattern may be noted with other British dress fasteners such as proto-handpins and zoo-morphic stick pins. Since Kilbride-Jones' publication in 1980, an increasing number are now being recog-nised from Roman contexts in southern Britain – handpins from *Tripontium* (near Churchover), War-wickshire and St Albans, Hertfordshire (Laing 1993, 75–7) and stick pins from Wroxeter (Barker *et al* 1997, fig. 310) and Ickham, Kent (Youngs, forthcoming). Although not closely dated, it cannot be possible that all of these brooches and pins represent residual post-Roman occupation on these sites as is com-monly supposed and some at least must date to the period when these sites were occupied, during the fourth and early fifth centuries. The presence of 'Celtic' dress-fasteners at these and other sites must not be seen as evidence of British 'mercenaries' or 'traders' at these Roman sites but rather reflect the Romano-British character of such objects.

The Irish find contexts of Class 1 penannular brooches are more equivocal. Of the 20, seven have no recorded findplace. By far the greatest number of contexted finds (five out of thirteen) come from rivers, some from the sites of important river crossings – from Toome, Co. Antrim and Ath-lunkard, Co. Limerick (Kilbride-Jones 1980, nos 3, 17). A further two come from bogs: Rathruane, Co. Cork and Shronebirrane, Co. Kerry (*ibid.*, no. 28; Newman 1995, fig. 6). The most obvious explanation for this is that they represent casual loss in transit but the relatively high proportion of wetland loca-tions for the Irish series ties in well with the deposition pattern of decorated Later Iron Age bronzes (Cooney and Grogan 1994, 195–99) so that their role as votive deposits cannot be ruled out. A few brooches, such as the examples from Knowth, Co. Meath and Navan Fort, Co. Armagh come from sites associated with important historical kingships (Kilbride-Jones 1980, nos 53, 26). Other possible settlement finds are two stray brooches from Ardagh, Co. Longford (*ibid.*, no. 30) and Tihilly, Co. Offaly (De Courcy Williams 1900, 371). Both are sites which were later to develop into significant churches but which may originally have been secular settle-ments which were later donated to the church.

Is it possible to pinpoint more accurately the source in Britain from which the Class 1 brooches were introduced into Ireland? I think we can. A greater proportion of Irish (10 out of 20) than British (4 of 33) examples are enamelled. It is only in the south that the enamelled British examples are found, at Abingdon, Calne and Bath (with an outlier at Keelby, Lincolnshire). Enamelled brooches are entirely absent from north Britain. The same pattern

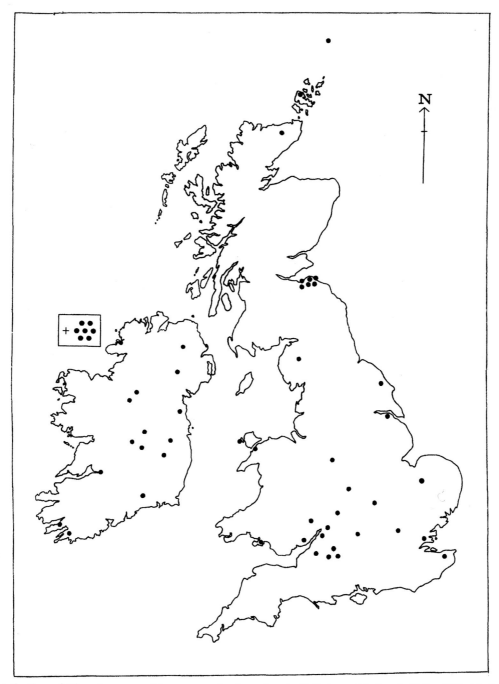

Fig. 1.1 *Distribution of Class 1 zoomorphic penannular brooches in Britain and Ireland. (After Kilbride-Jones 1980, fig. 8, with additions and corrections)*

holds true for hand-pins with decorated heads. It is therefore clear that the Irish series derives from those in south-west Britain, more specifically from an area around the lower Severn Valley. The brooches from Abingdon, Oxfordshire and Armagh, Co. Armagh (Kilbride-Jones 1980, nos 25–6) and those from High Down, Sussex and Shronebirrane, Co. Kerry (Newman 1995, fig. 6) are remarkably similar. Graham-Campbell (1991, 228) has suggested that enamelled brooches of this type developed in south-west

Britain in the fourth century. Youngs (1995, 130) has proposed a somewhat later date of 450–550 for the Class 1 series. The earliest Irish Class 1 brooches could therefore overlap chronologically with Bateson's (1973, 28) fourth- to early fifth-century group of 'Roman' finds from Ireland.

Parallel to this early group of zoomorphic brooches is a series of contemporary stick pins bearing related ornament. The first of these are zoomorphic pins, the pinheads of which mimic those

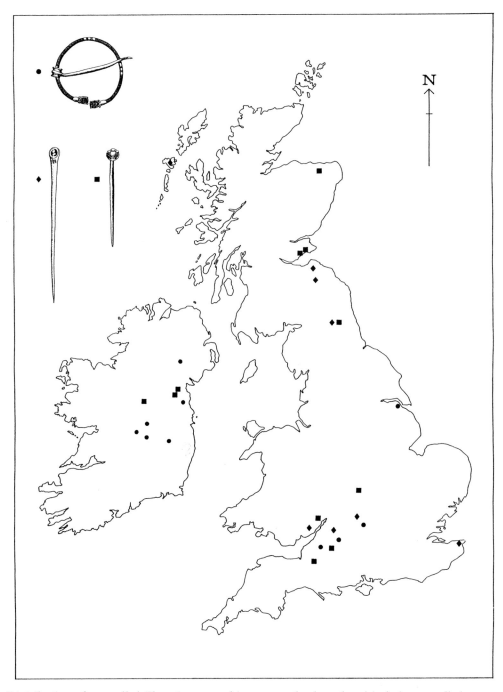

Fig. 1.2 *Distribution of enamelled Class 1 zoomorphic penannular brooches (circles), enamelled zoomorphic pins (lozenges) and enamelled hand-pins*

of the brooches. The distribution of these pins shows a concentration in the intramural area of Scotland with many being found at Traprain as well as at a number of Roman forts along Hadrian's Wall. Again, there is a second group in the lower Severn Valley. Of the five Irish examples, none is enamelled and only one is provenanced, that from Crumlin, Co. Dublin (Kilbride-Jones 1980, fig. 2,1). When one plots the enamelled examples of these pins we find that, as with the early zoomorphic penannulars, pro-portionately more southern British examples bear fine-line decoration and enamelling, 50% as opposed to 20% in the northern group (Fig. 1.2). These include the only two of the whole series with fine-line enamelling, from Cirencester (Brown 1976, fig. 3.1) and from an Anglo-Saxon grave at Cassington, Oxfordshire (Leeds and Riley 1942, fig. 16, b–d).

Another series of pins, which may be regarded as contemporary, are the so-called proto-handpins. Significantly, most are of silver and are enamelled,

Fig. 1.3 *Silver hand-pin from Newtownbond, Co. Longford. Front and back views of head. (Photograph: National Museum of Ireland)*

Fig. 1.4 *Two silver hand-pins from Castletown Kilpatrick, Co. Meath. That on the right has a replacement pin of tinned copper alloy. (Photograph: National Museum of Ireland)*

unlike other contemporary dress ornaments. The Scottish finds include a number of simple pins from Traprain as well as those from two hoards of silver ornaments from Gaulcross and Norrie's Law. Warner (1987, 20) suggested that the type was developed in the intramural zone in the late Roman period. To the south there is a group of silver pins from Romano-British contexts at *Tripontium*, Warwickshire, Oldcroft, Gloucestershire, St Albans, Hertfordshire (Laing 1993, nos 112–13, 118) and Atworth villa, Wiltshire. The Oldcroft pin was found with mid-fourth century coins, providing one of the few fixed dates for the whole series (most recently discussed by Graham-Campbell (1991) and Youngs (1995)).

In Ireland there are three provenanced pins of this type – all of silver. One is provenanced to Newtownbond, Co. Longford (unpublished, National Museum of Ireland, Reg. No. 1944:95; Fig. 1.3) and there are two pins from Castletown Kilpatrick, Co. Meath (Fig. 1.4) – all again in the east midlands area where the Class 1 brooches also occur. Although acquired separately, the find circumstances of the latter clearly indicate that they constitute a hoard (Youngs 1989, nos 2, 3). The findplace is significant as the place-name is and was only used to describe the church of Kilpatrick in the townland of Castletown, Co. Meath (Cogan 1867, 284) and the place-name and dedication suggests the site is of early medieval date. The recognition of the Castletown Kilpatrick find as a hoard has implications for

the dating of handpins. The hoard consists of a supposedly early proto-handpin along with a developed version of the same type. The latter (Youngs 1989, no. 3) is fitted with a silvered copper-alloy pin which is clearly a replacement. It is difficult to believe current art-historical arguments that these two handpins can be dated 200 years apart. The close similarity of the smaller, proto-handpin from the Castletown Kilpatrick hoard with that from Oldcroft suggests to me that all these silver handpins must be earlier in date than the sixth or seventh century normally attributed to them on the basis of the Scottish Gaulcross and Norrie's Law hoard associations (Youngs 1989, 26–7). As with the brooches, the newly published finds of silver handpins from southern Britain (Laing 1993, 75–7) argue persuasively in favour of a south-western British origin for the enamelled, fine-line decorated handpins and their occurrence in Romano-British contexts argues for a date of manufacture in the fourth/fifth centuries. The possibility that the pins from Gaulcross and Norrie's Law as well as those from Castletown Kilpatrick – all from hoards – represent imports from southern Britain must now be seriously entertained, given the absence of other Scottish enamelled objects of this date. The Norrie's Law hoard included silver objects of undoubted late Roman date and the handpins may also be residual. The distribution of these enamelled silver handpins (Fig. 1.2) indicates their currency in the Severn Valley with outliers in the Irish east midlands and in Pictland.

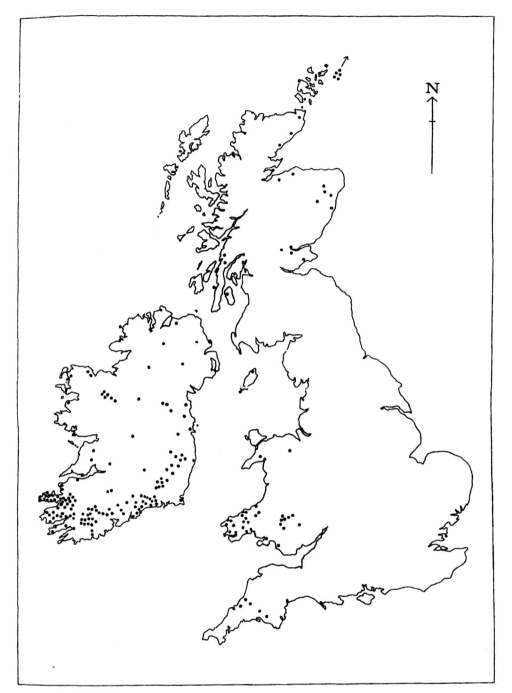

Fig. 1.5 *Distribution of ogam-inscribed stones in Britain and Ireland. (After Redknap 1995, fig. 37.7)*

From what I have said already, it is clear that the closest models in Britain for the earliest Irish brooches of Class 1 are to be found in the lower Severn Valley area and not in northern Britain and southern Scotland as has often been argued. This is also the region in which, I suggest, the fine-line enamelling seen on the later Irish series of brooches and pins was developed. The richness of this area is further emphasised by the number of silver hand-pins found here as well as the brooch from Bath with its uniquely rich decoration. This fact is best illustrated by a map which combines enamelled examples of all three brooch- and pin-types (Fig. 1.2). Only the two hoards of Gaulcross and Norrie's Law stand out in the north as examples of fine-line enamelling. None of the Class 1 Scottish penannular brooches is enamelled and the zoomorphic stick pins from Traprain and Newstead bear simple circular recesses of enamel.

The evidence outlined above suggests that the Irish series of fourth/fifth-century brooches and pins derives from a specific part of western Britain and that their Irish distribution is concentrated in the northern half of the modern province of Leinster. This is also the area where imported 'Roman' objects of the fourth/fifth centuries are found (Bateson 1973, 28). At the beginning of the historical period this would have formed part of the overkingship of the Laigin (Mac Shamhráin 1996, 51–7). Any explana-tion for contact between the lower Severn Valley (the territory of the Dobunni) and the territory of the Laigin must clearly be independent of the Irish settlement of western Britain as evidenced by the distribution of ogam stones. The distributions of ogam stones and Class 1 penannular brooches and related stick pins are mutually exclusive both in Britain and in Ireland. There are no ogam stones in the Severn Valley and only a few from north Leinster (Fig. 1.5).

If the British and Irish brooches and pins were found in areas opposite one another on either side of the Irish Sea, their distribution could be explained by geographical proximity. But the distributions in both regions are so confined and are mutually exclusive with the ogam-stone using areas which are located between them. Late Roman material in Ireland has been interpreted as the result of the activities of Romano-British traders, mercenaries or returned Irish auxiliaries (Swift 1996, 3–7). What the presence of these brooches and pins from the Severn Valley in the Irish east midlands suggests to me is nothing less than the adoption of a particular form of Romano-British dress. I would like to propose here that what these peculiar distributions may reflect is the actual presence of Britons in eastern Ireland in the later fourth or fifth to sixth centuries, perhaps introduced by kinship ties established through marriage with British-born women.

The connections perhaps follow on from links already established between the two areas in the fourth century, as evidenced by the few Irish finds of those penannular brooches which preceded the Class 1 brooches: Fowler's Type E brooches (equi-valent to Kilbride-Jones's (1980, 70–4) 'pseudo-zoomorphic penannular brooches'). All three Irish finds come from the Boyne Valley: from Knowth, Tara (Kilbride-Jones 1980, fig. 52, 3 and 21) and Newgrange (Carson and O'Kelly 1977, pl. VIIb). The Irish finds may represent votive deposits at shrines (Ó Floinn 2000, 26–7) and may be specifically linked with the cult of the Celtic god Nodens/Nuadu which is found in both areas. On the British side, this is best exemplified by the temple of Nodens at Lydney Park, Gloucestershire, in the Severn estuary, where a large number of brooches, including Type E penannular brooches, were placed as offerings (Wheeler and Wheeler 1932, Fig. 14; Woodward 1992, 76–8). The votive offerings of ornaments at Newgrange (which included imported Roman rings, brooches and coins) may well be linked with this

cult. At Newgrange, the ornaments were all found around the entrance to the tomb which was regarded as the otherworldly dwelling of the god Nuadu (Ó hÓgáin 1991, 326). In mythology, Nuadu was also strongly linked with the River Boyne, as the consort of its eponym, Boand (MacKillop 1998, 307). The source of the Boyne at Carbury Hill, Co. Kildare was known as Síd Nechtain, a pseudonym for Nuadu and at its foot was a spring known as *Linn Segais* (Gwynn 1991, 27; MacKillop 1998, 303), which invites comparison with the spring source of the Seine, *Fontes Sequana*. In a Dindshenchas poem on the Boyne, the river is compared with a number of rivers including, significantly, the River Severn, perhaps reflecting an ancient cult association bet-ween the two rivers on either side of the Irish Sea (Gwynn 1991, 29).

There is evidence in the very earliest Patrician writings of pre-Patrician missionaries in east central Ireland who are specifically of British origin. Pos-sible early British missionaries in Ireland include Lommán of Trim, Cairnech of Dulane, and Lonnán of Trevet, all in Co. Meath, Sanctán of St Anne's, Dublin, Mel of Ardagh, Co. Longford (from where an early Class 1 brooch is known) and Mochta of Louth, Co. Louth (Charles-Edwards 1999). A num-ber of these British saints were said to have been of noble birth, being the sons of British kings. One episode in the *Additamenta* of the Book of Armagh recounts how the family of the high king Lóeguire mac Néill could speak British. According to the text, Lommán – a Briton – accompanied St Patrick to Ireland and travelled up the River Boyne to Trim, Co. Meath, where he converted Lóeguire's son, grandson and their families. Lóeguire's wife is said to have been a daughter of the king of the Britons, while his son was also married to a Briton (Bieler 1979, 167–69).

We have, of course, no way of telling from what region, or regions, of Britain, these early missionaries came. It must, however, be noted that there is actually no evidence for the widely held belief that Patrick came from northern Britain. All we are told in the *Confessio* is that he was taken captive while at his father's *villula* which was near a place called *vicus bannavem taburniae*. Charles Thomas (1981, 311–14) and others have made the suggestion that this can be identified with a fort on Hadrian's Wall called *Banna* some 25km east of Carlisle. More recently, Byrne has proposed the reading *vicus Bannaventa Burriae*, containing the name of the Roman fort at *Burrium* on the site of the modern town of Usk in the lower Severn Valley (Byrne and Francis 1994, 71–3). *Burrium* is situated some 20km west of Lydney Park, which is located in the lower Severn Valley from where I propose that the Irish brooch and pin series originated.

For what it is worth, both in their recording of the arrival of Palladius and the return of Patrick, all early accounts have both landing on the east coast of Ireland around Wicklow and the Boyne area and in the case of Patrick, travelling *northwards* along the east coast, suggesting a more likely starting point in the south west rather than in northern Britain.

While not wishing to labour the point, it is possible that the adoption of Romano-British personal ornament types, and presumably Romano-British styles of dress, may well be linked in some way to this missionary activity. This activity may, as I have suggested, have travelled along routes already marked, perhaps through existing kinship and cultic ties.

High crosses

The Irish high cross series has now been made accessible by Harbison's (1992) monumental corpus. Like Kilbride-Jones's work on the brooches, however, its scope is limited – the main focus being on iconography: the original locations, specific site contexts, geological composition and wider politico-geographical contexts of the crosses are not explored. It is clear that the overwhelming majority are located on ecclesiastical sites of one kind or another and that many are from the most important monastic sites in the country – Clonmacnoise, Durrow, Kells and Armagh, for example. But it is equally evident that there are major monastic sites which have produced no known crosses – Devenish, Inisbofin, Killeshin, Lusk, Lismore, Rahan and Swords – and entire counties, such as Cork and Limerick, are without crosses. No doubt this can be explained in part as the result of selective loss and recovery but it would be instructive to analyse in greater detail those sites which have crosses. It is, in fact, extraordinary that this has not been done to date, especially as most of these sites can be identified in contemporary written sources. Why are there so many crosses from what are apparently relatively obscure foundations – for example, the two decorated cross-shafts and a base from Galloon, Co. Fermanagh (Harbison 1992, 91–4; figs 290–301)?

Problems of context are compounded in cases where the original provenance of the crosses has been obscured by their removal to other locations in relatively modern times. Although the original site of these is sometimes noted, it is still common practice to refer to these sculptures by their modern locations. How many are aware, for example, that the so-called north and south crosses at Graiguenamanagh, Co. Kilkenny are actually from churchyards at Ballyogan, Co. Kilkenny and Augh-

kilten, Co. Kilkenny respectively or that the cross at Caledon, Co. Tyrone came from nearby Glenarb? Rigorous examination of the original locations of these crosses and the identification of these sites in contemporary historical sources can reveal much about why and by whom they were erected. This is particularly rewarding in the case of crosses in reputedly obscure locations. Two examples will suffice to illustrate this – the crosses at Bealin, Co. Westmeath and Ahenny, Co. Tipperary.

The Bealin cross stands on a hill in the townland of Twyford, some 5km east of Athlone and 20km north east of Clonmacnoise in the Irish midlands. It is a ringed cross with panels of interlace and animal ornament which are stylistically linked to a number of crosses and pillars at Clonmacnoise and Banagher, Co. Offaly. Most scholars agree that the Bealin cross is a product of a workshop based at Clonmacnoise (Hicks 1980; Harbison 1992, 377–79; Edwards 1998, 106). In one of her earliest papers, Françoise Henry (1930) described the Bealin cross and provided a further link with Clonmacnoise by proposing that the person named on the cross's inscription, Tuathgal, could be identified with an abbot of Clonmacnoise of that name who died in 811 and a date of *c.* 800 for the whole group has been widely accepted since. Henry noted that the cross originally stood beside a well in Twyford Demesne some 500m distant. By the time her first volume on Irish art was published in 1965, however, Henry – led no doubt by the inscription – concluded that the cross was originally *located* at Clonmacnoise. She claimed it could be identified on a seventeenth-century view of Clonmacnoise and that it was subsequently removed to Bealin (Henry 1965, 143). This has received general acceptance despite the fact that there is no evidence whatever that the cross depicted can be equated with that at Bealin. Harbison (1992, 27) did not believe Henry's Clonmacnoise provenance and concluded that 'its original location must remain a mystery'. Henry need only have consulted the mid-nineteenth century *Ordnance Survey Letters* for Westmeath (vol. 1, 68) in which it is stated that the cross had been moved from an old graveyard in Twyford. The place-name Twyford had moreover been identified as *Tuath Buadha*, a place associated in the early sources with the kings of the petty kingdom of the Uí Chairpri (Hogan 1910, 650). Furthermore, in an article first published in 1932 and later revised, a local historian, Liam Cox, gave further information on the site's antiquity (Cox 1969). He referred to portions of the ruins of an ancient church incorporated in the buildings at Twyford and to a well dedicated to Saint Ciarán located near Twyford House. Cox went further, however, advancing many arguments in support of his contention that Twyford could be identified in the written sources as *Íseal Chiaráin* 'the low place of St Ciarán'. In the Life of the saint, Ciarán spent some time at *Íseal Chiaráin* before settling finally at Clonmacnoise. *Íseal Chiaráin* is otherwise mentioned in a number of eleventh-century annalistic references in connection with the presence there of one of Clonmacnoise's chief ecclesiastical families – that of Conn na mBocht. There also seems to have been a *Céle Dé* community and a hospital at the site. In 1093 it is recorded that the land was finally purchased by the family from the abbot of Clonmacnoise with the consent of the King of Míde. How far back the connection between *Íseal Chiaráin* and Clonmacnoise goes is uncertain. Genealogies in the *Book of Ballymote* and *MacFirbhisigh's Genealogies* record how one Cobhthach, of Tethbha and Feradach mac Duach, king of western Míde, granted *Íseal Chiaráin* 'to God and Ciarán' in perpetuity (Kehnel 1997, 68–71, 136–37). These purport to relate to the period of Clonmacnoise's foundation in the sixth century, but are clearly retrospective.

The site of *Íseal Chiaráin* would seem to have been a dependency of Clonmacnoise, perhaps serving at one time as the monastery's guesthouse (Kehnel 1997, 70). The references to it in the Life of the saint suggest that it held a special place in the early origin legends of the Clonmacnoise *paruchia*: according to one life, Ciarán's brothers devoted their lives to the service of God at *Íseal,* they were buried there and their relics venerated there (Cox 1969, 8). Tuathgal, described in his obit as *abbas sruithe Cluana* – 'abbot of the religious seniors of Clonmacnoise' (*AU* 811), may well be identified with the Tuathgal of the cross's inscription, as these 'seniors' appear to have been closely associated with the *Céle Dé* movement (Kehnel 1997, 45).

There can thus be established a connection bet-ween the site of Bealin/Twyford and Clonmacnoise which is independent of Henry's association through the inscription. In this context, it would thus not be surprising that an otherwise obscure church would have an elaborately carved cross erected by crafts-men from the monastic workshops at Clonmacnoise. A rigorous examination of the location of the Bealin/Twyford cross, therefore, has revealed that there is no reason to believe that it was moved there from Clonmacnoise; rather it was located at *Íseal Chiaráin* which is known from the early sources and was intimately connected with Clonmacnoise.

The crosses at Ahenny and the related examples in the immediate vicinity at Kilkieran, Killamery and Kilree, as well as others further afield, are among the most accomplished of the non-scripture crosses. Helen Roe, who wrote about this Ossory group of crosses 30 years ago confessed to some puzzlement at the fact that 'virtually no historical information is to be found relating to the religious foundations where the monuments remain' (1969, 9). Moreover, many do not appear to have any remaining up-standing church buildings. In her reassessment of the Ossory crosses, Edwards (1983) isolated the crosses of Ahenny, Kilkieran, Seir Kieran and Lorrha as a distinctive group. While the monastic sites of Seir Kieran – the principal church of the kingdom of Ossory – and Lorrha, founded by St Ruadhán, had known pedigrees, Ahenny and Kilkieran appeared to have no known history. Clearly, as with Bealin, these are not monastic foundations on the lines of Clonmacnoise or Durrow. They may rather be regarded as family or demesne churches which for some reason were endowed by a wealthy patron or patrons. What might be the context in which these crosses, all of a particular type, were erected and why were they located at such seemingly insigni-ficant locations?

The question of the identification of the sites in the historical record may be addressed first. As Roe (1969, 7) noted, the crosses lay within the western limits of the early historic kingdom of Ossory. They were, however, located in border territory, the Munster kingdoms of the Déisi and of the Eóganachta lay immediately to the south and west, respectively (Fig. 1.6). In fact, the River Lingaun, which separates Ahenny in Co. Tipperary from Kilkieran in Co. Kilkenny was the traditional border between Ossory and Munster (Meyer 1907, 141). The east-west range of low hills in which the crosses of Ahenny and Kilkieran are located were known collectively as *Sliabh Dile* (Hogan 1910, 607). The River Lingaun cuts through this range and formed a routeway, part of the *Belach Mór* or Great Pass of Ossory (Shearman 1876–8, 197, n.).

Kilkieran, which may be dedicated either to St Ciarán of Clonmacnoise or to St Ciarán of Saigher, patron saint of Ossory, is located in the townland of Castletown. It has a well dedicated to St Ciarán, but otherwise it appears not to be identifiable in early sources.

The church and graveyard in which the Ahenny crosses are located is called Kilclispeen, 'the church of St Crispin'. The name Ahenny is derived from the ford across the River Lingaun nearby and derives perhaps from *Áth Teine*, 'the ford of the fire' (Power 1952, 279). Although now the modern name of the townland in which the crosses stand, medieval documents clearly distinguished between it and the church, Kilclispeen. The latter name is suggestive of an Anglo-Norman re-dedication and that this is the case is clear from a deed in the Ormond archives dated 1359 which refers to lands in Aghenene once in the possession of one William Crispyn (Curtis 1932–43, II, 43). The Crispyn family held lands in and around the Ahenny area from about 1300 onwards and must have re-dedicated the church to

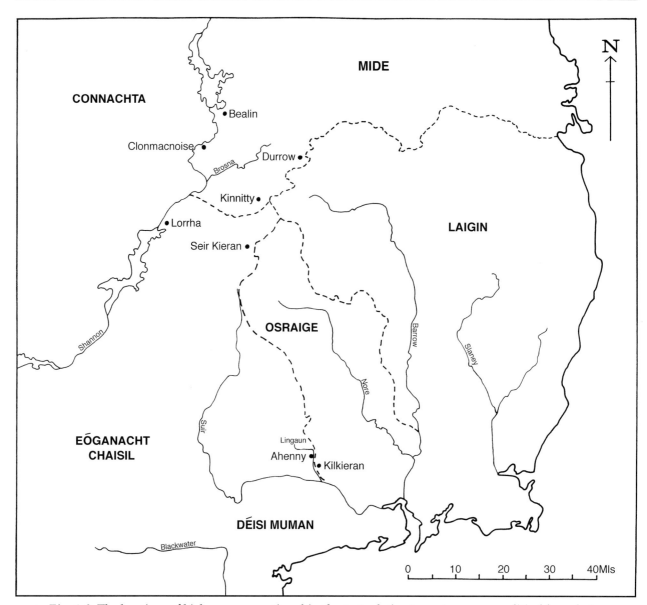

Fig. 1.6 *The locations of high crosses mentioned in the text relative to contemporary political boundaries*

their own patron saint, obscuring the earlier dedication in the process. Cillcrispyne as a place-name independent of Ahenny is first recorded in a deed dated 1429 (Curtis 1932–43, III, 273).

Having established Kilclispeen as an Anglo-Norman dedication, is it possible to identify the original, pre-Norman name of the church? A collection of Irish Litanies dating at least as early as the twelfth century contains one which lists the seven holy bishops of a number of churches. One line reads:

> Secht noeb epscoip Maigi Bolg, secht noeb epscop Maigi Brecmaigi, secht noeb nepscop Dromma Duin

> 'seven holy bishops of Magh Bolg, seven holy bishops of Magh Brechmagh, seven holy bishops of Druim Duin' (Plummer 1925, 68).

The last church mentioned, Druim Dúin, is glossed in a later hand, 'this is Cill Cnisbin on Sliab Dile' (*ibid.*). We can therefore confidently assert that the early name for the site at Ahenny was Druim Dúin. The name Druim Dúin seems otherwise unrecorded and its founder is unknown.

The group of crosses to which the Ahenny and Kilkieran crosses belong include those at Killamery, Kilree and Tibberaghny, all in south Kilkenny, as well as the crosses at Seir Kieran and Lorrha. The distribution of these crosses with respect to the borders of the kingdom of Ossory is of particular relevance here (Fig. 1.6). Those at Seir Kieran and Lorrha are in many senses geographically mirror images of the south Ossory group, being situated on the north eastern boundary of Ossory bordering the neighbouring kingdoms of Leinster, Munster and Mide.

Recent work on the inscriptions of the midland scripture crosses has shown that some were erected during the reign of the high king Máelsechnaill (846–862) – the crosses of Kinnitty, the South Cross at Clonmacnoise and the cross at Durrow – or that of his son Fland (879–916) – the Cross of the Scriptures, Clonmacnoise (Ó Murchadha and Ó Murchú 1988; de Paor 1987). In a recent article, Peter Harbison (1993) reassessed the Ossory group of crosses in the light of a new cross base from Cashel, Co. Tipperary and attempted to place them in an historical context. Harbison, following on a suggestion by Smyth, remarked that 'There is an apparent lack of any important political or ecclesiastical activity in the Ahenny area during the eighth and early ninth centuries [i.e. in the period to which these crosses are normally dated] which could help to create a suitable 'climate' in which the crosses could have been erected in their individual locations' (1993, 9). Setting aside the art-historical dates, he concluded that the Ahenny and related crosses could be attributed to Máelsechnaill, who in 859 succeeded in gaining the submission of Cerball mac Dúnlainge, the most powerful of all the kings of Ossory, wresting his kingdom from the overlordship of the king of Cashel and bringing it under control of the northern half of Ireland. Harbison thus saw the North Cross at Ahenny (and presumably by extension the other Ossory crosses) as physical reminders of Máelsechnaill's domination over the Osraige (*ibid.*, 20).

I think that it is more plausible however, that if the crosses are to be dated to the period when the kingdom of Ossory was of any consequence – during the reign of Cerball mac Dúnlainge (847–888) – then the erection of the crosses is to be attributed to Cerball himself.[1] Far from being the oppressed opponent of Máelsechnaill as portrayed by Harbison, Cerball was a skilled manipulator of political alliances. He was related by marriage both to Máelsechnaill and to the latter's successor as high king, Áed Findliath. His submission to Máelsechnaill in 859 was a political expedient which enabled him to concentrate his efforts against the Norse. This culminated in marriage alliances with the Norse dynasty of Dublin, of which he acted as protector from 870 until his death in 888 (Byrne 1973, 162). His control of Dublin would have provided him with the necessary resources to endow churches in Ossory, in particular churches affiliated with its patron saint, Ciarán, such as Seir Kieran and Kilkieran.

The River Lingaun, on either side of which Ahenny and Kilkieran are situated, holds a particular place in the origin legend of the Osraigi – the people who gave their name to the kingdom. In the eighth-century text 'The Expulsion of the Déisi' it is recounted how the Déisi of Co. Waterford were ceded additional territory to the north of the River Suir, in the present Co. Tipperary, provided they drove out the people of Ossory who then possessed it. The Osraige were duly expelled from the territory fleeing eastwards 'like wild deer' (hence the name Osraige – 'deer people') until they crossed the River Lingaun 'which is the boundary between the Déisi and the men of Ossory 'till doom'(Meyer 1907, 141; translation from Power 1914, 157). Just as *Íseal Chiaráin*, alias Bealin/Twyford, may have been provided with a decorated cross in view of its place in the early formation of the *paruchia* of Ciarán of Clonmacnoise, perhaps we might see Ahenny in the same light, being endowed by Cerball as a confident statement of his reclaiming of the territories east of the Lingaun lost ignominiously in earlier times.

Cerball's patronage of sculptors and erection of high crosses on the borders at each end of his kingdom would thus be a conscious imitation of Máelsechnaill's commissioning of scripture crosses at Clonmacnoise, Durrow and Kinnitty. Like the Ossory crosses, those linked to Máelsechnaill and his son Fland are located on the southern borders of the kingdom of Mide. However, the sculptors responsible for the Ossory crosses chose different models and designs which eschewed, for the most part, figure sculpture. This may have been a conscious decision, to distinguish them from the crosses erected by the kings of Mide.

It will of course be argued against this that the art-historical parallels for the Ossory crosses belong to the eighth and early ninth centuries and that the thesis proposed above cannot therefore hold water. The debt these crosses owe to metalwork prototypes is undoubted, but therein I suggest, lies the answer to the apparent chronological difficulty. These non-scriptural Ossory crosses are deliberate copies of a jewelled metalwork cross of the type described as having been erected on the Hill of Golgotha. Such a cross, symbolising Christ's victory over death, would be an appropriate form for a martial king such as Cerball to adopt. The metalwork cross which formed the prototype of the Ossory crosses must have been of some importance to warrant its copying in stone. One possibility is that the prototype may have been a relic of the True Cross. That such crosses were already known in Ireland in Cerball's time is indicated by a reference which is unique to the compilation of annals derived from a specifically Ossory source. This relates how the high king Áed Findliath defeated the Vikings at Killineer, Co. Louth in the year 868 (*FrA*, § 366). The annalist is at pains to point out that Áed was urged on by his wife Land, sister of Cerball, and that he was accompanied by his battle standards: a cross named 'the lord's cross' (*croch an Choimdheach*) and the *Bachall Íosa* or 'Staff of Jesus'. Áed is said to have encouraged his forces with the words 'Do not think of flight, but trust in the Lord who gives victory to the Christians'. This cross-reliquary must have been of sufficient merit to have been named along with the Staff of Jesus, one of the foremost reliquaries of the Irish Middle Ages. The use of a reliquary cross as a battle standard has immediate Constantinian resonances and this (or a similar) cross may well have served as the model on which the Ossory high crosses were based. In the absence of inscriptions, we can never know the precise circumstances under which the Ossory group of crosses was carved. What is clear is that they stand apart from the midland series of scripture crosses associated with Máelsechnaill and his son Fland. There are other factors which they have in common: they were erected in border areas of their respective kingdoms, many in relatively obscure or poorly documented church sites, and some sites have more than one cross.

The scenario proposed above for the erection of the Ossory high crosses is unlikely, in the absence of inscriptions from the crosses themselves, to be anything other than a best guess. All one can propose is that the political circumstances in Ossory in the mid-ninth century offer a more plausible background for these ambitious monuments than any period in the eighth century.

Conclusion

The reasons for the commissioning of a major piece of stone sculpture or ecclesiastical metalwork may often depend on immediately local factors, some of which may not be detectable due to the lack of detailed historical sources. Anniversaries, for example, may be commemorated by the translation of relics and their enshrinement and this may explain some annalistic references, such as the enshrinement in 1162 of the bones of Maeinenn and Cumméne Fota by the monks of Clonfert (*AFM*). Maeinenn cannot easily be identified in the sources but Cum-méne was the abbot of Clonfert whose death was reported in the annals exactly half a millennium earlier in 662 (*AU*). Similarly, the remains of St Manchán of Mohill, Co. Leitrim were enshrined by Ruaidrí Ua Conchobair in 1166 (*AFM*), probably marking the 500th anniversary of his death in the great plague of 665–6 (*AU*).

Before we consider the evidence from other disciplines, however, we must look at how we as archaeologists treat our own source material. An example of the casual use of primary archaeological source material is the recurrence of the use of imprecise or downright inaccurate find locations for important artefacts. The high crosses have been

mentioned in this regard above and there are many other examples. Although we all *know* that the 'Tara' Brooch was not found at Tara, we still persist in using the term – but how many have stopped to think of how such an object came to be deposited on the seashore at Bettystown, in Co. Meath? The 'Tara' Brooch is *not* a stray find; like all objects it has (or rather, had) a find context which can only partly be reconstructed today due to the lack of any detailed contemporary accounts of its discovery (Whitfield 1974).

What did the immediate landscape in which the 'Tara' Brooch was found look like in the eighth century? What lies in the vicinity of the find in terms of known contemporary or near contemporary monuments or artefacts? What was happening politically in this part of the kingdom of Brega at the time the brooch was made and when was it placed in the ground? We will probably never know why or when it came to be deposited but we cannot begin to know if we do not ask the right questions.

Notes

1 Smyth (1979, 287–8) has advanced a similar argument.

References

AFM = O'Donovan, J. (ed. and trans.) 1851, *Annála Rioghachta Éireann: Annals of the Kingdom of Ireland by the Four Masters from the earliest period to the year 1616*, 7 vols. Dublin.
AL = *Ancient Laws of Ireland* 1873, *Senchus Mor (conclusion), being the Corus Bescna or Customary Law and the Book of Aicill* (5 vols, 1865–1901) Vol. III . Dublin.
ATig = Stokes, W. (ed. and trans.) 1993, *The Annals of Tigernach*, 2 vols. (repr.). Felinfach.
AU = Mac Airt, S. and Mac Niocaill, G. (eds and trans.) 1983, *The Annals of Ulster (to AD 1131) part I, text and translation*. Dublin.
BARKER, P., WHITE, R., PRETTY, K., BIRD, H. and CORBISHLEY, M. 1997, *The Baths Basilica Wroxeter: Excavations 1966–90* (= Engl. Heritage Archaeol. Rep. 8). London.
BATESON, J. D. 1973, 'Roman material from Ireland: a re-consideration', *Proc. Roy. Ir. Acad.* 73C, 21–97.
BIELER, L. 1979, *The Patrician Texts in the Book of Armagh* (= *Scriptores Latini Hiberniae* 10). Dublin.
BOURKE, C. (ed.) 1995, *From the Isles of the North. Early Medieval Art in Ireland and Britain*. Belfast.
BROWN, D. 1976, 'Archaeological evidence for the Anglo-Saxon period', in A. McWhirr 1976 (ed.), *Archaeology and History of Cirencester* (= B.A.R. Brit. Ser. 30). Oxford.
BYRNE, F. J. 1973, *Irish Kings and High Kings*. Dublin.
BYRNE, F. J. and FRANCIS, P. 1994, 'Two lives of St Patrick: *Vita Secunda* and *Vita Quarta*', *J. Roy. Soc. Antiq. Ir.* 124, 5–117.

CARRIGAN, W. 1905, *The History and Antiquities of the Diocese of Ossory*, Vol. 4. Dublin (repr. Kilkenny, 1981).

CARSON, R . A. G. and O'KELLY, C. 1977, 'A catalogue of the Roman coins from Newgrange, Co. Meath and notes on the coins and related finds', *Proc. Roy. Ir. Acad.* 77C, 35–56.

CHARLES-EDWARDS, T. 1999, 'Britons in Ireland, *c.* 550–800', in J. Carey, J. T. Koch and P-Y. Lambert (eds), *Ildánach Ildírech: A Festschrift for Proinsias Mac Cana*, 15–26. Andover, Aberystwyth.

COGAN, A. 1867, *The Diocese of Meath Ancient and Modern. Vol. II.* Dublin (reprinted Dublin, 1992).

COOKE, T. L. 1852-3, 'The ancient cross of Banagher, Co. Offaly', *J. Roy. Soc. Antiq. Ir.* 2, 277–80.

COONEY, G. and GROGAN, E. 1994, *Irish Prehistory: A Social Perspective*. Dublin.

COX, L. 1969, 'Íseal Chiaráin, the Low Place of St. Ciarán, Where was it Situated?', *J. Old Athlone Soc.* 1, 6–14.

CURTIS, E. 1932-43, *Calendar of Ormond Deeds*, 6 vols. Dublin.

CUNLIFFE, B. (ed.) 1988, *The Temple of Sulis Minerva at Bath. Vol. 2. The Finds from the Sacred Spring*. Oxford.

DARK, K. R. 1994, *Civitas to Kingdom: British Political Continuity 300–800*. London, New York.

DAVIES, J. L. 1995, 'The early Celts in Wales', in Green (ed.), 671–700.

DE PAOR, L. 1987, 'The high crosses of Tech Theille (Tihilly), Kinnitty, and related sculpture', in E. Rynne (ed.), *Figures from the Past – Studies in Figurative Art in Christian Ireland in Honour of Helen M Roe*, 131–67. Dun Laoghaire.

DE COURCY WILLIAMS, W. F. 1900, 'Bronze brooch Durrow', *J. Roy. Soc. Antiq. Ir.* 30, 371.

EDWARDS, N. 1983, 'An early group of crosses from the kingdom of Ossory', *J. Roy. Soc. Antiq. Ir.* 113, 5–46.

EDWARDS, N. 1990, 'Some crosses of County Kilkenny', in W. Nolan and K. Whelan (eds), *Kilkenny: History and Society – Interdisciplinary Studies on the History of an Irish County*, 33–61. Dublin.

EDWARDS, N. 1998, 'A group of shafts and related sculpture from Clonmacnoise and its environs', in H. A. King (ed.), *Clonmacnoise Studies* 1, 101–18. Dublin.

FrA = Radner, J. N. (ed. and trans.) 1978, *Fragmentary Annals of Ireland*. Dublin.

GRACIE, H. S. 1970, 'Frocester Court Roman villa; first report', *Trans. Bristol Gloucestershire Archaeol. Soc.* 89, 15–86.

GRAHAM-CAMPBELL, J. A. 1991, 'Dinas Powys metalwork and the dating of enamelled zoomorphic penannular brooches', *Bull. Board Celtic Stud.* 38, 220–32.

GREEN, M. J. (ed.) 1995, *The Celtic World*. London, New York.

GURNEY, D. 1986, *Settlement, Religion and Industry on the Fen-edge; Three Romano-British Sites in Norfolk* (= East Anglian Archaeol. Rep. 31). Norfolk.

GWYNN, E. 1991, *The Metrical Dindshenchas, Part III* (= Roy. Ir. Acad. Todd Lecture Ser 10). Dublin (1913) repr. 1991.

HARBISON, P. 1992, *The High Crosses of Ireland. An Iconographical and Photographic Survey*, 3 vols. (= Römisch-Germanisches Zentralmuseum, Forsch-ungsinstitut für Vor- und Frühgeschichte Monographien 17, 1–3). Bonn.

HARBISON, P. 1993, 'A high cross base from the Rock of Cashel and a historical reconsideration of the 'Ahenny Group' of crosses', *Proc. Roy. Ir. Acad.* 93C, 1–20.

HENRY, F. 1930, 'L'Inscription de Bealin', *Rev. Archéol.* 32, 110–15.

HENRY, F. 1965, *Irish Art in the Early Christian Period to AD 800*. London.

HICKS, C. 1980, 'A Clonmacnois workshop in stone', *J. Roy. Soc. Antiq. Ir.* 110, 5–35.

HOGAN, E. 1910, *Onomasticon Goedelicum*. Dublin, London.

KEHNEL, A. 1997, *Clonmacnois – the Church and Lands of St Ciarán* (= *Vita Regularis*. Ordnungen und Deutungen religiosen Lebens im Mittelalter 8). Münster.

KELLY, E. P. 1993, 'The Lough Kinale book-shrine', in R. M. Spearman and J. Higgitt (eds), *The Age of Migrating Ideas, Early Medieval Art in Northern Britain and Ireland*, 168–74. Edinburgh, Stroud.

KELLY, F. 1988, *A Guide to Early Irish Law*. (= Early Irish Law Series, 3). Dublin.

KILBRIDE-JONES, H. E. 1937, 'The evolution of penannular brooches with zoomorphic terminals in Great Britain and Ireland', *Proc. Roy. Ir. Acad.* 43C, 379–455.

KILBRIDE-JONES, H. E. 1980, *Zoomorphic Penannular Brooches* (= Rep. Res. Comm. Soc. Antiq. London 39). London.

KNIGHT, J. K. 1984, 'Glamorgan AD 400–1100, archaeology and history', in H. N. Savory (ed.), *Glamorgan County History. Vol 2. Early Glamorgan Prehistory and Early History*, 315–64. Cardiff.

LAING, L. 1993, *A Catalogue of Celtic Ornamental Metalwork in the British Isles c AD 400–1200* (= B.A.R. Brit. Ser. 229). Oxford.

LASKO, P. 1994, *Ars Sacra*. New Haven, London.

LEEDS, E. T. and RILEY, M. 1942, 'Two early Saxon cemeteries at Cassington, Oxon.', *Oxoniensia* 7, 61–70.

MACKILLOP, J. 1998, *Dictionary of Celtic Mythology*. Oxford.

MAC SHAMHRÁIN, A. S. 1994, *Church and Polity in Pre-Norman Ireland: The Case of Glendalough* (= Maynooth Monographs 7). Maynooth.

MEYER, K. 1907, 'The Expulsion of the Déssi', *Ériu* 3, 135–42.

NEWMAN, C. 1995, 'The Iron Age to Early Christian transition: the evidence from dress-fasteners', in C. Bourke (ed.), 17–25.

O'BRIEN, E. 1993, 'Contacts between Ireland and Anglo-Saxon England in the seventh century', *Anglo-Saxon Stud. Archaeol. Hist.* 6, 93–102.

O'BRIEN, E. 1999, *Post-Roman Britain to Anglo-Saxon England: Burial Practices Reviewed* (= B.A.R. Brit. Ser. 289). Oxford.

Ó FLOINN, R. 1989, 'Secular metalwork in the eighth and ninth centuries', in S. Youngs (ed.), 72–91.

Ó FLOINN, R. 2000, 'Freestone Hill, Co. Kilkenny: a reassessment', in A. P. Smyth (ed.), *Seanchas: Studies in Early and Medieval Irish Archaeology, History and Literature in Honour of Francis J Byrne*, 12–29. Dublin.

Ó hÓGÁIN, D. 1991, *Myth, Legend and Romance: An Encyclopædia of the Irish Folk Tradition*. New York.

Ó MURCHADHA, D. and Ó MURCHÚ, G. 1988, 'Fragmentary inscriptions from the West Cross at Durrow, the South Cross at Clonmacnois, and the cross of Kinnitty', *J. Roy. Soc. Antiq. Ir.* 118, 53–66.

PLUMMER, C. (ed.) 1925, *Irish Litanies* (= Henry Bradshaw Soc. 62). London.

POWER, P. (ed.) 1914, *Life of St Declan of Ardmore and Life of St Mochuda of Lismore* (= Irish Texts Soc. 16). London.

POWER, P. 1952, *The Place-Names of Decies*. Cork.

REDKNAP, M. 1995, 'Early Christianity and its monuments', in Green (ed.), 737–78.

ROE, H. M. 1969, *The High Crosses of Western Ossory*. Kilkenny.

SHEARMAN, P. 1876-8, 'Loca Patriciana – Part XI – St Patrick's journey into Ossory', *J. Roy. Soc. Antiq. Ir.* 14, 188–245.

SMYTH, A. 1979, *Scandinavian York and Dublin*. Vol. 2. New Jersey, Dublin.

STEVENSON, R. B. K. 1959, 'The Inchyra stone and other unpublished early Christian monuments', *Proc. Soc. Antiq. Scotl.* 92, 33–55.

SWIFT, C. 1996, 'Pagan monuments and Christian legal centres in early Meath', *Ríocht na Midhe* 9, 1–26.

THOMAS, C. 1981, *Christianity in Roman Britain to AD 500*. London.

WARNER, R. B. 1987, 'Ireland and the origins of escutcheon art', in M. Ryan (ed.), *Ireland and Insular Art A.D. 500–1200*, 19–22. Dublin.

WHEELER, R. E. M. and WHEELER, T. V. 1932, *Report on the Excavation of the Prehistoric, Roman, and Post-Roman Site in Lydney Park, Gloucestershire* (= Rep. Res. Comm. Soc. Antiq. London 9). Oxford.

WHITE, R. H. 1988, *Roman and Celtic Objects from Anglo-Saxon Graves* (= B.A.R. Brit. Ser. 191). Oxford.

WHITFIELD, N. 1974, 'The finding of the Tara Brooch', *J. Roy. Soc. Antiq. Ir.* 104, 120–42.

WOODWARD, A. 1992, *Shrines and Sacrifice*. London.

YOUNGS, S. (ed.) 1989, *'The Work of Angels'. Masterpieces of Celtic Metalwork, 6th–9th Centuries AD*. London.

YOUNGS, S. 1995, 'A penannular brooch from near Calne', *Wiltshire Archaeol. Natur. Hist. Mag.* 88, 127–30.

YOUNGS, S. forthcoming, 'The stick pin', in I. Riddler, M. Lynne and Q. Mould, *The Roman Watermills at Ickham*, Canterbury Archaeol. Trust Occasional Papers.

2   The Cultural and Political Milieu of the Deposition and Manufacture of the Hoard Discovered at Reerasta Rath, Ardagh, Co. Limerick

Edel Bhreathnach

The circumstances of the discovery of the renowned hoard of fine ecclesiastical and secular metal objects close to the village of Ardagh, Co. Limerick in the nineteenth century were most reliably described by the Earl of Dunraven in his essay on the subject (Dunraven 1874, 433):

> In the parish, and close to the village of Ardagh, in the county of Limerick, there is a rath, called Reerasta. This rath is of the usual character, and of average size, its internal diameter being about fifty-seven yards. It is situated on a farm held by a widow of the name Quin, and has been partly levelled for the purpose of tillage ...Towards the end of September, 1868, her son was digging potatos (sic) in the fort at the south-western side. On reaching the base of the bank, and close to a thorn bush, he found the surface soft: he drove the spade down between the roots of the thorn, and felt it strike against something hard, like metal. While clearing the earth and roots to see what this could be, he thrust down his hand, and laid hold of the long pin of a fibula. He then excavated to the depth of about three feet, and found a most beautiful cup laid in the earth, with a rough flagstone on one side of it, and inside the cup was a smaller cup and four fibulæ. The small cup was the only article broken by the stroke of the spade. Excavations have been since made in the immediate vicinity of the spot where these articles were found, but nothing has turned up.

While Dunraven's account was dependent on the evidence of the widow Quin, a most unreliable source, who changed her story about the finding of the hoard in the hope of obtaining more money as a reward (Ó Floinn forthcoming), two essential elements of the story for the purpose of this paper are consistent. The find consisted of a hoard and was found either within or in the vicinity of a fort in the townland of Reerasta South near Ardagh.

The many commentaries on the most spectacular object from this hoard, the Ardagh chalice, have not alluded in any great detail to the composition of the hoard as an entity (for a comprehensive bibliography see Ryan 1990, 352–56). The brooches have been treated in a manner similar to the chalice, in that observations are usually confined to the attributes of individual brooches or pairs of brooches (Youngs 1989, nos 76, 81). It is important, however, to maintain the context of the chalice as part of a hoard since its find circumstances fixes the components in a more specific cultural milieu of origin and deposition. The complete hoard consisted of:

(i)   A copper-alloy chalice, its closest parallel being an unprovenanced copper-alloy vessel now in the Ulster Museum, Belfast (Ryan 1990, 290–92).

(ii)   A large two-handled silver chalice, the closest parallel for which is the other great Insular example known as the Derrynaflan chalice (Ryan 1990, 289–90; 1997, 1005–6).

(iii) A silver brooch of 'Tara-Hunterston type' which may be the earliest datable object in the hoard. The current view of art historians would date the production of variants of this type of brooch to the eighth and ninth centuries (Youngs 1989 no. 76; Whitfield 1992, 9–15; 1997, 228). An important feature on the Ardagh brooch is the presence of a nick on its pinhead that is characteristic of Viking Age silver (Graham-Campbell 1995, 47–8).

(iv)   Two silver brooches of 'Ardagh type'. These are the prototype. They are silver annular brooches of a type with a notable North Munster provenance. It is important in the context of this study to note that a similar brooch was found in the stone fort at Cahercommaun in north Clare (Ó Floinn 1999, 77–8). These brooches are dated to the early ninth century (Graham-Campbell 1972).

(v) A silver thistle brooch, parallels for which come from either side of the Shannon Estuary. Similar brooches have been found at Newmarket-on-Fergus, Co. Clare and Ballynolan, Co. Limerick. The Ardagh thistle brooch is small in size with solid, brambled terminals and is thus typologically early. Similar brooches occurred in the Cuerdale hoard, Lancashire, deposited *c*. 903, and in the Goldsborough hoard, Yorkshire, deposited *c*. 920 (Graham-Campbell 1983, 310–12). This type was replaced by the mid-tenth century by larger brooches with hollow-cast terminals. The absence of brooches generally dated to the tenth century, such as bossed penannular and kite-shaped brooches known to have been in circulation in the region (Cahill and Ó Floinn 1995, 65–82), may offer a *terminus ante quem* for the date of deposition of the Ardagh hoard.

Assessed as a single unit, therefore, the Ardagh hoard is composed of metal objects which, on the basis of art-historical evidence, could have been manufactured at any time from the early eighth century to the late ninth century, and therefore, could have been buried in the late ninth century. This possibility is strengthened because none of the objects belonging to the hoard show much evidence of deterioration due to wear and tear. Ryan has argued on similar grounds for a date no later than the tenth century for the deposition of the Derrynaflan hoard (Ryan 1997, 998–1000).

Some of the objects in the hoard came from a church of high standing. Others belonged either to eminent churchmen, craftsmen or secular rulers. The closest parallels for the majority of the objects come from north and mid Munster and it would appear that the 'Tara-Hunterston type' brooch passed through Viking hands.

The deposition of the Ardagh hoard

Any hoard usually has three parts to its story: the circumstances of deposition, origin and production of the individual pieces. The question as to who buried these objects, why and when, is best addressed by analysis of the hoard's contents and the location of its burial. Reerasta Rath, the enclosure in which the hoard was found, was described by the antiquary Thomas J. Westropp (1916–17, 28) as follows:

> A deep fosse, nearly straight, runs along the north face, and is over 6 feet deep and 10 feet wide, which, with its massive mound, show it to be a place of

importance; the east and west are levelled. The place measures about 300 feet across, being somewhat oblong, and is only interesting from the find in its rampart of the beautiful chalice which has spread the obscure name of Ardagh round the antiquarian and artistic groups of the world.

The Earl of Dunraven also noted that 'formerly a large stone, called Reerasta Cloch, stood on, or formed part of, the external face of the bank' (1874, 434). This stone was broken up in the nineteenth century. It is possible that this was an inauguration or ceremonial stone. Its existence led Liam Gógan in his monograph on the Ardagh chalice to suggest, on the basis of the name Reerasta, or the local variant thereof *Royrastia*, that the stone was *Cloch Riaráiste* 'The Stone of Rearage or Arrears' and hence was a tribute stone in the medieval period (Gógan 1932, 26). The enclosure is recorded as having three names, most commonly Reerasta Rath, Ravenstar Fort and Ardagh Fort. Two adjacent townlands are called Reerasta North and South, the fort being located in Reerasta South. The origin of Reerasta is chronologically established in the Ordnance Survey Place-Names Commission survey of County Limerick as deriving from *riaráiste*, the Irish word from Anglo-Norman or English 'rearage' (Ó Maolfabhail 1990, 240). A fiant[1] dated 1595 granting lands to a certain Captain Robert Collum in Co. Limerick refers to land in the parish of Ardagh, including 33 burgage acres at Rerage Ruddery, Minsters and the Spitall (Fiant no. 5957). The name 'Rerage Ruddery' is understood to be a translation of *riaráiste an ridire* 'the rearage of the knight', the knight in question being the Knight of the Valley of the house of Desmond. This sixteenth-century reference appears to be the earliest allusion to the townland of Reerasta. While the official explanation is perfectly acceptable, it is possible – considering that it is a relatively late record – that the name is a highly corrupt version of an earlier Irish place-name. There are other instances in the vicinity that testify to a tendency – not uncommon throughout Ireland – to transform Irish place-names into apparently highly anglicised names. The townlands of Dunganville Upper and Lower derive from *Dún gConmhaoile* 'the fort of Cú Maoile', a large enclosure in the vicinity of Rath Reerasta (Westropp 1916–17, 23–7; Ó Maolfabhail 1990, 168). The first reference to Dún gConmhaoile in the sources occurs in a deed of 1298 relating to the extent of the manor of *Novo Castro* (Newcastle, Co. Limerick) (*CDI* IV, 257). Of more immediate relevance are the names Glenstar, which derives from *Gleann Eas Dáire* 'the glen of the waterfall of the Dáir', the *Dáir* (Daar) being the local river, or even more spectacularly the Morningstar River which comes from Irish *Samhaír* (Ó Maolfabhail 1990, 81, 188). In both instances early references exist, Asdare also occurring in the '*Novo Castro*' deed of 1298, and Samaír in the pre-Norman codex *Lebor na hUidre*. It is possible that the alternative name for Reerasta Rath, Ravenstar, contains the elements *Eas Dáire*. One possible derivation might be *Ráithín Eas Dáire*.

If one were to speculate, mindful of the dangerous pitfalls involved in such topographic fantasies, an alternative derivation of the name Reerasta Rath might be a corruption of *Ráith Ríg Ressada*, 'the fort of the king of Ress or Ressad'. The title 'King of Ress or Ressad' is a metaphor used very occasionally to describe the ruler of the kingdom in which Ardagh was located prior to the coming of the Anglo-Normans, the kingdom of a people known as the Uí Fhidgeinti. Ress or Ressad may have been a territory in the kingdom of Uí Fhidgeinti that had a ceremonial significance. Archaeological evidence suggests that the area around Ardagh saw considerable activity during the Bronze Age and early medieval period. Ballylin, a substantial hillfort, is located on the slopes of the Slíab Lúachra mountain range overlooking Ardagh. An Old Irish text on the kings of Cashel, known as 'Conall Corc and the Corcu Loígde', alludes to the destruction of the walls of the fort of Ress (*muri ciuitatis Ressad*) as a result of the malediction of St Colmán of Cloyne (Meyer 1910, 60; Hull 1947, 900). The Annals of Inisfallen record the death of Donnubán of the Uí Fhidgeinti *ríg Ressad* in 980. The twelfth-century O'Brien propaganda text, *Cogadh Gáedhel re Gallaibh*, mentions one Flaithrí mac Allmaráin *ríg Ressad* (*CGG*, 72). The Uí Fhidgeinti consisted of a group of dynasties, linked together by various common ancestors in the pre-Norman genealogies, which included the Uí Chonaill Gabra, Uí Chairpri Aebda, Uí Chormaic, Áes Raigni and Fir Thamnaig (O'Brien 1962, 230–3). Their influence at the height of their power, prior to the tenth century, extended from the Shannon Estuary as far north as the Aran Islands (Plate I). Such was their status in Munster that they were regarded as part of the Éoganacht confederation that dominated the south of Ireland. The Uí Fhidgeinti were occasionally described as Éoganacht Gabra, Éoganacht Ninussa and Éoganacht Árann. The king of Uí Fhidgeinti was close in status to the king of Cashel, the provincial king of Munster (Ó Corráin 1972, 112; Byrne 1973, 178). Our earliest historical records even suggest that Uí Fhidgeinti kings were somewhat of an irritant to the kings of Cashel, as the genealogies preserved in the manuscript Laud Miscellany 610 caustically remark that they lost the sovereignty of Munster as a result of a deed perpetrated against the descendants of Corc, ancestor of many of the kings of Cashel (Meyer 1912, 309). Despite a gradual loss of power to Dál Cais from the tenth century onwards, the Uí Fhidgeinti retained a special status in Munster. The

late eleventh- or early twelfth-century text on the rights and privileges of the kings of Ireland, *Lebor na Cert*, states that the king of Uí Chonaill Gabra was not required to render hostages to the king of Cashel as a mark of loyalty or submission. He simply swore an oath of fealty (Dillon 1962, 30). In return, the king of Cashel intriguingly gave him an *errid Cásc*, translated by the editor as 'an Easter cloak' (*ibid.*, 138).

Ardagh is in the heartland of the kingdom of Uí Chonaill Gabra. Place-name evidence confirms as much. The barony of Connello retains the name Uí Chonaill (Ó Maolfabhail 1990, 139), Reens derives from Áes Raigni (Ó Corráin 1969–70), and Mahoonagh from Mag Tamnaige (Ó Maolfabhail 1990, 215). An early seventeenth-century petition from William Collum to the Lord Deputy describes Ardagh as 'Ardagh O'Connell, co. Limerick, situate (sic) near the mountain foot of Straflogher'(Hastings MSS vol iv, 40). The reference to Straflogher, or Slíab Lúachra, the mountain range which rises at Ardagh and runs southwards into the modern counties of Cork and Kerry characterises similarities between the locations of Ardagh and Derrynaflan. Slíab Lúachra was a border territory that marked the division between the kingdoms of Uí Fhidgeinti and Cíarraige Lúachra to the west, and Uí Fhidgeinti and Éoganacht Locha Léin to the south. Derrynaflan lay in the lands of Éoganacht Chaisil, but close to the border with the Éli to the north and Osraige to the east. Derrynaflan, an island in bogland, flourished as a monastery from the mid-eighth to mid-ninth centuries and was affiliated to the Céli Dé ascetic movement (Ó Muraíle 1983). As a church of some importance in its own right, fine altar plate could have been commissioned for Derrynaflan itself (Ryan 1997, 1000). However, the possibility that it was used as a safe haven by a more important church cannot be ruled out. Ardagh may have performed a similar function. A sixteenth-century account of the Desmond rebellion against Tudor authority in Munster describes this region in the following terms: 'This country of Connilloe is a large and woody yet fertile country, and was part of the sayd Earle of Desmonds partimony' (Hayman 1870, 32) and 'the greatest refuge and strength the Rebells had' (*ibid.*, 33).

What occasioned someone to bury the hoard in Rath Reerasta in the heartland of the kingdom of Uí Chonaill Gabra in the late ninth or early tenth centuries? The theory postulated in the nineteenth and early twentieth century, particularly by Canon John Begley in his history of the diocese of Limerick (Begley 1906, 107–8), that the hoard was buried by a fugitive priest in the early eighteenth century along with a Penal cross, can be dismissed for a number of reasons. Firstly, Ardagh is well documented as a bishop's manor from the thirteenth century (Mac-Caffrey 1907, 116 (CXLII)). If the chalice had been in circulation through the centuries, it is likely that it would have become part of the plate of the diocese or even have come into the possession of the Earls of Desmond. Nor would it have easily survived up-heavals such as the Desmond Rebellion or Crom-well's visit to Limerick. Secondly, it is highly unlikely that a hoard of such significance kept by a parish priest or local church as late as the eighteenth century would have gone unnoticed in the sources. Finally, the chalice and brooches do not exhibit signs of considerable wear and repair that other pieces of metalwork that remained in circulation show. As noted above, Ryan has postulated an early medieval date for the deposition of the Derrynaflan hoard for a similar reason (Ryan 1997, 998–1000).

Archaeological evidence from the Limerick region suggests that there was an upsurge in the conceal-ment of brooches in the ninth and tenth centuries. Cahill and Ó Floinn (1995, 80), in their discussion of two kite-shaped brooches from near Limerick city, have remarked on the number of brooches of gold and silver, along with the hoards and single finds of Scandinavian character, all of ninth- and tenth-century date, from Co. Limerick. These include the brooches from the Ardagh hoard, two kite-shaped brooches from near Limerick, a bossed penannular brooch from Kildimo, a thistle brooch from Bally-nolan, a gold brooch-pin from Kilfinnane and a silver ringed pin from Adare. To this list may be added the pair of mid-ninth century silver brooches from Scattery Island in the Shannon Estuary (*ibid.*, 81). The reasons why so many objects were con-cealed in north Munster in the late ninth or tenth centuries may lie in the complex relationships between the kings of Uí Fhidgeinti, their political masters, the kings of Cashel, the rising dynasty of Dál Cais, the Vikings who were establishing their bases on the Shannon and important ecclesiastics of north Munster. At a local level, two main dynasties, the Uí Chonaill Gabra and the Uí Chairpri – whose territory lay further east towards Limerick – fought among themselves for the overkingship of Uí Fhidgeinti. In 860, for example, Áed mac Dub-dá-bairenn of the Uí Chairpri seized (*do gabáil*) the kingship, but was killed in the same year. The overkingship of Munster was also somewhat un-stable with the ailing dynasty of Éoganacht Chaisil finding it difficult to hold on to the kingship due to severe pressure coming from three quarters: the northern dynasties of Uí Néill, the Vikings of Limerick and Waterford and the ascendant dynasty from across the Shannon, the Dál Cais. A notable feature of the kingship of Munster at that time was the number of ecclesiastics who became kings: Ólchobur mac Cináeda, abbot of the pre-eminent

church of Munster, Emly (died 851); Cenn Fáelad úa Mugthigirn, abbot of Emly (died 872); Cormac mac Cuilennáin, king-bishop of Cashel (it is not clear what his ecclesiastical jurisdiction was) (died 908); and Flaithbertach mac Inmainén, abbot of Inis Cathaig (died 944). Inis Cathaig was the primary church of the Uí Fhidgeinti, although it appears that Flaithbertach was one of the few abbots of the monastery not to have belonged to them. He may have originated from among the Múscraige, whose territories lay south of those of the Uí Fhidgeinti (Byrne 1973, 279), or even to the Dál Cais (Book of Ballymote fol.184a 49[2]). The Uí Ionmhainéin (*anglice* O'Noonan) were coarbs in the church of Tullylease, Co. Cork to the mid-seventeenth century (MacCotter and Nicholls 1996, 202–5, n. 151).[3]

The symbiotic relationship between the kings of Cashel and important churches such as Emly and Inis Cathaig needs to be considered, not only in the context of the ecclesiastical and secular polity of Munster of the ninth and tenth centuries, but also in relation to their position as guardians of church and royal treasuries, particularly during turbulent times, and also as patrons of sculptors and metalworkers. The twelfth-century poem *Mithig techt tar mo thimna* in which Cormac mac Cuilennáin, king-bishop of Munster, draws up his will before he departs for the battle of Belach Mugna Leinster in 908, depicts him as granting gifts to various churches (Poppe 1999, 300–11). A later prose version is found in Geoffrey Keating's *Foras Feasa ar Éirinn* (Dineen 1908, 198–99), in which the church at Mungaret near Limerick is singled out as having been particularly dear to Cormac:

> …just before he set out he left legacies for the sake of his soul to the principal churches of Ireland, to wit, an ounce of silver and an ounce of gold and his trappings [*a earradh*] and his steed to Drom Abhrad, that is Ard Fionain. A chalice of gold [*corn óir*] and a satin chasuble [*cochall sróill*] to Lis Mór; a chalice of gold and silver and four ounces of gold and a hundred ounces of silver to Cashel; three ounces of gold and a missal [*leabhar aifrinn*] to Gleann dá Loch; trappings and a steed, an ounce of gold, and a satin cope [*brat sróill*] to Cill Dara; twenty-four ounces of silver and of gold to Ard Macha; three ounces of gold to Inis Cathaig; three ounces of gold and a satin chasuble to Mungairid and the blessing of Cormac.

If king-bishops or king-abbots donated gifts to treasuries, did they also actively engage in dispers-ing such treasuries to safe havens when important churches were endangered? What happened, for example, around the time of attacks by the Vikings on Emly in 847 and *c*. 866 (Etchingham 1996, 64, 69)? We might envisage a scene similar to that depicted by the Annals of St-Bertin in 882 (Nelson 1991, 225–26):

...the Northmen came as far as the neighbourhood of the fortress of Laon, and ravaged and burned all the fortresses in the surrounding area. They planned to move to Rheims and from there to come back by way of Soissons and Noyon and storm the fortress mentioned above and bring the kingdom under their control. Bishop Hincmar [of Rheims, author of the annals and distinguished bishop and courtier] found out for certain that this was their plan: since the fighting-men in the command of the see of Rheims were away with Carloman, he only just managed to escape by night, taking with him the body of Remigius and the treasures of the church of Rheims. His physical weakness meant that he had to be carried in a portable chair. While the canons, monks and nuns scattered in every direction, he fled across the Marne and only just managed to reach a villa called Épernay [a villa of the church of Rheims].

Hincmar escaped from the centre of his see, Rheims, to a presumably safer location, away from the path of danger. When Carloman caught up with them the Northmen fled back north, well away from Épernay. Furthermore, one finds the episode in the *Orkneyinga Saga* (Pálsson and Edwards 1978, 189) in which Svein and Hákon, son of Earl Harald plundered the *Sudreyar* [Hebrides, the southern islands]: 'All the inhabitants were so afraid of him that they hid all their moveable property in the ground or in heaps of stones...'. The tendency to bury valuables in the ground is also attested in early Irish literature. An episode in the Middle Irish tale *Talland Étair* 'The Siege of Howth' relates how the satirical poet Aithirne came to Ard mBrestine in Mag Fea in south Leinster (Best and O'Brien 1956, 427):

> Now there was a horseman riding his horse on the hill. He would move towards the assembly. He would leap away from them. And once, while turning the horse over shanks(?), the horse flung a large sod from two of his hooves. No one in the assembly noticed it until it landed in the lap of the king, namely, Fergus Fairge. And he saw the brooch in the face of the sod, on the side from the ground, wherein were eighty ounces of red gold. "What is this in my lap, o Aithirne" said the king... "That is the brooch I have desired," says Aithirne. "My father's brother left it, and buried it in the ground after the breaking of a battle-slaughter on the Ulstermen, namely, the Battle of Brestine.

The deposition of the Ardagh hoard might have happened in similar circumstances. In spite of the local inter-dynastic rivalry, both main dynasties of the Uí Fhidgeinti were allies of the kings of Cashel in their efforts to counter pressure from the north and the Vikings. The king of Uí Chonaill Gabra was killed at the battle of Belach Mugna fought by the joint kings of Munster, Cormac mac Cuilennáin and Flaithbertach mac Inmainéin, in 908 against the king

of the northern half of Ireland, Flann Sinna and his allies. More significantly for the context of the Ardagh hoard, the king of Uí Chonaill Gabra, Gebennach mac Áeda was killed by the Vikings in 916, an action which brought immediate vengeance (perhaps twice over?) from his people and their relations. The Annals of Inisfallen 917 record *Ár nGall la Hú Conaill Gabra* 'a slaughter of the foreigners by Uí Chonaill Gabra' and this is supported by a reference in *Cogadh Gáedhel re Gallaibh* (*CGG*, 33) to a slaughter of the foreigners by an alliance of Éoganacht Locha Léin, Ciarraige Lúachra and the Uí Chonaill Gabra.[4]

While no exact date can be given for the concealment of the Ardagh hoard, the cultural, ecclesiastical and political clues evident from its contents coincide generally with this very period. In sum, the hoard consists of the contents of an important church's treasury presumably hidden as a consequence of pressure on that church: i. a 'Tara-Hunterston'-type brooch which would only have been the property of the highest stratum of society (ecclesiastic or secular) and which significantly has the nick (possibly loot recovered from a Viking looter); ii. the thistle brooch with a north Munster distribution; iii–iv the two 'Ardagh-type' brooches which are similar to a brooch found at Cahercommaun, the early medieval stone fort in north Clare. The Cahercommaun brooch may offer a regional or dynastic context for the Ardagh brooches because it appears that this stone fort was subject to another branch of the Uí Fhidgeinti until the mid-eighth century at least, when it may have fallen into the hands of the rising Dál Cais (Bhreathnach 1999, 83–91). The 'Ardagh-type' brooches may be Uí Fhidgeinti brooches and their presence in the Ardagh hoard would fit correctly with its deposition in the heart of the kingdom of Uí Chonaill Gabra.

The circumstances of the production and origin of the Ardagh chalice: a hypothesis

If these are the circumstances of concealment, what of the production and origin of the hoard's objects? Unlike the Derrynaflan hoard, which could conceivably have come from the one place, the Ardagh hoard appears to be a composite hoard, namely, a collection of objects some of which could have been family heirlooms (the 'Ardagh-type' brooches), a brooch which went through Viking hands (the 'Tara-Hunterston type' brooch) and the most elaborate object – the silver chalice – which came from an important church. What of the origin of the Ardagh chalice? In the absence of a dedicatory inscription suggestions as to the origins of chalices such as the Ardagh and Derrynaflan chalices can never be certain. However, I do not follow the cautious view adopted by Michael Ryan concerning the possible association between Feidlimid mac Crimthann, king of Cashel (died 847) and the Derrynaflan chalice where he claims that 'This sort of particularism is dangerous as hypotheses of this nature tend to be elevated into 'facts''(Ryan 1997, 997 n. 6). We cannot constantly avoid speculation on the origins of fine objects without dedicatory inscriptions on the basis that there may have been many other examples, some of which may yet be recovered, and that such a recovery could totally change our assessment of the subject to date. To adopt this purist approach confines discussion of these objects[5] to art-historical or liturgical studies bereft of an immediate local context. Ardagh, or at least the kingdom in which it is located, and Derrynaflan are sufficiently well-represented in the sources to allow us to surmise quite safely as to the possible cultural, ecclesiastical and political context in which the chalices were produced. The task of identifying this milieu can be approached from two angles. Firstly, we can identify the churches or royal residences (or other centres) in the north Munster region *likely* to have had the capacity to produce such fine altar plate. Secondly, we can begin to understand the circumstances in which these objects *might* have been commissioned.

Despite the design flaws evident in the construction of the Ardagh chalice (Ryan 1997, 1005–6), only a small number of craftsmen could have produced altar plate of this standard. The law-tract *Uraicecht Becc* (Mac Neill 1921–4, 265–81) demonstrates clearly that like most of society, there were grades of craftsmen with the top grade being accorded the most noble of title *ollam*, a title also accorded the highest grade of poet, lawyer, historian and bishop (Kelly 1988, 318). Notably, the king of Munster is described as *ollam ríg* 'master or chief of kings' (Mac Neill 1921–4, 281; Binchy 1966, 22 §2). The work of these high-class craftsmen is undoubtedly reflected in the standard of work produced, as was the case among the poets. It is likely that they, also in a manner similar to the literary class, worked in conditions that were conducive to the production of high-class material: relatively comfortable and stable conditions where a tradition of craftsmanship was well-established. Centres of excellence ranged from monasteries (e.g. Clonmacnoise: Bradley 1998, 46) and royal residences (e.g. Moynagh Lough: Bradley 1994–5) to workshops inhabited only by artistic communities (as has been suggested for the Mote of Mark; but see Longley, *in this volume*), and sites which point to intensive periodic activity.[6] A master craftsman was sufficiently prized and of high enough rank to have lived the relatively comfortable life of a noble, and not the precarious life of an itinerant journeyman. According to the law-tract *Uraicecht Becc*, the blacksmith, silversmith and coppersmith were entitled to seven *séts*, food provision for four men and three days' protection, the same entitlements as an *aire déso*, the average middle-ranking lord (Mac Neill 1921–4, 278). It would appear from the Middle Irish glosses to the law-tract, that in a manner similar to the literary classes these craftsmen could rise to higher ranks, a possibility which is likely to have developed with the increased complexity of their craft and the ensuing added value attached to it by patrons (Mac Lean 1995, 131–32). The craftsmen commissioned to produce luxurious items such as the Ardagh and Derrynaflan chalices lived in comfortable and stable environs, did not want for much and had patrons – ecclesiastical or secular – who had occasion to need fine altar-plate and were willing to provide materials, protection and sustenance to the *cerd* 'silversmith, goldsmith'.

The Ardagh chalice could have originated locally or could have been brought from a distant church treasury when it was under pressure. A number of important churches were located in the kingdom of Uí Fhidgeinti itself: Druim Lías (Tullylease), Cell Íte (Killeedy: Íte was their *matrona* 'mother saint'), Mungairit (Mungret) and Inis Cathaig (Scattery Island). St Senán, founder of Inis Cathaig, was patron of the Uí Fhidgeinti and the abbots of the monastery were often related to kings of Uí Fhidgeinti, the most notable of which was Ólchobar mac Flainn (died 797). Inis Cathaig was in the path of Viking fleets as they entered the Shannon and was subject not alone to raids, but also to Viking settlement (*AI* 977). At the time of the possible concealment of the Ardagh hoard in the late ninth or early tenth centuries, Flaithbertach mac Inmainéin, abbot of Inis Cathaig, was joint king of Cashel. If the Ardagh hoard was an Uí Fhidgeinti hoard, it is conceivable that the chalice was brought from the treasury of Inis Cathaig to a safe haven at the centre of the kingdom (the territory of Ress or Ressad) when the monastery was under pressure from the Vikings of Limerick or when Flaithbertach mac Inmainén was possibly imposed as abbot contrary to the wishes of the Uí Fhidgeinti.

A model similar to Hincmar's *villa* at Épernay could also be postulated for Ardagh. In such a context it was a safe haven for items brought from a royal or ecclesiastical treasury in troubled times. If so, what churches in Munster could have been the repositories of such fine altar plate? Given the location of Ardagh in relation to Cashel and the special status of the Uí Fhidgeinti in the polity of Munster, did the chalice come from Cashel itself or from one of the eminent churches of Munster: Cork, Cloyne, Emly or Lismore? If one were to consider Emly, the primary church of Munster in the eighth

and ninth centuries, as a *possible* place of origin, what circumstances would have given rise to the production of fine altar plate for such a church and to its subsequent dispersal elsewhere? As noted previously, the conditions that could have caused the dispersal of Emly's treasury could have occurred in the mid-ninth century, when the monastery was attacked in 847 and *c.* 866. Two kings of Cashel were abbots of Emly during this period, namely, Ólchobar mac Cináeda (died 851) and Cennfáelad úa Mugthigirn (died 872). Although there is no known surviving metalwork or carving from Emly, partially due at least to its complete destruction in the nineteenth century, there are many hints that Emly was a centre of excellence in a number of fields, and that this could have included metalworking. The Annals of Inisfallen were compiled there during the tenth century (Mac Niocaill 1975, 25). It may have been a law-school, if the reference to it in the law-tract detailing the status of craftsmen, *Uraicecht Becc*, is accepted as evidence of provenance (Mac Neill 1921–4, 281; Kelly 1988, 246). A curious entry in the Annals of Inisfallen in 947 offers indirect evidence that precious liturgical objects were kept there: 'a leaf descended from heaven (*duilend do nim*) upon the altar of Emly'. This is a metaphor for a *flabellum*, which appears in another text in relation to a *flabellum* (*cuilebad*) on the altar at Kells during the same period (Ó Floinn 1997, 155–58).

If Emly was the repository, an episcopal or royal treasury, what occasioned the commissioning of a chalice as fine as the Ardagh chalice? Many of the surviving early medieval Continental chalices would appear to have been abbatial or episcopal grave chalices (Ryan 1990, 336–49) or were given to churches by secular lords, as in the cases of the Tassilo chalice and one of the Galognano chalices. Indeed the composition and circumstance of the Ardagh hoard suggest great similarities with royal treasuries of barbarian successor states and medieval kingdoms on the Continent (Hardt 1998, 255–80). That the abbot-bishops of Emly were of sufficiently high standing to commission chalices in their own right like their Continental counterparts is evident from the recurrence of contenders for the kingship of Cashel among their ranks. Important secular rulers were probably patrons of Emly. A verse added to the *obit* of Cathal mac Finguine, king of Munster (died 742), in the Annals of Inisfallen suggests that the king was buried at Emly. When Armagh's expansionist policy flourished throughout the eighth century and culminated in Munster in 823 with the imposition of the Law of Patrick (*AU*), Emly responded at one point to this pressure by promulgating the Law of Ailbe, the church's founder saint, in 784 (*AU*). The Life of Ailbe, which in origin possibly dates to the eighth century (Herbert 1996,

89) represents Ailbe as a pre-Patrician saint – hence weakening Patrick's authority over him – and also subjects eminent saints including Enda of Aran to him. If one were to seek reasons for the commissioning of luxurious chalices of the standard of Ardagh by the ecclesiastical authorities at Emly, the promulgation of the Law of Ailbe in 784 might have been celebrated in such a fashion. Among the other unusual occasions which happened during the late eighth century in Munster which might given rise to the production of fine altar-plate was the 'ordination' (*ordinatio*) of Artrí mac Cathail as king of Cashel and the possible re-affirmation of the Law of Ailbe in 793 (*AU*). While the absence of an inscription on the Ardagh chalice militates against anything but a hypothetical theory as to the origin of the chalice, ecclesiastical and political activity in Munster in the period *c.* 750–800 would have been conducive to the commissioning and production of fine altar-plate similar to the Ardagh chalice. It is noteworthy that this period tallies with the dates suggested for the style of filigree animal panels on the piece (Whitfield 1997, 229–32).

I conclude the paper with a dedication. The late Liam de Paor in his collection of essays *Ireland and early Europe* travelled a similar path to mine in a paper he wrote on the discovery of the Derrynaflan hoard (de Paor 1997, 137–43). He mused that the Ardagh hoard might have been a thief's hoard, while Derrynaflan was a custodian's hoard and commented on the 'manifest relationship' between the two (*ibid.*, 143):

> This work [Derrynaflan] would seem to require a royal patron, and by far the most likely place to look for such patronage is Cashel. The great figure in early eighth-century Cashel is Cathal mac Finguine [king of Cashel, died 742], who seems to have taken a Carolingian view of kingship and to have been one of the first to do so. It would be totally in keeping with this to provide a magnificent set of liturgical equipment to a major church – Emly, perhaps, or Lorrha, or Lismore.

This paper is dedicated to the memory of that great scholar, Liam de Paor.

Acknowledgements

I wish to thank Eoin Grogan, Raghnall Ó Floinn, Michael Ryan and Niamh Whitfield for their comments on various aspects of this paper.

Notes

1   A warrant addressed to the Irish Chancery for a grant under the Great Seal.

2   The name Inmainéin occurs in the genealogy of the Dál Cais dynasty of Uí Ailgile. Despite Flaithbertach's intrusion into Inis Cathaig, the Uí Fhidgeinti held onto their claims to the monastery to the twelfth century (Ó Corráin 1973, 54).

3   Late medieval sources support the claim that Flaithbertach mac Inmainéin was of the Múscraige in that the Uí Ionmhainéin superseded another family, the Uí Donnacáin, as lords of the Gaelic remnant of Múscraige (MacCotter and Nicholls 1996, 203). It is also noteworthy that one Cú Duilig Ua Inmainéin and his sons were responsible for the enshrinement of St Patrick's bell at Armagh in the eleventh century (Macalister 1949, 112-13).

4   Similar Viking activity can be detected around Derrynaflan, although it happened in the 850s. *The Fragmentary Annals of Ireland* (Radner 1978, para 254) record that Cerball mac Dúngaile, king of Osraige (died 888) defeated the Vikings at Crúachan Maige Abnae (Crohane, east of Killenaule, Co. Tipperary) in the barony of Slievardagh, the same barony in which Derrynaflan is situated (Ó Corráin 1998, 442).

5   I would cite the Ardagh chalice, the Derrynaflan chalice and paten, the Tara brooch and the Lough Kinale book shrine as examples.

6   For a comprehensive survey of the likely structure and environment of workshops, see O'Meadhra 1987, 99-104.

7   A similar case may be made for the origin and deposition of the Derrynaflan hoard. It is more likely that the contents of the hoard were not produced at Derrynaflan, but were brought there for safe keeping. Whatever is concluded about Ardagh, Derrynaflan's extensive and distinguished connections are well-documented (Ó Muraíle 1983). Flann mac Fairchellaig (died 825) is described in the *óentu* of Máelruain of Tallaght as *Fland Find m. Fairchellaig i nDaire na Fland*. Elsewhere he is accorded the titles of coarb of Ailbe (Emly), Mochuda (Lismore) and Barra (Cork) (*ibid.*, 56-7). If the Ardagh chalice was a response to late eighth-century events in Munster, the Derrynaflan chalice could have been commissioned to celebrate events of the following decades such as the imposition of the Law of Patrick on Munster in 823.

References

AI = MAC AIRT, S. (ed. and trans.) 1951, *The Annals of Inisfallen (MS. Rawlinson B503)*. Dublin.

AU = MAC AIRT, S. and MAC NIOCAILL, G. (eds and trans) 1983 *The Annals of Ulster (to A.D. 1131)*. Dublin.

BB = The Book of Ballymote, Royal Irish Academy, Dublin (facsimile).

BEGLEY, J. 1906, *The Diocese of Limerick Ancient and Medieval*. Dublin.

BEST, R. I. and O'BRIEN, M. A. 1956, *The Book of Leinster formerly Lebar na Núachongbála*. Vol. 2. Dublin.

BINCHY, D. 1966, 'Bretha Déin Chécht', *Ériu* 20, 1-66.

BRADLEY, J. 1994-5, 'Excavations at Moynagh Lough, Co. Meath, 1988-1994', *Ríocht na Midhe* 9, no.1, 158-69.

BRADLEY, J. 1998, 'The monastic town of Clonmacnoise', in H. A. King (ed.), *Clonmacnoise Studies* 1, 42-55. Dublin.

BREATHNACH, E. 1999, 'The construction of a stone fort at Cahercommaun: a historical hypothesis', *Discovery Programme Reports* 5, 83-91.

BYRNE, F. J. 1973, *Irish Kings and High-Kings*. London.

CAHILL, M. and Ó FLOINN, R. 1995, 'Two silver kite brooches from near Limerick City', *N. Munster Antiq. J.* 36, 65-82.

CDI = SWEETMAN, H. S. 1881, *Calendar of Documents relating to Ireland preserved in Her Majesty's Public Record Office, London, 1293-1301*. London.

CGG = Todd, J. H. 1867, *Cogadh Gaedhel re Gallaib: the Wars of the Gaedhil with the Gaill, or the Invasions of Ireland by the Danes and other Norsemen* (= Rolls series 48). London.

DE PAOR, L. 1997, *Ireland and early Europe. Essays and Occasional Writings on Art and Culture*. Dublin.

DILLON, M. 1962, *Lebor na Cert. The Book of Rights*. Dublin.

DINEEN, P. S. 1908, *The History of Ireland by Geoffrey Keating, D.D.* Vol. 3 (= Irish Texts Society 19). London.

DUNRAVEN, EARL OF 1874, 'On an ancient chalice and brooches lately found at Ardagh in the County of Limerick', *Trans. Roy. Ir. Acad.* 24, 433-54.

ETCHINGHAM, C. 1996, *Viking Raids on Irish Church Settlements in the Ninth Century*. Maynooth.

FAIre = Radner, J. N. 1978, *Fragmentary Annals of Ireland*. Dublin.

FIANT = *The Irish Fiants of the Tudor Sovereigns during the Reigns of Henry VIII, Edwards VI, Philip & Mary and Elizabeth I*. 1994 reprint, with a new introduction by K. Nicholls and preface by T. G. Ó Canainn, 3 vols. Dublin.

GÓGAN, L. S. 1932, *The Ardagh Chalice. A Description of the Ministral Chalice found at Ardagh in County Limerick in the year 1868; with a Note on its Traditional Conformity to the Holy Grail of Legend and Story*. Dublin.

GRAHAM-CAMPBELL, J. 1972, 'Two groups of ninth-century Irish brooches', *J. Roy. Soc. Antiq. Ir.* 102, 113-28.

GRAHAM-CAMPBELL, J. 1983, 'Some Viking-Age penannular brooches from Scotland and the origins of the 'Thistle-Brooch'', in A. O'Connor and D. V. Clarke (eds), *From the Stone Age to the 'Forty-Five*, 310-23. Edinburgh.

GRAHAM-CAMPBELL, J. 1995, *The Viking Age Gold and Silver of Scotland (AD 850-1100)*. Edinburgh.

HARDT, M. 1998, 'Royal treasuries and representation in the early middle ages', in W. Pohl with H. Reimitz (eds), *Strategies of Distinction. The Construction of Ethnic Communities, 300-800*, 255-80. Leiden, Boston and Köln.

HASTINGS MSS = BICKLEY, F. (ed.) 1947, *Report on the Manuscripts of the late Reginald Rawdon Hastings, Esq. of the Manor House, Ashby de la Zouch*. Vol. 4. (= Historical Manuscripts Commission 78). London.

HAYMAN, S. 1870, *Unpublished Geraldine Documents*. Dublin.

HERBERT, M. 1996, 'Hagiography', in K. McCone and K. Simms (eds), *Progress in Medieval Irish Studies*, 79-90. Maynooth.

HULL, V. 1947, 'Conall Corc and the Corco Luigde', *Publications of the Modern Language Association of America* 62, 887-909.

KELLY, F. 1988, *A Guide to Early Irish Law*. Dublin.

MACALISTER, R. A. S. 1949, *Corpus Inscriptionum Insularum Celticarum,* Vol. 2. Dublin.

MACCAFFREY, J. 1907, *The Black Book of Limerick.* Dublin.

MACCOTTER, P. and NICHOLLS, K. (eds) 1996, *The Pipe Roll of Cloyne (Rotulus Pipæ Clonensis).* Cloyne.

MAC LEAN, D. 1995, 'The status of the sculptor in Old-Irish law and the evidence of the crosses', *Peritia* 9, 125–55.

MAC NEILL, E. 1921–4, 'Ancient Irish Law. The Law of Status or Franchise', *Proc. Roy. Ir. Acad.* 36C, 265–316.

MAC NIOCAILL, G. 1975, *The Medieval Irish Annals.* Dublin.

MEYER, K. 1910, 'Conall Corc and the Corco Luigde', *Anecdota from Irish Manuscripts* 3, 57–63.

MEYER, K. 1912, 'The Laud genealogies and tribal histories', *Zeitchrift für celtische Philologie* 8, 291–338.

NELSON, J. (trans. and notes) 1991, *The Annals of St-Bertin. Ninth-century histories,* Vol. 1. Manchester and New York.

O'BRIEN, M. A. 1962, *Corpus Genealogiarum Hiberniae,* Vol.1. Dublin. (Reprint 1976).

Ó CORRÁIN, D. 1969–70, 'Raigne, Roigne, Mag Raigni', *Éigse* 13, 81–4.

Ó CORRÁIN, D. 1972, *Ireland before the Normans.* Dublin.

Ó CORRÁIN, D. 1973, 'Dál Cais – church and dynasty', *Ériu* 24, 52–63.

Ó CORRÁIN, D. 1998, 'Viking Ireland – afterthoughts', in H. B. Clarke, M. Ní Mhaonaigh and R. Ó Floinn (eds), *Ireland and Scandinavia in the early Viking Age,* 421–52. Dublin.

Ó FLOINN, R. 1997, 'Insignia Columbae I', in C. Bourke (ed.), *Studies in the Cult of Saint Columba,* 136–61. Dublin.

Ó FLOINN, R. 1999, 'The date of some metalwork from Cahercommaun reassessed', *Discovery Programme Reports* 5, 73–9.

Ó FLOINN, R. (forthcoming), 'The finding of the Ardagh hoard' (to be published in a memorial volume for Liam de Paor edited by E. Rynne).

Ó MAOLFABHAIL, A. 1990, *Logainmneacha na hÉireann. Imleabhar 1. Contae Luimnigh.* Dublin.

O'MEADHRA, U. 1987, *Motif-Pieces from Ireland 2. A Discussion.* Stockholm.

Ó MURAÍLE, N. 1983, 'Notes on the history of Doire na bhFlann', in M. Ryan (ed.), *The Derrynaflan Hoard. A Preliminary Account,* 54–61. Dublin.

PÁLSSON, H and EDWARDS, P. (trans.) 1978, *Orkeyinga Saga: the History of the Earls of Orkney.* London.

POPPE, E. 1999, 'Cormac's metrical testament: 'Mithig techt tar mo thimna", *Celtica* 23, 300–11.

RADNER, J. N. 1978, *Fragmentary Annals of Ireland.* Dublin.

RYAN, M. 1990, 'The formal relationships of Insular early medieval eucharistic chalices', *Proc. Roy. Ir. Acad.* 90C, 281–356.

RYAN, M. 1997, 'The Derrynaflan hoard and early Irish art', *Speculum* 72, 995–1017.

WESTROPP, T. J. 1916–17, 'On certain typical earthworks and ring-walls in County Limerick', *Proc. Roy. Ir. Acad.* 33C, 9–42.

WHITFIELD, N. 1992, 'Animal ornament on Insular metalwork of the late 7th–8th centuries: its character and development', *Medieval Europe 1992: Art and Symbolism, Pre-printed Papers* 7, 9–15.

WHITFIELD, N. 1997, 'Filigree animal ornament from Ireland and Scotland of the late-seventh to ninth centuries', in C. E. Karkov, M. Ryan and R. T. Farrell (eds), *The Insular Tradition,* 211–43. Albany.

YOUNGS, S. (ed.) 1989, *'The Work of Angels'. Masterpieces of Celtic Metalwork, 6th–9th Centuries AD.* London.

Part II

National and Regional Identities

3 National and Regional Identities: the 'Glittering Prizes'

James Graham-Campbell

This paper seeks to address various aspects of the identity of selected Insular metalwork from Ireland and Northumbria, as well as from the kingdoms of the Picts and the Scots, but it commences in Norway as the repository of so much eighth- and ninth-century ornamental metalwork of Insular origin – the 'glittering prizes' of the Vikings.

Trøndelag, in western Norway, is an area of rich agricultural land in a sheltered location, with excellent communications by both land and water. It was consequently a region of advanced economic and social development – one which supported the wealthy earls of Lade, who were amongst the most powerful families in Norway in the early part of the Viking Age (Foote and Wilson 1970, 40–2). It is no surprise therefore that Trøndelag was one of the main regions involved in the Viking expeditions to the West, judging by the quantity of Insular metalwork which was deposited there as grave-goods (Sognnes 1991, 260, fig. 6; Myhre 1998, 23, fig. 1.9; Wamers 1998, 54, fig. 2.6). The chieftain-centre and pagan cult-site of Lade itself is situated on the southern side of Trondheimsfjord, not far from the modern city of Trondheim itself – or Nidaros to give it its medieval name – which celebrated its millennium in 1997 (Fig. 3.1). Nidaros was a royal foundation of the late Viking Age on the site of a trading centre which had grown up at the mouth of the river Nid; it soon boasted not only a mint, but also a cathedral containing the relics of Norway's martyred king, St Olaf (Christophersen 1999, 114–15, with references).

King Olaf met his death at the battle of Stiklestad in 1030. Stiklestad is located in the inner region of Trøndelag (Inn-Trøndelag), to the north of the central assembly-place at Frostating and to the south of the documented chieftain-centre and pagan cult-site of Mære (Lidén 1969). This is an area with a marked concentration of Insular metalwork from its

Viking Age graves – a rich corpus to which must now be added four, or perhaps five, pieces from a single female burial excavated in 1986 at Skei in Sparbu. These particular 'glittering prizes' have (so far) appeared only once in print, in a popular publication, while they were still undergoing conservation (Stenvik 1991). Now that conservation is complete, research by Lars Stenvik in Trondheim is nearing publication, but the following observations, which owe much to his draft report, must necessarily be regarded as provisional.[1]

The richly-furnished grave in question was covered by a mound (Mound 40), one of over 90 of varying types which together constitute a large late Iron Age cemetery on the farm of Skei. The cemetery, however, borders the adjacent farm of Dalem, and it seems most probable that these two farms once formed a single unit. The potential significance of this relates to the fact that some of Norway's richest grave-finds of early Iron Age date were discovered on Dalem's territory in the 1870s. Lars Stenvik (forthcoming) proposes therefore that Dalem/Skei may represent an undocumented chieftain-centre. This suggestion is supported by the presence within the cemetery of one of the distinctive 'court sites' which are known from at least eleven locations along the coast of northern Norway (Myhre 1998, 19–23).[2] These consist of a series of substantial buildings radiating around a central courtyard and, although their exact functions are debated, they appear to have served administrative and military purposes. At Skei, nine houses are arranged in an oval pattern and a couple more may have been destroyed by road construction; they are associated with huge cooking-pits, one of which has been excavated and has produced two radiocarbon dates, that from the bottom of cal. AD 670–870 (1 sigma; T-7985, 1260 BP) and that from the top of cal. AD 685–890 (1 sigma; Tua-56, 1220 BP).

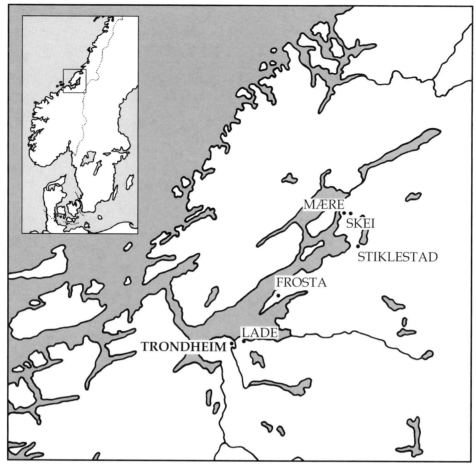

Fig. 3.1 Map of Trøndelag

Skei grave 40: the Insular metalwork

Grave 40 was disturbed by road improvements at Skei in the 1980s which necessitated its rescue excavation; however, it had already been damaged earlier in the twentieth century when an electricity pole was inserted into the head-end of the grave, disturbing the woman's jewellery in the process which, doubtless, also involved the loss of some grave-goods. The long mound had covered a stone cist (something of a rarity in Viking Age Norway), although the body itself was contained within a wooden coffin or chest. Only part of one oval brooch survives (of what should have been a pair); this is of the so-called 'Berdal type 1a', with gripping-beast ornament (Brinch Madsen 1984, 37–9, fig. 12). The Skei brooch is almost identical to a find from Hjallese Torp, Dalum, Odense in Denmark (Brøndsted 1936, 143, fig. 53), which Lars Stenvik (forthcoming) suggests was made in the same workshop. Berdal-type oval brooches began production in Southern Scandinavia during the mid-eighth century, as is demonstrated by workshop finds in Ribe, Jutland (Myhre 1998, 5, for a recent discussion with references).

What would have been the woman's third brooch, for a cape or cloak, was found in the disturbed part of the burial. This is made from a piece of Insular metalwork in the form of a gilt copper-alloy mount, incomplete at one end, converted into a brooch by the addition of pin-fittings (Fig. 3.2). At the foot end of the grave had been placed a whalebone plaque, on which there were the remains of horse-equipment, including an iron bit and a circular copper-

Fig. 3.2 Skei grave 40: brooch made from an Insular mount. (NTNU Vitenskapsmuseet, Trondheim; photograph: Per E. Fredriksen)

Fig. 3.3 *Skei grave 40: Insular bucket. (NTNU Vitenskapsmuseet, Trondheim; photograph: Per E. Fredriksen)*

alloy mount (Fig. 3.5), together with a triangular copper-alloy hanging-bowl (Stenvik 1991, 12, fig.). Adjacent to this group of grave-goods lay a copper-alloy ladle (Stenvik 1991, 12, fig.), associated with a fine wooden bucket covered with decorated copper-alloy sheets (Fig. 3.3).

The rectangular mount converted into a brooch is ornamented with a well-executed, standard interlace design (Fig. 3.2). In general, it clearly relates to the well-known series of Irish-style harness-mounts of eighth/ninth-century date (*cf.* Youngs 1989, nos 113–17; Wamers 1998, 38), but this example may well have been a shrine-mount because, instead of lugs for attachment, it has an original rivet neatly incorporated into the design at the complete end (*cf.* Wamers 1998, 41–2). Its simple rectangular form and interlace decoration are well matched by a narrow oblong mount from a Viking Age female grave at Sogge, Møre og Romsdal, Norway (Wamers 1985, no. 39). Its interlace pattern is also paralleled, for example, on the edge of the late eighth/early ninth-century finials from a house-shaped shrine, now at St-Germain-en-Laye in France (Mahr 1932, pls 26–7; Youngs 1989, no. 138), with their matching pair

having been found, together with Irish harness-mounts, a bowl and a pair of drinking-horns etc., in a rich female grave of ninth-century date at Gausel, Rogaland, Norway (Wamers 1985, no. 90; Bakka 1993).

More certainly of Irish origin is the hanging-bowl from Skei which is remarkable both for its triangular shape and its massive size, its sides having an average length of 410mm, as compared to about 240mm of its only close parallel – the triangular copper-alloy hanging-bowl from Kilgulbin, Co. Kerry (Raftery 1966).[3] Whereas the Kilgulbin bowl only retains traces of the attachment of a strainer, the strainer-plate of the Skei bowl remains *in situ*; this has a pattern of perforations, in the form of a central rosette between a pair of roundels, which recalls that of the strainer-ladle from the Derrynaflan hoard, Co. Tipperary (Youngs 1989, no. 126), as well as that of the ovoid hanging-bowl from Ballinderry Crannog No. 1, Co. Westmeath (Henry 1967, 112–14, fig. 14). The interior of the Skei bowl, which has been patched, is decorated with ridges, whereas the exterior is mounted with three bird-shaped escutcheons, having tinned wings and a three-feathered tail, of a type familiar on more conventional examples of the late hanging-bowl series, as known from other Viking Age graves in Norway (*cf.* Petersen 1940, figs 99, 106, 112). The Skei bowl represents therefore a most important addition to the corpus of eighth/ninth-century hanging-bowls.

The Skei ladle, on the other hand, is a standard representative of its eighth/ninth-century type. As described by Ó Floinn (in Youngs 1989, no. 122): 'Plain ladles, of which over thirty examples are known from Ireland, Britain and Scandinavian graves, can be divided into two groups: those with long handles and small bowls and those with short handles and relatively large bowls'. The Skei example belongs to the latter group, with a handle length of 145mm and a bowl diameter of 175mm.

In the Skei grave, the ladle partly overlay an eighth-century Insular bucket of the highest quality workmanship, almost matching that of the well-known bucket from Birka grave 507, Sweden (Bakka 1984; Youngs 1989, no. 120), and certainly above that of the other two examples of this type known from Norway which will be discussed below.

The Skei bucket, which stands 165mm high, is made from a single piece of yew fitted with a baseplate (Stenvik 1991, 13, fig.). This wooden pail is covered with three copper-alloy sheets, forming three ornamental bands, as well as having a plain rim binding and a decorated foot-ring (Fig. 3.3; Plate II). It is fitted with a copper-alloy handle, attached by means of two cast triangular escutcheons bearing engraved geometric ornament.

The central ornamental band is filled with a double row of diagonal fret pattern which is repeated in a simpler version around the foot-ring; the latter is also used to decorate the handle. The lower band contains a running spiral and trumpet pattern. This lightly incised ornament has background patterning in the form of alternating oblique hatching which is also employed on the other two bands.

The upper band is decorated with plants, formed of paired scrolling tendrils, inhabited by birds and animals (Stenvik 1991, 14, figs; Plate III). The design is repeated on either side of the handle escutcheons and comprises a symmetrical arrange-ment of two confronted quadrupeds, each with its hind-quarters being bitten by a bird. The animal heads have open jaws and drooping tongues which meet to form a pelta; their bodies are double con-toured and have spiral hips. The front legs extend forward to interlace with the plant-scroll, but a certain stiffness is evident in the rendering of the hind legs and looping tails in comparison with the fluidity of the treatment of the highly stylised birds. There is a particular elegance to the line of the single elongated bird's leg as it interweaves with the spiral which terminates the plant-scroll.

By way of comparison, the Birka bucket, which stands 185mm high (Bakka 1963, 27–33, fig. 23; 1984; Youngs 1989, no. 120), has not only the same method of construction (although in this case the pail is turned from birchwood), but also the same tripartite arrangement of the ornament on two copper-alloy sheets (plus rim-binding and foot-ring), executed in the same technique of lightly incised decoration against a similarly hatched background (Fig. 3.4).

The central ornamental band contains a procession of biting birds enmeshed in a horizontal plant-scroll, as opposed to the Skei fret-pattern, but both buckets have a running trumpet scroll in the lower band and geometric ornament on the foot-ring. The 'Tree of Life' motif in the upper band consists of bush-like plants inhabited by two-legged birds (Wamers 1998, 39–41). The Birka designs are the more sophisticated and fluently executed of the two, although a close connection is evident. The Skei inhabited plant-scroll would appear to be a combination of the Birka bushes (with their paired tendrils) and its scrolled birds (with their biting beaks) into a single composition – to which animals have been added. Furthermore, the treatment of the sinuous Skei birds' legs bears a striking resemblance to that of the looping tendrils which issue from below the Birka bird-scroll.

The bucket from Hopperstad, Sogn og Fjordane, has likewise a tripartite scheme of ornament in the same technique as both the Birka and Skei buckets, as well as a handle-plate like that on the latter (Bakka 1963, 28–9, fig. 24). The Hopperstad example has an upper band of bird-inhabited plant-scroll, but this is a much simplified version of that on the Birka bucket. Its central band is decorated with spiral ornament, but this is crudely designed, employing compass-drawn closed circles (Bakka 1963, 29–32, fig. 25).

The bucket from Farmen, Vestfold, is also somewhat crude in comparison with the Birka and Skei examples (Petersen 1940, fig. 93), having an even simpler bird-only frieze, as well as fret-pattern (Bakka 1963, 28–31, figs 26–7). On the other hand, the well-known fragment from Torshov, Akershus (Petersen 1940, fig. 2; Wamers 1985, no. 138), which presumably derives from a similar bucket, is of superior quality and regularity in design, with its tightly-spiralled animal-only frieze (Bakka 1963, 28–31, fig. 28). The Torshov fragment therefore provides a stylistic link to the Skei bucket, although the Torshov animals differ in having closed jaws. The Skei bucket is, however, the only one known to combine animals, birds and plants into a single design.

Bakka (1963, 28) has argued that 'the Birka and Hopperstad pails are so similar – in shape, handle mounts, handles, rim binding, tripartite arrange-

Fig. 3.4 *Birka grave 507: Insular bucket ornament (after Arbman 1940)*

ment of the bronze bindings of the body, and in ornamentation in particular – that they must have come from the same workshop'. For all the same reasons – and noting, in particular, the shared depiction of animals and/or birds in plant-scrolls – it may now be suggested that the Skei bucket is also to be regarded as a product of this same workshop.

Bakka also observed (1963, 31) that 'different types of background patterning are, *inter alia*, criteria for different workshop groups'. Given that the background patterning of alternating oblique hatching, which is common to all three of the Birka, Hopperstad and Skei buckets, is also used on both the Farmen bucket and the Torshov fragment (Bakka 1963, 29), they are also to be placed in the same group of workshops, as is also indicated by the nature of their bird and animal ornament respectively. Another feature shared by this group as a whole, as Bakka pointed out (1963, 29), is that ribbon interlace is missing.

To the products of this group of workshops should now be added two reused fragments, both excavated in Britain: one from a Viking Age grave at Machrins on Colonsay (Ritchie 1981, 268–69, fig. 6), with coiled animal ornament, and the other from the Anglian settlement at Flixborough, Lincolnshire, with a spiral/trumpet pattern (Youngs forthcoming).[4]

Bakka (1963, 32) advocated a Northumbrian location within 'the Hiberno-Saxon art province' for the manufacture of these particular buckets,[5] but David Wilson, in the context of his work on the St Ninian's Isle hoard, has since proposed (1970, 9) that they might rather be of Pictish origin – or that it was even 'just possible that these objects were manufactured in the west of Scotland, where a few technically similar decorated objects of sheet metal have been found in Viking graves'. Amongst these, the object displaying the closest technical similarity to the buckets is the Insular buckle-plate from Bhaltos, Lewis, because it also utilises alternating oblique hatching, but as a background to ribbon interlace (see Paterson, *this volume*).

Wilson's proposal of Pictish production for this group of buckets has to date remained really no more than a suggestion, although one strongly supported by Dr Isabel Henderson (pers. comm.) in the context of her study of Pictish vine-scroll ornament (Henderson 1983). In the meantime, Leslie Webster has repeated the case for the Birka bucket being of eighth-century Northumbrian manufacture (in Youngs 1989, no. 120) and thus the regional attribution of the group remains a matter for debate.

There remains one further copper-alloy object from Skei grave 40 for consideration. This is a circular openwork mount (39mm in diameter),

Fig. 3.5 *Skei grave 40: openwork cruciform mount. (NTNU Vitenskapsmuseet, Trondheim; photograph: Per E. Fredriksen)*

which is slightly convex in form; it is cruciform in design and plain, except for a central ornamental boss (Fig. 3.5). On the reverse are three lugs, but not at right angles, so that the object is neither a strap-connector nor a strap-crossover (pers. comm. Angela Care Evans). It was, however, seemingly in use as a harness-fitting because it was placed in the grave together with the iron bit, as well as about 67 small nails with copper-alloy coated heads. This mount may therefore have been made as a frontal ornament with Christian symbolic intent. In any case, it is certainly not of Scandinavian eighth/ninth-century manufacture and, although just possibly Continental, an Irish origin seems the most probable at this stage of its investigation, given that it has a close parallel in an unpublished openwork mount, of simpler cruciform design, but with central boss, from the late ninth/early tenth-century hoard from Shanmullagh, Co. Antrim (Bourke 1993, 24–39).[6] A further general comparison can be made with the more elaborate cruciform roundels, also with central boss, on either side of the Ardagh chalice (Ryan 1983, no. 51, a; Plate I).

In interim conclusion, Skei grave 40 contains a remarkably rich assemblage of Insular metalwork in an undoubtedly high-status female grave, located in the heart of Inn-Trøndelag. The combination of the Berdal-type oval brooch with this concentration of eighth/ninth-century Insular artefacts suggests that we are dealing with one of those graves which helps to define archaeologically the beginning of the Viking Age in Norway (*cf.* Myhre 1993; 1998, 6–8) – and which exhibits a clear expression of Norwegian ethnic identity.

There is good reason to suppose (*pace* Myhre 1993, 187–88; 1998, 7) that this assembly of Insular metalwork represents loot from the earliest Viking raids on Britain and Ireland which took place at end of the eighth and the beginning of the ninth century – the foreign exotica brought home to Skei for festive use by the chieftain's family.[7] These 'glittering prizes' are the status symbols which proclaim the prestige of an unknown Viking leader from Trøndelag.

Scandinavian status symbols and 'national' dress

Successful raiding on Western Europe clearly produced a desire for trophies, such as those from Skei grave 40, to be used in status display, whether on the person or on high-table. When some such were at the height of fashion, Scandinavian copies were produced, as is most clearly demonstrated by the well-known example of the trefoil brooch (Petersen 1928, 93–114), which was worn by some women as their third brooch for an outer garment, whether a cape or cloak. Those who were successful Vikings on the Continent brought home with them, amongst other things, Carolingian baldrics which had trefoil-shaped strap-distributors suitable for conversion into brooches or pendants for their women to wear (e.g. Wamers 1985, pl. 39),[8] in the same manner that the Skei lady was equipped with a brooch made from an Insular shrine-mount. Not everyone had access to original pieces of booty, so the trefoil mounts were copied as brooches (e.g. Wamers 1985, pl. 41), becoming in turn a standard type of Scandinavian female jewellery (e.g. Petersen 1928, figs 97–115). Norwegian men seem to have behaved in a somewhat similar manner in respect of their cloak-fasteners by adopting Insular types of brooch and pin (Graham-Campbell 1987) – and so it is here that we encounter the matter of the display of ethnic and/or regional identity, as well as status, in the wearing of Insular and/or Scandinavian brooches.

The special dress of a wealthy western Scandinavian woman during the early part of the Viking Age, when regular contact was established between the Norse and the Picts, Scots and Irish, was completely unlike the dress worn by Pictish, Scottish and Irish women. It required the wearing of a pair of substantial oval brooches which were used to fasten the shoulder straps of a tunic worn over a shift (for summaries and references, see Graham-Campbell 1980, 27–30, and Kaland in Roesdahl and Wilson 1992, 192–93). This represents therefore a distinctively Scandinavian type of 'national' dress, involving the wearing of brooches which were completely unlike those in use anywhere else in Europe.

It is inherently probable therefore that those female burials in Scotland and Ireland (as in Iceland), in which oval brooches have been found *in situ* on or near the shoulders of the skeleton, are normally the graves of Norse women, dressed in their native manner. However, as Myhre has observed in this context (1993, 193), 'ethnicity is not a static phenomenon' and it is clearly possible that a native Christian woman might have felt it appropriate, perhaps for her marriage to a Norse chieftain, to dress in a costume belonging to his family and was subsequently buried in it in the pagan manner. For the most part, however, it would seem unlikely that such was a common scenario.

Picts and Scots: some pins and brooches

Next to be considered are aspects of the manner in which the Picts might have asserted ethnic and/or regional identity, as well as status, through the wearing of ornamental metalwork, but passing over the so-called 'Pictish' chains of sixth/seventh-century date in view of their recent discussion by Charles Thomas (1995, 5–6). In order to approach this matter, it is necessary to turn from grave-goods, which are lacking from Pictish burials, to the evidence of hoards and workshop sites. Pictish hoards are characterised by the presence of pins and brooches and during the late Pictish period there appears to have been no interest in the wearing of rings (Graham-Campbell 1985, 256–7, table 2). This use of pins and brooches to denote status, rather than rings, is also well attested in Ireland, where law-tracts accord varying status/significance to brooches of differing values (Nieke 1993, 128–29).

The most notable type of pin is the hand-pin which, at this stage of its development (Youngs 1989, nos 3–7a), represented a widespread Insular Celtic fashion and the wearing of such a pin would certainly not have served to promote a particularly Pictish identity, although one of those from the Norrie's Law, Fife, hoard has been engraved, on the reverse, with the culturally distinctive Z-rod symbol (Youngs 1989, no. 8a; Graham-Campbell 1991, 253; see also Laing 1994, 25–30).

It is often stated that the Norrie's Law hoard contains a pair of silver penannular brooches (e.g. Graham-Campbell 1991, 246), but Lloyd Laing's interpretation of these rings as torcs is to be preferred, not for wearing around the neck in the Celtic tradition, but in the manner of the Roman army worn as insignia on the chest (1994, 24–5). This leaves only the plain silver penannular brooches in the Tummel Bridge, Perthshire, hoard by way of background for the eighth/ninth-century series of brooches which dominate the late Pictish period hoards, most notably that from St Ninian's Isle in Shetland (Wilson 1973, 81–105), with related moulds having been excavated on the Brough of Birsay in Orkney (Curle 1982, 27–9, illus 13–15).

The origins of this series must therefore have lain outside Pictland and Laing once proposed (1976, 17) that its starting point may have been in south-west Scotland. Since then, however, Alan Lane's 1980/81 excavations at Dunadd, in Mid Argyll, have provided clear evidence for the manufacture there of penannular brooches with sufficient so-called 'Pictish' features to have led him to suggest that it was no longer possible to identify any such thing as a truly Pictish brooch (Lane 1984, 52–5). Although Raghnall Ó Floinn (1989, 90) has briefly restated the case for the existence of a distinctive Pictish series of penannular brooch during the mid-eighth to early ninth centuries, Lane's suggestion has remained unanswered, thus encouraging others to follow in his footsteps. His revisionist approach to Pictish brooches was, however, promulgated when it was thought that the Dunadd workshop dated to the early ninth century (Lane 1984, 49–56). However, now that it is known to be of seventh-century date (Campbell and Lane 1993, 60), the situation is clearly different. This phase of brooch production at Dunadd thus preceded the *floruit* of the main series of Pictish brooches which can now be seen to have drawn on this earlier Dalriadic fashion for small penannular brooches which were enlarged and elaborated on in Pictish workshops during the eighth century.

The Carronbridge brooch: a case-study

In their publication of the silver penannular brooch found at Carronbridge in Dumfriesshire (Fig. 3.6), Owen and Welander state (1995, 763) that it 'falls clearly into a series identified as "Pictish" by Stevenson (1959, 256), followed by Wilson (1973, 81–105) and others'. They further comment that: 'Today, there is an increasing trend to abandon such ethnic labels in favour of less subjective terminology and, here, the term "Insular Celtic" is preferred' (Owen and Welander 1995, 763). 'Insular Celtic' is, however, a label so broad at this period as to suggest that

brooches belonging to this series might have been manufactured anywhere, not only in Northern and Western Britain, but also in Ireland.

It may be proposed, however, that the Carronbridge brooch should *not* be classified as belonging to the main series of Pictish penannular brooches, as defined by Wilson (1973), Stevenson (1985) and Ó Floinn (1989, 90), but that it is merely a relation – as, for example, are several 'hybrids' from Ireland, including that from Ervey Crannog, Co. Meath (Youngs 1989, no. 86), which is similar in various respects to the Carronbridge brooch. As Owen and Welander point out (1995, 763), the use of a raised bar, or collar, at the junction of hoop and terminals on the Carronbridge brooch is not a feature typical of 'Pictish' brooches in general, occurring only once (and then in what might best be described as embryonic form) on a brooch from the Rogart hoard, Sutherland (Wilson 1973, pl. xxxvii, d; Youngs 1989, no. 112). However, on the Carronbridge brooch this collar replaces the raised crescentic moulding (or cusp) which is one of the standard features of the main series of what are here considered to be truly Pictish penannular brooches.

By supposing that the Carronbridge brooch forms part of the main Pictish series, even if renamed 'Insular Celtic', Owen and Welander (1995, 764) were led to suggest that 'the pin on the brooch is not of the usual type with engraved, lentoid head; instead it is rather crude and undecorated. There is, therefore, a strong possibility that this pin replaced the original brooch pin'. It thus followed that this brooch, which is otherwise to be dated typologically to the late eighth/early ninth century, might have been deposited as late as the tenth century (Owen and Welander 1995, 764).

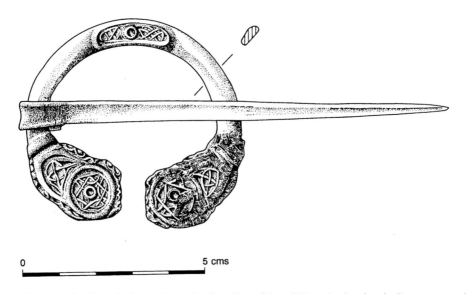

0   5 cms

Fig. 3.6 *Penannular brooch from Carronbridge, Dumfries. (Historic Scotland; Crown copyright)*

Fig. 3.7 *Brooch design from Dunadd, Argyll. (Trustees of the National Museum of Scotland)*

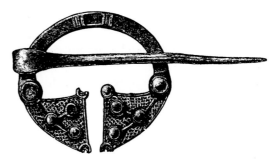

Fig. 3.8 *Penannular brooch (lost) from the island of Coll (after PSAS)*

If, however, this brooch is removed from the main Pictish series, there is no reason to suppose that its simple pin is necessarily out of place. All the more so, given that the XRF-analyses of the hoop and pin demonstrated that they both have 'similar compositions of relatively impure silver' in the form of 'a copper-rich silver alloy' (Owen and Welander 1995, 756), even if the pin seems to have a slightly higher copper content, 'perhaps to impart additional strength since it would have been subject to higher stress when in use than the hoop' (Owen and Welander 1995, 759). Laboratory examination also revealed that the surfaces of both have been 'highly polished' to a similar degree (Owen and Welander 1995, 759).

To have argued, therefore, that the Carronbridge brooch 'gives a south-west Scottish dimension' (Owen and Welander 1995, 767) to the distribution of 'Pictish' brooches is fallacious. It belongs instead to the group of Pictish/Irish 'hybrids' (Ó Floinn 1989, 90) and so may as well have been in the possession of an Irish traveller as anyone else.

Scots and Picts: panelled brooches

The Dunadd excavations demonstrated the production there of large panelled brooches, although in their discussion of these finds Campbell and Lane (1993, 57–8, 60–1, figs 6.8–10) did not mention the old Dunadd find of a design, incised on a piece of slate, for what might be another such brooch (Fig. 3.7). However, Wilson (1973, 87–8) compared the Dunadd design to the St Ninian's Isle brooch series, before concluding that it was later in date, as a possible missing link to the ninth-century bossed brooches of Ireland, a view subsequently endorsed by myself (1975, 43).

This was, however, at a time when the extant mould material from Dunadd appeared 'to bear no relation to the St Ninian's Isle series' (Wilson 1973, 88). It is now worth raising the possibility, at least, that the Dunadd design might have derived from the seventh-century workshop, even if on balance a later date still seems preferable for this motif-piece. At the same time, it is important to recall an unusual brooch from Dalriada which was found in the nineteenth century on the island of Coll, Argyll (Fig. 3.8). This is generally overlooked because it is now lost, but Wilson (1973, 88) considered it to be the brooch most closely related to the Dunadd design. Nevertheless, these two have never been illustrated together before which means that it may not have been appreciated that both share the same small size (with a hoop diameter of about 40mm). The Coll brooch is penannular in form and is reported to have been of gilt bronze with green glass settings (*Proc. Soc. Antiq. Scotl.* 15 (1880–81), 79–81, fig. 1).[9] This suggests that the proposed link between the Dunadd design and the large Irish brooches with their silver bosses may be less convincing than previously suggested.

Campbell and Lane (1993, 58, fig. 6.9c) have linked the Dunadd moulds for panelled brooches to those from the Pictish workshop at Clatchard Craig, in Fife, which have been dated to the eighth century (Close-Brooks 1986, 162–64), as well as to the extant brooch from Clunie in Perthshire (Campbell and Lane 1993, 58, fig. 6.10). Here again, there is evidence for Dalriadic inspiration behind the development of Pictish brooches, but in this case it appears to have been for a regional fashion, one confined to Southern Pictland.

Envoi

By way of conclusion, it is proposed that the Picts should be given back their brooches. If, however, ethnic labelling is no longer considered to be acceptable, one might consider reverting to Wilson's original (1973) label: 'the St Ninian's Isle type'. On the other hand, if it is accepted that the St Ninian's Isle brooches themselves are indeed of Pictish manufacture, on the basis of the Brough of Birsay moulds (Wilson 1973, 105; Curle 1982, 27–9), there will doubtless be those who will choose to continue to refer to 'the Pictish brooch series'.

Such brooches have been found in Norway, as also in Ireland (as well as the Pictish/Irish hybrids, referred to above). In Norway, the Pictish type of brooch with animal-head terminals (*cf.* that from Freswick, Caithness: Wilson 1973, pl. xlix, d) was actually copied by Norse craftsmen (Graham-Campbell 1987, 237–8, figs 6–8), in the same manner that Irish 'thistle' brooches were copied and elaborated (Graham-Campbell 1987, 238–42, figs 11–13).

But what did the Norse intend when they adopted Pictish and Irish brooch-types for their cloak-fasteners? It seems self-evident that they were not trying to masquerade as Picts or Irishmen, so we come full circle to the concept of 'glittering prizes' – that is to the use of the exotic to make statements, not about ethnicity or regionality, but concerning status. It is surely this factor which muddies these particular waters, for however much different groups of people may have chosen to express their identity by wearing varying types of standard brooches, there was always the lure of the exotic, whether a piece of loot or a gift, which might then in turn set a new fashion. Even so, other possible explanations remain for hybridisation leading to innovation, particularly the movement of craftsmen, for example in the retinue of Anglo-Saxon princes in exile, as Campbell and Lane have speculated for Dalriada (1993, 61) and, as suggested by Henry (1962, 64), Pictish and Scottish craftsmen may well have taken flight to Ireland on account of the inroads being made by the Vikings (see also Graham-Campbell 1974). The traffic in ideas was clearly continuous, whatever the mechanisms which brought it about.

Notes

1   I am most grateful to Lars Stenvik, of the Institute of Archaeology at the Norwegian University of Science and Technology, Trondheim, for allowing me to draw on his draft excavation report on the Skei cemetery and 'court site' (Stenvik, forthcoming) for publication here, as well as for having taken me to Stiklestad to examine the Insular objects when they were on display there; a joint paper on Skei grave 40 is planned for publication in English.

2   This 'court site' is to be identified with that labelled 'Steinkjer' on Myhre's map (1998, fig. 1.6), after the name of the *kommune* in which the farm of Skei is located.

3   Henry (1967, 114, n. 1) refers to the existence of a further triangular hanging-bowl in Stavanger Museum, but what remains of this fragmentary bowl (from Hegreberg, Rogaland) indicates that it would have been of normal semi-spherical shape.

4   I am most grateful to Susan Youngs of the British Museum for informing me about the Flixborough fragment, which has been folded to form a strap-end, and for showing me a draft of her forthcoming publication.

5   There exists a closely related group of Irish buckets which are characterised by having decorative bands with engraved or openwork interlace and geometric patterns, e.g. Derrymullen, Co. Laois (Ryan 1983, no. 58) and Clonard, Co. Meath (Youngs 1989, no. 119).

6   I am most grateful to Cormac Bourke of the Ulster Museum for information about this piece; the Shanmullagh hoard also contains a somewhat different, but nevertheless related, pair of circular openwork crosses which 'may be mounts from satchels or shrines' (Bourke 1993, 30, fig.).

7   Christians did not trade in ecclesiastical treasures and would not have willingly offered them as gifts to their pagan visitors (Wormald 1982, 133), as recently emphasised by Wamers (1998, 42–4), who draws particular attention to the fragmentary nature of the majority of the Insular ecclesiastical metalwork found in Scandinavia.

8   The classic example is the magnificent gold strap-distributor in the ninth-century hoard from Hoen, Buskerud, Norway, which was fitted with a silver pin for conversion into a brooch (Wamers 1985, pl. 39, 1; Roesdahl and Wilson 1992, no. 26).

9   The late Robert Stevenson was of the opinion that the Coll brooch dated to the late eighth or early ninth century (pers. comm.).

10 In this paper, I suggested that the small penannular brooch from Clogh, Co. Antrim, with bird-headed terminals, should be regarded as a Pictish/Irish hybrid of ninth-century date (Graham-Campbell 1974, 55). This attribution must now be abandoned (as Youngs 1989, no. 182) in the light of the seventh-century Dunadd metalworking material which includes seven moulds for bird-headed brooches (Campbell and Lane 1993, 54–5, figs 6.3 and 6.4, b–c).

References

ARBMAN, H. 1940, *Birka I. Die Gräber.* (Tafeln). KVHAA. Stockholm.

BAKKA, E. 1963, 'Some English decorated metal objects found in Norwegian graves: contributions to the art history of the eighth century A.D.', *Årbok for Universitetet i Bergen, Humanistik Serie* 1, 1–66.

BAKKA, E. 1984, 'Der Holzeimer von Bj 507', in G. Arwidsson (ed.), *Birka. Systematische Analysen der Gräberfunde*, Vol. 2:1, 233–35. Stockholm.

BAKKA, E. 1993, 'Gauselfunnet og bakgrunnet for det', *Arkeologiske Skrifter, Historisk Museum i Bergen* 7, 269–79.

BOURKE, C. 1993, *Patrick. The Archaeology of a Saint.* Belfast.

BRINCH MADSEN, H. 1984, 'Metal-casting: techniques, production and workshops', in M. Bencard (ed.), *Ribe Excavations 1970-76*, Vol. 2, 15-189. Esbjerg.

BRØNDSTED, J. 1936, 'Danish inhumation graves of the Viking Age', *Acta Archaeologica* 7, 81-228.

CAMPBELL, E. and LANE, A. 1993, 'Celtic and Germanic interaction in Dalriada: the 7th-century metalworking site at Dunadd', in Spearman and Higgitt, 52-63.

CHRISTOPHERSEN, A. 1999, 'Royal power, state formation and early urbanisation in Norway ca. AD 700-1200', in C. E. Karkov, K. M. Wickham-Crowley and B. K. Young (eds), *Spaces of the Living and the Dead* (= American Early Medieval Studies 3), 107-17. Oxford.

CLARKE, H. B., Ní MHAONAIGH, M. and Ó FLOINN, R. (eds) 1998, *Ireland and Scandinavia in the Early Viking Age.* Dublin.

CLOSE-BROOKS, J. 1986, 'Excavations at Clatchard Craig, Fife', *Proc. Soc. Antiq. Scotl.* 116, 117-84.

CURLE, C. L. 1982, *Pictish and Norse Finds from the Brough of Birsay 1934-74* (= Soc. Antiq. Scotl. Monogr. Ser.1). Edinburgh.

FOOTE, P. G. and WILSON, D. M. 1970, *The Viking Achievement.* London.

GRAHAM-CAMPBELL, J. 1973-4, 'The Lough Ravel, Co. Antrim, brooch and others of ninth-century date', *Ulster J. Archaeol.* 36-7, 52-7.

GRAHAM-CAMPBELL, J. 1975, 'Bossed penannular brooches: a review of recent research', *Medieval Archaeol.* 19, 33-47.

GRAHAM-CAMPBELL, J. 1980, *Viking Artefacts: A Select Catalogue.* London.

GRAHAM-CAMPBELL, J. 1985, 'A lost Pictish treasure (and two Viking-age gold arm-rings) from the Broch of Burgar, Orkney', *Proc. Soc. Antiq. Scotl.* 115, 241-61.

GRAHAM-CAMPBELL, J. 1987, 'Western penannular brooches and their Viking Age copies in Norway: a new classification', in J. Knirk (ed.), *Proceedings of the Tenth Viking Congress, Larkollen, Norway, 1985* (= Universitetets Oldsaksamlings Skrifter, Ny Rekke, 9), 231-46. Oslo.

GRAHAM-CAMPBELL, J. 1991, 'Norrie's Law, Fife: on the nature and dating of the silver hoard', *Proc. Soc. Antiq. Scotl.* 121, 241-59.

HENDERSON, I. 1983, 'Pictish vine-scroll ornament', in A. O'Connor and D.V. Clarke (eds), *From the Stone Age to the 'Forty-Five, Studies Presented to R.B.K. Stevenson,* 243-68. Edinburgh.

HENRY, F. 1962, 'The effects of the Viking invasions on Irish art', in B. Ó Cuív (ed.), *The Impact of the Scandinavian Invasions on the Celtic-speaking Peoples c. 800-1100 AD: International Congress of Celtic Studies held in Dublin, 6-10 July, 1959,* 61-72. Dublin.

HENRY, F. 1967, *Irish Art during the Viking Invasions, 800-1020 A.D.* London.

LAING, L. 1976, 'Penannular brooches in Ireland and Scotland', *Ulster J. Archaeol.* 39, 15-19.

LAING, L. 1994, 'The hoard of Pictish silver from Norrie's Law, Fife', *Studia Celtica* 28, 11-38.

LANE, A. 1984, 'Some Pictish problems at Dunadd', in J. G. P. Friell and W. G. Watson (eds), *Pictish Studies: Settlement, Burial and Art in Dark Age Northern Britain* (= B.A.R. Brit. Ser. 125), 43-62. Oxford.

LIDÉN, H.-E. 1969, 'From pagan sanctuary to Christian church', *Norwegian Archaeol. Rev.* 2, 3-32.

MAHR, A. (ed.) 1932, *Christian Art in Ancient Ireland,* Vol. 1. Dublin.

MYHRE, B. 1993, 'The beginning of the Viking Age – some current archaeological problems', in A. Faulkes and R. Perkins (eds), *Viking Revaluations: Viking Society Centenary Symposium, 14-15 May, 1992,* 182-216. London.

MYHRE, B. 1998, 'The archaeology of the early Viking Age in Norway', in Clarke *et al.,* 3-36.

NIEKE, M. R. 1993, 'Penannular and related brooches: secular ornament or symbol in action?', in Spearman and Higgitt, 128-34.

Ó FLOINN, R. 1989, 'Secular metalwork in the eighth and ninth centuries', in Youngs, 72, 89-91.

OWEN, O. and WELANDER, R. 1995, 'A travellers end? – an associated group of early historic artefacts from Carronbridge, Dumfries and Galloway', *Proc. Soc. Antiq. Scotl.* 125, 753-70.

PETERSEN, J. 1928, *Vikingetidens smykker.* Stavanger.

PETERSEN, J. 1940, *British Antiquities of the Viking Period, found in Norway* (= Shetelig, H. (ed.), *Viking Antiquities in Great Britain and Ireland* 5). Oslo.

RAFTERY, J. 1966, 'The Cuillard and other unpublished hanging bowls', *J. Roy. Soc. Antiq. Ir.* 96, 29-38.

RITCHIE, J. N. G. 1981, 'Excavations at Machrins, Colonsay', *Proc. Soc. Antiq. Scotl.* 111, 263-81.

ROESDAHL, E. and WILSON, D. M. (eds) 1992, *From Viking to Crusader. The Scandinavians and Europe 800-1200.* Copenhagen, New York.

RYAN, M. (ed.) 1983, *Treasures of Ireland. Irish Art 3000 B.C.-1500 A.D.* Dublin.

SOGNNES, K. 1991, 'Sentrumsdannelser i Trøndelag i yngre jernalder', in B. Wik (ed.), *Sentrum-periferi. Sentra og sentrumsdannelser gjennom førhistorisk og historisk tid* (= Gunneria 64:1-2), 251-62. Trondheim.

SPEARMAN, R. M. and HIGGITT, J. (eds) 1993, *The Age of Migrating Ideas. Early Medieval Art in Northern Britain and Ireland.* Edinburgh, Stroud.

STENVIK, L. F. 1991, 'Fabeldyr på vandring – litt om vikingtidens ornamentikk- og dekorasjonskunst', *Spor* 11:1, 12-14.

STENVIK, L. F. forthcoming, *Skei – et maktsenter fram fra skyggen.* Trondheim (published 2001).

STEVENSON, R. B. K. 1959, 'The penannular brooches: discussion', in A. C. Dell *et al.,* 'The St Ninian's Isle silver hoard', *Antiquity* 33 (241-68), 255-57.

STEVENSON, R. B. K. 1985, 'The Pictish brooch from Adclune, Blair Atholl, Perthshire', *Proc. Soc. Antiq. Scotl.* 115, 233-39.

THOMAS, C. 1995, 'The artist and the people, a foray into uncertain semiotics', in C. Bourke (ed.), *From the Isles of the North. Early Medieval Art in Britain and Ireland,* 1-7. Belfast.

WAMERS, E. 1985, *Insularer Metallschmuck in wikingerzeitlichen Gräbern Nordeuropas. Untersuchungen zur skandinavischen Westexpansion* (= Offa-Bücher 56). Neumünster.

WAMERS, E. 1998, 'Insular finds in Viking Age Scandinavia and the state formation of Norway', in Clarke *et al.*, 37–72.

WILSON, D. M. 1970, *Reflections on the St Ninian's Isle Treasure* (= Jarrow Lecture for 1969). Jarrow.

WILSON, D. M. 1973, 'The brooches', in A. Small, C. Thomas and D. M. Wilson, *St. Ninian's Isle and its Treasure*, 2 vols, 81–105. Oxford.

WORMALD, C. P. 1982, 'Viking studies: whence and whither?', in R. T. Farrell (ed.), *The Vikings*, 128–53. London, Chichester.

YOUNGS, S. (ed.) 1989, *'The Work of Angels'. Masterpieces of Celtic Metalwork, 6th-9th Centuries AD*. London.

YOUNGS, S. (forthcoming), 'Insular Metalwork from Flixborough, Lincolnshire', *Medieval Archaeol.* 45.

4   Strap-ends and the Identification of Regional Patterns in the Production and Circulation of Ornamental Metalwork in Late Anglo-Saxon and Viking-age Britain

Gabor Thomas

Introduction

The multi-purpose strap-end has long been recognised as one of the type fossils of ornamental metalwork from Late Anglo-Saxon and Viking-age contexts, here broadly defined as *c.* 750–1050 (Brønsted 1924, 129–32; Wilson and Blunt 1961, 97–8). Their discovery from a range of settlement sites across mainland Britain, combined with their great diversity in form, decoration, and quality, suggests that the popularity of strap-ends during this period transcended a range of geographical, political and social boundaries. The research summarised below draws upon 1,500 strap-ends discovered through recent archaeological and metal-detecting activity, a total which represents a sixteen-fold increase since the extant number of strap-ends was last quantified over thirty-five years ago (Wilson in Wilson and Blunt 1961, Appendix 2).

Analysis of this significant addition to the surviving corpus of Late Saxon ornamental metalwork has provided a new insight into several aspects of contemporary metalworking and its wider artistic, social and economic context. In art-historical terms, the sheer diversity of these artefacts affords an unprecedented opportunity to trace the full repertoire of decorative techniques and motifs at the disposal of the contemporary artisan (see, for example, Thomas 1996). Meanwhile, as this paper seeks to demonstrate, an exploration of the defined regional groupings within the database of these artefacts contributes to our understanding of contemporary manufacturing systems and the cultural and artistic climate in which they functioned.

Standardisation versus experimentation: the ninth-century Anglo-Saxon series

The most popular and widely distributed class of Late Anglo-Saxon strap-end, accounting for over 60 per cent of recorded examples, is characterised by its convex form, zoomorphic terminal and split attachment end. Decoration is restricted to the front surface within two zones: a main, centrally placed panel and a second subsidiary fan-shaped field located at the split-end which is commonly occupied by a trilobate foliate motif (Fig. 4.2a). The central panel of decoration displays great diversity in terms of stylistic composition and ornamental technique, ranging from simple incised geometric patterns through to more complex representational designs, often enhanced with vitreous or precious-metal inlays. In accordance with contemporary fashions in metalworking, a large percentage, including the majority of high-status silver examples, is representative of the Trewhiddle style which flourished throughout Anglo-Saxon England during the ninth century (Wilson 1964, 21–35; Wilson 1984, 95–105).

Their occurrence in broadly contemporary coin-dated hoards, such as Sevington, Wiltshire (*c.* 850); Trewhiddle, Cornwall (*c.* 868); Talnotrie, Dumfries and Galloway (*c.* 875); and Cuerdale, Lancashire (*c.* 905), provides firm grounds for a general ninth-century dating (Blackburn and Pagan 1986), a dating that has been augmented by several recent archaeological discoveries (e.g. Hinton 1996a, 37–44; Nicholson and Hill 1997, BZ19a; Moulden, Logan and Tweddle 1999, no. 78). The class is represented on a range of contemporary settlement types, from *emporia*, royal *vills* and monastic sites through to rural settlements, with and without an ecclesiastical component. These strap-ends are also particularly common finds on 'productive sites' such as Cottam on the Yorkshire Wolds, so named because they are invariably identified on the basis of metal-detected scatters of Middle and Late Saxon coins and ornamental metalwork (Richards 1999; Ulmschneider 2000). While, at a superficial level, the class's distribution covers much of Britain, from Cornwall to Anglian Scotland, more detailed spatial analysis of decorative sub-groups as well as stylistic features such as their terminals has shown distinct regional groupings.

One of the broadest regional distinctions relates to the style of their zoomorphic terminals of which there are two standard versions. The predominant terminal type, characterised by oval ears with lunate incisions in association with incised eyes, has a dispersed distribution across much of Britain (Fig. 4.2a). Strap-ends with heads featuring curly, comma-shaped ears and bulging eyes, however, have a much more restricted spread focusing on a region north of the Wash broadly concomitant with the neighbouring Anglo-Saxon kingdoms of Lindsey and Northumbria (Fig. 4.2c). This same geographical area is also home to a small number of strap-ends displaying a distinctive looping palmette which replaces the conventional fleshy-leafed trilobate motif common to the majority of the class (Fig. 4.2d). Moreover, of the few strap-ends which display both these stylistic variants, over half come from find-spots in the extreme north of the country (Fig. 4.1a).

Further evidence for the restricted circulation of variant motifs in this northern region has been revealed through analysis of the corpus of Trewhiddle-style strap-ends. Prominent amongst this material is a previously identified group decorated with an unusual loop-eared version of a Trewhiddle-style animal (Bailey 1993) (Fig. 4.2a, b). More recent discoveries have to some extent reinforced the attribution of the group to a 'York-based' workshop, proposed on the basis of its uniformity and defined geographical distribution (*ibid.*, 90), although a small number from Cheshire and Cumbria point to a wider circulation (e.g. Philpott 1999, fig. 4d) (Fig. 4.1b, Type 1). One possible explanation for such outliers, which are also present in the distribution of ninth-century Northumbrian stycas, is that they reflect contemporary patterns of redistribution targeting trans-Pennine routeways and coastal trading sites on the Irish Sea littoral (Metcalf 1987, 364, fig. 1; Higham 1993, 168).

The discovery of a fragmentary strap-end mould during excavations at Carlisle, however, suggests that the location of Northumbrian production sites may have extended beyond a region centred on York and its hinterland (Taylor and Webster 1984). This evidence for a Carlisle-based workshop or craftsman has recently been augmented by the discovery of a strap-end just outside the city which is closely related to the mould in its use of certain stylistic traits, notably the looping form of palmette (Richardson 1990, 40–1). This example also displays a number of other variant characteristics indicative of its provincial origins, including the comma-eared terminal and a contorted Trewhiddle-style animal enmeshed in interlace (Fig. 4.2c and d). Further examples of this type have since come to light revealing the existence of yet another highly uniform group from the Northumbrian region (Fig. 4.1b, Type 2).

Before discussion progresses, it should also be noted that some of the stylistic traits characteristic of these 'northern' groupings, and individual strap-ends to which they are related, can be paralleled more widely on other classes of Trewhiddle-style metalwork from the region (Webster in Taylor and Webster 1984, 180; Webster in Webster and Backhouse 1991, nos 159 and 249b and c). Such parallels indicate that Northumbria was home to a vibrant school of provincial metalworking during the ninth century, a proposition that accords with other evidence for sustained economic and cultural activity within the kingdom, in spite of internal political conflicts and the ravages of the Vikings (Yorke 1990, 97; Hinton 1990a, 65–7).

Evidence for regional production during the ninth century is not solely confined to the corpus of Trewhiddle-style strap-ends. One of the most striking regional patterns relates to a decorative style with a much more restricted sphere of influence in terms of the range of objects on which it appears and its geographical range. The 90 or so strap-ends most recently identified as exponents of this style, characterised by decorative settings of niello inlaid with silver-wire, constitute the primary evidence for a distinctive ninth-century metalworking tradition based within the Anglo-Saxon kingdom of East Anglia (Fig. 4.3; Thomas 1996; 2000). The only other contemporary class of ornamental metalwork on which this decoration occurs, though with much less regularity, is the hooked-tag (Web-ster in Webster and Backhouse 1991, no. 188g; Thomas 1996, fig. 4d).

The core of this metalwork's distribution, comprising nearly 85 per cent of find-spots, is confined to the modern counties of Norfolk and Suffolk (Fig. 4.1c). Apart from a scatter of finds to the west and south-west, notably from high-status and ecclesiastical sites such as Repton, Derbyshire (pers. comm. M. Biddle) and Hamwic (Hinton 1996a, 40, fig. 16), the majority of outliers are strung along the east coast, north into Lincolnshire and Humberside, and south into Essex and Kent (Thomas 1996, 83, fig. 1). The predominantly coastal distribution of outliers,

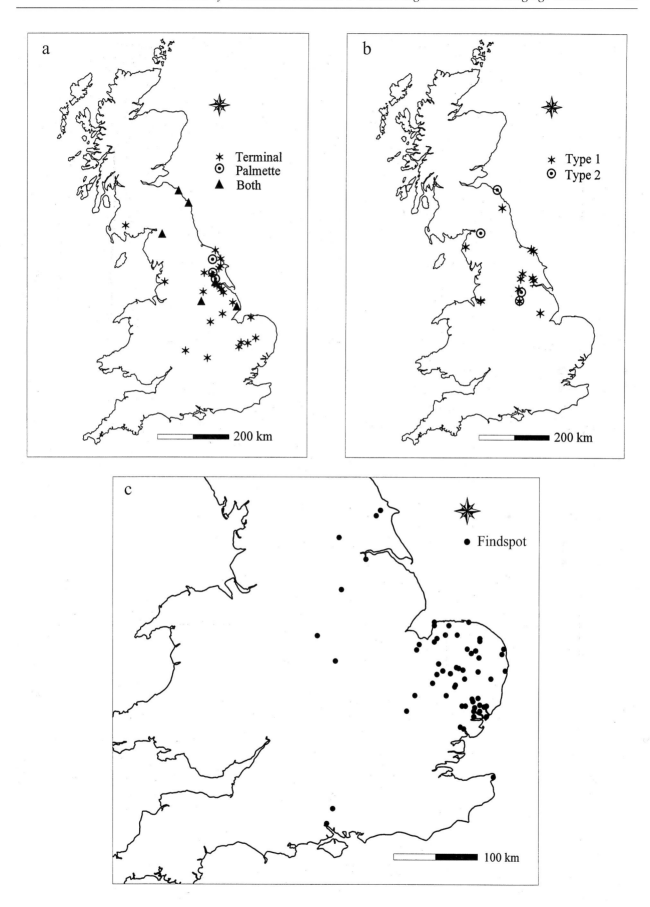

Fig. 4.1 *(a) Distribution of strap-ends displaying terminal and palmette variants; (b) distribution of Northumbrian groups of Trewhiddle-style strap-end; (c) distribution of silver-wire and niello strap-ends*

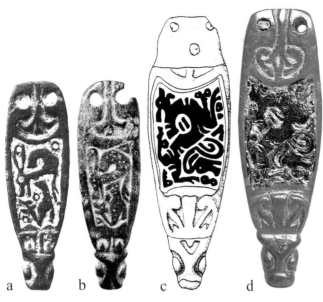

Fig. 4.2 *Representatives of two Northumbrian groups of Trewhiddle-style strap-end: (a) Goldsborough, North Yorkshire, now in Ripon Cathedral; (b) York, North Yorkshire, Yorkshire Museum 717.48; (c) Wetheral, Cumbria (after Richardson 1990, fig. 21), Tullie House Museum, Carlisle, 71–1986; (d) Thorpe Salvin, South Yorkshire, Sheffield City Museum 1987.202. Scale 1.5:1*

Fig. 4.3 *Silver-wire and niello strap-ends: (a) Nacton, Suffolk, Ipswich Museum 1987.150.2A, scale 1.5:1; (b) West Caister, Norfolk, Norwich Castle Museum 454.978, scale 2:1*

mirrored by the spread of other distinctly East Anglian products such as Ipswich-type ware, is likely to be a reflection of trade and exchange along the eastern seaboard coast trading networks (Blinkhorn 1999, fig. 2). The variability of the strap-ends associated with this East Anglian metalworking 'tradition' suggests that their manufacture was relatively decentralised, perhaps focusing upon the activity of itinerant craftsmen or several small low-output production sites (Hinton 1990b, 32–33). One possible location for such a production site may have been the *wic* at Ipswich where strap-end moulds and other non-ferrous metalworking debris were recovered from ninth-century contexts at the Buttermarket excavation (Wade 1993, 148; Newman 1999, 37).

Cultural diversity and assimilation: tenth-century strap-ends

By the beginning of the tenth century a new, more robust, tongue-shaped form of strap-end, based upon an established Continental Carolingian prototype, had replaced the zoomorphic variety in much of the country (Wilson 1964, 62, no. 148). The discovery of an increasing number of these Carolingian examplars from south and south-east England

highlights a direct source of influence from mainland Europe (Fig. 4.4a). However, their occasional presence in Viking graves, such as Aspatria, Cumbria (Edwards 1992, fig. 5.1d), and Balladoole on the Isle of Man (Bersu and Wilson 1966, pls VII b, VIII a), combined with the use of the form in the Viking homelands (Arbman 1940–3, Taf. 87, no. 9), suggests that Viking activity may also have played an important role in the class's adoption in Britain. During the course of the tenth century these strap-ends proliferated into a number of decorative types, examples decorated in what is now recognised as the 'Winchester style' being the most common. This is particularly so in the area corresponding with the heartland of late Anglo-Saxon Wessex, where the style may have first evolved under strong Continental influence (see Wilson 1984, 154–94; Hinton 1996b). More surprising in light of past art-historical interpretation, which has stressed this region's monopoly on the production of the style (Kendrick 1949, 1; Wilson 1984, 160), is the increasing number of Winchester-style strap-ends from the Eastern Danelaw, a distribution which suggests that the style was more widely adopted than hitherto thought.

The Danelaw assemblage also comprises examples decorated with motifs derived from the repertoire of contemporary Viking art styles. The most influential of these in respect to strap-ends, as

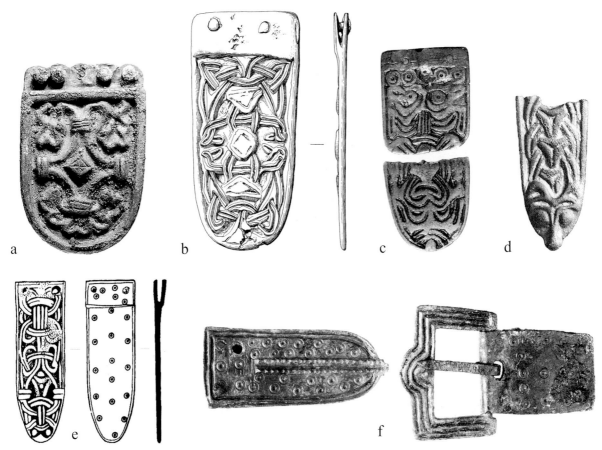

Fig. 4.4 *Representatives of tongue-shaped strap-ends: (a) Claydon, Suffolk, in private possession;*
(b) Great Walsingham, Norfolk (after Margeson 1997, Fig. 7), on loan to Norwich Castle Museum;
(c) unprovenanced 'Essex', in private possession; (d) Weston, Hertfordshire, in private possession; (e) St Mary
Bishopshill Senior, York, North Yorkshire, Yorkshire Museum 1973.24 (after Wilson 1965, fig. 29a); (f) Carlisle
Cathedral, Cumbria, strap-end (Ae 183), matching buckle (Ae 269), © Carlisle Archaeological Unit. Scale 1:1

well as a wide variety of other artistic media within the British Isles, was the Borre style which was current during the later ninth and tenth centuries (Wilson in Wilson and Klindt-Jensen 1966, 87–94). The style is represented in its purest form on a small number of tongue-shaped strap-ends likely to be of Scandinavian origin. For example, a strap-end from Great Walsingham (Fig. 4.4b) is decorated with a standard Borre-style ring-knot design, composed of raised lozenges and interlacing strands, paralleled widely on Scandinavian metalwork including a very closely related strap-end from Birka, Uppland, Sweden (Arbman 1940–3, Taf. 87, no. 9) and the zoomorphic strap-ends from both the Borre and Gokstad burials in Norway (Wilson and Klindt-Jensen 1966, pls XXVIIh, XXXb).

More numerous are strap-ends decorated with stylised or debased motifs characteristic of the distinctive Anglo-Scandinavian artistic tradition which evolved within the Danelaw and other regions of Viking settlement in Britain (Graham-

Campbell 1989, 73). Among them is a uniform group displaying a novel combination of two debased Borre-style motifs, the ring-chain and the cat-like animal mask (Fig. 4.4c; Thomas 1996, fig. 3C). Its East Anglian concentration (Fig. 4.5a), also displayed by a uniform series of contemporary Borre-style disc-brooches, identifies this region as an important tenth-century base for the serial production of Anglo-Scandinavian metalwork (Graham-Campbell 1989, 73, fig. 6; Richardson 1993, 31; Thomas 1996, 88).

Further examples of this tradition, including a fragmentary strap-end from Weston, Hertfordshire, are decorated with versions of the 'vertebral ring-chain', an interlace motif characterised by a central midrib formed from truncated triangles resembling a spine (Fig. 4.4d). This motif is particularly common on Viking-age sculpture, especially in north-west England and the Isle of Man, and is interpreted by Viking-age specialists as an essentially Insular adaptation of a Scandinavian Borre-style motif (Bailey 1980, 217; Richardson 1993, 180).

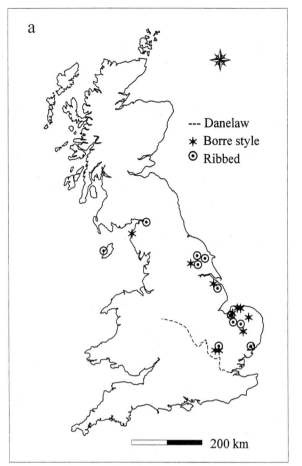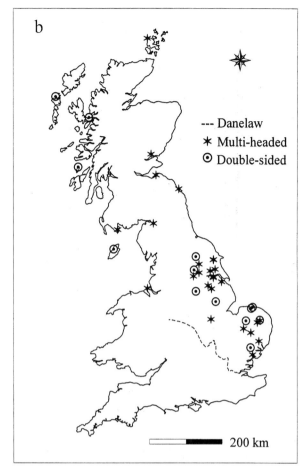

Fig. 4.5 *(a) Distribution of Borre-style and ribbed strap-ends; (b) distribution of multi-headed and double-sided strap-ends*

Amongst the considerable corpus of Anglo-Scandinavian finds from York, is a fine Borre-style strap-end from St Mary Bishopshill Senior, North Yorkshire, decorated with a complex looping ring-knot design and vestigial animal-head terminal (Fig. 4.4e). While the best parallels for both the form and decoration of this strap-end come from Scandinavian contexts (Graham-Campbell 1980, 53, no. 187; Arbman 1940–3, Taf. 87, no. 10), an Insular Anglo-Scandinavian origin is more likely in view of the stamped ring-and-dot design on its underside. This technique of ornamentation was popular within Anglo-Scandinavian Britain, not least on strap-ends such the aforementioned East Anglian Borre-style series which display a row of five ring-and-dots below the attachment end (Fig. 4.4c).

The use of ring-and-dot decoration extends to a further group of tongue-shaped strap-end present among the Danelaw assemblage, characterised by a centrally placed, longitudinal rib (Fig. 4.4f). This distinctive form appears to have been popular amongst Viking communities in the Irish Sea region, as evidenced by their discovery in association with matching buckles, from Viking graves at Peel on the

Isle of Man (Graham-Campbell forthcoming) and Cathedral Green, Carlisle Castle (Keevil 1989, fig.3, no.2; pers. comm. M. McCarthy). Stray detector finds indicate that the class was also adopted within the Eastern Danelaw (Fig. 4.5a), a pattern no doubt related to increasing contacts with the Irish Sea region precipitated by the Norse take-over of York in 919 (Higham 1992, 24–7).

The origins of this class are somewhat enigmatic; outside Britain two examples have been found in Scandinavia (Graham-Campbell forthcoming) and a third is published from the site of Domburg in Holland (Capelle 1976, Taf. 18, no. 307). The use of matching buckle-sets, however, is in itself a likely indicator of external foreign influence considering the general scarcity of buckles from contemporary Anglo-Saxon contexts (Hinton 1990c, 507). This is in contrast to the wider evidence provided by Viking graves from Scandinavia and Britain which reveal that this fashion was widespread in both Carolingian territories and the Viking homelands during the ninth and tenth centuries. For example, the Carolingian strap-ends from Balladoole (Bersu and Wilson 1966, pls VII b, c and VIII a, b) and Aspatria,

Fig. 4.6 *Multi-headed strap-ends: (a) Hurly Hawkin, Grampian, Scotland, National Museums of Scotland, Edinburgh HHA 30; (b) unprovenanced 'North Yorkshire', in private possession. Scale 1.5:1*

Cumbria (Edwards 1992, fig. 5.1 c and d) were found with corresponding buckles, or sets of buckles and strap-slides, used to fasten waist-belts or spur straps.

Two further groups of strap-end, united by their use of zoomorphic terminals and split-ends, circulated alongside the tongue-shaped variety within the Danelaw. The first may be differentiated from its ninth-century Anglo-Saxon antecedent by having additional animal masks on its shaft, often manifest as pairings in a confronted or opposed disposition (Fig. 4.6; Haldenby 1990, fig. 4, no. 7; Taylor 1982, fig. 6, no. 30). A different pedigree is also indicated by the style of these heads which, in their crispest guise (Fig. 4.6a), closely resemble the curving-eared examples, with pellet eyes, which occur widely on Borre-style metalwork from Scandinavia, including several of the mounts from the Borre find itself (Wilson in Wilson and Klindt-Jensen 1966, 90, pl. XXVII, g, h, i). On debased examples, such as that from St Mary's Abbey, York (Moulden *et al.* 1999, fig. 71, no. 58, misidentified in the publication as Anglian) (Fig. 4.6b), the facial features of each head are simplified to a series of punched dots and arcs – a stylistic trick also paralleled on contemporary Scandinavian metalwork, such as a strap-distributor from Västergötland, Sweden (Bersu and Wilson 1966, pl. XVIII, c).

Despite the existence of a few related examples from Scandinavia, including that from the Viking-age site of Trelleborg, Denmark (Nørlund *et al.* 1948, pl. XXII, no. 1), the greater number of findspots from Britain suggests that the form was being manu-

factured on this side of North Sea (Fig. 4.5b). Within Britain, a few examples from sites in Scotland (Curle 1982, fig. 39, no. 432) and the Irish Sea region (Bu'lock 1960, fig. 4e) indicate that they were being circulated, if not manufactured, in these areas of Norse or Hiberno-Norse settlement. More conclusive evidence for a production zone, however, comes from the Danelaw region where several examples carrying debased facial features have been discovered both within York and its hinterland.

Members of the second group display a number of shared characteristics which identify them as relatives of a contemporary class of Insular Irish strap-end. Most distinctive is their double-sided decoration comprising incised roundels, sometimes perforated centrally through the thickness of the metal, and panels of interlace enclosed within obliquely hatched or beaded borders (Fig. 4.7a). The predominant terminal form, often incorporating triangular or rounded eyes in conjunction with incised 'whiskers', is also very different in character to those employed on other classes.

Stylistic traits, including the use of Insular-derived interlace motifs, combined with the discovery of examples from the interior of Ireland, provide strong grounds for attributing the origins of the class to a ninth-century Irish milieu (Crawford 1923, fig. 8). Their wider circulation within the Irish Sea region suggests that the class was subsequently adopted by Scandinavian settlers, a cultural association attested by a number of archaeological discoveries. An example from Cronk Moar, Jurby, on the Isle of Man, for example, was discovered embedded in the remains of some textiles from a Viking burial mound (Bersu and Wilson 1966, 68, pl. XVI, b), whereas that from the excavated multi-period settlement at the Udal, North Uist, came from one of the Viking-age levels (Graham-Campbell 1973). Viking Dublin, meanwhile, is a likely candidate for a production centre, given the several examples from tenth-century habitation contexts encountered during various excavations within the town (Lang 1988, fig. 118; Wallace and Ó Floinn 1988, 18). Visual testimony to this Viking influence is also supplied by examples which share an Insular version of a Borre-style ring-chain motif closely paralleled on a number of Scandinavian finds including that on the strap-end from Borre, Vestfold, Norway (Fig. 4.7a; Graham-Campbell 1973, fig. 51; Richardson 1993, 152–57).

In their use of perforations, incised roundels and panels of interlace, the strap-ends are closely related to other metalwork from the Irish Sea region. This material includes a group of bridle-mounts from Viking warrior-graves, such as those from Kiloran Bay, Colonsay (Bersu and Wilson 1966, pl. 7a), and a series of buckles, one of which was recently dis-

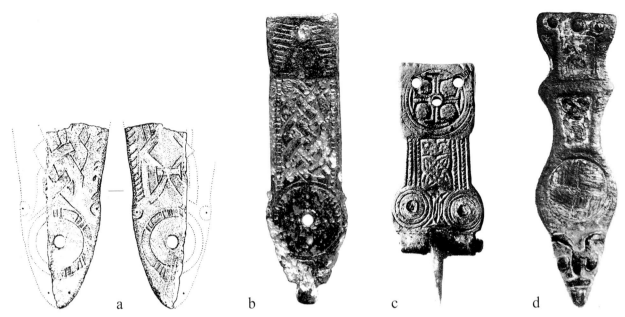

Fig. 4.7 *Double-sided strap-ends and buckle; (a) The Udal, North Uist, Scotland (after Graham-Campbell 1973, fig. 51); (b) Ashby-de-la-Launde, Lincolnshire, Scunthorpe Museum 1991.458.2; (c) Eynsham Abbey, Oxfordshire, © Oxford Archaeological Unit; (d) Polstead, Suffolk, Ipswich Museum 1992.11.4. Scale 1.5:1*

covered during excavations at Whithorn, Dumfries and Galloway (Nicholson and Hill 1997, fig. 10.57, BZ 18). The cross-current activity of Irish Sea Vikings during the later ninth and tenth centuries may have had a major influence on the formation of this wider metalworking tradition, of which the strap-ends were one product (Nicholson 1997; Graham-Campbell 1995, 68).

As alluded to above, versions of this class have also been discovered within England, their findspots clustering within a region corresponding to the Eastern Danelaw. A small number, including an example from Ashby-de-la-Launde, Lincolnshire (Fig. 4.7b), are sufficiently akin in form and style to examples from Ireland and the Irish Sea area to attribute their manufacture to these regions. These 'English' discoveries should be compared with a variety of other contemporary metalwork of Insular origin discovered in this region, including several ring-headed pins (Fanning 1993) and, most pertinent to the current discussion although discovered ouside the Danelaw territory, a buckle closely related to the series of Insular strap-ends from excavations at Eynsham Abbey, Oxfordshire (Fig. 4.7c).

Because of their deviant characteristics, most of the English examples are more likely to represent contemporary copies made within the Danelaw rather than being imports from the west. The most obvious difference displayed by the English variant is the lack of the central perforation, though the vestiges of the roundel survive as a circular field of decoration in the usual location above the terminal

(Fig. 4.7d). Together with the aforementioned series of ribbed strap-ends, the initial circulation and subsequent emulation of this distinct form within the Danelaw is redolent of the contacts existing between Viking communities in the Eastern Danelaw and the Irish Sea region during the tenth century, contacts also revealed by comparative research on Viking-age sculpture and place-names (Graham-Campbell 1995, 74–5).

Conclusions

This overview of the corpus of Late Anglo-Saxon and Viking-age strap-ends has presented some of the main regional variations highlighted by recent research. An assessment of the range of mechanisms that gave rise to these variations is more than can be attempted here, though a few relevant considerations can be advanced. Firstly, the size and homogeneity of the regional groupings identified varies greatly. Within the ninth-century series, for example, one can make a distinction between larger groups representative of broad metalworking traditions and smaller ones which may be attributed to individual workshops or craftspeople. The East Anglian series of silver-wire strap-end, notable for its quantity and variability (Thomas 1996), is likely to be representative of the former, while the activity of the latter is manifest in small, and highly uniform, groups of Trewhiddle-style strap-end identified in the north of the country.

Secondly, an evaluation of the factors underlying this observed product diversity must also take into account the influence of varying manufacturing techniques. The details preserved on the mould fragment from Carlisle suggest that the decoration on some strap-ends was cast to near completion, with only minor ornamental features needing to be applied by hand after casting. As a process, casting could have attained a high level of product standardisation, especially if several identical moulds were produced from a solid reusable model, as suggested for some members of one of the Yorkshire groups of Trewhiddle-style strap-end (Bailey 1993, 90). The increased levels of product diversity encountered elsewhere in the class may be a reflection of alternative methods of manufacture most likely associated with wrought technology. The production of strap-ends using techniques other than casting has been revealed through detailed examination of the series of unfinished examples from the Sevington hoard (La Niece in Thomas 2000), and the fine ninth-century silver pair decorated with gold filigree from Ipsden Heath, Oxfordshire (MacGregor 1994).

Thirdly, discussion has highlighted the mobility of some of the strap-ends associated with Viking settlement and colonial activity. The diverse Danelaw assemblage, which embraces strap-ends originating from Anglo-Saxon England, the Celtic West, Scandinavia and the Carolingian Continent, is testimony to the considerable range of external contacts exploited by Viking settlers in the British Isles. The same assemblage also provides an important body of evidence for exploring the influence of contemporary Viking art styles on indigenous metalworking. As with other representatives of Anglo-Scandinavian art, these strap-ends reflect the process of artistic assimilation through which mainstream Scandinavian motifs were subtly transformed to create a native stylistic tradition (Richardson 1992).

Acknowledgements

This paper has drawn upon the results of the author's doctoral research into Late Saxon and Viking-age strap-ends. My special thanks to Professor James Graham-Campbell who guided my research with diligence and a critical eye and to whom I am grateful for initially suggesting that I present a paper to the conference. Thanks also to Caroline Paterson for sharing her considerable knowledge and expertise on Viking-age metalwork with me. Although too great in number to list here individually, I would also like to thank the many detectorists, museum staff and archaeologists who kindly gave me access to view and record the strap-ends held in their possession, and without whose co-operation such a study would have been impossible.

References

ANDERTON, M. (ed.) 1999, *Anglo-Saxon Trading Centres; Beyond the Emporia*. Glasgow.

ARBMAN, H. 1940–43, *Birka I: Die Gräber*. Tafeln (1940). Text (1943). Stockholm.

BAILEY, R. N. 1980, *Viking Age Sculpture in Northern England*. London.

BAILEY, R. N. 1993, 'An Anglo-Saxon strap-end from Wooperton', *Archaeol. Aeliana* 5, 87–91.

BERSU, G. and WILSON, D. M. 1966, *Three Viking Graves in the Isle of Man* (= Soc. Medieval Archaeol. Monogr. Ser. 1). London.

BIDDLE, M. 1990, *Object and Economy in Medieval Winchester*, Winchester Studies, 7 ii (2 Vols), *Artefacts from Medieval Winchester* Vol ii. Oxford.

BLACKBURN, M. A. S. and PAGAN, H. E. 1986, 'A revised check-list of coin hoards from the British Isles c. 500–1100', in M. A. S. Blackburn (ed.), *Anglo-Saxon Monetary History*, 291–314. Leicester.

BLINKHORN, P. 1999, 'Of cabbages and kings: production, trade, and consumption in Middle-Saxon England', in M. Anderton, 4–24.

BRØNSTED, J. 1924, *Early English Ornament*. London, Copenhagen.

BU'LOCK, J. D. 1960, 'The Celtic, Saxon and Scandinavian settlement at Meols in Wirral', *Trans. Hist. Soc. Lancashire Cheshire* 112, 1–29.

CAPELLE, T. 1976, *Die frühgeschichtlichen Metallfunde von Domburg auf Walcheren 1 & 2* (= Nederlandse Oudheden 5).

CRAWFORD, H. S. 1923, 'A descriptive list of Irish shrines and reliquaries – Part II', *J. Roy. Soc. Antiq. Ir.* 53, 151–76.

CURLE, C. L. 1982, *The Pictish and Norse Finds from the Brough of Birsay 1934–74* (= Soc. Antiq. Scotl. Monogr. Ser. 1). Edinburgh.

EDWARDS, B. J. N. 1992, 'The Vikings in north-west England: the archaeological evidence', in Graham-Campbell (ed.), 43–63.

FANNING, T. 1994, *Viking Age Ringed Pins from Dublin*, Medieval Dublin Excavations 1962–81, Series B, vol. 4, Royal Irish Academy. Dublin.

GRAHAM-CAMPBELL, J. 1973, 'A fragmentary bronze strap-end of the Viking period from The Udal, North Uist, Invernesshire', *Medieval Archaeol.* 17, 128–31.

GRAHAM-CAMPBELL, J. 1980, *Viking Artefacts: A Select Catalogue*. London.

GRAHAM-CAMPBELL, J. 1989, 'The archaeology of the Danelaw: an introduction', in H. Galinié (ed.), *Les Mondes Normands (VIIIe–XIIe Siècles)*, 69–76. Caen.

GRAHAM-CAMPBELL, J. (ed.) 1992, *Viking Treasure from the North West. The Cuerdale Hoard and its Context* (= National Museums and Galleries on Merseyside Occas. Pap. 5). Liverpool.

GRAHAM-CAMPBELL, J. 1995, 'The Irish Sea Vikings: raiders and settlers', in T. Scott and P. Starkey (eds), *The Middle Ages in the North-West*, 59–83. Oxford.

GRAHAM-CAMPBELL, J. (forthcoming), 'Tenth-century graves: the Viking-age artefacts from the Peel Castle cemetery and their significance', in D. Freke, *Peel Castle Excavation, 1982–7*. Liverpool.

HALDENBY, D. 1990, 'An Anglian Site on the Yorkshire Wolds', *Yorkshire Archaeol. J.* 62, 51–63.

HIGHAM, N. J. 1992, 'Northumbria, Mercia and the Irish Sea Norse, 893–926', in Graham-Campbell (ed.), 21–31.

HIGHAM, N. J. 1993, *The Kingdom of Northumbria AD 350–1100*, Stroud.

HILL, P. 1997, *Whithorn & St Ninian. The Excavation of a Monastic Town 1984–91*. Stroud.

HINTON, D. A. 1990a, *Archaeology, Economy and Society: England from the Fifth to the Fifteenth Century*. London.

HINTON, D. A. 1990b, 'The medieval gold, silver, and copper-alloy objects from Winchester', in Biddle, 29–35.

HINTON, D. A. 1990c, 'Buckles and buckle-plates', in Biddle, 506–23.

HINTON, D. A. 1996a, *The Gold, Silver and other Non-Ferrous Alloy Objects from Hamwic*, Southampton Finds Vol. 2. Stroud.

HINTON, D. A. 1996b, 'A Winchester-style mount from near Winchester', *Medieval Archaeol.* 40, 214–17.

KEEVIL, G. D. 1989, 'Early medieval finds from Carlisle Cathedral', *Bull. CBA Churches Comm.* 26, 16–18.

KENDRICK, T. D. 1949, *Late Saxon and Viking Art*. London.

LANG, J. T. 1988, *Viking-Age Decorated Wood: A Study of its Ornament and Style*. Medieval Dublin Excavations 1962–81, Series B, vol. 1, Dublin.

LA NIECE, S. 2000, 'A report on the scientific examination of a group of Late Saxon strap-ends from Sevington, Wiltshire', in G. Thomas, 2000.

MARGESON, S. 1996, 'Viking settlement in Norfolk: a study of new evidence', in S. Margeson, B. Ayres and S. Heywood (eds), *A Festival of Norfolk Archaeology*. Huntstanton, Norfolk and Norwich Archaeol Soc., 47–57.

MACGREGOR, A. 1994, 'A pair of Late Saxon strap-ends from Ipsden Heath, Oxfordshire', *J. British Archaeol. Ass.* 147, 122–27.

METCALF, D. M. 1987, 'A topographical commentary on the coin finds from ninth-century Northumbria (*c.* 780 – *c.* 870)', in D. Metcalf (ed.), *Coinage in Ninth-Century Northumbria. 10th Oxford Symposium on Coinage and Monetary History* (= B.A.R. Brit. Ser. 180), 361–82. Oxford.

MOULDEN, J., LOGAN, E. and TWEDDLE, D. 1999, 'Catalogue of Anglian sites', in D. Tweddle, J. Moulden and E. Logan, *Anglian York: A Survey of the Evidence* (= The Archaeology of York, Anglian York 7/2), 231–94. York.

NEWMAN, J. 1999, 'Wics, trade, and the hinterlands – the Ipswich region', in Anderton, 32–47.

NICHOLSON, A. 1997, 'Metalwork and sculpture: design and patronage in *c.* 900 A.D', in Hill, , 621–23.

NICHOLSON, A. and HILL, P. 1997, 'The non-ferrous metals', in Hill, 360–404.

NØRLUND, P. 1948, *Trelleborg*, Nordiske Fortidsminder IV, I Hefte, Copenhagen.

PHILPOTT, R. A. 1999, 'Recent archaeological finds from Merseyside and Cheshire and their archaeological significance', *Medieval Archaeol.* 43, 194–202.

RICHARDS, J. D. 1999, 'What's so special about 'productive sites'? Middle Saxon settlements in Northumbria', in T. Dickinson and D. Griffiths (eds), *The Making of Kingdoms, Anglo-Saxon Stud. Archaeol. Hist.* 10, 71–80.

RICHARDSON, C. 1990, 'A catalogue of recent acquisitions to Carlisle Museum, and reported finds from the Cumbria area', *Trans. Cumberland Westmorland Antiq. Archaeol. Soc.*, 2nd ser. 90, 1–99.

RICHARDSON, C. 1992, 'Form, function and assimilation: the impact of the Borre Style in the British Isles', *Medieval Europe*, Pre-Printed Papers, Vol. 5, 121–23. York.

RICHARDSON, C. 1993, The Borre style in the British Isles and Ireland: A Reassessment, Unpublished MLitt thesis, Newcastle University.

TAYLOR, D. B. 1982, 'Excavation of a promontory fort, broch and souterrain at Hurly Hawkin, Angus', *Proc. Soc. Antiq. Scotl.* 112, 215–54.

TAYLOR, J. and WEBSTER, L. 1984, 'A Late Saxon strap-end mould from Carlisle', *Medieval Archaeol.* 28, 178–81.

THOMAS, G. 1996, 'Silver-wire strap-ends from East Anglia', *Anglo-Saxon Stud. Archaeol. Hist.* 9, 81–101.

THOMAS, G. 2000, A Survey of Late Saxon and Viking-age strap-ends from Britain, unpublished PhD thesis, University of London.

ULMSCHNEIDER, K. 2000, *Markets, Minsters and Metal-Detectors* (= B. A. R. Brit. Ser. 307). Oxford.

WADE, K. 1993, 'The urbanisation of East Anglia: the Ipswich perspective', in J. Gardiner (ed.), *Flatlands and Wetlands: Current Themes in East Anglian Archaeology* (= E. Anglian Archaeol. Rep. 50), 144–52.

WALLACE, P. F. and Ó FLOINN, R. 1988, *Dublin 1000: Discovery and Excavation in Dublin, 1842–1981*. Dublin.

WEBSTER, L. and BACKHOUSE, J. (eds) 1991, *The Making of England. Anglo-Saxon Art and Culture AD 600–900*. London.

WILSON, D. M. 1964, *Anglo-Saxon Ornamental Metalwork 700–1100 in the British Museum, Catalogue of Antiquities of the Later Saxon Period I*. London.

WILSON, D. M. 1965, 'Two 10th-century bronze objects', *Medieval Archaeol.* 9, 154–56.

WILSON, D. M. 1984, *Anglo-Saxon Art*. London.

WILSON, D. M. and BLUNT, C. E. 1961, 'The Trewhiddle Hoard', *Archaeologia* 98, 75–122.

WILSON, D. M. and KLINDT-JENSEN, O. 1966, *Viking Art*. London.

YORKE, B. 1990, *Kings and Kingdoms of Early Anglo-Saxon England*. London.

5 Irish Monumental Sculpture: the Dating Evidence Provided by Linguistic Forms

Catherine Swift

In 1987, Dr Isabel Henderson published a paper entitled 'Early Christian monuments of Scotland displaying crosses but no other ornament'. In this she emphasised the testimony of cross-inscribed stones as indicators of the existence of Christian faith in areas for which we often lack documentary evidence. She also stressed the major difficulties in dating these monuments. In both of these observations, as she herself makes clear, she was preceded by Dr Ann Hamlin in her 1982 article on similar stones from Ireland. Within the Irish corpus, however, is a sub-group consisting of those stones which both display crosses and are carved with inscriptions in the ogam script. About these, Hamlin wrote 'it is from language that the best hope of dating comes' (Hamlin 1982, 283). My purpose in this article is to look at the particulars of such a dating technique in the hopeful expectation that the results from such a study might be applied to monuments without inscriptions – either in Ireland or elsewhere.

For historical reasons, the class of ogam stones ornamented with cross forms, amounting to rather more than 10% of R. A. S. Macalister's 1945 corpus, has been underestimated, partly, it must be said, because of the approach of Macalister himself. In both the ogam stone corpus (1945, iv–ix) and in his book *The Archaeology of Ireland* (1949, 328–43) Macalister argued that the ogam alphabet was invented by druids who had learnt the Chalcidic version of the Greek alphabet in the sixth and fifth centuries BC, probably in northern Italy. At this stage, however, the alphabet consisted of a series of hand signals based on the five fingers. For Macalister, it was not until approximately the sixth century AD that ogam began to be inscribed on stones (1949, 334) but even at this stage, the primary purpose of such inscriptions was a magical invocation of the deceased rather than a simple commemoration. In addition, he accepted Eoin MacNeill's argument that

a number of inscriptions referred to gods rather than to human ancestors (Macalister 1949, 339; *cf.* MacNeill 1906).

According to Macalister's hypothesis, as Christianity began to spread, the missionaries of the new faith occasionally accommodated the pagan script. More commonly, the Christians came into conflict with the pagans and with what Macalister termed 'implacable hostility' (1949, 338) set about neutralising the pagan magic of the stones by carving the sign of a cross upon them. Macalister did acknowledge that in some cases the cross was carved contemporaneously with the inscription (a feature he saw as a later development in the ogam stone-carving tradition) and in such instances, he felt, the cross would be found at the head of the stone. In others, however, where the cross is cut about 4 ft (1.25m) from the ground, he saw this as subsequent carving on an already erect stone. In still others, he felt that the stone must have been thrown down, the cross carved on the butt-end and then re-erected with the inscription reading downwards into the ground and the cross triumphant above it (Macalister 1949, 338–39).

Several features of this model were criticised by both linguists and archaeologists of Macalister's own day, including Kenneth Jackson (1946), Daniel Binchy (1946) and M. J. O'Kelly (1945). In 1961, Eoin MacWhite suggested that some ogam letters might derive from Christian symbols and drew attention to the existence of what linguists had identified as an Irish vernacular version of the Christian *hic iacit* formula – the word ><OI or KOI (MacWhite 1960–1; Marstrander 1911; Pokorny 1915). In 1982, Hamlin argued that 'in at least ten cases' of the some 44 cross-ornamented ogam stones, there was evidence that the cross had been added later. 'In others, there is no indication or priority of ogham or cross and they may be contemporary' (Hamlin 1982, 285).

Amongst historians, Macalister's views still remain influential and have recently been endorsed by Daibhí Ó Cróinín in his 1995 book *Early Medieval Ireland*, the first general textbook on early Irish history to be written in 25 years. Ó Cróinín states (1995, 35):

> In some instances, of course, crosses appear on monuments but the evidence suggests that most, if not all, of these were added much later to monuments erected in the fifth and sixth centuries, monuments which originally only bore inscriptions... But though the evidence cannot be pushed too far, there is no escaping the fact that the ogam stones reflect a society in which the pre-Christian practice of memorial in stone has remained totally impervious to the influence of Christianity and this despite the fact that the epigraphic habit is usually believed to have derived from contact with the Roman world.

In archaeological circles, in contrast, there has been a tendency to follow Hamlin's lead: both Michael Herity and John Sheehan have published dates for certain cross forms deriving from the existence of ogam inscriptions upon the same stone. Sheehan (1990, 168) sees the presence of ogam as indicating a sixth-century date while Herity (1995, 90, 150, 156, 310) argues for the first half of the seventh century. Nancy Edwards (1990, 103–4) quotes Hamlin *in extenso* in her account of ogams in her 1990 textbook while Harold Mytum (1992, 38, 54–6, 66–9, 96), without referring explicitly to either Hamlin or Macalister, places the ogam stones within the transitional phase between paganism and Christianity and agrees that in some cases the crosses are contemporary with the inscriptions. In an important article, which adds much new data to the debate, Fionnbarr Moore endorses Hamlin's views while pointing out that 'linguistically early ogham stones are, in the main, not cross-inscribed', and, contrariwise, that the absence of explicitly Christian features on a slab 'does not necessarily indicate a monument with a pagan background' (Moore 1998, 26–7).

The position of Charles Thomas in relation to the paganism or otherwise of ogam monuments has varied over the last fifteen years although it should be said that his view that the *invention* of the ogam script was a pagan one has remained constant. (I deal with this issue below.) In 1987 Thomas wrote:

> The proposition now is that the single, marked, memorial stone by an actual burial (or not) arose in fifth-century Ireland *because* of the spread of Christianity. The overall distribution of the Ogham stones is in the broad region most affected by *romanitas* and the non-Patrician spread of Christianity in Ireland. The common formulaic epitaph with name and origin – 'Of A, of the son of B' – fulfilled a need, perhaps no more than social assertion, arising

out of the Christian and Roman contact... (Thomas 1987, 8)

He then points out that in Roman Britain, the inscribed tombstone was by no means universal and only four (and those dubious) have ever been claimed as Christian. This he sees as undermining the proposition that the appearance of Latin-inscribed memorials, which he views as making their appearance in western and northern Britain by 500, automatically come from Gaul. He continues:

> ...Reconsidering this puzzle, the writer would air a suspicion that use of Christian memorial stones in late fifth- and sixth-century Atlantic Britain may actually have been inspired from Ireland and not vice versa ... Is it just possible that the Late Roman personal memorial, tenuously conveyed as an idea to Ireland, took root there for particular reasons and was later reconveyed to the provinces where it had originated. (Thomas 1987, 8–9)

And finally:

> In those parts of Ireland where Ogham memorials are least common (that is, the north and extreme west) we encounter another and ultimately more important form: the uninscribed cross-ornamented stone. Its genesis is obscure as is the chronology ... By the sixth century we should have Oghaminscribed stones that, like British memorials, exhibit simple crosses. (Thomas 1987, 9)

These various statements are not (to me) entirely explicit – what are the precise connotations of the word 'should' in the last sentence for example? – and they involve certain very large assumptions about a range of issues which are the subject of much scholarly debate. It does appear, however, that in this article, Thomas is following Hamlin's line in assuming that a percentage of the ogam stones had crosses which were carved contemporaneously with the inscriptions. In 1994, however, in his book *And Shall These Mute Stones Speak?*, Thomas reverts to the Macalister doctrine: Irish ogam stones are too early to be affected by Christianity and 'anything else on these stones, like incised crosses, represents later additions unconnected with the epitaphs' (1994, 69). A different formulation, found in his latest article on the subject, appears to represent a mixture of Macalister's views on the role of pagan *literati* in creating ogam monuments and Jane Stevenson's article (1989) on the evidence for pre-Christian literacy in Ireland:

> The first applications of ogham to stone, in the form of simple memorials to individual dead, saying no more than *A son of B; of A, of a son of the tribe of B; A son of B of the tribe C* (and further variations thereof) are not in themselves datable; only context may sometimes provide a clue ... If the inferred and partly recorded minor settlements of Munster Déisi in

south-west Wales began near the end of the fourth century AD, there are a few menhir-like pillars in Pembrokeshire with ogham script (alone) and demonstrably Irish names that are probably for non-Christians and should be assigned to the early fifth century ... I want to present ogham as, to all intents, a parallel to Roman writing; and the latter as an innovation already entrenched in a large part of pre-400 Ireland. Any distribution of literacy is not automatically also a distribution of contemporary Christianity (Thomas 1998, 10–11).

And in conclusion:

> Our growing awareness of the impact of *romanitas* on early Ireland must reinforce the view that the very idea of the inscribed memorial, the stone proclaiming the name and filiation of the deceased for those who could read to read and appreciate, was taken from the pagan Roman empire (and various ways in which this could have happened can be left aside) ... Ogham was surely invented by *fili* [sic – presumably for O. Ir. nom. pl. *filid*], the Irish *literati*, before and beyond Christianity and originally for this precise end ... All in all, one could very well argue that Ireland's literary revolution began in Munster, within the Roman period and that only such a revolution could have enabled the surprisingly early eremitic monasticism of the fifth century to have taken root (Thomas 1998, 15).

As I understand it, this last interpretation sees the invention of ogam as being the result of (pagan) contacts between the Roman world and Ireland and that the pattern of ogam stone distribution reflects a pagan Irish world affected by *romanitas*. At some subsequent point, the 'romanisation' of this area results in its early adoption of an extreme form of Christianity. The argument seems to imply a belief that the majority of all Irish ogam stones precede and are separated chronologically from the arrival of Christianity, an event which is said to have occurred in the fifth century or before. Such a suggestion would imply an extremely early date for the creation of the vast bulk of Irish ogam stones and one which is at variance with all other recent scholarship on the subject (see, in particular McManus 1991, 40–1 where the most probable date for the vast bulk of ogam inscriptions is said to be the fifth and sixth centuries). It is tantalising, therefore, that Thomas has left the 'various ways in which this could have happened' to the reader's speculations.

I should point out here a potential source of confusion; Anthony Harvey (1987) (by implication) and Jane Stevenson (1989) have argued that the invention of the ogam alphabet might be as early as the third century AD. Whether or not this is the case (and the heavy degree of Roman influence in Ireland which both authors postulate was not substantiated by the conclusions of a recent 1997 conference on the subject of Romans in Ireland), there is a clear

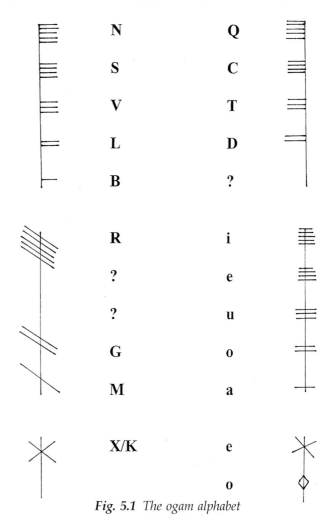

Fig. 5.1 The ogam alphabet

distinction between the date for the invention of the alphabet and the date of the first stones. The earliest version of the alphabet on the stones is one which has already been modified from the presumed original sequence of four groups of five strokes (Fig. 5.1). Some groups do not occur at all and already on the earliest pre-apocope stones, there are *forfeda* or letters which have been added. This would indicate a lapse of some, unquantifiable, time between the invention of the alphabet and the earliest monuments as we have them. In other words, it is perfectly plausible that Thomas's dating of the *invention* of ogam script to a pre-Christian period is correct; I do not accept, for reasons well rehearsed elsewhere, that the bulk of the surviving stones themselves belong to a pre-Christian period (Swift 1996; 1997, 27–69). This is not, of course, to say that the stones necessarily commemorate Christians; merely, that Christianity had been introduced to Ireland and had made an impact on the Irish language by the time the surviving ogam stones were created. We see this impact in the adoption of Christian Latin loan words such as *axal* 'apostle', *cásc* 'Easter' or *cruimther* 'priest' which by their form indicate that they were borrowed into Irish *before* the various linguistic changes which occurred during the period of ogam production and which are traceable in the ogam inscriptions (McManus 1983, 48).

My own view on the subject of contemporaneity or otherwise of cross forms on ogam stones is a slightly modified version of Hamlin's thesis, expanding on some points which she dealt with only summarily and discussing evidence which has become apparent since her article was written. I would concur that a percentage of ogam stones have crosses which are contemporary or indeed earlier than the ogam inscriptions. Amongst these, the most important is probably the stone from Church Island where the ogam inscription clearly overlies the cross (O'Kelly and Kavanagh 1954). There are also a number of stones in which, though it is impossible to detect a physical relationship between the cross and the inscription, the existence of the Irish vernacular version (><OI) of the largely Christian *hic iacit* burial formula or the reference of a Latin-named individual on a stone, with both cross and inscription, increases the likelihood that the cross is contemporary (Swift 1997, 96, 107). I would also agree that there is some degree of overlap between the ogam period and that of the cross-carved pillar stones (Hamlin 1982, 285; Swift 1997, 70–83).

In parenthesis, it should, perhaps be noted here that any argument based on Macalister's corpus without examination of the stones themselves cannot be a conclusive one. It is clear from the fieldwork done to date that Macalister's identification of cross forms is not always convincing. The stone from Lecan, Co. Kilkenny, for example, is identified by Macalister as having a Latin cross at its head (1945, 38–9); examination suggests that while there is some possible pocking running in a north-south line, the transverse arm is a natural fissure.

There appear to be cases where ogam stones have been reused at a later date as cross-ornamented pillars, with no cognisance being taken of their original function. An example of this would be Kilfountan in the Dingle peninsula. A pillar on which the ogam EQO(?)DD is carved on one of its narrow sides was subsequently decorated with a cross and Latin letter inscription 'Fintan'.[1] This, to my mind, is a matter of practicality rather than ideology; many of the ogam stones are of the same size and basic shape as the cross-marked pillars and, as Hamlin points out (1982, 285), many ogams, amounting to some 34% of Macalister's corpus, are found on ecclesiastical sites and would thus be a ready resource for later stone-workers. Moore (1998, 23) has now refined these figures: a national figure of 133 stones from 65 ecclesiastical sites and a Munster figure of 108 from 54 ecclesiastical sites.

Without going into details which I have argued elsewhere (Swift 1997, 34–48), I would see the function of the cross-marked ogam stones as being frequently (though not consistently) different from that of the cross-marked pillar stones without inscriptions. The former I see as being for the most part grave markers and as such influenced by contemporary Christian burial inscriptions in northwest Europe. The latter – or at least a percentage of them – I see as Christian estate-markers, the inspiration for which stems from Old Testament references to boulders being used as estate and boundary markers.

As Hamlin pointed out, there are a large number of stones where the cross is not clearly associated with the inscription and many of these have no other indication of Christianity such as ><OI or Latin-named individuals. On such stones, distinctions between crosses which might mark the Christian faith of the deceased or landowner, and crosses which represent reuse of earlier orthostats whose original purpose had been forgotten, are not easy to draw. They can only be established through examination of the stones themselves and not always then (Hamlin 1982, 293).

The corpus of Irish cross-carved stones for which Hamlin called in 1982 has not yet materialised and is an increasingly urgent priority given at least two recent cases when early medieval stones, lying unsupervised in rural sites, were removed by thieves.[2] Giant steps, however, have been made in recent years in the systematic linguistic analysis of ogam inscriptions. Unlike Latin, the Irish language goes through a chronological series of identifiable linguistic changes during the period in which ogam inscriptions were written. The evidence for these changes has been explored in detail by Damian McManus in *A Guide to Ogam* (1991), developing and occasionally superseding Kenneth Jackson's (1953) similar work on British stones. Though written for linguists in a manner which can be somewhat opaque for those outside a highly-specialised field, McManus's work is crucial for archaeologists and art-historians. In it, he provides clear sub-divisions of the Irish ogam inscription corpus, allowing us for the first time to say, not merely that a cross form belongs to the period of the ogam stones, but that a particular cross form is attested early in that sequence, on what are probably fifth-century stones, while another cross form could appear late in the sequence, probably late sixth- or early seventh-century. In these islands, where so many of our early Christian monuments displaying crosses but no other ornament are divorced from their original context, this provides a fundamental chronological bench-mark of a kind often lacking.

In brief, the three basic linguistic sub-divisions of the ogam-inscription corpus are entitled: pre-apocope, pre-syncope and post-syncope and I outline the

Pre-apocope

COLOMAGNI

Pre-syncope

COLOMANN

Post-syncope

COLMAN

Fig. 5.2 *The three basic linguistic sub-divisions of the ogam-inscription corpus: pre-apocope, pre-syncope and post-syncope*

sequence in Fig. 5.2. Apocope is the term for the loss of the final syllable of words and it is the first major linguistic development which we can detect in the inscriptions; McManus dates its onset to the beginning of the sixth century although it takes some time to be accepted by all carvers. Syncope is the loss of middle syllables in three-syllable words: something which begins around the middle of the sixth century and which spreads during the second half of that century. Inscriptions where there is no trace of the pre-syncope spelling are termed post-syncope and are dated to the end of the sixth and early seventh century and it is Irish of this post-syncope type which is revealed in the earliest manuscript evidence of later seventh-century Old Irish (such as the place-names and personal names in the Patrician lives by Tírechán and Muirchú: McManus 1991, 92–7).

There are complications, of course. The system is predicated on the accuracy of Macalister's readings which have still to be consistently rechecked; it must be a worrying consideration that M. J. O'Kelly in his review of the *Corpus* states (1945, 152) that of the 30 readings he checked, he felt eight were incorrect and a further ten were dubious. Some carvers appear to have been conservative and kept to the old spelling while their contemporaries were moving on to new forms. Formula words such as the word for 'son' – pre-apocope MAQQI, subsequently MAQ(Q) or MAC(C) – which occurs on the vast majority of inscriptions, seem to have retained an old spelling long after personal names had evolved. Moreover, while the system is a relatively convincing method of sub-dividing the ogam stone corpus into early, middle and late, it is at its weakest when proposing specific dates for any particular stone. Furthermore, although the end of the sequence can be established from the forms extant in seventh-century texts, the beginning of the sequence is very difficult to establish. All we can say to date is that the stratum of Irish found in the earliest or pre-apocope stones is one in which a number of ecclesiastical Latin terms has already been borrowed into the Irish language. This would imply a late fourth- or fifth-century starting date; this allows time for Constantine's establishment of Christianity as a major religion in the early fourth century to percolate through to an island beyond the north-western Roman frontier.

Despite these complications, McManus's linguistic dating system provides us with the only clear subdivisions of the Irish corpus and, in the absence of any excavated Irish ogam stone in an original context, it provides our only hope for dating the cross forms with which they are sometimes associated. Elsewhere I have argued that it is probably also a better method of sub-dividing the whole ogam corpus than the rather too specific dates sometimes put forward on the basis of epigraphical analysis of Latin-alphabet inscriptions on the Welsh ogam stones by Jackson (1953) and Nash-Williams (1950) (given the large number of unprovable assumptions on which their chronology is predicated; Swift 1997, 56–62). For the rest of this paper, therefore, I would like to examine some of the archaeological conclusions which one might draw, using the linguistic dating system.

I begin with the stone from Emlagh East, Co. Kerry, which is first recorded by Edward Lhuyd at the beginning of the eighteenth century when it stood upright in a field near the beach where it now lies (Brash 1879, 173–74). The inscription runs up the left-hand side of the stone to a point at the head where the edge of the stone is somewhat rough. Macalister argued (1945, 173; Fig. 5.3) that this was subsequent damage which eliminated part of a longer inscription; I would agree with the Dingle Archaeological Survey (Cuppage 1986, 255) and Damian McManus (1991, 66) who saw no such indication on the stone. The extant inscription reads

Fig. 5.3 *Inscription on the stone from Emlagh East, Co. Kerry*

BRUSCCOS MAQQI CALLIACI or in English 'belonging to B*, son of C*'. All three words are pre-apocope i.e. they have not lost their final syllables. Thus it belongs to the earliest sub-division of the ogam corpus, a group which probably belongs to the fifth century.

The importance of this date for the inscription lies in the relationship between the cross and the ogam scores of the letter L. It seems quite clear on examination of the stone (Macalister 1945, 173; Cuppage 1986, 255; McManus 1991, 54; Swift 1997, 108) that the second score of the letter L has been shortened in order not to run into the arm of the cross, a feature which indicates that the cross is earlier than the ogam (though how much earlier we cannot tell.) Here, then, we have a plain Latin cross which appears to be fifth century or earlier.

A similar cross is found on one of the stones from Ballintaggart, also in Co. Kerry. Macalister argued (1945, 157) that the cross was inverted with respect to the writing – in other words the upper arm is longer than the lower one. Examination of the stone indicates that Macalister was not making allowances for a natural fissure in the face of the stone which runs along its entire length (see Cuppage 1986, fig.147; Swift 1997, 109, pl.). The carver apparently used this fissure to guide him in creating the north-south line and exact dimensions of the latter are therefore extremely difficult to ascertain. The scores representing N do not run into the cross, indicating some care on the part of the carver of either the inscription or the cross given their close proximity. Most importantly, the inscription includes the

Primitive Irish word ><OI – seen by McManus and his predecessors as a vernacular reflection of the Christian *hic iacit* burial formula. There is, therefore, good evidence for assuming that this cross is broadly contemporary with the inscription. Again it is a pre-apocope formulation which suggests a fifth-century date for the cross.

Another two stones from Ballintaggart have equal-armed crosses in the middle of the face. There is no physical relationship between the inscriptions and the crosses to indicate their relative date but one inscription includes ><OI (Macalister 1945, 152, 155; McManus 1991, 65). In both instances, the inscriptions are pre-apocope or probably fifth century in date.

The stones, collected together today in the recently walled enclosure at Ballintaggart, were found in and around this site and all are of the local, water-rolled boulders from Minard beach, immediately to the south. Given this, the two stones with ><OI inscriptions, the two pre-apocope stones with plain Latin or Greek crosses and a fourth stone to be discussed below, with a different cross type and also associated with a pre-apocope inscription, it seems clear that at Ballintaggart, we have evidence of a Christian community of the fifth century. The graves of this community could be marked by boulders with ogam inscriptions and plain Latin or Greek crosses. It seems likely that the fifth-century cross and inscription at Emlagh East, the next townland to the east of Ballintaggart, is another indication of the existence of fifth-century Christians on the south coast of the Dingle peninsula. This would coincide

with the evidence from Reask towards the north of the Dingle peninsula where the earliest radiocarbon date, apparently contemporaneous with the first phase of the cemetery was cal. AD 410–600 (1 sigma: UB 2167, 1565±90 BP) (Fanning 1981, 79–86, 113–15, 121, 164).

This is not to say that all plain Latin or Greek crosses found on ogam stones are necessarily of fifth-century date. An ogam stone from Whitefield, near Killarney has a pre-apocope inscription with a Greek cross which might, therefore, correspond in date to the fifth-century Ballintaggart stones, but there are also four stones from Coolineagh, Co. Cork, Curraghmore West, Killogrone and Ratass, Co. Kerry, all of which include the word ANM in their inscription. This is a post-apocope version of the Old Irish word *ainm*, 'name'; therefore these four inscriptions are at least of sixth-century date (Moore 1998, 28–9). The use of this word in ogam inscriptions has been compared by Vendryes with Christian inscriptions, particularly those from North Africa, but possibly also two examples from Wales (Vendryes 1955).

The position of the crosses on these ANM stones differ. At Killogrone, in south Kerry, the cross is at the base of the stone, reading the inscription up the right-hand side of the cross. Brash tells us that on first recording, the pillar was inverted with the cross at the top and stood as the headstone of a grave (Brash 1879, 239–41). It is not clear that Brash himself had seen the stone in this location. Here, then, there might be evidence of Macalister's theory that the crosses were added subsequent to the inscription. Having said this, however, there are examples of later Irish Latin-letter inscriptions where crosses occur below the writing (Lionard 1960–1, 102). Looking at the Killogrone monument with the cross in the middle of the broad face at its base, the inscription runs from the bottom of the right-hand side up towards the top. Normally, the inscriptions run from the viewer's left hand to the top (McManus 1991, 47) but if one reversed the pillar so that the inscription read in this fashion (with the cross now positioned at the top of the pillar) the scores of the ogam would be reversed – reading Q for N and so forth (Fig. 5.1). The resultant reading would not make sense. It cannot be stated conclusively, therefore, that the position of a cross towards the base of a pillar must automatically be seen as post-dating the accompanying inscription. The only date that can be put forward for the Killogrone stone is a date for the inscription which can simply be dated to the end of the sixth century or beginning of the seventh.

At Ratass, in north Kerry, Thomas Fanning also argued that the cross was inverted with respect to the inscription and should therefore post-date it. In this case, however, there was evidence that the pillar

was used for sharpening and polishing blades subsequent to its use as an ogam memorial, and that the cross in turn overlay some of the polished area (Fanning and Ó Corráin 1977). The inscription is post-apocope but pre-syncope, indicating a date towards the middle of the sixth century for the inscription and a somewhat later date for the cross.

In the case of the Curraghmore West inscription, in south Kerry, there is no relationship between the inscription and the cross, but the cross is located in the middle of the broad face about two thirds of the way up, with the ogam inscription running up the left edge. Moore (1998, 29) takes it that the two are contemporary. The inscription is certainly post-apocope and may possibly be post-syncope. However the last person to publish a reading (McManus 1991, 176) had considerable doubt about Macalister's reading which, if it were correct, would indicate a date well into the seventh century. Making allowances for this possibility, it seems best to argue that simple Latin and Greek crosses, as witnessed on these various stones, probably occur throughout the date range of the ogam corpus, from the fifth century to the seventh.

Other cross forms can be more distinctive and may, therefore, have had a shorter lifespan. The shape of the stone from Drumconwell, Co. Armagh, makes it fairly clear that the monument was designed to be looked at from the same side as is currently on view. Here, a simple ringed cross with stem extending below the lower line of the circle, lies in the centre of the upper face (Fig. 5.4). The inscription is unusual in layout, running in two lines from bottom to top: first on the left-hand side and then on the right. There is no physical relationship between cross and inscription. My reading agrees with that of all commentators other than Macalister in ways which are crucial for dating purposes; Macalister's reading (1945, 298) would indicate a pre-apocope or fifth-century reading; I found that like William Reeves, John Rhys, Ann Hamlin and Richard Warner, I could not see the crucial final letter in QETAI(S) (see Warner 1991, 45 for references to all of the above). The lack of such a letter indicates the onset of apocope (McManus 1991, 82, 85–7; Swift 1997, 51), implying a sixth-century date. I should add that I found no evidence in favour of Richard Warner's suggested emendation of seven scores of the inscription to produce the name of the eponymous Ulster hero Conmáel whose name is incorporated in that of the townland (Warner 1991, 45–6). As Warner himself states, the consonant scores are all clear and while wholesale spelling errors on the part of an Archaic Irish carver transcribing his native tongue are of course possible, it does not appear probable to me.

The fact that this cross type is associated with

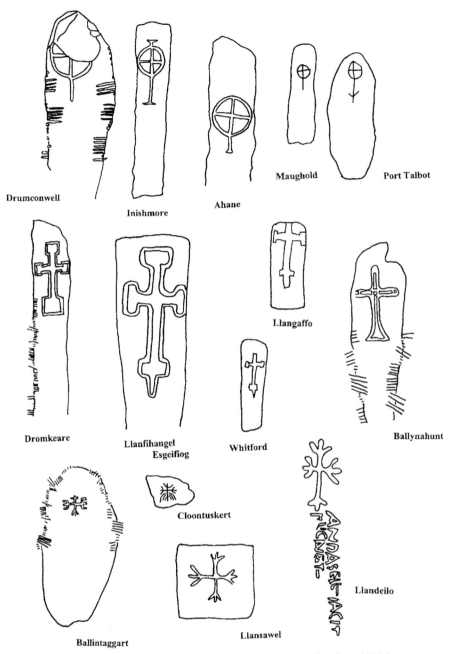

Fig. 5.4 Cross forms occurring on stones from Ireland and Wales

what is probably a sixth-century inscription is particularly interesting, in that it is a form which is widespread on cross-marked pillars from both Ireland and western Britain. From Ireland there are examples from Aghacarrible (from a souterrain site which also contained two ogam stones), Ahane, Ballydarrig, Ballymorereagh (a church site with ogam stones), Beginish, Illauntannig, Skellig and Glin North, all in Co. Kerry (Cuppage 1986, 103–4, 268–69, 290–92, 295–96; O'Sullivan and Sheehan 1996, 251, 259, 261–63, 281) as well as a closely related type from Inishmore, Co. Galway (Higgins 1987, ii, 125). From Wales there are examples of similar stones from Llantrisant and Port Talbot in Glamorgan, Llawhaden, Morvil and St David's in Pembrokeshire amongst others (Nash-Williams 1950, nos 219, 262, 342, 350, 372).[3] There is also an example from Maughold on the Isle of Man (Kermode 1994, pl. VII:10) and another from Iona (RCAHMS 1982, 180–81).

In one example, from Trallwng in Brecknockshire the cross is accompanied by both ogam and Latin-letter inscriptions; Nash-Williams suggested that the cross post-dates the Latin letters (Nash-Williams, 1950, no. 70). Looking at the stone with the circle in the middle of a broad face, at the top of the shaft, the ogam inscription runs along the right-hand side from top to bottom while the Latin-letter inscription, apparently referring to the same person, runs 'upward facing right', i.e. with the bottoms of the letters to the right-hand side of the viewer. (The terminology is that of Okasha 1993, 28.) The arrangement of both the ogam-scores and the Latin-letter inscription is not the norm and for the ogam scores to parallel the Latin letters in their present position one must reverse the scores, reading C for S, N for Q etc. (Such a reading would not make sense.) If one assumed, however, that the stone was inverted and the cross added later, the arrangement of both the ogam and the Latin-letter inscription would be both normal and consistent with each other. In other words, as Nash-Williams pointed out, the ogam inscription lies on the original left-hand edge, reading upwards with the Latin inscription in two vertical lines reading downwards, facing left. Subsequently, the stone was inverted and reused, with the upper part being incised with a ring-cross (*ibid.*; Lewis and Redknap, in prep.).

If the father's name refers to an Irishman, it is a pre-apocope form of fifth-century date; if it is British, Jackson (1953, 185) suggested the early sixth century (McManus 1991, 98, 113). A dating range later than the early sixth century is congruent with that suggested for Drumconwell (before end of the sixth century). A third example of this cross form, from Llanllŷr in Cardiganshire, is on an opposing face to an inscription which includes post-apocope and probably post-syncope forms of Irish names (Nash-Williams 1950, no.124). If this inscription is to be associated with the cross, on the other side of the stone, it would extend the dating range of this cross form into the seventh century and beyond.

A cross on the Ballynahunt stone, Co. Kerry, is carved in double lines with square terminals and what appears to be a triangular base (Macalister 1945, 164–65; Cuppage 1986, 253–54). It seems to be a case where the cross is not contemporary with the inscription, for if it is right to read the triangle as base, the inscription is inverted, running from the top downwards along the right-hand side and continuing around what is the bottom of the stone in this position. This is not a case where a small cross may lie either above or below the inscription as argued above for Killogrone, Co. Kerry; rather, the inscription is unreadable when viewed with the cross apparently upright and the reader must reverse all scores in order to make the two compatible (reading D for L, N for Q etc.). Such a 'reversed' reading does not make sense. Thus Macalister is probably right (1945, 164) when he states that the cross is later than the inscription. The words still have final endings and the inscription is, therefore, of pre-apocope or probable fifth-century type. This would mean the accompanying cross could be dated to some period after that date – a rather open-ended dating.

A cross potent with rectangular terminal at Dromkeare, Co. Kerry, is associated with a cross of similar form. Here the inscription runs from bottom left to top as normal and is of post-syncope form, i.e. late sixth or early seventh century. As with Drumconwell and Curraghmore West, the cross is positioned in the middle of a broad face, about two-thirds of the way up the shaft and – without being associated physically with the inscription – there is nothing problematical about seeing the two as contemporaneous. This single example, with the ambiguous parallel at Ballynahunt, may mean that we should see the cross-potent on this Irish stone as being a late sixth or early seventh century phenomenon.

Another example from the collection of stones at Ballintaggart, Co. Kerry, has a more complex cross, with trident-shaped trifid terminals (Fig. 5.4) than the plain Greek or Latin crosses from that site discussed previously. This is a stone with two inscriptions. Looking at the face with the cross in the centre of a broad face in the upper third of the shaft, one of the inscriptions runs from bottom left to middle of head according to the normal convention and is a unique memorial to the three sons of *Mailagnas*; the form of the name suggests a pre-apocope date in the fifth century. The other runs from bottom right to middle of head and, as with Ballynahunt, demands that the reader reverses scores, reading C for apparent S and so forth, if it is to be made compatible with an upright cross facing the onlooker. It is a single name inscription but the name form *Curcitti* is not clearly diagnostic and could be of any period within the ogam-inscription range. The two inscriptions do not appear to be related to each other. On the whole, it appears more likely that the cross is to be associated with the pre-apocope *Mailagnas* inscription which would suggest a fifth-century date; if it is to be associated with *Curcitti*, one must either reverse the scores as already mentioned or assume the cross is carved on the back of the monument.

John Sheehan (1994, 28) has drawn attention to the Merovingian parallels for this particular cross form, citing the evidence of the fifth- to seventh-century sarcophagi from Poitou, discussed by Edward James (1977, 71). It is also a style which occurs on a variety of cross-inscribed boulders both from Co. Kerry and Co. Galway (Sheehan 1994, 29), from Cloontuskert, Co. Longford (Fanning and Ó hÉailidhe 1980, 15) and from elsewhere in the British Isles (see, for example, Nash-Williams 1950, no. 118 from Llanddewi-brefi, Cardiganshire). A Welsh example, from Llandeilo in Pembrokeshire is accompanied by both an ogam and a Latin-letter inscription (Nash-Williams 1950, no. 313). If the cross is viewed in the middle of the broad face, at the upper end of the shaft, the ogam inscription runs up the left-hand side from bottom to top. The Latin-letter inscription is also vertical but reads 'downwards facing left'. Both of these positions represent the norm for ogam and Latin-letter inscriptions respectively. It is inscribed in Roman capitals for which Nash-Williams suggested a fifth- or early sixth-century date; the names – (A)NDAGELLI MACU CAV(ETI) – include one, ANDAGELLI, which is pre-syncope and possibly pre-apocope. Another stone from the same churchyard is dedicated to another son of *Cavetus*, called *Coimagnas* but inscribed only in Latin letters. The name on this second stone is a pre-apocope form of the Old Irish name, *Coéman* and is probably fifth century.

In short, the names associated with this particular cross form indicate that this type of cross was apparently being produced in these islands by the end of the fifth century. Furthermore, there is no clear distinction in age between the Welsh example and that from Co. Kerry, indicating the probability of contemporary contact between the two areas. The manuscript spelling system of the Old Irish vernacular, as found in late seventh- and eighth-century texts, differs from that used in ogam and instead derives from the spelling conventions of Vulgar Latin as spoken by British speakers. It has been a long-standing dictum of early Irish ecclesiastical history that the manuscript spelling system which had replaced ogam orthography by the classical Old Irish period in the eighth century was brought to Ireland by Welsh missionaries, during the later fifth and sixth centuries (MacNeill 1931; O'Rahilly 1957, 40–6; Stevenson 1989, 144–47). Archaeologically, however, we have not, as yet, investigated in any detail the possibility of links between the two islands in the cross forms on the memorial stones.

This brings me my last category of cross forms associated with ogam stones and that is the cross type known as the Maltese cross or cross-of-arcs. In 1991, Peter Harbison suggested that the Irish version of this cross type was associated with pilgrimage and possibly belonged to an eighth- or ninth-century date. The pilgrimage associations were based in the first instance on the Maumanorig inscription from Dingle which Macalister read as ANM COLMAN AILITHER or 'the name of COLMAN the pilgrim' (Harbison 1991, 75, 84; Macalister 1945, 191). Unfortunately this is one of Macalister's odder transcriptions; subsequent commentators, such as the Dingle Archaeological Survey (Cuppage 1986, 333–34) and Damian McManus (1991, 67) are agreed that there is no evidence for recognisable letters beyond ANM COL... The evidence for an eighth- or ninth-

century date range is also based on what is now an outdated linguistic analysis by Donnchadh Ó Corráin of the Ratass stone in 1977 (Fanning and Ó Corráin 1977, 18; see now McManus 1991, 71). Finally, it is worth noting that Harbison's map of this cross type (1991, 193) includes the simple cross-of-arcs together with a number of highly developed and ornate forms whose chronological relationship to the plainer forms is not clear.

In a recent study (1997, 70–83) I argued that where the simple cross-of-arcs is found associated with ogam inscriptions, they are all associated with later inscriptions of later sixth- or seventh-century date; the classic example being that of the pre-syncope stone at Arraglen, Co. Kerry, which is a rare example of an ogam memorial where the role of the commemorand is recorded: 'of the priest, *Ronann* son of *Comogann*'. I suggested that the origin of such designs might be sought in the Christian memorial stone tradition as represented in Iberia, Merovingian France and as far away as Egypt. Since this suggestion was made, Derek Craig's publication of the Whithorn stones has indicated that not only is there a collection of these stones from Whithorn, but a fragment of one such was found in a mid- to late seventh-century grave (Craig 1997, 439), dated through stratigraphical analysis. The excavator suggested this may have been debris from the adjacent shrine of an earlier seventh-century date – a date which is arrived at totally independently of the linguistic analysis of the ogam associations, but one which has produced a remarkably similar result.

Craig's work also draws attention to the collection of similar cross-of-arc stones from Man and the two stones from Wales while other examples of this cross type are found in St Boniface's Church, Papa Westray, Orkney (see current exhibition in the Museum of Scotland, Edinburgh). In Ireland, the traditional picture of the distribution of these crosses has been one which has focussed very strongly on the west coast, although Lionard pointed out that there was a collection of the type from Gallen (1960–1, 110–12) and other stones have been identified from both the north and east midlands. To this one might add that the current *Dúchas* inventory of some 700 graveslabs from Clonmacnoise includes at least seven examples of the cross-of-arcs as well as other examples of the associated marigold type. On one of these, an uncial inscription in horizontal lines, beneath a cross-of-arcs, calls for a prayer for somebody called Muirethach; the medial TH indicates that this is likely to be of late seventh- or early eighth-century date preceding the later spelling with medial D (Lionard 1960–1, 111). Two of these Clonmacnoise monuments, including the Muirethach stone, are pillar-shaped; possibly indicating a continuity of form from the ogam period into a phase when erect burial markers were produced with uncial inscriptions. Such a continuity is also indicated by the Inchagoill pillar, Co. Galway, where the Latin-letter inscription reflects a stage of Irish belonging to the first half of the seventh century and which is best paralleled in the ogam inscriptions (McManus 1991, 96).

The Irish evidence for crosses-of-arcs thus indicates at this preliminary stage that this cross-type is associated with late sixth to early eighth-century inscriptions, dated through linguistic analysis of the Irish vernacular. This is important, not just for the history of Christianity in Ireland, but also for the wider ecclesiastical history of these islands. Like the cross with trident-shaped terminals or the simple ringed cross, the cross-of-arcs is of a type found in both these islands and apparently at very similar dates. Not only then do cross-marked stones provide evidence for the existence of Christianity in otherwise undocumented areas; they also appear to provide us with evidence for the close links between the various regional churches. Of course, it is important to recognise the relative scarcity of ogam inscriptions associated with (possibly) contemporaneous crosses. Clearly one or two crosses dated through their associations with ogam inscriptions are not sufficient in themselves to date the entire corpus of such cross types. I would contend, however, that in providing us with chronological anchor points for even a minority of instances, the ogam inscriptions can be used to provide us with a more secure underpinning of an archaeological chronology than has been possible to produce to date.

In the context of the sixth-century ecclesiastical history of these islands, the missionary work of Columba in Iona is well known; the contacts between Gildas and the Irish have been much discussed (Kenney 1929, 170–73; Ó Cróinín 1995, 18–19); the exact nationality of Finian as either an Irishman working in Britain or a Briton working in Ireland has occasioned some debate (see, for example, Ó Riain 1981 versus Dumville 1984). The Irish linguistic evidence allows us to date not only stones with inscriptions and crosses, but also provides some possiblity of narrowing the chronological range accorded to cross-marked pillar-stones without inscriptions. If further study substantiates the preliminary suggestion made here that similar designs from different parts of these islands are likely to be broadly contemporary, we will be in a position to locate these few historical references in a much broader context of inter-regional contact. A combined study of Irish, Welsh and Scottish early Christian monuments displaying crosses but no other ornament may eventually lead us to the point where we will be able to produce a more nuanced archaeological account of sixth- and even fifth-

century ecclesiastical contacts in the Irish Sea region and beyond.

Notes

1 See however, M. J. O'Kelly's (1945) review of Macalister where he argued that the ogam inscription could be coeval with or later than the Latin-letter inscription and associated cross. He does not state the reasons for this belief. Although there is no clear physical relationship between the two, I would agree with McManus (1991, 54) that the carving technique used for the ogam contrasts with that used for the Latin alphabet inscription and with Macalister (1945, 179) that the most likely explanation is that the cross represents reuse of an earlier ogam pillar.

2 In both these cases, the stones, removed from sites in Co. Kerry and Co. Longford, were recovered subsequently through the agency of the National Museum of Ireland.

3 At Llantrisant, a smaller incised Latin cross with bifid terminals and trifid foot is also to be found on either side of the main cross stem (Nash-Williams 1950, no. 219). The stone from Port Talbot was redressed in the ninth or tenth centuries with a low relief ring-cross on the back. I am indebted to Mark Redknap for these details.

References

BINCHY, D. A. 1946, Review of *Corpus Inscriptionum Insularum Celticarum*. *J. Roy. Soc. Antiq Ir.* 76, 56–7.

BRASH, R. 1879, *The Ogam Inscribed Monuments of the Gaedhil in the British Islands; with a Dissertation on the Ogam Character*. London.

CRAIG, D. 1997, 'The sculptured stones', in P. Hill, *Whithorn and St Ninian. The Excavation of a Monastic Town 1984–91*, 433–41. Stroud.

CUPPAGE, J. 1986, *Archaeological Survey of the Dingle Peninsula: Suirbhé Seandálaíochta Chorca Dhuibhne*. Ballyferriter.

DUMVILLE, D. 1984, 'Gildas and Uinniau', in D. Dumville and M. Lapidge (eds), *Gildas: New Approaches*, 207–14. Woodbridge.

EDWARDS, N. 1990, *The Archaeology of Early Medieval Ireland*. London.

FANNING, T. and Ó CORRÁIN, D. 1977, 'An ogham stone and cross-slab from Ratass church, Tralee', *J. Kerry Archaeol. Hist. Soc.* 10, 14–18.

FANNING, T. and Ó HÉAILIDHE, P. 1980, 'Some cross-inscribed slabs from the Irish midlands', in H. Murtagh (ed.), *Irish Midland Studies. Essays in Commemoration of N. W. English*, 5–23. Athlone.

FANNING, T. 1981, 'Excavation of an early Christian cemetery and settlement at Reask, Co. Kerry', *Proc. Roy. Ir. Acad.* 81C, 67–172.

HAMLIN, A. 1982, 'Early Irish stone carving' in S. M. Pearce (ed.), *The Early Church in Western Britain and*

Ireland. Studies presented to C. A. Ralegh Radford (= B.A.R. Brit. Ser. 102), 283–96. Oxford.

HARBISON, P. 1991, *Pilgrimage in Ireland: the Monuments and the People*. London.

HARVEY, A. 1987, 'Early literacy in Ireland: the evidence from ogam', *Cambridge Medieval Celtic Stud.* 14, 1–15.

HENDERSON, I. 1987, 'Early Christian monuments of Scotland displaying crosses but no other ornament' in A. Small (ed.), *The Picts: a New Look at Old Problems*, 45–59. Dundee.

HERITY, M. 1995, *Studies in the Layout, Buildings and Art in Stone of Early Irish Monasteries*. London.

HIGGINS, J. 1987, *The Early Christian Cross-Slabs, Pillar Stones and Related Monuments of County Galway, Ireland*, 2 vols (= B.A.R Suppl. Ser. 375). Oxford.

JACKSON, K. H. 1946, Review of *Corpus Inscriptionum Insularum Celticarum Vol. 1.* by R. A. S. Macalister, *Speculum* 26, 521–23.

JACKSON, K. H. 1953, *Language and History in Early Britain. A Chronological Survey of the Brittonic Languages First to Twelfth Century A.D.* Edinburgh.

JAMES, E. 1977, *The Merovingian Archaeology of South-West Gaul*, 2 vols (= B.A.R. Suppl. Ser. 25). Oxford.

KENNEY, J. F. 1929, *The Sources for the Early History of Ireland*, Vol. 1. *Ecclesiastical*. New York, reprint 1979, Dublin.

KERMODE, P. M. C. 1994, *Manx Crosses* (reprint of 1907 vol.). Balgavies.

LEWIS, J. M. and REDKNAP, M. in prep., *Corpus of Early Medieval Inscribed Stones and Stone Sculpture in Wales, fascicule 1, South and South-East Wales*.

LIONARD, P. 1960–1, 'Early Irish grave-slabs', *Proc. Roy. Ir. Acad.* 61C, 95–170.

MACALISTER, R. A. S. 1945, *Corpus Inscriptionum Insularum Celticarum* Vol.I. Dublin.

MACALISTER, R. A. S. 1949, rep. 1996, *The Archaeology of Ireland*, 2nd ed. Dublin.

MACNEILL, E. 1906, 'The ancient Irish genealogies', *The New Ireland Review* 26, 129–45.

MACNEILL, E. 1931, 'Beginnings of Latin culture in Ireland part I', *Studies* 20, 39–48.

MACWHITE, E. 1960–1, 'Contributions to a study of ogam memorial stones', *Zeitschrift für Celtische Philologie* 28, 294–305.

MCMANUS, D. 1983, 'A chronology of the Latin loan-words in early Irish', *Ériu* 34, 21–71.

MCMANUS, D. 1991, *A Guide to Ogam*. Maynooth.

MARSTRANDER, C. 1911, 'Ogham XOI', *Ériu* 5, 144.

MONK, M. A. and SHEEHAN, J. (eds.) 1998, *Early Medieval Munster: Archaeology, History and Society*. Cork.

MOORE, F. 1998, 'Munster ogham stones: siting, context and function', in Monk and Sheehan, 23–32.

MYTUM, H. 1992, *The Origins of Early Christian Ireland*. London, New York.

NASH-WILLIAMS, V. E. 1950, *The Early Christian Monuments of Wales*. Cardiff.

Ó CRÓINÍN, D. 1995, *Early Medieval Ireland 400–1200*. London, New York.

OKASHA, E. 1993, *Corpus of Early Christian Inscribed Stones of South-West Britain*. Leicester.

O'KELLY, M. J. 1945, Review of R. A. S. Macalister's *Corpus Inscriptionum Insularum Celticarum* Vol. 1, *J. Cork Archaeol. Hist. Soc.* 50, 152–53.

O'KELLY, M. J. and KAVENAGH, S. 1954, 'An ogam inscribed cross-slab from County Kerry', *J. Cork Archaeol. Hist. Soc.* 59, 101–10.

O'RAHILLY, T. 1957, *The Two Patricks: a Lecture on the History of Christianity in Fifth-Century Ireland*. Dublin.

Ó RIAIN, P. 1981, 'The Irish element in Welsh hagiographical tradition', in D. Ó Corráin (ed.), *Irish Antiquity: Studies Presented to Professor M. J. O'Kelly*, 291–303. Cork.

O'SULLIVAN, A. and SHEEHAN, J. 1996, *The Iveragh Peninsula: an Archaeological Survey of South Kerry*. Dublin.

POKORNY, J. 1915, 'Ogom CI "hier" ', *Zeitschrift für Celtische Philologie* 10, 403.

RCAHMS 1982, Royal Commission on the Ancient and Historical Monuments of Scotland, *Argyll, An Inventory of the Monuments*, Vol. 4, *Iona*. Edinburgh.

SHEEHAN, J. 1990, 'Some early historic cross-forms and related motifs from the Iveragh peninsula', *J. Kerry Archaeol. Hist. Soc.* 23, 157–74.

SHEEHAN, J. 1994, 'A Merovingian background for the Ardmoneel stone?' *J. Cork Archaeol. Hist. Soc.* 99, 22–31.

STEVENSON, J. 1989, 'The beginnings of literacy in Ireland', *Proc. Roy. Ir. Acad.* 89C, 127–65.

SWIFT, C. 1996, 'Christian communities in fifth- and sixth-century Ireland', *Trowel* 7, 11–19.

SWIFT, C. 1997, *Ogam Stones and the Earliest Irish Christians*. Maynooth.

THOMAS, A. C. 1987, 'The earliest Christian art in Ireland and Britain', in M. Ryan, (ed.), *Ireland and Insular Art AD 500-1200*, 7–11. Dublin.

THOMAS, A. C. 1994, *And Shall These Mute Stones Speak ? Post-Roman Inscriptions in Western Britain*. Cardiff.

THOMAS, A. C. 1998, 'Early medieval Munster: thoughts on its primary Christian phase', in Monk and Sheehan, 9–16.

VENDRYES, J. 1955, 'Sur un emploi du mot AINM 'nom' en Irlandais', *Études Celtiques* 7, 139–46.

WARNER, R. 1991, 'The Drumconwell ogham and its implications', *Emania* 8, 43–50.

6 Neo-Pelagianism, Early Insular Religious Art, and the Image of Christ

Shirley Ann Brown and Michael W. Herren

In surveying Insular religious art from the seventh to the tenth century, two main categories emerge: the ornamented and symbolic, and the realistic and/ or representational. These categories obtain irrespective of the medium employed (manuscripts, metalwork, stone). The first, the ornamental and symbolic, is usually connected to the Irish Church, while the second, the more representational, is seen as a development owed to the Rome-oriented Anglo-Saxons. In this view, artistic style and choice would seem to be connected to national religious allegiance. This standard view seems to be correct, but the ecclesiological and theological bases for these national differences have not been fully explored. This paper is an attempt to do just that.[1]

In approaching this problem, it is essential to develop an historical model. Post-Roman Christianity in the British Isles was embodied in an institution that may conveniently be called the common Celtic Church,[2] whose origins occur at some point in the fifth century and extend into the seventh. The original geographical area embraced by this institution included western Britain, all of Ireland, and parts of Scotland. The unity of this institution was shattered at the start of the seventh century with the establishment of the Anglo-Saxon Church from Rome and, a little later, with the break-up of the Irish Church into two regions: a southern region more closely aligned to the Roman Church, and a northern (and Scottish) region loyal to the traditions of the common Celtic Church. By the middle of the seventh century we encounter the ecclesiastical map drawn by Bede: an English Church aligned with Roman ecclesiastical law and practice, an Irish Church split into two factions, and a British Church pursuing a policy of isolation and non-involvement.

To best understand the development of religious artistic traditions in the entire region it is essential to

understand the character of the common Celtic Church, which by the seventh century was geographically marginalised and losing influence, but whose ecclesiastical and artistic traditions continued to be formative. The common Celtic Church originated in western Britain (Wales, Cornwall, Strathclyde) and survived there long after the Irish branch divided into *Romani* and *Hibernenses*. One may imagine this Church as a kind of 'low Church' – biblicist and 'untheological', not given to pomp and ceremony in its liturgy, and very modest in its physical expressions (buildings, artefacts). This Church set store on following the precepts of the Bible to attain salvation; good works and obedience to the law were the key. It had little use for miracles, relics or other manifestations of divine interference with nature. The sacraments were administered out of respect for tradition, but not viewed as a panacea for human weakness. A generous place was made for the monastic movement because monks (living in the community rather than in isolation) provided the best example of the Christian way of life. Christ himself came to be identified with the perfect monk. The essential point of the Christian message was this: to follow Christ meant to live a life of self-denial and mortification in full obedience to the law. This, in turn, leads to salvation.

The leaders and members of the common Celtic Church surely did not think of themselves as heretics; if anything, they would have held a 'holier-than-thou' attitude and would have been contemptuous of the 'superstitions' emanating from the Continent. Evidence from Gildas, Adhelm and Bede shows that they readily excommunicated dissenters and generally avoided Christians of other persuasions. Their formation was surely influenced by the teachings of Pelagius (*c.* 350–430) and his successors. It has been rightly pointed out that Pelagius's views on the relation of grace to effort were probably widely shared in his day, that they were similar, but not identical to the views of the eastern Church, and that it was Augustine and his allies who were the real extremists in the battle over grace and free will in the early fifth century (Morris 1965; Markus 1986). Some modern scholars seem embarrassed by the fact that Britain and Ireland were associated with a heresy, and have struggled to explain away the evidence for a continuing connection between the Insular world and Pelagianism once the Pelagian heresy had been formally suppressed in the fifth century (e.g. Ó Cróinín 1985). But the evidence cannot be easily dismissed. It is now argued that Pelagius himself was a Briton,[3] as was Faustus of Riez, the semi-Pelagian author of *De gratia*; there was certainly one, and possibly two, outbreaks of 'the Pelagian heresy' in Britain in the fifth century; British monks (such as Faustus of Riez) were formed in the semi-Pelagian centres of southern Gaul in the fifth century; the writings of Pelagius and some semi-Pelagian writers were used extensively in Ireland in the eighth and ninth centuries (Kelly 1978) and also survived in Britain (Dumville 1985). A formal charge of Pelagian heresy was brought against the Irish just before the middle of the seventh century (Ó Cróinín 1985).

We introduce the term 'neo-Pelagian' here to describe the 'mindset' of Insular Christians who certainly did not think of themselves as heretical, but consciously or unconsciously accepted views and attitudes, which, for better or for worse, had been labelled as heterodox. The Christians in Britain who formed the common Celtic Church were affected by both the first wave of Pelagius's teachings and by the writings of the semi-Pelagians. Indeed, the semi-Pelagian movement was closely bound up with the southern Gaulish form of monasticism which claimed British adherents such as Faustus, and whose writings are quoted favourably by Insular writers such as Columbanus. If one agrees with the proposition that there was at least a recognisable Pelagian strain within the common Celtic Church, then the vicissitudes of the early development of religious art in the British Isles, and especially the imaging of Christ, can be more easily accounted for.

Let us now pose three basic questions.

The first basic question, rarely asked, underlies the study of Insular religious art. Given the fact that Christianity existed in Celtic Britain and Ireland from the fifth century, how does one explain the lack, until the middle of the seventh century, of contemporary religious artefacts upon which deliberate artistic attention and care had been consciously devoted? The rest of the Christian world was creating a wealth of objects decorated with religious images, or liturgical objects that were richly ornamented. When a separate Celtic Christianity began in western Britain in the fifth century, it would have been surrounded by a sophisticated repertoire of artistic forms from Roman Britain. Yet, apparently, it did not see fit to transpose any of this to the objects needed for ritual purposes, or for Christian instruction. Primitive stone monuments with incised crosses continued the earlier tradition of carved uprights. But these cannot be construed as a concerted effort to produce a Christian art. The accidents of survival and post-Roman economic decline may be invoked as explanations for the apparent lacuna.[4] However, can these fully account for a 200–year hiatus in artistic production not only in Britain, but also in Ireland, which was a province of the British Church for much of this period? In both regions there is no decorated religious artefact of interest to the art historian from *c.* 450 to *c.* 650.

The second basic question is: when religious art finally makes its appearance in Ireland around the middle of the seventh century, why is it non-representational, and why does it remain so for so long? Can the ornamental tradition of Celtic art alone provide the answer? This question is highlighted when one realises that other barbarian peoples, such as the Franks and Lombards, recently converted to Christianity and given to a non-representational artistic tradition more eagerly embraced the production of representational religious art (Hubert, Porcher and Volbach 1969).

The third basic question is: what factors determined the choice of themes depicted, once strictures against pictorial art had been removed and we begin to see religious images in manuscripts and stone carving around the turn of the eighth century? This question is particularly relevant to the situation in Northumbria, where Roman traditions mingled with those of the common Celtic Church (embodied in the *Hibernenses*).

Let us take each question in turn and start with the striking problem of the lacuna. One of the most important tenets of Pelagianist thought is an unflinching hostility towards every expression of luxury. Possession or use of material things other than the bare necessities of life is designated by the word *avaritia*, the root of all evil (*De divitiis* in PLS 1, 1380–82). Gold and silver may be God's creation, but the possession of them is not needful to existence (*ibid.*, 1397). The imitation of Christ commences with the imitation of his poverty (*ibid.*, 1393). Moreover, God himself is displeased with the use of luxury items in his worship (*ibid.*, 1391). Pelagian teachings on this point almost certainly helped to fashion the outlook of the common Celtic 'low Church'. Survivals of this attitude can be detected as late as *c.* 700. In the late seventh century Tírechán notes that Patrick had brought the required liturgical items across the Shannon: bells, chalices, patens, altar stones, books of the law and gospel books (Tírechán II.1 in Bieler 1979, 123). None of these is described as luxurious or decorated. This stands in contrast to Aldhelm's contemporary description of the very luxurious vessels used at Bugga's church in Anglo-Saxon England (Lapidge and Rosier 1985, 49). Thus Patrick's mission is seemingly credited with an austerity coinciding with Pelagianist ideals, perhaps reflecting their continuity in the Celtic Church as late as the early eighth century.

The second question entails the possibility that the common Celtic Church was not merely sumptuary, but also iconoclastic. Pelagius's friend Coelestius claimed that the law was as important as the gospels in attaining salvation (Rees 1988, 136), and thus a strict adherence to the Ten Commandments would constitute the minimum observance. The First Commandment is explicit about images: it forbids the representation of not only God, but of created nature as well (Exod. 20.4). While Pelagians allowed allegory for narrative portions of the bible, particularly of the Old Testament, they were literalists when it came to the law (*De divitiis* in PLS 1, 1394). Again, Tírechán provides a contrast between Ireland and Anglo-Saxon England. He describes Patrick preaching to the Irish while holding up written tablets in his hands like Moses (Tírechán II.2 in Bieler 1979, 123), whereas Bede portrays Augustine of Canterbury showing an image of Christ on a panel to the English he hoped to convert (HE I. 25 in Colgrave and Mynors 1969, 75) – a practice in line with Gregory the Great's own policy on the use of images for teaching and conversion (Harting-Correa 1996, 229). Strict adherence to Old Testament law is also evidenced by a number of seventh- and eighth-century canon collections associated with the *Hibernenses* (i.e. the Irish adherents of the common Celtic Church) (Kottje 1970). This retention of the customary thinking of the common Celtic Church may help to explain why, once sumptuary strictures had been eased, so many of the earliest religious artefacts of Irish manufacture remained limited to the decorative and symbolic.

One of the probable factors contributing to the easing of restrictions against luxurious religious objects in Ireland was the influence of the Irish *Romani*, detectable from the 630s. The *Romani* are best known for their support of the current Roman method of dating Easter, but their influence spread in many other directions. This movement introduced orthodox sources such as Augustine – possibly to counteract the Pelagianist authorities favoured by the *Hibernenses* (O'Neill 1984). They were probably also responsible for introducing saints' lives, a genre much in favour on the Continent, but apparently eschewed by the common Celtic Church on the ground that miracles interfere with free will – there are no early British examples of saints' lives, and the earliest Irish example is dated to the middle of the seventh century (Sharpe 1991, 14). Irish biblical studies and the production of commentaries and works on *quaestiones* may also have been started under *Romani* impetus. The texts ascribed to Irish authorship in the seventh and eighth centuries frequently employ allegory, an interpretative tool repugnant to literalists.[5] Note that no scriptural commentary emanated from the British Church.

It is interesting to observe that the beginnings of religious art production in Ireland may coincide with the heyday of *Romani* influence, namely the second half of the seventh and first half of the eighth centuries. In this period we see the creation of the first surviving instances of religious art meant to be lavish and long lasting, items such as the earliest standing decorated stone crosses, including those at Ahenny, Co. Tipperary (Roe 1969, 9) and possibly the Iona crosses (RCAHMS 1982; Sharpe 1995, 66, 80), and highly decorated liturgical items such as the Ardagh and Derrynaflan chalices.[6]

The decision, taken in Insular centres with a strong Celtic tradition, to retain the native repertoire of abstract ornament rather than to imitate the representational art of the Continental Church may signal an attitude which retained the neo-Pelagian prejudice against representational art. The Book of Durrow contains no realistic representations of natural beings and certainly no pictorial scenes. The Lindisfarne Gospels may contain the classically-inspired Evangelist portraits, but otherwise is non-representational. The Moylough belt-shrine (Youngs 1989, col. illus. p.37) and the Ardagh chalice have toothy dragon heads incorporated into the decoration, but these do not represent truly natural creatures and may, or may not, bear iconographical references. In the instances where figures were used, as on the otherwise non-pictorial Ahenny crosses (Fig. 6.1), they were relegated to the bases.

There were many ways of symbolising Christ without representing him in corporeal form. The Cross itself remains the primary substitute for Christ, and, as such, is capable of incorporating multiple references to his Incarnation, Death, and Second Coming within its form. The *nomen sacrum*, the sacred name in the shape of the Chi-Rho of Matthew 1:18, is decorated in the Insular gospel books, responding to exegetical tradition and perhaps the writings of Isidore of Seville which relate the chi to the Cross and iota to Christ-Ichthys (Lewis 1980). The Insular Chi-Rhos exhibit a common iconography, but in several cases individual gospel

Fig. 6.1 *North Cross, West Face at Ahenny , Co. Tipperary. (Photograph: S. A. Brown)*

books have incorporated idiosyncratic motifs. These range from the little cross of the Book of Durrow (Fig. 6.2), to the fish of the Book of Armagh (Fig. 6.3), to the inhabited vine of the Barberini Gospels (Henry 1974, 179, fig. 28), to the panoply of the created nature seen in the sacred monogram in the Book of Kells (Fig. 6.4).

The adoption of representational art in the Insular area was rather slow and regionally determined. In the case of the Anglo-Saxon Church, images were present from the very beginning, and there was never a theological question regarding their use. However, the facts that several important Northumbrian centres had been founded by Irish missionaries from Iona, and that Irish presence in the region remained strong, help to explain the continuing force of the non-representational and the relatively slow development of representational art. The Irish (in Ireland and on Iona) were the last to adopt a fully representational art. This seems to have begun in the period of *Romani* influence, that is, at the point when the whole panoply of *Romani* ideas had won acceptance – the effects of grace as manifested in saints' lives, miracles, relics, sacramentalism and liturgical display.

Let us turn now to question 3, the choice of themes. Despite the attempts of both Irish and English Romanisers to propagate a theology of grace, miracles and sacramentalism, the over-riding Christological images are those of Christ crucified and Christ as the ideal monk, as opposed to the resurrected or triumphant Christ. This was certainly the case in Northumbria, whose own *Romani* – Benedict Biscop, Wilfrid and Bede – had been active in reversing the agenda of the common Celtic Church represented by the Irish. However, even though Bede may have fought the good fight on the Paschal question, his spirituality remained rooted in the old Celtic ideal. Nothing exemplifies this better than his Life of Cuthbert, written at the turn of the eighth century. There Bede depicts Cuthbert's imitation of Christ as the desire for perfect mortification to be achieved in solitude (*Vita Sancti Cuthberti* XVII-XXII in Colgrave 1985, 215–31). The pages of the *Historia Ecclesiastica* are filled with similar portraits. The message remains the neo-Pelagian teaching that salvation is achieved through spiritual training and application. The properly-formed will of the *miles Christi* is the important thing. Grace is secondary; it is shown in the miracle of the otters which dry Cuthbert with their breath after his vigil in cold water (*ibid.*, 189–90). The otters validate the penitential ideal, and thus exhibit divine approval of the meritorious.

All of this places the eighth-century monuments at Ruthwell and Bewcastle in a new light. Located in remote areas which intervene between the territory

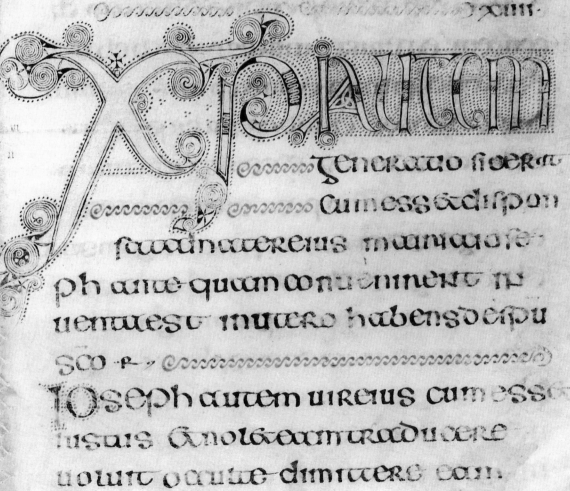

Fig. 6.2 *Book of Durrow, Dublin, Trinity College Library, MS 57, fol. 23r. (Photograph: by permission of The Board of Trinity College Dublin)*

Fig. 6.3 Book of Armagh, Dublin, Trinity College Library, MS 52, fol. 33v. (Photograph: by permission of The Board of Trinity College Dublin)

Fig. 6.5 The Ruthwell Cross, Dumfriesshire: St Anthony and St Paul of Thebes. (Photograph: S. A. Brown)

Fig. 6.4 The Book of Kells, Dublin, Trinity College Library, MS 58, fol. 34r. (Photograph: by permission of The Board of Trinity College Dublin)

of the 'reactionary' *Hibernenses* and the more Rome-oriented Northumbrian monasteries, these two monumental crosses reflect the desire to introduce a representational religious art which emphasises Christological iconography. The choice of subject and the manner of presentation on the Ruthwell Cross express the synthesis of Romanising Christology and sacramentalism with the older common Celtic penitential emphasis. The over-riding emphasis on the Crucifixion as the essential component for salvation is represented by the Cross itself and by the poem inscribed on it, a version of the *Dream of the Rood*. This is augmented by the scene showing the meeting of two desert fathers, St Anthony and St Paul of Thebes (Fig. 6.5), and by the representation of Mary Magdalene at Christ's feet (Fig. 6.6), both scenes typifying the ideal ascetic life. Christ is portrayed with beasts, an indication of his 40 days in the desert (Fig. 6.7), and hence, as the ideal monk. Added to these is the figure of John the Baptist, who led the exemplary life of mortification.

Fig. 6.6 *The Ruthwell Cross, Dumfriesshire: Mary Magdalene at Christ's feet. (Photograph: S. A. Brown)*

Fig. 6.7 *The Ruthwell Cross, Dumfriesshire: Christ standing on the Beasts. (Photograph: S. A. Brown)*

In contrast to the penitential images on the Ruthwell Cross are the inhabited vines (Fig. 6.8) with their Eucharistic symbolism on the narrow sides, indicating the essential role of the sacrament in redemption. The presence of this motif is crucial theologically. There is considerable ambivalence towards the Eucharist in the literature of the common Celtic Church (e.g. in the early British and Irish penitential handbooks) and also in the somewhat later literature of the Irish Culdees. There one finds a tension between the idea of the Eucharist as necessary sustenance for spiritual struggle as against

the Eucharist as a privilege to be earned. The iconographer of the Ruthwell Cross found the perfect synthesis between the unmediated penitential portraits and the assertive sacramentalism of the inhabited vines: he depicted the two desert fathers breaking the bread which had been miraculously brought to them by God's raven (Fig. 6.5). Reflecting the *confractio dominici corporis* of the Mass (Ó Carragáin 1978, 136–37), the image symbolises the Eucharist and grace and, at the same time, points to a penitential context.

Thus it was the Romanising movement – at first

Fig. 6.8 *The Ruthwell Cross, Dumfriesshire: Inhabited Vine. (Photograph: S. A. Brown)*

We do not see any changes in literary and artistic representations of Christ until around the middle of the ninth century, when a new impetus to representational art was provided by the synod of Paris (825) which condemned iconoclasm. New works of art, emanating from the Continent, brought a new balance between Christ's divinity and humanity and allowed scope for greater emphasis on his divinity. The older, Pelagianist thinking of the common Celtic Church, with its emphasis on only those acts of Christ which might reasonably be imitated by mankind, gives way to a fuller reading of the Christ portrayed in the Scriptures. Thus it becomes possible to portray the miracles of Christ and also his supermundane acts: the Second Coming, the Last Judgement and Christ in Glory, acts or states which are represented on a number of the Irish high crosses, such as those at Monasterboice (Fig. 6.13). In one particular, however, the old thinking persisted. In the Insular material up to and including the tenth century which we have surveyed, there are no direct representations of Christ's Resurrection. The Resurrection is the greatest miracle of them all, but it cannot be imitated. Men cannot raise themselves, they must be raised by God, thereby losing their freedom of the will. The absence of this motif in the Insular world may represent the last hurrah of neo-Pelagianism and the common Celtic Church.

represented in England alone, but gradually gaining strength in Ireland and its spiritual territories – that opened the door for the full flowering of Insular religious art, combining indigenous traditions of abstract design with the depiction of figures and narrative themes. The Crucifixion was an especially popular theme which took on a peculiar Insular form: the crucified Christ, together with Stephaton, Longinus, and two angels, appears in gospel books, on plaques and on stone carvings. It is presented either symbolically as in the Lindisfarne Gospels, fol. 2v (Fig. 6.9) where the blocks of design appropriate the figures, or directly, although with abstracted form, in the Durham Gospels, fol. 38v (Fig. 6.10), the St Gall Gospel Codex, p. 266 (Fig. 6.11; Plate XIV), the Athlone plaque (Fig. 6.12), and the slab from the Calf of Man. The image of the crucified Christ on the Athlone plaque indicates the complexity of the Christology that can now be displayed for all to see: Christ as the sacrifice, but also Christ robed as the high priest (Roe 1960, 204–5), and Christ as the *lorica*, or protective breastplate of the faithful Christian. Christ enthroned on the Cross is also the exalted Christ of the Second Coming (O'Reilly 1987–88).

Notes

1   This paper is a précis of *Christ in Celtic Christianity*, a forthcoming book-length work that attempts to trace the development of the images of the Insular Christ in both literature and art (*c.* 500–*c.* 1000). We hope that readers will understand that it is impossible to provide the detail of argumentation and annotation that will form part of this study. We are grateful to members of the Cardiff Conference for many helpful comments and references.

2   We use the term 'common Celtic Church' quite specifically to refer to the British Church and the Irish Church in the period between the mid-fifth century and approximately AD 600, when contacts between Ireland and Rome are known to have begun. After 600 the ideology of this formative period was preserved in Britain for at least two more centuries and was represented in Ireland by the *Hibernensis* party, influential in Northern Ireland, Scotland and Northumbria. The authority for the initial unity of the two churches rests on Bede, *HE* II.iv. The concept is treated extensively in our forthcoming work *Christ in Celtic Christianity* (Studies in Celtic History, the Boydell Press).

3   Most patristic writers refer to Pelagius as a Briton, while Jerome alone calls him Irish. One should perhaps consider the possibility that Pelagius was among the *Scotti* resident in south-west Britain.

Fig. 6.9 *The Lindisfarne Gospels, London, British Library, MS Cotton Nero D.IV, fol. 2v. (Photograph: by permission of the British Library)*

Fig. 6.10 *Durham Gospels, Durham Cathedral Library, MS A.II.17, fol. 38v. (Photograph: courtesy of the Dean and Chapter of Durham)*

Fig. 6.12 *Athlone Crucifixion Plaque. (Photograph: National Museum of Ireland)*

Fig. 6.11 *Gospel Book, St Gall, Stiftsbibliothek, Cod. 51, p.266. (Photograph: by permission of the Stiftsbibliothek, St Gallen)*

Fig. 6.13 *Tall Cross, East Face at Monasterboice, Co. Louth. (Photograph: S. A. Brown)*

4   While we acknowledge the weight of these arguments, we also feel that it cannot be argued that the 'missing' decorated liturgical objects must have existed. New finds and a means of securely dating existing objects can always lead to a revised thinking, but the current perception of a lacuna is too strong to ignore.

5   The matter of Hiberno-Latin exegesis is controversial. See most recently Gorman (1997) and Herren (1998).

6   The dating of these items is a much debated question and arguments can be based on possible political activity of the mid-eighth century or later, or, in our case, on the appearance of similar artistic motifs on other items, such as the Lindisfarne Gospels of *c.* 700.

References

BIELER, L. (ed. and trans.) 1979, *The Patrician Texts in the Book of Armagh* (= *Scriptores Latini Hiberniae* 10). Dublin.

COLGRAVE, B. (ed.) 1985, *Two Lives of Saint Cuthbert: A Life by an Anonymous Monk of Lindisfarne and Bede's Prose Life*. Reprint, Cambridge.

COLGRAVE, B. and MYNORS R. A. B. (eds) 1969, *Bede's Ecclesiastical History of the English People*. Oxford.

DUMVILLE, D. 1985, 'Late seventh- or eighth-century evidence for the British transmission of Pelagius', *Cambridge Medieval Celtic Stud.*10, 39–52.

GORMAN, M. 1997, 'A critique of Bischoff's theory of Irish exegesis: the Commentary on Genesis in Munich Clm 6302 ("Wendepunkte" 2)', *J. Medieval Latin* 7, 178–233.

HARTING-CORREA, A. L. (ed.) 1996, *Walafrid Strabo's "Libellus De Exordiis Et Incrementis Quarundam In Observationibus Ecclesiasticis Rerum"*. Leiden, New York, Köln.

HENRY, F. 1974, *The Book of Kells*. London.

HERREN, M. W. 1998, 'Irish Biblical Commentaries before 800', in J. Hamesse (ed.), *Roma, Magister Mundi: Itineraria Culturae Medievalis. Mélanges offerts au Père L. E. Boyle à l'occasion de son 75e anniversaire*, 391–407. Louvain-la-Neuve.

HUBERT, J., PORCHER, J. and VOLBACH, W. F. 1969, *Europe of the Invasions*. New York.

KELLY, J. F. 1978, 'Pelagius, Pelagianism and the early Christian Irish', *Mediaevalia* 4, 99–124.

KOTTJE, R. 1970, *Studien zum Einfluss des alten Testamentes auf Recht und Liturgie des frühen Mittelalters (6–8 Jahrhundert)*. Bonn.

LAPIDGE, M. and ROSIER, J. (eds) 1985, *Aldhelm, The Poetic Works*. Cambridge.

LEWIS, S. 1980, 'Sacred calligraphy: the Chi-Rho page in the Book of Kells', *Traditio* 36, 139–59.

MARKUS, R. A. 1986, 'Pelagianism: Britain and the Continent', *J. Eccles. Hist.* 37/2, 191–204.

MORRIS, J. R. 1965, 'Pelagian literature', *J. Theological Stud.* n.s. 16, 26–60.

Ó CARRAGÁIN, É. 1978, 'Liturgical innovations associated with Pope Sergius and the iconography of the Ruthwell and Bewcastle crosses', in W. A. Farrell (ed.), *Bede and Anglo-Saxon England* (= B.A.R. Brit. Ser. 46), 131–47. Oxford.

Ó CRÓINÍN, D. 1985, 'New heresy for old: Pelagianism in Ireland and the papal letter of 640', *Speculum* 60/3, 505–16.

O'NEILL, P. 1984, 'Romani influences on seventh-century Hiberno-Latin literature', in P. Ní Chathain and M. Richter (eds), *Irland und Europa/Ireland and Europe*, 280–90. Stuttgart.

O'REILLY, J. 1987–88, 'Early medieval text and image: the wounded and exalted Christ', *Peritia* 6–7, 72–118.

PLS = HAMMAN, A. (ed.) 1958–74, *Patrologiae Latinae Supplementum*. 4 vols. Paris.

RCAHMS 1982, Royal Commission on the Ancient and Historical Monuments of Scotland, *Argyll, An Inventory of the Monuments*, Vol. 4, *Iona*. Edinburgh.

REES, B. R. 1988, *Pelagius: A Reluctant Heretic*. Woodbridge.

ROE, H. M. 1960, 'A stone cross at Clogher, Co.Tyrone', *J. Roy. Soc. Antiq. Ir.* 90, 191–206.

ROE, H. M. 1969, *The High Crosses of Western Ossory*. Kilkenny.

SHARPE, R. 1991, *Medieval Irish Saints' Lives: An Introduction to "Vitae Sanctorum Hiberniae"*. Oxford.

SHARPE, R. (trans.) 1995, *Adomnán of Iona: Life of St Columba*. London.

YOUNGS, S. (ed.) 1989, *'The Work of Angels'. Masterpieces of Celtic Metalwork, 6th-9th Centuries AD*. London.

Part III

Art and Archaeology

7   The Mote of Mark: the Archaeological Context of the Decorated Metalwork

David Longley

Introduction

The Mote of Mark is a small stone-walled hill-fort occupying the summit of a granite crag on the north Solway coast. During the early medieval period the hill was the focus of a high quality metalworking workshop, whose products included, among other items, elaborately decorated cast bronze mounts and fasteners. The purpose of this paper is to examine the archaeological context of the metalworking evidence and, in particular, the chronological range of the decorated metalwork. This paper will therefore begin by describing the topographical setting of the site and the nature of the archaeological investigations undertaken; the evidence for structures including that of the defences and the evidence for associated artefacts are also considered. The evidence for metalworking in general and non-ferrous metalworking in particular are discussed and a chronology for the site sequence and the place of the decorated metalwork in that sequence are proposed.

The topographic setting of the site

The Mote of Mark is a small granite knoll rising 45m above the eastern shore of Rough Firth, the estuary of the Urr Water (Fig. 7.1). Rough Firth is one of the more prominent of the many indentations to the northern coastline of the Solway, occurring approximately midway between Carlisle and the Rinns of Galloway. The estuary is constricted at its southern, seaward, end by the two headlands of Castlehill Point and Almorness Point. The Mote of Mark is not a particularly conspicuous landmark from the sea; nevertheless, the site commands an extensive panorama of the estuary and its coastline with unbroken views across the Solway to the Cumbrian coast.

The uneven summit of the crag occupies an area of approximately one third of an acre, comprising two eminences that flank a central depression. The seaward slopes are rocky and precipitous; the landward approach is less severe.

Archaeological investigations at the site

The Mote of Mark has attracted antiquarian attention from at least the eighteenth century, drawn by the site's drystone defences and the surface evidence of vitrification. A number of casual discoveries, observations and, it would seem, limited excavations are recorded from that date (Coles 1893, 92–6). The first serious work at the site, however, was undertaken in 1913, when Alexander Curle excavated extensively in the central depression, sectioned or exposed the rampart at nine locations and undertook more limited excavation elsewhere on the summit (Fig. 7.2). Curle's work was exceptionally productive in recovering a very large assemblage of occupation and industrial debris of almost exclusively early medieval date. This material included clay mould fragments, crucibles, slag, bronze objects, wheel-thrown pottery and imported Continental glass. He also recorded the presence of large quantities of animal bone. A number of the clay moulds had been used to cast elaborately decorated ornaments and attachments, pins and brooches. The artefacts were published with photographic illustration in a detailed account of the excavations in 1914 (Curle 1914, 125–68).

The identification of a metalworking workshop, seemingly in association with potentially datable imported artefacts and in the context of a defended settlement, with structural evidence is of primary importance in our understanding of metalworking and stylistic developments in north western Britain in the early medieval period. This, of course, is particularly so in that the broken moulds relate to

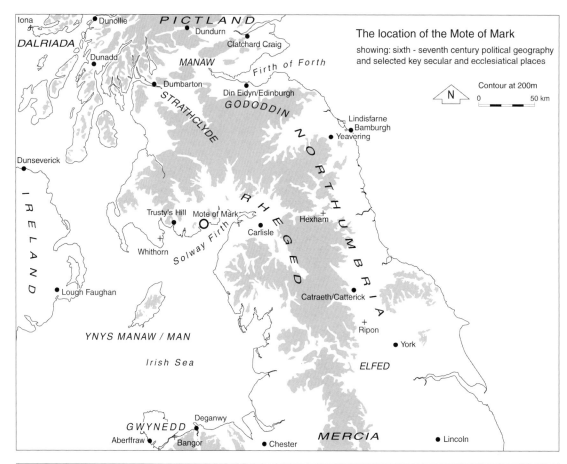

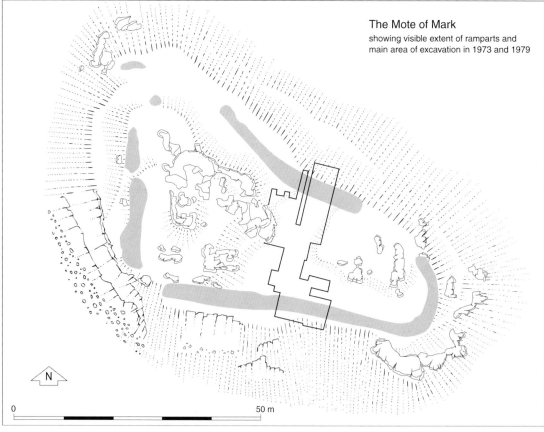

Fig. 7.1 *The Mote of Mark: location and site plan*

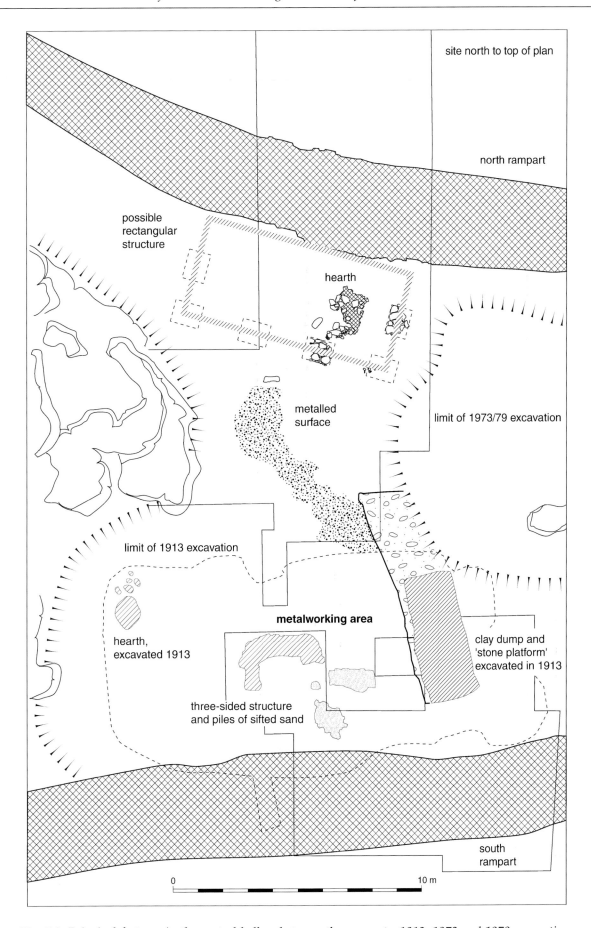

site north to top of plan

north rampart

possible
rectangular
structure

hearth

metalled
surface

limit of 1973/79 excavation

limit of 1913 excavation

metalworking area

hearth,
excavated 1913

clay dump and
'stone platform'
excavated in 1913

three-sided structure
and piles of sifted sand

south
rampart

0   10 m

Fig. 7.2 *Principal features in the central hollow between the ramparts: 1913, 1973 and 1979 excavations*

the process of manufacture of items, and their dating at the point of manufacture, rather than to the process of loss of finished products.

In 1913 Curle relied entirely on typological considerations in suggesting a date for the products from the Mote of Mark. More recent research on comparable material and on the chronology of imported pottery and glass allows some refinement of his analysis. More particularly, however, the published site record of 1913 does not permit the association of the metalworking sequence with the imports. Nor can the structural sequence of the occupation and the defences be established with complete confidence.

Curle's interpretation of his investigations proposed two phases for the construction of the defences (Curle 1914, 164). He postulated an initial massive drystone rampart that he believed could be associated with a brief occupation in the early centuries AD on the basis of two unassociated sherds of apparently Roman pottery. A second rampart, partially vitrified, was thought to have defended the main phase of occupation, encompassing the metalworking evidence and the imported artefacts, which Curle placed in the ninth century on the basis of a stylistic consideration of the decorated moulds. Unfortunately the published record does not present sufficient detail to allow the rampart sequence to be accepted with complete confidence; nor is the relationship between the defences and the occupation horizons demonstrably established. Furthermore, excavations on comparable sites and stylistic analyses of related material in the intervening period permit a reassessment of the proposed chronology. Accordingly, further excavations were undertaken in 1973 (by Laing) and in 1979 (by Longley) to address certain of these questions. In particular, the more recent excavations sought, firstly, to clarify the structural history of the defences, secondly, to establish how many phases of activity might be represented by the evidence for early medieval occupation and its associated metalworking and, thirdly, to address the relationship of the occupation to the defences. In each case, evidence was sought which might set the sequence within a chronological framework.

The defences

New cross-sections were recorded across the rampart on both the north and the south sides. In both cases the excavated area was extended to include a sufficiently large area of the interior to allow the relationship between the defences and the interior to be established (Fig. 7.1).

The rampart on the north side, although denuded, was intact. The rampart on the south side, however, had been encroached upon by Curle's extensive excavations in the southern part of the central hollow (Fig. 7.3). Both cross-sections displayed evidence of burning but the nature of the burning differed in each. On the north side masses of solidified vitrified stone were recorded immediately behind the front face of the rampart and in tumbled stone in front of the rampart. On the south side, burning had caused stonework in the core of the rampart to redden, crack and degrade but, except in a small number of isolated instances, not to vitrify. Burnt timber was identified at the base of both rampart sequences and a lateral beam was recorded in tumble beyond the front face on the north side. The build of the rampart was structured but there is no evidence to suggest more than one phase of construction. Quarried granite blocks were laid to provide a front and rear revetment defining a rampart 4m wide. Further granite blocks were placed behind the front revetment. The core comprised small beach pebbles and some granite blocks with a coping of large boulders brought up from the beach below.

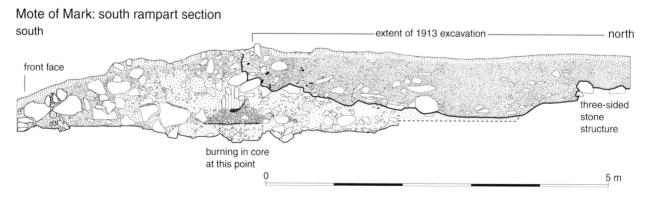

Mote of Mark: south rampart section

Fig. 7.3 The rampart on the south side showing Curle's incursion onto the rampart

The metalworking evidence

Iron, copper alloy, gold and silver were all worked on site. The presence of haematite ore and dense slag may be indicative of iron smelting, but the evidence is not conclusive. However, smithing is represented by smithing hearth cakes, a billet and bars (Crew, in Laing and Longley forthcoming). The identification of possible cupels and parting vessels is more certain evidence for the refining of metal. Copper alloy and gold were melted in crucibles; bivalve moulds, ingot moulds, casting debris and unfinished objects are clear evidence of casting.

It is clear from the distribution of metalworking debris that Curle's excavations in the southern part of the central hollow uncovered the metalworking focus (Fig. 7.4). A three-sided stone structure was identified here in 1913 and re-excavated in 1973. This structure was permeated with a loose and dusty grey-black sooty soil. It is best interpreted as a low bench or, perhaps, as a revetment or protection for a hearth. It subsequently became the focus of a substantial midden accumulation. A large deposit of clay measuring 5m by 2m and 305mm thick, in the immediate vicinity of the stone structure, was interpreted in 1913 as a floor. It is more likely to represent the raw material used in the manufacture of moulds and crucibles and itself overlay a series of dumps which had accumulated during the process of metalworking. Nearby lay two beds 'of pure sea sand … remarkably free of foreign matter' (Curle 1914, 138–39). These too may have been used in the industrial process, as a filler in the manufacture of crucibles or, alternatively, or perhaps additionally, as a bed to support moulds during casting.

The non-ferrous metalworking

One hundred and twenty one crucible fragments are recorded from the Mote of Mark. The majority are small, thin-walled and roughly triangular in plan view, with rounded or ovoid bases. Most crucibles were used to melt metal for casting. Some, however, were used for cupellation or parting. The largest category has distinct characteristics that identify its representatives as parting vessels.

Four hundred and eighty two fragments of clay mould are recorded. No complete moulds survive as the method of construction, assembly and casting requires that these bivalve moulds be broken to retrieve the finished product. Over 50% of the total

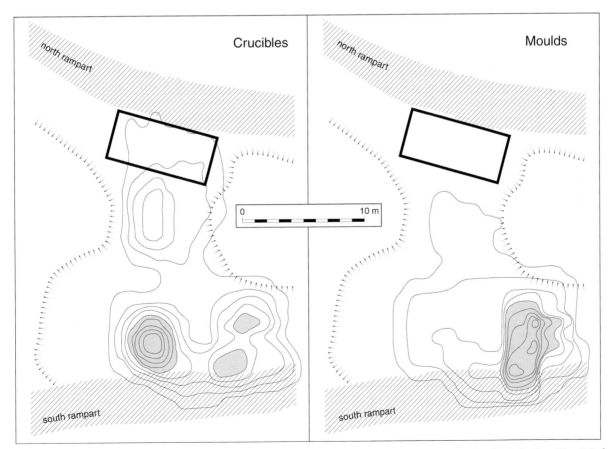

Fig. 7.4 *Artefact distributions: moulds and crucibles (trend surfaces with highest densities shaded). See Fig. 7.2 for location and relationship to features*

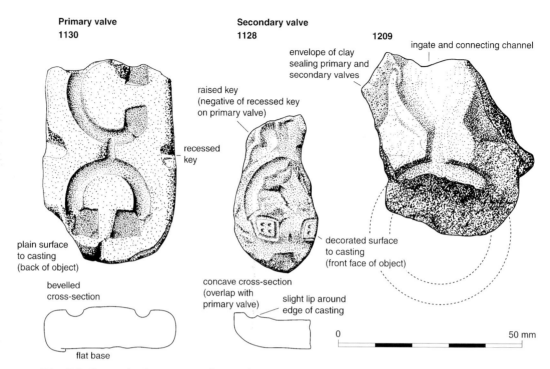

Fig. 7.5 *Stages in the process of manufacture and casting, illustrated by selected moulds*

are very small fragments with no diagnostic features. Nevertheless, 207 fragments are capable of interpretation, bearing information on the method of construction, the casting process and the objects cast (Fig. 7.5). The principal diagnostic artefacts cast in the moulds include penannular brooches, buckles, pins, studs, decorative mounts and a number of plain objects that may be the backs of decorative pieces (Fig. 7.6).

Penannular brooches (6 moulds)

The brooches are small (about 250mm in diameter) and plain, embellished only by a raised rim bordering a circular or lozenge terminal containing four raised pellets or, in one example, a lunate collar and design of concentric circles with one raised pellet at the centre. It is possible that the recessed fields on the terminals of these brooches were designed to take enamel. The backs are entirely plain.

Buckles and strap fittings (25 moulds)

The distinguishing characteristics of the buckles cast at the Mote of Mark are their small size (between 200mm and 250mm in diameter at the hoop) and that they were cast in one piece with their plate and not hinged. The openings of the loops on surviving examples range from 8mm to 16mm. They must have operated on very narrow straps or have been set in pairs or some other multiple arrangement on wider straps as is the case with, for example, modern harness and saddlery.

The upper faces of the loops and plates were decorated. The loops of three buckles were decorated with a pellet and tramline motif. A third loop bore sinuous linear decoration. On one of the buckles, the pellet and tramline motif terminated in the heads of two confronted, open-mouthed beasts. The plates of at least three buckles were decorated with serpentines in relief set within a recessed panel (Fig. 7.6). One plate has linear interlaced decoration and may be related to the linear decorated loop. The backs of all buckles are plain.

Studs (27 moulds)

All but the largest tanged studs or rivets (one example is more appropriately described as a shafted disc than a stud) were cast in strips of multiples, capable of being separated and trimmed for individual use. With the exception of the shafted disc, the size range incorporates small examples with heads of 6.5 – 8mm in diameter and large studs at 8 – 10mm in diameter. The average shaft length is 8mm. They may have been used to attach items to leatherwork or simply to decorate or strengthen the surface of leatherwork. These moulds represent one of the few categories where actual artefacts of copper alloy cast in the moulds survive on site.

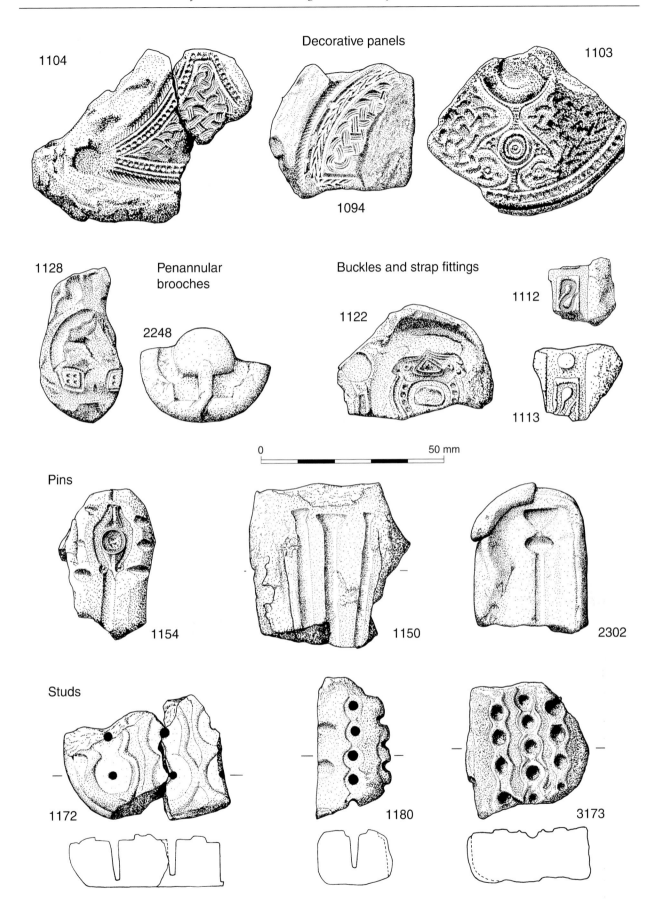

Decorative panels

1104

1103

1094

Penannular
brooches

1128

2248

Buckles and strap fittings

1122

1112

1113

Pins

1154   1150   2302

Studs

1172   1180   3173

Fig. 7.6 Moulds representative of the principal classes of artefact cast on site. Scale 1:1

Pins (35 moulds)

A range of pins were cast. No complete moulds survive. Consequently the total lengths are not ascertainable, although a bone pin with a length of 35mm was found which may have been a model for a knobbed type. The maximum surviving length of shafts in a mould is 36mm. Pin heads were embellished to a greater or lesser degree and include nail, drum, knob (with collar), disc (with collar) and thistle forms. One pin shaft terminated in a disc head flanked by confronted gaping-mouthed animals with curling tails (Fig. 7.6).

Decorative plates and their backs (80 moulds) and bosses (8 moulds)

A number of moulds were employed in the manufacture of decorative objects which do not fit into the above categories. The precise nature of the majority of these objects cannot now be determined because of the fragmentary condition of the moulds. Nevertheless, the character of the decoration is generally clear and, in some instances, the objects themselves may be reconstructed. The predominant decoration is a tight, regular interlace, often three-stranded and apparently symmetrical. Many of the pieces were bordered with running scrolls, pellet and tramlines, plait and rope-work or a combination of these motifs. Both curvilinear and straight edges to the designs are represented. Other motifs which occur, but less frequently, include palmettes and related 'late Celtic' designs. Certain of the objects cast in these moulds were clearly roundels; others were axe-blade plates.

Taken as a whole, while some of the items produced at the Mote of Mark were relatively mundane – the plainer pins for example – the assemblage is of very high quality. Gold was worked on the site: droplets were recognised embedded in the vitrified surfaces of crucibles and a small off-cut of gold, perhaps a stage in the process of drawing wire, has been identified. The small buckles are reminiscent, at a number of stages removed, of military belt sets, but might equally be part of prestigious horse harness. Horse 'brasses' are one, but not the only, interpretation of the roundels and axe-blade plates (Carver 1998, 110–13, pl. V). Even the small studs might be taken to be indicative of the manufacture of prestigious items in less durable materials such as leather. One rectangular panel with pelta and circle decoration in a cruciform arrangement might plausibly be interpreted as an applied decorative mount from the cover of a reliquary or gospel book.

Associated artefacts

The imported pottery and glass (comprising the fourth largest collection of such material from western Britain and Ireland) provides important information on the network of trading connections established between western France and the Irish Sea coastline during the sixth and seventh centuries (Campbell, in Laing and Longley forthcoming). Nevertheless, for our present purpose the significance of this material is in the light it casts on the chronology of the site (Figs 7.7, 7.8).

The stratigraphic evidence and associated chronological markers

The chronological sequence may be reconstructed from the relationships of, on the one hand, diagnostic artefacts, principally imported pottery and glass, and, on the other hand, radiocarbon determinations, with significant horizons in the stratigraphy of the site.

The relationships of the core area of metalworking activity to the construction and use of the rampart had been severed by the excavations of 1913 and by the encroachment of those excavations on to the rampart. Nevertheless, pockets of intact stratigraphy survived in the immediate vicinity of structures that were uncovered and partially excavated by Curle in 1913, and within and beneath the south rampart. In the northern part of the central hollow the relationship between the rampart on the north side and the occupation surface within the rampart was established. However, in this part of the site, artefacts associated with the metalworking process were very much more scarce, being located away from the focus of production. This was particularly the case with clay mould fragments (Fig. 7.4).

Pre-rampart activity

There is evidence to demonstrate activity on the hill, either pre-dating the rampart or contemporary with the phase of construction. This evidence comprises: (1) the presence of animal bone fragments incorporated in the rampart make-up and in contexts sealed by the rampart; (2) fragments of slag in a deposit incorporated in the rampart and (3) the presence of a small number of artefacts in contexts sealed by the rampart. A large fragment of imported glass, broadly datable to the sixth/seventh centuries and, more particularly, a basal sherd of E ware datable to the second half of the sixth century (although perhaps as early as 550: Campbell, in Laing and Longley forthcoming) occur in contexts which suggest that the rampart was built during the

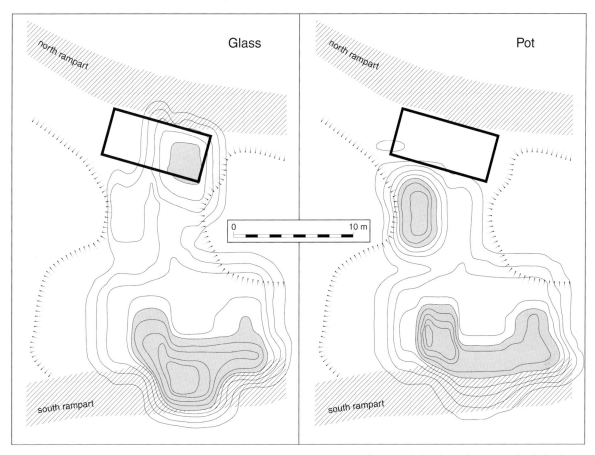

Fig. 7.7 *Artefact distributions: imported pottery and glass (trend surfaces with highest densities shaded). See Fig. 7.2 for location and relationship to features*

second half of the sixth century or later. It is possible that this material was associated with the process of clearance, laying out and construction on site. On the other hand, three imported sherds from less securely stratified contexts in the interior potentially indicate a longer pre-rampart chronology. These are two joining but very abraded sherds from a Bi amphora datable to the first half of the sixth century and a single sherd of D ware mortarium datable to the mid-sixth century. The latter was recorded by Curle at the bottom of a compact deposit of 'forced earth', which would appear to have been close to the base of the observed stratigraphic sequence (Curle 1914, 161).

The rampart

The rampart has a degree of complexity in its make-up, but is, nevertheless, of one phase of construction. Radiocarbon determinations were obtained from contexts sealed by the main body of rampart core and from a carbonised beam lying horizontally and longitudinally in tumbled rampart stone outside the front face of the rampart on the north side. Further

determinations were obtained from carbonised timber beams lying horizontally, both longitudinally and transversally, at the base of the rampart sequence on the south side of the central hollow. It was considered a possibility that these timbers, associated with the south rampart, might have been redeposited with backfilled material in 1913. It will be argued elsewhere (Laing and Longley forthcoming) that this is less likely than the possibility that they represent an *in situ* deposit constituting an initial phase of construction. The radiocarbon determinations are presented in Fig. 7.8 as calibrated dates at 95% confidence.

The radiocarbon determinations are compatible with the evidence of the stratified artefacts supporting the suggestion that the rampart may have been built towards the end of the sixth century. The destruction of the rampart was accompanied by fire, causing local vitrification and, elsewhere, burning and cracking of the rampart core. A considerable amount of stone, presumably from the ramparts, was spread within the interior of the site, sealing occupation horizons. The defences may have been deliberately levelled.

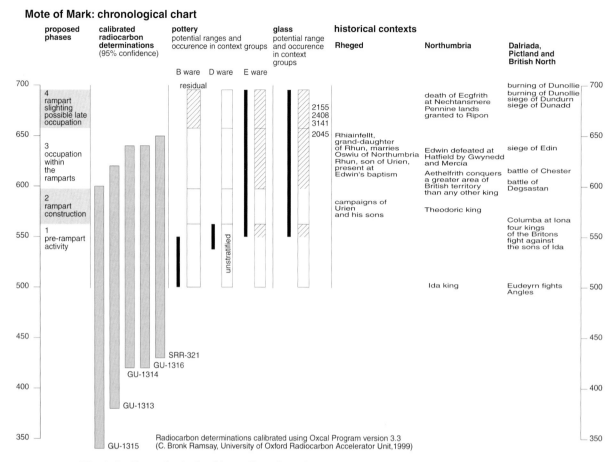

Fig. 7.8 *Chronological table: radiocarbon determinations, imported pottery and glass*

The final phase of occupation

The clay dump and sand piles which were discovered immediately behind the south rampart appear to have been abandoned at the time the ramparts were slighted. Stone debris, some of which corresponded to the beach boulder coping of the rampart (Curle 1914, 138), lay adjacent to the clay and over the sand piles. Curle believed that the large quantity of animal bone which overwhelmed the three-sided stone structure (also situated in the lee of the south rampart) represented the levelling of an adjacent midden after the demolition of structures and abandonment of occupation (Curle 1914, 166). This might be seen to be associated with the process of slighting, otherwise represented by the levelling of the ramparts. The deposits which overlay the clay dump and stone debris were described by Curle as distinguished by an 'almost complete absence of bones and relics' (Curle 1914, 137). The re-excavation of the southern part of the central hollow in 1973 confirmed, as far as the evidence allowed, the general contemporaneity of the clay dump/sand pile/three-sided structure horizon. Chronologically these features represent the latest phase of activity

immediately pre-dating the destruction of the rampart. However, a relatively high incidence of both imported pottery and glass occurs amongst the material interpreted as having been derived from the slighting of the ramparts. While it seems reasonable to suppose that these artefacts represent the disturbance of the latest occupation horizon in the interior, the possibility remains that some activity continued amongst the debris of the fort.

The assemblage of imported Continental pottery and glass represents one of the richest groups of this material from western Britain. The E ware spans the period from the middle of the sixth century to the later seventh century. Similarly much of the glass may be dated broadly within the range sixth/ seventh century. The latest glass on the site has been compared to material in later seventh-century contexts at Whithorn (Campbell, forthcoming). Examples of late seventh-century vessels are recorded on the latest occupation horizon and in the contexts associated with material derived from the destruction of the ramparts referred to above. It is likely, therefore, that occupation continued into the second half of the seventh century at the Mote of Mark.

In summary, the chronology of early medieval activity at the Mote of Mark may have developed along the following lines.

1 There is a possibility that the hill was occupied during the first half of the sixth century. This is suggested by the very small quantity of early to mid-sixth century pottery.

2 There was certainly activity on the hill before the rampart was built or, at least, before the rampart was completed. This activity included metalworking and is indicated by the presence of animal bones and slag, including furnace or hearth lining found in contexts sealed by the bulk of the rampart.

3 The rampart was built after the middle of the sixth century but probably before the end of that century. Imports of E ware ceramics and Continental glass were present before construction began and continued to form accessories to the activities on the hill through much of the seventh century.

4 High quality non-ferrous metalworking was carried out within the defences of the fort until the middle or the second half of the seventh century.

5 Destruction of the hill-fort defences by fire brought an abrupt end to the occupation of the hill and to metalworking in the later seventh century. The ramparts were deliberately demolished or slighted and no further occupation can be conclusively demonstrated.

A possible context for the decorated non-ferrous metalworking

The chronological scheme outlined above allows us to identify the first half of the seventh century as the heyday of the Mote of Mark with the defences in commission and high quality metalworking in production. The nature of the non-ferrous casting process, with constant breakage and discard of moulds and, to a lesser degree, crucibles, would be conducive to the accumulation of a considerable amount of rubbish. There is also evidence for the accumulation of a domestic midden in the immediate vicinity of the metalworking focus. The debris of metalworking, therefore, is likely to include material spanning a wide chronological range. If, however, it would seem reasonable that this rubbish should be disposed of periodically, then, while an inevitable residue might be anticipated, the greater part of the recorded assemblage should represent the later phases of production and discard.

There is no suggestion in the assemblage of stratified material from the 1973 and 1979 excavations that more than one tradition of non-ferrous metalworking is represented at the Mote of Mark, despite the identification of successive production phases. Equally, there is nothing across the assemblage as a whole to suggest the replacement of one tradition with another. The casting technology is consistent, as are the small details, such as the method of creating registration marks which might be considered to be a more sensitive indicator than technology.

The bulk of the diagnostic moulds (in terms of the artefacts cast in them or the decoration represented on them) were recorded in 1913 and, for the purposes of the present discussion, lack stratigraphic association. Nevertheless, the observations of Curle are relevant. Curle recorded clay moulds throughout the stratigraphic sequence (expressed in depth below the 1913 ground surface). However, the majority occurred in the upper levels (Curle 1914, 140), with particular concentrations adjacent to the clay dump. Curle's descriptions are not sufficiently precise to allow firm conclusions to be drawn. Nevertheless, there is an implication that the highly decorated moulds were recovered from the upper strata with only plainer items (including that for a Class G penannular brooch) occurring in the lower levels of the sequence (Curle 1914, 144). However, while the majority of clay moulds excavated in 1973 and 1979 were recovered from the redeposited backfill of the 1913 excavations, pockets of stratified contexts were identified which allow us to establish that decorated items were being produced prior to the final phase of production as well as, in all likelihood, during the last phase. These pieces include those bearing interlace decoration, as well as strap fittings, studs and pins.

The 'axe-blade' plate moulds – one aspect of stylistic influence with external associations

I do not propose to discuss the diversity of style represented on the moulds in any detail here (see Laing and Longley forthcoming). However, one component of decoration and its application to a particular group of artefacts is remarkable for the cultural associations implied by its presence. Of the 189 mould fragments which exhibit features indicative of the artefacts cast from them, a significant proportion (44%) were formed to produce the decorated fronts or plain backs of rectangular and curvilinear panels or plates. The predominant decoration applied to these panels was interlace (60%). Few of these fragmentary moulds are capable of satisfactory reconstruction. Nevertheless a small group display diagnostic features characteristic of a class of artefact better known from Anglo-Saxon England. This class comprises discs, sometimes compartmentalised into four segments and 'axe-blade' plates. The segments of the discs and the 'axe-blade' plates are typically decorated with interlace. The group has been discussed by Speake (1989, 75–80, fig. 68).

At the Mote of Mark indisputable examples of an axe-blade plate and a segmented disc, respectively, are represented by nos 1103 and 1104 (Fig. 7.9). The axe-blade plate bears tight three-strand, non-zoo-morphic interlace bordered by pellets within tram-lines with an outer border of rope-work; the disc bears apparently plain, tight, interlace with vestigial animal head and tail terminations, bordered by pellets within tram lines. Each of these decorative components is represented on other moulds, al-though not necessarily in the same relationship or on similar artefacts. Both plain and 3-strand, tight, interlace occurs on plates with running scroll bor-ders. The pellet-and-tramline and rope-work borders are related to Anglo-Saxon filigree and granular work and the contexts of the currently recognised comparanda for the Mote of Mark 'axe-blade' plates are predominantly Anglo-Saxon. The Mote of Mark craftsmen would, therefore, seem to have been familiar with such material in circulation in the Anglo-Saxon areas and to have been prepared to produce similar pieces. Speake has referred to the complexity of influences at work in the creation of decorated metalwork in this period and Campbell and Lane have drawn attention to the Anglo-Saxon influences present in the metalworking repertoire at Dunadd (Dalriada) in the seventh century (Speake 1989, 76; Campbell and Lane 1993, 52–63). Never-theless, one wonders what particular circumstances, or market demand, could have given rise to the manufacture of such artefacts at the Mote of Mark.

While the precise context of some of the Anglo-Saxon pieces is obscure, numerous axe-blade plates in association with discs were recorded as horse brasses in a grave under Mound 17 at Sutton Hoo, which has been assigned a date in the first quarter of the seventh century (Carver 1998, 183, 132–36). The bed burial at Swallowcliffe Down has been dated by Speake to the later seventh century where axe-blade foils were reused in the manufacture of a roundel on a satchel. It should be remembered, however, that both contexts involve deposition at some period later than the date of manufacture and that, in the case of Swallowcliffe Down, the 'axe plates' had been recycled from an earlier object. At Mote of Mark the context is the point of manufacture.

A possible historical context for the Mote of Mark?

The archaeological evidence suggests that the Mote of Mark was occupied from about the middle of the sixth century until the later seventh century. What very little we know, or think we know, of the kingdom of Rheged may be bracketed within the same chronological range.

The *Historia Brittonum* describes, from a ninth-century perspective, the struggles of British leaders in the north against the growing power of the dynasty of Ida in Bernicia. Four kings, we are told, fought against Ida and his sons (*HB*, 63). These kings are named as Urien (in Rheged), Rhydderch Hen (in Strathclyde), Gwallawg (possibly in Elfed) and Morgant (possibly in Gododdin). The reigns of the Anglian leaders against whom they are said to have fought span the greater part of the later sixth century from Ida himself (547–559) to Hussa (585–692). Urien Rheged and his sons, however, are seen particularly as the adversaries of Theodric, placing this phase of the confrontation in the 570s.

It has been supposed that the British leaders acted in alliance (e.g. Smyth 1984, 21) but there is nothing in the *Historia Brittonum* to lead us inevitably to this conclusion. On the contrary, Welsh tradition em-phasises internal and intra-national dissension and confrontation (*HB* 63; Bromwich 1978, triad 33; *AC s.a.* 573; *AC s.a.* 595; Williams 1970, 16, l. 37–9). Fortunately, for our present purpose, it is not necessary to demonstrate that the core of early poetic material within the *Book of Taliesin* comprising eulogies, battle poems, the propitiation and the elegy addressed to Urien and his son Owain are the authentic sixth-century voice of the bard himself. We may be content to agree with Dumville that, 'if in any sense genuine, they constitute a capital source for the period' and that 'whatever the status of the poetry, the known transmission in traditional litera-ture of a societal context proper to the founding era of that literature justifies the use of it to describe the heroic ethos of the sub-Roman northern Britons' (Dumville 1993, 6).

The society described is warlike and aristocratic. We hear of battles against an English enemy whose leader is known by his nickname Fflamddwyn – 'the Flamebringer' – much as Aethelfrith (593–616) was known to the *Historia Brittonum* as 'The Artful Dodger' and Oswald as 'Whiteblade' (Williams 1960, VI.7; X, II; *HB*, 57, 64). As a counterpoint to the splendour at court and the generosity of Urien, 'golden king of the north', there are war bands, musterings of men and border-crossing armies. At Argoed Llwyfain, Urien urges his men to 'raise a rampart high on the hilltop' in response to an incursion by the English (Williams 1960, VI.15). Such

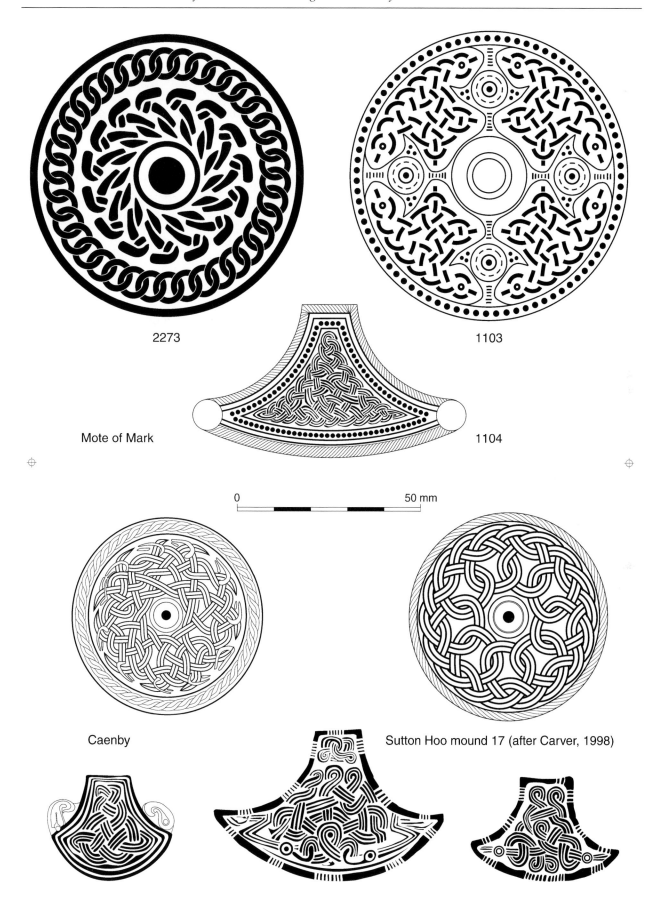

2273

1103

Mote of Mark   **1104**

0   50 mm

Caenby   Sutton Hoo mound 17 (after Carver, 1998)

Fig. 7.9 *Axe-blade plates and roundels: the Mote of Mark and selected comparanda from Caenby, Lincolnshire, and Sutton Hoo, Mound 17, Suffolk. Scale 1:1*

an atmosphere of conflict provides background context for, although, of course, not necessarily an explanation of, the defence of the Mote of Mark.

Aethelfrith became king in Bernicia in 593. In 603 he defeated Aedán mac Gabráin and his Scottish army at Degsastan. Two years later his expansionist policies drove Edwin and the Deiran nobility into exile. In 615 he won a notable, if infamous, victory against the Britons at Chester and probably weakened Mercian power in the process. He may have claimed overkingship in Mercia (Higham 1995, 195) and, after the death of Æthelberht of Kent, began to put pressure on Raedwald of East Anglia (*HE* II,12). Bede remarked that Æthelfrith ravaged the Britons more cruelly than all other English leaders; he overran a greater area than any other king, making their lands either tributary or ready for English settlement. We hear nothing directly of Rheged during Aethelfrith's reign but it would seem unlikely that he had not turned his attention to such a near neighbour.

Not all contact between Rheged and Northumbria was so directly confrontational during this period. The Welsh annals and the *Historia Brittonum* both preserve a tradition that Rhun son of Urien Rheged was, in some capacity involved in the baptism of Edwin of Northumbria's daughter Eanfled and, in the following year, Edwin himself. (*HB*, 63; *AC s.a.* 626). Oswiu, king in Northumbria from 642 to 670, appears to have first married Rhiainfellt, granddaughter of Rhun before taking Eanfled as his second wife. It is just chronologically possible that he met and married his British wife during his years of exile as his brother Eanfrith appears to have married a Pictish woman while similarly exiled from Northumbria (Dumville 1993, III, 12; Hunter-Blair 1954, 160).

Dynastic marriages and youthful relationships forged in exile are not guarantees of continuing cordiality between kingdoms. Edwin's later career ('one of the three Great Oppressions of Anglesey, nurtured within'; Bromwich 1978, 48, 54) and his feud with Cadwallon of Gwynedd is a case in point. Neither would such marriage ties lead obviously to the political assimilation of one or other kingdom as has been suggested for Rheged in the 630s or 640s. On the other hand, Thomas Charles-Edwards has considered the way in which the queen's household or retinue within a kingdom, separately from that of the king or other royal officials, might provide a point of access to royal favour and influence. In particular, it is suggested, Rhiainfellt, Oswiu's British wife, may have provided a focus of loyalty for the British nobility of Rheged (Charles-Edwards 1989, 32). While it is possible that both Edwin and Oswiu claimed some degree of overlordship in Rheged (*HE* II, 5) there is no evidence that Rheged had been absorbed by Northumbria at this date. Nevertheless, such relationships might very well provide a context for the assimilation of external influences including, perhaps, the appearance of Anglicising characteristics.

During the consecration of the church at Ripon in the 670s, Wilfrid read a long list of lands granted by Ecgfrith, Aelfwine and their predecessors. These included areas of Elmet and Pennine Rheged 'that the British clergy, fleeing from our own hostile sword, had deserted' (Eddius Stephanus, *Life of Wilfrid*, 17). Smyth has detected a certain immediacy in Eddius's account of these events which led him to suggest that the dismemberment of Pennine Rheged had occurred relatively recently (Smyth 1984, 24). Smyth has gone further, to suggest a significant dislocation in the power base of north Britain at this time (Smyth 1984, 25–6). If the political fragmentation of Rheged was achieved during the third rather than the second quarter of the seventh century, then such a date would accord with the archaeological evidence for the destruction of the Mote of Mark. Whether the hostile sword of Northumbria was in evidence, however, we are not able to say.

Acknowledgements

The excavations of 1973 were undertaken by Dr Lloyd Laing. I am very grateful to have had the opportunity of working on the material from that season as a student of Dr Laing in Liverpool. Following my own excavations at the Mote in 1979, I am particularly grateful to the staff of the then National Museum of Antiquities of Scotland, especially Trevor Cowie, in the 1980s and more recently Alison Sheridan, for their assistance in providing access to the material from the 1913 excavations and to Angela Care Evans of the British Museum for showing me the Sutton Hoo material. The work towards full publication of the recent excavations, together with a reassessment of Alexander Curle's results from 1913, has been a collaborative affair. This paper has benefited considerably from discussion with, and the work of, my co-author in that report, Lloyd Laing and the specialist contributors, Jennifer Bourdillon, Ewan Campbell, Peter Crew, Susan La Niece, R. I. Page, George Smith and Niamh Whitfield. The task of illustrating the large number of artefacts has been shared between the author and Andrew Smith.

The Society of Antiquaries of Scotland very generously contributed financial support for the radiocarbon determinations tabulated in Fig. 7.8 and towards the cost of completing the artefact illustrations in the final report.

References

AC: *Annales Cambriae*, in J. Morris (ed. and trans.) 1980, *Nennius. British History and the Welsh Annals*, 85–91. London, Chichester.

BROMWICH, R. 1978, *Trioedd Ynys Prydein*. Cardiff.

CAMPBELL, E. and LANE, A. 1993, 'Celtic and Germanic interaction in Dalriada: the 7th-century metalworking site at Dunadd', in R. M. Spearman and J. Higgitt (eds), *The Age of Migrating Ideas. Early Medieval Art in Northern Britain and Ireland*, 52–63. Edinburgh, Stroud.

CAMPBELL, E. forthcoming, 'The Continental imports', in Laing and Longley, forthcoming.

CARVER, M. 1998, *Sutton Hoo, Burial Ground of Kings.* London.

CHARLES-EDWARDS, T. 1989, 'Early medieval kingship in the British Isles', in S. Bassett (ed.), *The Origins of Anglo-Saxon Kingdoms*, 28–39. London, New York.

COLES, F. R. 1893, 'The motes, forts and doons in the east and west divisions of the stewartry of Kirkcudbright', *Proc. Soc. Antiq. Scotl.* 3 (1892–3), 92–182.

CREW, P. forthcoming, 'The slags' in Laing and Longley forthcoming.

CURLE, A. 1914, 'Report on the excavation of a vitrified fort at Rockcliffe, known as the Mote of Mark', *Proc. Soc. Antiq. Scotl.* 48, 125–68.

DUMVILLE, D. 1988, 'Early Welsh poetry: problems of historicity', in B. F. Roberts (ed.), *Early Welsh Poetry: Studies in the Book of Aneirin*, 1–16. Aberystwyth.

DUMVILLE, D. 1993, 'The origins of Northumbria: some aspects of the British background', in D. Dumville, *Britons and Anglo-Saxons in the Early Middle Ages.* III, 1–14. Woodbridge.

EDDIUS STEPHANUS, 'Life of Wilfrid', in J. F. Webb (trans.) and D. H. Farmer (ed.), 1988, *The Age of Bede.* Harmondsworth.

HB: *Historia Brittonum*, in J. Morris (ed. and trans.) 1980, *Nennius. British History and the Welsh Annals*, 50–84. London, Chichester.

HE: *Historia Ecclesiastica Gentis Anglorum*, B. Colgrave and R. A. B. Mynors (ed. and trans.) 1969, *Bede: Ecclesiastical History of the English People.* Oxford.

HIGHAM, N. J. 1995, *An English Empire: Bede and the Anglo-Saxon Kings.* Manchester.

HUNTER-BLAIR, P. 1954, 'The Bernicians and their northern frontier, in N. K. Chadwick (ed.), *Studies in Early British History*, 137–72. Cambridge.

LAING, L. R. and LONGLEY, D. forthcoming, *The Mote of Mark, a Dark Age Hillfort in South-West Scotland*, Soc. of Antiquaries of Scotl.

SMYTH, A. 1984, *Warlords and Holy Men.* Edinburgh.

SPEAKE, G. 1989, *A Saxon Bed Burial on Swallowcliffe Down* (= Engl. Heritage Archaeol. Rep. 10).

WILLIAMS, I. 1960, *Canu Taliesin.* Cardiff.

WILLIAMS I. 1970, *Canu Llywarch Hen.* Cardiff.

8   A Fine Quality Insular Embroidery from Llan-gors Crannóg, near Brecon

Hero Granger-Taylor and Frances Pritchard

Introduction

Llan-gors Lake is near Brecon, in southern mid-Wales, not far from the border with England. The crannóg in the lake underwent an extensive programme of fieldwork and excavation from 1989 to 1993. This work was undertaken by the National Museums & Galleries of Wales and the School of History and Archaeology, Cardiff University, under the direction of Mark Redknap, Alan Lane and Ewan Campbell. The project resulted in a complete reassessment of the site and its place in Welsh history (Campbell and Lane 1988; Campbell and Lane 1989; Redknap and Lane 1994). It is now known from dendrochronological evidence that the timber for the crannóg palisade was felled between the years 889 and 893. The crannóg was probably a royal residence of the rulers of the kingdom of Brycheiniog. In the 880s and 890s, the king of Brycheiniog was Elisedd ap Tewdwr, who was, according to Asser, driven by the might of the sons of Rhodri (Mawr) to seek the overlordship of Alfred, king of Wessex. During Elisedd's reign, Brycheiniog also endured raiding from north-west England. A hostile expedition by a Mercian army sent into Wales by Æthelflæd (Alfred's daughter and wife of Ealdorman Æthelræd of Mercia) is recorded in the Anglo-Saxon Chronicle for the year 916. This resulted in the destruction of *Brecenanmere* (the Anglo-Saxon name for the site known in modern times as Llan-gors or Llyn Syfaddan); according to the Anglo-Saxon Chronicle, the king's wife was captured, as were 33 others (Whitelock 1961, *s.a.* 916). Welsh kings appear to have attended the Wessex court in the early tenth century, to judge from the witness lists to English charters, including king Tewdwr, son of Elisedd and ruler of Brycheiniog at the time of the Mercian attack (Davies 1982, 114).

During the five seasons of excavation a wide variety of artefacts was recovered from the site. They include some items of high quality, one being an enamelled hinge from a small portable shrine (Redknap 1995, 65–6, fig. 4a). The most remarkable find, however, was the charred (carbonised) remains of an embroidered linen garment. It is this which forms the subject of this paper.

Recovery and conservation

The textile was discovered in 1990 buried in waterlogged silts outside the north-facing palisade in Trench A (Redknap 1991, 24; Redknap and Lane 1994, 200). The textile had undergone a sort of double preservation process, being both carbonised and waterlogged; it had evidently been damaged by fire before being deposited in the water. When recovered lying on a piece of wood, it consisted of a lump of blackened textile, in places up to 40 layers deep interleaved with silt and charcoal. The textile itself, in this state, measured approximately 220 × 135 × 65mm. The embroidered design and the extent of the layering became apparent only as the mud and silt were cleaned away (Mumford and Redknap 1998–9, 53).[1]

The textile as found was a roughly folded bundle, which was broken away at the edges on three sides but remained intact along a thick fold on the fourth side. As the layers were separated and unfolded, the relative position of the different pieces was carefully recorded. The conservator responsible for this exacting and time-consuming work, Louise Mumford, writes that the textile now exists 'as a series of separate pieces, eleven of them plain, varying in size from a saucer to a dinner plate, and seven of them embroidered, giving an embroidered area of approximately 780 sq cm'.[2]

Fig. 8.1 *The Llan-gors textile: part of an embroidered panel, edged with the lion border, and plain linen beyond.*
(Photograph: National Museum of Wales)

The embroidery technique

Although the whole object is black and, in places, the surface is worn and damaged, it is easy to distinguish the embroidered parts from the areas of plain textile (Fig. 8.1). The embroidery, carried out in silk thread, completely covers the panels within which it is contained, and these panels are glossier and thicker than the adjoining plain areas of linen (all the textiles appear to be linen). The technique of the embroidery, although so far without known parallel, is relatively easy to work out, when viewed through a binocular microscope (Fig. 8.2). There appears to be one embroidery thread for every thread of base textile and, since the linen ground has approximately 25 threads per cm in both warp and weft, this means there are about 25 embroidery threads per cm in one or other direction. The execution is very fine and regular.

A number of colours was probably used though these are now all black. With difficulty, the design can still be deciphered by looking both at the direction of the stitches and at the type of thread. The thread used for the motifs – the lions, the vine-scroll framework and its contents (see below) – has a comparatively dull appearance. It is of reeled silk, S-plied from two elements, the initial slight twist possibly in the Z-direction (Z ?, 2S). By contrast, the thread used for the background is shiny. This is of reeled silk with a slight S-twist and no ply. The direction of the threads in the background is also always at right angles to the direction of most of the threads in the motif.

An added subtlety affecting the whole scheme is that the direction of all the embroidery threads changes in blocks from time to time. In the lion border, these changes take place relatively fre-

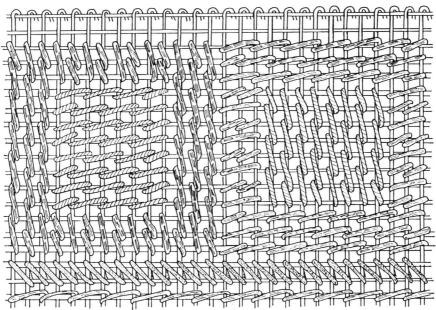

Fig. 8.2 *The Llan-gors textile: diagram showing needlework technique, the direction of stitches changing in blocks and the two types of silk thread. (Drawing by Grace Thompson after Hero Granger-Taylor)*

quently, with each little lion and its background block measuring approximately 12mm deep and 14mm wide. Contrasting blocks also occur in the main field of the design but after larger intervals. The change in the direction of the embroidery threads would have had the practical purpose of allowing the embroidered cloth to lie flat. It also gave, and still gives, a very interesting quality of contrast to the surface of the fabric, similar to that of a woven damask.

The technique can be categorised as 'stem stitch on counted threads'. The course of the embroidery thread follows the structure of the woven cloth, passing over three warp or weft threads and wrapping back under at the point where the warp and weft intersect (Fig. 8.2). The stitches are staggered row by row and, because they are all worked from left to right and have a slight slope due to the overlap, a diagonal emphasis is built up. The stitching is so regular that it almost appears to be woven. However, the setting of some wrapped threads at right angles to others would not have been possible in a woven textile. Also, for certain details (for example the lions' tails) we see that the regular pattern was broken, with some of the stitches set at approximately 45° to the regular stitches.

The place of the Llan-gors find in the history of Insular embroidery

As far as we know, this embroidery technique has no exact parallel. However, fine needlework is known to have been well established in the British

Isles by this period and, taking a broad view, the Llan-gors find can be seen to be a manifestation of one element in this gradually evolving tradition. The most famous examples of Anglo-Saxon embroidery are, of course, the embroidered vestments found in the tomb of St Cuthbert at Durham (Christie 1938, 45–52, pls 1–3; Plenderleith 1956, 375). It is apparent from the embroidered inscriptions that the stole and large maniple were made for Frithestan, Bishop of Winchester, between 909 and 916 (by chance, according to the Anglo-Saxon Chronicle, 916 is the same year that the royal residence at Llan-gors was apparently destroyed).

Although the Llan-gors embroidery is as fine as the St Cuthbert vestments, at first sight it seems to have little in common with the Durham pieces or with the earlier Anglo-Saxon embroidery preserved at Maaseik (Budny and Tweddle 1984). These have 'free-hand' designs, unrelated to the woven textile beneath, and use as much gold thread as coloured silk. Looking more closely at the Durham stole and large maniple, however, at least one important similarity emerges. This is the setting at right angles of areas of embroidery made up of parallel threads. More precisely, this occurs in the gold areas: the gold threads of the background are laid straight and parallel to the borders but at right angles to gold threads making up the haloes of the figures (the additional couched patterning in the haloes adds to the effect of contrast; Christie 1938, 48).

The similarity between the Llan-gors find's silk needlework ground and the treatment of gold thread in ecclesiastical embroideries becomes more obvious with later examples of *Opus Anglicanum* where areas of gold thread, often still organised in contrasting perpendicular fields, begin to have their own designs, in most cases in addition to a main pictorial composition in coloured silk. A prominent example is the Pienza cope of *c.* 1325 where, included among a variety of gold background designs, are plant scrolls containing birds and animals, reminiscent of Llan-gors in composition, if not in style (Christie 1938, 178–80, pls 139–42).

Another factor which makes the surface effect of these later gold embroideries closer to the Llan-gors fragments is that, from about the twelfth century, rather than being surface couched as at Durham, the gold thread in *Opus Anglicanum* was 'underside couched'. That is the gold thread was pulled through to the back of the cloth and secured there so that, in a manner reminiscent of the different Llan-gors technique, the 'binding point' is hidden (Christie 1938, 23). Underside couching, a characteristically English technique, had a practical as well as a visual purpose – the resulting fabric was more flexible than if surface couched. Is it too much to suggest that it grew out of a combination of the widespread technique of surface couching with a local tradition for counted stem stitch, even if the latter is now only represented by the Llan-gors find?

The absence of gold thread from the Llan-gors embroidery can at least be partly explained by function. As will be shown, the embroidered panels decorated a lightweight linen garment. Gold thread would have made the panels stiff and vulnerable to surface wear. It also should be remembered that the Llan-gors find is from a royal but secular context and as such cannot be directly compared to the Durham vestments or indeed to the overwhelming proportion of extant medieval embroidery which was made for church use.

Although we have referred to the Llan-gors find as an 'embroidery', a more correct description for it is 'needlework'; the English language traditionally discriminated between 'needlework', where a design is created akin to a woven design, and 'embroidery', which has the sense of enrichment and in the past usually involved the addition of pearls, beads, spangles and similar items (Levey 1998, 62). In fact, embroidery as it emerged in north-west Europe undoubtedly grew out of the woven decoration of textiles. In this it contrasts in particular with Byzantine embroidery which was based, not on weaving, but on the tradition of appliqué, specifically the attachment of precious stones, pearls and enamel plaques.

The textile origin of north-west European embroidery is best illustrated by looking at 'soumak-brocading', the woven technique which is closest to counted stem stitch. Soumak is a Turkish word which has been adopted in modern times as a general term

for a type of brocading weft which wraps back and around the warp elements with which it intersects (Burnham 1981, 127). In England, as in Scandinavia, soumak was used to decorate both full-width textiles and tablet-woven bands. A notable example is the so-called 'soumak braid' at Durham which is from the tomb of St Cuthbert, but which is earlier in date than the embroideries, probably *c.*800 (Granger-Taylor 1989, 316). The braid survives attached to the fragmentary white silk garment, probably an ecclesiastical dalmatic. Unusually, on the Durham soumak braid, the short floats of the wrapped thread are used for the front of the structure to build up a bricked effect across the centre of the border (the diagram of the technique by Mrs Crowfoot is very like the theoretical back view of the Llan-gors embroidery; Crowfoot 1956, 455, fig. 15). However, soumak brocading itself can only be worked in the direction of the weft and it is not possible to obtain, with soumak alone, the contrasting surfaces seen in the embroidery. The texture of the Llan-gors embroidery is closer to bands where the brocading only partly covers the surface and where the tablet-woven ground is also visible.

A band of this type forms the *infulae*, or lappets, on a mitre from the abbey of St Peter in Salzburg. The mitre dates to the twelfth century but the beautiful silk and gold lappets must be older, probably dating to the first half of the ninth century (Granger-Taylor 1991, 183). Their attribution as 'Insular, or Continental under Insular influence', is based on the technique of the band, together with the close connection known to have existed between the English church and Salzburg in the eighth century. The soumak brocading can be seen against, and at right angles to, the ribs of the tablet-woven ground – the two contrasting effects are particularly clear in old black and white photographs (Battiscombe 1956, pls 44–6). In detail, the soumak is worked from left to right and then, in the next row, right to left, so that a chevron, or herringbone, effect is achieved. This is unlike the Llan-gors embroidery, where all the stitching is worked from left to right. Nevertheless, the chevrons correspond in their own way to the band's ground, which, because the tablets were threaded alternately to the left and to the right, is itself made up of chevrons.

The design of the Durham soumak braid and the braid from Salzburg derive from a group of Central Asian silks in compound twill weave which have borders in this style (Granger-Taylor 1989, 312–16). For example, the well-known complete panel of silk from the shrine of St Lambert, Liège Cathedral, has borders of this type on all four sides (Musées Royaux d'Art et d'Histoire 1972, 173, B.4). The impression given is that such borders were commonly cut off the Central Asian silks and used as applied decoration on garments in a manner similar to the Western European tradition of using tablet-woven borders. There is now evidence for this practice: cut-off vertical and horizontal borders have been discovered recently in a Tibetan context in western China (Otavsky 1998, 33–5; Abb. 9; Zhao 1999, 115, fig. 03.08–1).

Soumak brocading was also used to decorate furnishing textiles. Here also a progression from weaving to embroidery can be traced which mirrors, on a larger scale, the progression seen in the woven bands. The brocading technique used on the hangings at Överhogdal (tenth/eleventh-century) and Skog (thirteenth-century), both in Sweden, is close to the embroidery stitch of the Llan-gors find (Franzén and Nockert 1992, 15, fig. 1; Grenander-Nyberg 1992, 124, fig. 7). The main difference is that, in the woven hangings, the wool threads used for the soumak pass chiefly over nine linen warp threads and back under three, whereas in the finer embroidery, the silk thread passes over three threads of linen ground and back under one.

The Bayeux 'tapestry' is a narrative hanging which relates to the Scandinavian friezes in materials and organisation but which is again embroidered rather than woven. Its 'laid and couched' embroidery technique, in its own way, can be seen also to have grown out of the earlier weaving tradition. By about the twelfth century, on the evidence of the Røn fragment and the Høyland hanging, this sort of textile had begun to be embroidered rather than woven in Norway also (Wilson 1985, 204–5; Svarstad Flø 1997).

Design and layout

A number of factors make deciphering the design difficult, in particular the absence of colour, the differing degrees of wear and degradation and the incomplete and fragmentary nature of the garment. Nevertheless, the overall layout and some of the principal features can now be established (Fig. 8.3).

There are two different border designs, running parallel to the seams. They are approximately 12mm deep and edged with a margin worked in a slightly different stitch. One design has pairs of small, confronting lions with a stiff stylised outline (Fig. 8.1; Plate IV). Each lion has only three legs, a raised tail and two spots on its body above its legs. These last two characteristics are significant as will be demonstrated presently, while the three-leggedness appears to be an individual foible. The second border has a geometric pattern of diagonal lines and opposing trefoils.

The main design is laid out symmetrically with motifs depicted in mirror image across both axes. It is divided into hexagon-like compartments, which are, in fact, angular plant scrolls springing from stylised vines. The scrolls sprout leaves and bunches of grapes on short side stems and are inhabited by long-necked birds (Plate V).

The design is considerably stylised, something that can be partly explained by the counted thread technique: this is one reason, for example, why the vine stems are so very straight. In addition, there is a certain naivety in the drawing and one might be tempted to describe this as 'provincial' if it were not for the great skill shown in the execution of the embroidery, as well as in the constructional details.

The inhabited vine-scroll is characteristic of Anglo-Saxon art from the eighth century. The symmetrical arrangement is less complex than vine-scrolls worked in other media, although it is a feature of the 'Rupertus' Cross, Bischofshofen parish church, Austria, which dates to the second half of the eighth century (Webster 1991, 171–73, no. 133). The closest parallels to the lions and birds are found on figured silks woven in weft-faced compound twill in Byzantium, Persia and Sogdiana (Central Asia), in the eighth to tenth centuries.

The little lions appear to be based on those portrayed in ninth- and tenth-century Byzantine lion silks, although their scale and stylisation is more akin to lions and other creatures on tablet-woven bands, such as the edging of the stole among the early tenth-century Durham embroideries (Crowfoot 1939, 70, fig. 9a; Crowfoot 1956, 443, fig. 8) and the late seventh-century wool girdle from the tomb of St Balthild (died *c.* 680) in Chelles (Laporte and Boyer 1991). Imperial Byzantine lion silks show pairs of confronted lions, up to 80cm in length, often with upwardly pointing tails and with a prominent spot, or foliate patch, positioned on either their leg joints or body (Plate VI). Body spots are visible on the lion silk removed from the tomb of St Julian in Rimini in 1911, which a recent study suggests dates to the late ninth century (Muthesius 1997, 46).

Bird designs are also very common on contemporary woven silks, some of Byzantine or Christian origin (Muthesius 1997, 47–9), but especially examples thought to be from Sogdiana (Shepherd 1981, 119–21; Watt and Wardwell 1997, 34–5; Otavsky 1998, 13–17, 28–30, 36–8; Zhao 1999, 114–19). Such Central Asian silk fabrics had a very wide distribution and at least two examples have been found from England, the textile used as facing strips on the 'dalmatic' fragments of *c.* 800 from the tomb of St Cuthbert (Granger-Taylor 1989, 311–12) and a fragment from a tenth-century pit fill at Milk Street, London (Pritchard 1984, 61). Documentary evidence also supports the popularity of bird silks in the West over many centuries. William of Malmesbury, writing in the early twelfth century, mentions that in the

Fig. 8.3 *The Llan-gors textile: all the embroidered and partly embroidered fragments in their relative positions with superimposed drawing showing the structural details and the design as far as it has been elucidated. (Drawing by Tony Daly after Mark Redknap and Louise Mumford)*

seventh century St Aldhelm wore in Rome a silk chasuble patterned with peacocks and also that in the early eleventh century Cnut placed a rich fabric woven with peacocks of various colours over the sepulchre of King Edmund in Glastonbury (Dodwell 1982, 145, 151). Other birds that recur on these exotic

silks are ducks woven in differing degrees of refinement, cockerels, pheasants, doves and eagles.

The designer of the Llan-gors embroidery must have been familiar with a range of woven silk designs and chose motifs to fit the commission. Undoubtedly the garment with its painstakingly fine needlework and distinctive technique was a specialised workshop product and would have been stitched by at least two people working on the separate panels. Copying woven designs was not only widespread in silk weaving centres, but also undertaken in other specialised techniques. These include the soumak-brocaded, tablet-woven band, mentioned above, decorating the silk 'dalmatic' from the tomb of St Cuthbert, which was modelled on a Central Asian floral design (Granger-Taylor 1989, 312–16). Details of silk designs were copied in other art forms as well, and close copies of Sassanian-style ducks have been identified in three decorated initials in the Sacramentary of Gellone, which was probably produced at the Monastery of the Holy Cross, Meaux, east of Paris, at the end of the eighth or in the early ninth century (Baldwin 1970, 3–5).

The garment

The Llan-gors fragments preserve a number of different constructional elements. The fragments fall into three categories: the panels entirely covered in embroidery, the plain areas beyond, and, thirdly, panels the same shape as the embroidered panels used to line the embroidery (Fig. 8.1). All these textiles are plain, tabby-weave linen and similar in quality. The threads in one direction, probably the warp, are Z-spun. By contrast, the threads in the other direction, probably the weft, are mostly S-spun but in places they are Z-spun. However, as there is no regularity in the grouping of the Z-spun yarn, the changes do not appear to be part of the sort of 'spin patterning' scheme seen on some early medieval linen (Bender Jørgensen 1992, 142).

A number of features point to the fragments being the remains of an item of clothing. One of these features is a hem, which is about 80mm deep and runs at right angles to the warp; it appears to mark the bottom edge of the garment. Another feature is a belt loop, 45mm long, made from a short piece of silk tape or ribbon in warp-faced tabby weave. A further detail, which appears to be functional rather than decorative, is a pair of eyelets worked in silk positioned at the broad end of a triangular panel of embroidery. At present it is unclear how these eyelets were used.

The constructional sewing is of a similar high quality to the embroidery and was carefully planned and executed. The embroidery was worked only on the areas intended to be left visible after the garment had been made up; this is seen most clearly on the triangular panel where all the embroidery ceases just in from the diagonal seams. The seams are covered on the front by a double cord of silk and a similar cord was stitched to the bottom edge of the hem

Fig. 8.4 The Llan-gors textile: detail of upper part of triangular panel or gore showing the double cords that cover the seams and one of the two reinforcing triangles. (Photograph: National Museum of Wales)

(Fig. 8.4). The cord was probably made by finger-looping and attached to the garment in the same process as the sewing of the seam (the seam would have been sewn from the outside). Similar double cords are found on some of the St Cuthbert relics – along both edges of the soumak braid, as well as at the sides of the narrow tablet-woven bands used to edge the later embroideries. In the 1956 publication of the relics, these cords are referred to as 'guilloches' (Crowfoot 1956, 447, 457). A further admirable detail on the Llan-gors find is that, where seams join, a little triangle in buttonhole stitch has been added as a reinforcement: two of these triangles are preserved (Figs 8.3, 8.4).

Evidence that the garment was used and worn occurs in the form of small, matted wads of silk formed from the floating ends of silk thread left at the back of the embroidery. Several of these wads were found between the embroidered panels and their lining during conservation. The embroidery is also worn away in places on the surface, particularly around the edges of the panels.

How did the fragments fit together? It is doubtful whether we will ever know the relationship to one another of the completely plain fragments, but it is possible to piece together most of the fragments with embroidery, and it seems that these came from a relatively limited area (Fig. 8.3). Two of the embroidered fragments can be seen to have belonged together on the evidence of the triangular panel, part of which appears in both. Two further substantial fragments of embroidery must have joined on below these first two, judging by the lay-out of their embroidery. The area of plain linen attached to these last two appears to have continued on into another fragment with plain linen, which itself has part of a panel of embroidery along the opposite side. If this piece joined up, as it seems to have done, with the embroidery above the triangle, the original construction must have been tubular or, more accurately, funnel-shaped or sleeve-like.

New problems arise, however, with the tentative identification of a sleeve. The triangular panel can be described as a gore. Such gores are often found under the sleeves of garments, at the armpit. But why would the embroidery be concentrated underneath the sleeve? If, however, the gore ran downwards from the top of the shoulder, the embroidery would be orientated with the little lions upside down, which is surely also incorrect.

Shirts and chemises made with gores represent a type of clothing construction that had originated in Central Asia, but which had reached the Eastern Mediterranean by *c.* 600 (Pfister 1951, fig. 3). It had probably spread into western Europe before *c.* 800. An early example is the so-called 'Dress of the Virgin' acquired by Charlemagne for Aachen Cathedral. It has recently been shown that rather than originating in first-century Palestine, this garment was made from a type of spin-patterned linen which was characteristic of early medieval western Europe (Verhecken-Lammens and De Jonghe 1995/1996, 23). This linen shirt, which has some embroidered whitework decoration as well as gores in the side seams and under the arms, might be considered a precursor of the Llan-gors garment.

By the time the Llan-gors garment was made, in the late ninth or early tenth century, gores may have been used more confidently and creatively in clothing construction. Evidence for this is an extraordinary linen gown preserved at Chelles in northern France. This is the so-called *Grande Robe*, which is recognised as being later in date than the relics of the two saints particularly associated with the abbey, Balthild and Bertila, who died around 680 and 704 respectively (Laporte 1988, 55, 62, 95). As well as gores in the sides of the skirt, the *Grande Robe* has a strange, triangular piece inserted in the middle of the back and half triangles coming down from either side of the neck (Laporte 1988, 93, 94, figs 18, 19). While this gown is not a direct parallel for the Llangors garment, it is a reminder that clothing construction towards the end of the first millennium was relatively fluid and that the Llan-gors garment may turn out to have been made in a way that has not before been reported.

Conclusion

A high status product made from fine linen and imported silk thread, the Llan-gors garment displays exceptional needlework skills combined with a familiarity with exotic silk designs. The embroidery and constructional sewing was carried out in the same place and, on the basis of technique, we know this was somewhere in the British Isles. Whether the garment was made locally in Wales or brought from England, more particularly Wessex, is a question best left until the design has been more completely read. However, there is no doubt that this unique discovery is enormously important for the history of early embroidery. It will also considerably enhance our picture of contemporary Welsh culture and court life.

Acknowledgements

The authors would especially like to thank Mark Redknap, Louise Mumford, Karen Finch, Monique King, Santina Levey and Kay Staniland for their help and advice.

Notes

1   The long and painstaking conservation work, carried out at the National Museums and Galleries of Wales and completed in 1997, was begun by Kate Hunter but has mainly been the work of Louise Mumford. The task of working out the design has been undertaken by Louise Mumford and Mark Redknap.
2   Louise Mumford, 'Observations on the Llan-gors textile', August 1998.

References

BALDWIN, C. R. 1970, 'Sassanian ducks in a Western manuscript', *Gesta* 9/1, 3–10.
BATTISCOMBE, C. F. (ed.) 1956, *The Relics of Saint Cuthbert*. Durham.
BENDER-JØRGENSEN, L. 1992, *North European Textiles until AD 1000*. Aarhus.
BUDNY, M. and TWEDDLE, D. 1984, 'The Maaseik embroideries', *Anglo-Saxon Engl.* 13, 65–96.
BURNHAM, D. K. 1981, *A Textile Terminology: Warp and Weft*. London.
CAMPBELL, E. and LANE, A. 1988, *The Llangorse Crannóg. Investigations in 1987 and 1988: An Interim Statement.* Cardiff.
CAMPBELL, E. and LANE, A. 1989, 'Llangorse: a 10th-century royal crannóg in Wales', *Antiquity* 63, 675–81.
CHRISTIE, A. G. I. 1938, *English Medieval Embroidery*. Oxford.
CROWFOOT, G. M. 1939, 'The tablet-woven braids from the vestments of St. Cuthbert at Durham', *Antiq. J.* 19, 57–80.

CROWFOOT, G. 1956, 'The braids', in Battiscombe, 433–63.

DAVIES, W. 1982, *Wales in the Early Middle Ages*. Leicester.

DODWELL, C. R. 1982, *Anglo-Saxon Art: A New Perspective*. Manchester.

FRANZÉN, A. M. and NOCKERT, M. 1992, *Bonaderna från Skog och Överhogdal och andra medeltida väggbeklädnader*. Stockholm.

GRENANDER-NYBERG, G. 1992, 'Soumak technique in Swedish medieval textiles', in L. Bender-Jørgensen and E. Munksgaard (eds), *Archaeological Textiles in Northern Europe*, 117–27. Copenhagen.

GRANGER-TAYLOR, H. 1989, 'The weft-patterned silks and their braid: the remains of an Anglo-Saxon dalmatic of *c*. 800?', in G. Bonner *et al* (eds), *St Cuthbert: His Cult and Community to AD 1200*, 303–27. Woodbridge.

GRANGER-TAYLOR, H. 1991, 'Fragment of a braid', in L. Webster and J. Backhouse (eds) *The Making of England. Anglo-Saxon Art and Culture AD 600–900*, 183–84. London.

LAPORTE, J.- P. 1988, *Le Trésor des Saints de Chelles*. Chelles.

LAPORTE, J.- P. and BOYER, R. 1991, *Trésors de Chelles: sépultures et reliques de la Reine Bathilde et de l'Abbesse Bertille*. Chelles.

LEVEY, S. M. 1998, *An Elizabethan Inheritance: The Hardwick Hall Textiles*. London.

MUMFORD, L. and REDKNAP, M. 1998/99, ' Worn by a Welsh Queen?', *Amgueddfa* 2 (= National Museums and Galleries of Wales Yearbook 1998/99), 52–4.

MUSÉES ROYAUX D'ART ET D'HISTOIRE 1972, *Rhin-Meuse: Art et Civilisation 800–1400*. Brussels.

MUTHESIUS, A. 1997, *Byzantine Silk Weaving AD 400 to AD 1200*. Vienna.

OTAVSKY, K. 1998, 'Stoffe von der Seidenstrasse: eine neue Sammlungsgruppe in der Abegg-Stiftung', *Riggisberger Berichte* 6, 13–41.

PFISTER, R. 1951, *Textiles de Halabiyeh*. Paris.

PLENDERLEITH, E. 1956, 'The stole and maniples: the technique', in Battiscombe, 375–96.

PRITCHARD, F. A. 1984, 'Late Saxon textiles from the City of London', *Medieval Archaeol*. 28, 46–76.

REDKNAP, M. 1991, *The Christian Celts. Treasures of Late Celtic Wales*. Cardiff.

REDKNAP, M. 1995, 'Insular non-ferrous metalwork from Wales of the 8th to 10th centuries', in C. Bourke (ed.), *From the Isles of the North. Early Medieval Art in Ireland and Britain*, 59–73. Belfast.

REDKNAP, M. and LANE, A. 1994, 'The early medieval crannóg at Llangorse, Powys: an interim statement of the 1989–1993 seasons', *Int. J. Naut. Archaeol*. 23, 189–205.

SHEPHERD, D. G. 1981, 'Zandaniji Revisited', in M. Flury-Lemberg and K. Stolleis (eds), *Documenta Textilia: Festschrift für Sigrid Müller-Christensen*, 105–22. Munich.

SVARSTAD FLØ, T. 1997, 'Høylandsteppet – en rekonstruksjon av midt-norsk middelalderteppe', *Spor* 12/2, 16–19.

VERHECKEN-LAMMENS, C. and DE JONGHE, D. 1995/1996, 'Technical report', in M. Paredis-Vroon, C. Verhecken-Lammens and D. De Jonghe, 'The major relics of Aachen cathedral', *Bulletin de Liaison du Centre International d'Étude des Textiles Anciens* 73, 14–26.

WATT, J. C. Y. and WARDWELL, A. E. 1997, *When Silk was Gold: Central Asian and Chinese Textiles*. New York.

WEBSTER, L. 1991, 'Metalwork, ivory and textiles', in L. Webster and J. Backhouse (eds), *The Making of England. Anglo-Saxon Art and Culture AD 600–900*, 131–43. London.

WHITELOCK, D. (trans.) 1961, *The Anglo-Saxon Chronicle. A Revised Translation*. London.

WILSON, D. M. 1985, *The Bayeux Tapestry*. London.

ZHAO, F. 1999, *Treasures in Silk: An Illustrated History of Chinese Textiles*. Hong Kong.

9 Glass Bangles as a Regional Development in Early Medieval Ireland

Judith Carroll

Introduction

Irish glass bangles of the early medieval period form a distinct group. There are 55 known. Of these, 52 have been found in Ireland, two on the west coast of Scotland, at Fraoch Eilean in Argyll and at Dumbarton in Strathclyde, and one in England, at Whitby on the Yorkshire coast. The main characteristics of this group are the wide, D-shaped cross-section, and dark blue, opaque glass body with white cable and dot decoration inlaid into and fused level with the surface of the bangle.

In Ireland, bangles predating this group are few and diverse, and appear to be sporadic imports from Britain and the Continent. The early medieval bangles appear not to have developed from an earlier Irish type. It may be suggested that they represent revival, rather than continuity, of a first/second-century AD Romano-British type. This revival, as part of the revival of Insular ornamental glassworking, is likely to have taken place through the Insular monastic interconnection. The initial development of the group and the main period of its manufacture occurred between the late seventh and ninth centuries. The group is a feature of the high status sites of the Brega area of Co. Meath, and is likely to have been developed under the aegis of the Brega kings.

Description and function

All 55 bangles in this group have D-shaped cross-sections on average measuring 8–12mm across the flat inner surface of the bangle and 4–6mm from the flat inner surface to the rounded outer surface. The bangles are either blue or green in colour, with white cable and dot decoration. The predominant colour of the glass is a deep, opaque to translucent purplish blue (Plate VII). In nineteen cases, the bangle has a different coloured 'core'. The core is generally of translucent, light blue glass, though in two examples it is of translucent, green glass.

The white cable and dot decoration is set in lines longitudinally along the rounded outer surface. It is level with the surface or placed just under the surface. The classic arrangement of decoration is two lines of dots alternating with three lines of cable. There are 16 examples of this typical arrangement. In addition to these, there are 11 examples in which an extra line of dots is either superimposed on the central cable line or arranged around it in groups of four. In one isolated case, there are three lines of dots but only one line of cable. In two cases, a double line of cable in a herringbone pattern forms the centre line of decoration.

Measurement of 42 bangles was possible and the average internal diameter was 58.5mm; this is very narrow for even a small adult hand to pass through and suggests that most of the bangles, if worn on the arm, were worn close to the wrist. Almost a quarter, however, were under 55mm in diameter – too small for an adult hand. Of these, half were under 50mm. It seems unlikely that such fragile bangles were made for children. A similar problem of size can be observed in the diameter of Romano-British bangles of the first and second centuries AD, though these appear to have been slightly smaller. In this group, the normal range of internal diameter is 40mm to 60mm while the average diameter is 50–55mm (Stevenson 1976, 50). However, many Romano-British bangle fragments have been cut and scored to be inserted into metal bracelet fittings (Kilbride-Jones 1937–38, 370). There is no evidence of this amongst the early medieval Irish bangles. Kilbride-Jones, discussing the function of Romano-British bangles (*ibid.*, 380) suggests that they may have been hung from torcs in the same manner as earlier

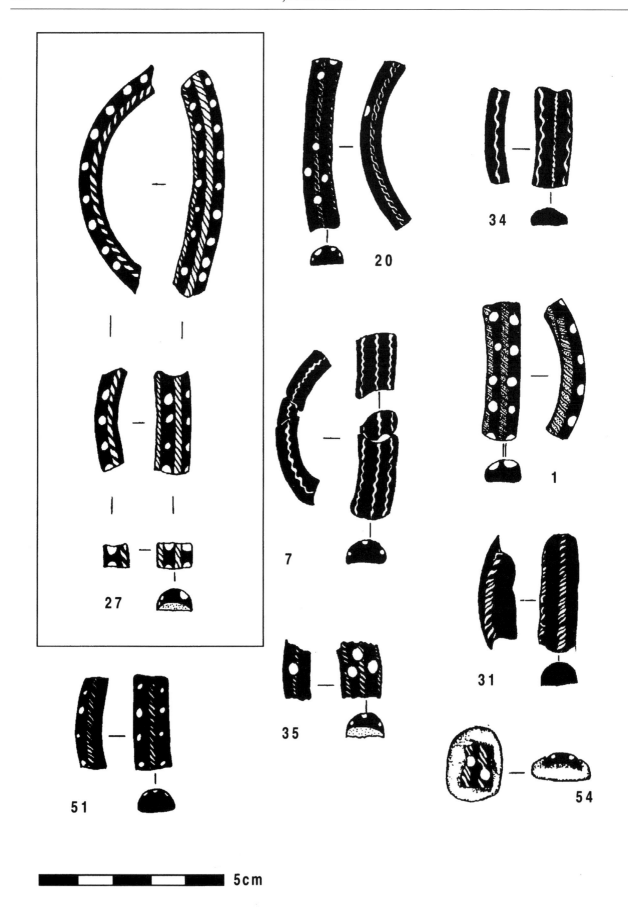

Fig. 9.1 *Glass bangles of early medieval date from Ireland and Scotland (See Appendix 1)*

examples, also of varying diameter, found in La Tène burial contexts on the Continent. The La Tène glass bangles were often found strung from torcs, in groups of three. They also appear to have been worn on the arm in the graves of women (Dechelette 1927, 830, fig. 578). It is therefore not impossible that the tradition of wearing both glass armlets and pendants continued into the early medieval period in Ireland. Stevenson, however, pointed out that if the Romano-British bangles were used as pendants rather than armlets, their outer surface, with its distinctive cable decoration, would be turned from view, leaving only the rough side visible (Stevenson 1976, 50). This argument, too, would apply to the Irish bangles. If the latter were used as pendants, they would look very rough from the side. Their light blue 'cores' would be untidily visible and their cable decoration layout would be unclear. The alternative suggestion that the bangles may have been used as hair rings is plausible, as a ponytail of hair could be pulled through the narrow ring, leaving the decoration clearly visible. However, there is no evidence for this use from any context, and whether or not they ever had another function remains unknown.

Technology

Theophilus, writing in the eleventh century, described the process of making a glass ring (Theophilus 1979, 74). He described how a rod of wood with an iron fitting should be prepared and how the molten glass should be allowed to drop onto a turning iron rod. In doing so, it forms a ring built up of layers of glass. The glass, when cool, distorts slightly as it contracts and can be gently shaken off the rod. Some experimentation has been carried out by the writer and it seems that a glass ring would achieve the same D-shaped cross-section if formed around any durable material, including baked or hardened clay. This is suggested by the rough and slightly porous undersides of most of the bangles.

Thin rods of glass with strands of another colour twisted round them, cable-fashion, have been found in early medieval monastic contexts at Iona (RCAMHS 1982, 15, fig. 14:1), Armagh (Lynn 1988, 82) and Movilla (Ivens 1984, 99). These were almost certainly used for the manufacture of beads and bangles, or for the embellishment of metalwork. They illustrate how cables were made by a strand of glass which was softened, drawn out by heat, and twisted around another thin rod of glass. For the glass bangles, white glass was twisted around a blue or clear glass rod, to make the cables which were to be incorporated in the glass ring.

Examination of the bangles shows how rods of clear glass wound with white double-twisted cable were incorporated in the glass ring. This was achieved in such a way as to give the illusion of a white interlace set into the blue glass body. The technique was quite simple and probably inspired by millefiori and the other types of intricate inlaid glasswork being manufactured on Irish sites at the same time.

The method of inlaying the decoration would seem to be as follows: the thin, clear or blue glass rod, wound with white cable, would be placed around the core of the glass ring while it was in a semi-molten state with the aid of an implement such as tweezers. The heat of the core glass ring would cause the thin, cable-decorated rod to soften as it was being applied to it. Two decorated cable rods would then be set to either side of it, resulting in a thin glass ring with three relief cables. The next step (in order to give the illusion of sunken cables) would be to drop dark blue, molten glass into the spaces between the cables as the glass ring was turning on the rod. The clear glass rod bearing the double-twisted white interlace would merge with the colorants of the dark blue glass to either side of it. This would leave the double-twisted white cable visible and the clear glass invisible. For a 'single-twisted inlaid cable' effect, a blue rod bearing the white cable, rather than a clear rod would probably have been used.

Classification and distribution

Of the 55 bangles (see Appendix 1), 53 can be divided into two classes; two are unclassified.

- *Class 1* comprises 19 bangles with an inner core of a different coloured glass, either translucent light blue or green, which forms approximately a third of the bangle. All these bangles have regularly twisted cable decoration.

- *Class 2* comprises 34 bangles without any visible inner core. These bangles often do not have cable decoration and are ornamented with dots alone or are plain. They tend to be more roughly made and this suggests degeneracy.

All but one of the 55 bangles are provenanced. Apart from three examples, two from Scotland and one from England, all the bangles are found in Ireland, where the distribution is concentrated in the north and east of the country (Fig. 9.6a, b). There is a particular concentration in the east midlands: over half the total number known are found in Co. Meath. There are a small number of outliers in the west and south, often in quite remote areas. Some 15 of the 19 Class 1 bangles are found in Co. Meath. Three of the remaining four are found in Offaly and Co. Dublin. One outlier is found in the west coast of Scotland

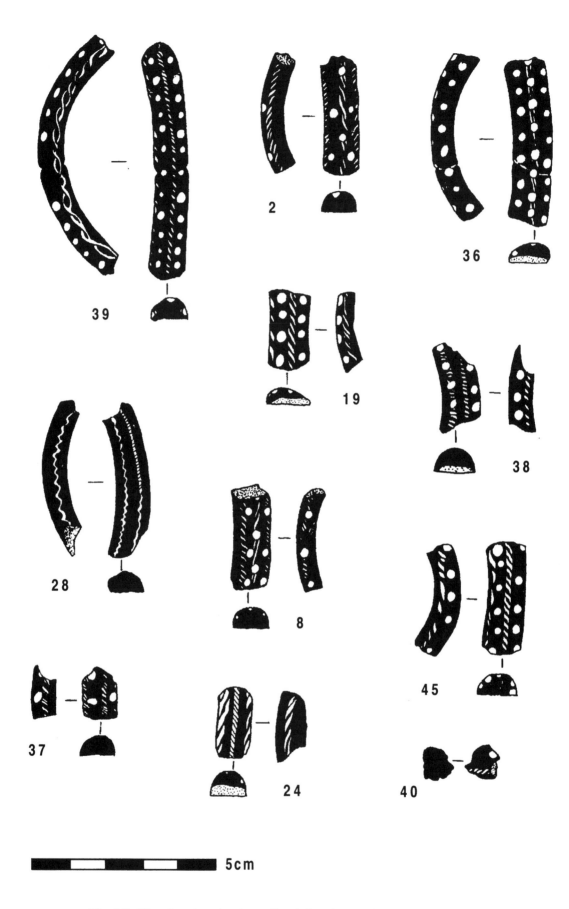

Fig. 9.2 *Glass bangles of early medieval date from Ireland (See Appendix 1)*

(Fig. 9.6a). In contrast, only 11 out of 34 Class 2 bangles are found in Co. Meath. All bangles found in the north and west of the country, and in the most outlying regions, are of this type (Fig. 9.6b).

Context and chronology

Out of the 54 provenanced glass bangles, 50 were found during the course of archaeological excavation or were stray finds from archaeological sites. There are 23 sites producing glass bangles and the dating evidence varies greatly in its type and reliability from site to site. The contexts yielding better evidence of date are discussed briefly below. Other contexts do not in any way suggest differing evidence to that given below. The radiocarbon and dendrochronological dates given below are quoted as given to the writer by the excavators of the sites where they were found.

Oughtymore, Co. Derry

The bangle (no. 8) was found stratified with Souterrain ware, and other less diagnostic material in a charcoal spread at the midden site of Oughtymore, Co. Derry. A calibrated radiocarbon date of cal AD 665–780 (at one standard deviation; UB 2442) and cal AD 630–880 (at two standard deviations) was obtained from the charcoal spread in which the bangle was found (Mallory and Woodman 1984, 51–62).

Knocksoghy, Larrybane promontory fort, Co. Antrim

The Larrybane bangle (no. 2) was associated with Souterrain ware which was stratified above and below the level in which the bangle was found (Childe 1936).

Moynagh Lough crannóg, Co. Meath

A dendrochronological date of 748 to 780 provides a beginning for Phase Y, which lasted until *c*. 780. This phase included deposits associated with the central house (Bradley 1991; pers. comm.). One stratified bangle (no. 41) was associated with these deposits.

Clonmacnoise, Co. Offaly

One of the three bangles (nos 46, 47, 48) from the site was stratified in a context yielding evidence of date. It was found during the excavation of F451 which is contemporary with F485. F485 produced a single charcoal sample which produced the uncalibrated radiocarbon date of AD 695±45 (GrN02753; 1255±45 BP; pers. comm. Heather King).

Christchurch Place, Dublin City

The bangle (no. 15) came from layer F335, which overlay the earliest post-and-wattle fence on the site. Wattle from this fence yielded a calibrated radio-

carbon determination of cal AD 872–1022 (2 sigma, 95% probability; GrN20246). However F335 lies *beneath* another fence, F674. Wattle from F674 gave an earlier radiocarbon date of cal AD 790–972 (2 sigma, 95% probability; GrN20247). This suggests an eighth- to tenth-century date for the context of the bangle (pers. comm. Claire Walsh).

Gortree, Langford Lodge, Co. Antrim

The bangle (no. 1) was found in the layer directly above a cobbled surface (Layer 3) and sealed by a clay layer (Layer 2). Souterrain ware and imported E ware were also found in Layer 3 (Waterman 1963, 52).

Garryduff 1, Co. Cork

The bangle (no. 7) was found just below the topsoil, in Phase 2 of the occupation. A large quantity of E ware came from both phases of occupation at the site (O'Kelly 1962, 74).

Lagore crannóg, Co. Meath

Out of 18 glass bangles found at Lagore (nos 23–40; Colour Plate 7), only two were stratified. One of these was found in Period 1a, the earliest phase of occupation on the crannóg. The other bangle was found in Period 2 (Hencken 1950, 145–57) above layers containing E ware. The bangles are both of Class 1; their close similarity suggests they are likely to be around the same date.

Assessment of the dating evidence

The radiocarbon dates suggest that the bangles date between the seventh and tenth centuries. The dendrochronological date for the beginning of the phase associated with the one stratified bangle from Moynagh Lough, Co. Meath, would suggest a mid- to late eighth-century date. Both Souterrain ware and E ware have been found associated with bangles. Souterrain ware is likely to be seventh- to eighth-century or later, though its earliest date is unknown (Ryan 1973). E ware is most likely to be late sixth- or seventh-century in date in Ireland (Thomas 1990) but may extend into the early eighth century (Campbell 1991; Warner 1985–86, 76). The date range recently attributed to E ware by Campbell is between the later sixth and the late seventh centuries (Campbell 1996, 92) From the above it is likely that the initial development of the bangles took place between the seventh and the ninth centuries, and probably in the late seventh or first decades of the eighth century.

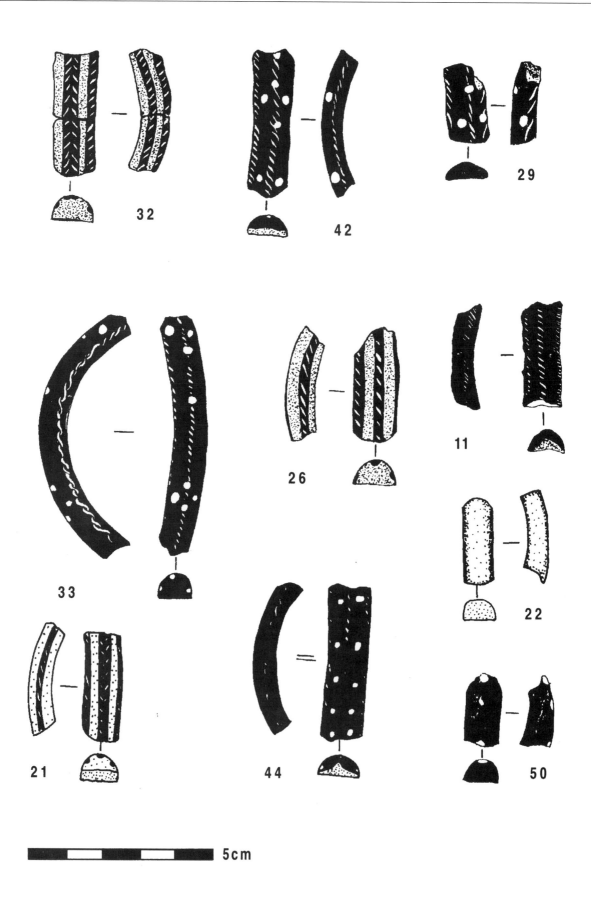

Fig. 9.3 *Glass bangles of early medieval date from Ireland (See Appendix 1)*

Discussion

The historical context

Twenty-six out of the group of 55 bangles were found at three sites in the area of the early medieval kingdom of Brega in Co. Meath: eighteen were found at Lagore crannóg, four at Knowth and four at Moynagh Lough crannóg.

The kingdom of Brega was one of the three territories of the Southern Uí Néill. It consisted of most of Co. Meath, part of north Co. Dublin and Co. Louth. The rulers of Brega were the Síl nÁeda Sláine branch of the Southern Uí Néill whose main period of dominance as a tribal group was from the seventh to the tenth centuries (Byrne 1968, 397). In Brega, the ruling family was divided into two groups. The northern branch of this family had their habitation site at Knowth from at least the beginning of the ninth century (Byrne 1967–68, 397). The southern branch had their main centre at Lagore crannóg, certainly from the eighth century (Price 1950, 26), though possibly from the seventh century or earlier (Price 1950, 32). Moynagh Lough crannóg has also been identified as a royal site associated with the Mugdorna (Bhreathnach 1998).

Class 1 bangles containing the core of lighter coloured glass are concentrated in Brega (15 out of 19). The core feature which is analogous with the earlier Romano-British bangle type (see below), is therefore likely to be a sign of their initial development. Outside Brega, the other examples of this type were found in Dublin, Clonmacnoise and Loch Awe, western Scotland. The concentration of the distribution also suggests that Brega was one of the areas for the initial production of the bangle type. The greatest variety of colour and cable decoration is found in the Brega region. The level of variety and technical skill contrasts greatly with bangles found outside this region. These factors suggest that patronage at the royal sites of Lagore, Knowth and Moynagh Lough was an important factor in the development of glass bangles as an Irish artefact type.

This development could have taken place through the political connection which historically existed between the Columban foundations and the royal Uí Néill family in Ireland (Herbert 1988, 90). Many of the monastic establishments founded by the successors of St Columba in Ireland were patronised by the Uí Néill. The monastic centre of Clonmacnoise, where bangles have been found, is known to have been patronised by the Uí Néill at the high point of their power (Herbert 1988, 54). Kells, Co. Meath also appears to have been a key political centre of the Southern Uí Néill before it was granted by them to the Columban *familia* from Iona

who founded a monastery there *c.* 807 (Herbert 1988, 68–9). It is very possible, therefore, that this connection between the secular and ecclesiastical worlds resulted in the development of the Irish early medieval glass bangle on Irish high status sites.

A reason for the development of luxury glass items on high status secular sites in Ireland may have been connected with the importance of gift-giving and reciprocity in the relationship between the over-king and his subject kings and clients. Doherty has illustrated the social implications of producing luxury goods as distinct from agricultural goods (Doherty 1980, 73–4) and how the distribution of luxury goods is likely to have been the prerogative of the over-king and a sign of his superiority. The eleventh/twelfth-century *Lebor na Cert* and the ninth/tenth-century *Frithfolad rig Caisil fria thuatha* 'The Counter Obligations of the King of Cashel and his Subject Tribes' appear to reflect this system. The lists of gifts given to subject kings by the over-king and vice versa depict the type of economy, society and aspirations which existed in early medieval Ireland. A need to produce luxury objects may therefore have resulted in the production of the glass bangles and the huge number and variety of colourful glass beads which we find on Irish high status sites of between the seventh and the tenth centuries. It is therefore not surprising to find strong evidence for the development and production of a luxury artefact type on the royal sites of the Southern Uí Néill, whose powerful occupants would have been vying for the high kingship at this time.

Romano-British glass bangles in Britain

Though glass bangles of the Iron Age and the earliest part of the medieval period are very few in number in Ireland, they were a distinctive and widely produced commodity during the first and second centuries AD in Britain, where they are found both on Roman and native sites well before the end of the Roman period (Price in Hayfield 1986; Price and Wilson 1988). Hundreds of bangles of the Roman period have been found and these are mainly concentrated in northern and eastern England and Scotland. These have been divided into three types by Kilbride-Jones (1937–38) and further studied by Stevenson (1954–56; 1976) and Price (1988, 353). It is Stevenson's *Type 2* which closely resembles the Irish bangles. This type was made either of translucent blue-green glass, or of dark blue opaque glass covering a core of blue-green translucent glass. The bangle is typically decorated with three lines of relief cables of blue and white glass placed longitudinally around the outer surface. The bangle is roughly D-shaped in cross-section, measuring on average around 12–13mm along the flatter inner side of the

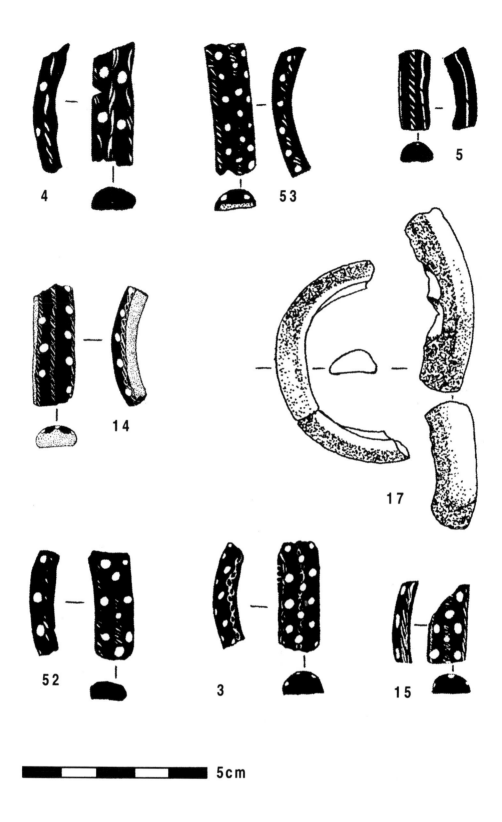

Fig. 9.4 *Glass bangles of early medieval date from Ireland and Scotland (See Appendix 1)*

D section by 8–9mm. The bangles of Roman Britain are concentrated in date in the first and second centuries AD and there is no continuity of the tradition into the post-Roman period. There may therefore be a 500–year gap between the Roman bangles and the early medieval Irish examples which closely resemble them.

Early medieval glass bangles in Britain

Very few glass bangles dating to the early medieval period have been found in Britain in stark contrast to the hundreds dating to the Roman period. As has been shown, two Irish early medieval glass bangles have been found on the west coast of Scotland[1] and one in Yorkshire (Peers and Radford 1943). Besides the Irish examples, a very small number of glass bangles have been found in Anglo-Saxon graves and monastic sites in England. The first group has been found in graves of the fifth and sixth centuries in Kent and the Isle of Wight. These are generally of flat section with moulded relief decoration on the outer surface (Tester 1968, 130–31; Arnold 1982, 57; Brown 1915, 458; Cook 1960, 81–2) and are in a different tradition from the Romano-British bangles. They do not resemble the Irish ones. These Anglo-Saxon glass bangles are not later than the early to mid-fifth century and probably originated in the Meuse Valley.

The second group of glass bangles which are comparable with the Irish group were found during the excavation of medieval monastic sites in north-east England. A dark blue bangle with a raised moulded cable rib was found during excavations at Jarrow, Tyne and Wear (Cramp 1961–2, 67). A similar dark blue bangle with a moulded ridge placed longitudinally along the centre of its upper surface was found at Monkwearmouth, Teeside (in a disturbed Saxon cemetery context; pers. comm. Rosemary Cramp). At both sites, there is other evidence of revived ornamental glassworking such as millefiori during their early medieval monastic occupation. During the excavation of the monastic site of Whitby, Yorkshire, a D-section bangle of opaque blue glass (no. 55) was found (Peers and Radford 1943, fig. 22). There is no description of its context or associated finds. The bangle, though undecorated, also fits into the group of Irish early medieval glass bangles. In the same levels at Whitby was a glass mount of fused blue and white twisted cables (Peers and Radford 1948, fig. 22). This mount is unique in Britain and demonstrates that experimentation with sunken cable decoration was taking place in this region.

There are, in addition, a few finds of Roman bangles from monastic sites at Whithorn (pers. comm. Peter Hill) and Mochrum, Barhobble, Dumfries and Galloway (pers. comm. William Cormack) and The Hirsel, Coldstream, Borders (pers. comm. Rosemary Cramp). Though these finds are considered to be Roman in date, their presence on monastic sites of the medieval period is of interest. It indicates that Roman bangles, plentiful as stray finds in the present day, could have been found in the medieval period in the vicinity of ornamental glassworking centres in the monasteries of the north.

Conclusions

Fragments of Romano-British glass bangles of a type which was manufactured in hundreds, were concentrated in distribution in north-east England and may have inspired a revival of the cabled bangles. From excavations in Northumbria, it appears that there was a revival of glass-working, as well as general experimentation in ornamental glass-working in Northumbrian monasteries of the seventh to ninth centuries. The revived idea of blue and white, cabled glass bangles, first experimented with in monastic houses in Northumbria, could have been transmitted to Ireland via monastic connections. The interconnected Columban monasteries in both Britain and Ireland are known to have been closely linked with royal sites. There was close contact in art, craftsmanship and learning from the mid-seventh century between the religious and the secular high status sites in Ireland, Dalriada and north-east England. These artefacts may have resulted in experimentation with the production of glass bangles and beads on Irish early medieval high status sites. It is of considerable interest that Class 1 bangles, the earliest of the two types, have been predominantly found in the Brega area of Co. Meath, suggesting that the glass bangle was developed here. In addition, the greatest variety of bangles with the greatest expertise in the rendering of the cable decoration, has been found here. Nearly half the total number of Irish early medieval bangles have been found in Brega and, of these, almost all are found on the royal sites of the Southern Uí Néill at Lagore and Knowth. Here, they appear to correspond with the historical date of the apex of power, the seventh to the tenth centuries, of this important tribal group, the Uí Néill, whose members were contenders for the high-kingship. This artefact type may reflect a need to produce luxury goods by a particular section of Irish early medieval society.

Acknowledgements

This paper is drawn from a study of the Irish early medieval glass bangles carried out as part of an M.A.

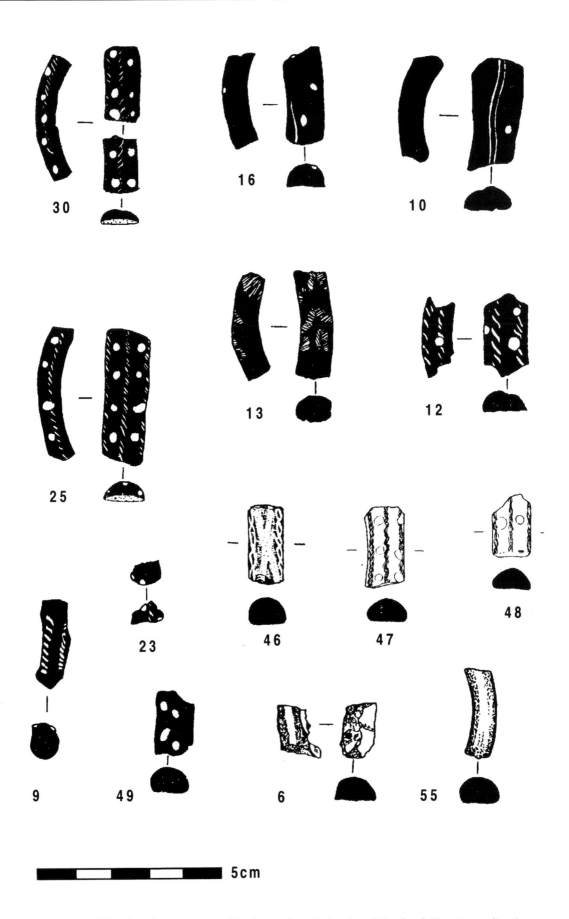

Fig. 9.5 *Glass bangles of early medieval date from Ireland and England (See Appendix 1)*

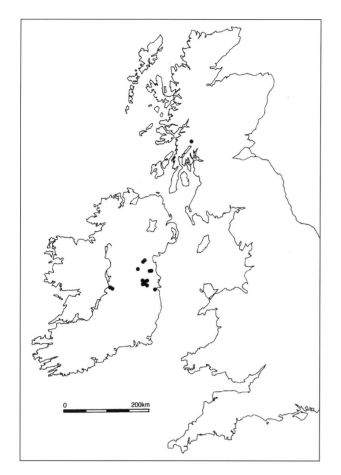

Fig. 9.6a *Distribution of Class 1 early medieval Irish glass bangles in Ireland and Britain*

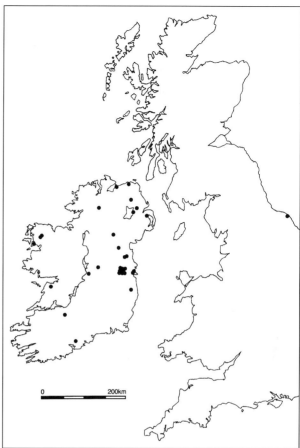

Fig. 9.6b *Distribution of Class 2 early medieval Irish glass bangles in Ireland and Britain*

thesis in University College Dublin in 1983. I would like to convey my thanks to those in the Department of Archaeology, University College Dublin, particularly Professor George Eogan, former head of department, and Dr Rhoda Kavanagh who supervised this study.

My thanks are due to the following institutions who made available the material in their care for examination and recording: The National Museum of Ireland; The Ulster Museum; The National Museum of Antiquities of Scotland; The Hunterian Museum, University of Glasgow; The British Museum; University College Cork; University College Dublin; Historic Monuments Section, Department of the Environment, Northern Ireland; National Monuments Service, Office of Public Works, Dublin/Dúchas. I am grateful to the following individuals for information on material in their care or for information on the findplaces of material treated in this paper: Professor Rosemary Cramp; Mr Peter Hill, Whithorn Trust; Mr William Cormack; Ms Heather King; Professor Peter Woodman; Mr John Bradley; Ms Claire Walsh; Mrs Susan Youngs; I am grateful to the National College of Art and Design, Dublin, for allowing me access to glassworking facilities and to Ms Elizabeth McClure, formerly of the National College of Art and Design. I also thank the following: Ms Patricia Johnson, Office of Public Works (Dúchas) for the drawings of the Clonmacnoise bangles; Ms Lisa Reardon, Department of Medieval and Later Antiquities (now Department of Medieval and Modern Europe), British Museum for the drawing of the Kells bangle; Ms Lucy Carroll for assisting me in the preparation of the other drawings of glass bangles.

Notes

1 Fraoch Eileann, Argyll (NMAS Fj156); Dumbarton Rock, Strathclyde (Hunterian Art Gallery, Glasgow 1982:52)

References

ARNOLD, C. J. 1982, *The Anglo-Saxon Cemeteries of the Isle of Wight*. London.

BHREATHNACH, E. 1998, 'Topographical note: Moynagh Lough, Nobber, Co. Meath', *Ríocht na Mídhe* 9 (4), 16–19.

BROWN, G. BALDWIN 1915, *The Arts in Early England. Saxon Art and Industry in the Pagan Period.* London.

BRADLEY, J. 1991, 'Excavations at Moynagh Lough, Co. Meath', *J. Roy. Soc. Antiq. Ir.* 121, 5–26.

BYRNE, F. J. 1967–8, 'Historical note on Cnoba (Knowth)', in G. Eogan, 'Excavations at Knowth, Co. Meath, 1962–5', *Proc. Roy. Ir. Acad.* 66C, 383–400.

CAMPBELL, E. 1991, Imported Goods in the Early Medieval Celtic West: with special reference to Dinas Powys. Unpublished PhD thesis, University of Wales Cardiff.

CAMPBELL, E. 1996, 'The archaeological evidence for external contacts: imports, trade and economy in Celtic Britain AD. 400–800', in K. R. Dark (ed.), *External Contacts and the Economy of Late Roman and Post-Roman Britain*, 83–96. Woodbridge.

CHILDE, V. G. 1936, 'A promontory fort on the Ulster coast', *Antiq. J.* 16, 179–90.

COOK, J. M. 1960, 'Two glass bangles from Milton Regis', *Archaeol. Cantiana* 74, 181–82.

CRAMP, R. 1961–2, 'Jarrow', in 'Medieval Britain in 1961', *Medieval Archaeol.* 6–7, 315.

DECHELETTE, J. 1927, *Manuel d'Archaeologie Prehistoric, Celtique et Gallo-Romaine.* Paris.

DOHERTY, C. 1980, 'Exchange and trade in early medieval Ireland', *J. Roy. Soc. Antiq. Ir.* 110, 67–90.

HAYFIELD, C. 1986, 'Wharram Grange Roman Villa 1975–82', in P. Rahtz *et al.*, unpaginated.

HENCKEN, H. O'NEILL 1950, 'Lagore crannog: an Irish royal residence of the 7th to the 10th century AD', *Proc. Roy. Ir. Acad.* 53C, 1–247.

HERBERT, M. 1988, *Iona, Kells and Derry – the History and Hagiography of the Monastic Familia of Columba.* Oxford.

IVENS, R. 1984, 'Movilla Abbey, Newtownards, Co. Down: excavations 1981', *Ulster J. Archaeol.* 47, 71–108.

KILBRIDE-JONES, H. E. 1937–38, 'Glass armlets in Britain', *Proc. Soc. Antiq. Scotl.* 72, 366–95.

LYNN, C. J. 1988, 'Excavations at 46–48, Scotch Street, Armagh, 1979–80', *Ulster J. Archaeol.* 51, 69–84.

MALLORY, J. P. and WOODMAN, P. 1984, 'Oughtymore: an early Christian shell midden', *Ulster J. Archaeol.* 47, 51–62

O'KELLY, M. J. 1962, 'Two ringforts at Garryduff, Co. Cork', *Proc. Roy. Ir. Acad.* 63C, 17–125

PEERS, C. and RADFORD, R. 1943, 'The Saxon monastery of Whitby', *Archaeologia* 89, 27–88.

PRICE, J. 1986, 'Roman glass (including a note on the production of Type 2 glass bangles)', in C. Hayfield, 'Wharram Grange Roman villa 1975–82', in P. Rahtz *et al.*, unpaginated, section 12.18.

PRICE, J. 1988, 'Romano-British glass bangles from east Yorkshire', in J. Price and P. R. Wilson (eds), *Recent Research in Roman Yorkshire* (= BAR. Brit. Ser. 193), 339–66. Oxford.

PRICE, L. 1950, 'The history of Lagore from the annals and other sources', in Hencken, 18–34.

RAHTZ, P., HAYFIELD, C. and BATEMAN, J. 1986, *Two Roman villas at Wharram le Street* (=York University Archaeological Publications 2).

RCAHMS 1982, Royal Commission on the Ancient and Historical Monuments of Scotland, *Argyll, An Inventory of the Monuments*, Vol. 4, *Iona*. Edinburgh.

RYAN, M. 1973, 'Native pottery in early historic Ireland', *Proc. Roy. Ir. Acad.* 73C, 619–33.

STEVENSON, R. B. K. 1954–56, 'Native bangles and Roman glass', *Proc. Soc. Antiq. Scotl.* 88, 8–21.

STEVENSON, R. B. K. 1976, 'Native bangles and Roman glass', *Glasgow Archaeol. J.* 4, 45–54.

TESTER, P. J. 1968, 'An Anglo-Saxon cemetery at Orpington', *Archaeol. Cantiana* 83, 125–50.

THEOPHILUS 1963, *On Divers Arts* (trans. J. G. Hawthorne and C. S. Smith, reprinted 1979). New York.

THOMAS, C. 1990, '*Gallici Nautae de Galliarum provinciis* – a sixth-seventh century trade with Gaul', *Medieval Archaeol.* 34, 1–26

WARNER, R. B. 1985–86, 'The date of the start of Lagore', *J. Ir. Archaeol.* 3, 75–7.

WATERMAN, D. M. 1963, 'A Neolithic and Dark Age site at Langford Lodge, Co. Antrim', *Ulster J. Archaeol.* 26, 43–54.

Appendix 1

Summary list of glass bangle decoration

Ireland

1   GORTREE (Langford Lodge rath), Co. Antrim (Fig. 9.1)
    Three light blue strips bearing cable of regular twist which are level with the dark blue opaque glass body of the bangle. These light blue strips bearing cable alternate with two parallel lines of dots.

2   KNOCKSOGHY (Larrybane), Co. Antrim (Fig. 9.2)
    Three lines of cable of loose diagonal twist and three lines of dots which are placed to the left and right of, and upon, the central cable line.

3   MOYLARG (crannóg), Co. Antrim (Fig. 9.4)
    Three lines of cables and three lines of dots. The lines of dots are placed to either side of the central cable line and upon it. The cables, formed by two strands, are twisted in opposite directions to form an interlace.

4   SEACASH (ringfort), Co. Antrim (Fig. 9.4)
    Three lines of cable of rough diagonal twist alternating with two lines of large and widely spaced dots.

5   TULLYCOMMON (Cahercommaun), Co. Clare (Fig. 9.4)
    Three lines of cable. The central line is regularly twisted but the two side lines are barely twisted at all.

6   TULLYCOMMON (Cahercommaun), Co. Clare (Fig. 9.5)
    No decoration.

7   GARRYDUFF (Garryduff 1), Co. Cork (Fig. 9.1)
    Translucent dark blue glass with cable formed by the twisting of a single strand. The cable is set immediately below the surface of the bangle covered

by a thin film of glass so that the decoration appears light blue. Slightly warped ring.

8   OUGHTYMORE, Co. Derry (Fig. 9.2)
Three lines of cable, the central line of which is diagonally twisted, and three lines of dots. The central line of dots is imposed on the central cable line.

9   BALLYKILBEG (Lough Faughan crannóg), Co. Down (Fig. 9.5)
Translucent dark blue, very badly heat damaged with a roughly circular section. Only two lines of cable, one of which is above the surface of the bangle. This, however, looks like distortion during manufacture. Found during the excavation of the crannóg.

10   SCRABO (Scrabo Hill), Co. Down (Fig. 9.5)
Opaque grey blue with a green tinge. One dot and faint traces of white lines where rough cable decoration had obviously been attempted.

11   CHRISTCHURCH PLACE, (Dublin City), Dublin (Fig. 9.3)
Three lines of closely twisted, single stranded cable decoration. Light blue core.

12   FELTRIM (FELTRIM HILL), Co. Dublin (Fig. 9.5)
Three lines of cable, loosely twisted and alternating with two lines of dots. The line of dots are not placed regularly between the cable lines, but almost imposed on them.

13   FELTRIM (FELTRIM HILL), Co. Dublin (Fig. 9.5)
Heat damaged with a rough oval section. Decorated with short feathery lines of cable at angles to each other and placed at random on the surface. Found during the excavation of the stone fort.

14   KELLS, Co. Meath (Fig. 9.4)
Three lines of cable alternating with two of dots. The cable lines are double twisted, fairly closely, to form an interlace pattern. The two lines of dots are moving onto the two side lines of cable. Light blue core.

15   LOUGH GUR (Carrig Aille 2), Co. Limerick (Fig. 9.4)
Three lines of cable, the central line of which is of a tight and clumsy twist, and three lines of dots of irregular size. The central line of dots is placed on the central cable line.

16   LETTERKEEN, Co. Mayo (Fig. 9.5)
A line of dots, widely spaced, on the surface of the bangle is combined with a faint white line which suggests that cable decoration had been attempted. Found during the excavation of the earthen ringfort.

17   LETTERKEEN, Co. Mayo (Fig. 9.4)
No decoration.

18   MALLARANNY, Co. Mayo (not illustrated)
Dots are placed at random on the surface. Found at the midden site at Mallaranny.

19   KNOWTH, Co. Meath (Fig. 9.2)
Three lines of cable of fairly broad and regular twist, alternating with two lines of dots. Light blue core.

20   KNOWTH, Co. Meath (Fig. 9.1)

Three lines of cable twisted together in opposite directions to form an interlace, very skilfully rendered. The dots are spaced in pairs at long intervals along the central cable line, while another dot is placed to either side of each pair to form a simple cruciform pattern.

21   KNOWTH, Co. Meath 1 (Fig. 9.3)
Bright green opaque glass. Two strips or 'rods' of very dark blue glass are placed in the centre of the bangle. Each strip bears cable twisted in opposite directions so that an herringbone pattern is created when the two strips are placed together. A single dark blue strip bearing cable is also placed to either side of the bangle. Light blue core.

22   KNOWTH, Co. Meath (Fig. 9.3)
Translucent to opaque dark blue glass. No decoration.

23   LAGORE, Co. Meath (Fig. 9.5)
Tiny fragment on which a line of regularly twisted cable and a dot is detectable. Light blue core. -247).

24   LAGORE, Co. Meath (Fig. 9.2)
Three lines of cable, the central line of which is closely and regularly twisted, the side cables being wider and more loosely twisted. Light blue core.

25   LAGORE, Co. Meath (Fig. 9.5)
Three lines of cable, regularly twisted, alternating with two lines of dots. Light blue core. Unstratified in the crannóg where it was found during excavation.

26   LAGORE, Co. Meath (Fig. 9.3; Plate VII)
Opaque light blue-green body, decorated with three dark blue rods bearing cable.

27   LAGORE, Co. Meath (Fig. 9.1)
Formed of three separate broken pieces. Three lines of cabling, regularly twisted alternating with two of dots. Translucent green glass core.

28   LAGORE, Co. Meath (Fig. 9.2)
Translucent dark blue glass. Three lines of cabling formed by the twisting of one strand and varying in type of twist from very tight to very loose.

29   LAGORE, Co. Meath (Fig. 9.3)
Three lines of cabling, regularly twisted, with dots which appear to be arranged around the central cable line in groups of four, cruciform fashion. Light blue core.

30   LAGORE, Co. Meath (Fig. 9.5)
Three lines of cabling, regularly twisted, alternating with two lines of dots. Light blue core.

31   LAGORE, Co. Meath (Fig. 9.1)
Translucent dark blue glass with three lines of cable, each one formed by the twisting of a single strand. Unstratified in the crannóg where it was found during excavation

32   LAGORE, Co. Meath (Fig. 9.3)
Opaque light green glass decorated with four strips or rods of dark blue glass. Two of these strips or

33 LAGORE, Co. Meath (Fig. 9.3)
Three lines of cable, each composed of two strands, twisted in opposite directions to form an interlace. The cable decoration is skilfully rendered. Dots are placed in groups of four around the central cable line in a simple 'cruciform' pattern.

34 LAGORE, Co. Meath (Fig. 9.1; Plate VII)
Translucent dark blue glass. Three lines of cable formed by a single strand and placed directly under the surface. These are covered by a film of dark blue glass and so appear light blue.

35 LAGORE, Co. Meath (Fig. 9.1)
Small fragment. With three lines of cable, regularly twisted, with large dots placed among them. It is difficult to say what pattern the dots formed around the cable.

36 LAGORE, Co. Meath (Fig. 9.2; Plate VII)
Only one line of cable, diagonally twisted, and three lines of dots. The dots are placed to either side of, and upon, the central cable line. Light blue core.

37 LAGORE, Co. Meath (Fig. 9.2)
Small fragment. Three lines of cable alternating with two of dots.

38 LAGORE, Co. Meath (Fig. 9.2)
Three lines of cable alternating with two of dots, one line of which is merged with one of the side cable lines. Light blue core.

39 LAGORE, Co. Meath (Fig. 9.2; Plate VII)
Three lines of cable alternating with two of dots. The cables are formed by two strands twisted in opposite directions so as to form an interlace. The central cable is small and skilfully handled while the two side cables are looser in twist.

40 LAGORE, Co. Meath (Fig. 9.2)
A very small fragment but enough remains of the line of cable to show that it was regularly twisted. To the side of the cable is placed a dot. Light blue core.

41 MOYNAGH (Moynagh Lough), Co. Meath (not illustrated)
Dark blue glass badly heat damaged, though two lines of regularly twisted, double stranded interlace cable are visible.

42 MOYNAGH (Moynagh Lough), Co. Meath (Fig. 9.3)
Three lines of cable of broad and regular twist. Dots are arranged in groups of four around the central cable line, forming a simple cruciform pattern. Light blue core.

43 MOYNAGH (Moynagh Lough), Co. Meath (not illustrated)
Very tiny fragment. Dark blue translucent glass. Two lines of cable are discernible and these are fused immediately below the surface.

44 MOYNAGH (Moynagh Lough), Co. Meath (Fig. 9.3)
Three lines of cable alternating with two lines of dots. Light blue core.

45 DRUMMOND OTRA (Loughnaglack), Co. Monaghan (Fig. 9.2)
Three lines of cable, regularly twisted, alternating with two of dots.

46 CLONMACNOISE, Co. Offaly (Fig. 9.5)
Three lines of interlaced cable decoration. The two side lines are of a standard regular twist but the central line is so large and wide that it almost takes up the whole body of the bangle. Blue/green core of translucent glass.

47 CLONMACNOISE, Co. Offaly (Fig. 9.5)
Three lines of interlaced cable decoration alternating with two lines of dots. The translucent greenish glass rods which the cables are wound around are clearly visible within the body of the bangle. The core is made of the same type of translucent greenish glass.

48 CLONMACNOISE, Co. Offaly (Fig. 9.5)
Three lines of interlaced cable decoration alternating with two lines of dots.

49 BARONSCOURT (Island MacHugh), Co. Tyrone (Fig. 9.5)
Decorated with white dots placed at random on the surface of the bangle.

50 BALLINDERRY (Crannóg no. 1), Co. Westmeath (Fig. 9.3)
A single line of dots spaced at intervals along the centre.

51 LACKAN (ringfort no. 2), Co. Wicklow (Fig. 9.1)
Three lines of cable alternating with two of dots. Neatly twisted cable with regular spacing of dots.

52 UNPROVENANCED (Fig. 9.4)
Three lines of cable alternating with two of dots. These are placed to right and left of, and upon, the central cable line.

Scotland

53 GLENORCHY (Fraoch Eilean), Argyll (Fig. 9.4)
Three lines of cables, regularly twisted, and three lines of dots. These are placed to the right and left of, and upon, the central cable line.

54 DUMBARTON (Dumbarton Rock), Strathclyde (Fig. 9.1)
Set in a lead weight measuring 15mm x 20.5mm. Most probably there are three lines of cable though only two are visible due to the way the fragment is set in the lead. These alternate with two lines of widely spaced dots.

England

55 WHITBY, Yorkshire (Fig. 9.5)
No decoration

Part IV

The Implications of Scientific Analysis
for Insular Art and its Production

10 The Rapid Qualitative Analysis of Groups of Metalwork: Making a Dream Come True

Paul T. Craddock, Jonathan M. Wallis and John F. Merkel

Introduction

It is 30 years since Hanson gave his paper, famously titled 'The curator's dream instrument' to the *Application of Science in Examination of Works of Art Conference*, held at Boston in 1971 (Hanson 1973). The particular dream instrument he had in mind was energy dispersive X-ray fluorescence (hereafter XRF) – its task being the rapid non-destructive analysis of materials, especially metals. One thing XRF could and can still do is rapidly to identify the components of most of the non-ferrous metals used in the past, enabling them to be correctly described. Yet, 30 years on, most copper-based artefacts are published without an identification of the metals. Instead they are routinely described as being of 'copper alloy', an analytical admission of defeat if ever there was one.

This paper considers why more use is not made of XRF for the routine identification of non-ferrous metals, and reports on an experiment carried out to test a procedure for the rapid identification of the metals used in large groups of metalwork.

For most artefacts, for most purposes, one needs to know what they are made of and, by extension, what to call them – that is, a simple identification. The procedures described here are very simple, involving minimal pre-treatment and only a very short exposure to X-rays, and thus it is preferable to describe the results as being identifications rather than as qualitative analyses, and nowhere are figures given.

The practical problems are twofold: analysis is expensive and the analytical facilities are normally remote from the archaeologist/curator. Analysis will always be expensive; the cost of the apparatus and of its housing and servicing, combined with the specialist staff costs, regrettably ensure that. Even if analytical facilities are provided free for a particular project, someone, somewhere is footing the bill. Also, projects undertaken on a grace and favour basis tend to be at the bottom of the list of priorities; one may wait a long time for a 'quick' analysis! Thus, the problem of cost cannot be removed, but can at least be ameliorated by ensuring a rapid throughput and thereby reducing the unit cost considerably.

Common experience shows that no matter how quick an analytical operation, the unpacking and inspection of the material, together with recording the data of registration and other information, take up considerable quantities of time – time that the archaeologist/curator is probably paying for.

Analytical facilities are normally remote from the archaeologist/curator and thus the analyses are conducted in isolation. This can mean that the potential significance of particular identifications is not realised nor followed up at the time of the analysis, but only becomes apparent months later when there is little opportunity to carry out confirmatory or additional analyses.

The obvious solution is to involve the archaeologist/curator in the identification process. This can reduce costs and produce a more interactive and thereby useful programme of identifications. It enables decisions to be made on the spot regarding additional analyses, following up interesting results or carrying out more work on pieces that turn out to be more complex than previously thought.

Alternatively, it might be possible for the archaeologist/curator, after some training, to undertake the XRF identifications unaided. However, having only one operator would considerably slow down the work, and as discussed below, there are many pitfalls in the interpretation of the data. It really is essential to have someone who is experienced in the scientific examination of antiquities as part of the team.

In practice most large groups of non-ferrous artefacts, with the exception of coins, tend to be of copper and its alloys. The need for identification of the metal is particularly acute for Roman and post-Roman material due to the wide range of compositional possibilities, compared, for example, to the British Bronze Age. There, the very early material is of copper, the overwhelming majority of the Early and Middle Bronze Age material is of real bronze, that is copper alloyed with tin, and in the Late Bronze Age these are joined by leaded bronzes. With the introduction of brass, the alloy of copper and zinc, in the Roman period the range of compositional possibilities becomes much wider (for more on the history of the nomenclature of the alloys and the vexed question of the varied use of the terms 'brass' and 'bronze' by art historian and artisan in the recent past, see Craddock (1996, 848) and Blair and Blair (1991)). The colours of the polished metal surfaces give only a very rough guide to the composition, and the corroded surfaces are not reliable at all, not even for an identification as 'copper alloy'. For example, base silver that has corroded or ordinary silver that has been in contact with corroding copper, can look like corroded bronze, as exemplified by the well-known silver chalice (see the front cover of Ryan 1983), found with other metalwork all inside a large bronze vessel at the ancient monastic site at Derrynaflan in the township of Lurgoe, Co. Tipperary, believed to be of ninth-century date. In addition, from the Roman period on, there are many more composite pieces that are often held together by solders and are plated and decorated with a variety of materials that can be quickly identified by XRF.

Rapid surveys such as that proposed here create the potential to carry out analytical surveys on very large numbers of objects and so quite quickly establish broad patterns of alloying. This is especially relevant for the first millennium AD when, as noted above, brass was replacing bronze as the usual copper alloy. Some of the surveys currently being carried out on British Museum material are showing that the adoption of brass was not a uniform phenomenon across Europe, and the situation in the Celtic West is especially interesting (see below).

The technique of energy dispersive XRF is well established (Hall *et al* 1973; Hackens 1977; Cowell 1998) and there should not be too much difficulty in locating a suitable XRF facility in the science departments of most universities or similar higher education establishments. There is also a growing number of instruments in laboratories attached to museums, some of which have been specially adapted to accommodate antiquities (see below).

XRF is especially useful for the routine survey of unknown materials because it automatically seeks a wide range of elements, and thus one does not have to search specifically for each metal that could

conceivably be in the artefact; if it is present in detectable quantities the relevant peak will appear, and with experience an unexpected peak is instantly recognised.

The procedure described here allows for a rapid throughput of samples and thus the additional funding necessary for analysis should not be too onerous. However there are many practical problems to be considered before it is possible to produce routinely reliable results from the surface analysis of metalwork that is often corroded. Phenomena such as the enhancement or depletion of metals at the surface, together with the possibilities of various surface treatments including plating, have to be considered (see below). Surface analyses that were wrongly interpreted would be very much worse than no analyses at all.

To investigate these problems, and to evaluate the feasibility of carrying out routine materials identification, a group of about 100 pieces of metalwork from the multi-period site of Highdown in Sussex was selected for examination.

Bronze Age, Roman and Saxon metalwork from Highdown, Sussex: a case study

Highdown, situated close to the south coast of England near Worthing, is a site which includes a fortification of the first millennium BC as well as a well-known Saxon cemetery. It was first investigated in the 1890s (Read 1894; 1896). It has been more recently re-excavated by the then Institute of Archaeology (University College London) Sussex Field Archaeological Unit,[1] under the direction of Mark Gardiner, in the wake of the storm of October 1987, which uprooted many mature trees on the site, causing extensive disturbance to the archaeological features.[2]

The metalwork included fragments of Anglo-Saxon jewellery and fittings, prehistoric pieces, Roman coins, as well as abundant unidentifiable fragments. The last included a considerable number of very rough lumps of cast metal, which are probably of Bronze Age date. Some of these had areas of recognisable deliberate cast shape but other pieces were clearly just droplets and spills of metal.

The metalwork from the excavation turned out to be excellent for this exercise as it included a wide range of typically corroded metals together with examples of plated and composite objects. Many of the objects had been sectioned for metallographic examination and thus comparison between the corroded surface and the clean body metal was possible.

The method: surface analysis by X-ray fluorescence (XRF)

The investigation was carried out at the Department of Scientific Research using a Links System 290 XRF spectrometer. Since this work was carried out, the Institute of Archaeology has acquired an XRF spectrometer. Most commercial XRF instruments have enclosed sample chambers. These are not large, typically about 150mm high and 300mm in diameter, but should accommodate the majority of small metalwork usually encountered without the necessity of taking a sample, although there may be problems positioning the object to determine the composition at a specific location. The area analysed may be up to 2.5mm across. Some instruments, such as the one used in this project, are enclosed within a much larger chamber or cabinet and on these so-called open-architecture instruments the object is positioned freely in front of the beam, and there is almost no size restriction. The area analysed is also somewhat smaller, being about 1 to 2mm across. There are open-architecture instruments at several other laboratories devoted to the study of antiquities such as the Oxford Laboratory for Archaeology and the History of Art, The Victoria and Albert Museum, the National Museums of Scotland, and the Royal Armouries in Leeds. It should be stressed that, in common with the British Museum and Institute of Archaeology, none of these institutions routinely undertake scientific examination or analysis for outside bodies.

There are also portable XRF instruments which could be brought to the archive of material (Ferretti and Moioli 1998). However their hire is comparatively expensive, and being less powerful than standard instruments, tend to be rather slower in acquiring a usable spectrum. The use of such equipment must conform to the Ionising Radiation Regulations (1985). If a radioactive source is used to generate the X-rays, then this must be registered under the Radioactive Substances Act (1993).

The sample to be analysed is bombarded with X-rays emitted from a radioactive source or, more usually, generated from an X-ray tube. This project was carried out in 1989 using a modified Link Systems spectrometer fitted with a tungsten target X-ray tube. The incident X-rays of such a system typically have an energy of up to 50 kv, and on striking the sample eject electrons from inner atomic orbitals which are replaced by electrons from outer orbitals with higher energy. The difference in energy is released principally in the form of X-rays. The energy of these secondary X-rays is characteristic of the element analysed and the intensity of secondary radiation produced is proportional to the amount of that element present. The method is precise and accurate (assuming the material analysed is homogenous), but not very sensitive compared to some other analytical techniques. As a rule of thumb most of the metals and trace elements that occur in copper alloys are detectable down to about 0.1%, which is sufficient to allow a full description of the alloy and the principal trace metals. A more complete description of XRF and its application to the analysis of antiquities is given in Cowell (1998).

A major drawback of the method is the difficulty in detecting X-rays from light elements, as a result of absorbance of their X-rays by air. Thus for these practical purposes it is not possible to detect the first ten elements in the periodic table. This is not too serious a problem in the analysis of most ancient metals, but without using a vacuum chamber it does exclude metals such as aluminum and magnesium which are common constituents of twentieth-century alloys.

Using the open-architecture energy-dispersive XRF, the object to be analysed is placed in the path of the primary X-ray beam and the secondary X-rays are determined electronically using a solid state detector. The spectrally separated peaks are displayed visually and sufficient X-rays for a qualitative analysis have usually been collected within a minute. Thus the method is very quick, at least for qualitative work. The XRF spectra so produced can be stored as computer files and printed out to form a permanent record for future reference.

For quantitative analysis a longer count time is required and some surface preparation of the object to be analysed is usually required (Cowell 1998).

Practical lessons of the exercise

This project was carried out to test the feasibility of rapid, low-cost routine identification of groups of non-ferrous metalwork by XRF. In this project the artefacts were analysed directly without any cleaning or pre-treatment of the surfaces at all. We have found that a team of two, one to unpack and record and one to operate the apparatus, were able to process about 50 objects in a half day, during which about 65 actual analyses were performed. This half day included coffee breaks, telephone calls and the other minor interruptions that are inevitable in any real life situation, and is a better guide than the number of samples per hour. The work is fairly intensive and repetitive and we found that after half a day our concentration was waning and minor mistakes began to occur. Thus it would be correct to say that 100 objects, involving 130 separate analyses took two half days to complete, and that it might be counter productive to attempt longer runs.

Several of the pieces were shown to be composite and some were of sufficient interest to warrant analysis of the individual components to give valuable information for the description or even the identification of the object. However, carrying out a detailed survey of an individual piece is time consuming, not least because of the problems of precisely locating very specific areas of the object in the path of the X-ray beam. If repeated too often this could easily negate any estimate of the time or funds needed to complete the identification programme. If the person primarily responsible for the publication of the material is helping with the analysis, then a decision on the analytical detail needed can be made on the spot.

Most of the analyses were on unconserved corroded surfaces although abrading through the corrosion to expose the body metal beneath would not have appreciably delayed the operation. However, the identifications made from the surface analyses were correct in those instances where they were checked against the analysis of polished sections.

Analytical results

Approximately 130 analyses were carried out on about 100 items of metalwork. On the basis of visual inspection all the pieces would have been described as 'copper alloy', but XRF identification showed one to be of a gold-silver alloy, disguised beneath a layer of silver bromide corrosion product and some copper salts, presumably from an adjacent bronze; seven were of base silver, and five more (Roman coins) contained a small percentage of silver. A further two were of lead and four were of unalloyed copper. The remainder were of bronze or brass, usually leaded, and not infrequently the alloy contained all three metals mixed with the copper. Traces of silver, arsenic, nickel and antimony were regularly detected. As expected, the Bronze Age material was of leaded bronze, whereas the Saxon material tended to be of alloys containing copper with tin, zinc and often contained lead as well. Six items had traces of gilding and are discussed in more detail below.

These results are typical of the composition of metalwork likely to be found on multi-period sites except perhaps for the cast fragments and spills of heavily leaded bronze, which made up about a third of the total.

Surface analysis: problems and potentials

XRF is very much a surface analysis technique. Typically the X-ray beam, which is about 2mm in diameter, analyses only about 0.1mm into the surface, depending on the material analysed. This creates the serious problem for both qualitative and quantitative analysis of relating the composition of the surface with that of the object as a whole. Conversely, surface analysis also creates the valuable potential to discover and record the remains of deliberate surface treatments such as gilding. The problems will be discussed first.

Problems

Metals vary greatly in composition, especially at the surface, and ancient metals which have been buried are even more likely to have a surface composition which is very different from that of the metal as a whole.

Alloys are rarely homogeneous. For example, metals such as tin, lead or arsenic in a copper alloy tend to concentrate at the surface during casting, leading to the phenomenon known as sweating, which results in a grey or silvery surface. To some degree this will persist even after working, heat treatment and even polishing. Thus it can be difficult to differentiate between sweating and plating. However, grinding or carving the metal should remove the sweated layer and thus, if the grey or silvery layer extends over areas of the surface where it has been worked *after* casting, then this should indicate that sweating was not responsible. The problem can be further complicated because, during burial, the phases with high copper content in copper alloys with a high tin or arsenic content can sometimes be preferentially dissolved out from the surface, leaving the higher tin or arsenic phases and thereby creating an apparent plated surface (Meeks 1986; 1993a and b).

Metallographic sections had been prepared on a substantial proportion of the pieces analysed for this project, including almost all of the heavily leaded cast pieces, and this provided a good opportunity to compare the surface analysis with that from the interior. In every case except the heavily leaded pieces, the surface accurately reflected the bulk alloy type. Although there tended to be more tin, lead and sometimes zinc at the surface, the same alloy description would have been reported from either the surface or interior. In several of the heavier cast leaded pieces, the lead was the major element at the surface, although copper and tin were always present. More careful analysis of the polished section showed that the lead content of the main body metal itself varied between 20 and 50 percent, reflecting the extreme heterogeneity of these alloys due to the almost total immiscibility of copper and lead. Thus, these pieces do have an unusually high lead content, but to have described the alloy as being principally of lead would have been incorrect. However, the propensity of lead to concentrate at the surface of heavily leaded castings is well known and the experienced analyst should be aware of this and merely describe the alloy as containing lead, tin and copper without attempting to provide a more specific description.

Corrosion of the metal in most burial conditions will also tend to concentrate the more electro-negative elements in the patination and thus the corroded metal surface of a bronze will tend to be richer in tin and lead than the underlying body metal. In some burial conditions zinc can be almost entirely lost from the surface of an alloy. Only with experience will the analyst be able to predict that the surface composition may be very different from that of the body metal beneath. Where the surface appearance suggests that excessive surface change may have taken place it is advisable to clean a small area on a carborundum disc to reveal, if possible, the unaltered body metal beneath. Alloys are rarely of homogenous composition. Instead, they are made up of regions of differing structure known as phases, and these can have markedly different properties as well as composition. The problems of selective corrosion of different phases is outlined above.

Metal objects from existing collections have often received unrecorded conservation treatment in the past which may have involved the use of other metals or their salts. One of the most common treatments in use from the late nineteenth to mid-twentieth century was electro-chemical reduction in which hydrogen was generated by the reaction of caustic soda solution on zinc sheet or wool wrapped around the object (Plenderleith 1934, 51–2, Plenderleith and Werner 1971, 194–95; Gilberg 1988). All trace of this operation should have been removed by washing, but sometimes residual zinc salts persist on the surface. A less drastic method for 'bronze disease' was to treat the affected area with silver oxide, converting the active copper chlorides to stable silver chloride, thereby creating potential confusion between post-excavation conservation treatment and an original plating (Plenderleith and Werner 1971, 253; Gilberg 1988). The analyst must be alert to the possibility of these and other treatments on objects from museum collections.

Once again only with experience of dealing with antiquities can these problems be anticipated and circumvented. Ideally, on a small but representative selection of the material, the surface to be analysed should be abraded to assess the various potential surface problems. Manual abrasion of a small area of a few square millimetres takes a very short time and the damage caused to the object should be acceptable if this is confined to minor and fragmentary pieces. Having the archaeologist/curator present can enable instant decisions on surface preparation to be taken and carried out. Most of the material analysed in our survey was not prepared in any way, because of the pre-existing flat surfaces polished for metallographic examination, but with two people working together a little surface preparation could have been done without extending the time taken unduly.

The archaeologist and conservator in the field are often faced with the problem of deciding to what degree freshly excavated metalwork should be cleaned or conserved, because of the potential loss of technical detail from the surface before scientific examination. As a general rule the adhering mud and very loose corrosion can be mechanically removed without loss of information but where possible chemical treatments or vigorous cleaning should be avoided until scientific examination has taken place. If corrosion is active then, of course, the object must be treated.

Potentials

The most obvious potential of the method is the rapid identification of the alloy types in use across a given group or culture. The application of this method to some of the post-Roman groups across Europe is beginning to change our perception of changes in alloy use.

Previous analytical work on metalwork of the first millennium AD has concentrated on the Romans, and their Byzantine and Islamic successors, and to a lesser degree, the Germanic tribes of Western Europe (Craddock 1985). These studies suggested a change over from bronze to brass that was largely complete by the mid-first millennium (Craddock 1985, 63; Hook and Craddock 1996; 1998). However, ongoing and as yet largely unpublished identification studies, such as those described here, on a large number of copper alloys from other groups across Europe is showing that the situation is more complex and that amongst some groups, bronze continued as the prevalent alloy for much longer than previously believed (Craddock 2001). This is especially true of the Celtic West.

From the several hundred pieces recently examined for the forthcoming catalogue of the medieval Celtic metalwork collections in the British Museum coming predominantly from Ireland, the following simplified overview emerges. The very few items contemporary with Roman-Britain are of bronze and brass. Then, from the fifth to the ninth centuries, the approximately 180 items examined are predominantly of bronze or leaded bronze with only nine brasses or leaded brasses and 11 mixed alloys with both tin and zinc. In contrast, the approximately 80 pieces dated to the tenth to twelfth centuries are predominantly of brass or a mixed alloy with only 8 bronzes. The change over in alloy composition seems to have occurred in the ninth and tenth centuries, and is presumably related to Viking settlement in Ireland.

The continuing prevalence of bronze in the west of Britain had already been hinted at by the very limited number of analyses carried out, including those of hanging bowls and some other items found in Anglo-Saxon contexts, notably from Sutton Hoo (Oddy 1983, 945–61; Craddock 1989, 170). Zinc was much more prevalent in the contemporary Saxon copper alloys, raising the question of the sources for the Celtic bronze, and the possibility of local production of the metals. The main metals, copper, tin and lead, all occur in the Celtic West, and there is increasing evidence for their exploitation through the first millennium AD, long after the departure of the Romans. There are, for example, various Byzantine and Coptic references to a trade in tin from the far west in the sixth and seventh centuries (Craddock 1979), contemporary with the finds of imported pottery at sites in south-west Britain.

The evidence for copper production is more direct. The recent programmes of research into Bronze Age copper sources in the British Isles have resulted in many radiocarbon dates, which have shown that some mines have evidence of being worked in the post-Roman and early medieval periods (Craddock 1994). The most significant evidence comes from the important Copper Age copper mine of Ross Island on Lough Leane, near Killarney in Co. Kerry (O'Brien 1995; 1996). The 1995 excavations revealed a copper smelting site with slags and the remains of small clay furnaces, with radiocarbon dates in the second half of the first millennium AD.[3]

Only when large numbers of samples are examined do these trends in composition become clear; the strategy outlined here enables these large numbers to be processed. Another important potential for the method is in revealing evidence of surface treatments. Six of the pieces from Highdown, including a mount, two buckles and three square-headed brooches, were found to have residual gilding, including one brooch of base silver that had been leaf gilded; otherwise the presence of gilding would not have been suspected from appearance alone. The usual gilding technique used throughout the Anglo-Saxon period was fire or mercury gilding; although no mercury was detected in these pieces, analysis by a more sensitive technique, such as emission spectroscopy, might have confirmed its use.

Subsequent work on metalwork for the forthcoming catalogue of the medieval Celtic collection in the British Museum, covering several hundred items, revealed gilding on many artefacts where this was no longer visible and was not suspected. Mercury was detected in a number of instances and once again mercury gilding is likely to have been the technique used. The survey revealed one example of mercury silvering on what was thought to be a sixth-century 'latchet' dress fastener from Icklingham, Suffolk (Reg. No. BM MLA 1923,10–17,1; Laing 1993, no.143). This caused some interest at the time as it would have been the earliest example of mercury silvering to be recognised from the British Isles, if not Europe (see La Niece 1990, 108–9). However reconsideration of the object, prompted by the discovery of the unusual silvering technique, led to its identification as a pendant of the high medieval period when mercury silvering was quite common. This is an example where a knowledge of the materials used led to a more correct understanding of the nature and date of the piece.

On copper-based objects, the presence of gold, silver or mercury would normally indicate gilding or silvering, even where the plating was no longer visible, although the precious metals could be in the body metal. This can be checked by analysing an area hidden from view – for example, at the back of the artefact, as it is rare for an object to be plated with precious metal all over. Thus, if the precious metals are only in the front or other parts exposed to view, then this would be good evidence for plating. This could be checked further by analysing an extremity where plating could be expected to have worn away. Failing this, it may be permissible to abrade the surface over a small inconspicuous area and determine whether the precious metals are present or absent from the body metal. If the precious metals were present in the body metal, the possibility that this could represent a deliberate addition made to produce a black, *shakudo*-like patination, should be explored (see below).

Putative examples of arsenic plating or of tinning are more problematic because of the possibility of sweating, and other phenomena, discussed above. Once again, if the high arsenic or tin contents were found to be confined to the exposed regions then this could be taken as evidence of deliberate treatment. Here the converse is not true; various surface treatments, such as dipping would result in a continuous surface all over the object, and the only way to be sure would be to examine the surface topography under high magnification with a scanning electron microscope, or to examine polished sections (Meeks 1986; 1993b).

Solders can also be detected, although there is sometimes the practical difficulty of targeting the X-ray beam on to the solder which is often in an angle or recess of the object. A crozier arm terminal from Ireland (Reg. No. BM MLA 1883, 2–18,10) of leaded brass had a side panel attached with a solder containing silver, copper and zinc. This is the familiar silver solder, still recommended and used as a top quality hard solder for joining both silver and copper alloys (Maryon 1954, 11–15). This is an unusual and early example of its use on a copper alloy.

Rapid surveys of large numbers of artefacts hold out the prospect of discovering unusual materials and techniques. For example, there is a class of copper alloys containing small amounts of precious metals, treated to give a fine black patina, that were either inlaid with precious metal or were themselves used as inlays in polished metal. The best known and most recent examples are the Japanese *shakudo* pieces, but research has shown that the technique was in use from the late third millennium BC in the Middle East (Craddock and Giumlia-Mair 1993). Many examples are now recognised from the Roman period when the material was known as Corinthian bronze, but until recently there were no examples from post-Roman Europe. However a survey of some Anglo-Saxon metalwork, primarily carried out to study the enamelling techniques, revealed that on two strap-ends the black-headed rivets were of a Corinthian bronze alloy (Stapleton *et al* 1996). No examples are yet known from the Celtic West but it has been suggested that components of the 'Tara' brooch which have a black patina may be candidates (Whitfield 1997).

A survey of Avar metalwork of the eighth and ninth centuries, undertaken for a forthcoming catalogue of material from the Carpathian Basin, now in the British Museum, brought to light an openwork shield-shaped suspension mount which has a fine black patina and contains gold and silver in the leaded bronze alloy (Reg. No. BM MLA 1997, 2–9, 6). Here the cast leaded bronze pins contained no gold and the intended contrast would presumably have been between the black strap end and the golden bronze of the pins – the reverse of that found on the Anglo-Saxon pieces. Details such as this on relatively minor metalwork with no obvious precious metal would remain undetected forever unless identified in surveys such as this. Having detected their presence a drilled sample was taken for full quantitative analysis of the body metal.

usual copper alloy. Our examinations showed that a number of objects were not copper alloy at all and we suspect that this is quite a common situation. Similarly traces of plating are probably regularly missed and several unsuspected examples were found in this and subsequent surveys. The incidence of gilding on the Irish material in the British Museum, for example, was substantially increased, which is of some consequence in the consideration of the availability of exotic and precious metals such as gold and mercury in Ireland and Britain in the post-Roman world. Unusual materials and techniques were also discovered amongst the Irish early medieval and Avar material subsequently examined. The only way that such discoveries will be made and their histories documented is by large-scale surveys such as those described here using quick and simple strategies. The identification of more complex multi-component and inlaid pieces produced additional information of great interest for those pieces.

It is essential for the rapid identification of the material that the team includes someone who is familiar with the material as well as someone who is familiar with the analysis of ancient metalwork. Ideally the archaeologist or finds assistant should be working directly with the analyst. This creates a productive interaction, as well as reduction in costs. A further advantage for the archaeologist is that the results are available literally as they appear. There is no question of the long, frustrating delays that can occur with specialist reports from outside institutions. Nevertheless a written report of the procedures and summary results, compiled by the analyst, would be necessary for publication, so that the limitations of the data were fully apparent.

Comprehensive identification surveys of all the metalwork from excavations is not usual at present because there is a common perception that such a survey would be both expensive and time consuming. However using the modern analytical apparatus that is available in many laboratories it is possible to provide a quick, routine and relatively inexpensive identification of the metals and alloys used.

Conclusion

Material identifications do enable a much more accurate description of the object to be given. As one analyst of antiquities, Bob Brill, put it some years ago, 'if you don't know what it's made of, you don't really know much about it at all'. This is true of both individual and group identifications. Our work on this early medieval Celtic material has helped clarify the main alloys in use at given periods and documented the changeover from bronze to brass as the

Acknowledgements

The authors have discussed aspects of this paper with colleagues at their respective institutions, but in particular would like to thank Mike Cowell and Susan Youngs, both of the British Museum, for their advice and help.

Notes

1 Now South Eastern Archaeological Services.
2 The material was studied by one of us as part fulfilment of a BSc in Archaeological Conservation at the Institute of Archaeology, University of London (Wallis 1989).
3 Unpublished but announced by O'Brien at the British Museum conference on *The Prehistory of Mining and Metallurgy*, 13th–18th Sept. 1995.

References

BLAIR, C. and BLAIR, J. 1991, 'Copper Alloys', in J. Blair and N. Ramsay (eds), *English Medieval Industries*, 81–106. London.

COWELL, M. R. 1998, 'Coin analysis by energy dispersive X-ray fluorescence spectrometry', in W. A. Oddy and M. R. Cowell (eds), *Metallurgy in Numismatics 4*, 448–60. London.

CRADDOCK, P. T. 1979, 'The copper alloys of the medieval Islamic world', *World Archaeol.* 11, 68–79.

CRADDOCK, P. T. 1985, 'Three thousand years of copper alloying', in P. A. England and L. van Zelst (eds), *Application of Science in Examination of Works of Art*, 59–67. Boston.

CRADDOCK, P. T. 1989, 'Metalworking techniques', in S. Youngs (ed.), *'The Work of Angels'. Masterpieces of Celtic Metalwork 6th–9th Centuries AD*, 170–213. London.

CRADDOCK, P. T. 1994, 'Recent progress in the study of early mining and metallurgy in the British Isles', *J. Hist. Metallurgy Soc.* 28, 69–85.

CRADDOCK, P. T. 1996, 'Bronze', in J. Turner (ed.), *The Dictionary of Art*. Vol. 4, 848–55. London.

CRADDOCK, P. T. 2001, 'Conservative metal alloying traditions in the Migration Period', in B. Plesingerova (ed.), *Archaeometallurgy in Central Europe III*. Herlany, 175–81.

CRADDOCK, P. T. and GIUMLIA-MAIR, A. 1993 '*Hsmn Km*, Corinthian bronze, *shakudo*: black-patinated bronze in the ancient world', in La Niece and Craddock (eds), 1026–27. London.

FERRETTI, M. and MOIOLI, P. 1998, 'The use of portable XRF systems for preliminary compositional surveys on large bronze objects', *Metal 98*, 39–44.

GILBERG, M. 1988, 'History of bronze disease and its treatment', in V. Daniels (ed.), *Early Advances in Conservation* (= British Mus. Occas. Pap. 65), 59–70. London.

HACKENS, T. (ed.) 1977, *X-ray Microfluorescence Analysis Applied to Archaeology*, PACT 1. Council of Europe, Strasbourg.

HALL, E. T., SCHWEITZER, F. and TOLLER, P. A. 1973, 'X-ray fluorescence of museum objects: a new instrument', *Archaeometry* 15, 53–78.

HANSON, V. F. 1973, 'The curator's dream instrument', in W. J. Young (ed.), *Application of Science in Examination of Works of Art*, 18–30. Boston.

HOOK, D. R. and CRADDOCK, P. T. 1996, 'The scientific analysis of copper-alloy lamps', in D. Bailey, *Lamps of Metal and Stone and Lampstands. Catalogue of the Lamps in the British Museum IV*, 144–64. London.

HOOK, D. R. and CRADDOCK, P. T. 1998, 'The chemical analysis of copper alloy lamps', in G. Nicolini and N. Dieudonné-Glad (eds), *Les Métaux Antiques: Travail et Restauration*, 121–27. Montagnac.

LA NIECE, S. 1990, 'Silver plating on copper, bronze and brass', *Antiq. J.* 70, 102–14.

LA NIECE, S. and CRADDOCK, P. T. (eds) 1993, *Metal Plating and Patination. Cultural, Technical and Historical Developments*. London.

LAING, L. 1993, *A Catalogue of Celtic Ornamental Metalwork in the British Isles c AD 400–1200* (= B.A.R. Brit. Ser. 229). Oxford.

MARYON, H. 1954, *Metalwork and Enamelling: a practical treatise on gold and silversmith's work and their allied crafts*. London.

MEEKS, N. D. 1986, 'Tin-rich surfaces on bronze – some experimental and archaeological considerations', *Archaeometry* 28, 133–62.

MEEKS, N. D. 1993a, 'Patination phenomena on Roman and Chinese high-tin bronze mirrors and other artefacts', in La Niece and Craddock (eds), 63–84.

MEEKS, N. D. 1993b, 'Surface characterization of tinned bronze, high-tin bronze, tinned iron and arsenical bronze', in La Niece and Craddock (eds), 247–75.

O'BRIEN, W. 1995, 'Ross Island and the origins of the Irish-British metallurgy', in J. Eadell and E. Shee-Twohig (eds), *Ireland in the Bronze Age*, 38–48. Dublin.

O'BRIEN, W. 1996, *Bronze Age Copper Mining in Ireland and Britain*. Aylesbury.

ODDY, W. A. 1983, 'Bronze alloys in Dark Age Europe', in R. Bruce-Mitford, *The Sutton Hoo Ship Burial*, Vol. 1 (ed. A. C. Evans), 445–61. London.

PLENDERLEITH, H. J. 1934, *The Preservation of Antiquities*. London.

PLENDERLEITH, H. J. and WERNER, A. E. A. 1971, *The Conservation of Antiquities and Works of Art*. Oxford.

READ, C. H. 1894, 'On excavations of a cemetery of South Saxons on Highdown, Sussex', *Archaeologia* 54, 367–82.

READ, C. H. 1896, 'Further excavations of a cemetery of South Saxons on Highdown, Sussex', *Archaeologia* 55, 203–14.

RYAN, M. 1983, *The Derrynaflan Hoard I: A Preliminary Account*. Dublin.

STAPLETON, C., BOWMAN, S. G., CRADDOCK, P. T., LA NIECE, S. and YOUNGS, S. 1996, '*Corinthium Aes* and black bronzes in the early medieval period', *Antiq. J.* 75, 383–90.

WALLIS, J. M. 1989, The study of a group of copper alloy objects from Highdown Hill, Sussex. Unpublished report submitted in partial fulfillment of the requirements of the degree of BSc in Archaeological Conservation, University of London.

WHITFIELD, N. 1997, '"Corinthian Bronze' and the 'Tara Brooch'?', *Archaeol. Ireland* 11, 24–8.

11   Insular Belt-fittings from the Pagan Norse Graves of Scotland: a Reappraisal in the Light of Scientific and Stylistic Analysis

Caroline Paterson

Introduction

The following discussion of Insular belt-fittings has developed as a result of their recent cataloguing for the forthcoming publication of the *Pagan Norse Graves of Scotland* by the author together with Professor J. Graham-Campbell (Graham-Campbell and Paterson forthcoming). These Insular belt-fittings, with the exception of a pair of Anglo-Saxon strap-ends from a rich female grave at Westness, Rousay, which are not included in this discussion, have all been previously published, though they received only passing mention in articles on Insular belt-fittings by de Paor (1961) and Bakka (1965). Scientific analysis of these fittings, generated in part by the pagan Norse graves project and in part by a recent programme of conservation, has provided a substantial new body of information. Moreover, recent excavations in various locations, in particular Dublin, have recovered a vast range of comparative material, much of which is from stratified, datable contexts. This has provided additional information on the origin, date and function of some of these belt-fittings, which the contexts of the pagan Norse graves, many of which were excavated in the last century, were unable to supply.

Context

There are three main problems with the archaeological data associated with Insular finds recovered from pagan Norse graves. Firstly, there is the issue of provenancing such finds, since their pagan burial contexts can be far from their place of manufacture, and many of the closest parallels for the Scottish grave finds come from Norwegian burial contexts (Wamers 1985, Taf. 28). Although on stylistic grounds an Insular origin is often indisputable, such

contexts provide little help in deciding whether an object originated in Ireland, Northumbria or even the west of Scotland (a possibility raised in Wilson 1970, 9). Close parallels excavated from urban sites where metalworking is much in evidence are now providing a link between some of the Scottish grave finds and possible places of manufacture. Secondly, the conjectured date of burial cannot automatically be applied to all the objects in the grave; those of an Insular, as opposed to Scandinavian, origin often appear to be substantially earlier in date. There could be many reasons behind this, but it appears that prestigious Insular objects, such as the Westness brooch-pin could have been at least 100 years old at the time of their deposition (Stevenson 1968, 30). Finally, the function of these belt-fittings within the burial cannot automatically be assumed to be that for which they were originally intended; their ornamental details appealed to the Scandinavian taste for personal adornment and thus some of them may originally have been produced for a different purpose, possibly of an ecclesiastical nature.

Metallurgical analysis

Metallurgical analysis of the Insular belt-fittings was undertaken by Dr Katherine Eremin of the National Museums of Scotland. This formed part of a larger project in which all copper-alloy objects from the pagan Norse graves of Scotland were analysed in an attempt to help with their provenancing, as well as providing a useful set of data for comparison (there being a paucity of such analyses for the early medieval period). The results suggest that there were different alloy traditions for Insular and Scandinavian artefacts, with brass being largely confined to Scandinavian objects such as oval brooches, whilst most bronze objects are of Insular origin. Brass was relatively rare in the British Isles from the late Roman period until it was reintroduced by the Norse (Bayley 1992, 809–10), probably via their eastern trading routes. Ringed pins of brass were clearly manufactured under Norse influence (Mullarkey in Fanning 1994, 122), and some brass finds from the Scottish graves have low zinc levels, which indicates the careful recycling of brass imports, probably in Hiberno-Norse centres such as Dublin. The presence of gunmetal among the finds from the Scottish graves suggests that there was also a more random recycling of tin- and zinc-bearing copper alloys. Although some of these finds appear to be exclusively Insular in character, the zinc-bearing alloys in their composition probably came from recycled Scandinavian imports.

The methods employed in the analysis were non-destructive X-ray fluorescence (XRF), with some additional scanning electron microscopy (SEM). These non-destructive methods, when applied to corroded artefacts, have clear limitations as a result of the limited depth of penetration. However, although the compositions may therefore not correspond exactly with that of the original alloy, the basic identifications are accurate (see also Craddock, Wallis and Merkel, this volume). Where specific alloys are named in the text below, they have been analysed; otherwise the general term 'copper alloy' is used. The metallic composition of the belt-fittings is included in their discussions, which are done on an individual basis, as most of these fittings appear not to have been the result of mass production and are very individual, sometimes unique, in appearance.

The Gazetteer

Bhaltos, Lewis (Plate VIII).
The buckle and its associated plate were recovered from a female Norse grave discovered by school children eroding out of a field bank at Bhaltos (Valtos) in 1915 (MacLeod *et al.* 1916, 181). The grave goods included a pair of oval brooches of ninth-century type, this date being assumed to be approximately that of the burial itself. The buckle was not the only Insular object to have accompanied the burial, which also included a penannular brooch and a substantial gilded circular mount (Grieg 1940, fig. 43). In the absence of a pin, Curle (in Macleod *et al.* 1916, 187) identified the latter as a belt-mounting. However, its size and the presence of the above buckle would make such an identification unlikely, and it is more probable that the circular mount was reused as a brooch in its burial context, its pin having either corroded away or not been retrieved.

The buckle is in three pieces, comprising an elaborate D-shaped loop and most of the front and back plates. The loop has a flattened decorative surface with raised rectangular insets positioned to either side of the tongue-rest and filled with red enamel. Simple two-strand interlace is incised in the angles of the loop, which are slightly damaged. The buckle-plate is formed from a rectangular sheet of bronze folded in two around the bar of the loop, with a rectangular opening for the now missing tongue. The fold of the plate also appears to have been recessed at its outer edges, but is now damaged with the front and back plates having become separated from each other. The front of the buckle-plate is decorated with a crudely incised interlace pattern of two spiralled knots set within a plain border to either side. The interlace strands have a medial line of dots and are set against a distinctive background of oblique hatching arranged in triangular blocks of alternating direction. The tinned upper surface of the plate contrasts with the bronze beneath, which shows through where the surface has been incised. The back-plate is also tinned, but lacks incised decoration and has a perforation in its one surviving far corner, indicating the means by which the plates would have been riveted together, securing a strap between them.

This buckle belongs to the small series of Insular buckles characterised by their D-shaped loops, quadrangular sheet-metal plates and incised white-metal plating (Bakka 1965, 36–7). Close parallels occur in Norwegian Viking graves, though the loop with its enamel insets to either side of the tongue-rest is similar to that from Ballinaby, Islay (Plate IX), and an Irish gilt bronze buckle-loop of eighth-century date in the British Museum (Reg. No. BM MLA 53, 11–17, 13), which likewise has settings for enamel and panels of simple interlace. The background of oblique hatching is typical of Insular ornamental metalwork (Wilson 1973, 118), and also occurs on the tinned rectangular back-plate of a similar buckle from Islandbridge, Dublin (Coffey and Armstrong 1910, fig. 22), and a buckle-loop from Nordrum, Norway (Bakka 1965, pl. 1a). It appears as a background motif to ribbon interlace, in the same manner as on the Bhaltos buckle-plate, on parts of the back- and end-plates of the Copenhagen house-shaped shrine (Youngs 1989, 164: no. 131) and the side-plates of the Domnach Airgid book shrine (Raftery 1941, pl. 117), both of which are regarded as being of eighth- or early ninth-century workmanship and of Irish style, though the former may have been manufactured in Scotland (Youngs 1989, 136). Both these shrines display the same surprising irregularity in their crudely incised interlace schemes as the Bhaltos buckle-plate. However, their 'one-way' hatching is simpler than that on the Bhaltos buckle-plate, where the background patterning is composed of alternating triangular blocks of oblique hatching, which Bakka (1963, 29) regarded as the hall-mark for a group of Insular bronze-bound buckets (see Graham-Campbell, this volume). The bronze composition of the Bhaltos buckle, together with its form and ornament, suggests that it is of Insular, possibly Irish workmanship, as originally proposed by Curle (in Macleod *et al.* 1916, 188).

Ballinaby, Islay (Plate IX).

This buckle with its attached plate formed part of the grave assemblage of a pagan Norse warrior, which was discovered by a shepherd freeing a lamb trapped in what turned out to be a stone-lined cist (Edwards 1934, 74). The interred man was accompanied by a rich assemblage of weapons which help date the burial to the second half of the ninth century. Relating to his attire was both a ringed pin and the buckle discussed below.

The buckle comprises an elaborate D-shaped loop around which a tapering rectangular plate has been bent. The loop is cast with four raised settings for red enamel, now absent from one setting. There are lightly incised crosses in the surfaces of two of the enamel settings. These settings are positioned one at either end of the loop and one to either side of the tongue-rest, with sunken borders of pseudo-beading between. The bronze loop is mercury gilded. The bronze tongue has one leg bent around the rear portion of the buckle giving it the appearance of looping back on itself. Its surface is subtly ridged, and zoomorphic in appearance, terminating in a slight knop. The surface of the plain plate, which is bent around the bar of the loop with an opening for the tongue, is tinned, as is the tongue itself (Eremin and Wilthew 1997, 10). There are two medial perforations through the plate, one of which is riveted to the back-plate. The flat plate has a significantly lower lead content than the other cast components suggesting that it was worked as sheet metal (*ibid.*).

This buckle belongs to the same series as the smaller Bhaltos example discussed above, both having D-shaped loops with red enamel insets to either side of the tongue-rest. The pseudo-beading on its loop is paralleled by that on the buckle from Islandbridge, Dublin (Bøe 1940, fig. 24), which also shares the same unusual tongue construction and is likewise plated with a white metal. It is possible that in some respects the buckle-loop imitates Late Antique or Germanic models, with the enamel settings a weak reminder of garnet inlay, as proposed for the Lough Gara belt-buckle from Ireland (Youngs 1989, 58, no. 46). The Ballinaby plate is unusual in being devoid of ornament, especially as it is associated with such a fine loop, possibly suggesting that it was a replacement, particularly as its metallic composition is different from the other components. However, the impressive gilded bronze

loop with its enamel settings would suggest that the original buckle was of Insular, probably Irish manufacture.

Kildonnan, Eigg (Plate Xa, b).

This impressive buckle was recovered together with other grave goods, including a sword, from a male inhumation within a mound near Kildonnan in 1875 (Macpherson 1878, 591–92). The sword helps date the burial to the late ninth or beginning of the tenth century. The buckle comprises a loop and tongue, which are hinged together with an unusual composite buckle-plate, comprising a cast upper-plate with recessed sides, riveted to a sheet-metal backing-plate. The upper-plate was originally cast in bold relief, but has suffered from corrosion and wear. The ornamental sequence determines the plate's outline to some extent, with curved expansions in the areas of the two roundels, tapering to a triangular terminal decorated with an animal's snout. Both roundels have an outer margin decorated with billeted pellets, which have a rough angular appearance. The centres of the roundels are plain with the remains of projecting rivets, which suggests that they were originally capped with hollow domed bosses. Discolouration of the boss-platforms is consistent with the bosses having a different composition from the buckle-plate. The two roundels are separated by a panel of single-strand interlace formed in a knot, set within a concave-sided border. A single strand of interlace with two angular loops at either end fills the space between one roundel and the hinge arms. The *en-face* animal-head terminal has ears which curve around the border of the nearest roundel; they have sunken centres, with distinctive lobed terminals. The eyes are bulbous, though now quite worn, and may originally have had sunken dot centres (Grieg 1940, 69, fig. 40). Double-contoured brows meet to form a medial ridge to the snout, which is pointed with a snub end and decorated to either side with transverse lines. A third rivet is discreetly positioned between the creature's eyes at the top of the snout.

The upper-plate was cast with prominent rebated sides, which are decorated with a cast step-pattern extending 30mm from the loop end. The substantial cavity formed by these sides can be viewed from the back of the plate, where the backing-plate is slightly damaged at its upper end, but its full extent is revealed on X-ray. A strap would presumably have filled this space, being secured between the upper- and backing-plates by the three rivets. The backing-plate is formed from a separate sheet of metal. Unlike the cast upper-plate, it is lightly ornamented with incised decoration, comprising a double contour for the roundel closest to the loop and a single one for the other. The roundels are linked by a

Fig. 11.1 *Buckle, Bishops Lough, Co. Westmeath (1:1). (Photograph: National Museum of Ireland)*

double-contoured margin, the outer strand of which terminates before reaching the second circle. Between these concave borders is a diagonally incised cross, the ends of which have roughly incised, arrow-shaped terminals. The backing-plate is broken just beyond the rivet of the roundel nearest the terminal, but would appear to have originally extended the entire length of the upper-plate, mirroring its outline. The loop is D-shaped, but with a prominent triangular apex in the area of the tongue-rest. Its upper surface is cast with billeted pellets and the reverse with a step pattern. The tongue is cast with transverse incised lines, and its terminal is moulded. The arms which attach the loop to the hinge-bar are ornamented with billeted pelleting, as are the corresponding plate arms.

The composite form of this buckle-plate with its substantial cavity is most unusual, though there is an extremely close parallel from Bishops Lough, Co. Westmeath (Fig. 11.1) (Reg. No. NMI: E499:463). This buckle has the same form and construction as the Eigg example, with which it shares many ornamental details, including the billeted roundels, central interlace panel, stepped sides and zoomorphic terminal, making it highly likely that they originally came from the same workshop. This unusual composite form with a cast front-plate riveted to a sheet-metal backing-plate is similar to that of the hinge-plates used for securing the carrying straps of house-shaped shrines, as seen on the Monymusk shrine (Youngs 1989, 163, no. 129). Many of these hinge-plates are rectangular with subtriangular terminals, which are frequently zoomorphic in character. The zoomorphic terminals on the Bologna house-shaped shrine hinge-plates (Blindheim 1984, fig. 55) have several features in common with the Eigg buckle-plate terminal, suggesting that they probably share a common stylistic origin. The Bologna shrine is said to be of Irish style

(Youngs 1989, 139–40, no. 132) and is dated to the ninth century. The Eigg buckle-plate probably belongs to a similar period, but is made of gunmetal. This combination of zinc- and tin-bearing copper alloys suggests that it may have been produced in a Hiberno-Norse environment, in which brass of Scandinavian origin was combined with native bronze (Eremin and Wilthew 1997, 13). However, the stylistic inspiration behind the Eigg buckle is certainly Insular, and it was probably produced from somewhere within the Irish Sea region.

The basic layout of the buckle-plate with its zoomorphic terminal and two, originally boss-capped rivets set within incised roundels, between which is a concave-sided panel of interlace, closely parallels one of the incised sheet-bronze harness fittings from the Norse grave at Kiloran Bay, Colonsay (Fig. 11.2), which is of late ninth-century date. A fragmentary sheet-metal buckle-plate from Whithorn, Galloway (Hill 1997, 371, 10.57, no. 4) with finely incised decoration, perforated roundel and waisted interlace panel, is also clearly related. This is of sheet metal and as such is technically more akin to the backing-plate of the Eigg buckle. However, there is a series of strap-ends which have many stylistic parallels with the Eigg buckle-plate and which are solid single castings of copper alloy.

Fig. 11.2 *Harness fitting, Kiloran Bay, Colonsay (1:1). (Drawing: Marion O'Neil)*

Fig. 11.3 Strap-end, Colonsay (1:1). (Photograph: Trustees of the National Museums of Scotland)

Features held in common include their sub-rectangular form with ornament on both sides, zoomorphic terminals with expansions around perforated roundels, panels of interlace and finely incised borders. There are only three such strap-ends from Scotland, namely a small, fragmentary example from the Udal, North Uist (Graham-Campbell 1973, fig. 51), an ornate later version with closed-circuit knots from Ashaig, Skye (*Discovery and Excavation* 1994, 43–4, fig. 21), and a recent find from Colonsay (Fig. 11.3) (Argyll and Bute Council). The Colonsay find does not bear any striking resemblance to the Eigg buckle-plate, besides being decorated on both sides, having a zoomorphic terminal with a faintly pelleted roundel behind, and a panel of interlace. However, other strap-ends in the series display closer stylistic links; the detailing on the zoomorphic terminal of a recent find from Werburgh Street, Dublin (Reg. No. NMI: 94E25:298:2; Paterson, in prep.) is almost identical to the Eigg animal head, complete with its distinctive sunken-lobed ears. A find from Saxton, North Yorkshire (*The Searcher*, June 1992, 21: pers. comm. Kevin Leahy), even has cast decoration along its narrow sides, though of linked lozenges as opposed to the Eigg buckle's step pattern. There are to date over 30 examples of this strap-end type, their distribution focussing on the Irish Sea, and Dublin in particular. Recent excavations in Dublin suggest that the series was being produced in this Hiberno-Norse centre, where eight examples, including a fine strap-end from Christchurch Place (Lang 1988, fig. 118) have been excavated. Although most of the datable contexts for this strap-end series are later than that proposed for the Eigg burial, it is possible that the Kildonnan buckle type was an early forerunner for the series, and is in some way representative of the transition from an ecclesiastical carrying-strap to the mass production of secular belt-fittings in response to a demand, generated in part by the Norse influx.

Cnip, Lewis (Fig. 11.4).
In 1979 a belt set, comprising a strap-end and associated buckle, was recovered from a female inhumation eroding from sand dunes on the Cnip (Kneep) Headland, near Bhaltos, Lewis (Welander *et al.* 1987, 149–51). This is an unusually fine belt set to accompany a female inhumation, belt-fittings being more commonly associated with male burials. The fittings were located just above the woman's waist, and other grave goods included her personal effects and several items of jewellery, including a pair of tenth-century oval brooches. The strap-end and buckle are both probably made of strips of sheet metal, which have been bent double and secured by a medial line of boss-capped rivets, some of which are missing. The buckle-plate has the boss cappings on its upper surface only, but the rivets on the strap-end have cappings on both sides, presumably because, unlike the buckle-plate, the strap-end could swing freely from side to side. Their elongated forms have slightly expanded terminals, the final boss in each being of a larger diameter than the others, a factor emphasised by its border of two incised concentric rings. The slightly waisted borders are likewise decorated with double contouring, as is the rolled loop of the strap-end. The tongue and D-shaped loop of the buckle are decorated with small clusters of transverse lines.

The belt set's apparent sheet-metal construction, together with its simple, yet finely incised ornament which decorates both faces of the strap-end, and the functional, yet decorative bossed rivets suggest that these fittings are of Insular workmanship. All the above features are closely paralleled on the Insular bronze bridle-mounts recovered from the rich Viking boat grave of ninth-century date from Kiloran Bay, Colonsay (Grieg 1940, fig. 30). It is probably as a result of so many of these related sheet-metal fittings having been recovered from Norse contexts that Nicholson has described them, in his discussion of the related buckle from Whithorn, as being the work of Scandinavian craftsmen (in Hill 1997, 621). However, there is no Scandinavian tradition for the production of such finely incised, sheet bronze fittings, and their inspiration is clearly Insular. A closely related strip of perforated sheet bronze from Iona, probably originally forming a strap-end, has a saltire fret motif incised at one end (O'Sullivan 1994, illus. 5:114). The Cnip belt-fittings are made of gunmetal, with an unusually high percentage of lead for sheet metal. The gunmetal suggests that they were produced from the random recycling of metals of different origins, namely both zinc- and tin-bearing copper alloys, most probably within a Hiberno-Norse environment. Moreover, the imprint of a fine diamond twill of Norwegian origin on the reverse of the buckle-plate (Bender-Jørgensen 1987, 166–68) corroborates the suggestion that they were manufactured in a place with a Norwegian presence,

Fig. 11.4 Belt-set, Cnip, Lewis (1:1). (Photograph: Trustees of the National Museums of Scotland)

such as Dublin. Indeed, recent excavations within Dublin's city centre have produced numerous parallels to the Cnip belt-fittings, including a fragmentary, copper-alloy buckle from Fishamble Street (Reg. No. NMI: E172:8162) (Fig. 11.5), where metalworking is much in evidence. The sheet-metal plate attached to this buckle-loop has simple incised linear decoration and a medial line of perforations, each of which is surrounded by a discoloured circular ring, which together with four associated rivet shanks, indicates that this plate was likewise decorated with a line of bossed rivets. A further parallel has recently been excavated from a context of disturbed burials in the pre-Norman phase at St Michael's, Workington, Cumbria (Paterson, in prep.). It is probable that the Workington buckle accompanied a burial, just as the Cnip set, suggesting that, although production in the Irish Sea area is likely on both technical and stylistic grounds, the fashion for such belt-fittings clearly appealed to Scandinavian taste and Norse patronage may well account for the production of the type in ninth- and tenth-century Dublin.

Ardskenish, Colonsay (Fig. 11.6).
A strap-buckle found at Ardskenish, Colonsay in 1891 (Anderson 1907, fig. 7), is closely related to the strap-fittings from Cnip discussed above. Although there is no information surrounding its discovery, its possible association with a ringed pin, donated at the same time, suggests that both finds may have accompanied a pagan Norse burial. The buckle-plate is composed of a strip of bronze bent double with possible tinning to its surface. It has a narrow central midrib of D-shaped cross-section, with incomplete cross-ribbing cast in high relief. Its ends are splayed into terminals perforated by hollow hemispherical boss-capped rivets. The terminals are outlined with a finely incised contour line, as is the lower plate, which mirrors the upper plate's outline, but is otherwise undecorated. The D-shaped buckle loop is of circular section and ornamented with five, evenly spaced groups of transverse lines, with two or three notches in each. The tongue also has incised transverse lines at both its tip and prior to looping around the buckle, behind which are two medially-aligned incisions.

Although this strap-buckle shares several stylistic conventions with the Cnip strap-fittings discussed above, including its bent-double construction, the use of boss-capped rivets, incised borders and transverse lines, its exaggerated waisted form with

Fig. 11.5 Buckle and associated rivets, Fishamble Street, Dublin (1:1). (Photograph: National Museum of Ireland)

Fig. 11.6 Buckle, Ardskenish, Colonsay (1:1). (Photograph: Trustees of the National Museums of Scotland)

Fig. 11.7 *Buckles, Fishamble Street, Dublin (1:1). (Photograph: National Museum of Ireland)*

central midrib cast in high relief is rather unusual. However, this form, together with the cast cross-ribbing and splayed terminals, is characteristic of a series of ninth- to tenth-century bow brooches, known as the 'Birka brooch type', the distribution of which clusters around Birka, Sweden (Arrhenius 1984). Rather than proposing a direct link between the Ardskenish find and this series, it seems more likely that both share a common ancestry in late Roman military belt strap-slides (Bullinger 1969, Abb. 7: 1 and 2), which were formed from single cast strips of metal with decorated midribs set between splayed terminals. The Ardskenish strap-buckle is bronze and technical details confirm it as being of Insular workmanship. However, close iron parallels have been excavated from York (Ottaway 1992, fig. 296: 3746 and 3759; fig. 299: 3795 and 3796), and Fishamble Street, Dublin (Reg. Nos NMI: E172: 11740; E172:1538) (Fig. 11.7). A related strap-end from disturbed burials in the pre-Norman church at St Michael's, Workington, Cumbria (Paterson, in prep.) is of gunmetal. This, together with the Anglo-Scandinavian and Hiberno-Norse contexts of the iron parallels, suggests that, although the Ardskenish strap-buckle is bronze, some examples of this type of strap-fitting were being produced in the mixed ethnic communities of York and Dublin.

Conclusion

All the decorative belt-fittings recovered to date from the pagan Norse graves of Scotland, with the exception of a Carolingian example from Eigg (Macpherson 1879, fig. 11; Grieg 1940, fig. 39), are of Insular origin, with metallic compositions ranging from bronze to gunmetal. Their recovery from pagan Norse graves provides a dress context, and their popularity within the Scottish graves reflects a Scandinavian liking for the use of personal belts, which was probably influenced by the availability of Insular belts and may subsequently have stimulated production within such Hiberno-Norse centres such as Dublin. The gunmetal composition of several of the above examples would appear to corroborate the proposed production within such communities, where imported Scandinavian objects of brass were recycled together with native bronze, reflecting Hiberno-Norse interaction at a metallurgical level. It would be of great interest to investigate the metallic composition of some of the copper-alloy parallel finds from Dublin contexts to test whether such assumptions are valid.

Acknowledgements

My thanks go to Dr Katherine Eremin for kindly providing a summary of her analyses prior to publication. Dr Patrick Wallace and Dr Paul Mullarkey have kindly drawn my attention to the existence of related strap-fittings in the collections of the National Museum of Ireland over the years, and I am grateful for permission to refer to some of these in this article. Professor James Graham-Campbell's informed comments on my draft accounts of the finds and this article have been invaluable.

References

ANDERSON, J. 1907, 'Notice of bronze brooches and personal ornaments from a ship burial of the Viking time in Oronsay, and other bronze ornaments from Colonsay', *Proc. Soc. Antiq. Scotl.* 41 (1906–7), 437–50.

ARRHENIUS, B. 1984, 'Bügelfibeln', in G. Arwidsson (ed.), *Birka II:I Systematische Analysen der Gräberfunde*, 39–44. Stockholm.

BAKKA, E. 1963, 'Some English decorated metal objects found in Norwegian graves: contributions to the art history of the eighth century A.D.', *Årbok for Universitetet i Bergen, Humanistik Serie* 1, 1–66.

BAKKA, E. 1965, 'Some decorated Anglo-Saxon and Irish metalwork found in Norwegian Viking graves', in A. Small (ed.), *The Fourth Viking Congress 1961*, 32–40. London.

BAYLEY, J. 1992, *Anglo-Scandinavian Non-Ferrous Metalworking from 16–22 Coppergate* (= The Archaeology of York: The Small Finds, 17/6).York.

BENDER-JØRGENSEN, L. 1987, 'The textile remains', in Welander *et al.* 1987, 165–68.

BERSU, G. and WILSON, D. M. 1966, *Three Viking Graves in the Isle of Man* (= Soc. Medieval Archaeol. Monogr. Ser. 1).

BLINDHEIM, M. 1984, 'A house-shaped Irish-Scots reliquary in Bologna, and its place among the other reliquaries', *Acta Archaeologica* 55, 1–53.

BØE, J. 1940 *Norse Antiquities in Ireland*. In Shetelig (ed.) Part III.

BULLINGER, H. 1969, *Spätantike Gürtelbeschläge*. Brugge.

COFFEY, G. and ARMSTRONG, E. C. R. 1910, 'Scandinavian objects found at Islandbridge and Kilmainham', *Proc. Roy. Ir. Acad.* 27C, 107–22.

DE PAOR, L. 1961, 'Irish belt-buckles and strap-mounts', *Bericht über den V Internationalen Kongress für Vor- und Frühgeschichte Hamburg 1958*, 649–53.

DISCOVERY and EXCAVATION 1994, 'Ashaig (Strath Parish)', in C. E. Batey with M. Keys (eds), *Discovery and Excavation in Scotland 1994*, Council for Scottish Archaeology, 43–4.

EDWARDS, A. J. H. 1934, 'A Viking cist-grave at Ballinaby, Islay', *Proc. Soc. Antiq. Scotl.* 68 (1933–34), 74–7.

EREMIN, K. and WILTHEW, P. 1997, 'Analysis of copper-alloy artefacts from pagan Norse graves in Scotland', *National Museums of Scotland Analytical Research Report* 97/52.

FANNING, T. 1994, *Viking Age Ringed Pins from Dublin*. Medieval Dublin Excavations 1962–81 Ser. B, vol. 4. Dublin.

GRAHAM-CAMPBELL, J. 1973, 'A fragmentary bronze strap-end of the Viking period from the Udal, North Uist, Inverness-shire', *Medieval Archaeol.* 17, 128–31.

GRAHAM-CAMPBELL, J. and PATERSON, C. forthcoming, *Pagan Norse Graves of Scotland*. Edinburgh.

GRIEG, S. 1940, *Viking Antiquities in Scotland*. In Shetelig (ed.) Part II.

HILL, P. 1997, *Whithorn and St Ninian. The Excavation of a Monastic Town 1984–91*. Stroud.

LANG, J. T. 1988, *Viking-Age Decorated Wood: A Study of its Ornament and Style*. Medieval Dublin Excavations 1962–81, Ser. B, vol. 1. Dublin.

MACLEOD, D. J., GIBSON, W. J. and CURLE, J. 1916, 'An account of a find of ornaments of the Viking time from Valtos, Uig, in the Island of Lewis', *Proc. Soc. Antiq. Scotl.* 50 (1915–16), 181–89.

MACPHERSON, N. 1878, 'Notes on antiquities from the island of Eigg', *Proc. Soc. Antiq. Scotl.* 12 (1876–78), 577–93.

NICHOLSON, A. 1997, 'Metalwork and sculpture: design and patronage in *c.* 900 AD', in Hill 1997, 621–23.

O'SULLIVAN, J. 1994, 'Excavation of an early church and a women's cemetery at St Ronan's medieval parish church, Iona', *Proc. Soc. Antiq. Scotl.* 124, 327–65.

OTTAWAY, P. 1992, *Anglo-Scandinavian Ironwork from Coppergate* (= The Archaeology of York: The Small Finds, 17). York.

RAFTERY, J. (ed.) 1941, *Christian Art in Ancient Ireland*, Vol. II, Dublin.

SHETELIG, H. (ed.) 1940, *Viking Antiquities in Great Britain and Ireland* Parts I–V. Oslo.

STEVENSON, R. B. K. 1968, 'The brooch from Westness', in B. Niclasen (ed.), *The Fifth Viking Congress, Torshavn 1965*, 25–31. Tórshavn.

WAMERS, E. 1985, *Insularer Metallschmuck in wikingerzeitlichen Gräbern Nordeuropas. Untersuchungen zur skandinavischen Westexpansion* (= Offa-Bücher 56). Neumünster.

WELANDER, R. D. E., BATEY, C. and COWIE, T. G. 1987, 'A Viking burial from Kneep, Uig, Isle of Lewis', *Proc. Soc. Antiq. Scotl.* 117, 149–74.

WILSON, D. M. 1970, *Reflections on the St. Ninian's Isle Treasure*. (= Jarrow Lecture 1969). Jarrow.

YOUNGS, S. (ed.) 1989, '*The Work of Angels'. Masterpieces of Celtic Metalwork, 6th-9th Centuries AD*. London.

12 An Aspect of Seventh-Century Anglo-Saxon Goldsmithing

Michael Pinder

While there have been several valuable studies on models, casting, inlaying and alloys in Anglo-Saxon jewellery, none have been published on smithing or hand working, with the exception of Whitfield's work on filigree, granulation and wire making. This is in no small part due to the fact that we have very little direct evidence of the Anglo-Saxon jeweller in the sixth to eighth centuries. However, the few finds we have of tools, such as the early seventh-century smith's hoard from Tattershall Thorpe in Lincolnshire (Hinton and White 1993), give us confirmation of the existence of some conventional jeweller's techniques at this early period. The basic tools of the jeweller and silversmith have altered little since they were first developed in Roman times or earlier. Hammers, shears, tongs, stakes and anvils of comparable forms are known from a variety of cultures, and at various dates throughout Northern Europe. The hammers and tongs from Tattershall Thorpe (Hinton and White 1993, fig. 9) are very close in form to those from a roughly contemporary site at Staraja Ladoga, western Russia (Vierck 1983, fig. 2), as are those from the tenth-century find at Mästermyr, Sweden (Arwidsson and Berg 1982, nos 65–71, pls 20, 21; nos 43, 44 pl. 22). It is worth noting here that modern jewellers' hand tools show very little alteration during the ensuing centuries. Only the basic and easily recognised tools have so far been identified, although there are a few small files, for example the 'needle file' from Tattershall Thorpe (Hinton and White 1993, pl. IIIc), but many other small and specialised tools, which are likely to have become heavily corroded, could easily have passed unremarked, particularly in earlier excavations. We are thus left with the surviving jewellery as the main source of evidence for the working practices of the fine jeweller or goldsmith in seventh-century England.

Theophilus' excellent twelfth-century *Treatise* discusses a number of tools and techniques which remain virtually unaltered in modern times (Theophilus 1963). A number of the recipes given in the possibly much earlier *Mappae Clavicula* have been shown by McFadyen (1999) to be not only perfectly viable, but also directly comparable with those given by Theophilus. It is also the case that, perhaps as a result of the secrecy which the need for security engenders, jewellery and silversmithing are more rooted in tradition than most crafts. It is reasonable to assume, therefore, that many of the working practices of the Anglo-Saxon jewellers are the same as those used today. This is not to belittle the skills and knowledge of the individual Anglo-Saxon jeweller in any way, nor to forget that they had knowledge and skills now lost to us. It remains the case, however, that a great deal can be learned about how a piece of jewellery was made from a close examination by a modern practising jeweller, even under relatively low magnification.

The gold and garnet cloisonné work of late sixth- and early seventh-century England represents one of the goldsmiths' most remarkable achievements during the Pagan and Conversion periods. Of this, a good number of pieces survive for us to study, in various states of repair from near-perfect to vestigial. One of the most impressive types is the large composite disc brooch, of which some seventeen are extant (Avent 1975, nos 169–83 and the brooches from Boss Hall, Suffolk (in Ipswich Museum) and Harford Farm, Norfolk (in Norwich Castle Museum)). These are highly complex pieces of design and construction which embody a very wide range of technologies. The front of a composite brooch is a very ornate disc of gold or copper alloy and garnet cloisonné, while the back is another disc, usually of a silver alloy, which holds the pin and catch. A finely reeded strip of gold, silver or copper alloy binds the front and rear assemblages together (Pinder 1995,

11–13). The manufacture of such strips is the subject of this paper.

The Kennard brooch from Faversham, Kent (Fitzwilliam Museum, Cambridge, Inv. No. M/2/1904; Avent 1975 no. 181), one of the largest and most impressive of the composite disc brooches, has, in addition to its rim-strip, four reeded gold strips in a cruciform arrangement on its central boss (Avent 1975, pl. 71). It also has two small pieces of reeded strip used as extra 'washers' beneath two of the rivet heads holding the catch-plate onto the back. The use of such short lengths of reeded strip is a characteristic feature of many other surviving pieces of late sixth- and early seventh-century Anglo-Saxon gold jewellery. For example, a large number of pendants have suspension loops made from reeded strips. I have critically examined sixteen of these, including two which were investigated using the facilities of the British Museum Research Laboratories (see below). There are at least another 60 in existence which give every appearance of having such loops, although I have not yet been able to examine them all. A buckle from grave 16, Alton, Hampshire (Curtis Museum, Alton) has been repaired with long reeded strips of silver gilt riveted across it, while a rim mount in the same grave is held by four silver reeded strips (Speake 1980, pl. 6b; Evison 1988, cover, no. 16.2, 51–2)

Although the use of these strips is frequent in seventh-century Anglo-Saxon contexts, it appears to be rare during earlier and later periods. The comparison with Frankish and Merovingian composite-type brooches is of interest, since they generally appear to have plain rim-strips, but two large brooches from seventh-century contexts in Frisia have reeded strips joining their front and back sections. In her comprehensive assessment, Mazo Karras (1985) argued a hybrid status for these objects, between Anglo-Saxon England and Scandinavia. This technical relationship would seem to support that idea.

The use of reeded strips to make suspension loops and small decorative features is quite widespread over a much longer period on the Continent. It has not been possible to conduct an exhaustive survey for the purposes of this paper, but pendants which have reeded suspension loops come from several sites in Frisia, including over twenty from Wieuwerd alone (Webster and Brown 1997, pl. 53). Other examples can be seen from as far apart as Sweden and the Byzantine provinces. They are commonplace on Scandinavian gold bracteates, for example, and can be seen on at least six of the pendants on the mid-tenth century belt from Vårby, Sweden (Graham-Campbell and Kidd 1980, pl. 23). Whitfield illustrates an eighth-century Byzantine coin brooch, the back of which shows a piece of corrugated reeded strip used to make the catch (Whitfield 1998, 75, fig. 46). A gold medallion of similar date from Commachio, Italy (*ibid.*, 75, fig. 47) has a row of upright double rings, which may well be made by a reeding technique. Elsewhere in this volume, she illustrates a provincial Byzantine bird pendant with a number of loops of ribbed strips placed around its edge (*ibid.*, figs 12b, 12c).

The reeding on the collars of the composite brooches comprises closely spaced parallel ridges running along their length. There may be as many as ten such ridges, giving very fine lines which, with the frequently found addition of decorative features such as beaded wires, produce a fine silky play of light around the perimeter of the brooches. Varying from 4.5mm to 11mm wide, most of these reeded strips can be seen to be flat on the back (for example that from Sarre, Kent; Reg. No. BM MLA 60, 10–24, 1; Avent 1975, no. 177, pl. 66). A few, such as the brooch from Boss Hall, Suffolk (Ipswich Museum), are made of thinner metal and are corrugated, the back of the strip being the reverse of the front. Close examination of all these brooches showed that, in nearly all cases, the lines which make up the reeding run exactly parallel.

In order to reach any worthwhile conclusions about the method or methods used to produce the reeding, it is necessary to examine examples under a high-powered microscope. Doing so should reveal any tell-tale traces left by the tools that were used, from which those tools might be identified. I have examined a very large number of examples of seventh-century Anglo-Saxon gold jewellery, but only with the aid of a 10x hand lens. Through the good offices of the Department of Medieval and Modern Europe and Department of Scientific Research at the British Museum, it was possible to examine five pieces of gold work of seventh-century date from their collections, each of which exhibits reeding in one form or another (see appendix).

There are a number of possible methods by which these reeded strips might have been produced, given what we know of the tools and materials available to the seventh-century craftsman. These are chasing, swageing, carving and draw-swageing.

Chasing

To the jeweller and silversmith, this means the decoration of a metal surface by the use of small punches, to make linear designs. Unlike engraving, metal is not cut away but is displaced by the action of the punch, which is a short, slim bar of iron or steel with one narrow, shaped end. The other end is struck repeatedly with a hammer while the craftsman guides it along. The metal to be decorated needs to be held firmly while the chasing is being done, and this is normally done by sticking it into a hard, bitumen-based pitch. This melts easily, sticks to the metal, and yet is resilient enough to maintain its grip while the metal is worked on. If the metal being decorated is thick, then lines can be chased which will appear only on the front of the piece. If, on the other hand, it is thin, then a negative of the work done on the front will appear on the back. Although Lebecq (1997, 68) has shown that pitch was being traded at least as near as Marseilles in the late sixth century AD, and pitch was used as a supporting medium inside some classical Greek jewellery, there is no evidence of such use in Anglo-Saxon jewellery, where calcite or quartz pastes were the usual materials for this purpose. A constituent of modern chaser's pitch is, however, 'Swedish pitch', which is a conifer resin derivative, so it is possible that a suitable substance was available.

There is, therefore, a possibility that these reeded strips were chased, either by individually chasing each line with a fine single-edged punch, or by using one with some sort of multi-grooved end. The skill of the Anglo-Saxon goldsmith is beyond question, but the extreme accuracy of the parallel ridges tends to point away from this purely skill-based technique. A more practicable method would be to have a punch with the negative of the lines cut on its face (Fig. 12.1). By repeatedly punching along the length of the strip, this should produce the reeded effect. It is possible that such a punch would not need to have covered the full width of the strip; by having only two or three grooves on its surface, it should be possible to produce any number of parallel lines by overlapping by one groove in the punch, and using the previously made grooves as a guide (Fig. 12.2). This method would still require great skill, and it would have been very difficult to achieve the completely even, unblemished result which is still evident. Even so, if the lines had been chased, microscopic examination could be expected to reveal tell-tale signs of the process – closely spaced and repeated dents or facets from the punch. In fact, no such punch-marks were visible on any of the pieces examined for this paper, and were not apparent on any previously studied jewellery.

In this context, the brooch from Harford Farm, Caistor St Edmund, Norfolk has an interesting repair. In order to replace a lost section of pseudo-plait, a thin strip of gold has been somehow impressed with concentric lines, of about the same spacing as the rim-strip. The line-spacing is good, and of similar scale to that on the rim of the brooch (Penn 2000, 109). There are, however, some slight variations which are hard to explain. It was only possible for the writer to examine this piece through a 10x hand lens, and at this magnification, no individual punch marks could be seen. It may well be the case that a punch with several grooves in its face was used to produce this strip, but to do so on an arc would probably be extremely difficult.

Swageing

This is, in effect, the reverse procedure to punching. The negative of the reeding would be cut into a solid piece of iron, and this is known as a swage, or swage-block (Fig. 12.3). The strip of gold would simply be hammered along its length into the profile cut into the swage (Fig. 12.4). Only a short run of the profile is necessary, as long as it is greater than the width of the hammer being used, in order to avoid inadvertently hammering the strip against the edge of the block, thus impressing a deep and irredeemable step across all the lines. This is a very effective way of producing short lengths of 'moulding', and the swage is fairly easy to make. The evidence of the process is to be found on the back of the strip where the hammering is done (there would be no sign of it on the front of a well made strip). The only piece examined which enabled a good length of the back to be seen was the fluted strip from the wand found at mound 1, Sutton Hoo, Suffolk (Bruce Mitford 1978, 400, figs 284–85; inv. no. 31). This showed no sign of any hammer marks.

In an earlier paper, I showed that three of the composite brooches have rim strips which do not have flat backs, but are in fact corrugated (Pinder 1995, 11–13, 21–2). These are the brooches from Boss Hall (Ipswich Museum), Monkton (Ashmolean Museum Inv. No. 1972.1401; Avent 1975, no. 172)

Fig. 12.1 *Tip of multi-lined punch*

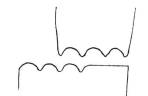

Fig. 12.2 *Using previous lines to guide multi-lined punch*

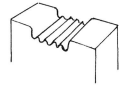

Fig. 12.3 *Swage block*

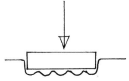

Fig. 12.4 *Hammering strip into swage block*

and Milton (Victoria and Albert Museum Inv. No. 82 2 13.1; Avent 1975, no. 183). It would be possible to produce this effect by swageing a thin strip using a soft mallet instead of a hammer, which would allow the metal to corrugate. Evidence for this technique is not easy to spot, especially in pieces where the back of the strip is largely obscured. If it is done well, as so much Anglo-Saxon work is, no traces of the making process would remain. There would certainly not be any of the rigidly parallel scratches which can be seen on most of the pieces examined at the British Museum (see below). Any faults in swageing would affect all the grooves in the area of the error, not individual ones, so the variations in line-width which can be seen on the very finely reeded Milton brooch, could simply be the result of over-enthusiastic filing. Even though this strip appears to be very thin gold, the reeding is so fine that even a very slightly misaligned file could cause the damage.

Carving

This method of making reeded strips was suggested during discussions with Dr Paul Craddock at the Department of Scientific Research in the British Museum. It involves the use of an adaptation of the silversmith's scraper. This tool normally comprises a heavy steel strip, with one end bent at right angles and sharpened (Fig. 12.5). It is used to clean up uneven areas of metal, such as those marred by poor soldering. Although little used nowadays, the principle of scraping has a long history. Theophilus (1963, 91) describes a small-scale scraper, related in form to an engraving tool. The description is open to interpretation, but he seems to suggest that it is the side of the tool which does the work, rather than the end. Cellini describes a much larger tool for cleaning the surfaces of cast silver plates (Ashbee 1883, 83). A scraper could be simply adapted by cutting the negative of the desired profile in its working edge. By repeatedly dragging this along a suitable width of gold strip the reeding could be carved into the surface (Figs 12.6, 12.7). This is a laborious process, requiring a sharp cutting tool. Tests carried out with a tool made of modern mild steel showed the need for frequent sharpening. This method leaves parallel scratches along the length of the grooves, similar to

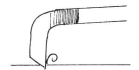

Fig. 12.7 *Carving along strip to produce reeding*

those found on some of the examples examined at the British Museum. The marks on the Anglo-Saxon pieces were much finer than on the test-piece, however, and the latter also showed some fine 'chatter' marks. Both of these phenomena could be ascribed to a lack of expertise on the part of the writer, but the laborious nature of the technique is probably the more significant point to note.

Draw-swageing

This is the most effective currently known hand method for producing fine, even reeding. Although well known in silversmithing for at least 300 years, there appear to be no early references to the technique; neither Cellini in the sixteenth century (Ashbee 1888) nor Theophilus in the twelfth century make mention of it. The process involves pulling a flat strip of metal through the gap between a shaped iron or steel die and a flat, hard surface. It is necessary to be able to make very fine adjustments to this gap, so that the strip can be pulled through a successively smaller opening, thus gradually transferring to it a negative of the profile on the die. If the surface opposite the profile is of an equally hard material, the completed strip will have the desired ridges on one side, the reverse remaining flat. If, on the other hand, this part is of a softer material, and the metal strip is thin, a corrugated strip will be obtained. The metal is normally pulled through the draw-swage assembly by hand, which is perfectly feasible for the small strips of silver and gold alloys we are concerned with here, but the apparatus needs to be firmly anchored to allow the metal to be drawn through it.

The modern draw-swage is made of steel, with a screw thread to enable adjustments to be made as work progresses (Fig. 12.8; Wilson 1902, 229–31, figs 152–54; Goodden and Popham 1971, 57, pls 20, 21). Clearly, since we have no evidence of screw-cutting at this early date outside the Byzantine world, some other means of clamping and adjustment would have been necessary. Possibly there was an adaptation of the type of locking tongs found at Staraya Ladoga (Vierck 1983, figs 2, 3), which could have been adapted by cutting a profile in the face of one jaw. The strip could have been drawn through while the jaws were held against two upright bars driven

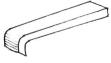

Fig. 12.5
Silversmith's scraper

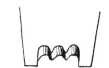

Fig. 12.6 *Scraper end, adapted to cut reeding*

Fig. 12.9 *Close-up of strip made using modern draw-swage*

Fig. 12.8 *A modern draw-swage, being used to produce corrugations along the length of a thin strip of copper, by drawing it against a small piece of plywood*

Fig. 12.10 *Close-up of rim strip on the composite disc brooch from Faversham (Reg. No. BM MLA 1028'70). Fine parallel scratches can be seen at the bottom of some of the grooves. (Reproduced by kind permission of the Trustees of the British Museum)*

into something solid, like a tree-trunk. It is, however, difficult to see how, even with very long handles, it would be possible to achieve the fine degree of adjustment necessary. Another possibility is some kind of adaptation of the small clamps found in Viking contexts such as those from Hedeby (Graham-Campbell 1980, 135, no. 472) These are usually of antler, which is probably not strong enough to withstand the kind of stresses involved in draw-swageing, but an iron one was found at Hedeby, and this would indeed be strong enough. These clamps are extremely similar to a modern type of jeweller's clamp, normally made of two hardwood jaws held together by a steel ring. The work is placed between them at one end, and a wedge driven in from the other end to provide the gripping pressure. The Viking clamps are of such similar form that it is very likely they were used in the same way. Wooden wedges would have been perfectly adequate, and although I know of none being found in association with these clamps, they may well be lost to us through decomposition. If the face of one jaw of such an iron clamp was cut with a suitable profile, then the wedge would provide very fine adjustability. How such a clamp would be held firmly enough to draw the wire through is not so easy to visualise, but like the tongs mentioned above, the tool does not need to be gripped, only prevented from moving in the direction in which the metal strip is being pulled through.

The modern draw-swage produces rigidly parallel scratches, best seen at the bottom of the grooves in the reeding (Fig. 12.9). Similar lines were clearly visible in the same position on several of the pieces examined microscopically, for example the rim on the brooch from Faversham (Reg. No. BM MLA 1028' 70; Fig. 12.10) and the strip from the Sutton Hoo 'wand' (Reg. No. BM MLA 1939, 10–10, 31; Fig. 12.11). The same examination revealed, however, that these pieces had been worked on subsequent to the formation of the reeding, probably with a fine file, with the result that the parallel scratches only run for short distances before being obscured by probable file marks. This filing may have been necessary to remove any blemishes in the reeding, such as accidental scratches made during assembly

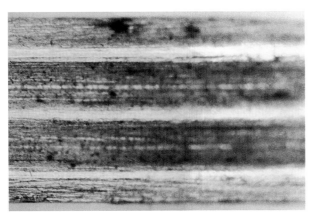

Fig. 12.11 *Close-up of the reeded strip from the Sutton Hoo 'wand' (Reg. No. BM MLA, 1939, 10–10, 31). Long parallel scratches are clearly visible. (Reproduced by kind permission of the Trustees of the British Museum)*

remains an unlikely choice, in my view, but no practicable alternative presents itself in this case.

The widespread use of reeded strips, even for seemingly mundane purposes, would suggest that they were not terribly difficult to produce. Had it been necessary to spend hours of concentration to produce such strips, the craftsman is hardly likely to have used them as washers on the back of a piece of jewellery, as on the Kennard brooch mentioned earlier. Examination of many pieces of reeding has made it obvious that there is much variation in width and proportion from one to another. This may indicate one of two things – either each goldsmith had his own individual tool, or that the tools were relatively easily made. The latter seems by far the most likely interpretation of the evidence. It may also be that the tools wore out quickly, which is quite likely if they were made of soft iron or bronze. The likelihood that knowledge and skill varied amongst jewellers must also be taken into account. This is most marked in the difference between the rim on the Boss Hall brooch already mentioned, and that on, for example, the Kennard brooch. The former is very thin, corrugated, and with relatively coarse reeding, while the latter has a flat back and extremely fine reeding.

The absence of any seventh-century tools which can definitely be assigned to the making of these strips means that the existence of any reeding technique in Anglo-Saxon England must be conjectural. There is, however, enough evidence to indicate that they were produced either by carving or by draw-swageing, and for the reasons given above, my preference rests with the latter. There is clearly a strong relationship between draw-swageing and wire drawing, and there is much debate about the beginnings of that technique in Anglo-Saxon metal working. More work needs to be done in this area of research, and it is obvious that a much broader sample needs to be considered before the definite existence of draw-swageing can be asserted.

of the brooch. It may also be the case that some 'chatter' occurred during the making of the strip, as happened with some of my early experiments. This occurs when the strip vibrates rapidly as it is drawn through the swage, and causes the strip to show very closely spaced undulations running at right-angles to the reeding. This would need to be removed, and filing is the most likely method by which this was done.

Discussion

There is clear evidence against two of these possible methods of manufacture. Chasing can be ruled out by the lack of evidence on the pieces examined, with the possible exception of the repair to the Harford Farm brooch, mentioned above. The lack of any hammer marks on the back of any of these strips, where visible, shows that they are unlikely to have been swaged. The scratch-marks in the troughs of the reeding are ambiguous, and are frequently disturbed by the marks left by filing. What they certainly tell us is that the process used was either draw-swageing or carving. The tendency to 'chatter', the coarseness of the parallel scratches and the laborious nature of the process all point away from carving and, while it cannot be ruled out, this seems the least likely of the two remaining options.

It is noteworthy that the fragmentary copper-alloy rim of a brooch from Chamberlain's Barn, Bedfordshire (Luton Museum), appears not to be produced by any of the methods discussed so far. The lines on this piece vary in width quite markedly, which is an impossibility with any of these techniques, with the exception of the first method discussed above – chasing with a single-point punch. This method

References

ARWIDSSON, G. and BERG, G. 1982, *The Mästermyr Find. A Viking Age Toolchest from Gotland.* Stockholm.

ASHBEE, C. R. 1888, *The Treatises of Benvenuto Cellini on Goldsmithing and Sculpture.* London (reprinted 1967, New York).

AVENT, R. 1975, *Anglo-Saxon Disc and Composite Brooches,* 2 parts (= B.A.R. Brit. Ser. 11). Oxford.

BRUCE-MITFORD, R. L. S. 1978, *The Sutton Hoo Ship-Burial,* Vol. 2. *Arms, Armour and Regalia.* London.

EVISON, V. I. 1988, *An Anglo-Saxon Cemetery at Alton, Hampshire* (= Hampshire Fld Club Archaeol. Soc. Monogr. 4). Gloucester.

GRAHAM-CAMPBELL, J. 1980, *Viking Artefacts: A Select Catalogue*. London.

GRAHAM-CAMPBELL, J. and KIDD, D. 1980, *The Vikings*. London.

GOODDEN, R. Y. and POPHAM, P. 1971, *Silversmithing*. London.

HINTON, D. and WHITE, R. 1993, 'A smith's hoard from Tattershall Thorpe, Lincolnshire: a synopsis', *Anglo-Saxon Engl.* 22, 147–66.

LEBECQ, S. 1997, 'Routes of change: production and distribution in the West (5th-8th century)', in Webster and Brown (eds), 67–78. London.

MAZO KARRAS, R. 1985, 'Seventh-century jewellery from Frisia: a re-examination', *Anglo-Saxon Stud. Archaeol. Hist.* 4, 159–77.

MCFADYEN, A. H. 1999, Aspects of the Production of Early Anglo-Saxon Cloisonné Garnet Jewellery. Unpublished PhD thesis, Manchester Metropolitan University.

PENN, K. 2000, *Norwich Southern Bypass Part II: Anglo-Saxon Cemetery at Harford Farm, Caistor St Edmund* (= East Anglian Archaeol. Rep. 92). Dereham.

PINDER, M. 1995, 'Anglo-Saxon garnet cloisonné, composite disc brooches: some aspects of their construction', *J. Brit. Archaeol. Ass.* 148, 6–28.

SMITH, C. S. and HAWTHORNE, J. G. 1974, 'Mappae Clavicula: a little key to the world of medieval techniques', *Trans. American Philosophical Soc.* New Series 64(4).

SPEAKE, G. 1980, *Anglo-Saxon Animal Art and its Germanic Background*. Oxford.

THEOPHILUS 1963, *On Divers Arts*. (trans. J. G. Hawthorne and C. S. Smith, reprinted 1976). Chicago.

VIERCK, H. 1983, 'Ein Schmeideplatz aus Alt-Ladoga und der präurbane Handel zur Ostsee vor der Wikingerzeit', *Münstersche Beiträge zur Antiken Handelsgeschichte* Band II, 2, 3–64.

WEBSTER, L. and BROWN, M. 1997, *The Transformation of the Roman World AD 400–900*. London.

WHITFIELD, N. 1998, 'The manufacture of ancient beaded wire: experiments and observations', *Jewellery Stud.* 8, 58–86.

WILSON, H. 1902, *Silverwork and Jewellery*. London (reprinted 1973).

Appendix

Observations on the jewellery examined microscopically at the Department of Scientific Research, British Museum.

1   The 'fluted strip' from the Sutton Hoo, Suffolk rod/wand. Reg. No. BM MLA 1939, 10–10, 31.
    Long parallel groups of scratches clearly visible in the grooves, but disturbed occasionally by groups of scratches running slightly diagonally. These appeared only to occur in single grooves.

2   The composite disc-brooch from Faversham, Kent. Reg. No. BM MLA 1028' 70.
    Parallel scratches clearly visible in the grooves on the rim strip, but overlaid, in single grooves, with groups of parallel scratches, probably file marks.

3   The composite disc-brooch from Sarre, Kent. Reg. No. BM MLA 60, 10–24, 1.
    Hints of parallel scratches visible in the grooves, but very worn and disturbed.

4   The pendant from Wye Down, Kent. Reg. No. BM MLA 93, 6–1, 189.
    No marks of any kind observable in the grooves on the suspension loops.

5   The pendant from Faversham, Kent. Reg. No. BM MLA 1145' 70.
    Clearly defined parallel scratches visible in the grooves on the suspension loop.

13   The Earliest Filigree from Ireland

Niamh Whitfield

Recent geological work has shown that native gold is relatively common in Ireland (McArdle *et al* 1987; Ixer *et al* 1990). It is puzzling therefore to find that while the art of goldsmithing, which included a knowledge of gold filigree work, flourished there in the prehistoric period, the working of gold seems to have been entirely forgotten in the early centuries of our era.[1] Some late Roman gold finger-rings decorated with filigree were left as a votive deposit at the prehistoric passage-grave at Newgrange in the fourth century AD (Kent and Painter 1977, nos 231, 232; Carson and O'Kelly 1977, 53–4, pl. III), but these were exotic imports which had no consequence for native metal smithing traditions. For centuries copper alloy was the chief metal used in Ireland for high-status ornaments, and while medieval and later historical records often refer to Irish native gold (Whitfield 1993a; 1993b; 1998a, 40–1), the earliest written evidence of its exploitation dates to the ninth century. The source is a ninth-century gloss on an eighth-century legal passage on the offence of digging in someone else's silver mine (*méin*),[2] amended to include references to the mining of gold, iron, copper and *créd* (?tin) (Kelly 1997, 435–36).[3]

However, in the sixth and seventh centuries the Irish travelled widely in Europe, and forged strong links with rich and powerful Anglo-Saxon and Continental Germanic royal dynasties. As a result of the stimulation which all these contacts afforded there was a great cultural flowering. One of the many changes which occurred was the reintroduction of the working of gold and simultaneously, it seems, gold filigree. This is a technique which uses fine wires and granules to depict minute motifs. The topic to be addressed here is how and when gold filigree began to be made in early medieval Ireland.

Special skills are needed, not only to manufacture wires and granules, but also to solder them in place, so an entirely new craft such as filigree would have

had to be learnt at first-hand from foreign goldsmiths. When learning such a craft from scratch, the novice is likely to imitate both the decorative techniques and style of the master. So one should expect the first generation of Irish filigree makers to produce work closely modelled on the style of the craftsmen who instructed them. Indeed, they are likely to have followed these masters' work so closely that it should be possible to identify the origin of the latter, and to say whether they were, for instance, Anglo-Saxons, Merovingian Franks or Lombards. Nevertheless, craftsmen from one culture rarely mimic in its entirety the style of craftsmen from another. They are influenced by their different visual training. Moreover, they may not always fully understand the subtleties of an alien technique, and there is scope for misunderstanding about the methods used to achieve particular effects. All these factors should be borne in mind when considering the origins of early medieval Irish filigree.

It is also important to emphasise that filigree is a very conservative craft. The style current in medieval Europe as a whole ultimately descends from the filigree of the Classical world. Many techniques are common to numerous cultures. For example, decorative elements such as block-twisted wire (made by twisting a square- or rectangular-sectioned metal rod and then rolling it between two flat surfaces to produce a smooth round-sectioned wire, see Fig. 13.1a) (Whitfield 1990b, 14–20), beaded wire (round wires specially treated to imitate the effect of rows of beads, see Fig. 13.1b) (Whitfield 1998b), rope-twists[4] (made by twisting two wires together, see Fig. 13.1c) appear on filigree from a variety of far-flung places, including early medieval Ireland. The classical roots of medieval filigree in general, and the number of shared techniques, mean that in the identification of a regional style what is significant is the combination of elements, rather than the

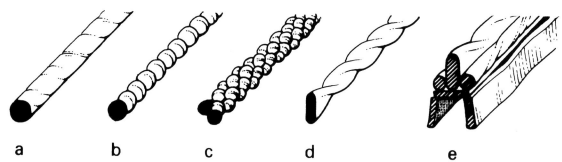

Fig. 13.1 *Schematic drawings of filigree wires: (a) block-twisted round wire; (b) beaded wire; (c) two-strand beaded rope-twist; (d) twisted ribbon; (e) profile of the combination found on Lagore filigree panel showing a twisted ribbon flanked by block-twisted wires, all resting on a flat gold support propped up on the edges of adjoining pseudo-cloisons. (Drawings: Nick Griffiths)*

occurrence of particular ones. This may involve the range of ornamental wires used, or the way wires are combined to form compound strands. It may also involve the forms of relief on the base-plate and the method used to attach the base-plate to the object to be decorated. Any attempt to characterise a regional filigree style should also, of course, include consideration of the type and style of motifs depicted by means of wires and granules.

The earliest large-scale filigree-decorated object in the early medieval Irish style is the Hunterston brooch. It was made in Ireland or perhaps the Irish kingdom of Dál Riata in Scotland,[5] at some time between the mid-seventh and early eighth centuries (Stevenson 1974, 28–40; Campbell and Lane 1993, 57–60; Whitfield 1993c, 126; Whitfield 2000, 211–47). While, as Stevenson (1983, 469–72) has shown, the treatment of the 'gap' between the two terminals shows a debt to Merovingian traditions, the pedigree of its filigree is clear. Both its techniques and motifs were clearly inspired by late sixth- to seventh-century Anglo-Saxon filigree. Anglo-Saxon filigree, in its turn, was heir to Germanic traditions developed in Scandinavia in the fifth century. So this particular filigree style is a Northern European, Germanic one (Whitfield 1997a, 211–25). Its presence on the Hunterston brooch and numerous later Irish pieces provides tangible proof of interaction between Irish and Anglo-Saxon goldsmiths. Nevertheless, while the Hunterston brooch filigree shows a heavy debt to these antecedents, it is too innovative for it to be mere imitation. The Anglo-Saxon filigree style has been absorbed and developed. So the Hunterston brooch hardly represents the efforts of a first-generation of goldsmiths experimenting with a new technique. This suggestion prompts the question, what evidence is there for earlier Irish filigree? This evidence is limited, and only three small objects survive which appear to predate the Hunterston brooch. In what follows these objects are discussed to see what they

reveal about the influences on Irish goldsmiths in the phase when the technique of filigree was being developed. The first two are described and analysed in detail; the third object is considered less closely here, due to lack of space in the present publication (see Whitfield forthcoming a).

The first object is a gold filigree panel from the crannog at Lagore (Figs 13.2a, 13.3). It was discovered during Hencken's excavations in the earliest level, in a stratum in which fragments of E ware pottery were also found (Hencken 1950, 86–7).[6] Ewan Campbell has proposed that this type of pottery carried goods, rather than being traded in its own right. Following his latest research, E ware originated in Western France in the later sixth century, had a *floruit* in the early seventh and continued to the end of the seventh century (Campbell 1996a, 80; Campbell 1996b, 92–3). So on the basis of the presence of E ware, the Lagore filigree mount can be assigned a dating bracket of late sixth to late seventh centuries.

The second object to be considered is the Garryduff bird (Fig. 13.11), discovered during O'Kelly's excavations of ring-fort no. 1 at Garryduff, Co. Cork. It also came from the earliest level of the site which likewise contained E ware (O'Kelly 1962, 27–30). So if we follow Campbell, a dating bracket of late sixth to late seventh centuries also applies.

The third is not well known, although it has been in the British Museum since 1849 (Reg. No. BM MLA, 1849, 3–1, 30). It is a gold finger-ring (Fig. 13.15) which was formerly in the collection of the Irish antiquarian, Redmond Anthony from Piltdown, Co. Kilkenny. Its Irish midlands provenance was recently established by Mary Cahill, who has discovered a nineteenth-century account which stated that it was 'found by a man cutting turf in a bog near Tipp[e]r[ary]' (Cahill 1994, 98–9, Appendix I, 18/40). In this case there is no stratigraphy to provide dating brackets but art-historical evidence suggests it dates to the sixth to seventh centuries (Whitfield 1990a, 341–52). As noted, this object is too complex to permit full discussion here.

Making sense of the Lagore filigree panel, the Garryduff bird and the Tipperary finger-ring is not straightforward. No two are alike. What is more, each is *sui generis* and lacks close analogues anywhere. Nevertheless, they each can be fitted into the general context of medieval European filigree. The question to be considered here is what each implies about the contacts of Irish goldsmiths in the late sixth to late seventh centuries. In this period Ireland was Christian and had widespread contacts in Europe as well as in Britain, so it is particularly interesting to consider whether the filigree on the objects in question stems from the same Northern European, Germanic tradition as does that on the Hunterston brooch, or whether other influences emerge. In other words, do we look only eastwards towards Anglo-Saxon England and ultimately northwards to earlier Scandinavian filigree work, or do we also look in a more southerly direction towards Frankish and Lombardic kingdoms or even further east towards the late Antique and Byzantine world? The answers may not be clear-cut, because matters are complicated by the numerous cross-cultural links in Europe in the sixth to seventh centuries. They are also complicated by the incomplete survival of filigree generally, which creates gaps in our knowledge of the background against which we must review these objects. With these *caveats* in mind, we will now consider each one in turn.

The Lagore filigree panel (Figs 13.1e, 13.2a, 13.3)

This panel (Fig. 13.3a, b), which was recovered in three fragments (Fig. 13.3c, d), consists of an incomplete, slightly asymmetrical, filigree-decorated, gold foil of roughly elliptical shape, with one end broken off. It was probably originally 48–50mm long.

In its centre (Fig. 13.3d) is a now empty, pointed oval, or vesica-shaped, *cloison* (about 12mm long) for garnet or glass, sub-divided by an empty transverse *cloison* (about 3.5mm long) of similar shape. On either side of this *cloisonné* work is interlace, delineated in filigree which stands proud of the back-plate. To use Adcock's terminology for interlace the pattern may be described as simple plaitwork with V-bends terminating in paired U-bends (Cramp 1984, fig 15b). Although the interlace on the narrower side of the foil (Fig. 13.3a, c) is incomplete, it seems to have been similar to that on the more intact, broader side (Fig. 13.3a, d). Each occupies a wedge-shaped space and consists of a six-strand

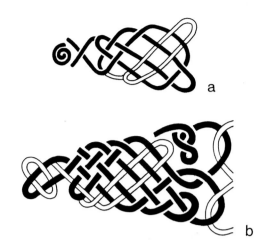

Fig. 13.2 *Schematic drawings of plaitwork: (a) motif on one side of the Lagore filigree panel; (b) motif on belt-buckle from Alton, grave 16, Hampshire. Scale approx. 2:1. (Drawings: (a) Nick Griffiths; (b) after Speake 1980, fig 4g)*

plait which shrinks to a four-strand plait, i.e. one where the pattern is spanned by three interlace crossings which reduces to two by the apex. The transition is accomplished by the introduction of an internal loop, linked to one of the U-shaped loops at the apex of the pattern (Fig. 13.2a). On the surviving apex of the panel an interlaced X-shaped link joins the plaitwork to a filigree spiral in whose centre is a rivet hole (Fig. 13.3c). Presumably this was matched by a spiral and rivet hole on the opposite end which would have allowed the panel to be securely riveted to the object it decorated. Although the shape of the panel is distinctive, it is not clear what type of object this was. It was not necessarily mounted in a decorative frame (*pace* Ryan 1989), but may instead have been directly attached to a wooden object such as a sword hilt or pommel (*cf.* Fig. 13.6).

The back-plate supporting this ornament is a (now torn) gold foil which is flat, apart from a little indentation caused by the filigree, visible as low ridges on the back. Two types of ornamental wire occur: (i) a central twisted ribbon (made by twisting a taut strip of gold) (Fig. 13.1d) and (ii) a far finer, block-twisted, round wire, which magnification reveals to have been insufficiently smoothed at various points and therefore it is sometimes more angular than the properly finished version shown in Fig. 13.1a.

These two types of wire are combined to create different effects. The panel as a whole is edged by a (now incomplete) two-wire border, which consists of an outer twisted ribbon inside which lies an inner block-twisted wire (Fig. 13.3c, d). This border stands proud, as it is attached to the top of the inside of a rim formed of the turned-up edge of the back-plate. On the outer wall of the large central *cloison* are

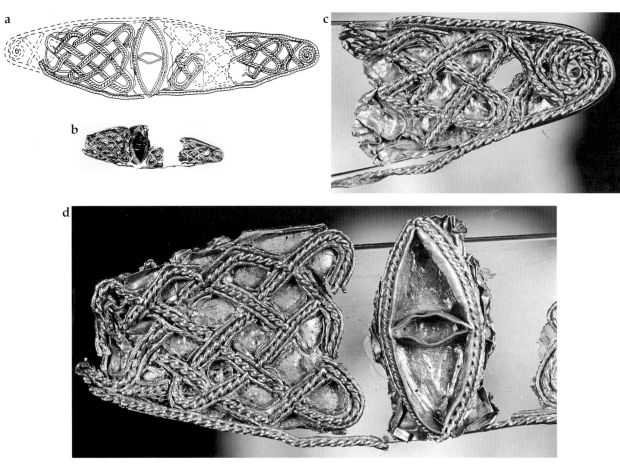

Fig. 13.3 Filigree panel from Lagore, Co. Meath (National Museum of Ireland, E14:216): (a) Reconstruction of the plaitwork pattern, scale approx.1.75:1; (b) front view, scale approx. 1:1; (c) detail of the filigree at intact tip of narrower side showing rivet hole in centre of spiral, scale approx. 5:1; (d) detail of filigree on broader side with damaged tip, mounted to show the locations of the breaks in the foil, scale approx. 5:1. (Photographs: (b) National Museum of Ireland; (c) & (d) author. Drawing: (a) Nick Griffiths)

instead three superimposed strands: a block-twisted wire above which are two twisted ribbons (Fig. 13.3d). A single, coiled, twisted ribbon delineates the spiral on the intact end of the foil (Fig. 13.3c).

The construction of the interlace pattern and X-shaped links is more complex (Figs 13.1e; 13.3c, d). They are each made of three-wire bands composed of a central twisted ribbon flanked on either side by a block-twisted wire (in fact, a single strand bent in two). The central twisted ribbon often extends beyond the flanking strands so as to close the gap at interlace crossing points. The wire bands all rest on flat gold supports which, in their turn, are propped up (with some overhanging) on the edges of small cells placed in the spaces between the interlace, each formed of a single strip of gold placed on edge (particularly visible by the broken edge in Fig. 13.3c). Hencken (1950, 87) called these background cells 'false *cloisons*', because they are too shallow and too irregular to have contained garnet or glass inlays:

their function is simply to raise the interlace pattern against its background. They also, in part, support the panel border, since the edges of those adjoining the border rest against the turned-up rim of the back-plate.

It is not possible to say how the flat gold supports for the filigree bands delineating the interlace were made. It may be that they rest on an upper foil which has been pierced so as to reveal the back-plate behind the 'false *cloisons*'. Alternatively, they may consist of a series of small horizontal strips of gold individually attached to the walls of the 'false *cloisons*' and running beneath each filigree band.

Discussion

At first sight the ornament on this filigree panel looks like a familiar Germanic combination of *cloisonné* and filigree interlace, and seems best

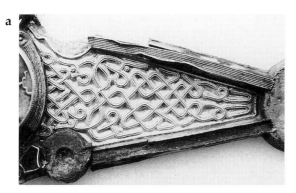

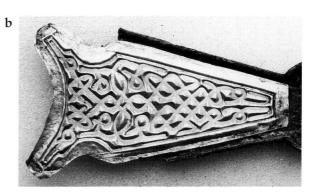

Fig. 13.4 *Belt-buckle from Wickambreux, Kent (British Museum, Reg. No. BM MLA 1905, 4–18, 14) with filigree mounted on impressed gold foil: (a) front view; (b) back view. Scale 1.3:1. (Photographs: author)*

Fig. 13.5 *Buckle from Faversham, Kent (British Museum, Reg. No. BM MLA 1094.1870) with filigree mounted on pierced impressed gold foil with flat back-plate beneath (so-called 'hollow platform technique'): (a) front view; (b)back view. Scale 2.25:1. (Photographs: author)*

paralleled by late sixth- to seventh-century Anglo-Saxon work. The use of riveting as a fastening technique (found also on the Hunterston brooch, see Whitfield 1993c, fig. 14.12), is also known, not only in Anglo-Saxon filigree work (e.g. Fig. 13.6), but also in Merovingian Frankish filigree (e.g. Fig. 13.12b, c). More specifically Northern European is the use of a three-wire band of wires raised above a sunken background to delineate interlace (*cf.* Figs 13.3c, d and 13.4a, 13.5a, 13.8). Tapered plaitwork with internal loops (*cf.* Fig. 13.2a, b) and vesica-shaped *cloisonné* cells also occur in this tradition (Fig. 13.7), although the latter are not sub-divided by central transverse vesicas in the Celtic manner. Initially, this detail, together with the spiral at the unbroken tip, are the only obvious features on the Lagore filigree panel that does not seem to have Anglo-Saxon antecedents, and they may be explained by an Irish origin – motifs from the native La Tène repertoire being added to domesticate a foreign design.

Yet, on closer inspection, the filigree on the panel is anything but conventional, and its manner of

construction finds no parallels in Anglo-Saxon or earlier Germanic filigree. Nor is it typical of early medieval Irish work.

One particularly distinctive feature is the composition of the three-wire band used to delineate the interlace (Figs 13.1e; 13.3c, d). While three-wire bands are also used in Northern European filigree for interlace, they are usually formed of a central beaded wire flanked by finer beaded wires (Figs 13.4a, 13.5a, 13.8). In such cases, twisted ribbons are never, to my knowledge, used to form the central element of such a band. In fact, twisted ribbons barely occur on sixth- to seventh-century Anglo-Saxon filigree.[7] They are far more common in Frankish work of the same period (e.g. Whitfield 1998b, fig. 53c), and this *could* be where Irish goldsmiths learned about this particular form of decorative wire. However, three-wire bands are not characteristic of Frankish filigree (which displays instead wire bands composed of two juxtaposed strands, usually a single wire bent in two). Moreover, the Lagore panel is the only surviving object in the Irish *corpus*

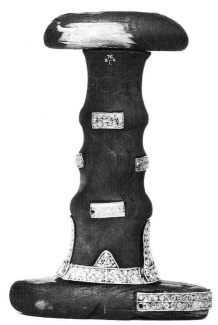

Fig. 13.7 *Head-plate from incomplete square-headed brooch from Faversham, Kent (British Museum, Reg. No. BM MLA 1096.1870), with vesica-shaped garnet* cloisonné *cells. Scale 1:1. (Photograph: author)*

Fig. 13.8 *Detail of disc-brooch from Grave 205, Kingston Down, Kent (Liverpool Museum, M 6226), showing* cloisonné *cells (some empty) and filigree panel with incomplete three-wire band of beaded wires resting on flat-topped ridges on impressed foil. Scale 2.5:1. (Photograph: author)*

Fig. 13.6 *Sword-hilt from Cumberland (British Museum, Reg. No. BM MLA 1876, 8–4, 1) with filigree panels attached by rivets. Scale 2:3. (Photograph: By permission of the Trustees of the British Museum)*

with a wire band of this precise type.[8] The other combinations of wire which occur on the Lagore filigree panel are also, to my knowledge, *sui generis*. What is particularly striking is that twisted ribbon takes over the decorative role played elsewhere by beaded wire (e.g Figs 13.4a, 13.5a, 13.6, 13.7, 13.8, 13.9, 13.11a, 13.14), a form of ornamental wire notably absent from this object.

Almost as unusual as the wirework is the way in which the relief on the foil is formed. Normally, in the Northern European tradition, and in Irish filigree derived from it, relief is created on the foil by hand-made repoussé or by stamping, and the filigree is mounted on the crests of the ridges created by one or other technique. This is the case whether an unpierced foil is used (Fig. 13.4a, b), or if alternatively, the sunken areas at the base of the filigree-bearing ridges on the impressed back-plate are pierced and a second flat foil inserted behind it (Fig. 13.5a, b), a method sometimes referred to as the 'hollow platform' technique (Whitfield 1987, 78; Whitfield 1997a, 224–25). On the Lagore filigree panel, in contrast, the wire is supported by pseudo-*cloisons*, a method which seems to reflect some confusion between filigree and *cloisonné* work (*cf.* Figs 13.3 and 13.8). This suggests that the Lagore panel was manufactured by a goldsmith who had some training in a novel technique (understanding, for instance, the art of soldering, the manufacture of round wire by block-twisting and the trick of closing the gap at interlace crossing points by extending the

central wire in a three-wire band) but with only a partial grasp of standard methods of achieving standard effects. He seems to have improvised to produce this curious hybrid, drawing on both *cloisonné* and filigree techniques.

The Lagore panel is not unique in the form of relief used, because some other pieces of Irish filigree have raised bands of wire supported in a similar way. One is an unattached panel from an unnamed crannog from Ireland, now at Alnwick Castle in the collection of the Duke of Northumberland (Fig. 13.9), which is impossible to date precisely, but which may also have been made in the seventh century (although a late ninth- to tenth-century date is also possible; Whitfield forthcoming b). This object was not examined under the microscope but only with a hand-lens and so details were difficult to see. However, it is clear that there a three-wire band is also supported by 'false *cloisons*' resting on a flat back-plate, though different types of decorative wire are used to 'draw' the pattern (a beaded wire flanked by fine spiral-beaded wires). It is difficult to know how to interpret the similar method of raising the filigree on both panels, but the more conventional wirework on the Alnwick panel makes it unlikely that they were made by the same individual.

Fig. 13.9 *Filigree panel from a crannog in Ireland (Alnwick Castle Museum. No. 530). Scale approx. 5:1. (Photograph: author)*

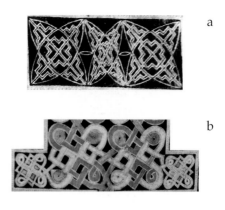

Fig. 13.10 *Folio 125v of the* Book of Durrow: *(a) detail of painted* cloisonné *work; (b) detail of interlace. Not to scale. (Photographs: The Board of Trinity College Dublin)*

It is a pity that the Alnwick filigree lacks a precise provenance within Ireland. The major part of the Irish collection at Alnwick was derived from that of Roger Chambers Walker of Sligo, who was probably responsible for the acquisition of the numerous objects from Ardakillen crannog in the Duke of Northumberland's collection. Ardakillen, or one of the other Roscommon crannogs, is thus also the most likely provenance of the filigree panel in question. However, it is just possible that it comes from Lagore, because another contributor to the Duke's collection, James Huband Smith, is known to have purchased items from Lagore (Whitfield forthcoming b).

A version of the technique reappears in later kite-brooches on one example, probably from Dublin (Reg. No. NMI 4W 27; Whitfield 1997b, no. 2, 502), and also on a newly-discovered panel from a lost kite-brooch from a tenth-century context at Temple Bar, Dublin (Simpson 1997, 28; Whitfield forthcoming c) – although in these cases the supporting base for the wire seems clearly cut from a single flat foil, which, as has been pointed out, may or may not be the mode of construction of the interlace patterns on the Lagore and Alnwick panels.

In any event, the scarcity of other examples of this Heath-Robinsonian way of raising filigree above its background suggests that this was a limited experiment, generally replaced by more conventional, and less fiddly, techniques.

The Lagore panel has some idiosyncratic decorative elements in common with another seventh-century object showing Anglo-Saxon influence, the Book of Durrow (Henderson 1999, 32–53). The following features on fol. 125v have counterparts on the filigree panel: (i) painted, vesica-shaped imitation *cloisonné* panels (albeit paired and overlapped to form an X-shaped motif on the manuscript) (Fig.

13.10a) and, in the attenuated lozenge-shaped fields between the latter; (ii) central transverse, miniature La Tène-style vesicas (Fig. 13.10a); (iii) plaitwork with U-bends and V-bends (Fig. 13.10b); (iv) interlaced X-shaped links between decorative units (Fig. 13.10b). The Lagore panel is unlikely to have been imported into Ireland and could well have been made at Lagore itself (Comber 1997, 110). The place of manufacture of the Book of Durrow, on the other hand, is hotly disputed, even though it is known to have been located at Durrow from at least the period 877 to 916 (Meehan 1996, 13). The above parallels support the evidence of the colophon which places the manuscript firmly in a Columban, and therefore culturally Irish, milieu (Meehan 1996, 22).

The Garryduff bird (Fig. 13.11)

The minute Garryduff bird is technically more accomplished than the Lagore filigree panel, and presents a different picture in other ways. It was an isolated find, but may originally have been one of a pair, or of a more complex grouping.

It consists of a minuscule piece of foil (Fig. 13.11c) cut in the shape of a bird (maximum dimensions: 15 x 10.5mm), whose proportions and sharply upturned tail indicate that it probably represents a wren, as O'Kelly (1962, 28) suggested. The foil has a flat rim, but is dished in the centre to suggest the rotundity of the bird's body. The front face (Fig. 13.11a, b) is covered with filigree decoration. Beaded wire divides the beak and edges the triangular projections denoting the legs (?) or ends of the wing (?). The flat rim edging the bird's body is more elaborately decorated with a three-wire band composed of a central rope-twist, composed of two beaded wires twisted together, which is flanked on either side by

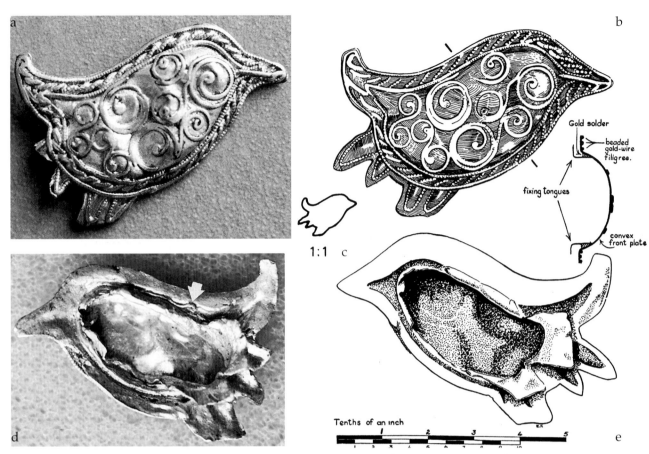

Fig. 13.11 *The Garryduff bird (Cork Public Museum L739): (a) & (b) front view, scale 5:1; (c) actual size; (d) & (e) back view, scale 5:1. Arrow on (d) indicates block-twisted round wire encircling strip of gold on edge. (Photographs: (a), (d) author. Drawings: (b), (e) after O'Kelly 1962; (c) Nick Griffiths)*

a single beaded wire. The bird's body is entirely covered by a scatter of S- and Z-scrolls 'drawn' by short lengths of beaded wire, now worn smooth on their upper surface. Each spiral has a club-shaped tip, formed by bending back the ends of the wire. The large spiral of the central scroll by the head seems to represent the bird's eye. The object was made for mounting on thin material such as metal, leather or cloth, because on the back (Fig. 13.11d, e) is a strip of gold on edge, soldered to the perimeter of the dished area. At its base the strip is encircled and buttressed by a block-twisted, round wire. The upper edge of the strip is nicked, so that tabs can be splayed out to fasten the bird on the thin material, like the eyelet on a boot. The 'fixing tongues' now vary in length, but O'Kelly (1962, 30) observed that they were damaged in antiquity.

Discussion

An important feature of the Garryduff bird is that its plump shape provides a surface for the display of scroll patterns. This contrasts with the Northern European Germanic filigree tradition where creatures, including birds (Haseloff 1981, Abb. 136m; Knape 1994, 94), have ribbon-like bodies which are extremely thin, sometimes so narrow that their trunk can fit only a single line of granules, which is the particular convention followed on animal ornament on the Hunterston brooch (Stevenson 1974, pls XII, XIII, XIVa; Whitfield 1997a, fig. 11.2). At present there is nothing like the Garryduff bird in the Anglo-Saxon filigree *corpus*, and its ornamental style points to other models. These are not hard to find if we look further eastwards. Indeed, small filigree creatures with bodies decorated with minute curvilinear motifs were fashionable over a wide area in the sixth to seventh centuries. The convention was known to the Merovingian Franks, who depicted a variety of creatures in this way, including birds and lions (Figs 13.12b, c). However, Merovingian filigree birds are not close cousins of the Garryduff bird. Their style is different. Moreover, the tiny motifs which ornament them may be more diverse than those on the Irish example, where just one pattern (an S-scroll) and its mirror image (a Z-scroll), appear.

Surprising as it may seem, there are better paral-

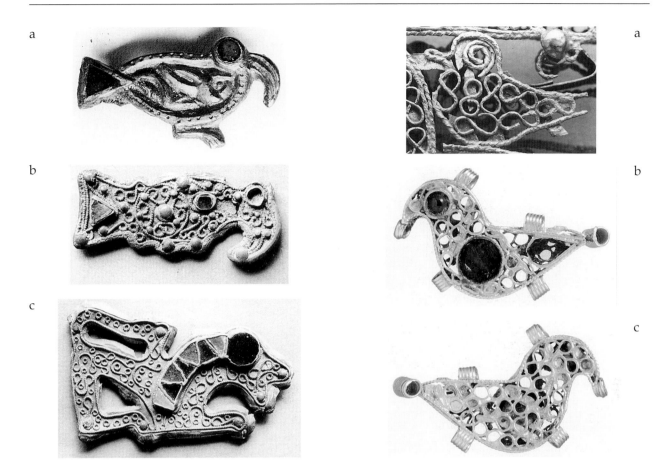

Fig 13.12 Bird- and animal-shaped brooches from France: (a) Bird-brooch from Herpes, Charente (Metropolitan Museum of Art, New York, 17,191.19) max. length 31.5mm; (b) incomplete eagle-shaped brooch from Sainte-Claire-sur-Epte, Val d'Oise (Musée des Antiquités Nationales, St-Germain-en-Laye, 72430), max. length 43mm; (c) incomplete lion-shaped brooch from Creul dans l'Oise (Musée des Antiquités Nationales, St-Germain-en-Laye, 50231), max. length 92 mm. (Photographs: (a) Metropolitan Museum of Art; (b), (c) author)

Fig. 13.13 Gold, openwork filigree birds: (a) bird with damaged tail on earring from Eastern Mediterranean (British Museum, Reg. No. BM MLA AF 349), max. length approx. 17.5mm; (b) front view of bird-shaped pendant from Maastricht (Rijksmuseum van Oudheden, Leiden 1 1995/12.2), max. length 20mm; (c) back view of Maastricht bird-shaped pendant. (Photographs: (a) author; (b), (c), Rijksmuseum van Oudheden, Leiden)

lels for the design of the Garryduff bird in provincial Byzantine gold filigree work from the Eastern Mediterranean, where the tradition may have originated. Fig. 13.13a illustrates one of a pair of birds from a sixth- to seventh-century gold filigree earring possibly from Egypt or Syria. Like the Garryduff bird, this little creature is minute. Other shared features are the similar chubby outline, the use of a scroll to denote the eye, and, most important of all, the repetition in the interior of the bird's body of the same minute motif (though a figure-of-eight rather than a scroll). The Garryduff bird's outline is more stylised, the curve on its back echoing that on its breast. The motif has also been adapted to native Irish taste by the use of club-shaped tips on the

spirals in the scroll patterns which replace the more usual granules. Nevertheless, its resemblance to Eastern Mediterranean examples is so close that its design has surely been influenced by provincial Byzantine models.

While church business sometimes took Irish clerics to Rome (Ó Carragáin 1994, 1–2) where such exemplars may have been seen, they could also have become acquainted with this convention closer to home, because minute gold filigree birds in this general style reached other parts of Western Europe. This is clear from the recent discovery at a site dating to *c.* 500–650 in Maastricht in the Netherlands of such a gold filigree bird (Peddemors 1996, no. a.3; Alkemade 1997, no. 23a, pl. 9.1).[9] This one is decor-

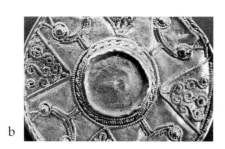

a   b   c

Fig. 13.14 *Three-wire bands composed of a beaded rope-twist flanked on either edge by a beaded wire: (a) pendant from Faversham, Kent (British Museum, Reg. No. BM MLA 1140.1870), height approx. 26mm; (b) detail of pendant from Milton Regis, Kent (British Museum, Reg. No. BM MLA 1926, 4–10, 2), diameter 38.5mm; (c) bracteate from Sønder Rind, Denmark (after Düwel et al 1975), diameter about 26mm. (Photographs: author)*

ated in addition with garnet or red glass and green stone or glass (Fig. 13.13b), and is suspended from a chain (not shown) perhaps attached to a jewel or, alternatively, to a cross in the manner of birds on fol. 132 of the mid-eighth century Frankish Gellesian Sacramentary (Nordenfalk 1988, 46). Though the Garryduff bird was never suspended in this way, the resemblance between it and tiny gold birds of this type is very striking, particularly when the back (Fig. 13.13c) rather than the front (Fig. 13.13b) of the Maastricht bird is considered.

Nevertheless, there are important technical differences between such filigree birds and the Garryduff example (*cf.* Figs 13.11 and 13.13). The former are executed in openwork and lack a gold foil back-plate. Moreover, ornamental wires other than beaded wire are used to 'draw' them. It is important to add that there are also technical differences between the Garryduff bird and Merovingian filigree creatures, which are often 'drawn' in spiral – (rather than right-angled) beaded wire (Whitfield 1998b, 76–9, figs 50, 51, 53a, 54–57).

In its manufacturing technique, as opposed to its style, the best parallels for the Garryduff bird occur on late sixth- to seventh-century Anglo-Saxon filigree. Firstly, on the bird (as is also standard in Irish work) the wires are firmly soldered to a foil back-plate edged by a filigree border (*cf.* Figs 13.11 and 13.4a, 13.5a, 13.6, 13.7, 13.8, 13.14b). Secondly, and significantly for dating purposes, the very distinctive three-wire band used on the rim of the Garryduff bird, a two-strand beaded rope-twist flanked on either side by a beaded wire, a device which seems to have originated in Scandinavia (Fig. 13.14c), is typical of late sixth- to seventh-century Anglo-Saxon filigree, where it also acts as edgings, either of an object as a whole (Fig. 13.14a), or of focal points such as studs (Fig. 13.14b). Thirdly, S- and Z-scrolls (used

to decorate the bird's body) also occur as space-fillers in Anglo-Saxon work, albeit inside geo-metrical patterns (Fig. 13.14b). Finally, the technique of mounting of the Garryduff bird has Anglo-Saxon parallels: little tubes splayed out at the bottom are reported by Avent (1975, 16) on some Anglo-Saxon disc-brooches, where they hold small garnets in place.[10] To conclude, all the techniques of manu-facture of the Garryduff bird can be matched on late sixth- to seventh-century Anglo-Saxon filigree.

How are the apparently different sources of inspiration in the design of the Garryduff bird to be interpreted? On the one hand, it may have imitated lost models which it resembled more closely, and if so, then it is not impossible that these were Anglo-Saxon. But on the other hand, it is to be remembered that the design of the Hunterston brooch incorpor-ates elements which seem to be of Merovingian origin, while its filigree derives from that of Anglo-Saxon England. The Garryduff bird may be similarly eclectic. Perhaps Irish goldsmiths on the Continent saw little Byzantine-style or Merovingian filigree birds whose bodies were covered with scroll-work and copied them using techniques of filigree manu-facture relatively recently acquired from the Anglo-Saxon England. An additional, if less immediate, source of inspiration may have been small chip-carved bird-brooches, fashionable in Francia from the mid-fifth to the late sixth century (Martin 2001, 237), which likewise depict minute birds with plump bodies. These lack scroll in the interior but some-times have prominent borders reminiscent of that on the Garryduff bird, as in the case of that illustrated in Fig. 13.12a. This is a particularly interesting example, because, although it is from a cemetery at Herpes, Charente, it belongs to a small group of such bird-brooches probably manufactured in Kent in the sixth century (Hines 2001, 283-84). It serves to em-

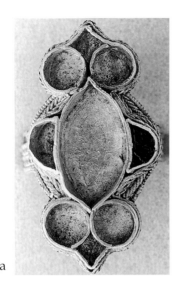

a   b

Fig. 13.15 The Tipperary finger-ring: (a) bezel (max dimensions approximately 33.5 x 19mm); (b) profile of bezel and hoop (max. internal dimensions: 18 x 17.5mm). (Photographs: author)

phasise how cross-channel contacts in this period led to the development of new designs in various regions, and is a reminder that the cosmopolitan character of the Garryduff bird is typical of its time.

The Tipperary Finger-ring (Fig. 13.15)

This ostentatious gold finger-ring, with its large bezel (about 33.5 x 19 mm) decorated with filigree and *cloisonné* and its filigree-decorated hoop (maximum internal dimensions: 18 x 17.5 mm) cannot be discussed in depth here but it is worth noting that it is the most puzzling of all three objects under review.

Its *cloisonné* work is eccentric (pers. comm. Noël Adams), which may mean that, like the Lagore filigree panel with which it shares the use of vesica-shaped *cloisons*, it was made by an Irish goldsmith who did not quite understand the models he followed. In Ireland in approximately the fifth to seventh centuries there was a vogue, influenced by late Roman fashion, for large, ostentatious finger-rings, usually made of copper alloy (e.g. Youngs 1989, nos 29, 30). The Tipperary finger-ring may represent an attempt to make an even more showy version of this type of jewellery, using a new material, gold, and the new-fangled techniques of *cloisonné* and filigree.

However, despite its Irish provenance, the finger-ring may not be Irish in origin. An alternative explanation is that it is an import, perhaps from the Merovingian kingdoms, where parallels for some details of its filigree can be found. This would be

equally interesting, given the current lack in Ireland of imported gold artefacts which inspired the Hiberno-Saxon style.

Conclusions

Study of the methods of manufacture of both the Lagore filigree panel and the Garryduff bird support the late sixth- to seventh-century date indicated by their stratification. What is more, as in the case of the Hunterston brooch, technically their filigree was most influenced by that of contemporary Anglo-Saxon England (although the goldsmith who made the Lagore filigree panel seems not to have fully understood his models). On both these objects, however, there are hints of influences from elsewhere. The use of twisted ribbon on the Lagore filigree panels may point to Merovingian contacts, while the design of the Garryduff bird seems influenced by Byzantine and Merovingian exemplars. The Tipperary finger-ring may also have Continental links. All this suggests that while the view that the Hiberno-Saxon style came into being as a result of contacts between Ireland, Scottish Dál Riata and Northumbria may be correct to a large extent, its origins are rather more complex. To suggest such contacts alone led to the new development of Irish art is to give a very thin base to a large structure, as Françoise Henry (1965, 53) remarked. Furthermore, the influences postulated here on technical and art-historical grounds are consistent with those suggested by studies of imported pottery and glass from sixth- and seventh-century Irish sites (Campbell 1996b).

Finally, the parallels between patterns on the Lagore filigree panel and the Book of Durrow should be taken into account in future debate about the origins of the manuscript. Françoise Henry (1965, 53) believed that the latter was made in a milieu

> 'where a fashion [was] setting in, a fashion based on the imitation of foreign models.'

Wherever the manuscript was illuminated, her remarks accurately describe the place in the history of Hiberno-Saxon art of the Lagore filigree panel and the Garryduff bird.

Acknowledgements

I would like to thank the following for facilitating examination of the objects under discussion: Mary Cahill and Raghnall Ó Floinn of the National Museum of Ireland and Michael Ryan, formerly of that institution; Stella Cherry and Samantha Melia of the Cork Public Museum; Leslie Webster, Dafydd Kidd, Virginia Smithson and Lisa Voden-Decker of the British Museum. For help with my research I thank Noël Adams, Barry Ager, Katharine Reynolds Brown, Mary Cahill, Alice Chadwick, Chris Entwistle, Cathy Haith, Andy Halpin, John Hines, Rebecca Lang, Arent Pol, Colin Shrimpton, Françoise Vallet, Richard Warner and Susan Youngs. I am, in addition, indebted to Nick Griffiths for his observations and for the patience and skill with which he drew Figs 13.1a-e, 13.2a-b, 13.3a and 13.11c.

Notes

1   The hiatus in gold working is perhaps explained by the fact that the most obvious gold sources had been depleted in prehistory, making the subsequent winning of gold more difficult. The hiatus perhaps also explains why the early Irish word for gold, *ór*, is not of archaic Celtic origin, but is a loan-word from the Latin, *aurum*, (Scott 1981, 117; McManus 1983, 42).
2   For discussion of the implications of the reference in the legal passage to gold mining, rather than to panning in streams and rivers, see Whitfield 1998a, 40–1.
3   The fine for illegal mining was five *séts* (*sét* = 'jewel, treasure, valuable': Kelly 1988, 114–15). In addition, the culprit had to restore the metal he had taken, even if it had been worked into a finished object.
4   This is the term used by jewellers to describe this particular combination of wires. In previous publications I have referred to it as 'twined wire' or 'cables'.
5   The term 'Irish' is here used to refer to objects, such as the Hunterston brooch, which are culturally Irish, and which may have originated in Ireland itself, in the Irish kingdom of Dál Riata in south-western Scotland or in an Irish monastery in Britain or Continental

Europe. For a new view of the origin of Scottish Dál Riata see Campbell 1999, 11–15.
6   Hencken's chronology has been the subject of extensive debate, conveniently summarised by O'Meadhra (1987, 61–3). Relevant to the gold filigree panel are: (i) suggestions that the occupation of Lagore may predate the 7th century (e.g. Raftery, 1981, 83–4) which have been convincingly countered by Warner (1985–6, 75–7); (ii) Lynn's interpretation of level Ia (where the foil was discovered) as the first phase of occupation (rather than that of construction, as Hencken suggested) (Lynn 1985–6, 69–73).
7   I have seen twisted ribbon on the following Anglo-Saxon pieces: (i) an incomplete jewelled disc-brooch from Ixworth (Stanton), Suffolk (MacGregor and Bollick 1993, no. 7.6; (ii) the Boss Hall (Ipswich), Suffolk, composite disc-brooch (Webster and Backhouse 1991, no. 33a); (iii) a gold openwork disc from Twickenham, Middlesex (Whitfield 1990b, fig. 9).
8   Twisted ribbons *are* used as the central element on three-wire bands on the Westness brooch from Orkney (Stevenson 1989, 250, illus. 11, 12). However, they do not appear on the Kilmainham brooch *pace* Hencken (1950, 87).
9   I am very grateful to Noël Adams for drawing this object to my attention.
10 The method used to mount the Garryduff bird also has parallels in the Irish filigree *corpus*. Tubes with tags like those reported by Avent on Anglo-Saxon work are used to attach filigree to studs on the 'Tara' brooch (R. Organ, pers. comm.), while tags are also used on the Ardagh chalice (to attach a ridged openwork foil to the flat foil beneath) (Organ 1973, 258, fig. 44).

References

ALKEMADE, M. 1997, 'Elite lifestyle and the transformation of the Roman world in Northern Gaul,' in L. Webster and M. Brown (eds), *The Transformation of the Roman World AD 400–900*, 180–93. London.

AVENT, R. 1975, *Anglo-Saxon Disc and Composite Brooches* (= B.A.R. Brit. Ser. 11). Oxford.

BROWN, K. R., KIDD, D. and LITTLE, C. T. (eds) 2001, *From Attila to Charlemagne. Arts of the Early Medieval Period in the Metropolitan Museum of Art.* New York.

CAHILL, M. 1994, 'Mr Anthony's bog oak case of gold antiquities', *Proc. Roy. Ir. Acad.* 94C, 53–109.

CAMPBELL, E. 1996a, 'Trade in the Dark-Age west: a peripheral activity?', in B. E. Crawford (ed.), *Scotland in Dark Age Britain*, 79–91. St Andrews.

CAMPBELL, E. 1996b, 'The archaeological evidence for external contacts: imports, trade and economy in Celtic Britain AD 400–800', in K. R. Dark (ed.), *External Contacts and the Economy of Late Roman and Post-Roman Britain*, 83–96. Woodbridge.

CAMPBELL, E. 1999, *Saints and Sea-Kings. The First Kingdom of the Scots.* Edinburgh.

CAMPBELL, E. and LANE, A. 1993, 'Celtic and Germanic interaction in Dalriada: the 7th-century metalworking site at Dunadd', in Spearman and Higgitt (eds), 52–63.

CARSON, R. A. G. and O'KELLY, C. 1977, 'A catalogue of the Roman coins from Newgrange, Co. Meath, and notes on the coins and related finds', *Proc. Roy. Ir. Acad.* 77C, 35–56.

COMBER, M. 1997, 'Lagore crannóg and non-ferrous metalworking in Early Historic Ireland', *J. Ir. Archaeol.* 8, 101–14.

CRAMP, R. 1984, *A General Introduction to the Corpus of Anglo-Saxon Stone Sculpture. Grammar of Anglo-Saxon Ornament.* Oxford.

DÜWEL, K., MÜLLER, G. and HAUCK, K. 1975, 'Zur Ikonologie der Goldbrakteaten IX: die philogische und ikonographische Auswertung von fünf Inschriftenprägungen', *Frühmittelalterliche Studien* 9, 141–85.

HASELOFF, G. 1981, *Die Germanische Tierornamentik der Volkerwanderungzeit. Studien zur Salins Stil I* (3 vols). Berlin, New York.

HENCKEN, H. 1950, 'Lagore crannog: an Irish royal residence of the 7th to 10th centuries AD', *Proc. Roy. Ir. Acad.* 53C, 1–247.

HENDERSON, G. 1999, *Vision and Image in Early Christian England.* Cambridge.

HENRY, F. 1965, 'On some early Christian objects in the Ulster Museum', *J. Roy. Soc. Antiq. Ir.* 95, 51–63.

HINES, J. 2001, 'Eclectic art of the early Anglo-Saxon jewelry', in Brown *et al*, 282–91.

IXER, R. A., MCARDLE, P. and STANLEY, C. J. 1990, 'Primary gold mineralization within metamorphosed iron ores, south-eastern Ireland', *Geol. Surv. Ireland Bull.* 4:3, 221–26.

KELLY, F. 1988, *A Guide to Early Irish Law* (= Early Irish Law Series, III). Dublin.

KELLY, F. 1997, *Early Irish Farming. A Study Based Mainly on the Law-texts of the 7th and 8th centuries AD.* Dublin.

KENT, J. P. C. and PAINTER, K. S. 1977, *Wealth of the Roman World. Gold and Silver AD 300–700.* London.

KNAPE, A. 1994, *The Magic of Gold in Life and Legend.* Stockholm.

LYNN, C. 1985–6, 'Lagore, County Meath and Ballinderry no. 1, County Westmeath crannogs: some possible structural reinterpretations', *J. Ir. Archaeol.* 3, 69–73.

MACGREGOR, A. and BOLLICK, E. 1993, *Ashmolean Museum, Oxford. A Summary Catalogue of the Anglo-Saxon Collections (Non-ferrous Metals)* (= B.A.R. Brit. Ser. 230). Oxford.

MARTIN, M. 2001, 'Early Merovingian women's broochs', in Brown *et al*, 226–41.

MCARDLE, P., MORRIS, J. H. and GARDINER, P. R. R. 1987, *Gold in Ireland. The Potential for Mineralization* (= Geol. Surv. Ireland Report Ser. RS 87/1 (Mineral Resources)).

MCMANUS, D. 1983, 'A chronology of Latin loan-words in early Irish', *Ériu* 34, 21–71.

MEEHAN, B. 1996, *The Book of Durrow. A Medieval Masterpiece at Trinity College, Dublin.* Dublin.

NORDENFALK, C. 1988, *Book Illumination. Early Middle Ages* (first paperback edn). Geneva.

Ó CARRAGÁIN, É. 1994, *The City of Rome and the World of Bede* (= Jarrow Lecture 1994). Jarrow.

O'KELLY, M. J. 1962, 'Two ring-forts at Garryduff, Co. Cork', *Proc. Roy. Ir. Acad.* 63C, 17–125.

O'MEADHRA, U. 1987, *Early Christian, Viking and Romanesque Art: Motif-pieces from Ireland, 2. A Discussion of Aspects of Find-context and Function.* Stockholm.

ORGAN, R. 1973, 'Examination of the Ardagh chalice: a case history', in W. J. Young (ed.), *The Application of Science in the Examination of Works of Art*, 238–71. Boston.

PEDDEMORS, A. 1996, 'Recent acquisitions IV.C. The Netherlands, Middle Ages', *Oudheidkundige Mededelingen uit het Rijksmuseum van Oudheden te Leiden* 76, 157–58.

RAFTERY, J. 1981, 'Concerning chronology', in D. Ó Corráin (ed.), *Irish Antiquity: Essays and Studies Presented to Professor M. J. O'Kelly*, 82–90. Blackrock.

RYAN, M. 1989, 'Filigree panel from Lagore crannog', in Youngs 1989, no. 222.

SCOTT, B. G. 1981, 'Some conflicts and correspondences of evidence in the study of Irish archaeology and language', in B. G. Scott (ed.), *Studies on Early Ireland. Essays in Honour of M. V. Duignan*, 115–19. Belfast.

SIMPSON, L. 1997, 'Researching Temple Bar's archaeology', *Archaeol. Ireland* 11:2, 26–8.

SPEAKE, G. 1980, *Anglo-Saxon Animal Art and its Germanic Background.* Oxford.

SPEARMAN, R. M. and HIGGITT, J. (eds) 1993, *The Age of Migrating Ideas. Early Medieval Art in Northern Britain and Ireland.* Edinburgh, Stroud.

STEVENSON, R. B. K. 1974, 'The Hunterston brooch and its significance', *Medieval Archaeol.* 18, 16–42.

STEVENSON, R. B. K. 1983, 'Further notes on the Hunterston and 'Tara' brooches, Monymusk reliquary and Blackness bracelet', *Proc. Soc. Antiq. Scotl.* 113, 469–77.

STEVENSON, R. B. K. 1989, 'The Celtic brooch from Westness, Orkney, and hinged-pins', *Proc. Soc. Antiq. Scotl.* 119, 239–69.

WARNER, R. 1985–6, 'The date of the start of Lagore', *J. Ir. Archaeol.* 3, 75–7.

WEBSTER, L. and BACKHOUSE, J. (eds) 1991, *The Making of England. Anglo-Saxon Art and Culture AD 600–900.* London.

WHITFIELD, N. 1987, 'Motifs and techniques of Celtic filigree: are they original?', in M. Ryan (ed.), *Ireland and Insular Art A.D. 500–1200*, 75–84. Dublin.

WHITFIELD, N. 1990a, *Celtic Filigree from the Seventh to the Ninth Century AD with Particular Reference to that on Brooches.* Unpublished PhD, University College London (4 vols), Vol 2.

WHITFIELD, N. 1990b, 'Round wire in the Early Middle Ages', *Jewellery Stud.* 4, 13–28.

WHITFIELD, N. 1993a, 'Some new research on gold and gold filigree from early medieval Ireland and Scotland', in C. Eluère (ed.), *Outils et Ateliers d'Orfèvres des Temps Anciens* (= Antiquités Nationales Mémoire 2), 125–36. Saint-Germain-en-Laye.

WHITFIELD, N. 1993b, 'The sources of gold in early Christian Ireland', *Archaeol. Ireland* 7:4, 21–3.

WHITFIELD, N. 1993c, 'The filigree of the Hunterston and 'Tara' brooches', in Spearman and Higgitt, 118–27.

WHITFIELD, N. 1997a, 'Filigree animal ornament from Ireland and Scotland of the late-seventh to ninth centuries: its origin and development', in C. E. Karkov, R. T. Farrell and M. Ryan (eds), *The Insular Tradition*, 211–43. Albany.

WHITFIELD, N. 1997b, 'The Waterford kite-brooch and its place in Irish metalwork', in M. F. Hurley, M. B.

Scully with S. W. J. McCutcheon (eds), *Late Viking Age and Medieval Waterford. Excavations 1986–1992*, 490–517. Waterford.

WHITFIELD, N. 1998a, 'Sources of gold in Ireland', *Archaeol. Ireland* 12:2, 40–1.

WHITFIELD, N. 1998b, 'The manufacture of ancient beaded wire: experiments and observations', *Jewellery Stud.* 8, 57–86.

WHITFIELD, N. 2001, 'The "Tara" brooch: an Irish emblem of status in its European context', in C. Hourihane (ed.), *From Ireland Coming*, 211–47. Princeton.

WHITFIELD, N. forthcoming a, 'A gold finger-ring found near Tipperary'.

WHITFIELD, N. forthcoming b, 'A gold filigree panel from an Irish crannog at Alnwick Castle, Northumberland', *J. Ir. Archaeol.* 10 (2001).

WHITFIELD, N. forthcoming c, 'A gold filigree panel from a lost kite-brooch', in L. Simpson (ed.), *Excavations at Temple Bar, Dublin*.

YOUNGS, S. (ed.) 1989, *'The Work of Angels'. Masterpieces of Celtic Metalwork, 6th–9th Centuries AD*. London.

Part V

Style: Analysis, Methodology and Meaning

14 The Barberini Gospels (Rome, Vatican, *Biblioteca Apostolica Barberini* Lat. 570) as a Paradigm of Insular Art[1]

George Henderson

The Barberini Gospels is a book the dimensions of which are within a very few millimetres the same as those of the Lindisfarne Gospels (London, British Library, Cotton Nero D.iv), the Durham Gospel fragments (Durham, Cathedral Library, MS A.II.16 and MS A.II.17), and the Echternach Gospels (Paris, Bibliothèque Nationale, Lat. 9389); also, interestingly, as the Salaberga Psalter in Berlin (Deutsche Staatsbibliothek MS Hamilton 553; Alexander 1978, nos 36, 9, 16, 10, 11, 14), that is 340 x 250mm. Except for its Barberini shelf number it oddly carries no extraneous marks that might indicate place of origin and subsequent history, although its style and content are loaded with indicators. The elegance and suavity of its design and colouring, and the curiousness and genuinely Antique flavour of some of its imagery explain why it might have appealed directly to Cardinal Francesco Barberini, the patron and founder of the great library to which it belongs (Osborne and Claridge 1998, 306). As the title of my paper suggests, it has, I believe, exemplary status with regard to Insular art.

The Fourth International Conference provided an opportunity to look again at what the parameters of the Insular style are, how the style informed itself and built and repaired its repertoire, and what visual ideas it invented and pursued. I have long taken the view that each and every Insular work of art, at least in the eighth century and probably before, was the result of choice and selection, and that quite widely different choice and selection were able to be made next time round by the same artists. Experiment and outreach were its essential qualities.

The fragmentary nature of the evidence relating to origin-centres and modes of transmission of motifs and ideas tends to give a claustrophobic feel to the discussion of the Insular style strictly on its home-ground. Many issues are indeed made clearer by consideration of the European dimension, as in Professor Nancy Netzer's recent study of the establishment and development of the scriptorium at Echternach (Netzer 1994a). There, in specific circumstances, we can observe the exercise of choice and selection: the direct influence on new works of respected models imported from the homeland – as when motifs in the Echternach Gospels are repeated in the Trier Gospels (Domschatz MS 61); also the programmatic significance of imported texts, as in Professor Netzer's important perception of the impact at Echternach and elsewhere of the seventh-century Irish exegete Ailerán's verses on the relationship of the Evangelists' beast symbols to the Eusebian Canon-tables (Netzer 1994b). We can see also in the Trier Gospels from Echternach the lively continuation of the characteristically Insular tendency to adapt, fuse, and co-ordinate traditional elements and, another typical tendency too, to acquire and exploit new decorative and figurative ideas from Continental models.

When an Insular artist-scribe, with his provision of material exemplars and mental attitudes, moved further east to Salzburg a bit later in the eighth century, we see the same fine tuning of various visual influences. Cutbercht's small but dynamically thrusting and sprawling *Christi autem* initial (Zimmermann 1916, pl. IV, 309) shows him in touch with the latest Insular scribal fashions, since the trick of using abruptly different forms of script within the first few phrases of the text has a number of striking Insular parallels in the mid-eighth century, and indeed is hard in some respects to differentiate from the *incipits* of the truncated Gospel texts in the Book of Cerne (Cambridge, University Library, MS Ll. 1.10; Brown 1996, pls II(b), III(b), I(b), IV(b)). Cutbercht is not the only Insular scribe-artist to be so carried away by his decorative efforts that he forgets to transcribe fully or intelligibly the sacred words of his text. Here he has had to come back, doubtless shamefacedly, to insert in minute script half of verse 18 of Matthew 1.

Cutbercht's first Canon-table is interestingly programmatic (Zimmermann 1916, pl. IV, 301), like Aileran's verses involving discussion, *uno ore loquentes*, among the Evangelists, but not here their symbolic beasts but the Evangelists themselves, captioned, two of them older, bearded, two younger, beardless and tonsured. The closest parallel I know for Cutbercht's images of these bust-length figures, engaged in debate, is back in Dumfriesshire in the now lost fragmentary cross-head from Hoddom (Henderson 1999, 170, pl. 72). However, he had many other ideas about the decorative construction of Canon-tables, including the opening with Canons 4 and 5 involving a Loch Ness monster-like design with a great beast head terminating an upright column (Zimmermann 1916, pls IV, 303–4). The opening with Canons 5 and 6 in the Book of Kells involves similar risers topped by fierce beast heads (Meehan 1994, 7, pl. 4). Some resemblance between the programmes of Cutbercht and Kells can be seen also in the brooch and belt design of their 'q' of *Quoniam* (Zimmermann 1916, pl. IV, 311; Meehan 1994, 73, pl. 95). What the points of contact or common factors are that led to these apparent similarities we can only speculate.

Close and specific, however, are the connections manifested by Cutbercht's portraits of the Evangelists, seated, at a pause from writing, on benches draped with skins or heavy textiles; the model from which these Evangelist portraits were copied was available also to the scribe-artist responsible for the Gospel book known as the Codex Millenarius, at Kremsmünster (Stiftsbibliothek, Cim.1; Wright 1964, 38–45, pls 1–8). In its spacious layout and handsome uncial script the Codex Millenarius aimed to reproduce the gravitas of a revered southern exemplar (Neumüller and Holter 1974), but in it the tug of Insular models, presumably *via* Cutbercht and Cutbercht's Echternach antecedents is seen in the elaborate initials which open the Gospels. The *Quoniam* of Luke on fol. 176 of Millenarius swells and flows with the authentic spirit of the Echternach Gospels (Alexander 1978, illus. 53) while the three other Gospel *incipits* on fols 19, 111, and 278, though comparatively narrow and upright, are equipped with the heads of their respective symbols, a merging of symbol and letter paralleled back in the Insular homeland in the remarkable initial to St Mark in Durham Cathedral MS A.II.16, fol. 37r (Zimmermann 1916, pl. IV, 327). In Durham MS A.II.16 the head of St Mark's lion terminates the stem of the letter. At the top of the letter is a human head, crested, blank and impassive in expression, like the head terminals on the ancient Aylesford Bucket (Brailsford 1975, 83–7), and very much part of the over-all design, constrained in its relation to the formal letter. In the Codex Millenarius, on the contrary, the human head which tops St Matthew's *Liber*, fol. 19, makes no concession to abstraction but is disconcertingly alive, with a blond coiffeur rivalling the classical Pleiades on fol. 4v of BL Harley MS 647 (Koehler and Mütherich 1971, pl. IV, 65a), but with an imperious glance worthy of an Ostrogothic or Lombard royal portrait.

That intensifying of expression is evidently what intrigued and stimulated the artist of the Barberini Gospels. In his *Initium* initial on fol. 51 (Plate XI) he too switches on this realism, in the midst of his excellent Insular spiral and interlace decoration and calligraphy. The drôle quizzical regard of these male heads derives, I take it, from a first-hand experience of Lombard or Roman wall-paintings and mosaics, involving the individualisation and animation of heads such as we see at Sant' Agata in Suburra in the fifth century and San Vitale at Ravenna in the sixth (Osborne and Claridge 1998, 49–53; Kitzinger 1977, pls 150–58).

Now we must note that the human heads in the initials in Durham MS A.II.16 and the Barberini Gospels are not St Matthew's symbol. They are attached to St Mark's *Initium*. The lion of St Mark roaring at the bottom of the initial in Durham MS A.II.16 aptly represents St Mark's reference to '*vox in deserto*'. The long rigid stem of the letter is a good evocation of the *rectas semitas*, the narrow way of the Lord which must be made straight, and the head at the top literally envisages the text '*ante faciem tuam*' of St Mark 1:2. Durham MS A.II.16 is evidently experimenting with the well known Insular contribution to book art, the historiated initial, in a much subtler sense than in the Vespasian Psalter, fols 31r, 53r (Wright 1967), which simply transfer narrative-history scenes from some exemplar and enclose them in the initial, at comparative random. In Durham MS A.II.16 the pictorial imagery of the initial literally illustrates words in the adjacent text.

The duplication of the face at the top of the Barberini Gospels *Initium* need not argue against both these faces referring to the one *facies* in the text. The Barberini Gospels, more than any Gospel book I know, signals, emphasises, puts frames round, the Eusebian or Ammonian sections in the margins. Parallel passages are a concern and preoccupation of the designer. In the right column on fol. 51, third line down, *ante faciem tuam* is aligned to the right face, and in the equivalent space in the lower margin, beside the cheek of the left face, are the references to the identical passages in Matthew and Luke, from Canon-table 2.

That this is an historiated initial of the same rare literal illustration category as I have indicated in Durham MS A.II.16, is proved by the bust-length figure of an angel in the base of the right down-stroke of N and I, illustrating the text also of St Mark 1:2, '*Ecce mitto angelum meum*'. I shall argue that the Barberini Gospels is in fact a leading exponent of this kind of literal textual illustration. A few other, contemporary, Insular manuscripts show similar tendencies very occasionally, and without coherence. The best known, though more historic than simply verbal, is the picture of St Gregory in the initial *His temporibus* at the beginning of Book II, chapter 1 of the St Petersburg Bede (Meyvaert 1964, pl. 1), the chapter which contains the account of St Gregory's life. Rather more surprising is the decision of the designer of the Salaberga Psalter to historiate the initial D of the great penitential Psalm *Domine exaudi* (Alexander 1978, illus. 63) with the fable of the wolf and the crane, or as Phaedrus tells the story, *Lupus et Gruis* (Mueller 1926, 4). Whatever allegorical sense this fable concerning ingratitude had where it is illustrated by a vignette in the margin of the Bayeux Tapestry under Harold's cross-Channel expedition (Stenton 1957, pl. 6; Hicks 1992, 253, n. 3), ingratitude is nowhere the theme of Psalm 101, the *Oratio pauperis* poured out in anxious supplication to God. Physiologus (or rather *physiologi*) is referred to by Cassiodorus in his Commentary on this Psalm (Adriaen 1958, 902), but not Phaedrus.

Can it be that the artist's stimulus was purely verbal? At verse 6 of the Psalm the text reads: 'Through the voice of my groaning, my bone hath stuck fast, cleaved to, my flesh: *adhaesit os meum carni meae*'. The wolf in the fable seeks help, *magno dolore*, when a bone sticks in his throat: '*os fauce cum haereret*'. As St Jerome remarks austerely about a particularly devious interpretation of a passage in the minor prophet Zacharias: 'I leave it to my readers to judge whether it could bear this meaning: *Hoc utrum ita accipiendum sit, lectoris prudentiae derelinquo...*' (Adriaen 1970, 898).[2] In another Insular psalter, the Lothian Psalter now in New York, the startled-looking half-length figure with arms flung up in the 'A' of *Salvum me fac* nicely catches the Psalmist's sinking feeling, 'Save me, O God! I stick fast in the mire. There is no sure standing: *Non est substantia. Tempestas demersit me...*' (Alexander 1978, illus. 148).

An example of this kind of literal textual illustration occurs also, I believe, on fol. 63 of the Book of Kells (Dublin, Trinity College Library, MS 58). Dr Bernard Meehan regards this initial as one of those interlinear animals 'outside the programme of established symbolism', as additions of 'an ornamental nature which demonstrate the range of models available to the artists and their proximity to nature' (Meehan 1994, 74, pl. 97). Meehan calls it a moth, and the letter a P. *Pharissaei* is spelt in Kells sometimes with a 'P', sometimes with an 'F', witness both spellings on fol. 100v, the text of Matthew's

Gospel 23:22–6 (Meehan 1994, 47, pl. 52, lines 3, 10, 15). It is an F in the moth initial. The text here is Matthew's Gospel 12:24, and reads 'The Pharisees say: This man did not cast out demons, except through Beelzebub, Prince of Demons.' As the diagnostically Insular series of interpretations of the Hebrew names which occur in the Book of Kells (McGurk 1994) and, incidentally, in the Barberini Gospels (fols 9v-10 and 48) makes clear, Beelzebub was known to mean 'having flies' or 'Lord of flies'. That the initial shows a fly, not a moth, judging from context but also from the bird-like form of its body and wings, is confirmed by comparison with the flies in the *Exodus* plague of flies represented on fol. 93 of the later Carolingian, Stuttgart Psalter (Eschweiler and Mütherich 1965–6).

In the matter of the historiation of initials, another contact between the thinking of the designers of the Book of Kells and the Barberini Gospels may be perceived in their treatment of the great *Quoniam* initial of St Luke, fol. 188, fol. 80r (Meehan 1994, 73, pl. 95; Zimmermann 1916, IV, pl. 315(a)). Technically both are masterpieces of Insular art. The Barberini Gospels terminates the 'q' with one of the largest, most savage, snarling and venom-dripping dragons in Insular art. Its formidable scale might suggest that this is the *magnus draco, serpens antiquus* of the Book of Revelation, and likewise the *draco* trampled by Christ in Psalm 90. This seems confirmed by the fact that the dragon is the victim of a vicious attack by a black snake. It streaks down from the top of the dragon's spiral crest, and strikes his nose. This enmity evokes the words of Luke 11:18, 'If Satan also be divided against Satan, how shall his kingdom stand?' Anglo-Saxon verse, notably *Christ and Satan*, represents the 'Old One', King of Hell, being bitterly reviled by the lesser demons (Krapp 1931, 136–37, lines 34–65). In his commentary on Luke chapter 11, Bede asks, in words borrowed from St Jerome, 'How can they have concordance between them, whose works are divisive?' (Hurst 1960, 232–34) and this divisiveness is emphasised again in Bede's comment on the *Quoniam quidem* preface whose purpose was to warn against pseudo-evangelists, false witnesses under the name of the Apostles, and the wide *multifariae diversitate* of heresy (Hurst 1960, 19–20). So a scene of hellish dispute and contention makes sense within the format of the 'q'. It is an interesting coincidence, therefore, that details of the *Quoniam* of Kells are often thought of as showing the torments of the damned in Hell (Henderson 1987, 165–68; Henderson 1996, 46–7), curious as such imagery in a great Gospel initial might seem to be.

The '*Christi autem*' initial in the Book of Kells is famously loaded with symbolism (Lewis 1980). The Barberini Gospels, with its magnificent whirlpools of spirals (Alexander 1978, illus. 170), inhabited by bird-head triplets elaborated on the tradition of Durham MS A.II.17 (Henderson 1987, pl. 79), seems more abstract, more strictly decorative. There is a curious circumstance about it, however, which may contradict this. After the modest sized *Liber* in Barberini (Alexander 1978, illus. 169) with its interesting on-the-spot adjustment of the small initial letters in the second column so as to isolate them from the text, like the leading letters of the acrostic poem in the Book of Cerne (Brown 1996, fig. 5), comes fol. 12v, the leaf leading to the *Christi autem* text, written by a scribe in a neat small hand, not the same used for Matthew's Hebrew names just before, on fol. 9v. The Matthean genealogy of Christ down to chapter 1:17, *generationes quattuordecim*, stops halfway down the right column, leaving a gap of a quarter of a page, in preparation for a full-page display initial, *Christi autem*.

On the reverse of *Christi autem* the text is continued at verse 19 in large handsome writing, but gets smaller, cramped, half the size, taking us to the Magi and their joy at seeing the star. This reduction of scale prepares us for the uniformly small writing of the continuation of the story of the Magi, at verse 11 of chapter 2, '*et intrantes domum*', on what is now fol. 13. The leaf with the *Christi autem* initial is a singleton, now displaced as fol. 18. It follows the text of Matthew 6 on fol. 17v. By happy chance, if chance it is, the panel of inhabited vinescroll at the left of the initial, with the four large birds biting grapes, remarkable by any standard in manuscript design, juxtaposes the text, at the top of the right column '*Pater vester caelestis pascit illa*', that is Matthew 6:26, 'Consider the birds of the air, they sow not, nor reap, and your heavenly Father feeds them.' The *Christi autem* initial as a singleton might have functioned as a moveable image, for meditation on the various blessings of the Incarnation, and so might have been planned iconographically in relation to texts beyond its own immediate vicinity in the Gospel narrative.

The most eye-catching and intriguing historiated initial in the Barberini Gospels is on a smaller scale, it is in fact the curvaceous Insular 'b' of the address to Pope Damasus of St Jerome's epistle beginning *Novum opus* (Fig. 14.1). The design of the 'b' is very close to the 'b' of *Liber* in the Lindisfarne Gospels, with the same panelling of the letter and crest of spirals at its apex (Alexander 1978, illus. 39), though the Barberini Gospels' letter's form is more flattened. The great difference is the content of the letter, the alert whiskered cat head with a mouse in its mouth – clearly not of the peaceful coexistence school of Kells (Meehan 1994, 45, pl. 49).

At the bottom of the oval picture space is a fat Silenus or satyr's head. This is similar to a series of grotesque mask-like heads, with pricked ears, flame-like hair or horns, with snakes hanging from their mouths on either side, which feature in the *incipits* to the Passion texts in the Book of Cerne (Brown 1996, pls III (b), IV (b)). He also has the look of the round-eyed, snub-nosed, grotesque actors' masks piled up on shelves prefacing Carolingian copies of Antique manuscripts of Terence's Comedies, for example Rome, Biblioteca Vaticana, Vat. lat. 3868, fols 3, 35, 77 (Koehler and Mütherich 1971, pls IV 30, 42, 56). If so, his big gaping mouth, hollowed and enlarged to make the actor's voice resound, has been covered up by the curve of the 'b' of '*beatissimo damaso*', the name of the patron and promoter of St Jerome's editorial efforts.

The epistle to Pope Damasus is a formal and nobly inscribed part of many earlier and contemporary Gospel books: Durrow (Dublin, Trinity College Library, MS 57), Lindisfarne, the Augsburg Gospels, and the *Codex Aureus* in Stockholm (Royal Library, MS A.135) start the epistle ornamentally with the words '*Novum opus*'; the Echternach Gospels has a long address phrase at the top, including the word '*beatissimo*'; the Trier Gospels has a large '*Beato*' above the large '*Novum*'; in BL Royal MS I.E.vi the epistle begins with an ornamental '*Beato*', like the Carolingian Tours Gospels, BL Add. MS 11848, and on a smaller scale, subsidiary to the '*Novum*', initial, in BL Harley MS 2788. Not one of these is historiated. Why, then, in the Barberini Gospels should the sober and business-like epistle to Damasus concerning the Gospel Canon-tables start with a frisky cat-and-mouse scene and a potentially loud-mouthed, but muzzled, bridled, satyr?

If we consider the text of St Jerome's epistle, there might be some sense in this imagery. St Jerome nervously anticipates that his watchful critics will with zestful appetite, '*a saliva*', eagerly snatch up his book and drink in its contents, '*inbibere*', and when they see that his edited texts depart from the norm they will shout out '*erumpat in vocem*', exclaiming, '*clamans*', that he is purveying false novelties. But St Jerome puts his faith in the Pope who commissioned the work and will presumably quell opposition, hence the stopping of the mouth of the satyr by '*beatissimo papae*'.

This attempt so to read the initial to the epistle to Damasus is up against one very practical problem. The epistle is a canonical part of the early medieval gospels. Its text is splendidly, and carefully, copied out, as I have remarked, in all the luxury *codices* of the period. But in the Barberini Gospels that portion of the epistle, and much more, a third of the entire text (presumably two sides of a leaf in the exemplar) is missed out, and the scribe sails on regardless from '*pariter vel*', the very point when ignorant protests might break out, to '*tramites ducit*', when the smooth waters of academic unity are restored. In respect of

Fig. 14.1 *The opening of St Jerome's letter to Pope Damasus, Barberini Gospels, fol. 7. (Photograph: Biblioteca Apostolica, Vatican, Rome)*

my attempted interpretation, three options are open. The first is that our initial is copied from an exemplar correctly aligned to the relevant text, which significantly demotes the Barberini Gospels itself. The second is that the initial was placed here to represent, in another form, the omitted text, which would significantly enhance the status of pictorial matter. And the third is that the initial is merely fantastical decoration, and not related to St Jerome's text. Again, '*Lectoris prudentiae derelinquo...*'.

It does, however, seem extraordinary in a book which is marked up as a lectionary, that there is no signal here of a correction or omission. The Barberini Gospels is not marked for lections anything like so heavily as, say, Durham MS A.II.17 (Turner 1931, 217). But there is a fair smattering of lection marks in the margins of St Matthew's Gospel, for example the reading of Matthew chapter 20 for *Septuagessima* Sunday marked at the top of fol. 33v. Old Testament references are inserted opposite the Temptation text on fol. 14. There are very few corrections, and much need for them, notably in Mark, with his '*vox*

clamantes' and his '*a Satanam*'. One careful correction is on fol. 32, where half of verse 18 of Matthew chapter 18 was omitted by homœoteleuton. I would like to think that the designer of the great *Initium* initial is making his own discrete protest, in the form of the face which casts a startled glance across to the bottom line of St Mark's text, where the scribe casually attributes to St John the Baptist the promise, 'I will baptise you with the Holy Spirit', omitting 'with water, but Christ will baptise you'!

The decoration and imagery of the Barberini Gospels is at its richest and most organised on the very first surviving leaf, fol. 1 (Plate XII), in Canon-table 1, '*in quo quattuor*', where the stylistic affiliations seem obvious (Zimmermann 1916, IV, pl. 317a). In basic decorative construction this first leaf resembles the equivalent page in the Lindisfarne Gospels (Alexander 1978, illus. 32), with pilaster columns packed with ornament and with stepped bases and capitals. In the Barberini Gospels the principal arch uniting the subsidiary arches is omitted. The infilled ornament consists of neat

Fig. 14.2 *Evangelist symbols on fol. 1v, as seen through from fol.1.*

regular interlace, and in the central column lacertines, skinny large-headed winged bipeds. The interlace, lacertines, and the tidy presentation of the ornament are akin in feeling to that of the Durham Cassiodorus (Bailey 1978, pl. 1) and very close to the frame of the Evangelist portrait in the first Maeseyck Gospels (Alexander 1978, illus. 87). At capital level are contained the names of the Evangelists, and in the inset of each arch is a bust-length Evangelist symbol, the two pairs turning to converse, winged, nimbed, holding books, and in zooanthropomorphic form, that is, with upright stance, human shoulders, but beast attributes. An important historical association is signalled by the rare representation of St Matthew's symbol as grizzled and bearded, shared by the Barberini Gospels with the Canon-tables of the second Maeseyck Gospel fragment (Alexander 1978, illus 104–7); the other symbols do not so exactly coincide, beyond their basic zooanthropomorphism – for example, the Maeseyck eagle has a heavy parrot-like beak whereas the Barberini Gospels version is more sea-gull like. The Maeseyck symbols have covered hands. The Brandon Evangelist St John (Webster and Backhouse 1991, 82–3, no. 66(a)), another example of this particular phase of Insular style and iconography, has human hands. In the Barberini Gospels the symbols grip their books with beasts' talons or hoofs.

A curious, typically quirky, feature of the Barberini Gospels' Canons is that the bull symbol of St Luke is placed second, over St Mark's numbers, and St Mark's lion is over St Luke's numbers. On the reverse (Plate XIII) the Evangelist symbols are not again represented. Their names are placed higher, within the arch, against a little landscape motif, a row of rounded boulders. However, thanks to the transparency of the parchment, the heads of the symbols drawn on the recto can be discerned on the verso, and although St Matthew's numbers are capped by St John's eagle, and St John's by the man,

St Mark's and St Luke's symbols are visible, correctly placed above their Evangelist's own numbers, thanks to their being incorrectly placed on the recto. As I have indicated, these symbols are not bust-length; only their heads can be seen, peering out above the row of boulders (Fig. 14.2). These truncated symbols, in cramped quarters, just peering over the sill of stones, have a curious parallel in a later Anglo-Saxon Gospel, the famous Eadui Codex now in Hannover, from Christ Church, Canterbury, of around 1020 (Temple 1976, illus 228–29). Curiously enough, in the Eadui Codex the symbols are, like those in the Barberini Gospels, in the wrong order and in the wrong place. In Canon 2, for example, on fol. 11v, the lion is over St Matthew's column of numbers, the bull over St Mark's, and the man over St Luke's. These tilted profiles or glowering frontally-placed Evangelist symbols, heads only, have an even closer parallel in the second series of Evangelist symbols in the Barberini Gospels, those which decorate the second and third parts of Canon 2, on fols 2v and 3 (Figs 14.3, 14.4).

On fol. 2v two profile beast heads, with open jaws, are placed on either side, the one at the right more vulpine than lion, with longer ears. The capitals of the middle columns carry frontal heads, two lugubrious human heads and an eager frontal lion head. On fol. 3 the side capitals carry a profile lion head, with projecting tongue, and an eagle. Of the three frontal heads two of them are distinctly ambiguous as to whether they are lions or men, and the third is a frowning squat head with bull's horns. The bull attributes are those of St Luke and the lions represent St Mark. The eagle is a make-weight, since Canon 2 does not include St John. These extraordinary symbols attempt a quite new, daring, zooanthropomorphism, fusing the character of men and beasts. It is to such a flight of fancy that one can imagine the patron/artist of the Book of Cerne was reacting, when he affirmed so unequivocally the separate

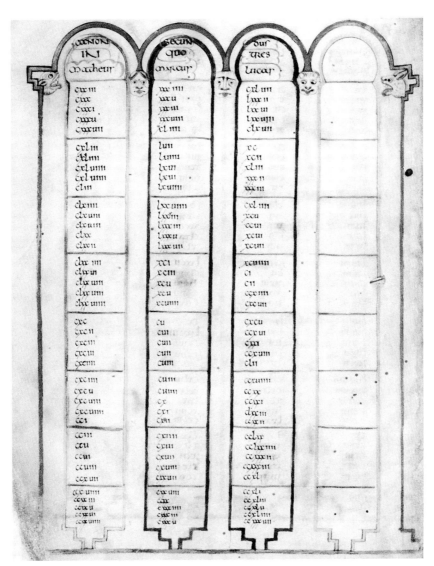

Fig. 14.3 *Canon 2, Barberini Gospels, fol. 2v. (Photograph: Biblioteca Apostolica, Vatican, Rome)*

identity of Evangelist and symbol (Brown 1996, pls II(a), III(a), I(a), IV(a)).

The odd, irreverent, tongue-in-cheek tone of these Barberini Gospels symbols might, I suppose, have non-Christian models. A rather similar series of heads of animals in profile, a ram, a dragon, an eagle, and a panther, and frontal heads of sinister horned men, occurs in fragments of friezes from a Roman sarcophagus excavated in the 1950s from the garden walls of a house at Neumagen near Trier (*Trierer Zeitschrift* 1945–58, I, 505; II, pl. 11; Fig. 14.5). Some such imagery might have been visible to members of the Echternach community, only a few kilometers further west, and somehow slipped into the repertoire of the designer of the Barberini Gospels. The horns and flaming hair of the Neumagen demigods are particularly suggestive of the kind of plumaged or horned heads which we have seen also in the Book of Cerne.

To return, however, to the recto of fol. 1 in the Barberini Gospels; the first Canon-table has an historiated or at least a pictorial appearance hard to parallel in this period, the Flavigny Gospels, now at Autun, being the one obvious analogy (Hubert, Porcher and Volbach 1967, 183, pl. 192). The iconography of the Flavigny Gospels is straightforward, its quotations from Sedulius's *Carmen Paschale*, and the rest, but that of the Barberini Gospels is much more obscure. The Flavigny Gospels example might suggest that Christ is an appropriate figure to place at the top centre of the Canon-table, so the solemn bearded head which fills the capital between St Mark and St Luke might be that of Christ. The Eadui Codex also places Christ above a Canon-table (Temple 1976, illus. 225).

The central column is filled with snaky biting beasts, and these surround, and actually attack, at throat and genitals, the naked figure who squats a little over half-way down the column. His antecedents lie not in the Anglo-Irish missionary lands abroad,

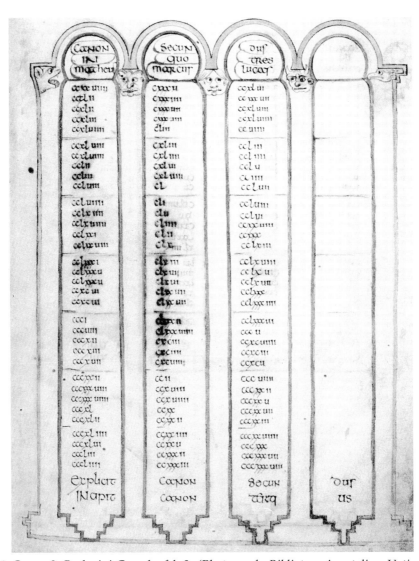

Fig. 14.4 *Canon 2, Barberini Gospels, fol. 3. (Photograph: Biblioteca Apostolica, Vatican, Rome)*

Fig. 14.5 *Roman frieze from Neumagen, Rheinland-Pfalz. (Photograph: Rheinisches Landesmusuem, Trier)*

but in various Insular projects at home. A figure in a virtually identical squatting pose, tugging his beard, appears on the flat end of a fragmentary cross-arm from Strathmartine in Angus (Henderson 1996, pl. VII(a)). Semi-naked figures in writhing poses pull one anothers' beards in the *Quoniam* initial of Kells (Meehan 1994, 71, pl. 93). Confronted wrestling men

in the recently found Pittensorn panel in Perthshire have their genitals bitten by serpents (Hall, Henderson and Taylor 1998, 129–44, illus 2, 3). The Barberini Gospels man seems to be in much the same place and predicament as the figure at the base of the bottom panel of the Rothbury Cross, recognised by Professor Rosemary Cramp as a representation of Hell

(Cramp 1984 vol. 1, 220; vol. 2, pl. 215, 1224). Why should our artist think it appropriate to display a doomed and punished inhabitant of Hell amidst the wholesome story of salvation encapsulated in the text references in the Gospel Canon-tables?

It is a curious, in my experience, unique, feature of the Barberini Canon-tables that the numbers on the recto of fol. 1 are written twice as large as those on the reverse, and as those on all the other Canon-table pages in the book. By contrast the Trier Gospels puts half of Canon 1 on fol. 11 and the second half on fol. 11v (Netzer 1994a, pls 5, 6). BL Royal MS I.E.vi puts the whole of Canon 1 on fol. 4 (Alexander 1978, illus. 162). But in the Barberini Gospels fol. 1v has reduced the size of the numbers by half, so of course gets more in. Was the generous scale of the numbers on fol. 1 just a miscalculation, afterwards corrected, or did the designer premeditate the disposition of the numbers in connection with the uncommon iconography of his page? I have already pointed out that this artist seems sensitive to the contents of the numbered lists, the Eusebian or Ammonian sections. If we look at the Gospel texts referred to by the numbers listed alongside the figure of the squatting man, Matthew 98, 133; Mark 96, 36; Luke 116, 77; John 40, 144, 129, 131, the gist of the sense of them is the repeated assertion of the essential equality and interaction of God the Father and Christ – 'Who honoureth not the Son, honoureth not the Father who hath sent him', and in addition a threat to the obdurate whose eyes are blinded and hearts hardened.

Might not these be pointers to the arch-heretic Arius, who notoriously disputed the relationship of Christ and the Father? The dread of Arianism did not go away. In the *Ecclesiastical History* Bede calls it 'madness', and writes of 'the deadly poison of its evil doctrine' (Colgrave and Mynors 1969, 35). Arius is specially picked out for condemnation in later Anglo-Saxon art. In the New Minster Miscellany, BL Cotton MS Titus D.27, he is in Hell, while in the Eadui Codex he falls under the feet of the Evangelist St John who is pointedly affirming Christ's Godhead (Temple 1976, illus 245, 227). One of the things which most impressed Arius's opponents was the singular manner of his death, recorded by St Athanasius and the historian Sozomen, and regarded as the judgement of God on perjury (Walford 1855, 99–100): our figure's squatting pose and hand gesture might not inconceivably refer to this case of acute colic. In the words of Gregory of Tours, '*interiora in successum deposita, infernalibus ignebus subditur*' (Krusch and Levison 1951, 96–7).

By happy chance, if nothing else, the squatting man in Hell shows through clearly on fol. 1v, precisely juxtaposed to the Canon-table references to Pontius Pilate's interrogation of Christ. The Anglo-Saxons were severe on Pilate. Echoing Eusebius, his death by suicide is recorded in the Anglo-Saxon Chronicle (Plummer 1899, I, 6), so he would be a reasonable candidate for damnation even if only at second hand, as it were.

Having contributed in a markedly sophisticated way to the history of Insular Evangelist symbols, the designer of the Barberini Gospels chose to omit the symbols from his Evangelist portraits (Alexander 1978, illus 174–78), thereby joining a select category of Insular Gospel books, including Maeseyck I, Cutbercht, Kells, Dimma, Macdurnan and Deer (Alexander 1978, illus 87, 181, 251, 222, 326, 335). The Barberini Evangelists sit looking over towards the *incipit* of their Gospels on the opposite recto. They are seated with a cushion, and drapery over the front of their seat. St Matthew's chair has a back with animal-headed terminals. All the Evangelists are busy working on their texts, two on scrolls, two on codices. The codex writers hold an eraser knife loosely in their left hand, with their little finger tucked below it. The four Evangelists are very similar to one another, solemn Judaic looking figures, all bearded, with long hair parted in the middle. They are unusual in that their heads are partly covered with a cloth, held in place by a looped fillet, giving a tallith-like effect. The only Insular parallel I know of is the vested head of Ezra in the *Codex Amiatinus* (Alexander 1978, illus. 27). Presumably the High Priest's head dress, in *Exodus* 39, crowned with the plaque engraved 'Holy to the Lord', could have been seen as a type of the name of Christ written on his servants' foreheads in the *Book of Revelation*, 22. The figures are naturalistic, calm and benign. The strongly muscled forearm and hand which St Matthew thrusts out to his inkwell indicates the onset of a proto-Romanesque phase of Insular art, which surely would have spread and developed had it not been for the Viking invasions. The musculature of the arm of Christ on the cross from Rothbury (Cramp 1984, 2, pl. 211, 1206) is no doubt part of the same story.

The pose of dipping the pen is an obvious pointer to sources shared with Continental artists such as Godescalc, working in the 780s (Rosenbaum 1956, 81–90). Like the Evangelists in Godescalc's Gospel Lectionary (Paris, Bibliothèque Nationale, MS Nouv. acq. Lat. 1203), the Barberini Gospels' Evangelists are seated out of doors, with a delimiting wall in the background. This wall is formed by the same row of boulders which block the base of the arches in the Barberini Gospels Canon-tables. Magnificent plants, placed on either side of the Evangelists, vouch for an out-of-doors setting, but also give the effect of a grand upright textile or brocade screening off the lower half of the picture. Except in St John's portrait, the plants are explored in isolation, not as part of a symmetrical pattern, and their sinuous upward movement is given a lurching top-heavy appearance by the big sprawling leaves, like bats with spread wings, large exotic flower-heads with long stamens, and bunches of long stalks with pellets at the end like drum sticks. The Bewcastle Cross, in the similarly isolated plant in the sundial panel, and in its carapace-like flower-heads with projecting stamens, closely parallels some of these features (Bailey and Cramp 1988, illus 99, 107). Acca's cross at Hexham is reminiscent of the elegant wiry interweaving of the plants in the portrait of St John (Cramp 1984, 2, pl. 169, 904; pl. 171, 907).

The frames on the Evangelist portraits, except for St Matthew's, are left blank. St Matthew's interlaces and lacertines are closely similar to the frame of the Evangelist portrait in the Maeseyck Gospels, and the segmented edges of the frame are related to the Durham Cassiodorus. The omission of the busy frames, in Saints Mark, Luke and John looks like an aesthetic judgement, to maximize the calm monumentality of the Gospel writers. Similar omission of distracting ornament occurs in the Valenciennes Apocalypse, after the initial picture (Alexander 1978, illus 302, 303).

The last of the frames is, however, not without interest. In his description of the illumination of the Barberini Gospels, Professor Jonathan Alexander comments on the portrait of St John on fol. 124v that 'The frame panels are again blank except for the central panel below, in which an animal is sketched apparently drinking. The date of this, as also its significance, is uncertain' (Alexander 1978, 61). Alexander further suggests that it might have been drawn when the later tracing-through of St Matthew was done – incidentally another symptom of the transparency of the Barberini Gospels' parchment.

The animal on St John's frame, a quadruped, is long and slender; it has a trefoil terminal to its tail. It wades in water and stretches down its long neck to drink. In arguing that this animal was planned from the start along with the portrait of St John and that its meaning is ascertainable, I turn first to another, earlier, work of art, the sixth-century ivory panel in the Fitzwilliam Museum, Cambridge, reputed to have come from the church of St Maximin in Trier (Weitzmann 1979, no. 486, 540), the designer of which chose to associate with his figure of St John the Evangelist a single scene chosen from his entire Gospel, namely the incident in chapter 4:7–26, when Christ offers salvation to the woman drawing water at the well in Samaria. In his commentary on the grand cosmic Psalm 103, *Benedic, anima*, 10–11, 'Thou sendest forth springs in the vales: between the midst of the hills the waters shall pass. All the beasts of the field shall drink,' Cassiodorus applies to these verses Christ's promise to the woman of Samaria: 'Who-

soever drinketh of this (well) water shall thirst again. But the water that I will give him shall become in him a fountain of water springing up into life everlasting' (Adriaen 1958, 929–30).

Cassiodorus regarded the *bestias silvarum*, the beasts of the field, as those who turn from their pagan beliefs, *idolorum cultura*, to drink of the promised waters of life. In the light of this, I suggest that the drinking beast at the foot of St John's portrait in the Barberini Gospels is richly significant. It illustrates a leading text of St John's Gospel, often no doubt in the minds of workers in the mission field, and illustrates it not directly, historically, but in terms of a visualisation of an associated Psalter text. Here we have unique evidence for the development in the British Isles in the eighth century of literal and Christological Psalm illustration. There are, as we have seen, several instances of the closeness of the Barberini Gospels artist's thinking to what was beginning to happen in Insular Psalter design, but here a specific and positive direction is indicated. The ground-work for the later great Continental literally illustrated Christological Psalters of Corbie, Stuttgart, and even Utrecht, may well have been laid on these shores, and fully illustrated Insular Psalters may have existed, now lost to us in the mischances of the Viking onslaught.

To sum up: I place the Barberini Gospels at the heart of the Insular achievement in its time. I like the implied open-mindedness of Lowe's entry on it in *Codices Latini Antiquiores*: 'written probably in England' (Lowe 1934, no. 63, 20). It undoubtedly has connections far and wide. As an exercise in copying out the Scriptures it drew on a wide pool of trained, and less-well trained scribes. On the last fol., 153, below the *explicit* of St John's Gospel, the scribe Wigbald invites our prayers. Judged by performance some of his colleagues seem in more need of them. In its artistic repertoire the Barberini Gospels gathered material from many sources. As I suggested in the design of the *Initium* initial and the decoration of Canon 2, it was constructively sensitive to Continental and Antique art. We see this again, markedly, in the uncommonly refined and sober acanthus capitals of Canon 4 (Fig. 14.6). At the same time it made sophisticated use of traditional Insular motifs, interlace, lacertines, trumpet and bird-head spirals. Decoratively it bestrides the conventional north-south divide, Northumbria versus Southumbria. In its bold handling of display letters and text layout it makes experiments and uses conventions running parallel with those of the Book of Kells, notably in the use by the scribe of St Mark's Gospel of space-fillers and snaky and other pictorial signals of over-spilt lines (Meehan 1994, 78–81, pls 108, 111, 112; Henry 1967, pl. V). It does not on the other hand equate to Kells in tying its art to a

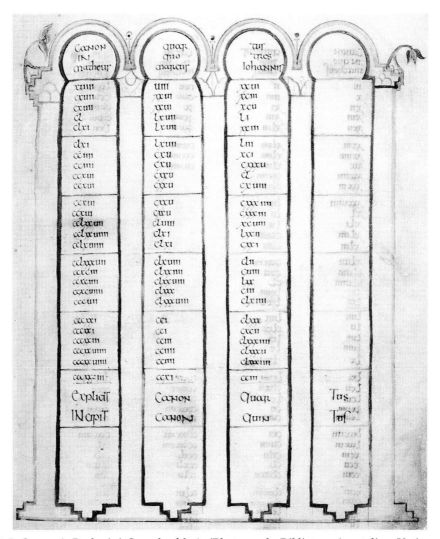

Fig. 14.6 *Canon 4, Barberini Gospels, fol. 4. (Photograph: Biblioteca Apostolica, Vatican, Rome)*

liturgical programme (Farr 1997). The Barberini Gospels has its own quality of combining sumptuousness of ornamentation with a certain fastidiousness, to which the peculiar elegance of its colouring contributes. It has its own special brand of laconic visual wit. Above all it records, I believe, an important new phase in the investigation of the relationship of word and image.

This list of its attributes confirms, to my mind, the role of the Barberini Gospels which I proposed in the title of this paper, a 'paradigm of Insular art'. It typically aims at, and delivers, synthesis, and yet the interesting tensions remain. As with so many Insular works, the polished performance does not exclude the sense of a surprise packet. The Barberini Gospels marries conscious artistry and masterly technique with impressive exegetical input, and yet conveys also a feeling of detachment, an almost anarchical undertow. As so often, this great work of Insular art faces us with intriguing questions regarding the personality of the artist. To whom was

he beholden? What was his brief, and how far was he licensed to drift away from it?

Notes

1　I dedicate this paper to the memory of my friend of long standing, Andrew Martindale. He was keenly interested in the interaction of art in England and the Continent. His views on any period were always acute, and I am very conscious of how much I would have enjoyed, and benefited from, discussing this material with him.

2　What had stuck, so to say, in St Jerome's throat was the interpretation of Zacharias 14:20 which resulted in the reported use by the Emperor Constantine of the nails from the Crucifixion as his horse's harness-bits. The Anglo-Saxon poet of *Elene* felt no such scepticism and fastidiousness, since he solemnly rehearses the story (Krapp 1932, 98–9, lines 1167–1200).

References

ADRIAEN, M. (ed.) 1958, *Magni Aurelii Cassiodori Expositio Psalmorum*, 2 vols. Turnhout. (= *Corpus Christianorum Series Latina*, XCVIII.).

ADRIAEN, M. (ed.) 1970, *S. Hieronymi Presbyteri Opera Pars I Opera Exegetica 6 Commentarii in Prophetas Minores: In Zachariam*, III. Turnhout. (= *Corpus Christianorum Series Latina*, LXXVIA).

ALEXANDER, J. J. G. 1978, *Insular Manuscripts 6th to the 9th Century. A Survey of Manuscripts Illuminated in the British Isles*, vol.1. London.

BAILEY, R. N. 1978, *The Durham Cassiodorus*. (= Jarrow Lecture for 1978). Jarrow.

BAILEY, R. N. and CRAMP, R. 1988, *Corpus of Anglo-Saxon Stone Sculpture. Cumberland, Westmorland and Lancashire North-of-the Sands* , Vol. II. London.

BRAILSFORD, J. 1975, *Early Celtic Masterpieces from Britain in the British Museum*. London.

BROWN, M. P. 1996, *The Book of Cerne. Prayer, Patronage and Power in Ninth-Century England*. London, Toronto.

COLGRAVE, B. and MYNORS, R. A. B. (eds) 1969, *Bede's Ecclesiastical History of the English People*. Oxford.

CRAMP, R. 1984, *Corpus of Anglo-Saxon Stone Sculpture*, Vol. I. 2 parts, *County Durham and Northumberland*. Oxford.

ESCHWEILER, J. and MÜTHERICH, F. (eds) 1965–6, *Der Stuttgarter-Bilderpsalter*. Stuttgart.

FARR, C. 1997, *The Book of Kells: Its Function and Audience*. London.

HALL, M. A., HENDERSON, I. and TAYLOR, S. 1998, 'A sculptured fragment from Pittensorn Farm, Gellyburn, Perthshire', *Tayside and Fife Archaeol. J.* 4, 129–44.

HARBISON, P. 1992, *The High Crosses of Ireland. An Iconographical and Photographic Survey*, 3 vols (= Römisch-Germanisches Zentralmuseum, Forschungs-institut für Vor- und Frühgeschichte Monographien 17, 1–3). Bonn.

HENDERSON, G. 1987, *From Durrow to Kells. The Insular Gospel-Books 650–800*. London.

HENDERSON, G. 1999, *Vision and Image in Early Christian England*. Cambridge.

HENDERSON, I. 1996, *Pictish Monsters: Symbol, Text and Image* (= H. M. Chadwick Memorial Lectures 7). Cambridge.

HENRY, F. 1967, *Irish Art during the Viking Invasions, 800–1020 A.D.* London.

HENRY, F. 1974, *The Book of Kells*. London.

HICKS, C. 1992, 'The borders of the Bayeux Tapestry', in C. Hicks (ed.), *England in the Eleventh Century. Proceedings of the 1990 Harlaxton Symposium*. Stamford.

HUBERT, J., PORCHER, J. and VOLBACH, W. F. 1969, *Europe in the Dark Ages*. Paris.

HURST, D. (ed.) 1960, *Bedae Venerabilis Opera*. Pars II *Opera Exegetica 3 In Lucae Evangelium Expositio* (= *Corpus Christianorum Series Latina*, CXX). Turnhout.

KITZINGER, E. 1977, *Byzantine Art in the Making. Main Lines of Stylistic Development in Mediterranean Art, 3rd-7th Century*. London.

KOEHLER, W. and MÜTHERICH, F. 1971, *Die Karolingischen Miniaturen IV. Die Hofschule Kaiser Lothars: Einzelhandschriften aus Lotharingien*. Berlin.

KRAPP, G. P. (ed.) 1931, *The Junius Manuscript*. New York.

KRAPP, G. P. (ed.) 1932, *The Vercelli Book*. London, New York.

KRUSCH, B. and LEVISON, W. (eds) 1951, Gregory of Tours, *Libri Historiarum X* (= *Monumenta Germaniae Historica: Scriptores Rerum Merovingicarum* I). Hanover.

LEWIS, S. 1980, 'Sacred calligraphy: the Chi Rho page in the Book of Kells', *Traditio* 36, 139–59.

LOWE, E. A. (ed.) 1934, *Codices Latini Antiquiores*, I. *The Vatican City*. Oxford.

MCGURK, P. 1994, 'An edition of the abbreviated and selective set of Hebrew names found in the Book of Kells', in O'Mahoney (ed.), 102–32.

MEEHAN, B. 1994, *The Book of Kells: An Illustrated Introduction to the Manuscript in Trinity College Dublin*. London.

MEYVAERT, P. 1964, *Bede and Gregory the Great*. (= Jarrow Lecture). Jarrow.

MUELLER, L. (ed.) 1926, *Phaedri Augusti Liberti Fabulae Aesopiae*. Leipzig.

NETZER, N. 1994a, *Cultural Interplay in the Eighth Century: The Trier Gospels and the making of a Scriptorium at Echternach*. Cambridge.

NETZER, N. 1994b, 'The origin of the beast Canon Tables reconsidered', in O'Mahony (ed.), 322–32.

NEUMÜLLER, W. and HOLTER, K. (eds) 1974, *Codex Millenarius*, Codices Selecti 45. Graz.

O'MAHONY, F. (ed.), *The Book of Kells. Proceedings of a Conference at Trinity College Dublin 6–9 September 1992*. Dublin.

OSBORNE, J. and CLARIDGE, A. 1998, *The Paper Museum of Cassiano dal Pozzo Series A-Antiquities and Architecture Part 2, Early Christian and Medieval Antiquities Vol 2, Other Mosaics, Paintings, Sarcophagi and Small Objects*. London.

PLUMMER, C. (ed.) 1899, *Two of the Saxon Chronicles Parallel*. Oxford.

ROSENBAUM, E. 1956, 'The Evangelist portraits of the Ada School and their models', *Art Bull.* 38, 81–90.

STENTON, F. M. (ed.) 1957, *The Bayeux Tapestry*. London.

TURNER, C. H. 1931, *The Oldest Manuscript of the Vulgate Gospels*. Oxford.

TEMPLE, E. 1976, *Anglo-Saxon Manuscripts 900–1066. A Survey of Manuscripts Illuminated in the British Isles*, Vol. 2. London.

Trierer Zeitschrift, Jahresbericht 1945 bis 1958.

WALFORD, E. (transl.) 1855, *The Ecclesiastical History of Sozomen, Comprising a History of the Church, from A.D. 324 to A.D. 440*. London.

WEBSTER, L. and BACKHOUSE, J. (eds) 1991, *The Making of England. Anglo-Saxon Art and Culture AD 600–900*. London.

WEITZMANN, K. (ed.) 1979, *Age of Spirituality: Late Antique and Early Christian Art, Third to the Seventh Century*, Metropolitan Museum of Art. (= Exhibition Catalogue.). New York.

WRIGHT, D. H. 1964, 'The *Codex Millenarius* and its model', *Münchner Jahrbuch der Bildenden Kunst*, 3rd Series, 15, 37–54.

WRIGHT, D. H. (ed.) 1967, *The Vespasian Psalter, British Museum Cotton Vespasian A.1* (= Early English Manuscripts in Facsimile 14). Copenhagen.

ZIMMERMANN, E. H. 1916, *Vorkarolingische Miniaturen*, 5 vols. Berlin.

15 Style: a History of Uses and Abuses in the Study of Insular Art

Nancy Netzer

To introduce the section of the conference proceedings devoted to questions of style, I was asked to discuss analysis, methodology and meaning of style in Insular art. Needless to say, this subject is too vast to treat comprehensively within the scope of a single paper. Rather, I have chosen to provide some historical context for the papers that follow, so that it might be possible to assess, on the occasion of this last-of-the-century, last-of-the-millennium International Conference on Insular Art, how our long and complex study of the style has affected the way we now view and analyse Insular art. In doing so, I am able to consider only a handful of key figures in this story, principally those who have written works dealing with large segments of the period. My selection has been influenced by both historical importance and a desire to include personages from various regional and ethnic backgrounds. Even after imposing such limitations, I am able to touch on only a fraction of the issues and implications raised by analysts of this style.

How many times have we been drawn to books by their cover images taken from the Lindisfarne Gospels (London, British Library, Cotton Nero D.IV; Alexander 1978, no. 9), the Book of Kells (Dublin, Trinity College Library, A.1.6; Alexander 1978, no. 52) or the 'Tara' brooch (Ryan 1983, no. 48) only to discover that the pictured object is not even discussed and that the book deals exclusively with history or literature? This use of the Insular style as a modern advertising lure implies much about the ability of the style to go beyond words in signifying an historical period or a nation. One of my tasks will be to concentrate on uncovering the meanings that have been attached to and projected onto the Insular style that encouraged such exploitations. I shall examine ways in which style has been used to interpret Insular art, especially when scholars have not restricted the issues raised exclusively to deter-mining formal relationships among works and historical precedents.

It is important to note at the outset that I have adopted the term 'Insular', as has this conference, in a narrow semantic sense, to refer to the style of art that flourished in Ireland primarily from the sixth century to the Viking defeat at Clontarf in 1014 and in Britain principally from the seventh century to the beginning of the age of Alfred in 871. The works were produced by people who today refer to themselves as English, Irish, Scottish and Welsh, or, at times, following modern political boundaries, as British and Irish. While the great majority of these works were produced in the British Isles, some were actually made in Insular foundations on the Continent. In the last quarter of this century the term Insular has been accepted to avoid disputed associations of certain sub-groups of the style with specific tribal groups like the Irish, Welsh, Picts or Anglo-Saxons. Such terms, as will emerge from the following discussion, were highly charged both politically and racially.

The first to write about what we now call the Insular style was a cleric of Cambro-Norman aristocratic descent, Gerald of Wales. On a visit to Ireland in 1185, he describes in his *Topographia Hibernica* (ch. 38) the illumination of a Gospel book in Kildare, which must have been similar to the Book of Kells, as 'drawn in a miraculous way' and copying an angel's designs. He continues 'you will notice such intricacies, so delicate and subtle, so exact and compact, so full of knots, so linked and bound together, so intricately illustrated with colours still so fresh, that you will not hesitate to declare that all this was designed by the diligence of an angel rather than that of a man. For myself the more often and the more carefully I inspect these things, the more I am amazed anew, and I always see things which I admire more and more'.[1]

Thus from the earliest descriptions, the Insular abstract ornamental style was viewed as intricate and exacting, repaying of close and prolonged inspection, all indisputable in objective terms. However, the notion that the style could seduce a viewer into reflection and meditation of miraculous events, and, most important, that it could be attributed to a miracle, that is, to the work of an angel, not a mere mortal, attaches meanings to the style that it does not inherently possess. Rather, although the idea may have derived from the decoration's placement within a gospel text, such meanings are in the commentator's mind, in this case filtered through the interpretive background of a medieval cleric and scholar which included both spiritual and political commitments.[2] Concerning the latter, it must be remembered that Gerald wrote the *Topographia Hibernica* for the glorification of Henry II, who used the image of the crude unreformed Irish masquerading as Christians as a rationale for invading Ireland in 1171. In keeping with this pretext, Gerald characterises the Irish as barbarous, cannibals and a 'filthy race ... more ignorant than all other nations of the first principles of the faith' (Wright 1863, 134–35). When in the same work Gerald lapses into rhapsodic praise of illumination in a Christian manuscript, he backs himself into a corner. Surely he could not attribute the style to an inferior heretical Irishman?

I would argue that most of the intricate abstract ornament found on Insular objects carries no Christian meditative connotation outside its audience's active participation. Nonetheless, Gerald's early interpretation of the style recurs like hiccups throughout the literature of the last 200 years and resonates to the present day, the most stunning witness being the title of an exhibition in 1989 '*The Work of Angels'. Masterpieces of Celtic Metalwork, 6th–9th Centuries AD* (Youngs 1989). Much of the staying power of this early interpretation may be attributed to the fact that, for the most part, the allegiances of the interpretative community for these works were Christian. I suggest that the perceived beauty and intricacy of the style, and its historical association with the miraculous and the Christian, have moved the interpretative community to assign additional meanings as national symbols to its very finest exponents, like the Books of Kells and Durrow (Dublin, Trinity College Library, A.4.5 (57); Alexander 1978, no. 6), the Lindisfarne Gospels and the Ardagh chalice (Youngs 1989, 160).

Although many of the deluxe manuscripts were thought from an early date to have been written by prominent saints like Columba and their texts subjected to scrutiny as early as the seventeenth century (e.g. Ussher 1639), appreciative descriptions of their decoration begin to appear only in the early nineteenth century (Dibdin 1817). Even though Sir William Betham, as early as 1826, shows enough interest in illuminations to include facsimile drawings in his discussions of the Books of Dimma (Dublin, Trinity College Library, A.4.23 (59); Alexander 1978, no. 48), Armagh (Dublin, Trinity College Library, 52; Alexander 1978, no. 53) and the Cathach (Dublin, Royal Irish Academy, S.n.; Alexander 1978, no. 4), his focus is the splendour of the manuscripts as evidence of a high state of civilization in early Ireland. Betham indulges neither in enthusiastic praise of the style nor miraculous assessment of its origin, as did Gerald, but, then again, Betham does not deal with the most sumptuous Insular manuscripts. In his view, the Cathach was written by St Columba and is chronologically the oldest of the three codices, but Dimma is 'the oldest in the pure Irish character' (1827, 243–44). That he fails to define or even describe this style, except in nationalistic terms, reveals more about the background and ideological perspective of the interpreter than about any objective property of the style. Indeed, Betham, like most of his Irish antiquarian colleagues in the nineteenth century, has virtually no interest in analysing style as a tool for establishing chronology. Betham absolves himself from this task even of analysing the script by declaring that, unlike the English or the Continental, 'the Irish written character' is 'nearly the same at the present day as at the earliest period' (1826, 42). Placing such methodological limitations on the analysis of style allows him to engage in his primary objective, that is, to assign early dates to the manuscripts as proof that '... Ireland, in the seventh century, was a cultivated and civilized country, and had been so for centuries' (1827, 245). He claims that 'Irishmen may be justly proud' of these manuscripts as 'evidences of the civilization ... of their country, at an age, when other nations of Europe, if not in utter ignorance and barbarism, were in their primers' (1827, 243). Thus, the manuscripts were essentially co-opted as weapons in combating the stereotypical image of the primitive, barbaric Irishman perpetuated in later English histories of Ireland, which often quoted the earlier statements of Gerald of Wales (Lebow 1973; Netzer 1999).

It is not until the middle of the nineteenth century that a more rigorously analytical study of the Insular style begins. John Obadiah Westwood, an English entomologist, imposed a method of systematic categorization on Insular ornament that he no doubt adopted from classifying insects. In 1845, in *Paleographia Sacra Pictoria*, he published coloured lithographs of decorations and miniatures in manuscripts of the Bible dating from the fourth to the sixteenth century to reveal the 'national character' of the book. He viewed Insular style from the seventh to the eleven century as 'more elaborate than that of any other existing; and which, having been carried by Anglo-Saxon missionaries to the Continent, became the origin of the styles employed in the finest MSS [sic], executed abroad in those ages; and even until the revival of art, in the thirteenth and fourteenth centuries' (Westwood 1845, vi). Of the ornamental initials in Insular manuscripts he argued 'the inventive skill displayed in the complicated flourishes, in which are generally intermixed the heads of strange lacertine animals, is both so singularly ingenious and elegant, that they far surpass in neatness, precision, and delicacy [an echo of Gerald of Wales's assessment of the style], all that is to be found in the ancient MSS executed by Continental artists; and as it is well known that missionaries from these countries carried their religion and arts to many parts of the Continent, it is not unreasonable to assert that many of the splendid capital letters of the Caroline period were executed in imitation of [and here he gives himself away] our earlier codices' (*ibid.*, x). Thus, Westwood's mission in characterizing the style was, at least in part, a form of cultural imperialism. He put Insular art on the map and sought a place for it within the context of medieval art as a whole.

The more elaborate the style of decoration, the more it reflected a 'national mannerism' (Westwood 1853, 275). To Westwood, style, quality, and nationalism are inextricably bound. He initiated the categorization of distinguishing elements of the Insular style – a technique of analysis that, through further elaboration by scholars like Romilly Allen (Allen and Anderson 1903), Rosemary Cramp (1984), and Gwenda Adcock (1978), remains a basic tool in the scholarly discourse about Insular art. Westwood distinguishes four principal groups: interlaced ribbon patterns; 'patterns formed by delicate straight lines, arranged obliquely, resembling Chinese work'; spiral patterns; and pattern forms of 'monstrously attenuated lacertine animals, or birds, with long interlacing tails, tongues, and topknots' (Westwood 1850, 17). These last forms he attempted to classify, as we might expect, according to his zoological training, as specific species; the quadruped in the Lindisfarne Gospels, for example, as the extinct Irish blood-hound (Westwood 1853, 293). Humorous as some of the identifications may be, Westwood's early attempts at species classification launched an avenue of productive stylistic analysis that carries on to the end of the twentieth century in the work of Gunther Haseloff (1987), Michael Ryan (1993) and, most recently, Suzanne Marx (1995) among other scholars.

Westwood (1845; 1868) reproduced drawings of ornamental details from various manuscripts in Ireland and Britain. Even to this day, such artistic renderings are generated as a key tool for studying the Insular style, especially metalwork. Although, by their very nature, such drawings introduce small inaccuracies that are alien to the originals, they continue to shape our conception of the Insular style and remain primary sources for scholars, many of whom write in offices far removed from the objects themselves.

Westwood compared such ornamental details among manuscripts, sculpture and the then rare specimens of metalwork in Britain and Ireland, which Westwood saw for the first time in the very influential Irish Industrial Exhibition of 1853, in Dublin (see Sproule 1854). This was before the founding of the 'Department of British and Medieval Antiquities and Ethnography' at the British Museum, for which he, like many other antiquaries of the period, lobbied in his publications (Westwood 1853, 296, n. 7). Comparing motifs among media, Westwood saw that he could show that artists were of the 'same school' and thereby shed light on relationships among the various Insular tribes. To Westwood, analysis of ornamental style was not an end in itself. Its true interest and significance lay in what he believed it could reveal about the long-standing ethnic and religious disputes of the day. He assesses the stylistic similarities among works from Ireland and Britain in this way: 'Such a further result necessarily proves the historic fact of the identity of the religious principles of both countries as completely as the assertion of the Venerable Bede himself; and it is this point of view ... that I consider may be rendered highly important, if fully worked out, with reference to the question of the introduction of Christianity, as well as the effects of intercommunication, among the various tribes which inhabited the islands from the first to the tenth century' (*ibid.*, 276).

Although he sees the style of ornament as technically superior, Westwood held a far different view of Insular figurative style. Here he could not free himself from the classical illusionistic ideal, criticising 'early British, Anglo-Saxon and Irish artists' for lacking even the 'slightest idea of the effects of light and shade' and calling the folds of drapery indicated by red lines on the Evangelist Matthew in the Lindisfarne Gospels (fol. 25v) 'ludicrous' (*ibid.*, 278). Westwood observed that 'notwithstanding the extraordinary skill manifested in the ornamenting of MSS, the art of miniature painting had fallen during the seventh and eighth centuries to its lowest ebb; it is, indeed impossible to imagine anything more childish than the miniatures contained in the splendid Hibernian and Anglo-Saxon MSS of this period. Neither can it be said to have improved between the eighth and eleventh centuries, the drawing of the human figure being rude, and the extremities singularly and awkwardly attenuated, and the draperies fluttering in all directions' (Westwood 1845, xiii). He reiterates this sentiment later, discussing portraits of the Evangelists in the Books of Kells, Dimma and Mulling, and the MacRegol and Ussher Gospels (Alexander 1978, nos 45, 48, 52, 54, 59) declaring that 'it is impossible to conceive of anything more barbarous .... The drawings, indeed, more resemble Egyptian or Mexican figures' (Westwood 1850, 18). Here he amplifies the slur by invoking comparison to what were then deemed clearly inferior colonial races. His hostility toward the figural style derives from its failure to provide 'archaeological information' such as the clerical garb of the time. He does admit that one should pay attention to 'the arrangement of the hair, destitute of tonsure' and 'the form of the shoes' (ibid., 18–19). Again, study of style is only the means to a greater end, namely, information about the early Christian past in Ireland and Britain.

Westwood reconciles his differing evaluations of the quality of Insular ornament and figures, not, as one might expect from the twentieth-century perspective, that is by arguing a division of labour similar to that found in later medieval manuscripts. Rather, he postulates an odd either/or situation, which he sees as an inevitable outcome of what he terms 'aesthetical development'. If the mind is occupied with the 'capabilities of higher art', which to him means figural art, it must neglect the technical aspect manifest in the execution of ornament. This seems to be a variant on the fairly common belief that truly creative people would not waste their time on mechanical details, and by Westwood's definition only those who practise the illusionistic style are truly creative people. Westwood believed that the mind of the Insular artist focused on ornamental details 'often with an astonishing perfection and intricacy' neglecting 'higher objects of art' as a result of the artists' 'ignorance' or 'religious or superstitious feelings' (Westwood 1853, 279).

Westwood then uses this principle to argue that similar working circumstances inevitably will produce similar styles. 'The British, Anglo-Saxon or Irish artist, living, as was the constant custom, in a monastery, and having, secularly, his mind and time fully occupied with this one subject, would work out these elements into elaborate results which could scarcely fail, in some instances at least, to be identical with those obtained by similarly occupied ornamentists in other countries' (ibid., 279). Is this just another twist on Gerald's theory that the Insular style results from angelic inspiration? If so, it seems – uncustomarily for the time – without anti-Irish sentiment, for Westwood's principle has the advantage of evading the question. On which side of the Irish Sea did the Insular style originate (ibid., 300–1)?

In applying his principle to the origins of interlace, he reveals an ulterior motive, that is, to reject the influence of the Romans in Britain. After all, if interlace patterns could rely on the ingenuity of the artist (Westwood mentions the twisting of twigs and strips of parchment), they need not depend on the influence of Romano-British mosaics, especially, as Westwood points out, because the form prevails in Ireland where no such mosaics exist (ibid., 280).

His theory of the formation of style is, however, inconsistent and merely convenient. He provides a different explanation for roots of ornament in Carolingian manuscripts when the artistic primacy lies in what was perceived as the Anglo-Saxon origins of modern Britain. He gives himself away when he says 'When we recollect the intercourse which was kept up between our Anglo-Saxon and Irish missionaries with those of France, it is not astonishing that the French artists should have adopted the fine features which they had seen employed in *our* [my italics] manuscripts and should have copied the very ornaments which they found in them, always, however, increasing their size and omitting much of their intricacy' (ibid., 280). In other words, the Carolingians may be bigger and more showy but they are not better than we. Here Westwood willingly admits the direct stylistic influence that he argued against within the British Isles. Then he adds that the addition of classical scroll ornament endows a 'gracefulness to [the Carolingian] pages which we look for in vain in the elaborate but often painfully intricate work of our artists' (ibid., 281). Inherent, then, in Westwood's nationalistic prejudice as he analyses Insular style and, indeed, in much of subsequent scholarship, is the belief that classical art is the ultimate attainment. As we shall see, many have failed fully to appreciate the potential of Insular style as an option within a larger range of artistic possibilities.

By the end of the nineteenth century, when the Welshman J. Romilly Allen, a civil engineer (Henderson 1993, fifteen) undertook a comprehensive history of early medieval decoration in Scotland, historians of art in general[3] had recognised applied ornament as a significant form of artistic expression in all media. This awareness was produced, in large part, by the array of new materials collected by archaeologists, ethnographers and antiquaries throughout the nineteenth century. Nonetheless, the study of early Christian art in the Insular world was still in its infancy. Following Westwood's introduction of a scientific approach to the Insular style, Allen's *The Early Christian Monuments of Scotland*, published in 1903, stands itself as a monument in the field. Allen's systematic drawing, classifying and analysing of hundreds of interlace, geometric, curvilinear and zoomorphic forms (following

Westwood's four categories mentioned above), was coupled with an introduction by Joseph Anderson, keeper of the National Museum of Antiquities of Scotland. Anderson plotted the geographical distribution of monuments that allowed him to distinguish two stylistic areas in Scotland (Allen and Anderson 1903, cii–ciii). He introduced the concepts of the relationship of style to geographic distribution as a 'relationship of race' and of the Scottish group of monuments as an 'offshoot, characterised by strong local or racial variations' of the early Christian style of the British Isles (*ibid.*, iv). He believed that the Picts used symbols 'for the same reason for which they were not used by the Irish in Dalriada, or by the Saxons in Northumbria, because they were a Pictish and not an Irish or Saxon mode of expressing whatever they were meant to convey' (Henderson 1993, twenty-three). Thus, we begin to see in variants within the overall Insular style more than nationalist associations; we also see racial codes or languages for which Allen had, in effect, codified the grammar and the dictionary.

Unlike Westwood nearly half a century earlier, Anderson calls the abstract ornament on Pictish monuments 'rigidly conventional', in contrast to the animal figures, which he sees as graceful, free and vital. Anderson perceives this difference, as well as the disparity between Pictish sculptured animals and those of lesser 'quality from the work of Irish illuminators' (was he thinking of the animals in the Book of Durrow?), which he sees as providing their 'inspiration' as an 'outcome of racial aptitude' (Allen and Anderson 1903, lxiv–lxv). In effect, style was explained as the result of racial propensity.

Anderson is perhaps the first to have identified the potential of the Insular style to examine significant parallels among its exponents in metalwork, sculpture and manuscripts throughout the British Isles. Calling it 'Celtic', he attributes its distinctive characteristics, in comparison to contemporary styles practised on the Continent, to isolation. The Insular church was largely cut off from foreigners and of 'necessity' turned to [unspecified] 'native handicrafts'. Anderson sees 'in the indigenous culture of the people a source of artistic potentiality which sufficiently accounts for the unparalleled efflorescence of their art in the Christian time' (*ibid.*, lxix). Furthermore, he continues 'throughout the pagan period this system of decoration was restricted in its scope by the restricted nature of the Pagan culture. But with the introduction of Christianity the scope of the art was widened, and under the influence of the higher culture, it was exalted in its aims and purposes'. Anderson then, describes Insular style as having emerged from a confluence of pagan stylistic tradition, racial potential and Christianity (*ibid.*, lxix–lxxvi). Such a theory of the origin of a style, which is, for the most part, not inherently Christian, tells us more about the way the British then constructed their ancestry than about the style itself.

As an outgrowth of his assumptions about the origin of the style, Anderson introduces a theory to trace the style's 'growth' based on the additions of interlaced patterns and frets to pagan spiral patterns. He suggests that as interlace and frets become increasingly prevalent, spiral patterns diminish and finally disappear. In simpler terms, he places closer to the pre-Christian period objects showing the greatest influence of the pre-Christian style, that is, objects on which spiral patterns have been least altered and encroached upon by other motifs. Thus, Anderson defends the Book of Durrow as early in the history of Insular art. The Book of Kells and Lindisfarne Gospels were viewed as later, marking the culmination of 'beauty and purity' in the art of Ireland and Northumbria. The introduction of floral elements, in the Book of Kells, is perceived as a 'turning point' marking the latest period, which commences in the early eighth century (*ibid.*, lxxvii–lxxviii). Anderson's chronology lingers, in part, to this day, although the underlying religious assumptions fueling his theory of development are never rehashed. He admits these 'interlaced and fretwork patterns and zoomorphic and foliagenous ornaments which the Christian art grafted on to the old stock' may not be native inventions but derived from Continental sources. Lest the latter possibility diminish the status of the Insular style, he cautions that:

> patterns are not art any more than words are poetry, or sounds are music. It is the methods of their selection and adaptation and combination that make a style … whether we regard the whole series of their [Scotland, Ireland, Wales and Northumbria] manuscripts, metal-work and monuments collectively as one great comprehensive manifestation of Celtic ornamentation of the early Christian period, or take them separately as national developments of a common style, it is equally true that … [the Insular style] presents a manifestation of artistic culture altogether unparalleled in Europe (*ibid.*, xcix–ci).

Again, we hear the *leitmotif* of style as a metaphor for the status of a culture. Such a construct was as much present-oriented, as it was historic evaluation.

In the twentieth century more systematic art-historical methods, based on detailed comparisons of styles found on objects of various media initiated by Anderson and Allen, gradually commanded primacy of place in the search for anchoring Insular works, especially those of the highest quality, to various national groups. The assumption was – and to a certain extent, still is – that, as individual styles developed within the Insular genre, they manifested themselves in all media simultaneously within a given geographic area. One cannot doubt that this operating principle in a broad sense is valid, but art historians may have gone astray in defining both the chronological and geographical limits, variously, too narrowly or too broadly to serve ulterior motives.

In 1934, the Englishman Sir Alfred Clapham (1934, 43–57), invoked what might be termed the 'negative' comparanda of manuscripts produced in two Continental Columban monasteries, Luxeuil and Bobbio. He saw the 'non-Irish' style of these manuscripts as proof that the Insular style, which he called 'Irish Christian art', was unknown in Ireland before the close of the seventh century. Clapham suggested instead, in an excessively convoluted argument, that the Insular style must have evolved through the hands of Irishmen, but only in Northumbria, citing as its best example the securely localised Lindisfarne Gospels. He speculated that Irish missionaries from Northumbria returned to Iona and Ireland, bringing with them the 'developed art of manuscripts', and produced the Book of Durrow probably at Iona.

The implicit assumption applied to this stylistic comparison, namely that a single style would have been practised at a given time in all Columban houses regardless of geographic proximity – an example of interpreting the geographic limits too broadly – emerges from hindsight as fuelled by the knee-jerk Anglocentric currents of the time.

Another Englishman, the Keeper of British and Medieval Antiquities in the British Museum, T. D. Kendrick, in 1938 published a survey of English art from the prehistoric phase of Celtic Art in Britain to the Viking Age. More limited in scope than are the contents of the book, the title, *Anglo-Saxon Art to AD 900*, probably reveals the vestiges of a nineteenth-century construction, wherein the Anglo-Saxon foundation of England was the dominant historiographic model. Kendrick seems principally concerned with using style to establish the continuity of an historical national narrative. He sees, for instance (in opposition to his compatriot Westwood of nearly a century earlier), the designs of the Durrow carpet pages as 'developed barbaric version[s]' of Romano-British pavements. Their ribbon-style animals with 'metallic edges', he rooted in metalwork like the Benty-Grange hanging-bowl escutcheon and the Crundale pommel.[4] In Kendrick's view, this 'Christian painting perpetuates in the seventh century a stage of animal-art that had already been achieved in Britain' (Kendrick 1938, 98–101).

Like Westwood, however, Kendrick divulges a preference for illusionism in his assessment of the Insular style. He introduces the concept of a 're-naissance' of Anglo-Saxon art as a correlate to the historical concept of the Golden Age of the English church (*ibid.*, 119). He lauds works like the majesty page of the Codex Amiatinus (Alexander 1978, no. 7) as showing 'no weakening whatsoever in the direction of a barbaric Celtic or English ornamental apparatus as seen in the Book of Durrow and the Lindisfarne Gospels' (Kendrick 1938, 113), thus exemplifying the argument that aesthetic judgments are not inherent to the works, but rather are culturally determined.

Kendrick derived national pride from his countrymen, who, albeit separated in time from him by more than a millennium, could produce works in the illusionistic style. He declares it 'one of the most remarkable events in the whole art history of England. For a brief moment, this country, rousing itself from its obsession with barbaric ornament, stands out bravely and is illumined in the sight of all Europe as the principal custodian of that immense and potent tradition that had found expression in Greek and Roman and Late Antique art' (*ibid.*, 119). No doubt Kendrick saw the illusionistic exponents in Insular art as supremely Christian visual manifestations of close contact of the Anglo-Saxon church with Rome. We should remember, however, that all these 'renaissance' works are English and not Irish, Scottish or Welsh. By placing them at the pinnacle of his qualitative hierarchy, Kendrick, in effect, grabs all of the glittering prizes for his nation. The imprint of Kendrick's hierarchy may have been felt in the disproportionate emphasis, primarily by American and English scholars, during the past 50 years, on the relatively few classicising manuscripts, like the Codex Amiatinus and the Vespasian Psalter (Alexander 1978, no. 29), and sculptures like the Ruthwell and Bewcastle crosses (Neuman de Vegvar 1987, 204–24). Indeed, Jonathan Alexander's comment in his introduction to his corpus of Insular manuscripts (1978, 12) all but proves the point. 'It is not surprising', Alexander declares 'considering the historical situation, that Anglo-Saxon artists should have attempted to render more faithfully their Mediterranean models, just as they regarded themselves as the true upholders of the tradition of the Roman church.' Thus through some considerable manipulation, the Insular style of these so-called Renaissance works has come to symbolise England and its Roman (non-Celtic) Christian heritage.

In general, Kendrick views the Insular style as 'the recital of a protracted series of conflicts between the mutually irreconcilable principles of the barbaric and the classical aesthetic systems'. The barbaric, he says, 'seeks to satisfy by means of dynamic abstract patterns and by the statement of organic forms in terms of inorganic and [here he chooses a word from his contemporary artistic ambiance] surrealist symbols; whereas classical art [to which he seems fiercely drawn] gives pleasure by means of a sympathetic and obvious naturalism' (Kendrick 1938, 1). Unlike those of his predecessors, Kendrick's chronological development of the Insular style assumes a progression toward greater naturalism. This allows him to place at the beginning the Book of Durrow, which he views as the only Insular manuscript whose ornament is 'wholly and relentlessly barbaric' throughout the book and unlike other Insular manuscripts 'makes no concession' to the 'classical figure-style' (*ibid.*, 97). This constitutes an early stage of development, an 'unashamed expression of an ancient barbarian style,' which Kendrick sees as 'completely outside the stage in which copies of classical paintings, or obvious adaptations of them, [here he is presumably alluding to works like the Lindisfarne Evangelists] interrupt the sequences of barbaric ornament' (*ibid.*, 97).

Coincident with this move toward naturalism is Kendrick's principle of gradual progression in the size of *incipit* monograms. His theory is cleverly and seductively illustrated by a page of four line drawings of *chi rho* pages from Durrow, Lindisfarne, the St Gall Gospels (Alexander 1978, no. 44) and Kells. The reasoning, which allows him to place Durrow 'typologically far behind' the others, reveals more about his projection onto the scribe-artist of his values pertaining to Insular art than about the style's development. Kendrick finds it 'incredible that a scribe so diligent and so expert in the most elaborate forms of ornament would have rejected the noble device of the Great Monogram had it been already conceived in his day'. Despite 'total ignorance of a naturalistic figural style', Kendrick continues, 'he did not neglect to insert the appropriate figures of the Evangelists and their symbols. He was working to a rule; but a rule that did not yet include the giant Monogram' (Kendrick 1938, 95–7). This line of reasoning had enormous allure, and is even adopted and amplified by the Swedish scholar Carl Nordenfalk (1977, 18). Nordenfalk postulates an inherent power of expansion for Insular ornament, visualising interlace as a liquid, pourable substance, that increases the ambition of artists to magnify the size of principal initials (*ibid.*, 14). Nordenfalk broadens Kendrick's scope to include in his schematic drawing of *Initium* initials (*ibid.*, 18) the Durham Gospel Fragment discovered subsequent to Kendrick's publication, and the Lichfield Gospels. Nordenfalk's allegiance to this theory is a mystery. He knew that manuscripts like the Echternach and Augsburg Gospels (Alexander 1978, nos 11, 24), the latter of which, incidentally, he published for the first time in 1947 with documents dating it to the early eighth century, rendered the theory untenable.

The discovery in 1939 (shortly before the outbreak of the Second World War) of the Sutton Hoo boat burial with its hoard of metalwork in East Anglia (Bruce-Mitford 1978), gave a huge boost to English scholars yearning to anchor dazzling exponents of the Insular style to their shores. To begin, a series of comparisons between the Durrow ornament and Sutton Hoo metalwork gave support to an early date, as well as to a Northumbrian origin for the Gospel Book. There is no denying some stylistic affinity between the two varieties of beasts on the Sutton Hoo purse and the symmetrically placed, short- and long-ribbon beasts forming the borders of one of the Durrow carpet pages (fol. 192v), but the conclusions reveal as much about the vantage point through which various scholars have looked as about any objective stylistic truth (Netzer 1999, 322–25).

In 1943, the Swedish scholar Nils Åberg concluded that the Sutton Hoo animals were of the same 'race' as those on the Durrow carpet page, and that this same race was also found on three other Anglo-Saxon works of the seventh century, the Kentish brooch from Faversham, the Kentish sword pommel from Crundale, and a silver foil from Caenby (1943, 63–4). Reflecting the *Weltanschauung* of the period, Åberg essentially deconstructed the style of the Durrow page as an inter-racial marriage of Celtic and Anglo-Saxon motifs.

In 1954, gazing from the other side of the Irish Sea, the French scholar Françoise Henry continued the geographical metaphor in discussing the style of the same Durrow carpet page. She viewed the animals 'not hitherto met with in Irish art' as an importation and acknowledged the close relationship already established to the animal interlacing on Anglo-Saxon and Merovingian jewellery. She was not surprised 'that an Irish illuminator should have had Saxon objects in his possession, and should have imitated them. What is more striking is the coherence and vivacity which he gave to animals that were lifeless and inert in his models. Starting from an almost amorphous system of animal-headed ribbons, he seemed to create a race of tiny skipping monsters with biting jaws and flexible limbs, which he combined not in a confused meander, but following a regular and intelligible rhythm. In doing so he subjects them to the general style of the manuscript' (Henry 1954, 32).

Stylistic comparisons of one object produce not only differing interpretations of the geographic limits in which a style might have been produced. More importantly, once again, systematic methods devised in the twentieth century did not free interpretations from cultural determinism. In some extreme cases, interpreters of the style, even seem to echo the kind of ethnic prejudice heard in statements made by their nineteenth-century antiquarian predecessors. A case in point is, François Masai, an anglophile Belgian, who in 1947, after placing all of the key manuscripts in Northumbria, declared that Irish illuminations revealed neither that the Irish people were highly civilized, nor their good taste; rather Masai perceived 'a profound barbarism, trying to imitate as well as possible, more civilized neighbours' (Masai 1947, 136). Equally revealing is Carl Nordenfalk's criticism (1977, 11) of Masai's argument, more because Masai deprived 'Ireland of the honor of having played an essential part in the creation of what has been considered its greatest national exploit', than for its factual evidence or its logic. Such were the meanings and stakes still attached to the Insular style only twenty years ago.

Nordenfalk (1977, 14–16) then explains the 'modest' Irish origin in his construct of the development of the Insular style. Beginning with the Cathach, he outlines a step-by-step process of an Insular initial liberating itself from the prison of 'reserved classicism' through the adoption of native Celtic forms. He sees this 'essentially anti-classical style' as brought to 'near perfection' almost overnight, in the Book of Durrow. He also incorporates Anderson's notion of a style's expression of racial aptitude in his explanation of the development of Insular carpet pages as presupposing an 'innate predilection' for 'free' decoration. In explaining the animal carpet page, however, Nordenfalk shifts his line of reasoning. He suggests that the Northumbrian prince Aldfrith's presence at Iona, where he thinks the book was probably written, would best explain the Anglo-Saxon beasts (*ibid.*, 9). Are we to assume that Aldfrith carried around with him a sketch-book of animals? Or that he had a few personal decorated objects, which a curious scribe-artist copied? While neither circumstance is impossible, there must have been ongoing undocumented contacts between Iona and Northumbria that would explain the confluence of style – that is, if he is even right in assuming the book was made in Iona. Nordenfalk falls into a similar trap, the trail to which was blazed by Westwood when he examined the introduction of new species of birds and quadrupeds in the Lindisfarne Gospels. He attributes them to the influence of the Anglo-Saxon nobility, whose favourite pastimes were hunting and hawking (*ibid.*, 17).

The real question is why art historians perpetuate the belief that theories concerning developments of Insular style have greater weight if they are attached, however arbitrarily, to the patronage or peregrinations of historically powerful and/or prominent persons. Such uses and abuses project additional, non-inherent meanings on the Insular style, meanings that are, consciously or unconsciously, adopted, adapted, altered and amplified throughout the history of the critical literature.

Why do we find images of the 'rock stars' of Insular art used as advertising lures to sell everything from history books to tea cups and scarves? The answer must at least in part have to do with appropriation of some of the meanings outlined here that have been projected onto various aspects of the Insular style, from as far back as the twelfth century. As a result, the Insular style endows the recipient object with higher status by prompting and exploiting the memory of assigned meanings. In different contexts, various exponents of the style may be made to signify an imagined glorious past of a specific nationality, the triumph or superiority of one ethnic group or culture over another, a connection to the Roman or Celtic church, and/or the ultimate attainments of Christian spirituality. Although such interpretations of visual style depend on memory, they are as present-oriented as their written counterparts.

The production of numerous books laying out methods for reconstruction and creation of Insular ornamental motifs, such as interlace, spirals, and key-patterns, based on various medieval models like the Lindisfarne Gospels and the Book of Kells has become a cottage industry over roughly the past fifty years.[5] These how-to books develop the legacy of Romilly Allen outside the scholarly sphere and aim to shape present and future visual styles. The hope expressed in the introduction to a motif book by George Bain first published in 1951 is for its use as a text book in Scotland's elementary and secondary schools to give instruction to students in a 'multitude' of crafts (Bain, G. 1977, 21). A more recent motif book by George's son Ian aims to 'bring forth a new expression of Celtic origin and supplant the tartan souvenirs in shops throughout Scotland and Britain' (Bain, I. 1986, 8).

One final question: are the observations and conclusions generated by individual analysts and interpreters of the Insular style outlined here so hopelessly skewed and distorted by culturally determining factors that they are interesting only from an historiographic point of view? At the end of the twentieth century, in the spirit of the times, I certainly acknowledge that interpretations of the Insular style are subject to the 'gaze' of the writer. And, although historians and art historians alike currently question assumptions of historical or cultural continuity and evolution, I would not plunge head-first into the present preference for rejecting all past scholarship in search of discontinuity, difference and fragmentation. After all, who is to doubt that in another time, this paper too will be seen to bear witness to a desire, engendered by august conferences of this type, to incite fashionable fin-de-millennium disruptions and innovations without fully acknowledging either the preservation of implied time-honoured art historical norms and methods, or my own American, baby-boomer gaze.

Notes

1   Wright 1863. I have used the translation of J. J. G. Alexander in Fox 1990, 266. Although many have thought that this is a description of the Book of Kells, the location of the manuscript in Kildare and a reference to its association with St Brigid reveal that Gerald's description is of another Gospel Book with elaborate decoration akin to that in the Book of Kells. For discussion see G. Henderson 1987, 195–98.
2   I am indebted here to a discussion of modern abstract art in Cernuschi 1997, 32–3.
3   Alois Riegl perhaps being the most prominent, see Riegl 1893.
4   This had earlier been recognised by Salin 1904.
5   The origins of this cottage industry are in the Celtic Revival that begins in the second quarter of the nineteenth century (see Sheehy 1980). The author is grateful to Nancy Edwards for this suggestion.

References

ÅBERG, N. 1943, *The Occident and Orient in the Art of the Seventh Century, I: the British Isles*. Stockholm.

ADCOCK, G. 1978, 'The theory of interlace and interlace types in Anglian sculpture', in J. Lang (ed.), *Anglo-Saxon and Viking Age Sculpture and its Context: Papers from the Collingwood Symposium on Insular Sculpture from 800 to 1066* (= B.A.R. Brit. Ser. 49), 33–45. Oxford.

ALEXANDER, J. J. G. 1978, *Insular Manuscripts 6th to the 9th century. A Survey of Manuscripts Illuminated in the British Isles*, Vol. 1. London.

ALLEN, J. R. and ANDERSON, J. 1903, *The Early Christian Monuments of Scotland*, 3 parts. Edinburgh (Reprinted 1993, 2 vols). Balgavies.

BAIN, G. 1977, *Celtic Art. The Methods of Construction*, 5th ed. London.

BAIN, I. 1986, *Celtic Knotwork*. London.

BETHAM, W. 1826 and 1827, *Irish Antiquarian Research*. London.

BRUCE-MITFORD, R. L. S. 1978, *The Sutton Hoo Ship Burial II: Arms, Armour and Regalia*. London.

CERNUSCHI, C. 1997, *Not an Illustration but the Equivalent: a Cognitive Approach to Abstract Expressionism*. Madison.

CLAPHAM, A.W. 1934, 'Notes on the origins of Hiberno-Saxon art', *Antiquity* 8, 43–57.

CRAMP, R. 1984, *Corpus of Anglo-Saxon Stone Sculpture*. Vol. 1, *County Durham and Northumberland*. Oxford.

DIBDIN, T. F. 1817, *The Bibliographical Decameron*, pt I. London.

FOX, P. (ed.) 1990, *The Book of Kells: MS 58 Trinity College Library Dublin*. Luzerne.

HASELOFF, G. 1987, 'Insular animal styles with special reference to Irish art in the Early Medieval period', in M. Ryan (ed.), *Ireland and Insular Art A.D. 500–1200*, 44–55. Dublin.

HENDERSON, G. 1987, *From Durrow to Kells. The Insular Gospel-Books 650–800*. London.

HENDERSON, I. 1993, 'Introduction, the making of *The Early Christian Monuments of Scotland*', in Allen and Anderson 1993, thirteen–forty.

HENRY, F. 1954, *Early Christian Irish Art* (3rd edition 1979). Dublin.

KENDRICK, T. D. 1938, *Anglo-Saxon Art to AD 900* (reprint 1972). London.

LEBOW, N. 1973, 'British historians and Irish history', *Eire-Ireland* 4, 3–38.

MARX, S. 1995, 'Studies in Insular animal ornament in late 7th and 8th century manuscripts', in C. Bourke (ed.), *From the Isles of the North. Early Medieval Art in Ireland and Britain*, 105–10. Belfast.

MASAI, F. 1947, *Essai sur les Origines de la Miniature dite Irlandaise*. Brussels, Antwerp.

NETZER, N. 1999, 'The Book of Durrow, the Northumbrian connection', in J. Hawkes and S. Mills (eds), *Northumbria's Golden Age*, 315–26. Phoenix Mill.

NEUMAN de VEGVAR, C. 1987, *The Northumbrian Renaissance*. Selinsgrove.

NORDENFALK, C. 1947, 'Before the Book of Durrow', *Acta Archaeologica* 18, 141–74.

NORDENFALK, C. 1977, *Celtic and Anglo-Saxon Painting, Book Illumination in the British Isles 600–800*. London.

RIEGL, A. 1893, *Stilfragen*. Berlin.

RYAN, M. (ed.) 1983, *Treasures of Ireland. Irish Art 3000 B.C. – 1500 A.D.* Dublin.

RYAN, M. 1993, 'The menagerie of the Derrynaflan Chalice', in R. M. Spearman and J. Higgitt (eds), *The Age of Migrating Ideas. Early Medieval Art in Northern Britain and Ireland*, 151–61. Edinburgh, Stroud.

SALIN, B. 1904, *Die altgermanische Thierornamentik*. Stockholm.

SHEEHY, G. 1980, *The Rediscovery of Ireland's Past: the Celtic Revival 1830–1930*. London.

SPROULE, J. (ed.) 1854, *The Irish Industrial Exhibition of 1853: a detailed catalogue of its contents*. Dublin.

USSHER, J. 1639, *Britannicarum Ecclesiarum Antiquitates*. Dublin.

WESTWOOD, J. O. 1845, *Paleographia Sacra Pictoria*. London.

WESTWOOD, J. O. 1850, 'On the peculiarities exhibited by the miniatures and ornamentation of ancient Irish illuminated MSS', *Archaeol. J.* 7, 17–25.

WESTWOOD, J. O. 1853, 'On the distinctive character of the various styles of ornamentation employed by the early British, Anglo-Saxon and Irish artists', *Archaeol. J.* 10, 275–301.

WESTWOOD, J. O. 1868, *Facsimiles of Miniatures and Ornaments in Anglo-Saxon and Irish Manuscripts*. London.

WRIGHT, T. (ed.) 1863, *The Historical Works of Giraldus Cambrensis*. London.

YOUNGS, S. (ed.) 1989, *'The Work of Angels'. Masterpieces of Celtic Metalwork, 6th–9th Centuries AD*. London.

16   The St Petersburg Gospels and the Sources of Southumbrian Art

Victoria A. Bruno

During the course of the eighth century, a style of art emerged in Southumbria commonly referred to as the 'Tiberius' school, which borrowed many features developed earlier in Northumbria (Webster and Backhouse 1991, 195). It can be difficult, therefore, to determine whether certain eighth-century manuscripts exhibiting Northumbrian features were written in Northumbria, or in Southumbrian scriptoria under Northumbrian influence. A notable example is the St Petersburg Gospels (St Petersburg, National Library of Russia, Cod. F.v.I.8; Alexander 1978, no. 39), considered to be Northumbrian by some scholars, and Southumbrian by others.[1] E. A. Lowe's assessment reflects the dichotomy inherent in the evidence: although noting that the St Petersburg Gospels shares a peculiar scribal feature with Kentish charters, Lowe felt, nevertheless, that its textual links to the Lindisfarne Gospels (London, British Library, MS Cotton Nero D.IV; Alexander 1978, no. 9) were strong enough to place it in Northumbria (Lowe 1971, XI, no. 1605). Despite this textual evidence, E. H. Zimmermann assigned the St Petersburg Gospels to his 'Southern English' group, which includes the Barberini Gospels (Rome, Biblioteca Apostolica Vaticana, Barb. lat. 570; Alexander 1978, no. 36), the Cutbercht Gospels (Vienna, Österreichische Nationalbibliothek, Cod. 1224; Alexander 1978, no. 37), and the Maeseyck Gospels (Maeseyck, Church of St Catherine, s.n.) (Zimmermann 1916, 137–45, 297–305). Although more recent scholarship has shown that the Cutbercht and Maeseyck Gospels were written on the Continent, at Salzburg and Echternach, respectively (Tholl 1986, 311–19; Netzer 1994a, 112–16), both exhibit many characteristic features of Southumbrian manuscripts. Because the scribe of the Cutbercht Gospels was trained in Southumbria, it is not surprising that he employed elements of the 'Tiberius' school. Similarity with the Maeseyck Gospels, on the other hand, illustrates the contribution of this manuscript, and others written at Echternach,[2] to Southumbrian art.

As the lack of scholarly consensus implies, a detailed examination of St Petersburg's textual and decorative features reveals a complicated conflation of models. The evidence suggests that the fusion of Northumbrian, Southumbrian and Echternach elements in its exemplar occurred in a Southumbrian scriptorium. Challenging traditional interpretations of the development of Insular art, recent studies have demonstrated that early medieval scriptoria were quite diverse and receptive to a variety of artistic traditions (Netzer 1994; Brown 1996). With a more complex view of these *scriptoria*, St Petersburg's numerous affiliations are no longer puzzling contradictions, but critical indications of the wealth of influences that shaped Southumbrian art in the eighth century.

The preliminary texts

In addition to the four gospels, most early medieval gospel books contained a variety of preliminary texts, such as general prefaces at the beginning of the manuscript, and prologues and lists of chapter summaries usually preceding each individual gospel. St Petersburg's preliminary texts belong to a distinct group, which includes the Lindisfarne Gospels, the Royal I.B.VII Gospels (London, British Library, MS Royal I.B.VII, Alexander 1978, no. 20), and the Gotha Gospels (Gotha, Forschungsbibliothek Cod. Memb. I.18; Alexander 1978, no. 27). These manuscripts are characterised by a specific set of textual features: (1) a series of general prefaces in the order *Novum opus*, *Plures fuisse*, and *Eusebius carpiano* (McGurk 1961, 110–12); (2) a certain type of chapter summary lists and corresponding chapter divisions (DeBruyne 1914); and (3) rare liturgical rubrics within the lists of chapter summaries preceding Luke and John (Brown 1960, 34ff.).[3]

The Lindisfarne Gospels is the oldest surviving manuscript with this combination of features which were copied directly from a sixth-century Neapolitan manuscript most likely owned by the scriptorium of Wearmouth-Jarrow (Brown 1960, 47–9). The St Petersburg Gospels very probably acquired these features from a copy of the same Neapolitan manuscript, for they do not appear to have been common in Southumbria, Echternach, or Ireland. Other extant Southumbrian manuscripts fall into two categories: the Stockholm Codex Aureus (Stockholm, Royal Library, MS A.135; Alexander 1978, no. 30) and the Codex Bigotianus (Paris, Bibliothèque Nationale, lat. 281 and lat. 298; Alexander 1978, no. 34) are prefaced by the *Novum opus* and *Plures fuisse*, but omit the *Eusebius carpiano*; whereas the Barberini Gospels and the Royal Bible (London, British Library, MS Royal I.E.VI; Alexander 1978, no. 32) contain only the *Novum opus*. Early manuscripts from Echternach – the Augsburg Gospels (Augsburg, Universitätsbibliothek Cod. 1.2.4°.2; Alexander 1978, no. 24), the Maeseyck Gospels, and the Trier Gospels (Trier, Cathedral Treasury, MS 61; Alexander 1978, no. 26) – possess a rare sequence of general prefaces in the order *Plures fuisse, Novum opus*, and *Sciendum etiam*. Many Irish manuscripts have no prefaces at all, and those that do, contain only the *Novum opus*. No other Southumbrian, Echternach or Irish manuscript, moreover, has lists of chapter summaries or chapter divisions of the same distinct type found in the St Petersburg, Lindisfarne, Royal I.B.VII, and Gotha Gospels; nor does any include the liturgical rubrics within the lists of chapter summaries of Luke and John.

Although St Petersburg's preliminary texts are Northumbrian in origin, a close examination proves that they were not copied from the Lindisfarne Gospels.[4] The omission from St Petersburg of all four lists of liturgical feasts found in Lindisfarne strongly suggests that there is no direct relationship between the two manuscripts. St Petersburg is also missing the liturgical rubric after the ninety-fourth chapter summary in the list that precedes Luke in Lindisfarne. Many of the variant readings in Lindisfarne's general prefaces, moreover, are not shared by St Petersburg. The combination of general prefaces *Novum opus, Plures fuisse*, and *Eusebius carpiano* is not found outside a small circle of manuscripts associated with the Northumbrian *scriptoria* of Lindisfarne and Wearmouth-Jarrow (Brown in Kendrick *et al.* 1960, 33); had St Petersburg copied these texts from Lindisfarne, one would expect a closer relationship between them. Particularly significant is the omission from Lindisfarne of several passages in St Petersburg's *Plures fuisse* preface, as well as the prologues to Matthew, Mark and John. Even variant readings in St Petersburg's lists of chapter summaries – of the type found only in the same limited group of Northumbrian manuscripts as the general prefaces – agree more often with the Royal I.B.VII and Gotha Gospels than with the Lindisfarne Gospels. In all likelihood, neither Royal I.B.VII (Brown 1960, 43–6) nor Gotha is a copy of Lindisfarne; rather, both probably represent independent copies of the sixth-century Neapolitan manuscript owned by Wearmouth-Jarrow. This is suggested by the presence of antique features in Royal I.B.VII and Gotha not found in Lindisfarne, but typical of uncial manuscripts from Wearmouth-Jarrow.[5] There are therefore enough differences between St Petersburg and Lindisfarne's preliminary texts to conclude that St Petersburg depends, likewise, on an independent copy of this Neapolitan manuscript.

Nevertheless, several distinctive features of the St Petersburg Gospels demonstrate that the Northumbrian model for its preliminary texts was most likely written at Lindisfarne. The St Petersburg Gospels faithfully copies the Lindisfarne Gospels in the numerical entries of its Canon-tables – a concordance of parallel passages in the four gospels, represented by numbers typically arranged in columns beneath an architectural arcade. Excepting minor differences resulting from scribal error, variants in the Canon-tables of St Petersburg and Lindisfarne are virtually identical: a simple misalignment of entries at the end of Canon X in St Petersburg accounts for the one major difference between them. St Petersburg could not have acquired its Canon-tables from the sixth-century Neapolitan manuscript, for it lost them before arriving in Northumbria (Brown 1960, 33–4, 48). The numerical entries of the St Petersburg and Lindisfarne tables are very similar to those of the Royal I.B.VII and Burchard Gospels (Würzburg, Universitätsbibliothek, M.p.th.f.68), a sixth-century Italian uncial manuscript, to which Canon-table entries were added at Wearmouth-Jarrow in the late seventh or early eighth century. Although the Canon-table entries of all four manuscripts probably descend from the same unknown archetype, differences between St Petersburg and Lindisfarne, on the one hand, and Royal I.B.VII and Burchard, on the other, preclude the possibility that St Petersburg's entries were copied from either of the second two manuscripts (McGurk 1993, 247–51). In this instance only does St Petersburg's Northumbrian model appear to be related directly to the Lindisfarne Gospels.

The chapter divisions

The combination of two different types of chapter

divisions in the main text of the St Petersburg Gospels also points to an origin at the Lindisfarne *scriptorium*. Most early medieval gospel books were divided into consecutively numbered chapters, usually marked by enlarged and/or decorated initials, and numbered with marginal Roman numerals. Brief summaries of the contents of each chapter were gathered into lists placed at the beginning of each gospel, or, occasionally, at the beginning of the manuscript. There were several systems of dividing the gospels, each yielding a different number of chapters, marked at different locations within the text. DeBruyne used these differences to classify manuscripts into families, with most Insular gospel books belonging to families B, C or I (DeBruyne 1914).

The lists of chapter summaries and divisions in the Lindisfarne Gospels, for example, correspond to the C family, which divides Matthew, Mark, Luke, and John into 88, 46, 94, and 45 chapters, respectively. Although all four lists of chapter summaries in the St Petersburg Gospels belong to the C family, the numerals marked in the margins of the main text are a combination of the B and C families. B-family chapter summaries and/or divisions are found in the Stockholm Codex Aureus, the Royal Bible, and the Barberini Gospels, and are thought to have been introduced into Southumbria via imported Italian models, such as the Gospels of St Augustine (Cambridge, Corpus Christi College, 286) (McGurk 1961, 113–14). It is unlikely, however, that any of these Southumbrian manuscripts is the source of B-family chapter divisions in St Petersburg, for each also contains I-family chapter summaries and/or divisions. If St Petersburg had copied any of these manuscripts, one would expect to find a similar combination of B- and I-family elements. Moreover, these manuscripts have only a small number of B-family divisions, and could not have provided St Petersburg with its nearly complete set in the gospels of Mark, Luke, and John. The possibility that St Petersburg's B-family chapter divisions were copied from an Italian manuscript, such as the Gospels of St Augustine, or a faithful Southumbrian copy of one, cannot be ruled out. Analysis of other Insular manuscripts with B-family chapter summaries and divisions, however, suggests an alternative Northumbrian source.

Although B-family chapter divisions are considered a Southumbrian attribute, the only early medieval manuscripts other than St Petersburg to combine B- and C-family chapter divisions – the Royal I.B.VII and Gotha Gospels – are Northumbrian.[6] The St Petersburg, Royal I.B.VII, and Gotha Gospels probably represent different branches of the same family tree, all descended from a single archetype – the sixth-century Neapolitan manuscript used as the exemplar for the Lindisfarne Gospels. Because B-family chapter divisions are not found in the Lindisfarne Gospels, this Neapolitan manuscript probably did not contain them either. Thus, at least one intermediary, with B-family chapter divisions, must stand between this Neapolitan manuscript and the St Petersburg, Royal I.B.VII and Gotha Gospels. This intermediary may have been the early eighth-century Durham Gospels (Durham, Cathedral Library, MS A.II.17; Alexander 1978, no. 10), or a close copy of it, because St Petersburg repeats errors specific to its system of B-family chapter divisions.[7] For example, both manuscripts mark B-family chapter division two in Mark, and B-family chapter division eighteen in Luke, at the same incorrect passages. The gospel of John in the B family should be divided into fourteen chapters; however, there are fifteen in the Durham Gospels because the scribe, for an unknown reason, included an extra chapter division at John 18:28. Although St Petersburg has only fourteen chapters, the last chapter is also marked incorrectly at John 18:28. Because none of these errors is found in the Stockholm Codex Aureus, the Royal Bible or the Barberini Gospels, it is all the more unlikely that any of these Southumbrian manuscripts was the source of B-family chapter divisions in St Petersburg.

On palaeographical evidence, Brown argued that the Durham Gospels was written at Lindisfarne *c.* 700 (Kendrick *et al.* 1960, 89ff.). Although this origin is not universally accepted (Ó Cróinín 1982), it has been shown that the Durham and Lindisfarne Gospels were corrected by the same scribe (Verey in Brown 1972, 243–45). If the Durham Gospels were at Lindisfarne in the eighth century, as the evidence of its corrections suggest, this would explain how, in the St Petersburg, Royal I.B.VII, and Gotha Gospels, B-family chapter summaries and divisions were conflated with those of the C family.[8] The presence of several rare liturgical notes in the main texts of both the Royal I.B.VII and the Durham Gospels supports this conclusion (Verey 1980, 26–8). Furthermore, an unusual *incipit* to the *Novum opus* preface in the St Petersburg Gospels is almost identical to that in the Echternach Gospels (Paris, Bibliothèque Nationale, lat. 9389; Alexander 1978, no. 11), which may also be from Lindisfarne (Brown 1960, 89ff.). The convergence of rare features of the Lindisfarne, Durham and Echternach Gospels[9] in a gospel book with preliminary texts derived from a sixth-century Neapolitan manuscript, borrowed from Wearmouth-Jarrow to be used as the exemplar for the Lindisfarne Gospels, cannot be a coincidence. The St Petersburg Gospels must have been copied from a manuscript written at Lindisfarne, or a Southumbrian copy of it.[10]

The main text

Although St Petersburg's preliminary texts can be placed firmly within a Northumbrian context, with ties to southern Italy, its main text has, for the most part, a different origin.[11] St Petersburg's gospel of Matthew is a close copy of the Vulgate, and the few variants it does have are related to the Lindisfarne Gospels and other members of the Italo-Northumbrian family.[12] Variants in the gospels of Mark, Luke and John, however, agree strongly with those

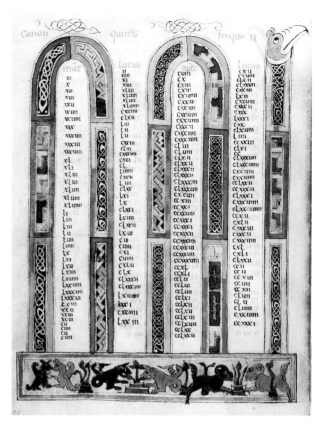

Fig. 16.2 *Cutbercht Gospels, fol. 19v. (Photograph: Österreichische Nationalbibliothek, Vienna)*

of Old Latin and Irish manuscripts. St Petersburg's main text appears to depend upon two distinct models. The first was a Northumbrian manuscript, similar to the Lindisfarne Gospels and other manuscripts of the Italo-Northumbrian family, perhaps even the model written at Lindisfarne, from which St Petersburg's preliminary texts and Canon-table entries derive. The second model descended from an Irish archetype, which may or may not have been written in Ireland. Recent scholarship has supported the existence of direct contacts between Ireland and Southumbria (Brown 1994; 1996), and St Petersburg's Irish model could have travelled this route. Alternatively, it could have been written in an English or Continental monastery founded by an Irish mission. The evidence favours the latter possibility: the Gospels of Mark, Luke and John in St Petersburg share many variants with the Southumbrian Stockholm Codex Aureus and the Barberini Gospels, as well as the Augsburg and Maeseyck Gospels from Echternach, which was founded by a mission from the monastery at Rath Melsigi in Ireland (Ó Cróinín 1984). This and other significant connections between Southumbrian and Echternach manuscripts have led to the suggestion that a model from Echternach, similar to the Augsburg, Maeseyck

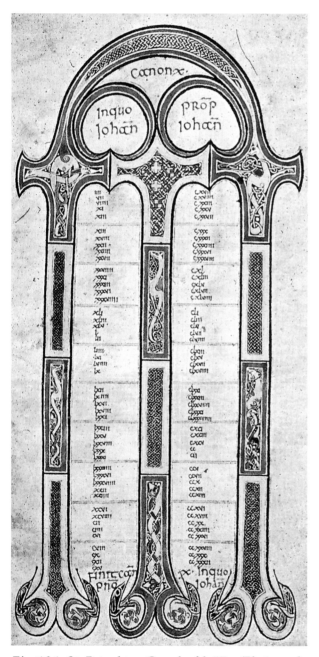

Fig. 16.1 *St. Petersburg Gospels, fol. 17v. (Photograph: National Library of Russia, St Petersburg)*

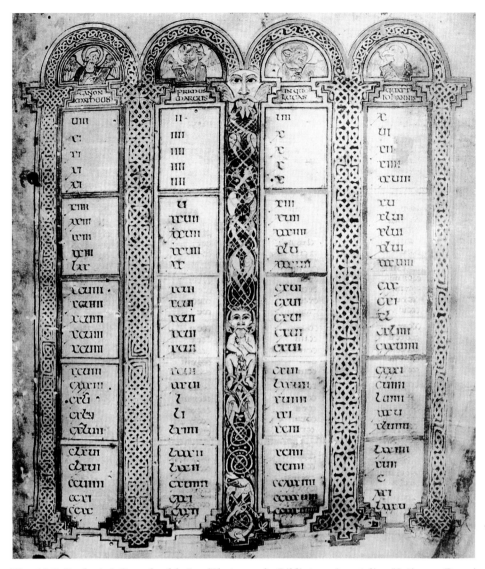

Fig. 16.3 *Barberini Gospels, fol. 1r. (Photograph: Biblioteca Apostolica Vaticana, Rome)*

and Trier Gospels, was available in Southumbria (Netzer 1994a, 26–7, 59, 62, 65–6, 83). Given that the Augsburg, Maeseyck, and part of the Trier Gospels were copied from an Irish manuscript with many Old Latin readings (Ó Cróinín 1988, 30–4; Netzer 1994b, 328), St Petersburg's dependence on such a model from Echternach would explain the decidedly Old Latin/Irish character of its Gospels of Mark, Luke and John.

The decoration of the Canon-tables

The Southumbrian conflation of models from Northumbria and Echternach in St Petersburg's textual features is also evident in the decoration of its Canon-tables. Although the unusual frames of these Canon-tables do not resemble any other surviving

set, the overall design is similar to the Canon-tables in the Cutbercht Gospels, written at Salzburg by a scribe trained in a Southumbrian, possibly Kentish scriptorium (Tholl 1986, 318–19). The artists of the St Petersburg and Cutbercht Canon-tables frequently departed from the traditional, strict distinction of base, column, capital and arch, in favour of whimsical variations, or even omissions, of these architectural elements. On St Petersburg's final table (Fig. 16.1), for instance, the fluid movement from the base of the column straight through to the arch is similar to examples in the Cutbercht Gospels (Fig. 16.2) and the Barberini Gospels (Fig. 16.3). Another rejection of architectural realism is the use of circular capitals to decorate the Canon-tables of the St Petersburg Gospels (Fig. 16.4), the Canon-tables and Evangelist portraits in the Stockholm Codex Aureus, and the Canon-tables and opening of the gospel of Luke in

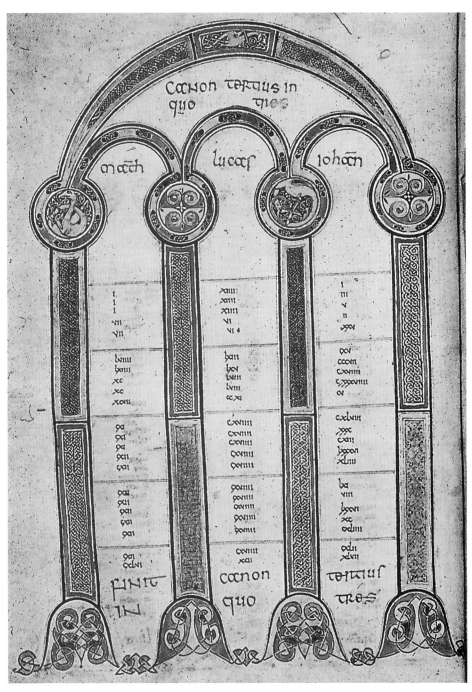

Fig. 16.4 *St. Petersburg Gospels, fol. 14v. (Photograph: National Library of Russia, St Petersburg)*

the Royal Bible. In all three manuscripts, circular capitals contain beasts or human busts, in addition to standard interlace designs. The alternating pattern of beasts entwined in interlace in the circular capitals of one of St Petersburg's tables (Fig. 16.4) has a parallel in the Royal Bible (fol. 4r, Alexander 1978, illus. 162). Circular capitals containing beasts and human busts are also found on two of the eight tables of a fragment attached to the Maeseyck Gospels. Given that the Canon-tables of the Stock-

holm Codex Aureus depend upon a model from Echternach, this feature may also derive from such a model.

A second type of circular capital in the St Petersburg Gospels (Fig. 16.5), however, is probably Northumbrian. The manner in which the bands of the inner and outer arches of this table are threaded through circular capitals recalls similar treatments on Mercian sculpture from Northamptonshire and Leicestershire, especially capitals on a wall panel

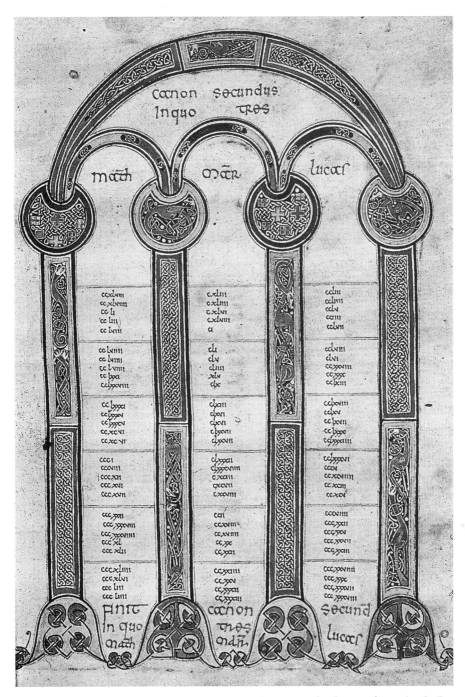

Fig. 16.5 *St. Petersburg Gospels, fol. 14r. (Photograph: National Library of Russia, St Petersburg)*

from Breedon-on-the-Hill (Cramp 1977, 217, fig. 58c). Possibly stemming from Northumbrian influence in Mercia, this feature appears to have spread further south: it is found in a modified form, in two Canon-tables in the Cutbercht Gospels. On these tables, the columns, rather than the arches are threaded through the capitals (Fig. 16.6). The way in which beast heads terminate the inner arches of Canon-tables in the St Petersburg Gospels (Fig. 16.7), the Cutbercht Gospels (Fig. 16.8), and the Royal Bible

(fol. 4r) may also have a Northumbrian origin, for the same feature is used on all the Canon-tables in the Royal I.B.VII Gospels. Other decorative similarities between the Canon-tables of Southumbrian manuscripts and the Royal I.B.VII Gospels attest to the presence of Northumbrian models in Southumbria. For example, the second Canon-table of the Royal Bible (fol. 4v, Alexander 1978, illus. 163) consists of three major columns from which spring the outer arches, alternating with two narrower

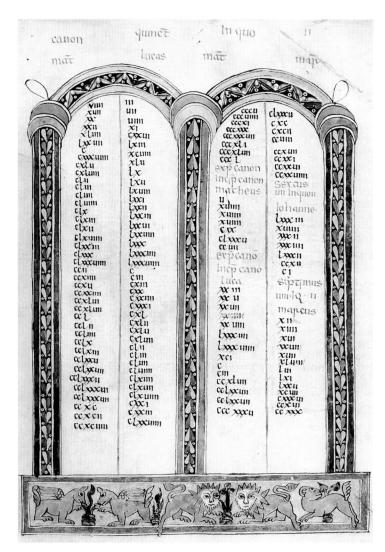

Fig. 16.6 *Cutbercht Gospels, fol. 20r. (Photograph: Österreichische Nationalbibliothek, Vienna)*

columns, on which the inner arches rest. Above the capital of the central column is a triangular wedge, formed by the intersection of the inner and outer arches. The frames of Royal I.B.VII's Canon-tables are identical, albeit more modest in design. Moreover, Royal I.B.VII's Canon-tables possibly inspired the unusual practice of replacing capitals with human and animal heads seen in the Southumbrian Barberini Gospels.

Conclusions

This analysis has not attempted to locate where St Petersburg's Southumbrian exemplar was created from Northumbrian and Echternach models, themselves ultimately dependent on Italian and Irish archetypes. The evidence does not suggest a definitive answer. The rare omission of a particular passage in the prologue to the gospel of Luke in the St Petersburg and Barberini Gospels, as well as the sixth-century Italian Gospels of St Augustine, may point to a common origin at Canterbury.[13] The Gospels of St Augustine are known to have been in England by the early eighth century (Webster and Backhouse 1991, 17–18). It was used as a model for the Stockholm Codex Aureus, possibly written at Canterbury and exhibiting elements of late Antique, Mediterranean script and decoration (Wright 1967). Past scholarship has emphasised the significance of Mediterranean influence on Southumbrian art and book production. Mediterranean models certainly played a seminal role in the development of Southumbrian art, but not to the exclusion of the native Insular tradition. Close examination of the St Petersburg Gospels indicates that Irish models were equally important in Southumbria in the second half of the eighth century, and the strongly Irish character

Fig. 16.7 *St. Petersburg Gospels, fol. 16v. (Photograph: National Library of Russia, St Petersburg)*

of the text of the Barberini Gospels supports this conclusion (Bruno forthcoming).

It is difficult to determine whether the St Petersburg and Barberini Gospels were written in Kent or Mercia. Both gospel books rely on a model from Echternach, which, at some point, must have been in the possession of a Kentish scriptorium, given its impact on the Stockholm Codex Aureus. Of course, this does not prove that either the St Petersburg or Barberini Gospels were written in south-east England, for this Echternach model, or a Southumbrian

copy of it, could easily have been taken to Mercia. Illuminations in the Book of Cerne, written in a Mercian scriptorium, demonstrate that models travelled from one Southumbrian region to another: Cerne's Evangelist portraits were copied from the same exemplar used for the illuminations in the Royal Bible from Canterbury (Brown in Webster and Backhouse 1991, 211, 217; Brown 1996, 73–5). Comprehensive study of other eighth-century manuscripts may help to locate the origin of the St Petersburg Gospels more specifically. Until then, it

Fig. 16.8 Cutbercht Gospels, fol. 18r. (Photograph: Österreichische Nationalbibliothek, Vienna)

is a reminder of the complexity of early medieval scriptoria, and of the need to expand our understanding of the sources of Southumbrian art.

Notes

1   The field has been divided between scholars who favour a Northumbrian origin for the St Petersburg Gospels (Kendrick 1938, 144ff.; Micheli 1939, 28; Henry 1940, 134; Brown 1972, 234–35; Lowe 1934–66 (*CLA* XI), no. 1605; Wilson 1984, 88–91), and those who favour a Southumbrian origin (Zimmermann 1916, 143–45, 304–5; Nordenfalk 1965, no. 398; Tweddle *et al.* 1995, 35ff.).

2   These are the Augsburg Gospels (Augsburg, Uni-

versitätsbibliothek Cod. I.2.4°.2) and the Trier Gospels (Trier, Domschatz MS 61). The Canon-tables of the Stockholm Codex Aureus contain rare decorative and textual features of the Augsburg, Maeseyck and Trier Canon-tables. According to Netzer, details of these features indicate that the similarities between the Stockholm Codex Aureus and the Echternach manuscripts were not the result of Southumbrian influence at Echternach, but rather demonstrate the presence of at least one model from Echternach in a Southumbrian scriptorium in Kent, possibly Canterbury (1994a, 26–7, 59, 62, 65–6, 83).

3   Although the Lindisfarne, Royal I.B.VII, and Gotha Gospels also possess lists of liturgical feasts for each gospel, these are not found in the St Petersburg Gospels.

4   My analysis of readings that vary from the Vulgate is

based on Wordsworth and White's edition of the four Gospels (1889–98), and Regul's study of Gospel prologues (1969).

5   In the Royal I.B.VII Gospels, red initials mark the start of each chapter summary and each entry in the list of feasts; entire lines in red signal the beginning of a new chapter within the main text (Brown 1960, 43–6). Similar treatments are found in the Gotha Gospels.

6   The list of chapter summaries prefacing John in the Gotha Gospels also belongs to the B family.

7   The fragmentary state of the Durham Gospels limits comparison with other manuscripts containing B-family divisions.

8   See Bruno, V. A. 1995, 'Audience and reception of early Insular Gospel books'. Unpublished paper delivered at the 30th International Congress on Medieval Studies, Western Michigan University, Kalamazoo.

9   These features are the Canon-table entries of the Lindisfarne Gospels, the errors in the B-family divisions of the Durham Gospels, and the *Novum opus incipit* of the Echternach Gospels.

10   There is a small number of variants in St Petersburg's preliminary texts corresponding to those in Southumbrian manuscripts. This suggests that these texts were not copied directly from the Northumbrian model.

11   My analysis of variants in St Petersburg's main text is based on Fischer's collations of pre-tenth century manuscripts (1988–91).

12   The Italo-Northumbrian family includes the following: the Codex Amiatinus (Florence, Biblioteca Medicea-Laurenziana, Amiatinus 1); the Stonyhurst Gospels of St John (Stonyhurst, College Library); the fragments of John in Durham A.II.16 (Durham, Cathedral Library A.II.16 [fols 103–34]); the Utrecht fragment (Utrecht, Universiteitsbibliotheek, 32); the uncial leaves at the end of the Durham Gospels (Durham, Cathedral Library, A.II.17 [fols 103–11]); and Luke 2:10–3:8 in the Burchard Gospels.

13   *Et in quo electus scriberet indicaret* (Wordsworth and White 1889–98, 270 l.4; Regul 1969, 45 l.15). This passage is also missing from two other manuscripts: the Livinus Gospels (Ghent, St Bavo Cathedral s.n.), written at St Amand *c.* 800, and a late ninth-century manuscript from Brittany (Bern, Burgerbibliothek, 85). The connection with the Livinus Gospels is significant, given McGurk's examination of its close textual relationship with the Stockholm Codex Aureus and the Barberini Gospels (1963, 165–75).

References

ALEXANDER, J. J. G. 1978, *Insular Manuscripts 6th to the 9th Century. A Survey of Manuscripts Illuminated in the British Isles*, Vol 1. London.

BROWN, M. P. 1994, 'Echoes: the Book of Kells and southern English manuscript production', in O'Mahony (ed.), 333–43.

BROWN, M. P. 1996, *The Book of Cerne: Prayer, Patronage, and Power in Ninth-Century England*. London.

BROWN, T. J. 1960, 'The nature of the Latin text' and 'The palaeography of the Latin text', in Kendrick *et al.*, Vol.II, bk I, pts II, III, 31–106.

BROWN, T. J. 1972, 'Northumbria and the Book of Kells', *Anglo-Saxon Engl.* 1, 219–46.

BRUNO, V. A. (forthcoming), The Barberini Gospels and the Development of Gospel Book Production in Southumbria in the Eighth Century. Unpublished PhD thesis, Cornell University. Ithaca.

CRAMP, R. 1977, 'Schools of Mercian sculpture', in A. Dornier (ed.), *Mercian Studies*, 191–233. Leicester.

DEBRUYNE, D. 1914, *Sommaires, Divisions, et Rubriques de la Bible Latine*. Namur.

FISCHER, B. 1988–91, *Die Lateinischen Evangelium bis zum 10 Jahrhundert*, 4 vols. Freiburg.

HENRY, F. 1940, *Irish Art in the Early Christian Period*. London.

KENDRICK, T. D. 1938, *Anglo-Saxon Art to A.D. 900*. London.

KENDRICK, T. D., BROWN, T. J., BRUCE-MITFORD, R. L. S., ROOSEN-RUNGE, H., ROSS, A. S. C., STANLEY, E. G., WERNER, A. E. A. (eds) 1960, *Evangeliorum Quattuor Codex Lindisfarnensis*, 2 vols. Olten, Lausanne.

LOWE, E. A. 1934–66, 1971, *Codices Latini Antiquiores*, 11 vols + supplement. Oxford.

MCGURK, P. 1961, *Latin Gospel-Books from A.D. 400 to A.D. 800*. Paris, Brussels.

MCGURK, P. 1963, 'The Ghent Livinus Gospels and the scriptorium of St Amand', *Sacris Erudiri* 14, 164–205.

MCGURK, P. 1993, 'The disposition of numbers in Latin Eusebian Canon-tables', in R. Gryson (ed.), *Philologia Sacra Biblische und patristische Studien für Hermann J. Frede und Walter Thiele zu ihrem siebzigsten Geburtstag*, 242–58. Freiburg.

MICHELI, G. 1939, *L'Enluminure du Haut Moyen Age et les Influences Irlandaises*. Brussels.

NETZER, N. 1994a, *Cultural Interplay in the 8th Century: The Trier Gospels and the Making of a Scriptorium at Echternach*. Cambridge.

NETZER, N. 1994b, 'The origin of the beast Canon-tables reconsidered', in O'Mahony (ed.), 322–32.

NORDENFALK, C. 1965, *Karl der Grosse*. Aachen.

Ó CRÓINÍN, D. 1982, 'Pride and Prejudice', *Peritia* 1, 352–62.

Ó CRÓINÍN, D. 1984, 'Rath Melsigi, Willibrord, and the earliest Echternach manuscripts', *Peritia* 3, 17–42.

Ó CRÓINÍN, D. (ed.) 1988, *Evangeliarium Epternacense (Universitätsbibliothek Augsburg, Cod. I.2.4°.2), Evangelistarium (Erzbischöfliches Priesterseminar St. Peters, Cod. ms. 25)* (= *Codices Illuminati Medii Aevi* 9). Munich.

O'MAHONY, F. (ed.) 1994, *The Book of Kells. Proceedings of a conference at Trinity College Dublin, 6–9 September 1992*. Aldershot.

REGUL, J. 1969, *Die Antimarcionitischen Evangelienprologe*. Freiburg.

THOLL, S. (ed.) 1986, The Vienna Cutbercht Gospels (Wien, Österreichische Nationalbibliothek, Codex 1224). Unpublished PhD thesis, Columbia University. New York.

TWEDDLE, D., BIDDLE, M. and KJØLBYE-BIDDLE, B. 1995, *Corpus of Anglo-Saxon Stone Sculpture in England: South-East England*. Oxford.

VEREY, C. D., BROWN, T. J. and COATSWORTH, E. (eds)

1980, *The Durham Gospels* (= Early English Manuscripts in Facsimile 20). Copenhagen.

WEBSTER, L. and BACKHOUSE, J. (eds) 1991, *The Making of England. Anglo-Saxon Art and Culture AD 600–900*. London.

WILSON, D. M. 1984, *Anglo-Saxon Art*. London.

WORDSWORTH, J. and WHITE, H. J. (eds) 1889–98, *Novum Testamentum Domini Nostri Iesu Christi Latine, Secundum Editionem Sancti Hieronymi*. Oxford.

WRIGHT, D. H. (ed.) 1967, *The Vespasian Psalter* (= Early English Manuscripts in Facsimile 14). Copenhagen.

ZIMMERMANN, E. H. 1916, *Vorkarolingische Miniaturen*, 5 vols. Berlin.

17   Bible Text and Illumination in St Gall Stiftsbibliothek Codex 51, with Special Reference to Longinus in the Crucifixion Scene

Martin McNamara

Introduction to the St Gall Codex 51

Codex 51 of the Stiftsbibliothek of St Gall contains the four Gospels in the usual order in Latin but in subdivisions marked off by larger initials, probably intended for liturgical reading (Kenney 1929, 649; Duft and Meyer 1954, 69–71). The Gospel text ends on page 265 (like most St Gall manuscripts, this one is numbered by pages, rather than by folios). The existence of these Gospels has been noted for a long time. More attention has been devoted to the illumination of the work than to an examination of the biblical text it carries, although this has not been forgotten.

The manuscript and its contents have been and need to be studied from at least three points of view: palaeographical, art-historical and from that of the biblical text. W. M. Lindsay examined the script in 1913 (Lindsay 1913, 304): the script was Irish (half-uncial or large minuscule). The scribe, he wrote, relapses at the conclusion of the text (*ibid.*, 265) into what we may suppose to have been his everyday hand. This is of the Continental type of minuscule, for Lindsay proof positive that the manuscript was not written in Ireland, for Continental minuscule did not appear in Britain or Ireland until the tenth century. He regretted that neither Chroust nor Steffens, who had published photographs of this manuscript, had selected this most interesting page. Perhaps, he surmised, this was because they thought (which seems unlikely) that the scribe left the text unfinished, and that the concluding lines were added later. Lindsay returned to a brief consideration of the manuscript two years later (Lindsay 1915, 483), maintaining basically the same positions: the last three lines of the text, which look like, but can hardly be, a later addition, are in Continental minuscule. He added that a clue to the (Continental) provenance of this manuscript is its use of the contraction *usi* etc. for 'vestri', etc. – these originally Visigothic/Spanish contractions being found in Continental, but not in Irish manuscripts. In his study of the illumination and the origin of the manuscript in 1916, E. H. Zimmermann (1916, 99–102; 240–42) took quite a different position. In his opinion, the manuscript contained no indication of a Continental origin. The script was free of Continental influence and the postscript which Lindsay held to be contemporary was much later (end of the tenth century). The abbreviations which Lindsay took as indications of Continental origin were too few to carry conviction and the field had not been sufficiently researched. Zimmermann argued for Irish origin and for a date *c.* 750–60 (*ibid.*, 101–2; 240). K. Löffler (1929, 13–15) reviewed earlier studies of the origin and date of the manuscript, including Zimmermann's, and noted the predominant opinion favouring an Irish origin and a mid-eighth century date. He returned to the end lines being in Carolingian minuscule, and noted that the minuscule is of the stamp to be found in St Gall at the time of Grimalt and Hartmut (*ibid.*, 841–72; 872–83). For him, the likelihood of the end lines of John having been forgotten and later added was as good as excluded. The possibility of St Gall as place of origin could not be excluded, and at a date of about 850. J. Kenney also summarised some of the earlier views on the work (Kenney 1929, 649).

J. J. G. Alexander included it in his study of Insular manuscripts of the sixth to the ninth centuries (Alexander 1978, no. 44, 66–7). He noted the presence of corrections and pen-trials in Carolingian minuscule (*ibid.*, 1, 128). He assigned it a date of the second half of the eighth century. In his view the manuscript was probably made in Ireland and brought to St Gall at a later date, no doubt in the ninth century. It was less likely to have been made by Irishmen on the Continent.

The most authoritative examination of the manuscript was made by Johannes Duft, librarian of the Stiftsbibliothek (Duft and Meyer 1954). He noted the studies of Zimmermann and Löffler and their differences with regard to the date and place of origin. Duft himself described the last two lines of the text (*testimonium eius ... libros*) as in Carolingian minuscule; below this in another charter-like, grotesque hand was written: 'Amen Amen DIgnus est operarius mercede SVA' (ibid., 69). The time of origin, Duft remarked, can only be decided on palaeographic and art-historical grounds and it was about, or more probably, later than 750. In his view, MS 51's place of writing was probably Ireland; at all events it was the work of an Irish scribe and of at least two book illuminators (*ibid.*, 69–70).

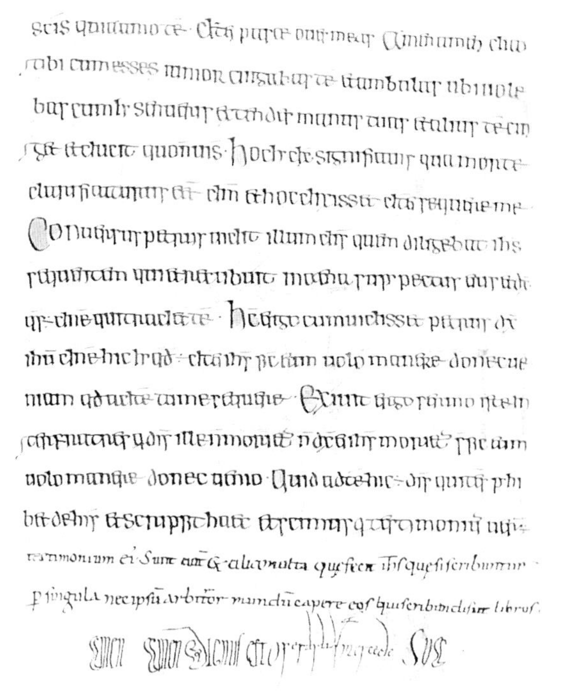

On palaeographic and art-historical grounds Zimmermann and Duft opted for a date about 750, or somewhat later. The arguments of Lindsay, Löffler and others for a later date and Continental origin derived mainly from the last two lines of text in Carolingian minuscule (the line below this in a charter-like, grotesque hand, with no bearing on the biblical text, is clearly a later addition). Given the importance of the last two lines it was unfortunate that attention had not been given to details of the biblical text they carried. We may here recall how the manuscript ends. Page 264 has 25 lines of text. On page 265 there are thirteen full lines in the normal hand of the manuscript, ending with an incorrect reading at the second-last verse of John's Gospel (John 21:24) as follows: '*et scimus quia testimonium uerum est*' (instead of '*quia uerum est testimonium eius*'). The St Gall reading is attested in no known manuscript and must be regarded as an error. Why this error, and why the original scribe did not write the final verse (21:25) we cannot say. The last verse is missing from the Greek original of the fourth-century Codex Sinaiticus, but from no other text. We can presume it was in the original of St Gall 51. In our manuscript the text, with the final verse of the Gospel, is completed in two further lines. This text in minuscule begins (after the erroneous '*testimonium uerum est*') with the correct ending of verse 24: *testimonium eius* (abbreviated as *ei*), and continues with verse 25 as follows: '*Sunt autem* (*aut*, with a stroke over the *t*) *et alia multa quae* (*que. e caudata*) *fecit Iesus quae* (*que, e caudata*) *si scribuntur* (Vulgate: *scribantur*) *per* (*p*, with a stroke through the lower part) *singula nec ipsum arbitror* (second *r* interlineated) *mundum capere eos qui scribundi* (sic, -*un*-; lege: *scribendi*) *sunt libros*'. In these two lines I draw attention to the different abbreviation and contraction system from that of the main text. Thus for *autem* we have *aut*, with a stroke over the *t*, for the horned *h* as in page 265, line 9 (21:21) (Fig. 17.1), and in general in St Gall 51. For *per* we have *p* with a

Fig. 17.1 *Final page of text in St Gall Gospel book (Stiftsbibliothek, MS 51, p. 265). The two lines in Carolingian minuscule which appear below the main text have featured in the redating of the manuscript. (Photograph: by permission of the Stiftsbibliothek, St Gall)*

bar through the downward shaft, instead of the horned *p* as in page 265, lines 7 and 12 (second last line of normal text) (21:20, 24) (Fig. 17.1) and *passim* in the manuscript. For *eius* we have *ei*, with a stroke over the *i*, while in St Gall 51 it is generally written in full, as in page 265, line 7 (21:20) (Fig. 17.1). *Quae* is written as *que*, with *e caudata*, for the usual *q* with three dots ('therefore'-sign, at John 20:33 and *passim*), although it occasionally has *quae* (conjoined *ae*, at John 2:24), even *e-caudata* (1:9), but with much longer '*cauda*' than here in end lines. We have no explanation as to why the principal scribe lapsed into textual error in the second-last verse of John's Gospel, or why the final verse (21:25) was omitted. The ending in minuscule, which presumes an awareness of the uncorrected error in verse 24, has all the hallmarks of a text coming from quite a different person than the main scribe. It appears to be an addition, not a continuation, and would seem to have no bearing on the date or place of origin of the main text.

The biblical text

What has just been said on the final verses indicates

the importance of paying attention to the biblical text for a satisfactory understanding of the manuscript. To my knowledge, until recently the biblical text has been generally neglected. The Gospels feature in Gregory's *Textkritik* (Gregory 1900, no. 1923, 708). Samuel Berger examined them for his study of the Vulgate in the early Middle Ages (Berger 1893, 56, 416). He observed that they have the mixed Irish type of text, particularly mixed in the first chapters of Matthew, noting some rare or unique readings: Matthew 1:25, *filium suum unigenitum*; 2:4, *et congregatis omnibus pontificis et scribis populi*; 2:6, *domus Iuda ... rex*; 2:7, *exquessiuit*; 3:3, *Hoc enim quod dictum est*; 3:7, *ab ira uentura*; 4:18, *Transens autem secus mare Galileae*; 10:31, *timere eos, multo magis passeribus*; 16:6, *Adtendtite uobis et*; Mark 1:42, *Inspiciens autem uultu iecit eum*; John 13:10: *non indiget ut lauet nisi pedes lauare* (doublet); 21:25 is omitted; end of verse 24: *quod testimonium uerum est*.

The first serious analysis is that of the sixteen passages (four from each Gospel) examined by Bonifatius Fischer in his four volumes on the Latin Gospels before 900 (Fischer 1988; 1989; 1990; 1991). For this work Fischer collated some 464 manuscripts (mainly from before the year 900), whereas J. Wordsworth and H. J. White in general used only 29 for their critical edition of the Vulgate Gospels, including Matthew (Wordsworth and White 1895). Fischer has given the siglum Hs (Hibernia, St Gall) to the biblical text of Codex 51. For his examination of the text of Matthew he collates four sections (*Probeabschnitte*) from it: Matthew 2:19–4:17; 8:2–9:8; 16:9–17:17 and 26:39–58 + 27:29–46 (taken as a single *Abschnitt*). In the first of these four sections, he says, the MS St Gallen 51 is as far removed from the Vulgate text as is the Vetus Latina side of Codex Bezae and scarcely less than the Bobiensis, which has the African text of the Vetus Latina (Fischer 1988, 6*).

In a work published in 1990 the present writer carried out a partial collation of chapters from all four Gospels of Codex 51. For all four Gospels, except for St Matthew (for which Fischer's partial collation was also used), this was made against the critical edition of the Vulgate alone. This partial collation indicates that in this codex we are in the presence of some curious phenomena, ranging from readings otherwise unattested in the early chapters of Matthew to an extraordinary correspondence throughout John with the Irish manuscripts the Book of Armagh and the Mac Regol Gospels.

In preparation for the present study a complete collation of John's Gospel has been made, except for chapters 8:17–59, chapters 9, 10, 11 and 16, that is except for four and a half of the Gospel's twenty-one chapters. This collation was first made against the critical edition of the Vulgate alone, and later also

against Fischer's complete collation for the four pericopes chosen by him for John's Gospel (John 2:18–3:31; 7:28–8:16; 12:17–13:6; 20:1–21:4). This first fuller collation shows that the agreement between St Gall 51 and Armagh runs right through the Gospel of John, from beginning to end. The same holds for the relationship of Codex 51 to Mac Regol.[1] The second stage of the collation against Fischer's much richer evidence showed that many of the variants of St Gall Codex 51 were shared by other manuscripts (Irish and sometimes from other text groups) beyond Armagh and Mac Regol. While this indicates the need for caution and for further research before we prove an overall special textual relationship between Codex 51 with Armagh and Mac Regol, the evidence does clearly show that for the Gospel of John Codex Sangallensis 51 has an Irish biblical text.

A further, but partial, examination of the text of Matthew's Gospel also indicates special affiliations with the so-called 'Celtic' or 'Irish' texts of the Book of Armagh, British Library Egerton 609, the marginal glosses of the Echternach Gospels, the Lichfield Gospels, the Book of Kells and Mac Regol.

For the Gospels of Matthew and John we may note interpolations in the crucifixion scene. Especially significant for our purpose is the addition in the Irish textual tradition at Matthew 27:49 (McNamara 1990, 25). In the Gospel scene the dying Jesus cries out (27:46): '*Heli heli lema sabacthani...* Some of the bystanders said: *heliam uocat iste*. And immediately one of them ran, took a sponge, filled it with vinegar, put it on a reed and gave him to drink. (49) *Ceteri uero dicebant sine uideamus an ueniat Elias liberans eum* (there are variant readings to the verse)'. Here the Irish tradition has an interpolation from John 19:34, found in St Gall 51 as follows:

> *Alius autem* (written in full, not with the Irish symbol as is usual in St Gall 51) *accepta lancea pupungit latus eius et exit aqua et sanguis* ('Another, however, having taken a lance pierced his side and water and blood came out').

This interpolation in Matthew is also found in the following Latin Gospel texts, almost all of which are Irish: the texts listed in the paragraph above; in addition to these (among the texts thus far examined) we have Usserianus Secundus (Irish; *CLA* 271); the Book of Mulling (Irish, dated to the eighth century; *CLA* 276); BL Additional 40618 (Ireland, dated to the ninth century; *CLA* 179); British Library Harley 1023 (Irish, dated to the tenth century), British Library Royal 1 E VI plus Canterbury, Cathedral Library Additional 16 (dated to the end of the eighth century; Kent; *CLA* 214). Thus, in Latin Gospel texts, this interpolation is transmitted almost exclusively in Irish manuscripts. The interpolated passage is a variant of the Vetus Latina text of John

19:34, with the inversion *aqua et sanguis* for *sanguis et aqua* as in the African text of the Vetus Latina.

The interpolation itself, however, is a very old one in Gospel texts. It is found in some earlier Greek Gospel books, such as Codex Sinaiticus (London, British Library, Add. 43725), Codex Vaticanus (Vat. graec. 1209), Codex Ephraim rescriptus (Paris, Bibliothèque Nationale, grec 9); Greek minuscule 1010 (dated to the twelfth century), in manuscripts of the Syro-Palestinian translation, in some of the Ethiopic translations, and in John Chrysostom (according to Severus, AD 538). The Greek interpolated text reads:

> '[auton]. *allos de labwn logchn enuxen autou thn pleuran kai exhlqen udwr kai aima*' (see John 19:34), 'another taking a lance pricked/stabbed his side and water and blood came out' (as against John 19:34: 'One of the soldiers pricked/stabbed [Jesus'] side with his lance and immediately there came out blood and water').

We have an extremely significant interpolation in St Gall 51 (chiefly from Matthew 27:51 or Mark 15:38) at John 19:30, again at the account of the death of Christ, added after the words 'He handed over the spirit':

> 19:30 (tradidit spiritum*). 'Cum ergo expirasset uelum templi scisum est a summo usque deorsum. (Iudei ergo...)'* ('When, then, he had breathed his last, the veil of the Temple was rent from the top right down to the bottom').

This addition is known otherwise in Latin only in Irish Gospel texts: in the Vulgate texts Armagh, Mac Regol, BL Egerton 609, BL Harley 1023, Harley 1802 (Gospels of Mael Brigte, AD 1138), Cadmug Gospels (Fulda); in the Vetus Latina only in Usserianus Primus, Irish. It is also found in some late (twelfth- and fourteenth-century) Greek minuscule texts, although it occurs as well in earlier Syriac and Syro-Palestinian translations (see the apparatus to John 19:30 in Merk 1948 and Tischendorf 1872).

With regard to these interpolated passages in the crucifixion scenes in the Gospels of Matthew and John, we may legitimately ask whether they have been preserved by textual transmission alone, or whether their presence is due to the prominence of the crucifixion scene in Irish devotion.

The textual evidence for John's Gospel in particular indicates that the St Gall codex 51 was written in Ireland or copied from an Irish exemplar, most probably the former. The significance of the St Gall manuscript for a knowledge of the Bible text in Ireland, and among Irish on the Continent, can only be assessed after a fuller examination of the whole evidence.

In this paper we will concentrate on the Crucifixion scene on page 266 of the St Gall Codex (Plate XIV), with reference to the other miniature facing it on page 267 (Plate XV). The biblical text, with the ending in Carolingian minuscule, we may recall ends on page 265.

Crucifixion scene: Longinus and Stephaton in Christian art and in Irish art

All we need examine here on the Crucifixion scene in Christian art are those exemplars which have a bearing on the understanding of the miniature in Codex Sangallensis 51. Of these the principal earlier depictions are that in the Rabbula Gospels, in a fresco of Santa Maria Antiqua, and in a miniature in a ninth-century Gospel manuscript in the Bibliothèque Nationale, Paris.

In the Rabbula Gospels (now in the Biblioteca Laurentiana, Florence), created in 586 in the monastery of Zaqpa in Mesopotamia by the Greek monk Rabbula, we have the well-known depiction of the Crucifixion (Fig. 17.2), with Christ clad in the *colobium* (a sleeveless garment signifying dignity, reaching to the knees or ankles, in this case to the ankles). At his right is depicted the lance-bearer (identified by the name *Loginos*) piercing his side, and on his left the (unnamed) sponge-bearer. There is a similar depiction of the Crucifixion in a fresco in the Chapel of Theodotus, in the church Santa Maria Antiqua in Rome (Fig. 17.3). It is from the time of Pope Zacharias (741–52), and is under Greek and eastern influence (de Grüneisen 1911; Romanelli and Nordhagen 1964, VII). Again, the lance-bearer (identified by the name Longinus) is on Jesus' right and the unnamed sponge-bearer on the left. The wound in Christ's right side is visible, with two streams pouring from it, the stronger one towards Longinus's face, but not reaching it (depicted in the reproduction in de Grüneisen 1911).

Another early related example occurs in the Gospel book in Paris, Bibliothèque Nationale, lat. 257 (Plate XVI) (already noted by Gougaud 1920, 135; it is Qd of Fischer's sigla, where Q designates Franco-Saxon manuscripts, with their chief centre as Saint Amand). This Gospel book, written in part in golden letters, is a ninth-century manuscript illuminated in the style of the Franco-Saxon school (Lauer 1939, 94–5). It has a full-page miniature of the Crucifixion (Louandre 1858b, pl. 14), with Longinus at Christ's right and Stephaton on his left. Longinus is depicted piercing Christ's right side. Four streams (of blood?) pour from the wound, the lowermost striking Longinus's knee, the uppermost his face at eye-level. There is a description of the miniature in Louandre (1858a, 36–8), with special interest in the clothing. The dress worn by Longinus (called the 'executioner' by Louandre) and the sponge-bearer recalls Gaulish dress; their long-sleeved tunic is an imitation of the

Fig. 17.2 *Crucifixion from the Rabbula Gospels. (Photograph: Florence, Biblioteca Medicea Laurenziana, MS Plut. 1. 56, fol. 13r. By permission of the Ministerio per i Bene le Attivita Culturali)*

ancient *sagum*, and the clothes covering their thighs and legs resemble the Gaulish breeches. It can be noticed that Longinus wears a kind of trousers buttoned at the legs. In Louandre's opinion, there are good grounds for believing that these items of clothing are the exact reproduction of some civil dress of the ninth century. From our point of view what is noteworthy is the blood issuing from Christ's

wound on to Longinus, one of the streams reaching his eyes, although there seems to be no indication of any healing. Both Longinus's eyes are open, and seem healthy. Unlike the St Gall miniature, and other Irish Crucifixion scenes, Longinus is on Jesus's right. The Crucifixion scene in Irish iconography has been extensively studied and written on by Gougaud and others (Gougaud 1920 (extensive, almost exhaustive,

Fig. 17.3 Crucifixion scene with Longinus and Stephaton, from the church of Santa Maria Antiqua, Rome

treatment); Henry 1965, 1970; Henderson 1987, 80–8 ('The Iconography of the Last Judgment-Crucifixion'); Ó Floinn 1987; O'Reilly 1987–8; Harbison 1992, vol. 1, 273–86).

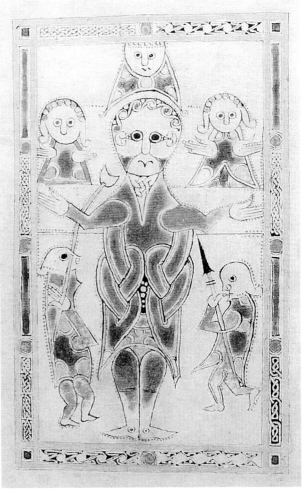

Fig. 17.4 Crucifixion scene from the Southampton Psalter (Cambridge, St John's College, MS C9 (59)). (Photograph: by permission of St John's College, Cambridge)

The Crucifixion scene in Codex St Gall 51 and its context

The illumination of the manuscript consists of Evangelist portraits with initial pages opposite, St Matthew (page 2), 'Lib' (page 3); St Mark (page 78), 'Ini' (page 79); St Luke (page 128), 'Q' (page 129); St John (page 208), 'In' (page 209) (Alexander 1978, no. 44, 66–7). In addition, a carpet page (page 6) precedes the genealogy of Christ with the initials 'Xpi' (page 7). At the end, after St John's Gospel (which ends on page 265) there are two miniatures – one of the Crucifixion (page 266), faced by another (page 267) which Alexander calls the Lord's Advent (1978, 66–7).

Alexander (1978, 67) describes the Crucifixion miniature as follows (with references to other manuscripts studied by him in the same volume):

> In the Crucifixion miniature (p. 266) the Christ is shown swathed in the colubium as in Eastern iconography (*cf.* the Durham Gospel Book, no. 10). Stephaton is on the left holding up the sponge and

Longinus with the spear is on the right with the blood from Christ's side spurting into his eye. A pair of frontal half-length angels holding books are on either side above the arms of the cross. The composition is very close to that of the Durham Gospel Book. A Crucifixion miniature was planned for the Book of Kells (no. 52). The scene is also shown on the Southampton Psalter (no. 74).

In Alexander's opinion the manuscript St Gall 51, which he dates to the second half of the eighth century, was probably made in Ireland and brought to St Gall at a later date, no doubt in the ninth century (1978, 67); it was less likely to have been made by an Irishman on the Continent and was the most important of the later Gospel books generally accepted as Irish. The Southampton Psalter (Cambridge, St John's College MS C. 9 (59)) was written in Ireland, probably in the early eleventh century. It has the Crucifixion miniature on fol. 38v, before Psalm 51, at the beginning of the 'second fifty'. In the Southampton Psalter (Fig. 17.4), Longinus is on the right (on Christ's left), as in St Gall 51. No blood is issuing from Christ's side.

The Durham Gospel Book (Durham, Cathedral Library, MS A.II.17, fols 2–102 and Cambridge, Magdalene College Pepysian MS 2981), of Northumbrian provenance (possibly Lindisfarne), is from the late seventh or early eighth century. Alexander thus describes the Crucifixion miniature as follows (1978, 40–1):

> The end of St. Matthew is framed (f. 38$_3$) by a broad panel with projecting squares at the centre of each side in a cross shape. . . The frame is filled with dotted interlace. On the verso, preceding the chapters to St. Mark, is a full-page miniature of the Crucifixion (f. 38$_3$^{v}). The Christ is bearded and swathed in a long robe (*colobium*). To left and right below the cross are Longinus and Stephaton, the former piercing Christ's side with the lance, the latter holding the sponge to His lips. Above the Cross on either side are six-winged Seraphim.

This miniature differs from St Gall 51, the Southampton Psalter and other Irish representations of the Crucifixion in the positioning of Longinus and Stephaton. The Durham miniature has inscriptions linking the Crucifixion scene with New Testament texts and with Christian life (Henderson 1987, 81–8).

Stephaton and Longinus stand on either side of Christ on the cross on almost all the Irish representations of the Crucifixion. This is also the case in the vast majority of non-Irish Crucifixion scenes of the first millennium. As Harbison notes (Harbison 1992, vol. 1, 277), in most of the examples outside of Ireland, Stephaton with the vinegar is on the right (facing the viewer; on Christ's left), where he is found in the Irish examples on the crosses at Moone, Castledermot South, Ullard and Arboe. The only non-Irish examples which place Stephaton on the left are found in England and Russia – in Russia in a silver plate found in the Perm Government, now in the Hermitage Museum, Saint Petersburg. In the St Gall Gospels (as in the Southampton Psalter) Stephaton's pole has a crescent-shaped vessel on top, which, Harbison says, finds its closest parallel in the Perm plate (Harbison 1992, vol. 1, 277). We may note, of course, that in one branch of Irish literary tradition Longinus pierced Christ's right side, and that Christ's arm-pit (not his heart) was pierced (thus, for instance, the Old Irish Tract on the Mass in the Stowe Missal, a text noted further below).

With regard to the Crucifixion miniature in St Gall 51 we should note in particular the liquid (blood; blood and wine; blood and water?) coming from Christ's pierced side to Longinus's right eye. Longinus's right eye is clearly depicted as open and healthy, while the left is a slit rather than with an eyeball. Longinus is represented as holding the lance

firmly with both hands. In this the difference with the Southampton Psalter is noticeable.

In the overall plan of this St Gall codex the Crucifixion miniature (on the left, on page 266) was intended to be viewed in conjunction with the other miniature of the Last Judgement facing it on page 267. Alexander (1978, 67) describes this miniature as follows:

> In the miniature on the opposite recto [to the Crucifixion picture] (page 267) the half-length Christ, above in the centre, blesses with His right hand and holds a cross and a book. On either side is a full-length angel blowing a trumpet. Below twelve half-length figures with haloes and books and looking up represent the twelve Apostles. The matching narrow frames filled with interlace and key pattern emphasize the connection between the two pictures. This is an early stage in the evolution of the iconography of the Last Judgement (*cf.* the Turin Gospel Book [Alexander 1987], no. 61). Christ suffering as Man is contrasted with His triumphant return as Lord and Judge.

Longinus and 'Longinus the Blind' in later Irish tradition

The earliest evidence we have on Longinus as a blind person and on his healing comes from the St Gall miniature and the Poem of Blathmac, the two texts generally regarded as of eighth-century origin. Irish evidence on Longinus became more plentiful in later centuries, although the date of origin of the material in these later texts remains to be determined.

In the Old Irish tract on the Mass in the Stowe Missal, added in the early ninth century, with reference to the symbolism of the particle which the priest breaks off from the wafer during the Mass, we read:

> The particle that is cut off from the bottom of the half which is on the (priest's) left hand is the figure of the wounding with the lance (*lágin*) in the armpit of the right side; for westwards was Christ's face on the Cross, to wit, *contra ciuitatem*, and eastwards was the face of Longinus; what to him was the left to Christ was the right. (Stokes and Strachan 1903, 254)

The Irish *Passion of Longinus*, found in the *Leabhar Breac* and other manuscripts, probably dates from the second half or end of the eleventh century (Atkinson 1887, 60–4; 300–4; Vendryes 1911, 351; Latin text *Acta Sanctorum* 1865, 377, 379–80). In general the Irish text of the *Passion of Longinus* seems to follow the Latin of the *Passio Longini* (McNamara 1975, 81, no. 69), apart from the very beginning. In some earlier manuscripts of the Latin *Passio*, the text begins:

In the days of Our Lord Jesus Christ, there was a certain soldier, a Centurion (*miles Centurio*), by name Longinus, who at that time was standing by the cross; at the command of Pontius Pilate he struck the side of the Lord with a lance, and seeing the signs which occurred (*signa quae fiebant*) – the sun darkened, and the earth quaking – he believed in the Lord Jesus Christ, and striking his breast said in a loud voice: 'This is truly the Son of God'. And afterwards, withdrawing from the army he was instructed in the precepts of the Lord. (*Acta Sanctorum* 1865, 377; other Latin texts, omitting the word *centurio*, *Acta Sanctorum* 1865, 379).

The beginning of the Irish text translates as follows:

When Christ was being crucified by the Jews, one of the soldiers who was at his crucifixion, called Cennturus, and also Longinus, came and brought a long spear (*laigin*) in his hand, with which he wounded Christ in his side and split his heart in twain (*co ro-ghon Crist i n-a shliss di, ₇ scoiltis a cride ar dó*), so that blood and wine (*fuil ₇ fín*) came out (Atkinson 1887, 60, 300; note: 'blood and wine', as in Blathmac's poem - not 'blood and water').

In a manner more faithful to the Latin, the Irish text goes on the speak of the great darkness that followed: the sun darkened, the rocks rent, the graves opened. Then we read:

When, therefore, Longinus saw that great miracle [*mírbuil*; translating Latin *signa?*; or referring to the blood and wine from Christ's wounded side?) he forthwith believed in the one God, Jesus Christ, and quitted his worldly military services.

Longinus is mentioned by name in the apocryphal *Gospel of Nicodemus* (*Acts of Pilate*) 16,7, as the soldier who pierced Christ's side with a lance. We have an Irish translation (or perhaps Irish translations) of the *Gospel of Nicodemus*, made probably in the twelfth century (Hughes 1991, where it is dated to the twelfth century, following Dottin 1913, xviii). The Irish translation makes no mention of Longinus in the rendering of 16:7. Earlier, however, at the account of the death of Christ in chapter 10 (where there is no mention of Longinus in the *Gospel of Nicodemus [Acta Pilati])* the Irish text reads (Hughes 1991, 16, 17):

Then Jesus said on the cross: 'I am thirsty'. The soldiers [lit. horsemen] filled a vessel with vinegar and gall and gave it to Jesus to drink. Then a certain soldier called Longinus *i.e.* blind one (*loinginus .i. dall*) came forward and thrust his lance (*buile da gaí*) into the side (*i slis*) of Jesus. There rushed out at once two streams from his side – a stream of blood and a stream of water – and they rushed along the shaft to his hand so that when he put his hand on his forehead, there appeared two eyes and he believed in Jesus thereafter.

There is also a more popular account on Longinus in *Leabhar Breac* page 159b, lines 30 to end (as yet unpublished and undated). It comes at the end of a piece on the Holy Places and is headed '*Longinus … ₇ egitianus*'. It ends saying that *Egitianus … uel cefaton* (= Stephaton) was the second man at the Cross. In the poem '*Caoin tú féin, a dhuine bhoicht*' ('Mourn for yourself, O unfortunate man') (O'Rahilly1977, no. 65, 222 who dates it to the seventeenth century at the earliest), the reader is asked to lament for Christ, his two hands and his two feet, '*s an croidhe do sgoilt an Dall,* 'and the heart that the blind one split'. *An Dall,* 'the blind one', in later Irish has become a name given to Longinus.

The healing of the blind Longinus by blood from Christ's side in Blathmac's poem to Mary (eighth-century)

The poems of Blathmac, edited by J. Carney (1964), are presented in the manuscript as follows: 'It is Blathmac son of Cú Brettan son of Congus of the Fir Rois has made this devoted offering to Mary and her Son'. The Fir Roiss are of the Airgialla; they were located in Co. Monaghan and extended into Co. Louth (*ibid.* xiv, n. 18). Carney (1964, xiv) notes that fortunately Blathmac is genealogically identifiable. Blathmac's father, Cú Brettan son of Congus of the Fir Roiss, is represented in the saga of the Battle of Allen (718) as the only prominent adherent of the high-king, Fergal, son of Mael Dúin, to escape alive, and he is shown as composing some quatrains on the battle. Cú Brettan's death is recorded in the *Annals of Ulster* at 739 (= 740): *Cú bretan mac Congusso mortuus est.* His name is found in the genealogy of the Uí Ségáin (BB [*Book of Ballymote*] 114 fol. 12): '*Ainbith m. Canannan m. Tigernaich m. Donngaili m. Duin[n] Bo m. Con Bretan m. Congasa m. Murgiusa…*' Donn Bó, son of Cú Brettan, mentioned in this pedigree, was a brother of Blathmac. According to the Four Masters, Congal, lord of Airthera, was slain in 743 by Donn Bo, son of Cú Brettan; and it is doubtless the same Donn Bó who was slain in the battle of Emain Macha (*Annals of Ulster* 758 = 759). With his father's death about 740 and his brother's about 759 the period of Blathmac is well established. We may take it that the period of his maturity, and consequently of the composition of these poems, fell at latest somewhere in the years 750–70.

Blathmac describes his poem as a keening, a keening of Christ in union with Mary his mother (quatrain 1). He speaks of the conception of Christ, of his public life, his Passion and Crucifixion, of the events at Calvary, in which context he describes the piercing of Christ's side as follows:

(q. 55) 'When they thought that Jesus could be approached, Longinus then came to wound him with the spear (*dïa guin cosind láigin*)'.

(q. 56) 'The king's son of the seven holy heavens, when his heart was pierced (*o fu-rócbath a chride*) wine was spilled upon the pathways (*do-rórtad fín fu roenu*; i.e. the declivities of his body?), the blood of Christ (flowing) through his gleaming sides'.

(q. 57) 'The flowing blood from the side of the dear Lord baptized the head of Adam, for the shaft of the cross of Christ had aimed at his mouth'.

(58) 'By the same blood - it was a fair occasion! - he instantly cured the fully blind man (*is trait ron-ícc in n-ógdall*) as he openly with his two hands was plying the lance (*ossé díb dornnaib co glé/ oc imbeirt inna láigne*)'.

(After Carney 1964, as changed by Dooley 1997)

As already noted, as in this poem, so also in the *Leabhar Breac* text of the *Passion of Longinus* (Atkinson 1887, 60, 300) we are told that 'blood and wine came out', flowed from Christ's wounded side.

Did the topos of Longinus the Blind One originate in Irish tradition?

A question arises as to the origins of the topos of the miraculous healing of Longinus. Did it originate in Ireland, or could it have come to Ireland from the east (Greek Church, Syria) through Rome or even Spain? The miracle is richly attested in European medieval translations of the Gospel of Nicodemus from the twelfth century onwards (Beggiato 1996, 6–7). The legend seems to have been popular in Wales and Brittany. *L'aveugle Longin* is mentioned in a French *Chanson de geste* (1210; Peebles 1911).

In an examination of the origins of the tradition (Longinus, the blind centurion healed by blood and wine/water from Jesus side) it will be as well to consider the individual elements involved.

The earliest iconographic evidence we have for the healing of Longinus of physical blindness seems to be the portrait of Codex St Gall 51 (probably of the eighth century), which has been the subject of this study. While it is not certain, it seems likely that quatrain 58 of the Poem of Blathmac also speaks of healing from physical, not mere spiritual, blindness. If so, this is the earliest attested literary evidence of this tradition, recorded in the mid-eighth century if one follows the generally accepted date for Blathmac's poem.

With regard to the liquid (blood, blood and water, or blood and wine) coming from Christ's wounded side towards or onto Longinus, this is present in the well-known fresco of Santa Maria Antiqua, Rome (741–52) and in the Gospel Book in Paris, Bibliothèque Nationale, lat. 257 (ninth century). The same theme, apparently, is to be found on the shaft of the

Fig. 17.5 Detail from shaft of the South Cross, Clonmacnoise. (Photograph: Peter Harbison)

west face of the South Cross at Clonmacnoise (Fig. 17.5) (Harbison 1992, vol. 2, fig. 156; vol. 3, fig. 899). Here, according to Harbison, we have the figure of Christ in comparatively low false relief placed against the background of a cross. Beneath Christ's right arm is Stephaton, who holds up on a pole a sponge or vessel containing the hyssop. Facing him on the other side of Christ in the lower right-hand corner of the panel is the figure of Longinus. In his left hand he holds the spear with which he pierces Christ's left side. The piercing of the left, rather than the right, side is in keeping with most of the Irish high crosses. What is unusual in this Clonmacnoise cross, however, is the representation of two streams of blood which spout out from Christ's left side onto the face of Longinus, who according to tradition, was thereby healed of his blindness (thus Harbison 1992, vol. 1, 56; see also Harbison 1988, 179–80). The South Cross dates probably from the mid-ninth century, possibly erected for the king Maelsechnaill who reigned 846–62.

The question arises as to the possibility of foreign influence on the Irish texts witnessing to the healing of Longinus from his blindness. Commenting on the blood from Christ's wound pouring on to the face of Longinus in the South Cross, Clonmacnoise, illustrating the apocryphal tradition in the Blathmac Poems, Harbison notes that since this is found not only in the St Gall 51 Crucifixion but also on a mid-eighth century fresco from Santa Maria Antiqua in Rome (with reference to Schiller 1972, fig. 328), and possibly on a tenth-century ivory from the collections of the Provinzial Museum (now Rheinisches Landesmuseum), Bonn, it is probably not an Irish feature, but one borrowed from Rome (Harbison 1992, vol. 1, 281–82). Harbison favours a ninth-century date for St Gallen 51 (Harbison 1988, 180; Harbison 1984b, 15). He notes that the Irish poet Blathmac, who according to him, probably lived in the ninth century, gives us in a long poem what sounds suspiciously like the description of an extensive Carolingian fresco cycle – not necessarily in Ireland, where churches of the time were perhaps too small to accommodate fresco cycles, but more likely in Rome – or perhaps in France (Harbison 1984a, 469, and note 181). Harbison instances the mention in Blathmac's poem of such fresco themes as the stoning of Stephen, Cyprian and Cornelius, the seven sons of Machabeus and Quiricus. On this one may remark that while the idea of Blathmac's dependence on a European original is attractive, it is difficult to accept the ninth-century date Harbison wishes to assign to both the St Gall manuscript and to Blathmac's poem. We have seen above that the basis for so dating St Gall 51 (namely the ending of the text of John's Gospel) has little to commend it, and, I may add, both the language of the poem and the genealogy of Blathmac argue in favour of an eighth-century date for this composition.

Beggiato opts for an Irish origin for the topos of the belief in the healing of Longinus. He notes Irish creativity in such matters (Beggiato 1996, 7–8). Ann Dooley also believes in an Irish origin: the Blathmac passage is but an indication of the artful weaving of different strands which Blathmac has brought together in his poem. She notes that in the poem the soldier who pierced the side of Christ with a lance, fused with the Roman centurion who testified to Christ's divinity after Christ's death, is named Longinus and described as having been cured of his blindness (1997, 366). She further writes (1997, 368):

> The quatrains quoted above (qq. 20–21) combine, in his [Blathmac's] mature yet impassioned expositional style, the apocryphal theme of Longinus with that of Adam's baptism at Calvary. They create an emotive link with the multi-faceted image of the wounded Christ in majesty, who resumes in himself the whole of time and the cosmos and who, by his

Passion, initiates the sacramental acts of the present age of salvation history. A link with the E[vangelium]N[icodemi] as a source is unlikely because the set of exegetical and meditative relations active here is much more complex than is suggested by the unremarkable centurion material in the EN.

She poses the question whether Blathmac's understanding of the story of Longinus might not be governed by an iconographic model: in numerous Irish depictions of the Crucifixion, as in the poem, the lance-bearer grasps the spear firmly with both hands.

While the earliest witnesses known for this topos are Irish, and probably both contemporary and of the eighth century, the question of the roots of the belief remain to be determined. One possibility is that the original lies in John 19:37: '*uidebunt in quem transfixerunt*' ('they shall look on him whom they have pierced'), or in the variant in the Book of Armagh '*quem transfixerunt uidebunt*' ('they shall see the one they have pierced'). However, the belief may have originated in a tradition that Longinus (the centurion) was cured from spiritual blindness, coming from paganism to belief in Christ. Such an origin would be in keeping with the *Passion of Longinus*, found in Irish translation in the *Leabhar Breac* (page 181b, 46–64; Irish translation, eleventh century?; Atkinson 1998, 60; 300), already noted, which says that when Longinus saw the miracles that followed Christ's death and the piercing of his side he believed in the one God, Jesus Christ. Such an origin is favoured by L. Gougaud (1920, 134–35).

Possibly this and other sources besides stand behind the origins of the cure of Longinus. One worth mentioning is a homily once attributed to John Chrysostom (*c.* 347–407), now recognised as the work of Severian of Gabala (*c.* 400; see Voicu 1983–84) on 'Zeal and the man born blind' (*Patrologia Graeca* 59, 543–54). The author passes from consideration of the man born blind to the good thief, who came to believe in Christ on the cross. He needed baptism for salvation, and was baptized by the blood and water from Christ's wounded side. Commenting on John 19:54 ('blood and water came out') the homilist says: 'The blood and water did not come out in the sense that they just flowed; they came with such force that they sprayed the body of the thief' (*Patrologia Graeca* 59, 553–54). It would be easy to transfer a belief such as this from the good thief to the centurion, and the healing from spiritual to healing from physical blindness.

The traditions behind the Blind Longinus tradition may have been many and complex. Future research may help clarify them. From some such literary and iconographic evidence early Irish tradition could have reached its own position with regard to Longinus. In any event the earliest attest-ation we have, whether literary or iconographic, of the healing of Longinus from his physical blindness comes from early Ireland, represented by what appear to be two eighth-century witnesses.

Notes

1   I intend to publish this new collation of John in the near future.

References

Acta Sanctorum 1865, *Acta Sanctorum* (Bollandists), March vol. 2, G. Henschenius and D. Papebrochius (eds). Paris, Rome.

ALEXANDER, J. J. G. 1978, *Insular Manuscripts 6th to the 9th Century. A Survey of the Manuscripts Illuminated in the British Isles*, Vol. 1. London.

ATKINSON, R. 1887, *The Passions and the Homilies from the Leabhar Breac*. Dublin.

BEGGIATO, F. 1996, 'Origine e diffusione del topos leggendario-narrativo del "Perdono di Longino" nelle letterature romanze'. Paper read at the III Colloquio internazionale medievo romanzo e orientale: "Il viaggio dei testi". Venice.

BERGER, S. 1893, *Histoire de la Vulgate* (reprinted 1961, New York). Paris.

BOURKE, C. 1993, 'Chronology of Irish crucifixion plaques', in R. M. Spearman and J. Higgitt (eds), *The Age of Migrating Ideas. Early Medieval Art in Northern Britain and Ireland*, 175–81. Edinburgh, Stroud.

CARNEY, J. (ed.) 1964, *The Poems of Blathmac Son of Cú Brettan* (= Irish Texts Society 47). Dublin.

CECCHELLI, C. 1959, 'The iconography of the Laurentian Syriac Gospels', in Cecchelli, Furlani and Salmi, 23–82.

CECCHELLI, C., FURLANI, G. and SALMI, M. (eds) 1959, *The Rabbula Gospels*. Facsimile Edition of the Miniatures of the Syriac Manuscript Plut. I, 56 in the Medicaean-Laurentian Library. Olten, Lausanne.

CHROUST, A. 1905, *Monumenta Palaeographica. Denkmäler der Schreibkunst des Mittelalters*. I. Abt. Schrifttafeln in lateinischer und deutscher Sprache. I. Serie, III. Bd., Lief. 19. (= Ser. 1, Vol. 3, fasc. 19). Munich.

CLA see LOWE, E.A.

DE WAAL, A. 1887, 'Die apokryphen Evangelien in der altchristlichen Kunst', *Römische Quartalschrift* 1,173ff.

DOOLEY, A. 1997, 'The Gospel of Nicodemus in Ireland', in I. Zbigniew (ed.), *The Medieval Gospel of Nicodemus. Texts, Intertexts, and Contexts* (= Medieval and Renaissance Texts and Studies 158), 361–401. Tempe, Arizona.

DOTTIN, G. 1913, *Manuel d'Irlandais Moyen*. Paris.

DUFT, J. and MEYER, P. 1954, *The Irish Miniatures in the Abbey Library of St Gall*. Olten, Berne, Lausanne.

FISCHER, B. 1988–1991, *Die lateinischen Evangelien bis zum 10. Jahrhundert* (Aus der Geschichte der lateinischen Bibel). 1988, I. Varianten zu Matthäus; 1989, II. Varianten zu Markus; 1990, III. Varianten zu Lukas; 1991, IV. Varianten zu Johannes. Freiburg.

GOUGAUD, L. 1920, 'The earliest Irish representations of the Crucifixion', *J. Roy. Soc. Antiq. Ir.* 50, 128–39.

GREGORY, C. R. 1900, *Textkritik des Neuen Testament*, Vol. 1. Leipzig.

GRILLMEIER, A. 1956, *Der Logos am Kreuz*. Munich.

GRILLMEIER, B. and HESBERT, R. J. 1940, *Le Problème de la Transfixion du Christ dans les Traditions bibliques, patristiques, iconographique, liturgique et musicale*. Paris, Tournai.

GRONDIJS, L. H. 1960, *Autour de l'Iconographie Byzantine du Crucifié sur la Croix* (= *Bibl. Byzant. Bruxellensis* 1) Utrecht, 1950; (in BAV/URBS: [1960]). Leiden.

GRÜNEISEN, W. de 1911, *Sainte-Marie Antique*. Rome.

GUREVICH, W. 1957, 'Observations on the iconography of the wound on Christ's side with special reference to its position', *J. Warburg and Courtauld Institutes* 20, 358–62.

GWYNN, J. (ed.) 1913, *Liber Ardmachanus*. The Book of Armagh edited with Introduction and Appendixes. Dublin, London.

HARBISON, P. 1984a, 'Earlier Carolingian narrative iconography - ivories, manuscripts, frescoes and Irish high crosses', *Jahrbuch des römisch-germanischen Zentralmuseums* 31, 455–71.

HARBISON, P. 1984b, 'The bronze crucifixion plaque said to be from St John's (Rinnagan), near Athlone', *J. Ir. Archaeol.* 2, 1–17.

HARBISON, P. 1987, 'The date of the crucifixion slabs from Duvillaun More and Inishkea North, Co. Mayo', in Rynne (ed.), 73–91.

HARBISON, P. 1988, 'The shield of Longinus', in *Bathron. Beiträge zur Architektur und verwandten Künsten* (Festschrift Heinrich Drerup), Saarbrücker Studien zur Archäologie und Alten Geschichte 3, 179–83. Saarbrücken.

HARBISON, P. 1992, *The High Crosses of Ireland. An Iconographical and Photographic Survey*, 3 vols (= Römisch-Germanisches Zentralmuseum, Forschungsinstitut für Vor- und Frühgeschichte Monographien 17, 1–3). Bonn.

HARBISON, P. 1994, *Irish High Crosses with the Figure Sculptures Explained*. Drogheda.

HARBISON, P. 1999, *The Golden Age of Irish Art. The Medieval Achievement 600–1200*. London.

HENDERSON, G. 1987, *From Durrow to Kells. The Insular Gospel-Books 650–800*. London.

HENRY, F. 1965, *Irish Art in the Early Christian Period to A.D. 800*. London.

HENRY, F. 1967, *Irish Art during the Viking Invasions, 800–1020 A.D.* London.

HENRY, F. 1970, *Irish Art in the Romanesque Period, 1020–1170 A.D.* London.

HESBERT, R.-J. 1940, *Le Problème de la Transfixion du Christ: dans les Traditions bibliques, patristique, iconographique, liturgique et musicale*. Paris.

HUGHES, I. (ed.) 1991, *Stair Nicoméid. The Irish Gospel of Nicodemus* (= Irish Texts Society 55). London.

KENNEY, J. F. 1929, *The Sources for the Early History of Ireland*, vol. 1. *Ecclesiastical*. New York (later reprints: Dublin).

KOEHLER, W. 1972, *Buchmalerei des frühen Mittelalters: Fragmente und Entwürfe aus dem Nachlass* (E. Kitzinger and F. Mütherich, eds), Munich.

LAUER, P. 1939, *Bibliothéque Nationale. Catalogue général des Manuscrits latins.* Tome 1er (Nos 1–1438). Paris.

LECLERCQ, H. 1931, 'Marie Antique (Sainte)', *Dictionnaire d'Archéologie Chrétienne et de Liturgie* 10, col. 2078.

LINDSAY, W. M. 1913, 'Irish cursive script', *Zeitschrift für celtische Philologie* 9, 301–8.

LINDSAY, W. M. 1915, *Notae Latinae. An Account of Abbreviations in Latin MSS. of the Early Minuscule Period (c. 750–850).* Cambridge.

LÖFFLER, K. 1929, 'Die Sankt Galler Schreibschule in der 2. Hälfte des 8. Jahrhunderts', in W. M. Lindsay (ed.), *Palaeographia Latina,* part 6 (= St Andrews University Publications 28), 5–68. Oxford.

LOUANDRE, C. 1857–58, *Les Arts somptuaires; Histoire du Costume et de l'Ameublement et des Arts et Industries qui s'y rattachent. Introduction générale et Texte exlicitatif.* Paris.

LOUANDRE, C. 1857, Vol. 1. *Introduction générale.* Paris.

LOUANDRE, C. 1858a, Vol. 2. *Texte explicatif.* Paris.

LOUANDRE, C. 1858b, *Planches du Ve au XIVe siècle:* vol. 1. Paris.

LOUANDRE, C. 1858c, *Planches du XV= au XVIIe siècle:* vol. 2. Paris.

LOWE, E.A. 1934–71, *Codices Latini Antiquiores,* vols I–XI, Supplement. Oxford.

MCGURK, P. 1961, *Latin Gospel Books from A.D. 400 to A.D. 800* (= Publications de Scriptorium 5). Paris, Brussels, Antwerp, Amsterdam.

MCNAMARA, M. 1975, *The Apocrypha in the Irish Church.* Dublin

MCNAMARA, M. 1990, *Studies on Texts of Early Irish Latin Gospels (A.D. 600 – 1200)* (= Instrumenta Patristica 20). Steenbrugge, Dordrecht.

MCNAMARA, M. 1995, 'The Celtic and mixed Gospel text: some recent contributions and centennial reflections', *Filologia Mediolatina* 2, 69–108.

MANNING, C. 1998, *Clonmacnoise Co. Offaly* (2nd ed.). Clonmacnoise.

MARTIN, J. R. 1955, 'The dead Christus on the cross in Byzantine art', in *Late Classical and Medieval Studies in Honour of A. M. Friend,* 189–96. Princeton.

MERK, A. 1948, *Novum Testamentum Graece et Latine,* edition 8. Rome.

MICHELI, G.-L. 1936, 'Recherches sur les manuscrits Irlandais decorés de Saint-Gall et de Reichenau', *Revue Archéologique* (6th ser.) 7, 193–207.

NEES, L. 1993, 'The Irish manuscripts at St Gall and their continental affiliations', in J. King (ed.), *Sangallensia in Washington: the Arts and Letters in Medieval and Baroque St Gall viewed from the Late Twentieth Century,* 95–132, 314–24. New York.

OCHSENBEIN, P., SCHMUCKI, C. and VON EUW, A. 1990, *Irische Buchkunst: die irischen Handschriften der Stiftsbibliothek St Gallen und das Faksimile des Book of Kells.* St Gall.

Ó FLOINN, R. 1987, 'Irish Romanesque crucifix figures', in Rynne (ed.), 168–88.

O'RAHILLY, T. (ed.) 1977, *Measgra Dánta. Miscellaneous Irish Poems* II. Cork.

O'REILLY, J. 1987-8, 'Early medieval text and image: the wounded and exalted Christ', *Peritia* 6-7, 72–118.

PEEBLES, R. J. 1911, *The Legend of Longinus in Ecclesiastical Tradition and English Literature and its Connection with the Grail* (= Bryn Mawr Monographs 9). Baltimore.

PORTER, A. K. 1931, *The Crosses and Culture of Ireland.* Newhaven, London, Oxford.

ROMANELLI, P. and NORDHAGEN, P. J. 1964, *S. Maria Antiqua.* Rome.

RYAN, M. (ed.) 1983, *Treasures of Ireland. Irish Art 3000 B.C. – 1500 A.D.* Dublin.

RYNNE, E. (ed.) 1987, *Figures from the Past. Studies on Figurative Art in Christian Ireland in Honour of Helen M. Roe.* Dun Laoghaire.

SAUSER, E. 1966, *Frühchristliche Kunst. Sinnbild und Glaubensaussage.* Innsbruck, Vienna, Munich.

SCHILLER, G. 1968, *Iconographie der christlichen Kunst. 2. Die Passion Jesu Christi.* Gütersloh.

SINTHERN, P. (ed.), 1925, *Roma Sacra. A series of one hundred and fifty-two views in colors.* Vienna, Munich, Biel.

STEFFENS, F. 1929, *Lateinische Paläographie,* 3rd ed. Berlin, Leipzig.

STOKES, W. and STRACHAN, J. (eds) 1903, *Thesaurus Palaeohibernicus,* Vol. 2. Cambridge. (reprint Dublin, 1973).

THOBY, P. 1959, *Le Crucifix des Origines au Concile de Trente. Étude iconographique.* Nantes.

THOBY, P. 1963, *Le Crucifix des Origines au Concile de Trente. Étude Iconographique. Supplément.* Nantes.

TISCHENDORF, C. (ed.) 1872, *Novum Testamentum Graece ad antiquissimos testes denuo recensuit apparatum criticum omni studio perfectum apposuit,* vol. I. Leipzig.

VENDRYES, J. 1911, Review of T. Ó Máille, *Contributions to the History of the Verbs of Existence in Irish,* Dundealgan Press, *Revue Celtique* 32, 350–52.

VEREY, C. D., BROWNE, T. J. and COATSWORTH, E. (eds) 1980, *The Durham Gospels* (= Early English Manuscripts in Facsimiles 20). Copenhagen.

VOICU, S. 1983–84, 'Nuove restituzioni a Severianodi Gabala', *Rivista di studi bizanti e neoellenici,* n.s. 20–21, 3–24.

WORDSWORTH, J. and WHITE, H. J. 1889, *Nouum Testamentum Domini Nostri Iesu Christi Latine. Pars Prior - Quattuor Evangelia, Matthew.* Oxford.

WORDSWORTH, J. and WHITE, H. J. 1895, *Nouum Testamentum Domini Nostri Iesu Christi Latine. Pars Prior - Quattuor Evangelia, John.* Oxford.

ZIMMERMANN, E. H. 1916, *Vorkarolingische Miniaturen,* 5 vols. Berlin.

18   Hidden Order, Order Revealed: New Light on Carpet-Pages

Emmanuelle Pirotte

Robert Stevenson (1981) was the first scholar to take a real interest in the intricate aspect of the carpet-pages.[1] He demonstrated that some carpet-pages from the Book of Durrow (Dublin, Trinity College Library, MS 57, fol. 1, 125v; Alexander 1978, cat. 6, illus. 21) and the Lindisfarne Gospels (London, British Library, Cotton Nero D.IV, fol. 26v, Alexander cat. 9, illus. 35) are built on a complex programme of cruciform designs, many of them hidden in the negative of forms and interlace or in the image's background. Stevenson proposed that these compositions were deliberately made to create visual ambiguities. The author seemed to have the intuition that the efficiency and function of carpet-pages had something to do with their complex appearance and the ambiguous delivering of the cross. I would like to advance the inquiry into these abstract surfaces and see if we can learn something about their functions and uses from their specific visual characteristics.[2]

I do not claim to propose a definitive interpretation of carpet-pages. No author from the Middle Ages has ever given any clue to an acute understanding of these images except Giraldus Cambrensis in the twelfth century (Dimock 1867, 123–24), who gave a vivid depiction of a now lost Irish Gospel Book and wrote about the mysterious 'shrines' – arcana – of Insular ornamentation. But what the reason for and purpose of these 'shrines' was is still problematic and has not been much debated.

This paper may seem quite insubstantial from an archaeological or historical point of view; but an art historian has inevitably to take some risk in interpretation if he or she wants to reach the smallest glimpse of truth about objects – the Gospel Book and its images – that embody so many cultural aspects of a society. A work of art is first of all a visual object and the power of carpet-pages, with their strong abstract and ornamental character, lies, as will be argued, in their very surface.

Psychology of visual perception, and particularly Gestalt Theory,[3] have demonstrated that visual perception is an active cognitive process by which the eyes try to organise the field of vision in the simplest way possible. According to Rudolf Arnheim (1954, 45), 'Any stimulus pattern tends to be seen in such a way that the resulting structure is as simple as the given conditions permit'. The recognition of a figure clearly delimited from a ground is the most important criterion of a good Gestalt which means the clearest possible structure.

Most carpet-pages that have survived do not offer this simple structure and the related clear perception, but the reverse. Folio 128a verso of the Turin fragments (Turin, Bibl. Nazionale cod. O.IV.20; Alexander 1978, cat. 61, illus. 277; Plate XVII) is a good example. The cross is not a figure lying on a bed of interlace but it is that bed of interlace itself, interrupted by four geometric figures, that creates a cruciform design. So the figure of the cross is here a ground, a situation which is not acceptable according to Gestalt Theory. As a matter of fact, analytical perception, according to these laws, sees the ground as something vague, without clear definition, meaningless (Arnheim 1954; Guillaume 1937). In contrast, Insular artists tend to give value to the ground, which becomes thick with meaning, and the cross is of course the most meaningful shape within the image and will therefore tend to be perceived as a figure. Perception will nevertheless not be able to stabilise itself, incapable of conceding a determinate position to the 'figure-ground' cross. So the cross will seem either to project itself towards the observer like a figure or move away from him like a ground.

The same kind of effect is obtained by the Augsburg carpet-page (Harburg über Donauwörth, Schloss Harburg, Fürstlich Öttingen-Wallerstein 'sche Bibliothek, Cod. I. 2. 4°. 2, fol. 126v; Alexander 1978, cat. 24, illus. 119; Plate XVIII). But there, the bed of fret patterns does not continue under the four panels and this enhances the visibility of the cross. Nevertheless, there is a high proportion of interplay between this cross and the four panels. The cross will be seen as coming towards us as the four panels move backwards and vice versa. In the Lindisfarne Gospels, however, fol. 94v is conceived according to the same principle as fol. 128a verso of Turin. The cross is a blue bed of interlace interrupted by four panels and a central circle, which have a clear visual definition, while on page 6 of the St Gall Gospel Book (St Gall, Stiftsbibliothek, Cod. 51; Alexander 1978, cat. 44, illus. 200; Plate XIX) the tension between the cross and the four panels of strange bone-like animal ornament is at a climax. But the situation is different here: the artist has not based the animation of the page on an ambiguous relationship between the figure and ground. Rather, the cross, confined in a very narrow space, seems to compete with the four panels. The powerful organic aspect of the internal spirals of the cross enhances this impression of competing forces. The page is therefore strongly animated and full of tension.

In fol. 85v of the Book of Durrow (Alexander 1978, cat. 6, illus. 20), the small yellow cross in the central medallion is surrounded by two other cruciform figures (an interlaced equal-arm cross and a cross of arcs). These three crosses are distinct motifs generated by one another, but at the same time, together, they form one compact motif in a circle. Analytical perception is forced to see one motif after the other (and the two others as ground-like elements). What we have here is a ternary composition, which could function as a purely formal exploration of the three-in-one, the one-in-three, according to the Christian doctrine of the Trinity. George Henderson (1987, 41) proposed an interesting symbolic interpretation of fol. 192v in Durrow (Alexander 1978, cat. 6, illus. 22). If it is correct that the book has lost a carpet-page, this folio would be the sixth carpet-page of the book. With its unique animal ornament, this image could have been an evocation of the sixth day of Creation, when God made all the animals that creep on the earth.[4]

But it is not often possible to decode such precise symbolic meanings in strictly ornamental compositions; it is not even certain that this meaning was clearly intended. However it is the property of ornament to have a great potential for semantic indetermination, which, inevitably, leads to 'over' determination (Bonne 1996b, 234). I am not thinking of the modern interpretation but of the medieval way of conceiving ornamental images. Ornamental compositions are more suggestive than prescriptive and therein lies their specific and unique power.

Most surviving Insular carpet-pages present an area of conflict, an animated, vibrating surface which could have functioned as a visual support for meditation and contemplation, being an equivalent to the *ruminatio* of sacred texts or *exercitatio mentis* of exegetical practice. According to Jean-Claude Bonne (1996b, 209), these images have not much to do with representation but with practice; in other words, what is important here is less the symbol of the cross itself, more the way it is worked out by ornament, the way it presents itself, the way it appears, disappears, hides completely (as in Durrow fol. 125v) or moves. What the observer is invited to do is to have a contemplative or meditative experience, supported essentially by a visual object that stimulates the desire to find the Christian sign wherever it is hidden, or to stare at the animated surface and follow the wave-motion of the cross. These movements of the eyes produce a kind of hallucination and give the cross an extraordinary and lively presence.

This sort of 'visual incantation' finds homologues in the recitation of charms or of *loricae*, these typical Insular 'breastplate prayers' with apotropaic powers. In the *Faid Fiada* ('The Deer's Cry') to St Patrick (Carey 1998, 130–35), dated to the eighth century, the suppliant asks for the help of Christ to protect him, which is very common, but in this text, he is not far from expressing a radical fusion with the divinity:

> May Christ be with me,
> Christ before me, Christ behind me,
> Christ within me, Christ beneath me,
> Christ above me, Christ to my right,
> Christ to my left, Christ where I lie down,
> Christ where I sit, Christ where I stand,
> Christ in the heart of everyone who thinks of me,
> Christ in the mouth of everyone who speaks to me,
> Christ in every eye who looks on me,
> Christ in every ear which hears me. (Carey 1998, 134)

It is highly probable that these incantations had the power to plunge the mind in an altered state of consciousness. The vision of carpet-pages could lead the medieval observer to a similar state of mind, as will now be explained.

Psychoanalysis of vision studies the modes of unconscious or syncretical perception, while Gestalt Theory is only concerned with laws that govern analytical, superficial, conscious perception. Anton Ehrenzweig (1953; 1967) demonstrated that analytical perception, with its focussing tendency, is always balanced by another kind of vision, which is scanning the entire visual field and not focussing on its specific elements. The primary processes at work in the unconscious mind guide this mode of unconscious perception. Syncretical, global perception is able to resolve conflicts and see harmony and coherence whereas analytical perception is only able

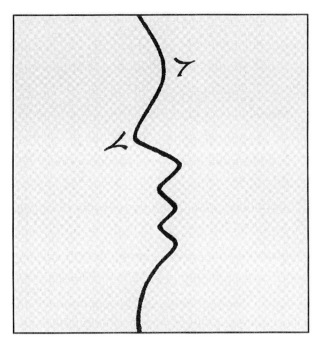

Fig. 18.1 Rubin's double profile.
(Redrawn from Ehrenzweig 1953, fig. 3)

to find conflict and fragmentation of surface. The 'Rubin's Two Profiles' (Ehrenzweig 1967; Fig. 18.1) illustrate perfectly the alternation of conscious and unconscious perception: conscious, analytical perception cannot see the two profiles at the same time, but one profile with the second like a meaningless ground (Ehrenzweig 1967, 56–7). Syncretical, unconscious perception is able to see two human profiles kissing each other.

Modern art, at least since Cubism, tends to challenge the rules of Gestalt and create a fragmented, ambiguous pictorial surface, which is an invitation to this unconscious scanning (Ehrenzweig 1967, 101–14). The words of Paul Klee illustrate this perfectly, 'I don't paint figures but space between figures' (Klee 1961). This sentence could have been expressed by Insular artists, who tackle so systematically the good Gestalt and stimulate alternation between analytical and syncretical modes of vision. When this syncretical perception happens, carpet-pages, full of tension, are seen as integrated wholes. In the Turin, Augsburg and Lindisfarne Gospels, the cross is perceived as a figure and ground at the same time, without any conflict. All the hidden crosses of Durrow fols 1 and 125v, which are impossible to discover by an analytical, focussing vision, will be integrated unconsciously by perception, like subliminal images.

The psychological effects of syncretical perception have been studied in laboratory conditions with people submitted to short time exposures (Varendonck 1923): these effects are described as

impressions of dissolution of time and space, disintegration of the frontiers of self-identity. A feeling of radical fusion with the image can emerge. I think these impressions could have been stimulated by carpet-pages, as they were stimulated by incantation songs or ritual gestures during the liturgy.

To summarise, such analytical perception could provoke ascetic, arduous efforts equivalent to what is commonly understood as meditation, while syncretical perception, that resolves tensions and gives a feeling of harmony, would be the higher state of contemplation, a moment of revelation, a glimpse at the hidden order of the image as well as an apprehension of the hidden order of things in Creation, the harmony and beauty created by God in the Universe, only partially accessible to man. So carpet-pages were potential visual treatises of cosmological character.

It is pertinent to recall here the great interest in cosmology expressed by Irish writers in the Early Middle Ages, in texts as old as the *Amra Columcille* and the beautiful *Altus Prosator* (Clancy and Marcus 1995) up to the *Saltair Na Rann* (Carey 1985). The harmonious correspondences and articulations between different orders in creation (human, angelical, divine, infernal) fascinated Irish scholars. Since Isidore of Seville, the Greek word 'cosmos' is often translated in Latin by *ornatus* ('ornament') and closely associated with the idea of beauty, harmony, and order (Bonne 1996a, 43, 48).[5] John Scotus more particularly expressed the links between cosmos, ornament and beauty.[6] Augustine speaks of the harmony of the universe in terms of measures and weight. Anglo-Saxon writers more than once compared the Creation or Nature to a jewelled ornamented work (Dodwell 1982, 27–9; Ehwald 1919, 146).

Carpet-pages are rigorously constructed. According to the work of Robert Stevick (1994), the inner design of the image is structurally linked to its frame by systems of measures and complicated geometrical designs. This feature clearly testifies to a particular preoccupation with harmony and correspondences. However, this underlying organisation is impossible to understand just by looking at the achieved work; it is veiled or totally hidden. Moreover, the intricacy of the composition, the principles of combination and interlacement of figures and forms is intelligible up to a certain threshold after which, according to Jean-Claude Bonne, 'the objective order that is foreshadowed by the phenomenal structures is looking like a sacred order, in other words, hidden to mankind' (Bonne 1996b, 236). Carpet-pages are constantly animated by that double and paradoxical requirement of an order, worldly and divine, visible and invisible, finite and infinite. I must emphasise here that these images are not mere translations or representations of concepts of theological and cosmological nature. Each carpet-page is a singular cognitive process, it is an exploration, on a purely aesthetic, visual and abstract mode, of articulations and correspondences between the orders of the world.

Carpet-pages are what J. M. Foley called 'immanent art' (Foley 1991) about texts from oral or semi-oral cultures. The principal characteristic of these textual productions is that meaning is not conveyed through words or structure but is created in them. This concept of immanent art forces us to get away from the traditional dichotomy between form and substance, both for verbal and visual productions.

Pauline Head (1997) has recently traced the hermeneutics of Anglo-Saxon poetry, 'a reading of Anglo-Saxon reading'. She demonstrates that the process of reading an Anglo-Saxon poetic text is like solving a riddle. It takes time and the reader actively participates in the text's meaning. 'Language is thick with meaning, and is seen as something substantial, in sound and appearance' (Head 1997, 87). This conception regarding language underlies creation and reception of images. Carpet-pages possess that opacity, where form and substance, signifier and meaning, are absolutely impossible to separate from one another.

This semiotic thought is very far from the one prescribed by the Carolingian doctrine of images, for which visual signifiers have to be transparent, rapidly transferred to the observer to convey the meaning. In Carolingian thought, a picture, without the *titulus* is incomplete (Ganz 1992, 27; Arnulf 1997). Images must be highly legible and not too visual. Carpet-pages on the contrary testify to a totally opposed conception and offer the inverse proportion of legibility and visuality, but one can ask if that strong visuality was really made to be visible.

Carpet-pages and all images contained in prestigious and sometimes relic-like Gospel Books, were maybe not primarily created to be seen. The ritual function of art, as Walter Benjamin (1971–83) has revealed, involves the presence of images which were sometimes more important than their visibility. This statement may seem in total contradiction with the perceptive approach I propose. But it is not. The fact that works of art are made partially to be hidden does not mean that they are crafted with no specific aesthetic purpose. Concealed art is visible to another kind of eye, and in the case of Insular *deluxe* Gospel books, this other eye was the eye of God. The purpose of the object then was to please the Creator, to intercede with him, to ward off Evil. To be able to accomplish all these tasks, the object must fill several aesthetic criteria. These were the ones brought from the artist's cultural background. What was regarded

the most exceptional act of virtuosity and devotion deserved to take place in a sacred book and enhanced that book's efficacy. Eadfrith or Mac Regol knew this, or more precisely, they lived in a society and culture where this anthropological dimension to sacred objects was commonly accepted.

However, we must recognise that we have yet to discover all the various functions of these great Gospel books. No doubt they were many. Some of these books had a liturgical function, and the works of Carol Farr (1997) and Éamonn Ó Carragáin (1994), have shown the symbolic dimension of iconic images in that context. We cannot deny that one and the same book could have had many different functions during its life in a monastic community. So it is impossible to restrict interpretations of these objects and their images. Carpet-pages, like Anglo-Saxon riddles, do not contain their solutions. Multiform as they are, they were also multifunctional and offered various modes of efficacy in various kinds of context, to various kinds of audience. Enclosed in the sacred words of God, away from human eyes, they continued to shimmer in the dark, and that is maybe the best reason why we can still admire them and wonder about them today.

Notes

1 As distinct from the interpretation of these carpet-pages as apotropaic or talismanic images in the Gospel book, see the most recent paper by J. Trilling (1996; Bischoff 1967).

2 This paper is part of an unpublished PhD thesis entitled 'La Chair du Verbe. L'image, le texte et l'écrit dans les évangéliaires insulaires (VII–IXèmes siècles)' presented in March 1999 at the Université Libre de Bruxelles under the direction of Professor Alain Dierkens.

3 A discipline with its origins at the end of the nineteenth century in Germany and illustrated by psychologists like Wertheimer, Kölher, Koffka and more recently by R. Arnheim (1956; 1966) and E. Gombrich (1979).

4 See also the recent iconological interpretation of this page in relation to fol. 291v in the Book of Kells by M. Werner (1997).

5 J-C. Bonne (1996a, b) is one of the scholars who has offered in some recent papers the most brilliant and refreshing contribution to the understanding of ornament in medieval art and thought.

6 *'Cosmos' quippe grace ornatus propie interpretatur, non 'mundus'* (Jeauneau 1972, 232).

7 This is attested by the riddle of the Gospel Book in the Exeter Book, when the object declares 'Now let the decoration and red die [*sic* dye] and wondrous settings proclaim far and wide protection for people...' (Mardsen 1998, 146).

References

ALEXANDER, J. J. G. 1978, *Insular Manuscripts 6th to the 9th century. A Survey of Manuscripts Illuminated in the British Isles*, Vol. 1. London.

ARNHEIM, R. 1954, *Art and Visual Perception*. London.

ARNHEIM, R. 1966, *Toward a Psychology of Art*. Berkley, Los Angeles.

ARNULF, A. 1997, *Versus ad Picturas. Studien zur Titulusdichtung als Quellengottung des Kunsgeschichte von der Antike bis zum Hochmittelalter*. Berlin.

BENJAMIN, W. 1971-83, *L'Oeuvre d'Art à l'Ère de sa Reproductivité Technique, Essai*, Vol. II, trans. M. de Gandillac. Paris.

BISCHOFF, B. 1967, 'Kreuz und Buch im Frühmittelalter und in den ersten Jahrhunderten der spanischen Reconquista', *Mittelalterliche Studien* 2, 284–303. Stuttgart.

BONNE, J-C. 1996a, 'Les ornements de l'histoire (à propos de l'ivoire carolingien de St Remi)', *Annales HSS* (janvier) 1, 37–70.

BONNE, J-C. 1996b, 'De l'ornemental dans l'art médiéval. Le modèle insulaire (VIIème–XIIème siècle)', in J-C. Schmitt and J. Baschet (eds), *L'Image. Fonctions et Usages des Images dans l'Occident Médiéval*, 207–51. Paris.

CAREY, J. 1985, 'Cosmology of Saltair Na Rann', *Celtica* 17, 33–52.

CAREY, J. 1998, *King of Mysteries. Early Irish Religious Writings*. Dublin.

CLANCY, T. O. and MARKUS, G. 1995, *Iona: The Earliest Poetry of a Celtic Monastery*. Edinburgh.

DIMOCK, J. F. (ed.) 1867, *Topographia Hibernica, Giraldi Cambresis Opera*, Vol. II. London.

DODWELL, C. R. 1982, *Anglo-Saxon Art. A New Perspective*. Manchester.

EHWALD, R. (ed.) 1919, *Aldhelmi Opera, M.G.H.* (= *Auctorum Antiquissimi Morum*, 15). Berlin.

EHRENZWEIG, A. 1953, *The Psychoanalysis of Artistic Vision and Hearing: An Introduction to the Theory of Unconscious Perception*. London.

EHRENZWEIG, A. 1967, *The Hidden Order of Art*. London.

FARR, C. 1997, *The Book of Kells. Its Function and Audience*. Toronto, London.

FOLEY, J. M. 1991, *Immanent Art: from Structure to Meaning in Traditional Oral Epic*. Bloomington.

GANZ, D. 1992, '"Pando quod ignoro". In search of Carolingian artistic experience', in L. Smith and B. Ward (eds), *Intellectual Life in the Middle Ages*, 25–32. Rio Grande.

GOMBRICH, E. 1979, *The Sense of Order*. Oxford.

GUILLAUME, P. 1937, *La Psychologie de la Forme*, Nouvelle Bibliothèque Scientifique, 7–9. Paris.

HEAD, P. 1997, *Representation and Design. Tracing a Hermeneutics of Old English Poetry*. Albany.

HENDERSON, G. 1987, *From Durrow to Kells. The Insular Gospel-Books 650–800*. London.

JEAUNEAU, E. (ed. and trans.) 1972, *Jean Scot. Commentaire de l'évangile de Jean* (= Sources Chrétiennes no.180). Paris.

KLEE, P. 1961, *The Thinking Eye*. London.

MARDSEN, R. 1998, '"Ask what I am called": The Anglo-Saxons and their Bibles', in J. Sharpe and K. Van Kampen (eds), *The Bible as Book. The Manuscript Tradition*, 145–76. London, Newcastle.

Ó CARRAGÁIN, É. 1994, '"Traditio evangeliorum' and 'sustentatio': the relevance of liturgical ceremonies to the Book of Kells', in F. O' Mahony (ed.), *The Book of Kells. Proceedings of a conference at Trinity College Dublin, 6–9 September 1992*, 398–436. Aldershot.

STEVENSON, R. B. K. 1981, 'Aspects of ambiguity in crosses and interlace', *Ulster J. Archaeol.* 44, 1–27.

STEVICK, R. 1994, *The Earliest Irish and English Bookarts. Visual and Poetic Forms before A.D. 1000*. Philadelphia.

THONNARD, F. J. (ed. and trans.) 1947, *Augustine. De Musica* (= Bibliothèque Augustinienne VII, t. IV). Paris.

TRILLING, J. 1995, 'Medieval interlace ornament. The making of a cross cultural idiom', *Arte Medievale* IX, no. 2, 59–86.

VARENDONCK, J. 1923, *The Evolution of the Conscious Faculties*. London.

WERNER, M. 1997, 'The Book of Durrow and the question of programme', *Anglo-Saxon Engl.* 26, 23–39.

19   Apocalyptic Elements in Irish High Cross Iconography?

Kees Veelenturf

I

Probably the most important iconographic type in early religious art to have originated in the Apocalypse of St John, commonly called the Book of Revelation, is the *Maiestas Domini*. A great many examples in painting, manuscript illumination and sculpture can be cited. Almost invariably these images show a mandorla with the enthroned Christ, raising his right hand in blessing, who is surrounded in some way by the four living creatures from John's vision which are often interpreted as 'evangelist symbols' (Van der Meer 1938, 315–97). Art historians seldom fail to tell us that this image type expresses the harmony of the four gospels. Much more about its 'core meaning' and its variants can be said, but here it must suffice to say that this image is charged up to a considerable degree with the notion of the Church of the *perfecti*, the perfect Christians in conformation to the mysteries of Christ (Veelenturf 1997, 27–57).

On the Cross of Patrick and Columba in Kells there is the well known carving on the west face of the cross-head (Fig. 19.1), which is held by some scholars to be such an image (*cf.* Veelenturf 1997, 64–6). Of course, this configuration is no *Maiestas Domini* in its proper sense, but it is evident too that the sculptor has adopted a composition which is very much akin to that of the *Maiestas Domini*. The presence of Christ on the head of this cross no doubt

Fig. 19.1 *The Cross of Patrick and Columba, Kells: the eschatological scene on the west face.*
(Photograph: Dúchas, The Heritage Service, Dublin)

has an eschatological meaning, for he appears as the Judge in his characteristic 'Osiris' pose which may be compared with the other Irish scripture crosses. The four living creatures, however, betray some ambiguity. Above Christ's head, the bust of a man raises a circular device with a lamb inside it, and this is not a detail typical of *Maiestas Domini* images. It is also very likely that the eagle beneath the feet of Christ was carved deliberately as the visual and symbolic *trait-d'union* between the figure of Christ the Judge and the Crucifixion image below (Veelenturf 1997, 64–6).[1]

None of the Irish crosses display the *Maiestas Domini* proper or the Apocalyptic Vision as Françoise Henry used to call it (*cf.* Henry 1967, 64ff.). In view of its absence we might ask ourselves whether there are any apocalyptic elements at all in Irish high cross iconography. This question is particularly relevant with respect to the more isolated animal figures on the North Cross, Duleek, that have been taken to be the so-called 'evangelist symbols' (Harbison 1992, figs 240, 242, 244; Porter 1931, 74, fig. 113; Roe 1959, 22).

In this somewhat lapidary way of setting the scene the word 'apocalyptic' has been used to indicate iconographic motifs which allegedly derive from the Apocalypse of St John. Another sense, relating to ultimate disaster, to eschatological accomplishment, will now be adopted.

Fig. 19.2 *The South Cross, Graiguenamanagh: the Crucifixion on the west face. (Photograph: Dúchas, The Heritage Service, Dublin)*

II

The cross-heads of the Irish crosses with a developed display of iconographic images are of an essentially eschatological nature. Typical examples are the Cross of Muiredach, Monasterboice, and the Cross of the Scriptures, Clonmacnoise (Harbison 1992, figs 473, 481, 134, 141). The Last Judgment or the Second Coming of Christ on one face correlates with the Crucifixion on the reverse, and the eschatological overtones of these Crucifixion scenes stress this interrelationship. The Crucifixion is not merely a narrative rendition of an historical event. The image, which is marked out by a high degree of conflation, tells the beholder that Christ was judged by humans in order to be their Final Judge, that he was sacrificed on earth in order to rule in glory for ever. In fact the Irish high cross Crucifixion is a theophany, a disclosure of the hypostatic union in Christ, and this revelation has an eschatological hue. The high cross itself can be understood as a Passion cross, because the figure of Christ is nearly always crucified *upon* the high cross itself, and there is no other cross indicated behind his body. At the same time, because of the eschatological image on the reverse and its interrelationship with the Crucifixion, the high cross

is also the cross of the *Parousia*, of the Second Coming, in which it will be the sign that leads the Judge. Of course not all of the crosses have images which render these motifs – the Last Judgment, the Second Coming and the Crucifixion – in as detailed a form as on the so-called scripture crosses.[2]

Sometimes we encounter more abridged or conflated forms which fit smoothly into the repertoire of high cross images that are tantalisingly hard to interpret. Among these carvings is an image of Christ, even an image type, which has an apocalyptic meaning. There are thirteen high crosses on which this representation is carved. A fine example is the South Cross, Graiguenamanagh, which on its west face has the Crucifixion (Fig. 19.2) and on its east face another one (Fig. 19.3) – or so it seems. On the west face we can discern the faint assistant figures of the lance and sponge bearers flanking Christ, but they are clearly absent from the counter-image. Do we see here two different types of Crucifixion scene? It will come as no surprise that the answer is in the negative. On this high cross the same principle can be recognised that rules the iconography of the more elaborately decorated crosses: eschatological theophany and Crucifixion scene are again correlated.

Fig. 19.3 *The South Cross, Graiguenamanagh: the cruciate eschatological Christ on the east face. (Photograph: Dúchas, The Heritage Service, Dublin)*

The figure of the crucified Christ with his extended arms on the west face has almost been replicated by the sculptor in the figure of Christ on the reverse. On the latter, however, we see him as he will appear in the apocalyptic setting of the end of time. His outstretched arms identify him as the Final Judge who first had to be crucified at the end of his life on earth. Doing justice to its form and to its iconographical setting, this specific type can therefore be designated as the cruciate eschatological Christ (Veelenturf 1997, 129–33, 182–83, Tables 4–6).

The Graiguenamanagh figure is not the only specimen in high cross iconography; nor is it without parallels in early medieval iconography from the Continent. The Continental images, which make up quite a long iconographical tradition, help to explain why Christ was depicted in this very compact cruciate pose which differs so much from the usual 'Osiris' attitude in the Irish Last Judgment scenes. In Continental eschatological images of Christ we often see him with outstretched arms beside or in front of a large *Parousia* cross. For example, on the tympanum sculpture of the abbey church of Saint-Denis dated *c.* 1137–40, Christ sits enthroned in front of the *Parousia* cross, while there is visual rhyme, as it were,

between his arms and the arms of the cross (Fig. 19.4). In a liturgical manuscript of the Ottonian emperor Henry II from *c.* 1007 we have a miniature of the Last Judgment, where there is a triple consonance of the *Parousia* cross with the extended arm and the cross nimbus of Christ (Fig. 19.5). These examples could easily be multiplied (*cf.* Veelenturf 1997, 138, n. 718).

The pose of Christ with outstretched arms has its roots in exegesis: at the end of time he will be seen as he was hung upon the cross at Golgotha. For artists this was an opportunity to depict Christ while displaying the wounds in the palms of his hands. We see this particularly in images of the Second Coming, for instance on Byzantine pectoral crosses (Wessel 1960, 99–102), and in images of the Ascension in which very often the *Secundus Adventus* of Christ is implied (Klein 1987, 125–27; Klein 1988, 129–30). On some pectoral crosses from Viking-age Scandinavia we encounter the same pairing of Christ figures as on the Irish crosses (Blindheim 1972, 92–3, no. 76; Graham-Campbell 1980, 157–58, 308, nos 530–32; Fuglesang 1981, 73–6). The interrelationship of Crucifixion and eschatological theophany is very much on the surface here, and we may therefore conclude that the type of the cruciate eschatological Christ has a solid foundation in both theology and comparative iconology (Veelenturf 1997, 131–39).

The two images of the cruciate Christ and the Crucifixion are not always juxtaposed in such an organised fashion as on the Graiguenamanagh South Cross and on the high cross of Kilgobbin (Harbison 1992, figs 381–82). The high cross at Moone has a Crucifixion scene on the cross-base, whereas on the cross-head we see a cruciate Christ figure, and on its reverse a whorl from which animal heads emerge (Harbison 1992, figs 515, 511, 516).[3] Nevertheless, it is hard to doubt that the carving on the east face of the cross-head is the eschatological Christ. We may assume the same identity or, perhaps better, quality of Christ for a number of images which show a formal resemblance to the cruciate figures which have already been mentioned. In these cases, the usual assistant figures of the sponge and lance bearers and the two robbers, who are relatively rare in Ireland, are always absent. Nor is there any clear indication that the Christ figures are depicted in a state of suffering. These erect human shapes often reveal a balanced poise which is combined with what might be called a quiet dignity (Veelenturf 1997, 132–34, 143–49, 182–83, Tables 5, 6).

Therefore, the cruciate figure of the eschatological Christ was not only known on the Continent. This type is also found on Irish sculpture as an alternative to the Christ with an 'Osiris' pose who figures in the more elaborate depictions of the events on Doomsday.

Fig. 19.4 *The eschatological Christ: sculpture of the western portal of the abbey church of Saint–Denis, France. (Photograph: Centrum voor Kunsthistorische Documentatie, Nijmegen)*

III

In the previous paragraph the semantic difference between the terms 'eschatological' and 'apocalyptic' has not been articulated clearly. These words are of course no synonyms. Nobody doubts that the early Irish were interested in eschatology. Apparently, they also believed in the acute imminence of an End, for we have evidence of the existence of apocalyptic tendencies.

According to the annals it was 'Apocalypse Now!' in 1096 because the Irish expected the final destruction of their island in that very year. Only through fasting, praying and so forth were they able to avert a catastrophe. This threat of complete downfall was due to the legendary Irish druid Mog Ruith. He had become notorious as the Irishman who had beheaded John the Baptist at the court of king Herod. It was this severe crime which had provoked the widespread prophecy that the destruction of Ireland would take place on the feast-day of the decollation of the Precursor, on the 29th August, in a year in which certain chronological conditions would be fulfilled. The Irish believed this

to be in 1096 (Kenney 1979, 749–53; McNamara 1984, 126–43; Veelenturf 1997, 155).

On the Continent comparable upheaval with a strong apocalyptic flavour has been recorded in connection with the first crusade, which was incited by Pope Urban II in 1095. Abbot Ekkehard of Aura wrote in his chronicle that a rumour was circulating during the summer of 1096 that Charlemagne had risen from his grave to lead the crusaders to Jerusalem (Ekkehard of Aura 1895, 19; Cohn 1970, 72, *cf.* 113). Guibert of Nogent suggested that the liberation of the Holy City would signal the coming of Antichrist (Guibert of Nogent-sous-Coucy 1879, 138–39, *cf.* 239). This is not to say that in 1096 expectations of an immediate End were general in Continental Europe, but these chronicles demonstrate that the Irish expectancy of final destruction was not without contemporary parallels (*cf.* Cohn 1970, 71–3). The Irish tradition, however, originated some centuries before, as is indicated by a cycle of Irish texts and lore concerning Mog Ruith.

In these early Irish apocalyptic expectations the 'wheel' plays an important role. The name Mog

Fig. 19.5 *The Last Judgment: miniature on fol. 202r in the* Perikopenbuch *of Emperor Henry II (München, Bayerische Staatsbibliothek, MS lat. 4452). (Photograph: Centrum voor Kunsthistorische Documentatie, Nijmegen)*

Ruith means 'Slave of the Wheel'. His wheel was 'an engine of destruction', which was prophesied to appear before the Last Judgment (O'Rahilly 1984, 521–22). In Irish tradition, the magic ravaging wheel of destruction connected with our druid has been explained to be such fancy things as a 'bull roarer' or a 'paddle wheel' or an 'oared wheel' (a ship in the air). It has also been associated or even equated with other apocalyptical motifs that were specific to Ireland. These were, for instance, the *Scúap a Fánait* or 'Broom out of Fanaid' which was apparently some kind of tornado or whirlwind, a snake, a dragon, a fiery bolt, or even Antichrist. All of these designations seem to refer to the same notion; they lack a sharp delineation, and appear to be to some extent interchangeable. Many of the horrors which we encounter in early Christian apocalypticism were rooted in ancient pagan tradition, and Mog Ruith with his accoutrements appears to be of pre-Christian descent too. It is very interesting that thunderstorms, and especially whirlwinds, are conspicuous in apocalyptic lore *and* in connection with the feast-day of John's beheading, and not only in Ireland.

Phenomena of the air were also associated with Mog Ruith; he was capable of raising a tempest and of forming a cloud by blowing his breath. His moving wheel, which like a thunderstorm would devastate the country before Doomsday, has therefore, not only a prominent position, but also a broad range of associations at the centre of apocalyptic expectations in early Ireland (Macalister 1919, 344–56; Müller-Lisowski 1923; 1938; O'Rahilly 1984, 519–22).

Is there any reflection of all this in high cross iconography? After considering the images derived from the Apocalypse which are *not* seen on the high crosses, and the cruciate eschatological Christ which *is* seen in a number of instances, we may now turn to one example of a small number of motifs which we find chiefly in an eschatological context.

It is found *inter alia* on the north face of the high cross at Castlebernard (Fig. 19.6) and on the east face of the Cross of Patrick and Columba in Kells, of which the central image on the other face was briefly discussed above. Both cross-heads are decorated with a composition of six interconnected spiral bosses grouped around a central boss (Harbison

Fig. 19.6 *The high cross from Kinnitty at Castlebernard, north face. (Photograph: Dúchas, The Heritage Service, Dublin)*

Fig. 19.7 *The North Cross, Duleek, east face. (Photograph: Dúchas, The Heritage Service, Dublin)*

1992, figs 99, 345–46). We find similar devices on the cross-heads of crosses at Duleek (Fig. 19.7), Tihilly (Fig. 19.8), Tynan (Fig. 19.9) and Eglish (Harbison 1992, fig. 266). Cognate configurations also appear on a fragment from Tybroughney (Harbison 1992, fig. 625) and, without bosses, on a slab from Carrowntemple (Wallace and Timoney 1987, 48–9, cat. no. 3, illus. 2:4–6). All of these devices consist of six bosses plus one, except for the East Cross, Eglish, which, inconveniently, numbers eight plus one. This non-figural composition has been the object of

scholarly attention before (Edwards 1987, 113, fig. 2; de Paor 1987, 145–46; Ó Carragáin 1988, 16–19;[4] Hamlin 1995, 191–92).

On the cross at Castlebernard, the North Cross, Duleek, and the Tihilly Cross this whorl of spiralling bosses is the counter-image of the Crucifixion. It therefore takes the place of a figural scene which is usually of an eschatological nature. This feature, taken together with its prominent position in the centre of the cross-head, leads to the question of what the significance of this particular composition

Fig. 19.8 *The high cross, Tihilly, east face.*
(Photograph: Dúchas, The Heritage Service, Dublin)

Fig. 19.9 *The Island Cross, Tynan, east face.*
(Photograph: Northern Ireland Tourist Board, Belfast)

might be. For clarity's sake, it is not the origin of the motif with which we are concerned, but the intended meaning within a Christian iconographic context.

The description 'whorl of spiral bosses' for the device would probably be fitting. The seven spirals make a strong impression of revolving movement; in this respect they very much resemble some sort of wheel or propeller. Does the bossed spiral device in the eschatological context of the high crosses belong to the complex of attributes and phenomena in Irish apocalyptic beliefs in some way associated with Mog Ruith?

There is nothing new in attempting to establish iconographical meaning for apparent decorative or non-representational devices in early medieval art. We only have to think of studies undertaken by

Elbern (*i.a.* 1955; 1962a; 1962b), and Stevenson (1974, 38–40; 1981). At the same time it is evident that such an enterprise is not without problems.

Adducing some of the interpretations suggested for fol. 192v in the Book of Durrow and for the Carolingian brooch from Dorestad in the Netherlands (Plates XX, XXI), these problems readily come to the fore. It is clear that the Trinitarian analysis of the central decoration of the manuscript page by Elbern (1955), which focuses on the combined application of quadrangle, circle, cross and triangle, has a considerable degree of plausibility. How are we to substantiate this sophisticated theory in a positivistic way? A derivative morphological problem presents itself in the interpretation of the Dorestad brooch by Van Es (1976, 261–64) and

Peddemors (1981, 61–2). The two crosses which determine its composition – a Greek cross (taken to stand for the *crux gemmata*) and a St Andrew's cross – were considered to represent an eschatological and a cosmological concept, and interpreted consequently as a *Parousia* cross and a triumphal cross. As forms, the particular cross shapes upon the brooch are explicitly distinct and of a composite nature, and we may wonder whether their respective symbolic contents are not wider apart or prone to different interpretation.[5]

Caution is therefore necessary, and in this context it may be wise to recall the words of Professor Ernst Kitzinger who has warned us that, 'Limits – very strict limits – must be imposed if floodgates are not to be opened to wild and reckless interpretations of every bit of knotwork and zoomorphic interlace in Insular art' (Kitzinger 1993, 3). In the case of the seven spiral bosses on the Irish crosses we may venture to move on solid ground, however, for it stands that the occurrence of this configuration is limited to the eschatological context of the cross-heads and crossings, at least in its Irish distribution.[6]

The number of spiral bosses in our device does not oppose an eschatological interpretation. Many years ago it was remarked that, 'The careful arrangement of raised bosses in high relief of some of the crosses is likely to be based on . . . language of numbers' (Richardson 1984, 31). There are six spiral bosses arranged around a central one, so we deal with the numbers six and seven. In Christian number symbolism six is a perfect number connected with the days of the Creation and also with salvation's history, from the creation of Adam to the Last Judgment: it is a number of completion (Meyer and Suntrup 1987, 442ff.; *cf*. Richardson 1984, 29–30). Seven is no less a perfect and holy number, especially in Scripture, and is of course often related to the seventh day. On account of the week cycle of six days plus one, God's rest day after the six days of Creation, and *sex aetates mundi* followed by the rest period of eternity, seven is particularly the sign of earthly circular time. In this respect seven also has significance because of its position after the number six (Meyer and Suntrup 1987, 479ff.). Perfect numbers that relate to the completion of time are, of course, especially suited to figure in an eschatological context.

It must be added that the seven spiral configuration is not the only one which we might suspect to have an apocalyptic association. The cross-head of Drumcullin and the Killamery high cross, for instance, display designs which also suggest whirling movement (Harbison 1992, figs 231, 411–12). But either these designs go without juxtaposition with the Crucifixion, or they do not recur in the same place on other crosses. We have,

therefore, other non-figural motifs on the high cross heads in which circle and spiral or spirals are combined, but they do not stand out as clearly as the seven spiral device. On some scripture crosses, like those of Durrow and Clonmacnoise, we also see carvings that are not dissimilar. Above the eschatological Judge of Durrow there are four bosses with animals emerging from them (Harbison 1992, figs 247–48), and we meet cognate decorations above the Crucifixion on the Cross of the Scriptures in Clonmacnoise (Harbison 1992, figs 132, 134) and above and below the crucified Christ on Muiredach's Cross, Monasterboice (Harbison 1992, figs 480–81).

Despite minor formal variations, which I take to be of subordinate significance when compared to their compositional cohesion and place, the seven spiral devices stand out as a distinctive group. However, it is likely that the sculptors used a much more extensive repertoire of 'non-representational' motifs to convey iconographic meaning of an eschatological or apocalyptic nature. The same complex way of expression may have been at work as in the figural iconography, where different subjects can represent or allude to one theological truth or concept.

An aspect typical of early Irish art is that iconography follows its own distinctive path. This has a negative side. The apocalyptic figure of Antichrist was a familiar figure in early Irish texts (McNamara 1984, 139; McGinn 1988, 11–13), but up to now nobody has managed to identify a convincing instance of the representation of Antichrist in the visual arts. Among the extensive body of Irish texts that betray a profound interest in eschatological and apocalyptical matters are expositions on the fifteen signs that will be seen before Doomsday. These signs were a popular subject in early Ireland (McNamara 1984, 128–38); therefore why do we not meet them in eschatological imagery? Or, perhaps better, why are we unable to detect or recognise them?

Let us move back from negative to positive. Everybody who has read early Irish narratives or apocryphal prose knows that the Irish were capable of fanciful explanations of things, of finding unusual metaphors, of filling in fantastic details in 'historical' accounts. If we consider these phenomena together with the Irish love of ornamentation in the visual arts – a more appropriate designation than *horror vacui* – as well as with the iconographic permeability of non-figural decoration, then an iconographical explanation of our seven spiral device does not strike us as awkward or impossible. In general I deem it very likely that the motifs suggesting whirling movement on the high crosses really *are* emblems of the turmoil that will occur before Doomsday – emblems, of course, not straightforward 'illustrations'.

It will be manifest, however, that this last part of my paper is just a first attempt to follow the thread through a Gordian knot. The iconographical analysis of so-called abstract decoration has a long way to go, but it looks as if such studies may be very rewarding.[7]

Notes

1 After my paper at the Cardiff conference, the question arose as to whether the image on the Cross of Patrick and Columba in Kells could indeed be called a *Maiestas Domini*. Of the two arguments I put forward against this, the first one, the generally accepted definition of the image type as formulated by F. van der Meer, is paramount and remains valid. However, I would no longer wish to question the resemblance of the winged animals flanking Christ to an ox and a lion as expressly as I did then.

2 The subject of the antithesis of Crucifixion and eschatological theophany on the Irish crosses is discussed at much greater length in chapter VI 'The crucified and the eschatological Christ' in Veelenturf 1997.

3 The high cross at Moone was re-assembled at the end of the nineteenth century, and the possibility that the present cross consists of parts from more than one monument cannot be ruled out.

4 In the opinion of Éamonn Ó Carragáin, the 'mat' with the spiral device on the east face of the Cross of Patrick and Columba in Kells refers to the *second* miraculous feeding of a multitude by Christ (Matt. 15:32–9; Mark 8:1–10), with the seven bosses representing loaves of bread which symbolise the gifts of the Holy Ghost, presented to the Church on Pentecost. The question of course is whether this interpretation would hold for all the instances of the spiralled boss design.

5 It is appropriate to quote the words of the main authority in the field of iconographic interpretation of non-figural motifs, in this case cross incisions on Merovingian artefacts: *Man wird gut tun, die 'ikonographische' Aussage der hier vorgelegten merowingischen Objekte mit christlichen Zeichen nicht zu pressen und zu viel hineingeheimnissen zu wollen. Es dürfte daher auch ratsam sein, von dem Versuch einer individuellen Deutung dieser Stücke abzusehen. Der Hinweis auf ihren allgemein christlich-geheiligten Charakter muß genügen* (Elbern 1962b, 220).

6 Outside Ireland the device occurs especially in Scotland, for which see the listing in de Paor 1987, 146.

7 The third section of this paper is meant to be a preliminary instalment of a more elaborate study of apocalyptic beliefs in early Ireland and their traces and correspondences in iconography.

Acknowledgments

I am grateful to the editors of these proceedings for the skilful correction of my English.

Appendix 1

The cruciate eschatological Christ on Irish high cross heads

HIGH CROSS	EAST FACE	WEST FACE
Balsitric, cross-head	boss (Face 1)	cruciate eschatological Christ (Face 2)
Durrow, cross-head	shepherd – guide of the soul (?)	cruciate eschatological Christ
Dysert O'Dea	cruciate eschatological Christ	lozenges
Graiguenamanagh, South Cross	cruciate eschatological Christ	Crucifixion
Kilfenora, 'Doorty' Cross	ecclesiastic (?)	cruciate eschatological Christ
Kilfenora, West Cross	cruciate eschatological Christ	fretwork circle
Kilgobbin, high cross	cruciate eschatological Christ	Crucifixion
Killaloe, limestone cross	cruciate eschatological Christ	interlace
Killesher, cross-head	boss (Face 2)	cruciate eschatological Christ (Face 1)
Monaincha, cross fragments	interlace	cruciate eschatological Christ
Monasterboice, head fragment	boss (Face 2)	cruciate eschatological Christ (Face 1)
Moone, high cross	cruciate eschatological Christ	whorl
Roscrea, sandstone cross	ecclesiastic (?)	cruciate eschatological Christ

Appendix 2

Device of seven bossed spirals on Irish high cross-heads

HIGH CROSS	EAST FACE	WEST FACE
Castlebernard, Kinnitty Cross	spiral whorl (N. Face)	Crucifixion (S. Face)
Duleek, North Cross	spiral whorl	Crucifixion
Eglish, East Cross	eight spiral whorl (Face A)	interlaced boss (Face B)
Kells, Cross of Patrick & Columba	spiral whorl	Second Coming of Christ
Tihilly, high cross	spiral whorl	Crucifixion
Tynan, Island Cross	spiral whorl	bosses

References

BLINDHEIM, M. 1972, *Norge 872–1972: Middelalderskunst fra Norge i Andre Land / Norwegian Medieval Art Abroad,* 2nd ed. Oslo.

COHN, N. 1970, *The Pursuit of the Millennium: Revolutionary Millenarians and Mystical Anarchists of the Middle Ages,* 3rd ed. London.

DE PAOR, L. 1987, 'The high crosses of Tech Theille (Tihilly), Kinnitty, and related sculpture', in Rynne (ed.), 131–58.

EDWARDS, N. 1987, 'Abstract ornament on early medieval Irish crosses: a preliminary catalogue', in M. Ryan (ed.), *Ireland and Insular Art A.D. 500–1200,* 111–17. Dublin.

EKKEHARD of AURA 1895, 'Hierosolymita, de oppressione, liberatione ac restauratione Jerosolymitanae ecclesiae', in *Recueil des historiens des croisades publié par les soins de l'Académie des Inscriptions et Belles-Lettres: historiens occidentaux* 5, 1–40. Paris.

ELBERN, V. H. 1955, 'Die Dreifaltigkeitsminiatur im Book of Durrow', *Wallraf-Richartz-Jahrbuch: Westdeutsches Jahrbuch für Kunstgeschichte* 17, 7–42.

ELBERN, V. H. 1962a, 'Kreuzritzungen auf einigen frühmittelalterlichen Geräten', in V. H. Elbern (ed.), *Das erste Jahrtausend: Kultur und Kunst im werdenden Abendland an Rhein und Ruhr,* Textband I, 216–22. Düsseldorf.

ELBERN, V. H. 1962b, 'Der fränkische Reliquienkasten und Tragaltar von Werden', in V. H. Elbern (ed.), *Das erste Jahrtausend: Kultur und Kunst im werdenden Abendland an Rhein und Ruhr,* Textband I, 436–70. Düsseldorf.

FUGLESANG, S. H. 1981, 'Crucifixion iconography in Viking Scandinavia', in H. Bekker-Nielsen, P. Foote and O. Olsen (eds), *Proceedings of the Eighth Viking Congress: Århus 24–31 August 1977,* 73–94 (= Mediaeval Scandinavia supplements 2). Odense.

GRAHAM-CAMPBELL, J. 1980, *Viking Artefacts: A Select Catalogue.* London.

GUIBERT OF NOGENT-SOUS-COUCY 1879, 'Historia quae dicitur Gesta Dei per Francos', in *Recueil des historiens des croisades publié par les soins de l'Académie des Inscriptions et Belles–Lettres: historiens occidentaux* 4, 113–263. Paris.

HAMLIN, A. 1995, 'The Blackwater group of crosses', in C. Bourke (ed.), *From the Isles of the North. Early Medieval Art in Ireland and Britain,* 187–96. Belfast.

HARBISON, P. 1992, *The High Crosses of Ireland. An Iconographical and Photographic Survey,* 3 vols (= Römisch-Germanisches Zentralmuseum, Forschungsinstitut für Vor- und Frühgeschichte Monographien 17, 1–3). Bonn.

HENRY, F. 1967, *Irish Art during the Viking Invasions (800–1020 A.D.).* London.

KENNEY, J. F. 1979, *The Sources for the Early History of Ireland: Ecclesiastical. An Introduction and Guide.* Dublin. (= Records of civilization: sources and studies 11). [Reprint of the 2nd ed., New York 1966, with Preface, corrections, and additions by Ludwig Bieler.]

KITZINGER, E. 1993, 'Interlace and icons: form and function in early Insular art', in R. M. Spearman and J. Higgitt (eds), *The Age of Migrating Ideas. Early Medieval Art in Northern Britain and Ireland,* 3–15. Edinburgh, Stroud.

KLEIN, P. K. 1987, "*Et videbit eum omnis oculus et qui eum pupugerunt*': zur Deutung des Tympanons von Beaulieu', in P. Bjurström, N. Göran-Hökby and F. Mütherich (eds), *Florilegium in Honorem Carl Nordenfalk Octogenarii Contextum* (= Nationalmuseums skriftserie n.s. 9), 123–44. Stockholm.

KLEIN, P. K. 1988, 'Le tympan de Beaulieu: Jugement Dernier ou Seconde Parousie?', *Les Cahiers de Saint-Michel de Cuxa* 19, 129–37.

MACALISTER, R. A. S. 1919, 'Temair Breg: a study of the remains and traditions of Tara', *Proc. Roy. Ir. Acad.* 34C, 231–399.

MCGINN, B. 1988, 'Portraying Antichrist in the middle ages', in W. Verbeke, D. Verhelst and A. Welkenhuysen (eds), *The Use and Abuse of Eschatology in the Middle Ages* (= *Mediaevalia Lovaniensia,* series 1, studia nr 15.), 1–48. Leuven.

MCNAMARA, M. 1984, *The Apocrypha in the Irish Church,* 2nd ed. Dublin.

MEYER, H. and SUNTRUP, R. 1987, *Lexikon der mittelalterlichen Zahlenbedeutungen* (= Münstersche Mittelalter-Schriften 56). München.

MÜLLER–LISOWSKI, K. 1923, 'Texte zur Mog Ruith Sage', *Zeitschrift für Celtische Philologie* 14, 145–63.

MÜLLER–LISOWSKI, K. 1938, 'La légende de St Jean dans la tradition irlandaise et le druide Mog Ruith', *Études Celtiques* 3, 46–70.

Ó CARRAGÁIN, É. 1988, 'The meeting of Saint Paul and Saint Anthony: visual and literary uses of a eucharistic motif', in G. Mac Niocaill and P. F. Wallace (eds), *Keimelia: Studies in Medieval Archaeology and History in Memory of Tom Delaney*, 1–58. Galway.

O'RAHILLY, T. F. 1984, *Early Irish History and Mythology*, 6th ed. Dublin.

PEDDEMORS, A. 1981, 'The Carolingian jewelled brooch from Dorestad', *Oudheidkundige mededelingen uit het Rijksmuseum van Oudheden te Leiden* 62, 59–62.

PORTER, A. K. 1931, *The Crosses and Culture of Ireland*. New Haven, London, Oxford.

RICHARDSON, H. 1984, 'Number and symbol in early Christian Irish art', *J. Roy. Soc. Antiq. Ir.* 114, 28–47.

ROE, H. M. 1959, *The High Crosses of Kells. s.l.*

RYNNE, E. (ed.) 1987, *Figures from the Past: Studies on Figurative Art in Christian Ireland in Honour of Helen M. Roe*. Dún Laoghaire.

STEVENSON, R. B. K. 1974, 'The Hunterston brooch and its significance', *Medieval Archaeol.* 18, 16–42.

STEVENSON, R. B. K. 1981, 'Aspects of ambiguity in crosses and interlace', *Ulster J. Archaeol.* 44, 1–27.

VAN DER MEER, F. 1938, *Maiestas Domini: théophanies de l'Apocalypse dans l'art chrétien. Étude sur les origines d'une iconographie spéciale du Christ* (= Studi di antichità cristiana 13). Città del Vaticano, Roma, Paris.

VAN ES, W. A. 1976, 'La grande fibule de Dorestad', in *Festoen: opgedragen aan A. N. Zadoks–Josephus Jitta bij haar zeventigste verjaardag* (= Scripta archaeologica Groningana 6), 249–66. Groningen, Bussum.

VEELENTURF, K. 1997, *Dia Brátha: Eschatological Theophanies and Irish High Crosses* (= Amsterdamse historische reeks, kleine serie 33). Amsterdam.

WALLACE, P. F. and TIMONEY, M. A. 1987, 'Carrowntemple, Co. Sligo, and its inscribed slabs', in Rynne (ed.), 43–61.

WESSEL, K. 1960, 'Die Entstehung des Crucifixus', *Byzantinische Zeitschrift* 53, 95–111.

20 High Cross Design

Robert D. Stevick

This paper discusses a single element of high cross design: the relations among the primary dimensions of individual crosses. These dimensions will be treated as extensional quantities.

According to Boethius, grammarians, and common usage, quantities are of two kinds: magnitude and multitude – 'how-much' and 'how-many'. Measure a cross with a ruler, and you get dimensions of the 'how-many' kind – so many meters, centimetres, millimetres nowadays, or so many of whatever units that have been marked along your ruler, medieval or modern. However, most numerals of multitude measure are opaque in representing design, which lies in relations among the dimensions. What does the ratio 97:71 mean to you, for example? Or 99:70? Taking measures in this way is the activity of the surveyor. On the other hand, work with dividers and straight-edge, and you can grasp dimensions relative one to another, entirely independent of some scale of measure that has every likelihood of being irrelevant. This is the activity of the geometer. All the measures will be of the 'how-much' kind, related as proportions in terms of a given magnitude. In the case of the early free-standing stone crosses of Ireland – just as in the case of the cross-pages in the Lindisfarne, Kells, and St Gall Gospels – this kind of measuring can provide a wonderfully transparent representation of the formal relations among the primary dimensions of many of these splendid crosses. It enables one to trace palpably many of the fundamental features of their designs.

While all the primary dimensions in a cross design stand in a fixed scheme of relations, one of the dimensions will nonetheless dominate. In viewing a plan, the dominant dimension is the one that anchors the relations among all the dimensions in the perceptual processing – something like the fundamental tone in a musical composition, the one around which the tonal activity takes place. In constructing a cross plan, the dominant dimension is the one usually called the 'given' dimension, the one from which the others take their respective measures.

The process of constructing a ringed cross design can be straightforward. It requires setting the size of the ring outside and inside, the height of the cross-arms and their length, the dimensions of the shaft, and the dimensions of the central re-entrant arcs (the 'armpits') that commonly are present. These are what I am calling the primary dimensions. By way of illustration, let us construct a simple plan for a ringed cross. Its general size will be determined by such non-design factors as the budget and the purpose and the materials available. Consistent with that size, the 'given' dimension must be set first. *Which* dimension will be the 'given' has to be decided, of course, before construction of the design is to begin. Let us select the ring diameter to be the given magnitude: it is the only large element in the form of many crosses that is symmetrical both laterally and inversely. We shall also need right angles. Both ring and right angle configurations are set initially by the most basic of the geometer's procedures (Fig. 20.1).

(a) Lay down the given measure and bisect it.
(b) Plot a circle on that same measure.
(c) Plot a concentric square with sides equal to the given measure.

And then proceed to set the scheme of related dimensions (Fig. 20.2).

(a) Plot the transverse measure of the arms and shaft by using the diagonal measure of single quadrants of the square (illustrated for one quadrant).
(b) Plot the length of the arms this time using the diagonal measure of two adjacent quadrants of the square.

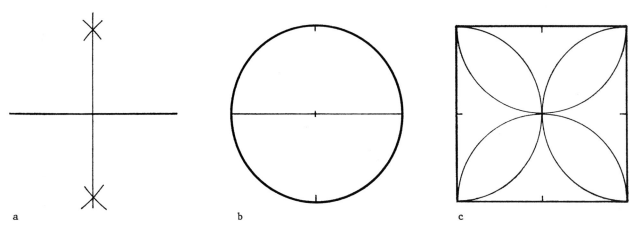

Fig. 20.1 *A practical method of constructing a concentric cross, circle and square*

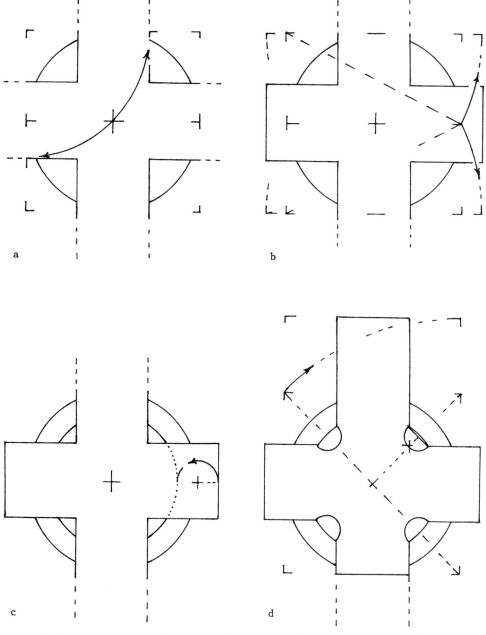

Fig. 20.2 *Constructing the primary dimensions of the South Cross, Castledermot*

*Fig. 20.3 South Cross, Castledermot, Co. Kildare.
(Photograph: Dúchas, The Heritage Service, Ireland)*

(c) Plot the inner radius of the ring using the difference between the diagonal measure of two quadrants of the square and one of its sides.

(d) Plot the height of the upper shaft by using diagonals of the underlying square. Plot the armpits with centres at intersections of diagonals with chords of the inner circle as shown, radii extending to intersections of cross and shaft lines in step (c).

The form constructed in this way is an accurate replication of the basic design of the South Cross at Castledermot (Fig. 20.3), as would be seen if a drawing of this form were laid on top of an appropriate photograph on the same scale.[1]

Suppose now we have been asked to design a second cross for the same community. It would not be right to offer the same design again. The two can be similar, however, and it would be appropriate if they were. So let us modify the first design for some of its derivative dimensions (Fig. 20.4). Keep the arm (the transom) height of the first cross (a), but use a new code for the ring thickness (b) and for the arm extension (c), and recompute the armpit arcs adjusting to the changes which have resulted (d). The operations are as follows:

(a) Same as for the preceding design.

(b) In step (a) the difference between the lengths of the diagonal and the side of a quadrant is used eight times; copy (or recompute) that measure from any corner of the square to mark a point along one of its sides. A straight line from that point to the nearest opposite corner will intersect the underlying cross, setting the radial measure for the inner circle of the ring.

(c) With dividers, copy the difference in radius length between the outer and inner circle to mark a point along an extension of the cross; this derives the radius of a still larger circle, which is used to set the length of the cross arms.

(d) The curves at the armpits of the cross are then plotted from markings already in place.

If a drawing of this form were to be laid on top of an appropriate photograph on the same scale as the North Cross at Castledermot (Fig. 20.5), it would show an accurate replication of the basic design of this second cross.

These two designs are easy ones – simple to construct and simple to grasp because their ratios of measure are basic and few, and their relations are direct. Several other better known crosses also have designs that are simple in this sense (Stevick 1999). So do many full-page illuminations in the early Insular Gospel manuscripts. The Castledermot South Cross, for example, uses a single ratio in setting dimensions of the length of the cross-arms (Fig. 20.2b), the one symmetrical extension from the given measure of the ring. The same ratio is used for setting the outer frame dimensions for two well-known cross-pages in the Lindisfarne Gospels, fol. 2v (Fig. 20.6), and fol. 138v. It takes only a rotation by a quarter turn of the one (Fig. 20.2b) to produce the other (Fig. 20.6a) in appropriate orientation. From those frame dimensions the other primary dimensions of the frame and the cross on this page are derived (Fig. 20.6b-f) by constructive geometry (Stevick 1994, 103–9), even as the other primary dimensions for the cross are derived in Figs 20.2c and d.

The less simple designs are not so easy. Reduce the symmetry anywhere in the plan and the layout is less easy to decode. I will describe two of these.

The Tower Cross at Kells (Fig. 20.7) adds a bit of schematic complexity by its armpits having complex arcs – that is, curves departing from simple circular paths. Even so, the design would have maintained a fine clarity if the lower shaft had not been made wider than the upper extension [2] – the finished face of it, that is. Its fundamental design again will evolve through direct derivations from concentric cross, circle, and square (Fig. 20.8). It seems to have begun with a radical clarity confined to proportional

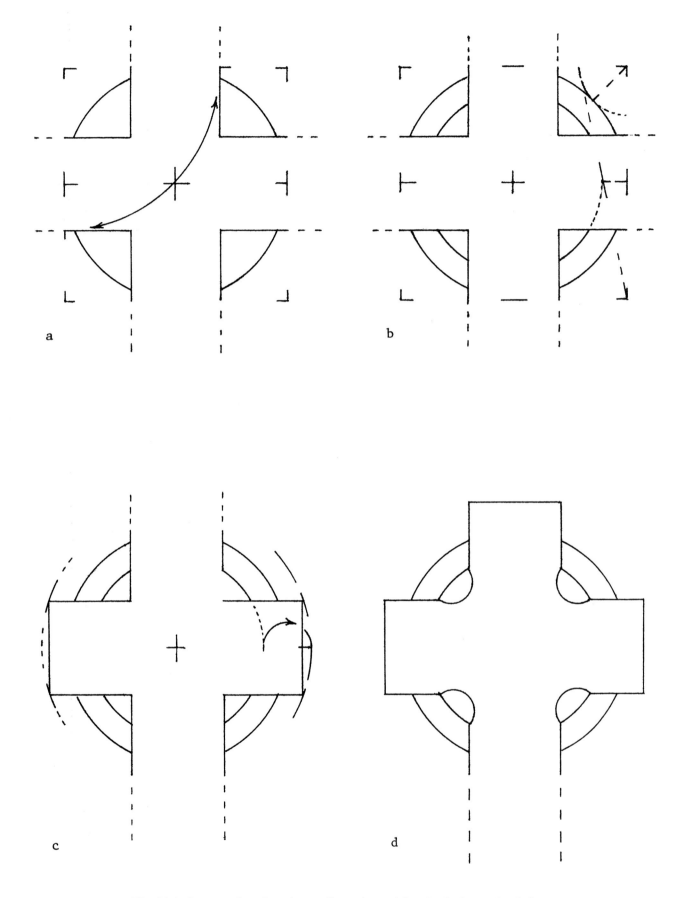

Fig. 20.4 *Constructing the primary dimensions of the North Cross, Castledermot*

Fig. 20.5 North Cross, Castledermot, Co. Kildare. (Photograph: Dúchas, The Heritage Service, Ireland)

measures derived from two of the simplest ratios – 2:1 and √2:1, in modern terms;[3] or in basic operational terms, proportional measures produced most readily by cutting a line in half and cutting a square in half diagonally.

(a) Intersections of diagonals of quadrants set the inner radius of the ring. Intersections of these diagonals also set the paths of straight lines for the cross-arm transverse measure and for the upper segment of the shaft (the measure for the lower segment has been augmented).

(b) The path of a circle whose radius measure is that of the diagonal of a quadrant of the underlying square sets the length of the cross-arms (length of the cross-arms in relation to the outer ring measure is the inverse of that of the outer and inner ring measures).

(c) The armpit arcs combine two circular arcs with beguiling simplicity. The inner segments of the armpits have centres at the intersections of the diagonals of the large quadrants (the same points as those that set the radius of the inner ring); their radii are the difference between those of the outer and inner circles of the ring. Also, the central square of the east face has its corners already set by intersections of the inner arcs of the armpits with diagonals of the quadrants.

(d) Semicircular arcs the size of the outer ring can be sketched when creating the underlying square (Fig. 20.1c), or they can be reset as arcs with centres at midpoints of the four sides of the underlying square: their paths are followed for the outer segment of the armpits (between the inner and outer circles of the ring). Also, the small circle enclosing the seven bosses at the centre of the cross can be plotted from points already in place.

If this plan were to be laid on an appropriate photograph of the east face of the Kells Tower Cross, there would be a good fit everywhere that it retains full measures – everywhere, that is, *except* the armpit configurations, which have been altered to accommodate the wider dimension of the lower cross-shaft; they have also been carved with less than average symmetry. The plan, though, matches some easily ignored aspects of the carved design, for example the original place where the arc ended at the join of cross-arm and armpit in the lower right quadrant. It shows, too, the extent of erosion, as well as the slight departure from symmetrical regularity, particularly in the outer elements of the arms.

Muiredach's Cross at Monasterboice (Fig. 20.9) is less than simple in two ways. Like the Kells Tower Cross, its shaft is tapered, again skewing slightly the symmetry of the re-entrant arcs, and with them the roll devices at the centres of these arcs. But unlike the radical confinement of ratios for the Tower Cross design, the plan of Muiredach's Cross uses a combination of √2, √3, √5 (as well as √4, which of course is 2) to set its proportions (Fig. 20.10). The transverse measure of the arms (Fig. 20.10a) is the same as that found in the two crosses at Castledermot (Figs 20.1, 20.3), based on √2. The arm length is a function of √3 (Fig. 20.10b), the same as Duleek North Cross.

The ring measure seems almost surely to be a function of √5 in one of its less common derivatives, the inner circle being the inverse of √φ in relation to the outer circle (φ represents the 'golden section' ratio); it is fundamental to the design of the Trier Gospels 'tetramorph' page, and occurs only seldom elsewhere (Stevick 1994, 133–36). The ratio √φ is only one step beyond φ in geometric derivation: in Fig. 20.10c, step 1 sets φ in relation to a quadrant of the square, step 2 sets √φ from that, and step 3 derives its inverse. (The radii of the armpit arcs reach to half the radius measure of the outer circle of the ring.)

The re-entrant arcs (Fig. 20.10d) have their centres and radii based on the same ratio that set the arm measure (Fig. 20.10a) – until those centres were shifted slightly to accommodate the asymmetry of the tapered shaft; in fact, the arcs are a bit too small to connect properly to the ring and cross *unless* the shaft is widened and their centres are shifted. The

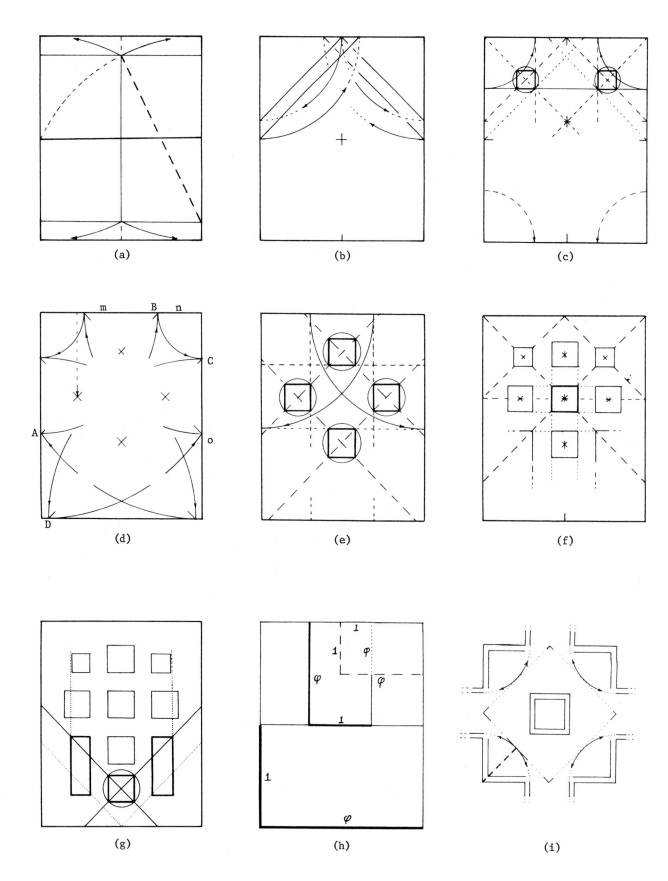

Fig. 20.6 *Constructing the primary dimensions of the Lindisfarne Gospels (London, British Library, MS Cotton Nero D.IV, fol. 2v)*

Fig. 20.7 *Tower Cross, Kells, Co. Meath. (Photograph: Dúchas, The Heritage Service, Ireland)*

rolls at the centre of the armpit curves are located asymmetrically, as well, but are consistent with the shifts in centres of the arcs.

Earlier, we rotated a drawing by a quarter turn to find identical ratios in the arm length and ring diameter of a stone cross and the frame extensions of a well known cross-page (Figs 20.2*b*, 20.6*a*). Rotating a drawing for the arm length and ring diameter of Muiredach's Cross (Fig. 20.10*b*) gives the frame extensions of the St John portrait in the Book of Kells, among others, in their appropriate orientation. From those frame dimensions derive all the other primary dimensions of the St John page (Stevick 1994, 231–33). In the vellum underlying this portrait is a puncture at its exact centre – not on any line in the portrait, nor at the centre of any element of decoration: it lies exactly at the centre of the design.[4] The design of the page cannot be created without computing that proceeds by graphic representation from that point, just as the design of Muiredach's Cross – like all the others – unfolds from a given dimension divided exactly at its centre.

Discussion

The premise of this paper has been that high cross design depends upon the methods of the geometer; specifically, the primary dimensions of particular crosses are developed in a continuous chain by constructive geometry proceeding from one given measure. The basic dimensions are expressible most naturally and accurately in relational terms as magnitudes and not as multitudes. The geometrical construction amounts to a graphic computation, in effect. This premise seems to be validated inductively by multiple replications of specific designs by the methods illustrated (see others in Stevick 1999). This is not the same as noting a geometrical ratio here, another one there, especially when there is a mix of primary dimensions and others such as those of panels enclosing surface decorations. It is critical that all the primary dimensions be linked first; further linking with dimensions of surface decorations may then follow on, if it can be demonstrated. It is this principle which distinguishes the analyses proposed here from those recently proposed by Kelly (1996).[5]

An obvious implication of the premise and the demonstrations based on it is that design of this kind is nearly impervious to number symbolism as it is usually understood, and as it is widely documented in medieval Latin Christianity. That tradition operates with numerals, i.e. in multitude measures of quantity which are integers (one, three, seven, twelve, forty . . .); or they are expressible as integer ratios even when given as sesquitertial, sesquialter, sesquioctave and such. A few quantities in magnitude measure of the crosses may be numerical – halves and sometimes thirds – but many are not. They are 'irrational', which is to say, the contrary of rational numbers, for being neither integers nor quotients of integers.

Not immediately obvious are other implications of the coherent geometry in these designs. These have to do chiefly with the conceptual difference of primary dimensions of the design from the decorative aspects, whether iconographic or only ornamental. The measures of the circles of the ring, the cross-arm thickness and length, the extensions of the shaft, the measure of the radii and location of the centres of the armpits – all of these are bound together in a closed system of extensional measure, with the consequence that its internal ratios will be non-representational in nature (being related only to each other). In contrast, a depiction of, say, the *Agnus Dei* or the sacrifice of Isaac is related to objects or events in a system of religious texts, which may have had any number of other representations. Decoration of this kind is representational and allusive, specific to a body of beliefs, history and dogma, and any

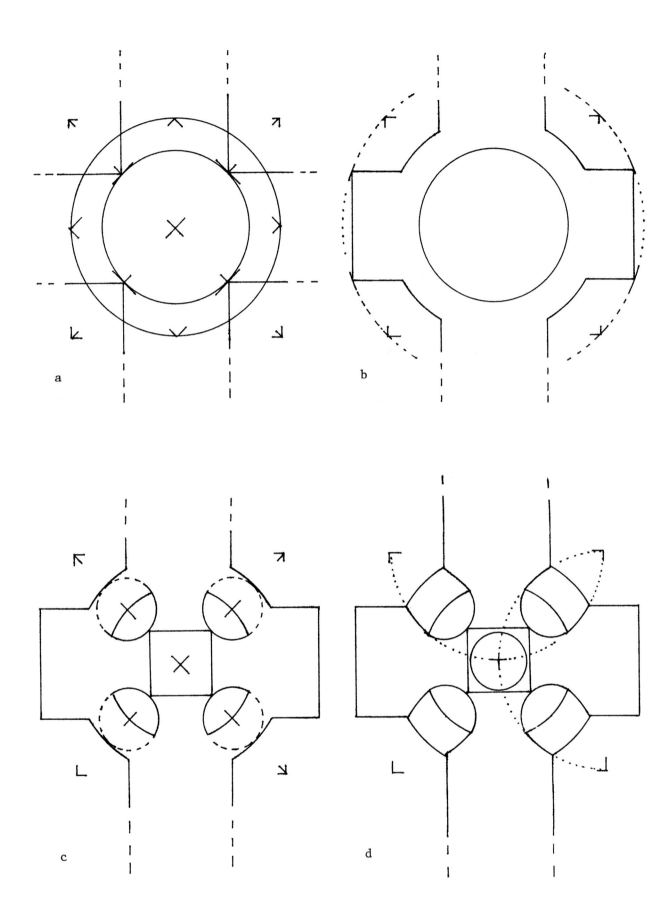

a

b

c

d

Fig. 20.8 *Constructing the primary dimensions of the Tower Cross, Kells*

Fig. 20.9 *Muiredach's Cross, Monasterboice, Co. Louth. (Photograph: Dúchas, The Heritage Service, Ireland)*

such item belongs to an essentially open set of representations of these topics, as well as all the others in the tradition. The geometrical abstract decorations such as interlace patterns, grilles, and circles-within-circles were presumably non-representational (non-signifying) when worked into cross designs but typically do not form a single closed system.

These differences in the designs of the cross shapes and the designs of their surface decorations in turn have implications for study of sources, influence, transmission and evolution in high cross design. When a depiction of Adam and Eve, for example, resembles other known depictions in orientation, posture, and attendant details, but not in still other respects, the resemblances and the differences are interpreted as locating that depiction in a scheme of transmission of the pictorial subject. Similarly, abstract patterns can be placed in an array of increasing complexity, which in turn may be interpreted as a developmental, usually simple chronological, sequence. The classic example is W. G. Collingwood's (1927) evolutionary integration of all the Northumbrian examples, which depends on the assumption that transmission was by imitation

of particular examples that had been observed, along with two other assumptions which are gratuitous. One is the notion that the earliest designs of a particular type are the best, the ones following inferior: 'nascent' stages are vigorous, later ones decadent. The second is that stone-cutters paid no heed to manuscript painters and metalwork designers. Otherwise we could not explain 'the taste or want of taste that hedged monumental art within such narrow lanes as we find it followed, while all the wealth of ornament in manuscripts and metal was open to any explorer who could have got his head above the fence' (Collingwood 1927, 184).

Whatever the uses – and abuses [6] – of this kind of approach to the historical study of the decoration of high crosses, it will be either inapposite or empty in the study of their basic forms. The primary dimensions of cross-plans do not offer these kinds of clustering and putative sequencing of data, so far as I can tell. Nothing makes $\sqrt{2}$ as a key ratio 'earlier' or 'later' than $\sqrt{3}$ or $\sqrt{5}$. Nor does a combination of any two of them necessarily follow the development of a design from a single one: it would not be easy to argue for the Kells Tower Cross being an earlier type than either the North Cross or the South Cross at

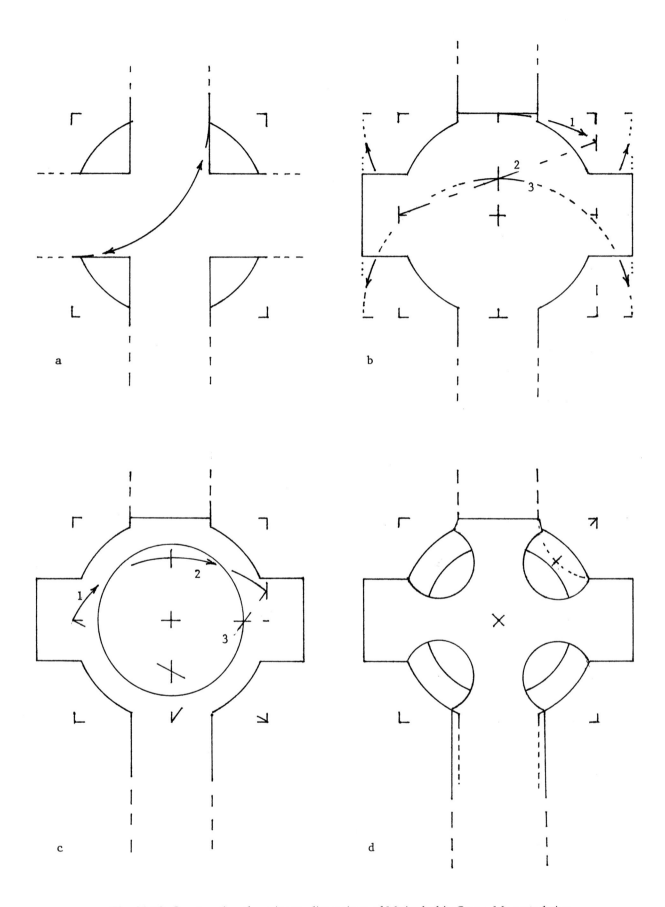

Fig. 20.10 *Constructing the primary dimensions of Muiredach's Cross, Monasterboice*

Castledermot. Ingenuity of design is something quite separate from single and compound geometrical ratios. Furthermore, the use of any of these ratios as the core of a proportional *schema* of a cross-page and a stone cross does not warrant connecting the two as model and copy, either direct or through intermediary instances. The ratios are too few and the variations are too many.

The cross shapes, I believe, would seldom have been drawn by imitation of particular observed models, whereas the pictorial images presumably were.[7] Rather, a cross shape would have been created anew each time, complete in itself, generated by constant principles of devising shapes that are symmetrical and commodular (*cf.* Mac Lean 1995). This would in no way preclude influence in some external respects – whether the ring should be slender or heavy, whether armpit curves would end at the inner circle of the ring, or the outer, or inside both. Or examples seen elsewhere could affect a decision on whether the arms of the cross should be heavier or lighter – or identical, as in the case of the North and South Crosses at Castledermot (Figs 20.2, 20.4). Neither would it preclude the transfer of the technique from rectangular framed designs on vellum (or stone or wood) to unframed circle-and-cross designs in wood or stone, or from metalwork to vellum, or from stone back to either of these. I am persuaded that the people who designed the stone crosses knew and used in their cross designs the same principles of creating form, as did those who created the forms of freestanding illuminations in the fine gospels manuscripts wrought in the same regions at about the same time. The cross designs, like the page designs, can be replicated from brief generative codes for magnitudes defined in the fundamentals of a geometer's art.

Notes

1 At the Fourth International Conference on Insular Art, transparencies of the drawing in Fig. 20.2 and the photograph in Fig. 20.3 were shown, first separately, then with the first superimposed on the second. Similar pairs of transparencies were shown for the other crosses discussed in this paper.

2 The wider measure of the lower shaft often found in high cross design is beyond the scope of this paper, but two observations will be made here. One is that while that measure was no doubt selected 'by eye', it must have been set out first by constructive geometry, just as the other primary dimensions were. For the Kells Tower Cross that measure seems to have been the complement of the measure selected for the Durrow Cross, $1-1/\sqrt{5}$ for the first, $1/\sqrt{5}$ for the second ($\sqrt{}$ = square root); from the underlying form illustrated in Fig. 20.1c the derivations of these measures are the same except for being in reverse directions.

3 Kelly (1996) provides measurements of several elements of this cross. Because her interest is in discovering the 'design structure' within the 'architecture' of Scottish and Irish crosses, she provides in fact two sets of measures. One set is 'Actual', based on fieldwork, and the other 'Ideal', inferred from 'blueprint' drawings proposed to illustrate the design features of this cross (measures given in cms). Both of these sets of measures for the Kells Tower Cross are given below (Table 1), alongside two others headed 'Linked' and 'Ratio'. The latter is commodular, computed as the ratios generated in Fig. 20.8 and listed here in modern numeral notation; the former gives cm measures computed from the 'Ratio' column on the basis of the outer circle of the ring being stipulated as 99. The ratios binding the design, it must be emphasised, are relations among magnitudes; the modern notation does not attempt to represent the processes by which they were developed in creating the design. The first five measures (140 to 35) form a single geometric progression.

Table 1 *Sets of measures for the Kells Tower Cross (in cm)*

Feature	Linked	Ratio	Ideal	Actual
Transom diagonal length	140	$99 \times \sqrt{2}$	–	140
Ring diameter, outer	99	Given	99	96/98.6
Ring diameter, inner	70	$99 \div \sqrt{2}$	70	70.5/71
		$(99 \times \sqrt{2}) \div 2$		
Transom height	49.5*	$99 \div 2$	46.5	46.5/47
Hollowed angles, largest	35	$99 \div 2\sqrt{2}$	34.8	34 – 35
Hollowed angles, smallest	29	$99 \div 2+\sqrt{2}$	29	27 – 28.5
Square, centre head	29	$99 \times (2-\sqrt{2}) \div 2$	29	28.5 – 29
Circle around bosses	20.5	$99 \div 2 + 2\sqrt{2}$	20.5	21.5 – 22

* See text

4   This puncture is not detectable in any of the facsimiles and does not show on the face of the St John page because of the thick paint. On the reverse side it does not appear to the unaided eye. However, when the leaf is viewed from the reverse with normal room light behind it, a small pin-point of light shows through. (A great many punctures are visible in other parts of the leaf, many of them in the facsimiles as well, guiding intricate decorative patterns.) I am grateful to Dr Bernard Meehan for permission to examine this portion of the manuscript in September 1996, with the assistance of Jane Maxwell.

5   For the Kells Tower Cross, Kelly notes the relation of the armpit inner curves to the outer circle of the ring, and to the central square of the cross face – the same relations generated here in Fig. 20.8c. However, she constructs an 'alternate explanation', taking 'the height of the transom' (the transverse measure of the cross-arm) as 'the basis of the geometrical layout'. This approach computes some larger measures from smaller ones (not the practical method of an artisan), omits the measure of the arm extension, and misses the key to commodular design – the complete binding of the primary dimensions in a proportional scheme (see note 3).

6   Stalley (1997) made wonderfully clear some of the pitfalls of a strict evolutionary interpretation of cross designs.

7   Abstract decorative patterns fall between cross shapes and images in this respect.

References

COLLINGWOOD, W. G. 1927, *Northumbrian Crosses of the Pre-Norman Age*. London.

KELLY, D. 1996, 'A sense of proportion: the metrical and design characteristics of some Columban high crosses', *J. Roy. Soc. Antiq. Ir.* 126, 108–46.

MAC LEAN, D. 1995, 'Technique and contact: carpentry-constructed Insular stone crosses', in C. Bourke (ed.), *From the Isles of the North. Early Medieval Art in Ireland and Britain* 167–75. Belfast.

STALLEY, R. 1997, 'The Tower Cross at Kells', in C. E. Karkov, R. T. Farrell and M. Ryan (eds), *The Insular Tradition*, 115–41. Albany.

STEVICK, R. 1994, *The Earliest Irish and English Bookarts: Visual and Poetic Forms before A.D. 1000*. Philadelphia.

STEVICK, R. 1999, 'Shapes of early sculptured crosses of Ireland', *Gesta* 38, 3–21.

21   Two Shrine Fragments from Kinneddar, Moray

Penny Dransart

The work reported here forms part of a larger pro-gramme of research on a collection of stones known in the literature as Drainie (Stuart 1856, 40; Allen 1903, III, 124, 142–49; Mack 1997, 142, addendum). Here they are considered under the old parish name of Kinneddar. Kinneddar was the location of an early stone castle and cathedral, as well as an early medi-eval site. In 1845 it was reported that a cist cemetery underlay ramparts or a ringwork, indicating that Kinneddar is a multi-period site (NSA 1845, 151–53). The castle seems to have been levelled during the nineteenth century. Resistivity surveys have suc-ceeded in locating the sites of both the castle (the Bishop's Palace) and the former cathedral/parish church (Aspinall, Bogdan and Dransart 1995).

Kinneddar is not the only site that was to become associated with the bishops of Moray at which Pictish stones were found. Birnie is also an ancient ecclesiastical centre with a Class I stone, and several Class III stones (now lost) (Allen 1903, III, 118–19, 156–57). At Elgin, a Class II stone was found 'a little to the north-east of the old church of St Giles' (Stuart 1856, 8); it has been placed in the cathedral. Kin-neddar is unusual in being associated with stones in all three classes of Romilly Allen's classification (Allen 1903, II, 4).

In the past, Kinneddar was situated on the shore of a sea loch, on the edge of a raised ridge which runs from Burghead to Roseisle and Covesea bet-ween the sea and Loch Spynie (Small 1976, 118–19). It had a lochside location like the monastery at Iona (Lochan Mór). The site of Iona was also protected by a vallum or rampart (RCAHMS 1982, 36–9). Early religious communities in north-western Europe were usually sited within a stone or earthwork enclosure, sometimes inside an already existing fortification (RCAHMS 1982, 12; Swan 1985, 97–100; Blair 1992, 231–35). On the Tarbat peninsula, an enclosure ditch has been located at Portmahomack (Harden 1995,

226). A similar arrangement might have existed at Kinneddar, but here the situation has been com-plicated by the building of the bishop's palace and a cathedral of cruciform shape on top of the site.

The discussion of two probable shrine fragments in this paper highlights stylistic parallels with St Andrews. MacQuarrie demonstrates that a Pictish royal founder established the religious community of St Andrews, and he suggests that in the eighth century, the founder transferred the episcopal residence to St Andrews from Abernethy or from Nechton son of Derilei's church of St Peter (Mac-Quarrie 1992, 120). From the evidence discussed here, it is possible to suggest that Kinneddar was also a royal foundation and perhaps the residence of an early bishop, although the first historically documented bishop of Moray is in 1120 (ibid., 133). The two Kinneddar fragments presented here for-med part of the religious equipment of a religious community. They display figurative and non-figur-ative imagery respectively, and they give some indication of the character of the stones recovered from the site.

The conventional use of the term 'sarcophagus' is perhaps misleading when applied to these Pictish stone structures. Charles Thomas prefers the term 'shrine' in his discussions of the sculptured stones from St Ninian's Isle and Papil (Thomas 1973, 20; 1983). The type of monument I have in mind is unlike the elaborately decorated sarcophagus from Govan, which measures 2.1m long, and would have been suitable for burying a deceased person in a supine position with the legs extended (Ritchie 1994, 147). In contrast, shrines often consist of four corner posts or blocks, which were set into the ground and supported the four side panels. Corner posts have been identified at various places including Iona, St Ninian's Isle, Papil and Portmahomack.[1] Corner blocks are also widely distributed; they are known

Fig. 21.1 *The David stone from Kinneddar, Elgin Museum 1855.1.14. (Copyright: T. E. Gray)*

from Burghead, Monifieth and St Andrews. Similar corner-block structures have been reported from Kilnaruane, Bantry and Kildrenagh, Valencia Island in Ireland, but Michael Herity sits on the fence by calling them 'tomb-shrines' (Herity 1993, fig. 23.5). Often the shrines have survived in a fragmentary condition. Where the evidence allows, the shrines are shorter, wider and deeper than the Govan sarcophagus. The Papil side panel is '3 feet 4 inches' (approximately 1m) in length (Moar and Stewart 1943–44, 92), while the internal dimensions of the St Andrews shrine are 1.55m long, by 0.9m wide, by 0.7m deep (Henderson 1998a, 20–1).[2] These structures were evidently not designed for containing the complete, extended burial of a person.

The David stone

The first Kinneddar fragment is carved in high relief (Fig. 21.1). It depicts a standing figure dressed in classical style clothing; the upper part of the body and the feet of the figure have not survived. The figure is evidently that of David, who is shown wrenching apart the jaws of a lion with his bare hands. The similarities between this fragment and the long panel of the St Andrews sarcophagus are numerous. In both, the figure is presented frontally, and the lion in profile. David holds the lower jaw of the lion in his right hand with the thumb in the lion's

mouth, while he grasps the upper jaw with his left hand. In both versions the lion is lithe, with the locks of the mane and the ribs carved in detail.[3]

Differences may be noted in the drapery flung over David's left forearm, since the cloth falls into folds depicted in a different manner on each stone, and in an extra length of drapery which can be seen below the raised foreleg of the lion at Kinneddar. Details in the scabbard hanging by David's thigh also vary, with grouped horizontal lines on the Kinneddar version and curvilinear decoration at St Andrews (Henderson 1998b, 162). However, in both cases the scabbard is attached by two straps.

In terms of composition, a striking difference may be noted. On the St Andrews panel, the sheep rescued by David appears above his right shoulder. The position of the sheep on the Kinneddar fragment was near David's left elbow, since the remains of two hind feet have survived. It is possible that the sheep was looking backwards toward David like its St Andrews counterpart – the feet are clearly pointing away from him (Fig. 21.2).[4] This has implications for the overall composition, since there is far more space to the right of David's left arm at Kinneddar than at St Andrews. This space is partially occupied by the lion's body, which adopts a slightly more horizontal posture than at St Andrews. Hence the Kinneddar David cannot have been placed at the extreme right of the panel as at St Andrews. Henderson's argument (1994, 71) that the St Andrews sarcophagus was

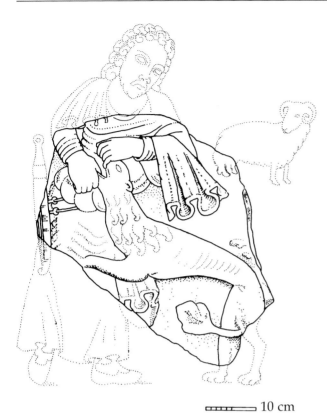

Fig. 21.2 *Partial, conjectural reconstruction of the David stone from Kinneddar. (Reconstruction: P. Dransart)*

placed at right-angles to the altar, with the figure of David wrenching apart the jaws of the lion nearest the altar itself, cannot necessarily be applied to Kinneddar, unless the composition was executed as a mirror image. In that case, the St Andrews sarcophagus might have been placed to the left of the altar, and the Kinneddar one to the right.

David is carved in high relief on both St Andrews and Kinneddar. They are standing figures dressed in classical-style clothing. Romilly Allen observed that the scene is likely to be confused with the reference to Samson rending the jaws of the lion in Judges 14:5–6 (Allen 1992, 203–4). Hence Pictish (and also Irish artists) incorporated images of a sheep or harp to indicate the presence of David rather than Samson. However, there are Byzantine or Syrian silks dating from the sixth to eighth centuries that have survived in western treasuries which are thought to show Samson. A fragment from Chur, Switzerland (Schmedding 1978, 85–8) shows Samson grasping the lion's head firmly with both hands.[5] He struggles with the animal by placing his knee over its back. The Kinneddar lion is a much more gracile creature than the lion of the woven silks, and David is shown effortlessly pressing down the lower jaw with his right hand and pulling up the upper jaw with his left.

Isabel Henderson has observed a similar use of the right thumb in an illuminated initial depicting David and the lion in the Vespasian Psalter (London, British Library, Cotton Vespasian A.I, fol. 53; Alexander 1978, illus. 144; Henderson 1986, pl. 5.4b). This Canterbury manuscript has been dated to the second quarter of the eighth century (Alexander 1978, 55), not long before the date Henderson proposes for the St Andrews sarcophagus. Although the Vespasian David uses his right thumb in a similar fashion to the Kinneddar and St Andrews Davids, the overall position of the hands is dissimilar. Other differences should be noted. David is clean shaven, unlike the St Andrews version, where he is bearded. Also, the Vespasian lion is a squat, stocky beast, indeed much more stocky than is the case with the Syrian silks. In contrast, the St Andrews and Kinneddar lions are lithe, almost exaggeratedly so in the case of the latter.

In this respect, the Kinneddar lion belongs to a pictorial form which serves as the symbol of St Mark in late seventh- and early eighth-century illuminated gospels. A rampant lion with an extremely narrow groin appears in the Echternach Gospels (*ibid.*, illus. 56). The treatment of the mane is comparable with Kinneddar, although the manuscript lion has the whole of its body covered with stylised locks of hair, and not just the neck and shoulders. Similar lions occur in other manuscripts, such as London, British Library, Cotton MS Otho C.V, fol. 27 (*ibid.*, illus. 57), the Book of St Chad (Lichfield, Cathedral Library, Gospel Book; *ibid.*, illus. 80), and Trier, Domschatz, Codex 61, fol. 1v (*ibid.*, illus. 114). All these lions are of the so-called 'terrestrial' type which can be traced back to the Book of Durrow (*ibid.*, 42). They are different from the winged lion symbol in the Book of Armagh, which is dated by inscription to *c.* 807 (*ibid.*, illus. 230). However, it should be noted that the Armagh lion retains the exaggeratedly narrow groin of the earlier manuscripts and also of Kinneddar.

Henderson dates the St Andrews sarcophagus to the middle of the eighth century, and associates the kingly figure of David with the Pictish monarch Oengus, son of Fergus, who died in 761 (Henderson 1986, 101; 1994, 80). In her interpretation, David is portrayed as King of Israel, and precursor of Christ the Saviour of human souls. Henderson stresses the importance of understanding the imagery as an expression of secular kingship (Henderson 1994, 79–81, 92–3). MacQuarrie interprets the figure of David as the portrait of a Pictish king on a shrine designed to hold the relics of a saint as important as St Andrew (MacQuarrie 1992, 119).[6]

In Leslie Alcock's interpretation of the scene, more emphasis is given to the illustration of God's saving grace and the presentation of David as a 'type' for the expected Messiah rather than David's secular position of authority (Alcock 1995, 1). Both

Henderson's and Alcock's interpretations reveal different levels of meaning that may be perceived in the David imagery. However, there is a more profound level of meaning that refers to the theme of the Resurrection of the body. David's plea in Psalm 22:21 comes to mind: 'Save me from the lion's mouth'. The image invoked is that of releasing saved souls from the maw of hell. The David iconography of the Kinneddar and St Andrews stones might contain a reference to the Harrowing of Hell, a visual theme that deals with Christ's descent into 'the lower regions of the earth' in order to rescue the righteous (Ephesians 4:9). The concept is included in fourth-century creeds; the earliest surviving depiction of the Harrowing of Hell is a fresco in Santa Maria Antiqua, Rome, dating from 705–7.[7] In later versions, St John the Baptist and the kings David and Solomon are included in the iconography.

Neuman de Vegvar (1997, 172–82) has explored the Christological references expressed by the lion symbol of the Evangelist Mark in the Echternach Gospels, which so resembles the Kinneddar lion.[8] She considers that the image of the lion evoked the presence of Christ in the minds of the viewers. Describing the Echternach lion as 'an upward-leaping lion the color of the rising sun' (*ibid.*, 177), she regards the image as an expression possibly of the Resurrection, but also a visualisation of the dual human and divine states of Christ. He was human and therefore constrained by death; equally he was divine and free of death. In the Kinneddar carving, a royal human personage is combined with the figure of a lion. The Christological references conveyed by images of David and a lion interact in a complex visual theme that reinforces the message of the dual nature of Christ, and of the Resurrection of the body as Christ releases souls from the jaws of hell. This imagery helps strengthen the conjecture that this admittedly fragmentary Kinneddar stone is a piece of a shrine, like its counterpart in St Andrews.

A hybrid shrine panel

More has survived of the second monument discussed here, and there is no doubt that it was a shrine panel (Figs 21.3, 21.4). This large, shaped panel, which now consists of four adjoining fragments, was recovered incomplete when a grave was dug towards the eastern centre of the cemetery (Corner nd). If the piece was originally symmetrical in design, the top edge would have formed a wide, rectilinear U-shape. There are projections at each end of the bottom edge, but the one on the left is more pronounced. Thus the piece probably served as a side of a shrine, with the projections inserted into the floor/ground. The overall size of the panel (height 650mm,

width 890mm, depth 75mm [at top], 90mm [at bottom]) is fairly similar to the surviving end panel of the St Andrews sarcophagus. At the back, a vertical groove runs from the base of each projection, towards the top (Fig. 21.5). The complete groove has been filled with modern cement; it was possibly 500 or 520mm long. At the bottom, it was 92mm wide and 25mm deep. The incomplete groove measures 105mm in width and 35mm deep.[9] This Kinneddar shrine was highly unusual as the 'corner blocks' and 'side panel' were carved in one piece. In Thomas's typology, it is of a hybrid form (1998, 84–5). The panel is grooved, like Thomas's Jedburgh type, but it was carved to resemble the separate end panel and corner blocks of a shrine such as St Andrews.

The surface of the stone is worn, but it can be seen that the design is arranged in three areas of low relief. The Reverend Corner (nd) noted that these areas are parallelograms rather than rectangles. This is a feature of the highest quality Pictish carving, also evident in the main panel of the St Andrews sarcophagus (Foster 1998a, 62). Romilly Allen's surface key-pattern no. 958 is used to fill the tall upright panels at the left and right. The central panel is wider than it is tall. It is filled with Allen's spiral-pattern no. 1029, consisting of two-coil spirals combined with straight-line spirals at the corners (Allen 1903, II). Narrow strips of plain dressed stone separate the three panels.

This tripartite organisation of the design is reminiscent of a wide rectangular panel from Rosemarkie (Groam House Museum ROMGH 1992.3; Allen 1903, III, fig. 83). The design consists of a central area of two-coil spirals flanked by Allen's surface key-pattern no. 974, another straight-line spiral design which is found at Kinneddar (Elgin Museum 1855.1.9, 1978.153 and 1978.155),[10] as well as at Burghead, Rosemarkie and Tarbat. On the Rosemarkie panel, there are no undecorated areas of stone in between the areas of key patterns as at Kinneddar. The surface key-pattern no. 958 is also used to cover the face of another wide panel at Rosemarkie (ROMGH 1992.2; Henderson 1990, no pagination), surrounded on three sides by a narrow border design. This surface key-pattern also occurs on three stones at Burghead (Allen 1903, III, figs 140, 142–3). In spite of these similarities, it is noteworthy that key-pattern no. 958 is more loosely conceived on the Kinneddar stone, where more background is visible between the strands of the design than the tightly packed patterning of the Rosemarkie and Burghead slabs. These strands are finished in a more rounded relief than on ROMGH 1992.2 at Rosemarkie (Henderson 1990), and Burghead nos 9 and 12 (Allen 1903, III, figs 140, 142). At Rosemarkie and Burghead, the design is very regular indeed, but the carving consists merely of punched lines of peck

Fig. 21.3 *The shrine panel from Kinneddar, Elgin Museum 1939.6. (Copyright: T. E. Gray)*

marks, which have not been abraded to present a smooth surface. Although the relief on the Kinneddar stone is not high, the carving corresponds with the category known as 'modelled technique' employed in the *British Academy Anglo-Saxon Sculpture Corpus*, since the strands have a rounded appearance and there is flat, smooth ground between them (Cramp 1984, xxii). In contrast, the Rosemarkie and Burghead stones were executed in a punched outline 'grooved technique' (*ibid.*, xxii). The impressive but monotonous regularity of ROMGH 1992.2 contrasts with the more organic flow of the Kinneddar sarcophagus panel.

The characteristic interplay in the transformation of key-pattern no. 958 from straight-line to two-coil spirals as used at Kinneddar and Rosemarkie is a feature which occurs beyond the Moray Firth and the Black Isle. Other instances occur at St Andrews (Hay Fleming 1931, fig. 8, no. 51) and Lindisfarne no. 5 (Cramp 1984, pl. 191 no. 1057). Two-coil spirals are characteristic of a stone from Lemanaghan, Ireland (Crawford 1911, 156).[11] This panel is comparable with a related fragment from Kinneddar (Elgin Museum 1855.1.10; Allen 1903, III, fig. 145).

Notwithstanding the widespread distribution of such key-patterning, there is a striking feature which

⌐_____⌐10 cm

Fig. 21.4 *Conjectural reconstruction of the shrine panel from Kinneddar. (Reconstruction: P. Dransart)*

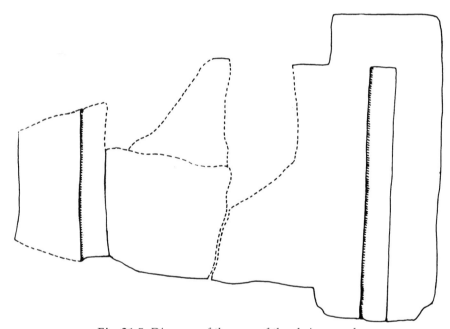

Fig. 21.5 *Diagram of the rear of the shrine panel*

is shared by the two Rosemarkie slabs (ROMGH 1992.2, 1992.3) and the Kinneddar panel. In these three pieces, round pellets have been inserted within the triangular spaces of the key-patterns. When *The Early Christian Monuments of Scotland* was published at the beginning of the twentieth century, Allen noted that Rosemarkie no. 2 (ROMGH 1992.3; Allen 1903, III, fig. 83) was the only instance in Scotland of a key-pattern with pellets. He mentioned parallel occurrences: the cross at Carew, Pembrokeshire (Nash-Williams 1950, no. 303) and the Gospel of

MacDurnan (London, Lambeth Palace, MS 1370; Allen 1903, III, 86). In another publication, Allen presented two further Welsh examples, on the cross at Nevern, Pembrokeshire (Nash-Williams 1950, no. 360), and on a cross-shaft from Llanfynydd, Carmarthenshire (*ibid.*, no. 159; Allen 1993, 191, 261). These Welsh crosses are dated from the late tenth to the eleventh centuries (Nash-Williams 1950; Redknap 1991, 22, 57, 66). However, the MacDurnan Gospel Book has been dated to the second half of the ninth century because it contains an inscription which associates it with Maelbrigt MacDurnan, Abbot of Armagh (Alexander 1978, 86). These stylistic parallels suggest that the second Kinneddar shrine was not contemporary with the first.

Concluding comments

Michael Herity (1984) has proposed that there are three main elements that formed the focus of western ecclesiastical foundations: a cross-slab, a saint's tomb or bed *(leaba)*, and a rectangular oratory. If the third element existed at Kinneddar, then the oratory probably lies beneath the cruciform church that we detected in our resistivity survey in the churchyard. However, we do have evidence for cross-slabs and the shrines discussed here for containing the relics of a saint or saints. Traditionally Kinneddar was the place where an Irish saint and miracle worker, known locally as St Gerardine, and as the Confessor Gervadius in the Aberdeen Breviary, 'had a stone bed' (Forbes 1872, 354; see also Cooper 1893).[12] His date in the Calendar is 8 November. Bishop Forbes (1872, 354–55) suggested that he died in 934, because the events contained in a legend in the Aberdeen Breviary might be taken to indicate the invasion of the north by 'Athelstane'. However, the evidence is circumstantial, and it is possible that he lived in the sixth or seventh centuries, the period that produced most of the Irish saints. If the David panel formed part of a shrine, a tenth-century date would be too late to suggest that Gerardine's relics were placed inside it.

Relics of the saints played a special role in early Christian understandings of the resurrection. Emerging in the late third century, the cult of saints was an important strategy for disseminating Christianity. Peter Brown wrote that Christians brought with them in their travels the 'presence' of the saints, '[w]hether this was unimaginably far to the north in Scotland ... or on the edge of the desert ...' (Brown 1981, 12). It would seem that Kinneddar had the relics of at least one very important saint for whom the shrine with the David imagery was designed, perhaps in the eighth century, possibly at the instigation of a royal patron. This shrine may have been replaced, perhaps in the late ninth or tenth century, by the later shrine with its non-figurative imagery and its unusual construction. Alternatively, the second shrine may have been erected to house the relics of another saint or saints.

Acknowledgements

I am grateful to the Moray Society for giving me permission to examine the Kinneddar stones, to Isabel Henderson for her advice and suggestions, and to the British Academy for financial support towards the work.

Notes

1 For a comprehensive listing, discussion and relevant literature, see Thomas (1998, 96).
2 I wish to thank Sally Foster for supplying these measurements in advance of the publication of the recent book on the St Andrews sarcophagus (Foster 1998).
3 Ferguson (1956, 225) thought that the ribs were absent on the Kinneddar lion, but they are in fact present.
4 The conjectural reconstruction is based on one published in Aspinall, Bogdan and Dransart (1995). An alternative one by Ian G. Scott has been published by Henderson (1998b, fig. 35). I take the curved line at the top of the fragment to be the remains of the garment neckline, whereas Scott takes it to be the chin of David – in which case David does not have a neck.
5 For other examples of these silks see Muthesius (1997, 67–8). The position of the knee over the animal's back has a parallel in the depiction of the Persian god Mithras sacrificing the bull (Henderson 1998b, 120). David, accompanied by a sheep, is shown at the end of a cross-arm with his knee on the lion's back on both the Tower and Market crosses at Kells. However, Stalley suggests a date of *c.* 900 for the former (Stalley 1997, 135). Harbison (1992) dates them to the second quarter of the ninth century, and Edwards (1986) to the mid-ninth century.
6 For a discussion of the royal associations, and literature therein, see Foster (1998a, 42–3).
7 *The Oxford Companion to Art* stresses that the Harrowing of Hell superseded the Resurrection in the iconography of the Greek church, and that it was more commonly employed in the east (Osborne 1970, 525). Representations of the Harrowing of Hell in western art included medieval mystery plays. When the theme gained currency in Britain is not known.
8 On lion imagery in Insular art, see also Edwards (1998, 113).
9 I wish to thank Susan Bennett of Elgin Museum for making it possible for me to see the back of the stones.
10 Stuart (1856) included 1855.1.9 as no. 12 in his pl. 129. Allen's identification of the key pattern on it is tentative and he did not illustrate it (no. 12 in Allen and Anderson 1903, III, 148). The other two stones have not, to my knowledge, been published.
11 I wish to thank Conleth Manning for drawing this parallel to my attention.
12 I wish to thank Nicholas Bogdan for the Cooper reference.

References

ALCOCK, L. 1995, 'What is David doing to a lion?', *Pictish Arts Soc. J.* 7, 1–2.
ALEXANDER, J. J. G. 1978, *Insular Manuscripts 6th to the 9th Century. A Survey of Manuscripts Illuminated in the British Isles,* Vol. 1. London.

ALLEN, J. R. 1903, Part II, General results arrived at from the archaeological survey of the Early Christian Monuments of Scotland; Part III, Archaeological survey and descriptive list, with illustrations of the Early Christian Monuments of Scotland. In J. R. Allen and J. Anderson, *The Early Christian Monuments of Scotland*. Edinburgh.

ALLEN, J. R. 1992 [1887], *The High Crosses of Ireland*. Facsimile reprint. Felinfach.

ALLEN J. R. 1993 [1904], *Celtic Art in Pagan and Christian Times*. London.

ASPINALL, A., BOGDAN, N. Q. and DRANSART, P. Z. 1995, Kinneddar. *Discovery Excav. Scotl*. 1995, 35–6.

BLAIR, J. and SHARPE, R. (eds) 1992, *Pastoral Care before the Parish*. Leicester.

BLAIR, J. 1992, 'Anglo-Saxon minsters: a topographical review', in Blair and Sharpe (eds), 226–66.

BROWN, P. 1981, *The Cult of the Saints: its Rise and Function in Latin Christianity*. London.

COOPER, J. 1893, St Gerardine, *Trans. Aberdeen Ecclesiastical Soc*. 8, 105–16.

CORNER, M. M. nd, Kinneddar as an early Christian settlement. Unpublished MS, National Monuments Record of Scotland, MS/131.

CRAMP, R. 1984, *Corpus of Anglo-Saxon Stone Sculpture*. Vol. 1 *County Durham and Northumberland*. Oxford.

CRAWFORD, H. S. 1911, 'The early slabs at Lemanaghan, King's County', *J. Roy. Soc. Antiq. Ir*. 41 (2), 151–56.

EDWARDS, N. 1986, 'The South Cross, Clonmacnois', in J. Higgitt (ed.), *Early Medieval Sculpture in Britain and Ireland* (= BAR Brit. Ser. 152), 23–48. Oxford.

EDWARDS, N. 1998, 'A group of shafts and related sculpture from Clonmacnoise and its environs', in H. A. King (ed.), *Clonmacnoise Studies* 1, 101–18. Dublin.

FERGUSON, W. 1956, 'Note on a fragment of sculptured stone in Elgin Museum', *Proc. Soc. Antiq. Scotl*. 88, 225.

FORBES, A. P. 1872, *Kalendars of Scottish Saints…* . Edinburgh.

FOSTER, S. M. 1998a, 'Discovery, recovery, context and display', in Foster (ed.), 36–62.

FOSTER, S. M. (ed.) 1998b, *The St Andrews Sarcophagus: A Pictish Masterpiece and its International Connections*. Dublin.

HARBISON, P. 1992, *The High Crosses of Ireland. An Iconographical and Photographic Survey*, 3 vols (= Römisch-Germanisches Zentralmuseum, Forschungsinstitut für Vor- und Frühgeschichte Monographien 17, 1–3). Bonn.

HARDEN, J. 1995, 'A potential archaeological context for the early Christian sculptured stones from Tarbat, Easter Ross', in C. Bourke (ed.), *From the Isles of the North. Early Medieval Art in Ireland and Britain*, 221–27. Belfast.

HAY FLEMING, D. 1931, *St Andrews Cathedral Museum*. Edinburgh.

HENDERSON, I. M. 1986, 'The 'David Cycle' in Pictish art', in J. Higgitt (ed.), *Early Medieval Sculpture in Britain and Ireland* (= B.A.R. Brit. Ser. 152), 87–123. Oxford.

HENDERSON, I. 1990, *The Art and Function of Rosemarkie's Pictish Monuments*. Rosemarkie.

HENDERSON, I. 1994, 'The insular and continental context of the St Andrews sarcophagus', in B. Crawford (ed.), *Scotland in Dark Age Europe*, 71–102. St Andrews.

HENDERSON, I. 1998a, 'Descriptive catalogue of the surviving parts of the monument', in Foster (ed.), 19–35.

HENDERSON, I. 1998b, '*Primus inter pares*: the St Andrews sarcophagus and Pictish sculpture', in Foster (ed.), 97–167.

HERITY, M. 1984, 'The layout of Irish early Christian monasteries', in P. Ní Chatháin and M. Richter (eds), *Ireland and Europe: The Early Church*, 105–16. Stuttgart.

HERITY, M. 1993, 'The forms of the tomb-shrine of the founder saint in Ireland', in R. M. Spearman and J. Higgitt (eds), *The Age of Migrating Ideas. Early Medieval Art in Northern Britain and Ireland*, 188–195. Edinburgh, Stroud.

KARKOV, C. E., FARRELL, R. T. and RYAN, M. (eds) 1997, *The Insular Tradition*. Albany.

MACK, A. 1997, *Field Guide to Pictish Symbol Stones*. Balgavies, Forfar.

MACQUARRIE, A. 1992, 'Early Christian religious houses in Scotland: foundation and function', in Blair and Sharp (eds), 110–33.

MOAR, P. and STEWART, J. 1943–44, 'Newly discovered sculptured stones from Papil, Shetland', *Proc. Soc. Antiq. Scotl*. 78, 91–9.

MUTHESIUS, A. 1997, *Byzantine Silk Weaving AD 400 to AD 1200*. Vienna.

NASH-WILLIAMS, V. E. 1950, *The Early Christian Monuments of Wales*. Cardiff.

NEUMAN DE VEGVAR, C. 1997, 'The Echternach lion: a leap of faith', in Karkov, Farrell and Ryan (eds), 167–88.

NSA 1845, *New Statistical Account of Scotland: Elginshire*. Edinburgh.

OSBORNE, H. (ed.) 1970, *The Oxford Companion to Art*. Oxford.

RCAHMS 1982, Royal Commission on the Ancient and Historical Monuments of Scotland, *Argyll, An Inventory of the Monuments*, Vol. 4, *Iona*. Edinburgh.

REDKNAP, M. 1991, *The Christian Celts. Treasures of Late Celtic Wales*. Cardiff.

RITCHIE, A. 1994, *Govan and its Early Medieval Sculpture*. Far Thrupp, Stroud.

SCHMEDDING, B. 1978, *Mittelalterliche Textilien in Kirchen und Klöstern der Schweiz*. Bern.

SMALL, A. 1976, 'Iron Age and Pictish Moray', in D. Omand (ed.) *The Moray Book*. Edinburgh.

STALLEY, R. 1997, 'The tower cross at Kells', in Karkov, Farrell and Ryan (eds), 115–41.

STUART, J. (ed.) 1856, *Sculptured Stones of Scotland*, Vol. 1. Aberdeen, Edinburgh.

SWAN, L. 1985, 'Monastic proto-towns in early Ireland: the evidence of aerial photography, plan analysis and survey', in H. B. Clarke and A. Simms (eds), *The Comparative History of Urban Origins in Non-Roman Europe*, I (= B.A.R. Int. Ser. 255), 77–102. Oxford.

THOMAS, C. 1973, 'Sculptured stones and crosses from St Ninian's Isle and Papil', in A. Small, C. Thomas and D. M. Wilson, *St Ninian's Isle and its Treasure*, 8–44. London.

THOMAS, C. 1983, 'The double shrine 'A' from St Ninian's Isle, Shetland', in A. O'Connor, and D. V. Clarke (eds), *From the Stone Age to the 'Forty-Five*, 285–92. Edinburgh.

THOMAS, C. 1998, 'Form and function', in Foster (ed.), 84–96.

22   The Date of the Aberlemno Churchyard Stone

Lloyd Laing

The Kirkton of Aberlemno stone, or Aberlemno 2, Angus, is justifiably considered to be one of the finest early medieval sculptures in Europe. In recent years there has been a growing tendency to see the stone as being one of the earliest, if not the first, of the surviving Class II Pictish sculptures, and to identify the battle scene on the reverse as a depiction of the battle of Nechtansmere fought between Bridei mac Bili and Ecgfrith of Northumbria in 685. This battle resulted in the death of Ecgfrith and the expulsion of the Angles from Pictland. This interpretation was first advanced by Graeme Cruickshank (1985; 1994; 1999), and has been followed, sometimes with a note of caution, by most later commentators, notably Ritchie (1989, 25), Laing and Laing (1993, 131), Sutherland (1994, 177) and Alcock (1993, 234); Isabel Henderson has been more cautious (1994, 51). If this were the case, and the Aberlemno stone can be assigned to a date not far removed from the battle, then it would be remarkable as the only commemorative monument of its kind in north-west Europe in the late seventh or early eighth century. In spite of the early date favoured recently, it might be noted that Radford (1942) dated it to the ninth century, Stevenson (1955, 115) to the mid-ninth, then subsequently to the late eighth (Stevenson 1971, 72), and Allen and Anderson (1903, 213) by implication to a date around 800.

Both sides of the stone are not necessarily contemporary, as Graeme Cruickshank (1994, 41) has noted. He has pointed out that 'If a case is to be made out for the Aberlemno battle scene being a representation of the Battle of Dunnichen, then the stone must be shown to date from the year 685 or not very long after' (*ibid.*). He has dated the battle-scene side of the slab to the 680s, and the cross-side to the 720s, on the grounds that the latter shows Northumbrian influence, notably from the Lindisfarne Gospels.

Aberlemno 2, reverse

The main feature on the back of the slab is the battle scene (Fig. 22.1). Before turning to consider the general affinities of this scene, it is worth looking at some details which may provide a clue to the date. These are the depictions of swords. The clearest of these is the outline sword apparently dropped by the figure at the top right. Although weathered, it can be seen that the sword has a down-turned lower guard and an up-curved profile to the pommel (Figs 22.1, 22.5d). A similar type of sword seems to be carried by the first of the advancing soldiers in the middle register on the left (Fig. 22.5e), and possibly (though the hilt is very eroded) is the type of sword represented discarded above the top left-hand figure in the battle scene.

In the ninth century English swords acquired guards that instead of projecting straight from the sword, as was the case with seventh- and eighth-century examples, curved downwards, the design sometimes being echoed by the reverse curve of the pommel (Davidson 1962, 63–4; Pollington 1996, 106–7). This design was taken up by the Danes, and developed further in Scandinavia. Pommels of this period have a lobed profile, and this type of sword persisted until after the Norman Conquest (and indeed appears to have survived late into the Middle Ages in the West Highlands of Scotland). In the ninth century the central lobe was more pronounced, but on tenth-century swords the profile is softer. The guards are of iron (the hilts are usually iron with inlays), and on the tenth-century swords the curve on the guard is less pronounced. A group of these late Saxon swords have silver pommels inlaid with niello and decorated in the 'Trewhiddle' style of late Saxon ornament. Among them is a sword from the River Witham at Fiskerton in Lincolnshire (Wilson 1965, 33–5) (Fig. 22.5f), an example from a stream

Fig. 22.1 Aberlemno 2, Angus: back. (Photograph: copyright T. E. Gray)

bed at Gilling Beck, Yorkshire (Watkin 1986) (Fig. 22.5h), one from the Palace of Westminster, London (Dunning and Evison 1961), one from Abingdon, Berkshire (Backhouse, Turner and Webster 1984, cat. no. 14) (Fig. 22.5g) and one from the River Seine (Wilson 1964, 166–67). Of these, the Gilling Beck, Abingdon and Seine swords have a high central peak, which appears to be the variety carried by the advancing soldier in the central register. This type has been seen as a late ninth-century form (*cf.* discussion in Webster and Backhouse 1991, 277). Davidson, following Wheeler, has assigned the swords with curved guards to the period 875–950, while also arguing for the survival of the type later (Davidson 1962, 63).

It may be noted that the same type of sword appears to be carried by a figure at the top right on the back of the slab from Nigg, Ross (Allen and Anderson 1903, fig. 81), though in the published drawing no pommel is indicated – I have not examined this detail myself, and it may well be that the pommel has been damaged. Isabel Henderson has noted the Nigg sword's similarity to those at Aberlemno, but has suggested that the Picts had their own form of sword hilts (Henderson 1998, 159). If this is the case, they must have anticipated developments in England and Scandinavia by half a century or more, and divergence in Pictish swords in this case seems at variance to the evidence afforded by the St Ninian's Isle chape, which is closely comparable to English designs.

Some other comparisons of details are useful for the scene on the back of Aberlemno 2. The type of pointed shield-boss found at Aberlemno can be matched in London, British Library, Harley MS 603, which, though a copy of a Carolingian manuscript of the Utrecht school produced at Canterbury around 1000, has been seen as English in points of detail. Folio 69r is particularly useful for comparison as is fol. 12, and Carver has suggested that all the details in this manuscript by hand 1F are native (Carver 1986, 129). Another battle scene in a late Anglo-Saxon manuscript can be seen in fol. 25r of London, British Library, Cotton Tiberius B.IV, of similar date.

Combat scenes are very rare in early medieval art, as indeed are any 'narrative' scenes which are not scriptural. The origins of the battle scene lie in Antique art – they are a feature of Roman battle sarcophagi, of which the Ludovisi Sarcophagus is a classic example, and they are also to be found on Roman public monuments, such as Trajan's Column. The battle scene can also be seen in another form in the fourth-century mosaics of Santa Maria Maggiore in Rome, and occasionally is found in Lombard art in Italy. There are no battle scenes elsewhere in the sculptural art of north-west Europe in the seventh

Fig. 22.2 *Aberlemno 2, Angus: front. (Photograph: copyright T. E. Gray)*

century; a mounted warrior appears on the famous Merovingian relief from Hornhausen, now seen to be part of a stone screen with other horsemen and figures from a church (Schmidt 1996, 296–97). This has been dated to the first half of the seventh century by German scholars, but the type of animal with interlocking jaws represented on the base has a long currency, and is apparent in the Book of Durrow in the second half of the century, or, in a variant form, on the porch of St Peter's church, Monkwearmouth, Co. Durham, of late seventh-century date. The Hornhausen relief is architectural sculpture, that is to say, not a free-standing monument, and may represent Christ as Warrior, rather than a secular combatant.

Fig. 22.3 *Aberlemno 2, Angus. Detail of back, showing swords. (Photograph: T. E. Gray)*

It has been cogently argued that the introduction of relief sculpture to Northumbria came about through the influence of Merovingian architectural sculpture in the late seventh century, the date currently assigned to the early frieze fragments at Hexham and the sculpture on the church of St Peter at Monkwearmouth (Bailey 1996a, 27–41).

The counterpart of the Hornhausen mounted warrior is apparent in metalwork, but again, with the possible exception of the horseman riding down the enemy on the Sutton Hoo helmet plaques, representations in metalwork are of isolated figures outside a narrative context. It is with the revival of interest in Late Antique art in the Carolingian period that the idea of a narrative battle scene becomes credible. Robert Stevenson drew attention to the occurrence of narrative in Carolingian fresco art, and was the first to see this as a possible inspiration for Aberlemno (Stevenson 1955, 114).

In Anglo-Saxon art the first occurrence of a secular warrior is on the Repton shaft, Derbyshire. The figure here has been identified by Biddle and Kjølbe-Biddle as a portrait of the Mercian king Æthelbald (died 757), and they have argued in favour of Carolingian inspiration (Biddle and Kjølbe-Biddle 1985). The figure carries a small round shield and is dressed in chain mail, which may be the case with some at least of the figures at Aberlemno.

Ann Carrington has discussed the use of the horseman motif in Pictish art (in the context of the Meigle sculptures), and has concluded that the model reached Pictland from Mercia, no earlier than the later eighth century, being ultimately derived from Antique sources (Carrington 1995, 34).

In terms of general style, the combat scene on Aberlemno 2 is best paralleled on the base of the Market Cross at Kells, where the warriors in some cases have shields with pointed umbos, similar to those on the Aberlemno stone (Harbison 1992, no. 126, fig. 338). It is to be noted that the apparently secular content of this scene at Kells is to be matched in the secular scenes on the other panels of the base of the Market Cross (notably a Pictish-looking hunt scene and mounted figures), and on the base of the Cross of Patrick and Columba (Henry 1964, pls 28, 30). A hunting scene is also to be found on the base of the South Cross at Castledermot, Co. Kildare

Fig. 22.4 *Aberlemno 2, Angus. Another view of the back, taken in different light, showing swords. (Photograph: copyright T. E. Gray)*

(Harbison 1992, fig. 977), which has been compared with a hunt scene on a stone at Cività Castellana in Italy (*ibid.*, fig. 978). Other examples of secular iconography appear on the base of the North Cross at Ahenny, Co. Tipperary (*ibid.*, fig. 17), and also on the base of the South Cross at Ahenny (*ibid.*, figs 28–9).

In his study of the iconography of the Irish high crosses, Harbison has pointed out that the details of the iconography of the Kells group of crosses can be matched very precisely in Pictland – he has matched details on the Market Cross at Kells with those on stones at Easterton of Roseisle, Kettins, St Vigeans 7, Dunkeld and Meigle, while details on the Cross of St Patrick and Columba can be matched at Burghead, Aberlemno 3, and Monifeith. These are not the only parallels, and Harbison has provided us with an impressive list of over a dozen Pictish monuments which display details matched very closely on Irish crosses (*ibid.*, 325–26).

Although the comparisons are generally well known, it has in the past been assumed that the main series of scripturally-decorated high crosses in

Ireland belongs to the tenth century rather than earlier, and that therefore the Pictish monuments pre-date them. The literature on the chronology is extensive, and has been usefully summarised by Stalley (1997). If it is accepted that Harbison is correct in assigning the main *floruit* of crosses to the period around the 830s or 840s, the chronological problems are diminished, and the Irish monuments may be viewed as models for the Pictish. Harbison has suggested that 'there would seem to be a reasonable case for suggesting that the eastern Scottish iconography came eastwards with St Columba's relics – perhaps to an already established centre at Dunkeld – sometime between 830 and 850, probably from Iona. However, in the absence of any surviving traces of the same iconography on Iona, it seems reasonable to assume that Iona was only the intermediary, and that it was Kells that was the real supplier' (Harbison 1992, 326).

Helmets appear on Irish high crosses, for example on the Cross of the Scriptures, Clonmacnoise, the Durrow Cross, Co. Offaly, the Drumcliff Cross, Co. Sligo, and the Cross of Muiredach, Monasterboice,

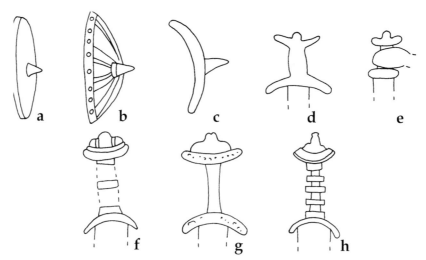

Fig. 22.5 Swords and shields depicted on Aberlemno 2, and some counterparts. (a) Harley 603, fol. 12 (Hand IB); (b) Harley 603, fol. 29 (Hand III); (c) Aberlemno 2; (d) engraved sword, Aberlemno 2; (e) sword carried by warrior, Aberlemno 2; (f) Witham, Lincolnshire, sword; (g) Abingdon, Berkshire, sword; (h) Gilling Beck, Yorkshire, sword. (Drawn by David Taylor; a, b after Carver 1986)

Co. Louth. The best parallel for the Aberlemno helmets can be found on the two soldiers at the base of the west face of the shaft at Durrow. Small round shields with central umbos are comparatively common on Irish crosses, and the spike-like form of the umbo, in keeping with Aberlemno 2, can be seen in the profile view of a shield on the base of the Market Cross at Kells (*ibid.*, fig. 338).

Before leaving the back of the Aberlemno stone, two other points are worth making. The first is that there appears to be a blank area at the base, which Allen and Anderson suggested may have been because earth was heaped up against it as a support (1903, 213–14). This seems very unlikely, since one would expect a similar panel left blank on the front, which is not the case. A greater probability is that the 'blank' area originally bore a painted inscription, relating to the dedicator – the existence of inscribed panels in Pictland is well known, and includes the panel on the 'Drosten' stone (St Vigeans 1) and the recently discovered panel on the cross at Dupplin, discussed below. In addition to these, there is a panel, perhaps for a painted inscription, on St Andrews 14, and a blank panel at the bottom of Sueno's stone that may have had an inscription (I am indebted to Mr Tom Gray for drawing my attention to this). This phenomenon is also to be found in Wales, for example on Carew, Pembrokeshire and Llandyfaelog-fach, Breconshire (Nash-Williams 1950, nos 303, 49). In both these cases there is an incised inscription and a space in which the inscription could have been painted. On that from St Ishmael's, Pembrokeshire, there is a blank panel at the base of a cross-shaft that is only explicable if it

were intended to have an inscription (*ibid.*, no. 397). It is noteworthy that an area of the 'blank' portion on Aberlemno 2 is roughly dressed, as though to take a plaster wash, while the area at the very bottom of the slab is undressed. Allen and Anderson suggested an inscription as a possible explanation for the blank panel (1903, 213).

The second feature of the back is the pair of confronted serpents which frame the composition. The treatment of the heads is exactly matched by the head of the 'wolf' on the fragmentary mount from the Viking burial at Westness, Rousay, which produced the Westness brooch (Stevenson 1968; Laing 1993, no. 179). The treatment of the head, with open jaws, suggests a closer affinity to the style of the 'dragons' on one of the St Ninian's Isle brooches (no. 28) or on the brooch from Freswick, Caithness, both datable to around 800, as probably is the mount from Rousay (for these brooches, see Laing 1993, nos 85–86). This zoomorphic frame is apparent on a number of other Pictish slabs, most notably on the Dunfallandy stone, Perthshire, which also displays, as will be seen, an unusual but almost identical animal to one which appears on the front of Aberlemno 2 (Fig. 22.6l). Dunfallandy is a 'boss style' monument, and, avoiding the issue of where the use of bosses on stone sculpture originates, it may be said that the earliest date suggested for any of them is at the very end of the eighth century.

Also displaying confronted framing beasts are the stones from Cossans, Farnell, Monifeith, Meigle 4 and Meigle 26. The last stone, which is a recumbent slab, possibly a cross-base, additionally employs a pair of hippocamps and a beast with convoluted hind-quarters of the type represented on the front of Aberlemno 2. It also has a swastika of four men, a device found in the Book of Kells.

The ancestry of the confronted dragons is a long one, and can be traced via the pair on the entrance to St Peter's, Monkwearmouth, backwards into pagan Germanic art. It may be seen as protective in function.

Aberlemno 2, front

The front of the stone (Fig. 22.2) is characterised by an interlace-decorated cross with quadrilobate arm sockets and with key and spiral patterns, and with animals flanking the shaft and on either side of the head. In view of the general similarity of some of these creatures to animals in the Lindisfarne Gospels and other Insular manuscripts of the earlier eighth century, there has been a tendency to see the ornament on the front of Aberlemno 2 as being derivative of Northumbrian art, and datable to the same period.

The flanking animals at the top are particularly useful in seeking comparative data. It can be seen at once that they are separate creatures (i.e. not linked with others), contorted to fit the available void. The deer (or horse) on the right has its legs folded under it, and its head bent back over its tail, which is similarly bent back over the line of its body and ends in a curl (Fig. 22.6b). Its feet are made up of a ball-and-claw, a feature shared by other animals on the slab. This type of discrete animal does not occur in 'Insular' manuscript art of the later seventh or earlier eighth centuries, where with certain exceptions, notably the evangelist symbols, the animals are interlinked as part of a pattern.

The individual animal is a motif which evolved in the eighth and ninth centuries, and passed into manuscripts and metalwork, notably the Anglo-Saxon 'Trewhiddle' style of the ninth century. Its development was studied by Brøndsted (1924, 127) and by Kendrick (1936, 196), both of whom saw the origins of the style in Merovingian and Carolingian manuscripts, a view refuted by Wilson and Blunt (1961, 102), who preferred to see a native English origin for the beasts. The starting point is perhaps provided by a creature very similar to that on the top right at Aberlemno on the reverse of an East Saxon series N sceatta, assigned by Metcalf to 715–25 (1994, 368). A type of discrete animal may have developed in Northumbria, perhaps starting with the that represented on the Bamburgh, Northumberland, mount (Bailey 1993) and the animal on the slab that Bailey has recent reassessed from Wamphray, Dumfries (1996b), probably of the earlier eighth century. These are however quite far removed from the simplified creatures on the Aberlemno slab.

In the 'Celtic' world the contorted 'Trewhiddle' animals undoubtedly influenced the evolution of a similar type of creature, though a native contribution, represented by the filigree dragons of the Dunbeath and Hunterston brooches, the 'Tara' brooch animals and the creatures that appear on the back of the ninth-century Killamery brooch, probably had a part to play in the development.

The most useful comparisons for the Aberlemno creatures can be found on the Crozier of Cú Dúilig (Fig. 22.6c, f, g), on the Bologna Shrine (Fig. 22.6e), and on items of the 'Trewhiddle' style, notably the Talnotrie strap end (Fig. 22.6k) and a ring from Selkirk in the collection of the Society of Advocates in Edinburgh (Fig. 22.6h), though they are also discernible on Irish motif pieces of the Viking period (Figs 22.6i, j), and on a motif piece from York in the 'Trewhiddle' tradition.

For the animal at the top left of the Aberlemno stone a useful parallel is provided by one on a motif piece from Christ Church Place, Dublin (O'Meadhra 1979, 40–1, cat. no. 278) (Fig. 22.6j). The features to note here are the lolling tongue, open mouth, foreleg twisted forward, the ear as a head lappet, the convoluted hindquarters and the ball-and-claw foot. Similar creatures appear on the Crozier of Cú Dúilig, for which the best parallel is provided by two animals on Knop 3 (MacDermott 1955, fig. 13, nos 2, 9), and by a creature on Knop 2 (*ibid.*, fig. 11, nos 15, 16). Again the ball-and-claw foot and lolling tongue is apparent, as is the forward-bent leg. The Crozier of Cú Dúilig also provides a model for the triquetra knot on the front of Aberlemno 2, the motif appearing on Knop 2. There is some disagreement about the dating of the crozier. Bourke has assigned the crozier to the end of the ninth century (1987, 171), but a recent study has argued that the inscription is datable to 1001–25, and while that inscription relates to a repair, the crozier itself is most probably of the early eleventh century (Michelli 1996, 19–20, and pers. comm. Dr Michelli). An early eleventh-century date is similarly to be assigned to the Dublin motif piece, in which O'Meadhra has seen Mammen-Ringerike influence (O'Meadhra 1987, 161–62), drawing particular attention to the forward pointing eye of the Irish animals. This can be seen on the animal at the top left on Aberlemno 2.

Anglo-Saxon 'Trewhiddle' comparisons are not as close, but the animal on the Talnotrie, Kirkcudbright, strap-end is generally closely related (Maxwell 1912–13, fig. 3, re-drawn by MacDermott 1955, as fig. 15), as is an animal on a gold ring found near Selkirk, now in the Faculty of Advocates collection in Edinburgh (Webster and Backhouse 1991, 237, no. 203). The creatures represented in the metalwork of the Trewhiddle hoard itself are less close, but one of

Fig. 22.6 *Animals on Aberlemno 2, and their counterparts. (a), (b), Aberlemno 2; (c), (f), (g), Crozier of Cú Dúilig; (d) Hereford Gospels; (e) Bologna Shrine; (h) ring from Selkirk, Roxburghshire, in collection of Society of Advocates, Edinburgh; (i), (j) details from motif pieces, Christ Church Place, Dublin; (k) animal on strap end, Talnotrie, Kirkcudbright; (l) Dunfallandy stone, Perthshire*

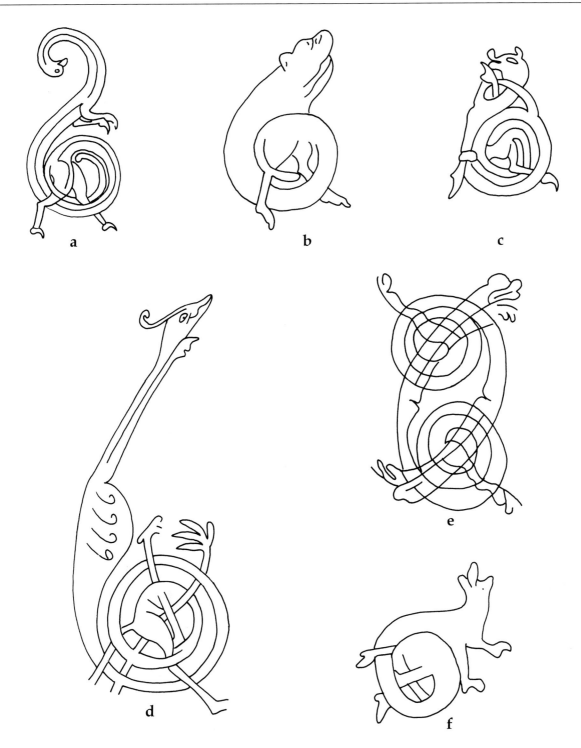

Fig. 22.7 Aberlemno 2 animals, and their counterparts. (a) Aberlemno 2; (b), (f) Meigle 1, Perthshire; (c) Crozier of Cú Dúilig; (d) Bealin Cross detail, Co. Westmeath ; (e) Duleek Cross detail, Co. Meath. (Drawn by David Taylor, not to scale)

the animals on the large mount displays general similarities (Wilson and Blunt 1961, fig. 1a, no. 3).

The head of the deer on the top right is distinctive (Fig. 22.6b), with its long nose slightly hooked at the end. Exact parallels are difficult, apart from the animal on the sceatta already described, but similar

heads appear in the Hereford Gospels (Hereford, Cathedral Library, MS P.I.2, fol. 102; Fig. 22.6d), on which can also be seen the use of spiral hindquarters related to those discussed below, and a long-beaked bird head reminiscent of those on the right side of the shaft on Aberlemno 2. This manuscript is usually dated to the late eighth century (Webster and Back-house 1991, 127 no. 91). The treatment of the 'nose' is very similar to that on the 'swimming elephant' that appears on Meigle 4, which arguably is one of the later stones from the site. The closest parallels for this creature as a whole, however, are at the bottom on the front of the Dunfallandy cross-slab, and on the Bologna Shrine which bears close similarities to the Monymusk Reliquary, but is generally regarded as a ninth-century work. The creature on Aberlemno 2 is most closely matched by the tiny animal crouched under the larger at each end of the ridge-pole (Blindheim 1984, fig. 53). The Bologna shrine, too, provides a parallel for the use of a triquetra knot for an infill (*ibid.*, 21).

The column of interlinked animals with contorted hindquarters that appears on the left of the shaft on Aberlemno 2 (Fig. 22.7a) has most often been cited as being derivative of the art of the Lindisfarne Gospels (London, British Library, Cotton Nero D.IV, e.g. fol. 26v) – a suggestion first put forward by Mrs Curle (1939–40, 76, fig. 5). While the device of spiral hindquarters does indeed occur for the first time in the Lindisfarne Gospels, the device was adopted into Insular art to remain fashionable for two centuries. The same device appears for example in the Book of Kells (Dublin, TCD MS A.1.6, fol. 40v), or again among the animals represented on the Crozier of Cú Dúilig (MacDermott 1955, fig. 13, 3 and 8) (Fig. 22.7c). They appear in sculpture on the Bealin Cross, Co. Westmeath (Fig. 22.7d) and on Meigle no. 1 (Fig. 22.7f) and Meigle 9. The treatment of the bird heads in a whorl at the top can be matched on St Vigeans no. 7.

The animals to the right of the shaft pose more problems. The pair of confronted hippocamps, which may be an echo of the the pair of confronted dragons on the back of the slab, have their slightly cruder counterparts on one of the corner posts of Shrine A at St Ninian's Isle, Shetland (Small, Thomas and Wilson 1973, pl. IVa; Thomas 1971, fig. 73, reconstruction). Confronted hippocamps also appear at Skinnet, Caithness, and single examples at Ulbster, Rosemarkie, Brodie, Mortlach, Meigle 1, 9 and 26, Murthly, Largo and Dogtown.

The ornament on Aberlemno 2 was noted by Allen as being particulary sophisticated, comparable only with Nigg and the Cross of Muiredach at Monasterboice in its complexity (Allen and Anderson 1903, 211). The spiral pattern on the head (Allen pattern no. 1091) can be matched on Aberlemno 3, Shandwick and Meigle 1; the design on the top arm of the cross (Allen pattern no. 739) can be matched on Meigle 1; the arms of the cross have key patterns (Allen pattern no. 971), matched on a number of stones, including St Vigeans 7 and Meigle nos 3 and 5; and the shaft has pattern nos 642 and 765,

otherwise without parallel. None of the other stones on which the patterns appear have features which suggest a date earlier than the ninth century.

Conclusions

None of the details on Aberlemno 2 are features that are diagnostic of the eighth century, much less the seventh. How much later than 800 the stone should be dated is another matter. The swords on the reverse point to a date no earlier than the mid-ninth century; some of the animal ornament on the front might be at home in a context in the early eleventh. It has to be admitted that the occurrence of ornament on the front of Aberlemno 2 normally associated with Insular manuscript art of the eighth century, is a problem which is not easy to resolve. The likeliest explanation is that there was a deliberate revival of designs associated with the Columban foundation at Iona, most notably those to be found in the Book of Kells. If a ninth-century (or later) date is accepted for Aberlemno 2, there is a case for arguing that the 'Early' low relief slabs of Eastern Pictland are in fact 'Late', and look back to the 'Golden Age' of Pictish sculpture rather than anticipate it.

Acknowledgements

I am extremely grateful to Mr Tom Gray, whose outstanding photographs clarified details on the reverse of the stone, and who has allowed me to reproduce them here, and to Dr Perette Michelli for discussing with me the dating of the Crozier of Cú Dúilig. I am also grateful to Mr David Taylor, of the Department of Archaeology, Nottingham University, for redrawing my figures.

References

ALCOCK, L. 1993, 'Image and icon in Pictish sculpture', in R. M. Spearman and J. Higgitt (eds), *The Age of Migrating Ideas. Early Medieval Art in Northern Britain and Ireland*, 230–36. Edinburgh, Stroud.

ALLEN, J. R. and ANDERSON, J. 1903, *Early Christian Monuments of Scotland*, 3 parts. Edinburgh.

BACKHOUSE, J., TURNER, D. H. and WEBSTER, L. (eds) 1984, *The Golden Age of Anglo-Saxon Art*. London.

BAILEY, R. 1993, 'Sutton Hoo and seventh-century art', in R. T. Farrell and C. Neuman de Vegvar (eds), *Sutton Hoo Twenty-Five Years After*, 31–42. Miami.

BAILEY, R. 1996a, *England's Earliest Sculptors*, Pontifical Institute of Medieval Studies. Toronto.

BAILEY, R. 1996b, *Ambiguous Birds and Beasts: Three Sculptural Puzzles in South-West Scotland*. Whithorn.

BIDDLE, M. and KJØLBYE-BIDDLE, B. 1985, 'The Repton stone', *Anglo-Saxon Engl.* 14, 233–92.

BLINDHEIM, M. 1984, 'A house-shaped Irish-Scots reliquary in Bologna, and its place among the other reliquaries', *Acta Archaeologica* 55, 1–53.

BONE, P. 1989, 'The development of Anglo-Saxon swords from the fifth to the eleventh century', in S. C. Hawkes (ed.), *Weapons and Warfare in Anglo-Saxon England* (= Oxford University Committee for Archaeology Monograph 21), 62–70. Oxford.

BOURKE, C. 1987, 'Irish croziers of the eighth and ninth centuries', in Ryan (ed.), 166–73.

BRØNDSTED, H. 1924, *Early English Ornament*. Copenhagen, London.

BURT, J. R., BOWMAN, E. O. and ROBERTSON, N. M. R. (eds) 1994, *Stones, Symbols and Stories, Aspects of Pictish Studies*. Edinburgh.

CARRINGTON, A. 1995, 'The equestrian motif in early medieval Pictish sculpture at Meigle, Perthshire', *Pictish Arts Soc. J.* 8, 28–43.

CARVER, M. O. H. 1986, 'Contemporary artefacts illustrated in Late Saxon manuscripts', *Archaeologia* 108, 117–45.

CRUIKSHANK, G. 1985, *Nechtansmere 1300: a Commemoration*. Forfar.

CRUIKSHANK, G. 1994, 'Explaining the Aberlemno battle-scene', in Burt *et al.* (eds), 39–42.

CRUIKSHANK, G. 1999, *The Battle of Dunnichen*. Balgavies

CURLE, C. L. 1939–40, 'The chronology of the early Christian monuments of Scotland', *Proc. Soc. Antiq. Scotl.* 74, 60–116.

DAVIDSON, H. E. 1962, *The Sword in Anglo-Saxon England*. Oxford.

DUNNING, G. C. and EVISON, V. I. 1961, 'The Palace of Westminster sword', *Archaeologia* 98, 123–58.

HARBISON, P. 1992, *The High Crosses of Ireland. An Iconographical and Photographic Survey*, 3 vols (= Römisch-Germanisches Zentralmuseum, Forschungsinstitut für Vor- und Frühgeschichte Monographien 17, 1–3). Bonn.

HENDERSON, I. 1967, *The Picts*. London.

HENDERSON, I. 1994, 'The Picts: written records and pictorial images', in Burt *et al.* (eds), 64–57.

HENDERSON, I. 1998, '*Primus inter pares*: the St Andrews sarcophagus and Pictish sculpture', in S. M. Foster (ed.), *The St Andrews Sarcophagus. A Pictish Masterpiece and its International Connections*, 97–167. Dublin.

HENRY, F. 1964, *Irish High Crosses*. Dublin.

KENDRICK, T. D. 1938, *Anglo-Saxon Art to AD 900*. London.

LAING, L. 1993, *A Catalogue of Celtic Ornamental Metalwork in the British Isles c AD 400–1200* (= B.A.R. Brit. Ser. 229). Oxford, Nottingham.

LAING, L. and J. 1993, *The Picts and the Scots*. Stroud.

MACDERMOTT, M. 1955, 'The Kells crozier', *Archaeologia* 96, 59–113.

MAXWELL, H. 1912–13, 'Notes on a hoard of ornaments, implements, and Anglo-Saxon and Northumbrian coins from Talnotrie, Kirkcudbrightshire', *Proc. Soc. Antiq. Scotl.* 47, 12–16.

METCALF, D. M. 1994, *Thrymsas and Sceattas*, 3. Oxford.

MICHELLI, P. 1996, 'The inscriptions on pre-Norman Irish reliquaries', *Proc. Roy. Ir. Acad.* 96C, 1–48.

NASH-WILLIAMS, V. E. 1950, *The Early Christian Monuments of Wales*, Cardiff.

O'MEADHRA, U. 1979, *Early Christian, Viking and Romanesque Art: Motif Pieces from Ireland*, 1. *An illustrated and descriptive catalogue of the so-called artists' 'trial-pieces' from c. 5th–12th cents. AD, found in Ireland, c. 1830–1973*. Stockholm.

O'MEADHRA, U. 1987, 'Irish Insular, Saxon and Scandinavian elements in the motif-pieces from Ireland', in Ryan (ed.), 159–65.

POLLINGTON, S. 1996, *The English Warrior, from Earliest Times to 1066*. Hockwold.

RADFORD, C. A. R. 1942, 'The early Christian monuments of Scotland', *Antiquity* 16, 1–18.

RITCHIE, A. 1989, *The Picts*. Edinburgh.

RYAN, M. (ed.) 1987, *Ireland and Insular Art A.D. 500–1200*. Dublin.

SCHMIDT, B. 1996, 'Das Königreich der Thüringer und seine Eingliederung in das Frankenreich', in A. Wieczorek, P. Périn, K. von Welck and W. Menghin (hrsg.), *Die Franken Wegbereiter Europas. Vor 1500 Jahren: König Chlodwig und seine Erben*, 285–97. Mainz.

SMALL, A., THOMAS, C. and WILSON, D. M. 1973, *St Ninian's Isle and its Treasure*, 2 vols. Aberdeen.

STALLEY, R. 1997, 'The tower cross at Kells', in C. E. Karkov, M. Ryan and T. Farrell (eds), *The Insular Tradition*, 115–41. Albany.

STEVENSON, R. B. K. 1955, 'Pictish Art', in F. T. Wainwright (ed.), *The Problem of the Picts*, 97–128. Edinburgh.

STEVENSON, R. B. K. 1968, 'The brooch from Westness, Orkney', in B. Niclasen (ed.), *Proceedings of the Fifth Viking Congress, Torshavn 1965*, 25–31. Torshavn.

STEVENSON, R. B. K. 1971, 'Sculpture in Scotland in the 6th–9th centuries AD', *Kolloquium über Spätantike und Frühmitterlalterliche Skulptur*, 65–74. Mainz.

SUTHERLAND, E. 1994, *In Search of the Picts*. London.

THOMAS, A. C. 1971, *The Early Christian Archaeology of North Britain*. Oxford.

WATKIN, J. R. 1986, 'A late Anglo-Saxon sword from Gilling Beck, North Yorkshire', *Medieval Archaeol.* 30, 93–99.

WEBSTER, L. and BACKHOUSE, J. (eds) 1991, *The Making of England. Anglo-Saxon Art and Culture AD 600–900*. London.

WILSON, D. M. 1964, *Anglo-Saxon Ornamental Metalwork 700–1100* (= Brit. Mus. Cat. of Antiquities of the Later Saxon Period I). London.

WILSON, D. M. 1965, 'Some neglected late Anglo-Saxon swords', *Medieval Archaeol.* 9, 32–54.

WILSON, D. and BLUNT, C. E. 1961, 'The Trewhiddle hoard', *Archaeologia* 98, 75–122.

23   Biblical Narrative and Local Imagery on the Kilnaruane Cross-shaft, Co. Cork

Jonathan M. Wooding

A sandstone pillar which stands in a field to the south of Bantry House, Co. Cork, is known variously as the Kilnaruane (after the townland) or Bantry pillar, stone or cross. The lower panel on its northeast face (E1), elements from which have been frequently reproduced in books as well as on religious and other artworks, contains the only recognisable early medieval illustration of the type of hide-covered boat which is known in Irish as a *curragh* or *naomhóg* (Figs 23.1, 23.2; Hornell 1937; 1938; Marcus 1980, 3–15; MacCullagh 1994).[1] The choice by an early medieval sculptor to depict this specific type of boat has generally been taken to be the simple adaptation of a local image of a boat, perhaps the type of craft most familiar to the artist, for a scene in which the church is represented metaphorically as a ship with Christ as the steersman (Hourihane and Hourihane 1979, 70; Mc-Gaughan 1998, 170–71), for a scene illustrating 'some

feature in the life of one of the Irish navigating saints' (Wallace 1940–41, 155), or the Biblical episode of 'Christ stilling the tempest' (Harbison 1992, 131–32, 254–55). It will be argued here that the last two possibilities are the more likely. The Kilnaruane pillar is in origin the shaft for a high cross. Scriptural panels are commonly found on such monuments and a strong case can be made that E1 represents the Biblical scene of Christ stilling the tempest on the Sea of Galilee (Matthew 8:23–7; Mark 4:35–41; Luke 8:22–5) or the verses of Psalm 107:23–32 concerning those who 'go down to the sea in ships'. This interpretation does not, however, exclude a parallel with the voyage tales of the Irish saints. The Galilee episodes and Psalm 107 were of especial interest to the eremitical monasticism of the early Irish church, engaged as it was with the search for 'hermitages in the ocean'. The hide boat was a specific part of the ethos of such monasticism. Monastic literature

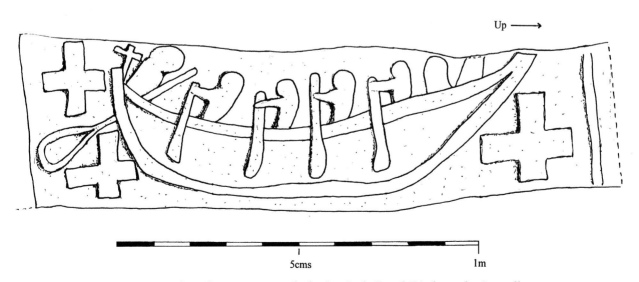

Up ⟶

5cms   1m

Fig. 23.1 *The Kilnaruane cross-shaft, Co. Cork. Panel E1 shown horizontally*

Fig. 23.2 *The Kilnaruane cross-shaft, Co. Cork. Panel E1*

represented the voyages of the *peregrini* in hide boats as consigning the voyagers to the protection of the Lord – at times making an implicit, sometimes an explicit, parallel with the episode of Christ's stilling of the tempest. The imagery of E1 may thus be explained as the representation of a Biblical scene, but one which has an especial resonance with the generally monastic subjects of the panels of the cross-shaft.

The site

The Kilnaruane pillar stands in a field to the south of the old main road from Bantry to Cork (OS 118:6:6, 387, 337; National Grid V988475). The site was first noted by the antiquary John Windele (1846, 313). The first element of the townland name is clearly Old Irish *cell* ('monastery', 'church'). The third element might be a dedication to St Ruadhán, though this is inconsistent with the plural article.

Rómhán ('Romans') has been suggested as an alternative (Hourihane and Hourihane 1979, 70–1), though this hypothesis is partly predicated on an unlikely theory as to the interpretation of the scene on the north-east face (see below). Earthworks visible on aerial photographs appear to have formed a small enclosure in which the pillar now stands – though only excavation could determine whether it stands on its original site (Hurley 1980; Pochin Mould 1981). The site also has remains of a burial ground and a *bullán* stone as well as several other stones which are not connected with the pillar (Power *et al.* 1992, 273, 276, 279, 305). On the basis of the generic name-element – leaving aside the obscure third element – along with the visible remains, we may assume that the remains are those of an early monastery.

The pillar

The pillar is approximately 2.13m high and has tapering sides averaging 280mm wide and 140mm deep. Two deep grooves (each 60mm long x 30mm wide and 40mm deep) near the top of the shaft strongly suggest that it once bore a transverse arm or cross-head at the top (Henry 1964, 63; Hourihane and Hourihane 1979, 71; Harbison 1992, 131–32). The pillar is evidently the shaft of a cross in the tradition of the high cross.

The two broader faces of the shaft, oriented approximately north-east (labelled by Harbison as 'E'[ast]) and south west (Harbison 'W'[est]), carry between them a total of seven illustrated panels. The panels depict (numbering from bottom to top): (W1) St Anthony and St Paul breaking bread in the desert; (W2) a decorated cross; (W3) an *orans* figure; (W4) simple interlace; (E1) a boat with its prow facing up the stone, surrounded by crosses; (E2) four beasts; (E3) two figures face-to-face.

The Kilnaruane cross-shaft forms a part of the somewhat indeterminate 'Munster' group of high crosses, many of which are undecorated (Harbison 1992, 382–83). On artistic criteria a date in the late first millennium AD would not seem to be in doubt (Henry 1940, 108; Harbison 1992, 131–32). Henry was inclined to date the illustration on the cross to the eighth century, on account of the naturalism of the image, which she saw as similar in this respect to the imagery of the Ahenny group (Henry 1940, 108). Harbison has taken a less evolutionary approach, preferring to date the monument with reference to a process of dissemination of the cross-form from the Midland-North Leinster group, which would place this cross roughly in the ninth century (Harbison 1992, 382–83). A ninth-century date is consistent with the general character of the site, though nothing categorically excludes a date within the range of around a century earlier or later.

The relations of the Munster group to other families of crosses make it unclear at this stage whether we should expect a greater or lesser proportion of Biblical subjects on such crosses, as opposed to other subjects from Patristic or even local history. Of the surviving portions of the Kilnaruane cross, the only definite attribution, the scene of SS Anthony and Paul the Hermit breaking bread in the desert (W1), is not Biblical in theme.

The boat image

Turning to the imagery of cross panel E1, this depicts a craft rowed by not less than four oarsmen (Fig. 23.1). Another figure is sitting or standing in a hunched position, leaning forward, in the stern and there is at least one further figure in the bow, or possibly two. These two shapes are no longer visible to the naked eye, but are visible in the Hourihanes' photograph (1979, 71, pl. 3). The stern-most of these two shapes may also be wielding an oar, but if so it is virtually butting into the back of the next oarsman. The second shape is at a different angle to the one aft of it and may be inanimate. It is possible that weathering at this point has removed part of the top of this shape.

Under the prow of the boat there is a cross, in the water. Two other crosses are depicted astern of the boat, one above and one below what would appear to be a steering-oar. These three crosses are nearly touching the sides of the boat – almost framing the curve of the prow and stern. A further, much smaller, cross rises from the stern of the boat, behind the back of the steersman. The indeterminate of the two figures/shapes in the bow may be a further cross, as it resembles the arms of the crosses which surround the boat – if so, this would at least provide balance to the scene. This side of the shaft is scalloped and loss of a portion is possible here – though the rest of the scene is clearly within the space now available.

The boat is certainly a hide boat. The sharp upward angle of sheer, starting around a quarter of the length of the vessel back from the prow, is almost identical with that of a modern curragh (Fig. 23.3; Hornell 1937, 160, 172, fig. 3, 173, fig. 4; 1938, 10, plan 1, 11, plan 2, 18, plan 3, 19, plan 4; MacCullagh 1992, 170–77). *Pace* Severin (1978, 25, 33), this medieval hide boat is almost identical to its modern counterparts. Like a modern curragh it is not double-ended, but appears to have a transom at the stern, rising at a sharp angle from the keel, though this has not always been correctly represented in reproductions (e.g. Wallace 1940, 153; Hourihane and

Hourihane 1979, 66). The boat image is without parallel in Irish iconography. Other sculptural images of boats clearly define planking, as in the boat on the Tall Cross at Monasterboice, or are in form of Scandinavian type, such as in the boat motif on the cross-shaft from Killary, Co. Meath (Johnstone 1964, pls XLVI–XLVII).

Why did the artist choose in particular to represent a hide boat? It would be unwise to assume that this was an issue of local preference. The hide craft was by no means the only type of craft known in early medieval Ireland. Finds such as the boat from Cummerstown, Lough Lene, Co. Westmeath (Brindley and Lanting 1991; Ó hEailidhe 1992; O'Sullivan 1998, 91–100) show that wooden ship-building techniques were known in prehistoric Ireland. Adomnán describes a *longa nauis* ('longship') as being built from timber (*Vita Columbae* II, 45; Anderson and Allen 1991, 174–75) and the Old Irish word for 'warship' (*long* < Latin *longa nauis*) might, by extension, be held also to describe a ship of wood (*cf. Uraicecht Becc*, where a *long* is distinguished in the same phrase from a *curach*; Binchy 1978, 1615.27–9; 2280.1–2; 2332.13–15). The hide boat was clearly one of a number of types of craft in use. We must assume that the different types served different functions or were chosen for use for various economic or ideological reasons. We cannot assume that the hide boat was the only possible option for either voyager or artist.

Biblical parallels

The cross in the stern of the boat adjacent to the steersman may be an indicator that this is Christ himself. Small, ambient crosses are, for example, drawn upon the tomb of Christ on the Cross of the Scriptures at Clonmacnoise (shaft W1). In that case they signify the presence of Christ. The number of crosses in the Kilnaruane scene itself hints at a Christ-centred scene. Paul Johnstone, however, has drawn attention to the presence of a small cross as a stern-mounting on the famous image of a hide boat in use, drawn by Captain Thomas Phillips in 1670 (Pepys Library, Magdelene College Cambridge; Johnstone 1976, 130; McGrail 1998, 178) and this might give pause to the argument that the stern cross is anything other than a traditional feature of Irish hide boats. For the Kilnaruane stern cross to be seen as part of such a tradition, however, would presume a long survival across time. In a religious artwork one is to assume that the cross has a symbolic function in the scene presented.

The 'steering-oar' held by the figure is a curious feature. From its position it is clearly to be interpreted as a steering-oar and not as, say, a trailing

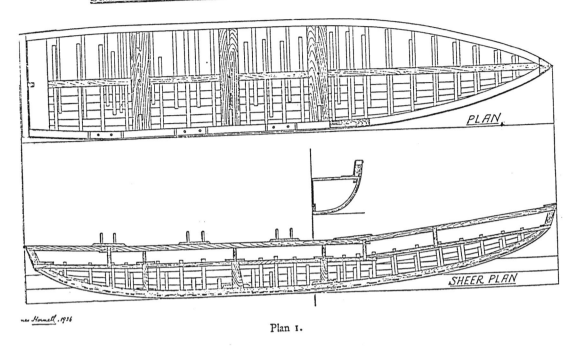

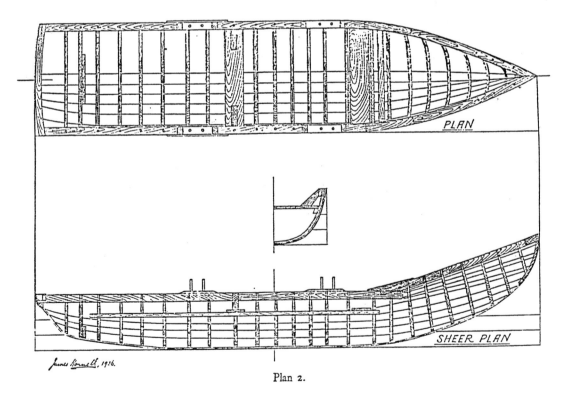

Fig. 23.3 Drawings of two modern curraghs from Achill Island (above) and Iniskea Island (below) by James Hornell. (Drawing: reproduced by permission of the Society of Nautical Research from The Mariner's Mirror 24 (1938), 10–11)

net. Yet it is unexpectedly depicted with a depression in its centre, as if it were hollow. Michael Ryan (pers. comm.) also has noted that it has parallels with baptismal spoons, but one may only say that, from its position, it is undoubtedly to be understood as a steering-oar.

Other scenes involving boats occur in high cross panels. Christ walking on the water is found on the Tall Cross at Monasterboice. In this example, Christ's body is clearly outside of the ship, however, whereas at Kilnaruane the figure is completely within the stern and most probably steering the vessel. Harbison suggests (1992, 132) as a subject for E1 the scene from Matthew 8:26: 'Then he rose and rebuked the winds and the sea; and there was great calm'. Such a scene is not depicted elsewhere in Irish iconography, though literary parallels may be adduced.

Christ's location within the boat is not described in Matthew 8:26, though it is in Mark 4:38–9:

> But he was in the stern, asleep on the cushion; and they woke him, and said to him, "Teacher, do you not care if we perish?". And he awoke and rebuked the wind, and said to the sea, "Peace! Be still!" And the wind ceased, and there was a great calm.

Here Christ is not explicitly steering the craft, but does rise up in the stern. It is of course possible that the scene is not explicit: Christ may simply be the steersman, or the Lord may be with the steersman, as in Psalm 107: 29–30, 'He made the storm be still, and the waves of the sea were hushed. Then they were glad because they had quiet, and he brought them to their desired haven'.

Parallels in voyage literature and Irish exegesis

I have argued elsewhere (Wooding 2001) that the hide craft is particularly chosen for monastic exile as a metaphor for the more perilous penitential voyage in the boat of one hide (Kelly 1988, 219–21). The boats used in the *immram* tales and in monastic voyages of exile are typically large vessels of two or more hides (*Immram Curaig Ua Corra* XXXIII, Stokes 1893, 38–9; Anglo-Saxon Chronicle *s.a.* 891; Plummer and Earle 1892, vol. 1, 82). This contrasts with a tradition of voyages of secular, punitive, exile in boats of one hide (Byrne 1932; an example is the exile of Macc Cuill in Muirchú's *uita* of St Patrick; Bieler 1979, 104). The common theme between the punitive and eremitical motifs is that of placing oneself on the ocean with a hide as a prophylactic between oneself and a perilous sea (*cf.* O'Loughlin 1995, esp. 22; Borsje 1996).

The theme of the perilous voyage in a boat of hide in which the voyager is protected by the vigilance of the Lord is one shared between the 'voyage' narratives in *uitae, immrama*, the *Nauigatio sancti Brendani abbatis* and in Irish Biblical exegesis. In the *Pseudo-Jerome Commentary on Mark* (Irish, seventh century, see Bischoff 1976, 81f.; Wooding 2001, 87–92; for a contrary view see Coccia 1967, 343–45) the exegete explicitly makes this equation:

> The ship made of dead skins, contains living beings. It holds off the waves and is strengthened with wood, that is to say, the church is saved by the cross and death of the Lord. The cushion represents the body of the Lord, on which divinity was bowed down like the head. The ship is the church at its beginning when Jesus sleeps in a bodily sense, because 'he never sleeps who guards Israel'. He rebukes the wind and the sea that it may be quiet. Concerning this, it is said, 'You control the might of the sea etc'. The wind and the sea are the demons and the persecutors (Cahill 1997, 27–8; 1998, 52–3).

The artist in E1 has reproduced the hide craft with sufficient care that it is immediately and unambiguously recognisable even to this day. This specific depiction of a hide boat, adjacent to the crosses, is probably to make the same point as the Pseudo-Jerome commentary. The wooden cross supports the craft of mortal flesh on its voyage through the ocean, as we are supported by the cross and death of Christ.

The crosses, often regarded as extraneous to the boat, are in fact crucial to the message of the boat motif – which is the same as that used in the monastic voyage narratives. Unlike the authors of the voyage tales, however, the artist was unable to draw a visible distinction between wood and hide *within* the substance of the hull. Instead, the artist has placed crosses externally, so that the contrast between the hide boat as a vehicle for the mortal soul – a metaphor for the body perhaps also – and the wooden cross which supports it, is clear. It is more difficult to decide whether this is also a representation of Christ stilling the tempest, or of a voyage of *peregrini*. Arguably the motifs are sufficiently indivisible to be impossible to distinguish.

The Hourihanes' explanation, that the image is a representation of the motif in which 'The body of the church is like a great ship carrying men of diverse origins through a violent storm' (Pseudo-Clement, Epistle to James, XIV), seems unlikely. This choice of theme is advanced by the Hourihanes as a metaphor for the so-called *Romani* controversies of the seventh century, in keeping with their rather forced explanation of the name of the site as **Cill na Rómhán* (Hourihane and Hourihane 1979, 70). This argument is unlikely both in terms of date and in the absence of literary analogues. The motif of the church as a ship remains possible as a source for the image. The pseudo-Constantinian image of the church as a ship in a sea of adversity gave way, in patristics, to an image of the church as the vehicle of salvation (Stuhlfauth 1942, 129). The pseudo-Clementine image of Christ as a *gubernator* would be consistent with the Kilnaruane depiction of Christ as a steersman (Pseudo-Clement, Epistle to James, XIV; Daniélou 1964, 60). In other early Christian uses of this motif the mast and yard is frequently used as a metaphor for the cross, though this is also true in general of the wood of the ship's hull (Rahner 1942; Daniélou 1964, 60-1). One can only say that the Kilnaruane image, if it is within this broader tradition, adds to the motif the further specific element of the hide of the boat, which may explain why the wooden cross needs to be made separate and adjacent.

Other panels on the Kilnaruane cross-shaft

The adjacent panel on the same face (E2) is clearly separate from E1. E2 would appear to contain four beasts, possibly cows or sheep, in an act of grazing. There is no logic in arguing that the boat is voyaging toward them as it would be upside-down. Another image can be vaguely seen in the left of the panel (i.e. higher up the stone than the animals), but it is illegible. The Hourihanes (1979, 69-70) have argued that E2 depicts the four beasts of Revelations 4-6, but they appear to be mostly uniform images, not evincing sufficient variety to represent, separately, the ox, lion, man and eagle.

Allowing for the illegibility of E2, a possible reading of the remaining panels of the cross as a whole is as an allegory of salvation through monastic life. St Anthony and St Paul the Hermit (W1) are archetypal monastic figures within the Irish tradition (Ó Carragáin 1988, 32) – the latter figuring in the *Nauigatio* (XXVI; Selmer 1959, 70f.). The *orans* figure (W3) in the early church may be simply a figure in prayer, but the implication in this case may be more one of deliverance (Roe 1970, 218). Ó Carragáin (1988, 14, 35) would suggest a more specifically liturgical context to the tableau, but this seems less likely than that the voyage (E1) is the voyage both of the monastic *peregrini* and of the Biblical disciples, in a hide boat guided and supported by the cross and death of Christ.

Acknowledgements

The assistance of Karen Jankulak with all aspects of this paper is gratefully acknowledged. I would also like to thank especially Gerald Bonner, George Henderson, Isabel Henderson, Tom O'Loughlin, Heather Pulliam and Michael Ryan for helpful discussion.

Notes

1   The terms now generally refer to canvas-covered craft; canvas has replaced hide in the modern form of the *curragh*.
2   The phrase is wrongly attributed by the Hourihanes to 'Homilies', a non-existent work (Hourihane and Hourihane 1979, 70).

References

ANDERSON, A. O. and M. O. (eds and trans.) 1991, *Adomnán's Life of St Columba* (revised ed.). Oxford.

BIELER, L. (ed. and trans.) 1979, *The Patrician Texts in the Book of Armagh* (= Scriptores Latini Hiberniae 10). Dublin.

BINCHY, D. A. 1978, *Corpus Iuris Hibernici*. Dublin.

BISCHOFF, B. 1976, 'Turning points in the history of Latin exegesis in the early Middle Ages', trans. C. O'Grady, in M. McNamara (ed.), *Biblical Studies: the Medieval Irish Contribution*, 73-160. Dublin.

BORSJE, J. 1996, *From Chaos to Enemy: Encounters with Monsters in Early Irish Texts* (= Instrvmenta Patristica 29). Turnhout.

BRINDLEY, A. L. and LANTING, J. A. 1991, 'A boat of the Mediterranean tradition in Ireland: preliminary note', *Int. J. Naut. Archaeol.* 20, 69-70.

BYRNE, M. E. 1932, 'On the punishment of sending adrift', *Ériu* 11, 97-102.

CAHILL, M. (ed.) 1997, *Expositio Evangelii Secundum Marcum* (= Scriptores Celtigenae 2, CCSL 82). Turnhout.

CAHILL, M. 1998, *The First Commentary on Mark*. New York, London.

COCCIA, E. 1967, 'La cultura irlandese precarolingia. Miracolo o mito?', *Studi Medievali* 8, 257-420.

DANIÉLOU, J. 1964, *Primitive Christian Symbols*. London.

HARBISON, P. 1992, *The High Crosses of Ireland. An Iconographical and Photographic Survey*, 3 vols (= Römisch-Germanisches Zentralmuseum, Forschungsinstitut für Vor- und Frühgeschichte Monographien 17, 1-3). Bonn.

HENRY, F. 1940, *Irish Art in the Early Christian Period*. London.

HENRY, F. 1964, *Irish High Crosses*. Dublin.

HORNELL, J. 1937, 'The curraghs of Ireland', *Mariner's Mirror* 23, 74-83; 148-75.

HORNELL, J. 1938, 'The curraghs of Ireland', *Mariner's Mirror* 24, 5-23.

HOURIHANE, C. P. and J. J. 1979, 'The Kilnaruane pillar stone, Bantry, Co. Cork', *J. Cork Archaeol. Hist. Soc.* 84, 65-73.

HURLEY, V. 1980, 'Additions to the 'Map of Monastic Ireland': the South-West', *J. Cork Archaeol. Hist. Soc.* 85, 52-65.

JOHNSTONE, P. 1964, 'The Bantry boat', *Antiquity* 38, 278-79.

KELLY, F. 1988, *A Guide to Early Irish Law*. Dublin.

MACCULLAGH, R. 1992, *The Irish Currach Folk*. Dublin.

MARCUS, G. J. 1980, *The Conquest of the North Atlantic.* Woodbridge.

MCCAUGHAN, M. 1998, 'Voyagers in the vault of heaven: the phenomenon of ships in the sky in medieval Ireland and beyond', *Material History Review* 48, 170–80.

MCGRAIL, S. 1998, *Ancient Boats in North-West Europe. The Archaeology of Water Transport to AD 1500.* London.

Ó CARRAGÁIN, É. 1988, 'The meeting of Saint Paul and Saint Anthony: visual and literary uses of a eucharistic motif', in G. Mac Niocaill (ed.), *Keimelia. Studies in Medieval Archaeology and History in Memory of Tom Delaney*, 1–58. Galway.

Ó HEAILIDHE, P. 1992, 'The monk's boat – a Roman period relic from Lough Lene, Co. Westmeath, Éire', *Int. J. Naut. Archaeol.* 21, 185–90.

O'LOUGHLIN, T. 1995, 'Living in the ocean', in C. Bourke (ed.), *Studies in the Cult of St Columba*, 11–23. Dublin.

O'SULLIVAN, A. 1998, *The Archaeology of Lake Settlement* (= Discovery Programme Monograph 4). Dublin.

PLUMMER, C. and EARLE, J. (eds) 1892, *Two of the Saxon Chronicles Parallel.* Oxford.

POCHIN MOULD, D. 1981, 'The monastery of Cill Ruán', *J. Cork Archaeol. Hist. Soc.* 86, 107–8.

POWER, D. with BYRNE, E., EGAN, U., LANE, S. and

SLEEMAN, M. 1992, *Archaeological Inventory of County Cork.* Vol. 1, Dublin.

RAHNER, H. 1942, 'Antenna Crucis III: Das Schiff aus Holz', *Zeitschrift für Katholische Theologie* 66, 197–227.

ROE, H. M. 1970, 'The *orans* in Irish Christian art', *J. Roy. Soc. Antiq. Ir.* 100, 212–21.

SELMER, C. (ed.) 1959, *Navigatio Sancti Brendani Abbatis.* Notre Dame.

SEVERIN, T. 1978, *The Brendan Voyage.* London, New York.

STOKES, W. 1893, 'The Voyage of the Húi Corra', *Revue Celtique* 14, 38–9.

STUHLFAUTH, G. 1942, 'Das Schiff als Symbol der altchristlichen Kunst', *Rivista di archaeologia cristiana* 19, 111–41.

WALLACE, J. N. A. 1941, 'Carved stone pillar at Bantry, Co. Cork', *N. Munster Antiq. J.* 2, 153–55.

WINDELE, J. 1846, *Cork and its Vicinity.* Cork.

WOODING, J. M. 2001, 'St Brendan's boat – dead hides and the living sea in Columban and related hagiography', in J. Carey, M. Herbert and P. Ó Riain (eds), *Studies in Early Irish Hagiography: Saints and Scholars*, 77–92. Dublin.

24   The Hillquarter, Co. Westmeath Mounts: an Early Medieval Saddle from Ireland

Eamonn P. Kelly

In 1988 the National Museum of Ireland came into possession of a number of decorated copper-alloy mounts and part of an iron boss found in the bed of the River Shannon in the Irish midlands (Fig. 24.1).[1] The find-place, a short distance north of the town of Athlone, is immediately below Lough Ree at a place known locally as Dead Man's Island.[2] It will be proposed here that the mounts in question are the decorative elements of a saddle of late sixth-to early seventh-century date. From remote times saddles were in use by the nomads of the Steppes and from that area their use spread westwards into Europe. By the sixth century AD, the use of distinctive wooden saddles with a high arched pommel and bindings in copper alloy and iron was concentrated in two areas of Europe. One group was found in the area of the River Danube between Hungary and the Black Sea and a second group occurred in Scandinavia. However, more widely distributed examples of the same general type are known, such as the saddle found in a woman's grave at Wesel-Bislich in the Rhineland (grave no. 446; Janssen 1981). It seems likely that the Hillquarter mounts were attached to a saddle of broadly similar construction. However, the decoration is Irish, suggesting that the Hillquarter saddle was a local copy of a Continental example.

Description

Not all the mounts survive and at least one component (which seems to have been a curved binding strip) was lost during the removal of the objects from the river bed. Apart from an iron boss, all the surviving components are of copper alloy. The boss, which is broken and survives in four sections, was approximately 120mm in diameter and had a broad flanged rim (Fig. 24.2a–d). It was attached – probably to the front of the pommel – by four, cast bronze, tripartite mounts placed at the cardinal points. Each of the mounts consists of a central cylindrical section flanked by two smaller cylinders. The same designs occur on each mount. On the central area, which has a diameter of 12mm, there is a relief design formed of three spirals, which spring from a small central ring. Each spiral ends in a clubbed terminal and each has a small ring attached. The two flanking areas are 7mm in diameter. Each bears a sunburst design consisting of a central ring with eight and nine emanating rays respectively. The mounts would have stood proud of the surface of the boss flange. They were each secured by means of a bar of rectangular section measuring 14mm in length. A small hole located approximately 3mm from the end of each bar originally held a transverse pin to secure the mounts in place. The section to which the ring or boss was fastened would, therefore, have been approximately 10mm thick.

There is a decorated circular cast mount measuring 34mm across and 1mm thick which may have been centrally placed on the iron boss (Fig. 24.2e). It has a convex cross-section and bears fine line ornament in low relief comparable to that on the tripartite mounts. At the centre there is a setting containing a blue glass stud, which projects from the underside of the mount. On the upper surface two rings, in low relief, encircle the stud. From the outermost of these spring four spirals which terminate in stylised bird heads. From each of the spirals springs a single smaller spiral with a clubbed terminal.

There are two semi-circular bronze mounts, of which one is broken (Fig. 24.2f–g). Originally each consisted of a semi-circular band of copper-alloy sheeting 0.3mm thick and 10.5mm wide and forming a circle with a diameter of approximately 268.5mm. The complete example is ornamented with 80 repoussé oval pellets arranged radially and it was

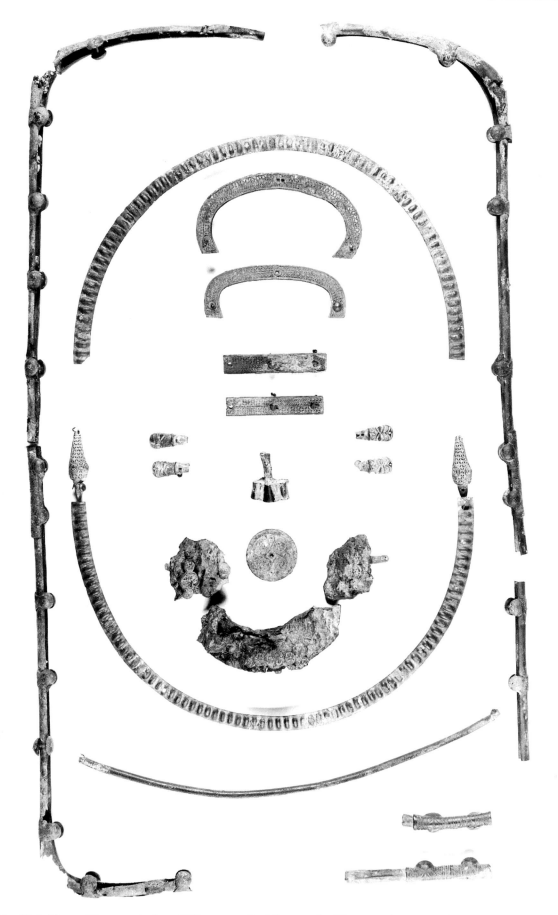

Fig. 24.1 *The saddle mounts from Hillquarter, Co. Westmeath. (Photograph: National Museum of Ireland)*

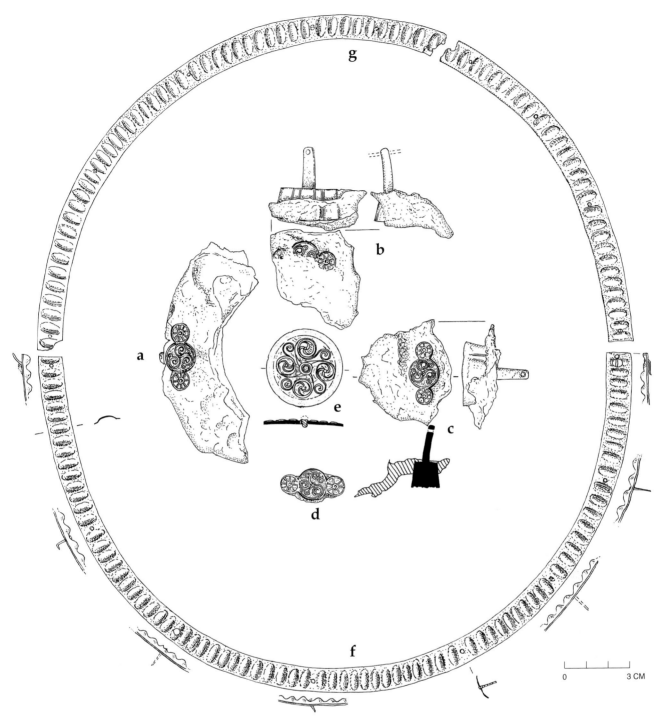

Fig. 24.2 *The pommel mounts from Hillquarter, Co. Westmeath. (Drawing: National Museum of Ireland)*

attached in at least eleven places, with five nails still surviving. The second mount had at least 75 repoussé pellets and was held in place by eight nails, of which seven survive.

There are two C-shaped cast mounts of different sizes. The overall dimensions of the larger piece are 111 x 56mm and it has a cross-section measuring 11 x 1mm (Fig. 24.3a). The centre of the mount is perforated by two nail holes 1.5mm in diameter and two nails survive in holes near the ends. The mount

has a border 1mm wide enclosing ten zones of ornament built up of small lentoids arranged in patterns. Two small zones at the ends, beyond the nails, contain lozenge and herringbone patterns respectively. The mount is divided longitudinally by a narrow relief border and laterally into segments of roughly equal length separated by the central nail-holes and two sunburst motifs. The panels contain herringbone, chevron and saltire patterns. The back of the mount is plain and corroded in places. Beneath

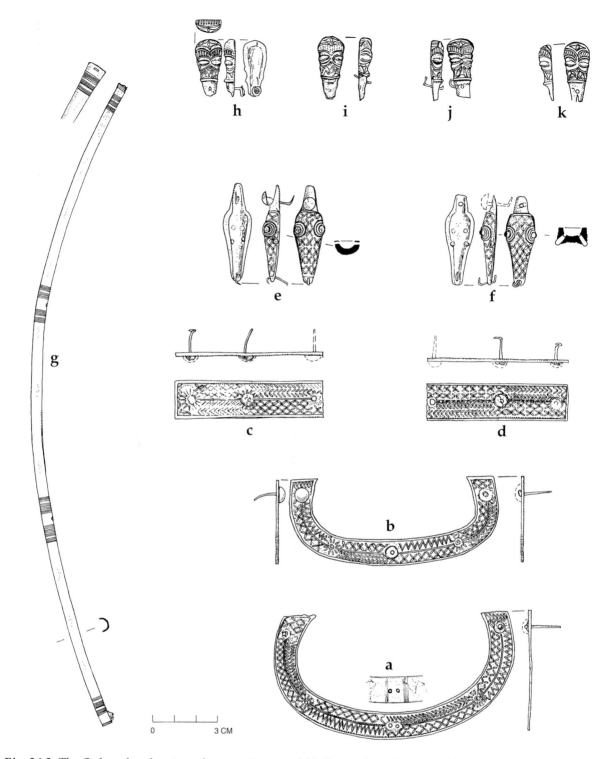

Fig. 24.3 *The C-shaped and rectangular mounts, curved binding strip and zoomorphic mounts from Hillquarter, Co. Westmeath. (Drawing: National Museum of Ireland)*

the two central nail holes there is a central segment 7mm long which has been filed down into a slight recess.

The smaller C-shaped bronze mount measures 94 x 40mm with a cross-section of 11 x 1mm (Fig. 24.3b). It has a single central nail hole measuring 2mm in diameter and two nails survive in holes near the ends. Ten panels of ornament are separated by the nail holes and by sunburst motifs. The patterns are the same as on the larger, C-shaped mount consisting of chevron, herringbone and saltire designs. The back of the mount is plain. An unidentified mastic-like material, to which copper-alloy bosses were secured, covered the heads of the nails by means of which both C-shaped mounts were attached. The purpose was entirely aesthetic in order to conceal the inelegant nail heads. One of the nail heads still retains its copper-alloy boss. On other examples, although the bosses are missing the domed mastic beneath has survived.

There are two similarly decorated, rectangular bronze mounts measuring 64 x 16 x 1mm and 68 x 16 x 1mm respectively (Fig. 24.3c–d). Three nails, one in the middle and two near the ends, were used to attach the mounts. Sunburst motifs are centred on the end nail holes of one of the mounts but these are absent on the other example. Otherwise, the ornament on each occurs in four, equal-sized, rectangular zones with rows of herringbone and saltire designs.

There are seven sections of semi-tubular binding strips (Fig. 24.4a–g). The fragments illustrated as a and b appear to have been joined, as were e and f (Fig. 24.4). This suggests that originally there were two continuous binding strips with right-angle bends at either end (Fig. 24.1). The strips expand at the corners where they are bent. The long sections were approximately 540mm in length and the short ones were at least 150mm in length. The binding strips were held in place by metal clips which were wrapped around them. These have domed ends and were secured by nails hammered through from the centre of one domed head through to the centre of the domed head opposite. Most of the binding strips are of sheet metal and are plain, but there are four decorated sections in which the binding strips were cast together with their attachment clips. These were then soldered to the sheet sections. The ornament is roughly the same in each case, consisting of four rows of lateral herringbone ornament flanked by lateral lines. A zone of triangles links the two halves of each domed attachment clip and in two of the four cases the triangles in the zones are punched at the centre (Fig. 24.4a, 4c and enlarged 24.4g).

Cast terminals, two of which survive (Fig. 24.3e–f), may have been attached at the ends of the binding strips. Each has a short perforated tang and the triangular head of a long-snouted animal. There is a hole at each end which contained rivets, three of which survive and one of which still has a domed cover attached. There are a further two holes half way along on either side of the mounts. The eyes of the animals are each formed of three concentric rings, rising pyramidally and crowned with a blue glass stud. The rest of the surface is decorated inside a plain border, up to 1mm wide, tapering towards the nose. The ornament consists of a lattice of satire motifs formed by opposed lentoids. The back of each head is slightly hollowed, following the exterior shape of the head. One of the mounts measures 44mm in overall length, 13.7mm wide and 7.4mm high. The second animal head measures 39.7mm in

length, 13.7mm wide and 6.5mm high. Despite one of the animal heads being slightly smaller, the two mounts must be seen as a matching pair.

There is a curved semi-tubular binding strip (Fig. 24.3g) and a second possible example was discarded before the importance of the find was recognised.[3] The surviving example measures 285mm in length with a maximum cross-section of 6mm. It is decorated with four zones of lateral lines located at the ends and along the main body of the binding strip. Four nail holes are present.

Four cast mounts in the form of highly stylised duck-heads (Fig. 24.3h–k) appear to have been attached at the ends of the curved binding strips. The best preserved measures 250mm long, 11mm wide and 5mm high. The terminals are roughly pear-shaped with a short perforated tang at the narrow end. At the broad end there is a band of short parallel lines in low relief. The forehead is decorated with two opposed triangles with deeply incurved sides and a punched dot at the centre. There is a Y-shaped moulding below with two curved bands of short parallel lines. The eyes are two bulging ovoids within a figure-of-eight. Below the eyes there is a zone containing five triangles with deeply incurved sides and punched dots at their centres. A low moulding, which separates the tang from the decorated surface appears to be a residual beak.

Discussion

The ornament on the Hillquarter mounts is characteristic of that found on a range of sixth- to seventh-century metalwork, and specific parallels can be drawn with the decoration found on objects such as latchets, penannular brooches, hand pins, bracelets and hanging bowls (Kilbride-Jones 1980a; 1980b). In general terms, the use of zones of transverse and cross-hatched lines that occur on the binding strips (Figs 24.3g, 24.4) can be compared with decoration found on a range of objects, such as the rings of penannular brooches and on the escutcheon frames of hanging bowls. Points of comparison may also be seen in the decoration found on the cheek pieces of Vendel harnesses (Arrhenius 1983, figs 16–18). There are a growing number of Irish mouldings bearing decoration similar to that on the binding strips found at Hillquarter. A number of examples were found in or near crannógs such as Ballinderry, Co. Westmeath, Toneymore North, Co. Longford (Farrell *et al* 1989, 126, fig 7:1) and Lagore, Co. Meath. A copper-alloy cylindrical bead with comparable decoration was found on a crannóg at Auburn, Co. Westmeath and a similar moulding was found at Clogher, Co. Tyrone (see Ryan 1992, 92).

In the collections of the National Museum of

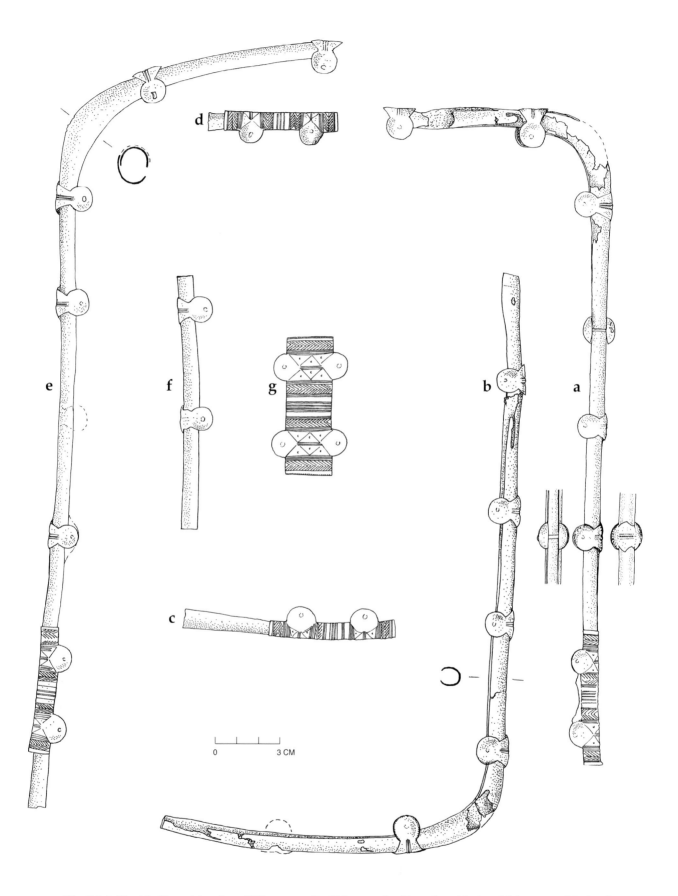

Fig. 24.4 *The binding strips from Hillquarter, Co. Westmeath. (Drawing: National Museum of Ireland)*

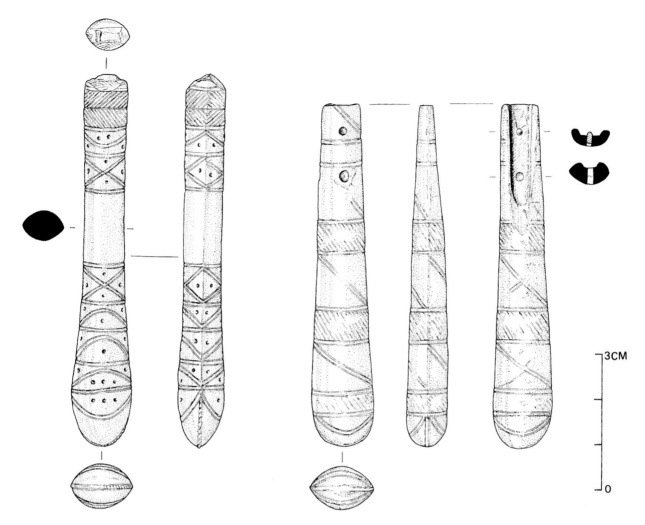

Fig. 24.5 *Decorated handles, possibly mirror handles. (a) unprovenanced. (b) from a crannóg in Lugacaha, Lough Sewdy, Co. Westmeath. (Drawing: National Museum of Ireland)*

Ireland there are two further objects, not published previously, on which the same decoration is present. Both are made of copper alloy and may have been handles.[4] One example,which is unprovenanced, has a waisted profile, a broad rounded end and a pointed elliptical cross-section throughout (Reg. No. NMI P.780; Fig. 24.5a). The narrow end is damaged and has been abraded since its discovery, perhaps with a file. The narrow central section is plain but the rest of the surface is ornamented with incised decoration that is similar along both main surfaces. At the broad end there is a low beaded moulding running around the extremity. There is also a series of panels defined by incised, double-contoured lines. Four semicircles occur. Two are opposed and separated by transverse lines while the other two semicircles are placed parallel to each other and are also separated by transverse lines. A saltire motif completes the decoration at the knobbed end. Within the two opposed semicircles there are three punched dots and all the other spaces have a single punch

mark centrally placed. At the broken end there is a saltire and a semicircle separated by transverse lines and with punched dots in the voids. There is also a panel of herringbone ornament. The overall length is 80.5mm and the maximum cross-section is 13.8 x 10.7mm. The second handle (Fig. 24.5b) is complete and was found on a crannóg at Lugacaha, Lough Sewdy, Co. Westmeath (Reg. No. NMI E499:352). It has a broad rounded end. At the other extremity there is a tapered groove where a tang was once held in place by two rivets, one of which remains. The surface is abraded and the decoration is difficult to see. There is a low moulding around the broad end. The rest of the decoration is placed in panels defined by incised, double-contoured lines. There is a plain semicircular panel at the broad end. There are also a series of alternating panels bearing saltire motifs and cross-hatching. The object measures 75.6mm in length and 14.4 x 9.6mm in maximum cross-section.

The early levels of a ringfort excavated at Gar-

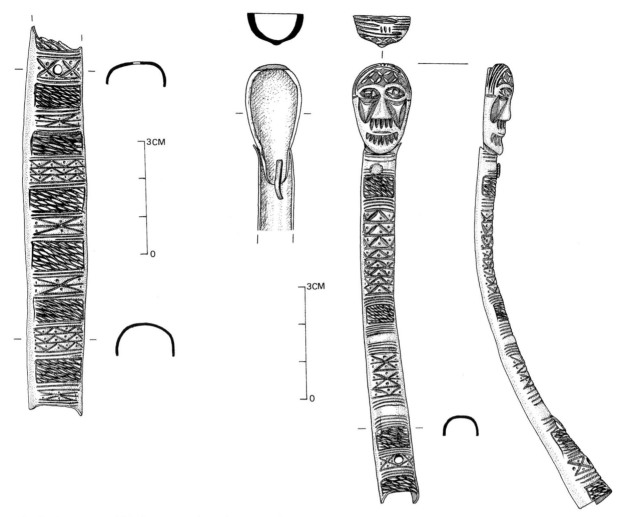

Fig. 24.6 *Decorated binding strips from the River Shannon at Athlone. The exact findplace is not recorded but it would have been within one mile of the findplace of the Hillquarter saddle mounts. (Drawing: National Museum of Ireland)*

ranes, Co. Cork yielded a binding strip of U-shaped cross-section that may have performed a function similar to that of the Hillquarter bindings. The Garranes example, which is decorated with transverse lines and saltires, measures 83mm in length and is a fragment of a larger binding strip (Ó Ríordáin 1942, fig. 4, 341). Two nail holes, 2mm in diameter, are located along the long axis.

The curved binding strip from Hillquarter (Fig. 24.3g), which bears four zones of transverse lines, may also be mentioned in connection with the objects and mouldings discussed above. It is comparable to another, similar curved binding found in the River Shannon at Athlone during drainage work in the nineteenth century (Fig. 24.6). Recovered in two fragments, it has an anthropomorphic cast terminal attached to one end. The decoration consists of a variety of transverse linear patterns including cross-hatched panels and rows of interlocking concave-sided triangles with a central dot (Ó Floinn 1989, 30).

In their overall shape the tripartite mounts, by means of which the iron boss was attached (Fig. 24.2a–d), bear obvious comparisons with hand pins. A recent unpublished find from a crannóg at Cappagh, Lough Garr, Co. Westmeath (Reg. No. NMI E499:368) may be a hand pin but its solid form suggests that it might be an example of a mount smaller but similar to the Hillquarter examples (Fig. 24.7). A positive identification of its purpose remains uncertain because what may have been either a pin or a rod for attachment was broken off and lost in antiquity. The Cappagh object consists of a solid cylindrical section flanked by two smaller but similar forms. The central portion formerly held a decorative stud surrounded by a low relief zone of herringbone patterns formed of lentoids. The flanking areas also bore studs. The object has a maximum width of 17.3mm and is 12.2mm thick.

Fine line spiral ornament, found on the Hillquarter disc (and on the tripartite mounts) is comparable with ornament found on latchets and on the

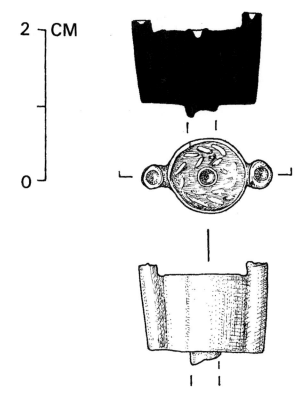

Fig. 24.7 Decorated bronze object from a crannóg at Cappagh, Lough Garr, Co. Westmeath. The object may be the fragment of a handpin or it may be a mount similar to those on the Hillquarter boss. (Drawing: National Museum of Ireland)

and on Vendel saddles where they may have had symbolic significance.[5]

The two cast animals with long snouts from Hillquarter (Fig. 24.3e–f) appear to be Germanic beasts and some comparisons can be drawn with long-snouted animals found on the Sutton Hoo helmet and shield. Even better comparisons can be drawn with pendant animals found on Ostrogothic cheekpieces from Apahida, Romania and on Vendel cheekpieces (Arrhenius 1983, fig. 16, 56). The same type of creature is represented on attachment clips that held the bindings of the Wesel-Bislich saddle (Janssen 1981, Abb. 5–7).

Rows of garnets set in gold cells are found on Continental saddle pommels such as that from a warrior's grave at Krefeld-Gellep (Pirling 1964, 188–91) and the so-called Theoderic's Harness from Ravenna (Vierck 1972, 213–17). The rows of pellets on the two semicircular Hillquarter mounts (Fig. 24.2f–g) may be skeuomorphs, representing an attempt to recreate something of the impression of such garnet inlays.

Suggested reconstruction

The Hillquarter mounts were likely to have been attached to a saddle of the same general type as that from Wesel-Bislich, which was made of wood decorated with copper alloy and iron. Like it, the Hillquarter saddle may have consisted of two angled sideboards bridged by a high arched pommel and cantle (Fig. 24.8). The decorated disc was probably placed centrally on the iron boss. In turn, this was likely to have been located prominently on the pommel and surrounded by the two semicircular strips arranged in the form of a circle. The two C-shaped mounts, which differ in size, may have been positioned above the arch of the pommel and cantle respectively. The two rectangular mounts may have been placed on the sideboards or, possibly, on the pommel. The binding strips may have been placed along the front and bottom of the sideboards. This would indicate that the sideboards were about 54mm long (which is around the same size as those on a reconstruction of the Wesel-Bislich saddle). The long-snouted animal mounts may have been attached at the ends of the binding strips. However, the ends of the binding strips are broken and missing and so there are no matching rivet holes present to prove this proposition.

The concave binding strips, which appear to have the cast bird-headed mounts attached at either end, may have been located along the upper edges of the boards where the rider sat (Fig. 24.9). A similar function can be proposed for the binding strip from the River Shannon at Athlone (Fig. 24.6).

terminals of penannular brooches (Fig. 24.2e). So too is the sunburst motif that occurs on the tripartite mounts and on the rectangular and C-shaped mounts. Further comparison with the ornament on penannular brooches and pins is to be found in the four duck-headed mounts from Hillquarter. Close comparisons can be made with birds' heads on pins from Ballyeagh, Co. Kerry and Horn Head, Co. Donegal (Newman 1995, fig. 2). The same bird appears on the terminals of an unprovenanced Irish penannular brooch (*ibid.*, fig. 4) and on an example from Shronebirrane, Co. Kerry (*ibid.*, fig. 6). A similar brooch was found in a grave at High Down, Sussex (*ibid.*, fig. 6). The Hillquarter birds bear triangular motifs with incurved sides and a punched dot at the centre and basically the same motif is inscribed on two of the cast mouldings (Fig. 24.4 a, c, g). This motif, which also occurs on the anthropomorphic mount from Athlone (Fig. 24.6), is used commonly on bracelet terminals and brooches. It is also found on handles in the Norrie's Law hoard (Ó Floinn 1989, 30). The choice of bird-headed motifs (on the disc and on four of the cast terminals) may not be coincidental, as bird designs are prominent among the decorative motifs on the Wesel-Bislich saddle

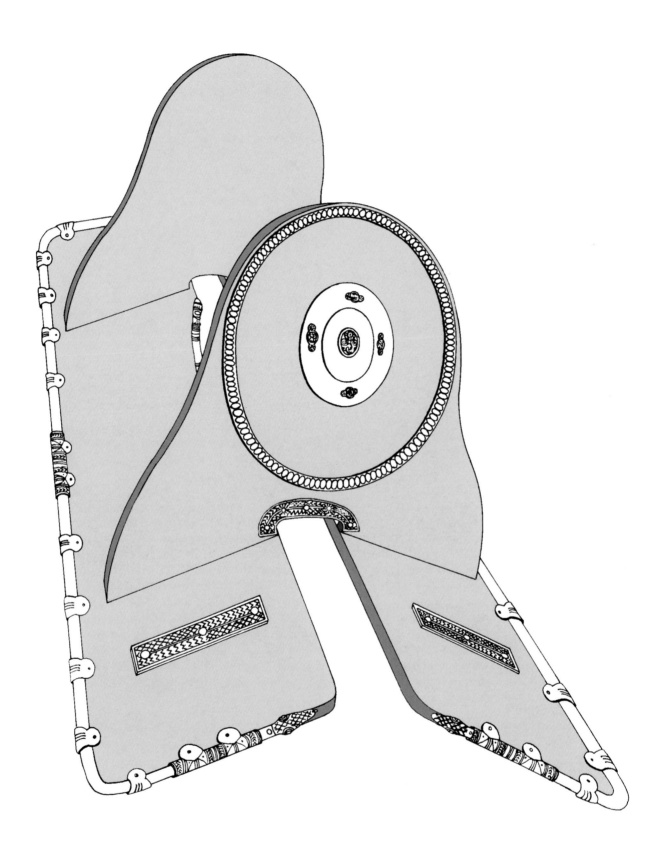

Fig. 24.8 *Suggested reconstruction of the Hillquarter saddle. (Drawing: National Museum of Ireland)*

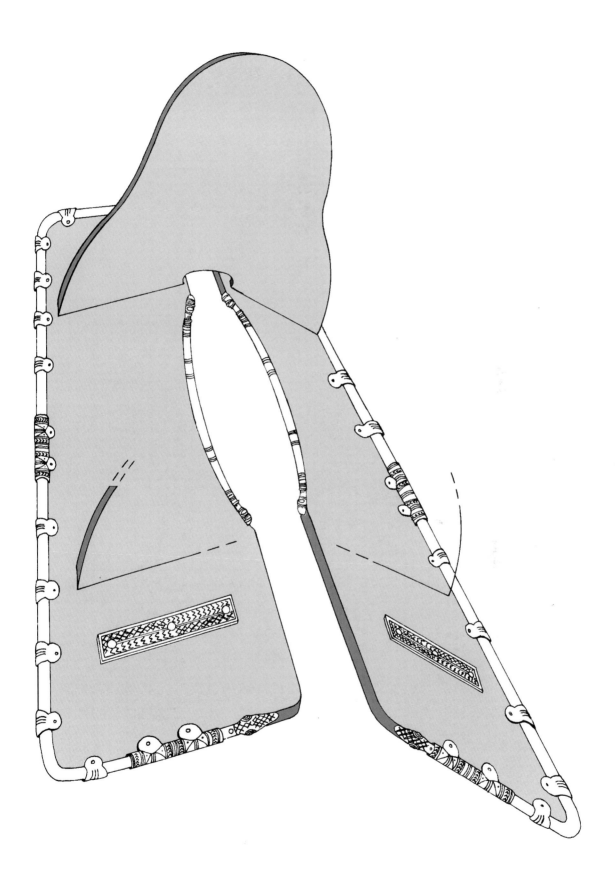

Fig. 24.9 *Suggested reconstruction of the Hillquarter saddle. The pommel has been omitted to show the curved binding strips in position. (Drawing: National Museum of Ireland)*

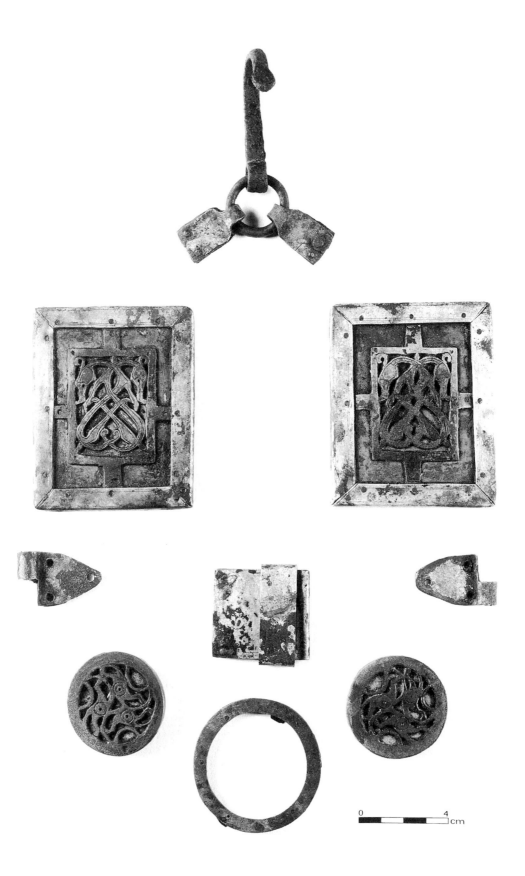

Fig. 24.10 *Harness mounts and strap distributors found near a crannóg in Templehouse Lake, Co. Sligo.*
(Photograph: National Museum of Ireland)

A reconstruction of the positions of the binding strips suggests that this may have been positioned without a particular practical purpose in mind, and consequently the Hillquarter saddle may have functioned mainly as a display object.

Conclusion

Assessment of the decoration on the mounts and comparison with the Wesel-Bislich saddle suggest that the Hillquarter saddle was made during the last quarter of the sixth century or the first quarter of the seventh century. The Hillquarter mounts and some of the other examples cited[6] might represent a phase when saddles were used in Ireland, reflecting a fashion then current in parts of Europe. If this was so, however, the use of saddles appears to have been of short duration. Writing in the twelfth century, *Giraldus Cambrensis* stated that the Irish used no saddles; this continued to be the case until the end of the Middle Ages when riding to saddle became a requirement of law to enforce English custom (Kavanagh 1988, 93). Instead of saddles, the Irish used a cloth placed over the horse's back known as a *dillat* – modern Irish *diallait* (Kavanagh 1988, 93). A number of items of early medieval Irish horse harness are known and these, presumably, were used in association with a *dillat* or blanket. The Irish harness mounts from a Viking grave at Navan, Co. Meath are well known (Ó Floinn 1989, 117–18). To these may now be added a recent discovery of harness mounts and strap distributors (Fig. 24.10), some decorated with openwork Insular animal ornament, found near a crannóg in Templehouse Lake, Co. Sligo (Kelly 1998, no. 235). A later harness mount of eleventh- or twelfth-century date is known from the excavation of a ringfort at Ballycatteen, Co. Cork (Ó Ríordáin and Hartnett 1949, 17–22, figs 5–6). Although the Vikings may have used saddles in Ireland (Kavanagh 1988, 109) the practice appears to have been largely ignored by the Irish. Four objects identified as Viking saddle pommels (or possibly straddles) have been found in Dublin (Kavanagh 1988, 105–9, figs 5:4.1, 5:5.1). A further similar object, elaborately decorated, found at Ballynagarbry, Co. Westmeath and dated to the tenth century (Ryan 1983, 153–54) may represent Viking activity in the midlands. Like the Dublin examples it is arched in a manner reminiscent of the earlier Vendel pommels.

The discovery of the Hillquarter saddle suggests that, around the period of its manufacture, Ireland had extensive contacts with Britain and the Continent. Parallels have been drawn with decoration on objects in the Norrie's Law hoard suggesting contact with Pictish Scotland. Judging from the ornament on the mounts and the overall form of the saddle, the maker of the Hillquarter saddle was an Irishman who possessed a good level of knowledge of Continental saddles. The find clearly implies that there were contacts with mainland Europe and, in this context, the activities of Irish churchmen on the Continent and Bede's reference to the presence in Ireland of Merovingian visitors (*HE* III, 7) must be seen to be of particular relevance. A trade item or a gift to an Irish king may have provided an exemplar. Such an object may even have formed part of a dowry, for in Continental and Asiatic traditions, saddles were given as bridal gifts. Perhaps noteworthy in this respect is the fact that the Wesel-Bislich saddle was found in a woman's grave. Viewed from an art-historical perspective the main significance of the Hillquarter find is the range of decoration present on the mounts which allows for comparisons to be drawn with almost the full range of contemporary, Insular decorated metalwork.

Acknowledgments

The drawings are by Albert Siggins and John Murray, National Museum of Ireland. I am grateful to Donal Boland for making available the drawings of the saddle components and to Michael Heffernan, National Museum of Ireland, for preparing them for publication. My thanks are due to Paul Mullarkey and Raghnall Ó Floinn, National Museum of Ireland, for advice and assistance.

Notes

1   Reg. No. NMI 1990:167
2   Off-shore from the townland of Hillquarter, parish of St Mary's, barony of Brawny, Co. Westmeath. O.S. 6" sheet 29.
3   The finder thought it was part of the windscreen wiper of a car. Once discarded it was swept away by the current.
4   There are a number of possible functions for the handles. They may have been attached to small iron pans used in glass working. Such pans have been found as stray finds or have been excavated on sites such as Lagore, Co. Meath (Ó Floinn 1989, 204–5). Another possibility is that they were the handles of small strainers, later examples of which are known from Moylarg Crannóg, Co. Antrim and from the River Suir at Doornane, Co. Kilkenny (*ibid.*, 120–21: 123). Given the finely decorated nature of these handles, a further and perhaps more likely possibility is that they were attached to small hand mirrors.
5   Birds are also depicted on saddles in the area of the Steppes. For a discussion of the significance of the depiction of birds on Anglo-Saxon metalwork see Wickham-Crowley 1992.

6 The Athlone binding strips (Fig. 24.6), the fragment from Garranes, Co. Cork and the possible mount from Cappagh, Co. Westmeath (Fig. 24.7).

References

ARRHENIUS, B. 1983, 'The chronology of the Vendel graves', in J. P. Lamm and H-Å Nordström (eds), *Transactions of the Boat-grave Symposium in Stockholm, Feb. 2–3, 1981, Vendel Period Studies* 2, 39–68. Stockholm.

FARRELL, R., KELLY E. P. and GOWAN, M. 1989, 'The Crannóg Archaeology Project (CAP), Republic of Ireland, 1: a preliminary report', *Int. J. Naut. Archaeol.* 18.2, 123–35.

FARRELL, R. and NEUMAN DE VEGVAR, C. (eds) 1992, *Sutton Hoo: Fifty Years After* (= American Early Medieval Studies 2). Oxford, Ohio.

GIESLER, J. 1996, 'Rekonstruktion eines Sattels aus dem fränkischen Gräberfeld von Wesel-Bislich', in A. Wieczorek, P. Périn, K. von Welck and W. Menghin (hrsg.), *Die Franken Wegbereiter Europas. Vor 1500 Jahren: König Chlodwig und seine Erben*, 808–11. Mainz.

HE: *Historia Ecclesiastica Gentis Anglorum*, B. Colgrave and R. A. B. Mynors (ed. and trans.) 1969, *Bede: Ecclesiastical History of the English People*. Oxford.

JANSSEN, W. 1981, 'Die Sattelbeschläge aus Grab 446 des fränkischen Gräberfeldes von Wesel-Bislich, Kreis Wesel', *Archäologisches Korrespondenzblatt* 11, 149–69.

KAVANAGH, R. M. 1988, 'The horse in Viking Ireland', in J. Bradley (ed.), *Settlement and Society in Medieval Ireland. Studies presented to Francis Xavier Martin O.S.A.*, 89–121.Kilkenny.

KELLY, E.P. Catalogue entry, in K. Hada (ed.), *Treasures of Celtic Art: A European Heritage, Metropolitan Art Museum, Tokyo*, no. 235, 195. English language supplement, no. 235, 56. Tokyo.

KILBRIDE-JONES, H. 1980a, *Zoomorphic Penannular Brooches* (= Rep. Res. Comm. Soc. Antiq. London 39). London.

KILBRIDE-JONES, H. 1980b, *Celtic Craftsmanship in Bronze*. London.

NEWMAN, C. 1995, 'The Iron Age to Early Christian transition: the evidence from dress fasteners', in C. Bourke (ed.), *From the Isles of the North. Early Medieval Art in Ireland and Britain*, 17–25. Belfast.

Ó FLOINN, R. 1989, Catalogue entries in Youngs 1989.

Ó RÍORDÁIN, S. P. 1942, 'The excavation of a large earthen fort at Garranes, Co. Cork', *Proc. Roy. Ir. Acad.* 47C, 77–150.

Ó RÍORDÁIN, S. P. and HARTNETT, P. J. 1949, 'The excavation of Ballycatteen Fort, Co. Cork', *Proc. Roy. Ir. Acad.* 49C, 1–43.

PIRLING, R. 1964, 'Ein fränkisches Fürstengrab aus Krefeld-Gellep', *Germania* 42, 188–91.

RYAN, M. (ed.) 1983, *Treasures of Ireland. Irish Art 3000 B.C.–1500 A.D.* Dublin.

RYAN, M. 1992, 'The Sutton Hoo ship burial and Ireland', in Farrell and Neuman de Vegvar (eds), 83–116.

VIERCK, H. 1972, 'Prunksattel aus Gellep und Ravenna', *Archäologisches Korrespondenzblatt* 2, 213–17.

WICKHAM-CROWLEY, K. 1992, 'The birds on the Sutton Hoo instrument', in Farrell and Neuman de Vegvar (eds), 43–62.

YOUNGS, S. (ed.) 1989, *'The Work of Angels'. Masterpieces of Celtic Metalwork, 6th–9th Centuries AD*. London.

25   Survival and Revival of the Insular Style in Later Medieval Scottish Art

Virginia Glenn

Introduction

There are 120 pieces of decorative metalwork and ivory carving in the National Museums of Scotland which were made in the country or imported during the period 1100–1500.[1] Of these, roughly ten per cent have a distinctive Insular or at least West Highland character. Some come with elaborate family mythologies; others have well recorded archaeological provenances.

There is not a straightforward geographical grouping of find sites for this material. Scots in the east of the country were not averse to objects with Insular features. A corpus very similar to that on the bell shrine found at Kilmichael Glassary in Argyll comes from a grave at Tibbermuir in Perthshire (Fig. 25.1), while another now known only from a late eighteenth-century drawing was discovered in the ruins of Dunfermline Abbey (Fig. 25.2). The elegant late thirteenth-century seal of the chapter of Dunkeld (Birch 1907, figs 73, 74) shows a crozier reliquary

Fig. 25.1 Corpus from a crucifix, from a grave in Tibbermuir churchyard, Perthshire, copper alloy with gilding. National Museums of Scotland H.1995.680

Fig. 25.2 A 'brass' crucifix figure found at Dunfermline Abbey (now lost) from an album of Drawings in Scotland *collected by Francis Grose, late eighteenth century. National Museums of Scotland Library, Society of Antiquaries of Scotland MS 476*

resembling that of St Fillan in the Museum collection, and the library of the Cistercians at Coupar Angus included a twelfth-century psalter in full Insular style (Bannister 1910).

Equally, enamels imitating standard thirteenth-century Limoges types have turned up on Benbecula (Caldwell 1977) and Islay (Caldwell forthcoming), and an elegant gold thirteenth-century brooch in the mainstream of European fashion has a provenance in Bernera (Stevenson 1961). 'Hibernicity' was not the only norm, even in the far west.

The Guthrie bell shrine

To illustrate these points I shall concentrate on aspects of the dating and context of just two of our West Highland objects. The Guthrie bell shrine (Plate XXII) was acquired by the Museum in 1925 from Guthrie Castle, east of Forfar (Eeles 1926). The eighteenth- and nineteenth-century literature simply says it had 'been there since time immemorial' (Warden 1882, 400).

The Guthries are documented in Lower Leslie and Forfar from the mid-fifteenth century onwards (Thomson 1882, no. 868 (25 March 1466)). They included numerous churchmen both before and after the Reformation, among them two Richards, abbots of Arbroath (Arbroath Liber 1856, 80–5, 165–67). By the early twentieth century family tradition (Guthrie 1906, 35), based on what Warden calls 'conjecture only', assumed that the curious old bell among the relics at the castle had belonged to John Guthrie (1577–1649), who was made bishop of Moray. As a prominent Royalist Episcopalian, who shocked adherents of the kirk by preaching at the coronation of Charles I in Edinburgh in 1633 adorned in a rochet, John Guthrie could reasonably be expected to have tolerated the imagery of the shrine. However, the bell shrine cannot be identified among the detailed inventories of his household belongings – including his silver – at Spynie Palace, or the possessions he was allowed to remove when he fled to Dundee in 1642 (National Archives of Scotland GD 188 2/9, 19/1 and 24/12/2).[2] Nor did the bishop have any recorded contact with the west of Scotland whence the object very evidently originates.

A more likely candidate is Alexander Guthrie, who was appointed to act as commissary to his cousin John Leslie, bishop of the Isles in 1628 (National Archives of Scotland GD 188 24/3/7).[3] In this capacity he would have overseen the legal affairs of the church and had access to any remnants of the western church treasuries which had weathered the Reformation. Some of the sixteenth-century appointees to Iona never set foot there, although the abbey church functioned as the cathedral (Dillworth 1971), but Alexander would have had to go to the island to carry out his legal duties and it is said that Leslie toured his diocese three or four times yearly, complaining to the king that no proper residence had been provided for him (Craven 1907, 84).

Alexander died without issue in 1637, the same year as he made his will in Dundee (National Archives of Scotland GD 188/24/12). Assuming it was he who graduated *scriba civitatis Edimburgensis* in 1609 (Edinburgh Graduates 1858, 24), Alexander Guthrie was a lawyer of scholarly and antiquarian interests sufficiently concerned about the Greek and Latin books and the volumes of the Acts of Parliament in his house to name them as specific bequests to Richard Guthrie, writer to the signet and his executor. Otherwise, apart from numerous monetary legacies, he left to his brother Francis 'the haill utensils and domiceills with my abilyamentis of my body with my haill scots buikis' and his armour. These are the only chattels mentioned.

The family had spread out into a senior and a junior branch in the early sixteenth century, Alexander and Francis belonging to the former. According to the occasionally inaccurate pedigree pasted into the back of D. C. Guthrie's *History* (1906), after various vicissitudes, the lands and barony of Guthrie were disponed to Bishop John of the junior connection by a distant cousin. However, the whole clan continued to live in the same area and members of both branches were remembered in Alexander's testament. Finally, Francis took the prudent step of marrying Bethia, daughter and sole heiress of the bishop, becoming laird of Guthrie in right of his wife. Consequently, heirlooms from both sides were reunited at Guthrie Castle.

As with some of its Irish equivalents, the 'shrine' has been created by applying successive layers of ornament to the iron bell itself (Mahr and Raftery 1932; 1941, 56–7, 157, 165, pls 68–70, 81, 83, 124–25). The whole piece is now 198mm high, 144mm wide and 124mm deep. The top edges of the back and front sheets are rounded and roughly bent back against the bell inside. It would originally have had a cresting which concealed the handle and descended to cover the protuberant shoulders of the early iron bell. These resemble the animal head terminals noted on late eleventh- and twelfth-century Irish bell reliquaries by Ó Floinn (1990, 26).

A combination of stylistic and scientific analysis allows us to assign some dates and artistic context to the layers.[4] The earliest is the copper-alloy plate behind the silver front. This is just visible through the damage to the left of the central top figure and at the end of the cross-arm. It has some relief decoration which does not quite correspond with that on the silver and it dictates the shape of the crucifix.

The alloy of this plate is very close, but not identical in composition to that used to cast the figures of Christ and St John, which are now applied to the side of the shrine (Fig. 25.3). They in turn match each other exactly in major, minor and trace elements. These two highly stylised figures can be broadly described as 'Romanesque', but do not wholly fit into the context of either Irish or Continental art. Like Ó Floinn writing on Irish twelfth-century crucifix figures (1987a, 178), I have difficulty in categorising this example alongside any of the catalogued European types (Bloch 1992).

The very vertical stance, the almost horizontal arms, the clinging knee length loin-cloth with heavy girdle straight across the stomach, the long strands of hair on the shoulders, the slightly inclined head with large, oval, open eyes and the schematised rib patterns compare with Bloch VI A 12, 13 and 14 which he describes as Franco-Flemish and dates to the first half of the twelfth century. What the Continental examples do not share, however, are the jug ears, the crossed feet with one nail or the strange flat head-dress of the Guthrie bell shrine crucifix figure. All three Franco-Flemish examples wear low, but conventional crowns.

The ears of both these Guthrie figures, the short squared off beard of Christ and the very conventionalised frontal poses are, however, reminiscent of the saints on St Manchan's Shrine from Co. Offaly. So also is the way the square shouldered St John has one arm at right angles across his body and the other flattened against his book. St Manchan's Shrine is again early twelfth century (Ó Floinn 1994, 16).

The crossed feet do not appear in either Bloch's assemblage of crucifix figures or those mentioned in Ó Floinn's 1987 article, although his example from Kilkenny West, Co. Westmeath (Ó Floinn 1987a, illus. 10.3) does have conjoined feet below converging ankles pierced with one rivet hole. There is, however, another with a Scottish provenance, the detached crowned bronze figure found at Dunvegan Castle and now in the British Museum (Edinburgh 1982, 25, cat. no. B34). Purely on stylistic grounds, it too is given a twelfth-century date. Crossed feet and Crucifixion figures with only three nails may be a peculiarity of West Highland art of this period, as the type does not normally occur elsewhere for more than a hundred years.

Another isolated incidence now in the Brussels Musée d'Art et d'Histoire occurs on the font from Saint-Germain de Tirlemont which bears the date 1144. The museum handbook describes it as reproducing Mosan themes, but employed by a dissident of lesser talent or an itinerant (Muller 1983). The same can be said of some Hebridean artists, aware of European norms but working in isolation and following their personal inclinations. The head-dress

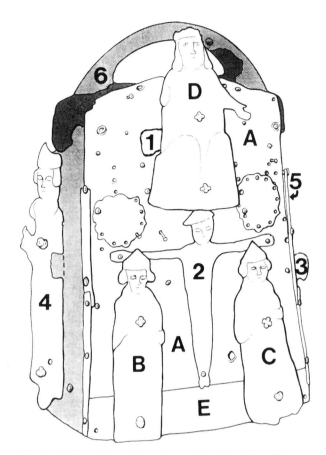

Fig. 25.3 *Drawing of the front of the Guthrie bell shrine by Marion O'Neil 1998*
Analysis of the metals:
Copper alloy:
1 is very similar, but not identical to 2 and 3 (St John)
2 and 3 match in both major, minor and trace elements
4 and the sheets encasing the sides and back, the handle on the back and the framing strips (except 5) are a broadly similar type of zinc brass alloy
5 differs from everything else
6 differs from everything else
Silver:
A has trace elements similar to B and C, but a lower copper content, which is possibly the result of surface depletion, but more probably a genuine difference indicating a separate phase of workmanship
B and C are very similar and likely to be from the same batch of silver
D is not inconsistent with B and C, but the analytical results are clouded by the gilding
E has a high lead content due to the application of niello, is higher in gold than the rest of the silver parts and is definitely different in origin

on the bell shrine is also highly idiosyncratic and may represent part of Christ's hair, a flattened halo or a totally misconceived version of the flat-topped crown or *camelaucium* noted by Ó Floinn on some

Fig. 25.4 *Reconstruction of the front of the Guthrie bell shrine about 1200 by J. S. Richardson. Proceedings of the Society of Antiquaries of Scotland 1926*

Fig. 25.5 *Gold fillet found in the Nunnery at Iona. National Museums of Scotland H.HX 36*

contemporary Irish crucifix figures (1987, 180). To summarise, the figures of Christ and St John belong with the front bronze plate which is now largely hidden. They were carried out in the first half of the twelfth century by an artist influenced by both Irish and European styles, but outside the mainstream of either.

The next layer to be added to the Guthrie bell shrine was the embossed silver sheet to which the two figures are now attached. J. S. Richardson produced a drawing which reconstructed this to illustrate an article by Francis Eeles (1926, 414, fig. 4). He subtracted the bishops, God the Father and the bottom inscription (Fig. 25.4). This sheet has a lower copper content than the three silver figures now applied to it, which may be the result of surface depletion, but more probably indicates a genuine difference in manufacture. All the silver on the shrine has similar trace elements, implying that the raw materials came from the same source, but at different times.

Eeles noted (1926, 412) that the embossed scrolls down each side of the crucifix match a gold fillet found under the floor of the Nunnery on Iona (Fig.

25.5) (Curle 1924). More elaborate versions of this scroll evolved to become a recurrent motif on sculptured grave-slabs and crosses, not only of the 'school of Iona', but also of Kintyre, Loch Awe and even sixteenth-century Oronsay (Steer and Bannerman 1977, 16, 49, 54, figs 3, 10, 12). Similarly placed embossed scrolls also survived or were revived in a Gothic form with flower head and oak leaf terminals down each side of the crucifixion scene on the fifteenth-century front of the Bearnán Conaill bell now in the British Museum (Ó Floinn 1994, 31, pl. 16).

I would add that another clearly recognisable Iona motif on the Guthrie bell shrine is the foliated cross embossed in two horizontal bands of four above the Crucifixion on the same silver sheet. Steer and Bannerman (1977, 19, fig. 4) detect the origins of similar foliated crosses in twelfth-century Kerry and Tipperary stone carving and plot their development through to Iona masons working on Oronsay about 1500. The examples on the shrine are of a less evolved type and indicate an early stage of the sequence.

Attempts to date the embossed scrolls on the

Guthrie bell shrine depend on the period ascribed to the gold fillet excavated at Iona. Ó Floinn has suggested that it was part of a related group recorded in Ireland and western Scotland, and pointed out that two of the fillets found in Scotland were associated with finger rings of a Scandinavian type (Ó Floinn 1983, 7). Lightbown, on the other hand, says that along with other examples found on Iona and Bute they are a representation of the head-bands worn by great ladies in twelfth-century Scotland and England and 'possibly elsewhere as well' (1992, 109–10).

Two other, plainer, complete gold fillets, and a part of a third which can be dated to the mid-twelfth century on the basis of the coins in the same hoard, were found on Bute in 1863 (Pollexfen 1864, 215, 373). They resemble a further fragment of a gold band found at a second Iona site, St Ronan's Church, whose only decoration is a beaded border and embossed zigzag. In agreement with Lightbown, I think the scrolled fillet is a more developed example and somewhat later than the others. The gift of such secular ornaments to religious houses was not uncommon. Lightbown quotes the bequest of Matilda, queen of William the Conqueror, of two gold *ligaturae* (head bands) to the abbey of La Trinité at Caen (1992, 109).

The scrolled fillet was found carefully wrapped in textile with four silver spoons. The date and provenance of these has also been the subject of debate. Stratford considered that they were made at least 50 years before the foundation of the Iona nunnery (Zarnecki 1984, 280), but his comparisons with other metalwork and manuscript decoration involve Romanesque motifs too generalised to be entirely convincing. Spoons with comparable features have been found in Taunton and Pevensey (How 1952, 28–31), Dublin (Ryan 1991, 157) and on Gotland (Hildebrand 1894, 188) and assigned dates in the first half of the thirteenth century.

The existing St Ronan's Church is a completely unembellished structure built around 1200 (RCAHMS 1982, 21). Recent excavations have uncovered earlier burials and the foundations of a small previous building on the site (O'Sullivan 1994); the gold band was probably associated with these. Ranald, son of Somerled, who died probably about 1210, founded the nunnery in whose precincts the church stands, and his sister Bethag was prioress (McDonald 1997, 222). The architecture of the nunnery church places it in the first quarter of the thirteenth century and suggests that it was strongly influenced by Irish models (RCAHMS 1982, 22). The stylistic evidence suggests that it was during this era of great activity – the first abbey church of the Iona Benedictines was also built between 1200 and 1220 (RCAHMS 1982, 23–4) – that the Guthrie bell shrine underwent this first renovation. It was also around

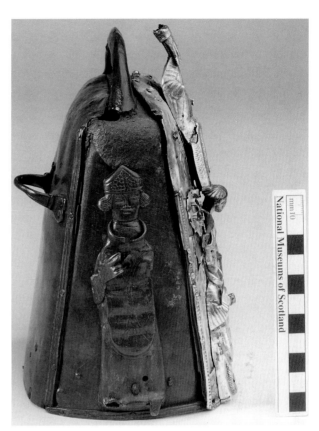

Fig. 25.6 *Guthrie bell shrine, side view with copper-alloy figure of bishop. National Museums of Scotland H.KA 21*

1210 that the Iona psalter (National Library of Scotland MS 10000) described by Morgan as 'a product of the highest quality' (1988, 76) was illuminated in Oxford for a patron on the island.

The three silver figures on the front of the shrine take little cognizance of the previous programme of decoration, hiding parts of it. They are worked up from thick sheet metal into shallow relief and their arms are flat, diagrammatic cut-outs tucked under their sides. Exactly the same technique has been employed for the bronze bishop on the side (Fig. 25.6). His vestments, face and the style of engraving match the silver bishops so precisely that they must be by the same craftsman. Steer and Bannerman convincingly relate them to early fourteenth-century grave-slabs, again at Iona (1977, 29).

The copper alloy of the bishop on the side is a match for all the visible bronze sheets, the edging strips and the carrying handles on the back. This implies that the casing – or recasing – of the bell with bronze and the addition of the three figures on the front are all from one major overhaul in the first half of the fourteenth century.

The panel of interlace, I believe, also belongs to this phase. It contrasts sharply with the refinement of the embossed ornament, but has the same kind of blunt crudity as the engraving on the bishops' chasubles. It obviously pre-dates the inscription plaque which covers part of it. The shape of the motif is ungainly and it resembles neither the graceful zoomorphic meshes developed in Ireland from Ringerike and Urnes (Ó Floinn 1987b; Stalley 1994, pls 2, 5, 7, 8), nor the accomplished fleshy interweaving scrolls on the Lewis chessmen (Stratford 1997, 13–14). Equally, it cannot be compared with the neatly plaited ornaments of West Highland stone sculpture (Steer and Bannerman 1977, 187) or late fifteenth-century ivory carving (Edinburgh 1982, 58–60, nos D17, D18). The bottom section has most in common with the latter, but unravels into a formless asymmetrical upper part filled with haphazard hatching. My conjecture is that it is the work of an early fourteenth-century craftsman, attempting to revive a style in which he was untrained, perhaps under the influence of an earlier object then surviving in the Iona treasury. Why it was not balanced by an engraved panel on the other side of the shrine is difficult to say; perhaps even its author found it rather unsatisfactory.

The niello inscription in poorly formed black letter reading IOHANNES ALEXAN/DRI ME FIERI FECIT is on a strip of silver with a higher gold content than any other part of the shrine. It is now attached upside-down to the bottom of the front behind the lower parts of the two bishop figures. It was designed for this position, as the flaring vestments of the figures would have left slightly more space for the upper line of text than the lower and that is exactly how it is laid out. The engraver and his patron, one assumes, were literate enough to attach their plaque the right way up, so this may be part of a botched repair when the object entered Guthrie hands after the misadventures of the Reformation. The bruised condition of the lower quatrefoil-headed rivets holding each bishop in place is consistent with them having been loosened and hammered back more than once. At this stage too, the loss of the upper part may have been roughly made good by flattening the top of the front and back and encasing the exposed iron bell handle with an alloy differing in composition from everything else present. The two silver-gilt ornaments attached above the cross-arms also belong to the sixteenth century when donations of jewellery to favourite shrines were not unusual.

Steer and Bannerman (1977, 145) rather wistfully equated Iohannes Alexandri with John II, Lord of the Isles (died 1498) and his father. However, they also maintain (1977, 5–6) that black letter inscriptions only appear on West Highland sculpture after about 1500, so given John's turbulent and ultimately ruinous later career, this is inherently unlikely. A more convincing candidate is John MacIan of Ardnamurchan, the heads of whose family had styled

themselves Iohannes Alexandri and Alexander Iohannis for generations (Munro 1986, 284–86). There is also some evidence that they were artistic patrons. John, who died in 1517–18, has an elaborate grave-slab at Iona Abbey with a long inscription, again in black letter, erected by his sister Mariota (Steer and Bannerman 1977, 112–14, no. 24, pl. 25D). She was married to Malcolm MacDuffie whose imposing cross attributed to the Iona School stands at Oronsay Priory (Steer and Bannerman 1977, 119–20, no. 32, pl. 13).[5]

The Reformation was a gradual and peaceful process at Iona and seventeenth-century accounts of major acts of iconoclasm can be largely discounted (Stevenson 1928). The bell with its living Christ figure and barely identifiable St John, its bishops and God the Father without haloes and purely secular inscription may well have been allowed to pass almost unnoticed into private hands. A more cataclysmic fate presumably befell the arm reliquary of Columba donated by Donald, Lord of the Isles (died 1421), to the Iona treasury and recorded in the Book of Clanranald (Cameron 1894, 160–3). It would have been regarded as thoroughly idolatrous.

The Kilmichael Glassary bell shrine

The Kilmichael Glassary bell shrine, found near the church of the same name in Mid Argyll, was dug up by labourers in 1814 (Fig. 25.7). The circumstances of the find are somewhat obscure as it did not enter the museum until 1827 (Campbell and Sandeman 1961, 82, no. 501). It is a considerably smaller object than the Guthrie bell shrine at 148mm high.

The construction is very interesting. The robust framing and the Christ figure are cast in a more yellow alloy than the flat engraved panels. This may have been because a coppery metal was softer and easier to engrave as the whole would almost certainly have been gilded, so concealing the effect of the colour difference. The entire top, including the handle, the *Manus Dei* and the four corner pieces approximately a third of the way down, are a single casting. Perhaps the craftsman knew that bell shrines normally had some kind of distinct cresting but not exactly what form they took.

The parish of Kilmichael Glassary, which is particularly rich in sculptured stones of the later medieval period, lies a few miles inland from the western coast (RCAHMS 1992, 143–49, no. 69). For most of the twelfth century it was in the very large diocese of Dunkeld, but in the 1180s it became part of the newly created bishopric of Argyll. Modern writers question Bower's view that this division was because of language differences between east and west (Watt 1991, 11–13), but for most of the twelfth

Fig. 25.7 *Kilmichael Glassary bell shrine, front view. National Museums of Scotland H. KA 4*

Fig. 25.8 *Kilmichael Glassary bell shrine, side view with strapwork ornament. National Museums of Scotland H. KA 4*

century, Kilmichael Glassary would have had much more cohesive links culturally and by way of the many short sea crossings with the neighbouring diocese of Sodor, or the Isles, which in 1153 was finally placed under the authority of Nidaros (modern Trondheim). The latter was very far flung, with many conflicting political forces and, as R. A. McDonald recently pointed out (1997, 207), the 1219 bishop of the Isles was sent to Dublin for consecration, while in 1244 Innocent IV noted that his successors sometimes went to York and sometimes to Nidaros.

This duality is clearly apparent in the Kilmichael Glassary bell shrine. The very practice of enshrining a bell as a relic is peculiar to Ireland and the Hibernian seaboard (Harbison 1991, 157–58). The handle with its zoomorphic terminals and the animal-head feet, two of which are missing, are in a recognisable Insular style. There is also a small patch of interwoven ornament on one side consisting of four panels of plain plaited straps against a ground

punched with dots (Fig. 25.8). They slightly resemble the lower section of the interlace motif engraved on the Guthrie bell shrine, but are much more irregular than Scandinavian work of the twelfth century (Roesdahl and Wilson 1992, 362, no. 517).

Unlike Guthrie, this is not a shrine created by attaching layers of enrichment to the bell itself in the Irish manner. It is not even particularly bell shaped. It is a box inside which the small, unadorned relic, which has survived with it, had a separate existence. The early hand bell was not attached, but held in by a panel forming a floor to the reliquary (Bourke 1980, 66).

It is in Scandinavian metalwork one finds the influences which produced a bell shrine so far removed from previous tradition. The angularity, the tidy geometrical layout and the border patterns of the Eriksberg reliquary from Västergötland in Sweden (Fig. 25.9), attributed to the second half of the twelfth century, are very similar (Roesdahl and Wilson 1992, 212, 350, no. 469; Langberg 1992, 56,

Fig. 25.10 Copper-alloy crucifix figure found in Copenhagen. Kopenhagen Nationalmuseet D 78/1963

Fig. 25.9 End view of the Västergötland reliquary. Stockholm Statens Historiska Museet 5561

1992, pls 13, 14), making it unmistakably Danish. Although its condition is poor, the crown, facial features and hair are strikingly like the Scottish example. So too are the schematised arm muscles (though the arms are more raised on the Copenhagen figure), the stylised rib cage and the low slung loin-cloth below a slightly convex stomach. Many of these details of both are commonplaces of Romanesque art, but German, French or English crucifix figures do not relate so closely to either.

The very stylised treatment of the loin-cloth with the plunging 'V' at the top, the frilly hem and the scrolling knot on one hip seems peculiarly Scottish. The fact that two more incidences of it occur in the east coast area of Scotland testify that here too there were trading and political links with Scandinavia (Figs 25.1, 25.2). The Kilmichael Glassary bell shrine is sufficiently idiosyncratic for one to assume that it was not itself an import to Scotland, but the strength of the Scandinavian influence is so strong, and it forms such a striking contrast with all the phases of the Guthrie bell shrine, that it is possible that the craftsman may have been an immigrant. Set against neighbouring European art in this way, one can reasonably date it to the second half of the twelfth century.

figs 26–28). The Swedish shrine has traces of niello in the framing pieces and Kilmichael Glassary may well have done so too.

Outwith Scotland, the bronze crucifix figure I have found which most nearly compares with that on this bell shrine is now in the Nationalmuseet in Copenhagen (Fig. 25.10), having been discovered during road works there in 1963 (Bloch 1992, 209, no. V A 13, pl. 91). This in turn derives many of its characteristics from the large twelfth-century wooden crucifixes covered with metal from Åby (Roesdahl and Wilson 1992, 348, no. 460), Lisbjerg (*ibid.*, 350, no. 467), Odder and Tirstrup (Langberg

Conclusion

Elements of both survival and revival are apparent

Fig. 25.11 *Kilmichael Glassary bell shrine, detail of the top front. National Museums of Scotland H. KA 4*

Fig. 25.12 *Kilmichael Glassary bell shrine, detail of the design above the* Manus Dei, *drawn by Marion O'Neil 1998. National Museums of Scotland H. KA 4*

on the bell shrines. In conclusion I would indicate two possible instances either of these phenomena or simply of Highland conservatism.

It has been pointed out that the Christ figure on the *c*. 1500 stone cross at Kilmartin, the adjacent parish to Kilmichael Glassary, very much recalls his ancestor of three centuries before on the Guthrie bell shrine (RCAHMS 1992, 14, 138–39). Was this an Iona carver sticking firmly to his very long held traditions?

Finally, on the Kilmichael Glassary bell shrine, just above the *Manus Dei*, cast into the metal, is a set of squiggles which at first sight appear to be incompetent egg and dart. However this is a pretty competent metalworker otherwise, and egg and dart is rather surprising in this very un-Classical vocabulary (Fig. 25.11). In the same position at the back of the bell shrine, this area is left entirely blank. The overriding effect of the squiggles, in their rectangular panel emphasised by bold horizontal borders, is that of some kind of label or inscription. The general appearance, at least, is evocative of cursive Arabic script, imitated by someone unfamiliar with its actual meaning. This feature was noticed by Daniel Wilson (1884, 86–93). He rejected the opinion of several eminent Orientalists, who with Victorian self confidence, read it as a reference to 'Allah'. Wilson was unable to accept the presence of an infidel reference on a sacred Christian object.

Could this be the survival of another cultural strain transmitted through all the silver – including the hundreds of thousands of inscribed coins and other metal objects imported by the Vikings from the East and still abounding in Scandinavia (Arne 1914, 97, 113–203; Roesdahl and Wilson 1992, 74–8; Jansson 1996)?

Acknowledgements

I should like to thank the following for their assistance: Clara Jane Anderson, National Archives of Scotland; Cormac Bourke, Ulster Museum; David Caldwell, Ulrike al Khamis, Jackie Moran and Jennifer Scarce, National Museums of Scotland; John Cherry, British Museum; Jane Dawson, University of Edinburgh; James Graham-Campbell, University College London; Poul Grinder-Hansen, Nationalmuseet, Copenhagen; Raghnall Ó Floinn, National Museum of Ireland; Roger Stalley, Trinity College, Dublin; Göran Tegnér, Statens Historiska Museum, Stockholm.

Fig. 25.10 is reproduced by permission of the Danish National Museum, Copenhagen; Fig. 25.9 by permission of the Riksantikvarieämbetet och Statens Historiska Museer, Stockholm (photo G. Hildelrand). All other illustrations reproduced by permission of the Trustees of the National Museums of Scotland, Edinburgh.

My research in Scandinavia, Ireland and London was financed by a generous grant from the British Academy.

Notes

1   A catalogue of this material is scheduled for publication in 2002 (Glenn, V. 2002, Romanesque and Gothic Decorative Metalwork and Ivory Carvings in the Museum of Scotland. Edinburgh).
2   I am indebted to Dennis Gallagher, who generously gave me access to his full transcripts (as yet unpublished) of these difficult documents.
3   This possibility was pointed out by Ian Fisher, Royal Commission on the Ancient and Historical Monuments of Scotland.
4   The silver and bronze were analysed by Paul Wilthew, Department of Conservation and Analytical Research,

National Museums of Scotland. A detailed scientific report by Catherine Eremin will be published in the forthcoming National Museums of Scotland catalogue (See note 1).

5   Geoffrey Barrow, University of Edinburgh, proposed this hypothesis.

References

ABROATH LIBER 1856, *Liber S.Thome de Aberbrothoc*. (Bannatyne Club). Edinburgh

ARNE, T. J. 1914, *La Suède et l'Orient*. Uppsala.

BANNISTER, H. M. 1910, 'Specimen pages of two manuscripts of the Abbey of Coupar-Angus in Scotland', *Codices e Vaticanis Selecti Phototypice Expressi. Series Minor*, (II) 7–13, figs I–IV. Rome.

BIRCH, W. de G. 1907, *History of Scottish Seals*, II. Stirling.

BLOCH, P. 1992, *Romanische Bronzekruzifixe* (= Bronzegeräte des Mittelalters 5). Berlin.

BOURKE, C. 1980, 'Early Irish hand-bells', *J. Roy. Soc. Antiq. Ir.* 110, 52–66.

CALDWELL, D. H. 1977, 'An enamelled plaque from Borve, Benbecula', *Proc. Soc. Antiq. Scotl.* 109, 378–80.

CALDWELL, D. H. (ed.) forthcoming, *Recent Excavations at Finlaggan*.

CALLANDER, J. G. 1926, 'Notes on (1) a casket of cetacean bone and (2) a Highland brooch of silver', *Proc. Soc. Antiq. Scotl.* 60, 105–17.

CAMPBELL, M. and SANDEMAN, M. L. S 1961, 'Mid Argyll: an archaeological survey', *Proc. Soc. Antiq. Scotl.* 95, 1–125.

CAMERON, A. 1894, *Reliquae Celticae, texts, papers and studies in Gaelic Literature and Philology* (2), 138–309.

CRAVEN, J. B. 1907, *Records of the Dioceses of Argyll and the Isles 1560–1860*. Kirkwall.

CURLE, A. O. 1924, 'Note on four silver spoons and a fillet of gold found in the nunnery at Iona', *Proc. Soc. Antiq. Scotl.* 58, 102–111.

DILWORTH, M. 1971, 'Iona Abbey and the Reformation', *Scottish Gaelic Studies* 12 , 78–109.

EELES, F. 1926, 'The Guthrie Bell and its shrine', *Proc. Soc. Antiq. Scotl.* 60, 409–20.

EDINBURGH 1982, *Angels, Nobles and Unicorns – Art and Patronage in Medieval Scotland* (= D. H. Caldwell (ed.), exhibition catalogue, National Museum of Antiquities of Scotland). Edinburgh.

EDINBURGH GRADUATES 1858. *A Catalogue of the Graduates in the Faculties of Arts, Divinity and Law of the University of Edinburgh since its Foundation*. Edinburgh.

GUTHRIE, D. C. 1906, *The Guthrie Family 1178–1900*. Northampton.

HARBISON, P. 1991, *Pilgrimage in Ireland – the Monuments and the People*. London.

HILDEBRAND 1894. *Sveriges Medeltid*. Stockholm.

HOW, G. E. P. and J. P. 1952, *English and Scottish Silver Spoons – medieval to late Stuart*. London.

JANSSON, I. 1996 (ed.), *The Viking Heritage – a Dialogue between Cultures*. Stockholm.

LANGBERG, H. 1992, *The Lundø Crucifix*. Copenhagen.

LIGHTBOWN, R. W. 1992, *Mediaeval European Jewellery*. London.

MCDONALD, R. A. 1997, *The Kingdom of the Isles*. East Linton.

MAHR, A. and RAFTERY J. 1932, 1941, *Christian Art in Ancient Ireland*. Dublin.

MORGAN, N. 1988, *Early Gothic Manuscripts [I] 1190–1250*. Oxford.

MULLER, J. 1983, *Laiton – Dinanderie*. Musées Royaux d'Art et d'Histoire. Brussels.

MUNRO, J. and . R. W. (eds) 1986, *Acts of the Lords of the Isles, 1336–1493* (Scottish Historical Society). Edinburgh.

Ó FLOINN, R. 1983, 'A gold band found near Rathkeale, Co. Limerick', *North Munster Antiq. J.* 25, 3–9.

Ó FLOINN, R. 1987a, 'Irish Romanesque crucifix figures', in E. Rynne (ed.), *Figures from the Past. Studies on Figurative Art in Christian Ireland*, 168–188. Dun Laoghaire.

Ó FLOINN, R. 1987b, 'Schools of metalworking in eleventh- and twelfth-century Ireland', in M. Ryan (ed.), *Ireland and Insular Art A.D. 500–1200*, 179–187. Dublin

Ó FLOINN, R. 1990, 'Two ancient bronze bells from Rath Blathmach. Co. Clare', *North Munster Antiq. J.* 32, 19–32.

Ó FLOINN, R. 1994, *Irish Shrines and Reliquaries of the Middle Ages*. Dublin.

O'SULLIVAN, J. 1994, 'Excavation of an early church and a women's cemetery at St Ronan's medieval parish church, Iona', *Proc. Soc. Antiq. Scotl.* 124, 328–65.

POLLEXFEN, J. H. 1864, 'Notice of the coins of David I of Scotland, Henry I and Stephen of England, found with gold ornaments & c at Plan in the island of Bute, in June 1863', *Proc. Soc. Antiq. Scotl.* 5, 372–84.

RCAHMS 1982, Royal Commission on the Ancient and Historical Monuments of Scotland, *Argyll, An Inventory of the Monuments*, Vol. 4, *Iona*. Edinburgh.

RCAHMS 1992, Royal Commission on the Ancient and Historical Monuments of Scotland. *Argyll - An Inventory of the Monuments*, Vol. 7, *Mid Argyll and Cowal*. Edinburgh.

ROESDAHL, E. and WILSON, D. M. (eds) 1992, *From Viking to Crusader. The Scandinavians and Europe 800–1200*. Copenhagen, New York.

RYAN, M. (ed.) 1991, *The Illustrated Archaeology of Ireland*. Dublin.

STALLEY, R. A. 1994, 'The Romanesque sculpture of Tuam', in R. A. Stalley, *Ireland and Europe in the Middle Ages*, 127–63. London.

STEER, K. A. and BANNERMAN, J. W. M. 1977, *Late Medieval Monumental Sculpture in the West Highlands*. Edinburgh.

STEVENSON, J. H. 1928, 'Iona and the 'Reforming Synod'', *Scott. Hist. Rev.* 25, 393–400.

STEVENSON, R. B. K 1962, 'The Kames brooch', *Proc. Soc. Antiq. Scotl.* 95, 308–9.

STRATFORD, N. 1997, *The Lewis Chessmen and the Enigma of the Hoard*. London.

THOMSON, J. M. (ed.) 1882, *Registrum Magni Sigilli Regum Scotorum*, ii. Edinburgh.

WARDEN, A. J. 1882, *Angus or Forfarshire III*. Dundee.

WATT, D. E. R. 1991, *Ecclesia Scoticana*. Stuttgart.

WILSON, D. 1884, 'The Kilmichael-Glassrie bell-shrine', *Proc. Soc. Antiq. Scotl.* 18, 79–93.

ZARNECKI, G. (ed.) 1984, *English Romanesque Art 1066–1200*. London.

Plate I. *The Ardagh hoard. (Photograph: National Museum of Ireland)*

Plate II. *Skei grave 40: Insular bucket.*
(Photograph: NTNU Vitenskapsmuseet, Trondheim)

Plate III. *Skei grave 40: detail of upper band on Insular bucket. (Photograph: NTNU Vitenskapsmuseet, Trondheim)*

Plate IV. *Detail of an embroidered lion border on the Llan-gors textile. (Reconstruction: National Museum of Wales)*

Plate V. *Detail of an embroidered panel on the Llan-gors textile. (Reconstruction: National Museum of Wales)*

Plate VI. *Inscribed lion silk woven in weft-faced compound twill, Constantinople 976–1025, church of St Heribert, Cologne. (Photograph: Helmut Stahl)*

Plate VII. *Glass bangles of early medieval date from Ireland (from top, nos 34, 26, 36, 39). (Photograph: National Museum of Ireland)*

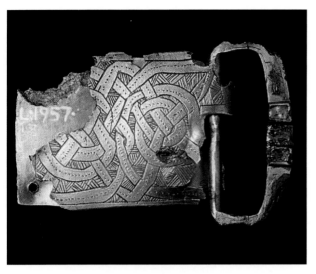

Plate VIII. *Buckle, Bhaltos, Lewis (length 52mm).*
(Photograph: Trustees of the National Museums of Scotland)

Plate IX. *Buckle, Ballinaby, Islay (length 65mm).*
(Photograph: Trustees of the National Museums of Scotland)

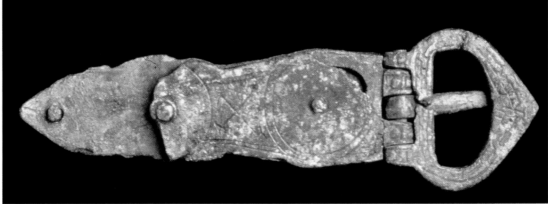

Plate X a, b. *Buckle, Kildonnan, Eigg (length 82mm). (Photograph: Trustees of the National Museums of Scotland)*

Plate XI. The opening of St Mark's Gospel, Barberini Gospels, fol. 51. (Photograph: Biblioteca Apostolica, Vatican, Rome)

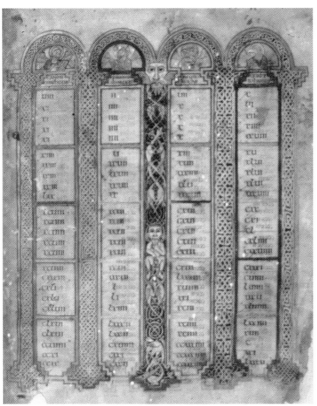

Plate XII. Canon1, Barberini Gospels, fol. 1. (Photograph: Biblioteca Apostolica, Vatican, Rome)

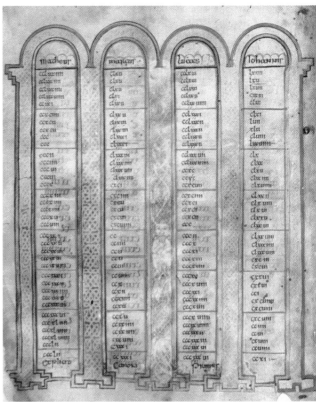

Plate XIII. Continuation of Canon 1, Barberini Gospels, fol. 1v. (Photograph: Biblioteca Apostolica, Vatican, Rome)

Plate XIV. *Crucifixion miniature, St Gall Gospel book (Stiftsbibliothek, MS 51, p. 266). (Photograph: by permission of the Stiftsbibliothek, St Gall)*

Plate XV. *Christ in Glory miniature, St Gall Gospel book (Stiftsbibliothek, MS 51, p. 267). (Photograph: by permission of the Stiftsbibliothek, St Gall)*

Plate XVI. *Crucifixion scene from Gospel book (Paris, Bibliothèque Nationale, lat. 257, fol. 12v.). (Photograph: by permission of the Bibliothèque Nationale, Paris)*

Plate XVII. *Carpet-page, Turin, Bibliotheca Nazionale, cod. O.IV.20, fol. 129 (Photograph: by permission of Bibliotheca Nazionale, Turin)*

Plate XVIII. *Carpet-page, Augsburg , Cod. I, 2.4°.2, fol. 126v. (Photograph: by permission of the Fürstlich Öttingen-Wallerstein'sche Bibliothek)*

Plate XIX. *Carpet-page, St Gall Gospel Book (Stiftsbibliothek, Cod. 51, p.6). (Photograph: by permission of the St Gall Stiftsbibliothek)*

Plate XX. *The decoration of fol. 192v in the Book of Durrow (Dublin, Trinity College Library, MS 57). (Photograph: The Board of Trinity College Dublin)*

Plate XXI. *The Carolingian brooch from Dorestad near present-day Wijk bij Duurstede, The Netherlands.*
(Photograph: © Fotografie Rijksmuseum van Oudheden, Leiden)

Plate XXII. *The Guthrie bell shrine. National Museums of Scotland H.KA 21.*